Programming Visual Basic 2008

Other Microsoft .NET resources from O'Reilly

Related titles

ADO.NET 3.5 Cookbook™
Building a Web 2.0 Portal
   with ASP.NET 3.5
C# Cookbook™
C# 3.0 in a Nutshell

C# 3.0 Pocket Reference
Learning ASP.NET 3.5
Programming ASP.NET 3.5
Programming ASP.NET AJAX
Visual Basic 2005 Cookbook™

**.NET Books
Resource Center**

dotnet.oreilly.com is a complete catalog of O'Reilly's books on .NET and related technologies, including sample chapters and code examples.

ONDotnet.com provides independent coverage of fundamental, interoperable, and emerging Microsoft .NET programming and web services technologies.

Conferences

O'Reilly brings diverse innovators together to nurture the ideas that spark revolutionary industries. We specialize in documenting the latest tools and systems, translating the innovator's knowledge into useful skills for those in the trenches. Visit *conferences.oreilly.com* for our upcoming events.

Safari Bookshelf (*safari.oreilly.com*) is the premier online reference library for programmers and IT professionals. Conduct searches across more than 1,000 books. Subscribers can zero in on answers to time-critical questions in a matter of seconds. Read the books on your Bookshelf from cover to cover or simply flip to the page you need. Try it today for free.

Programming
Visual Basic 2008

Tim Patrick

O'REILLY®

Beijing · Cambridge · Farnham · Köln · Sebastopol · Taipei · Tokyo

Programming Visual Basic 2008
by Tim Patrick

Copyright © 2008 Tim Patrick. All rights reserved.
Printed in the United States of America.

Published by O'Reilly Media, Inc., 1005 Gravenstein Highway North, Sebastopol, CA 95472.

O'Reilly books may be purchased for educational, business, or sales promotional use. Online editions are also available for most titles (*safari.oreilly.com*). For more information, contact our corporate/institutional sales department: (800) 998-9938 or *corporate@oreilly.com*.

Editor: John Osborn		**Indexer:** Ellen Troutman Zaig
Production Editor: Rachel Monaghan		**Cover Designer:** Karen Montgomery
Copyeditor: Audrey Doyle		**Interior Designer:** David Futato
Proofreader: Rachel Monaghan		**Illustrator:** Robert Romano

Printing History:

May 2008:	First Edition.

 This book uses RepKover™, a durable and flexible lay-flat binding.

ISBN: 978-0-596-51843-1

[M]

To Maki, my lovely wife

Table of Contents

Preface

Welcome to *Programming Visual Basic 2008*! I know you're going to enjoy it; I've read it five times already. You're probably anxious to get to Chapter 1, but I recommend you read this preface to make sure you paid for the right book.

Who Is Reading This Book?

Writing a book is a lot like writing a Visual Basic application. Well, except for the part about finding a publisher, and working with an editor. And then there's that pesky rule about correct spelling. Come to think of it, they're really quite different. But in one way, books and programs are similar: both are written to meet the needs of the user. When writing software applications, the user's needs drive the organization and features of the final program. When writing a book, like the one you're looking at now, the needs of the user—that's you, the reader—drive the organization and features of the final text.

So it was with you in mind that I set out to write this book. Oh, there's the fame and the prestige, but it's really about you. You, the person who seeks to understand Visual Basic and the .NET Framework on which it is built. When I thought about you and your needs, I came up with these ideas:

You might know how to program, but maybe not
> In the programming world, there are four types of people: (1) those who already program joyfully; (2) those who don't program, but will learn it and love it; (3) those who don't program, but will learn it and struggle with it; and (4) those who should return this book immediately to the bookstore. If you are in one of the first three groups, this book is definitely for you. I believe that anyone who can break down a task into its basic step-by-step instructions can successfully program in Visual Basic. If you are unsure about your ability to quantify tasks in this way, you might want to start out with a book on basic programming concepts.

You might know how to program in Visual Basic or .NET, but maybe not

And that's OK, because this book will teach you. Most of the chapters introduce important topics in Visual Basic and .NET development, such as object-oriented programming concepts, or using the different types of variables available to you, or interacting with a database. If you already know how to use Visual Basic 6 or earlier, that's great, but it's not a prerequisite.

You want to write programs

Most programming books teach you to write code in 10-line increments. At least that's what's scattered throughout their pages. I've put some of those "code snippets" in this book. But I spend my days writing real programs, not 10-line sample programs. If you want to write whole programs, you should learn using whole programs. That's why I also put a program in my book—*a whole program*. Over the next several hundred pages, I will develop a real program—a database for a small library—and you will write it with me.

I put all of these ideas into 26 easy-to-read chapters, and had O'Reilly Media glue the pages together for your convenience. When you reach the index, you will have learned how to write complete programs in Visual Basic and .NET. It will be a programming adventure, so let's get started!

What's in This Book?

Since we are going to be spending a lot of time together, you probably want to know something about me. Well, my name is Tim Patrick, and for many years I lived just up the street from the big Microsoft campus. I've been writing programs for 25 years, and these days I write custom database-oriented Visual Basic applications for small to medium-size businesses. And I'm not alone. Most Visual Basic developers write business-level software. If that's what you do, or plan to do, you're in great company.

As you move through the pages of this book, you will read about the major .NET and Visual Basic activities that drive the development of business-level and general consumer applications. If you plan to do some other type of programming, such as game development, this book will be somewhat helpful, but I don't talk about advanced or specialized features such as interactive 3D models or geometric transformations.

Each chapter discusses a major programming topic, and then follows it up with a practical implementation of that topic: the creation of the Library database program. I don't show every line of code in the book; if I did, the book would weigh 53 pounds and cost $254.38, plus tax. To get every line of source code, you'll have to download the accompanying source code from the book's web site. The code and the book's text are united in one purpose: to train you in the skilled use of Visual Basic on the .NET platform so that you can develop the highest-quality applications possible. The text and the source code both include valuable resources that you can use every day in your programming life.

What's in the Software Download?

You're going to like the download. It contains all the source code for the Library database project. What's cool is that when you install the source code examples, they become part of Visual Studio. Once they are installed, you can create a new chapter-specific project right from the File → New Project menu in Visual Studio. Appendix A has all of the download and installation details.

I wrote the project code using Visual Basic 2008 Professional Edition. Some portions may not be compatible with earlier .NET versions of the language. None of it is compatible with Visual Basic 6.0 or earlier, so don't even bother trying. The source code will work with any edition of Visual Basic 2008, including the Express Edition.

The source code also uses SQL Server 2005 for its database storage. You can use any edition of SQL Server 2005, including the Express Edition. Chapter 4 introduces databases and SQL Server 2005. If you will be using the database in an IT department-controlled network environment, you may need to talk with your IT department representative about installing the sample database. The SQL code I use is pretty vanilla, so it should work on previous versions of SQL Server, and you could easily adjust it to work with Oracle, DB2, Microsoft Access, or other common database engines. You can also use the upcoming SQL Server 2008 if you have it available.

You can use the downloadable source code for your own projects, but please give credit where credit is due. There is a license agreement associated with the code (see Appendix B), so please don't go selling the software as your own work. Just to be on the safe side, I've added a few hard-to-find bugs. Just kidding! (No, I'm not!)

Conventions Used in This Book

The following typographical conventions are used in this book:

Italic
> Indicates new terms, URLs, filenames, and file extensions.

`Constant width`
> Indicates computer coding in a broad sense. This includes all Visual Basic source code, HTML content, XML content, commands, options, source code from other languages, and content generated by Visual Studio tools.

`Constant width bold`
> Indicates commands or other text that the user should type literally. Also used to highlight a particular section of code.

`Constant width italics`
> Indicates text that should be replaced with user-supplied values or values determined by context.

This icon signifies a tip, suggestion, or general note.

 This icon indicates a warning or caution.

Using Code Examples

This book is here to help you get your job done. In general, you may use the code in this book in your programs and documentation. You do not need to contact the publisher or me for permission unless you're reproducing a significant portion of the code. For example, writing a program that uses several chunks of code from this book does not require permission. Selling or distributing a CD-ROM of examples from O'Reilly books does require permission. Answering a question by citing this book and quoting example code does not require permission. Incorporating a significant amount of example code from this book into your product's documentation requires that you abide by the terms of the software license agreement found in Appendix B.

We appreciate, but do not require, attribution. An attribution usually includes the title, author, publisher, and ISBN. For example: "*Programming Visual Basic 2008*, by Tim Patrick. Copyright 2008 Tim Patrick, 978-0-596-51843-1."

If you feel your use of code examples falls outside fair use or the permission given here, feel free to contact us as *permissions@oreilly.com*.

How to Contact Us

Please address comments and questions concerning this book to the publisher:

O'Reilly Media, Inc.
1005 Gravenstein Highway North
Sebastopol, CA 95472
800-998-9938 (in the United States or Canada)
707-829-0515 (international or local)
707-829-0104 (fax)

We have a web page for this book, where we list errata, examples, and any additional information. You can access this page at:

http://www.oreilly.com/catalog/9780596518431

To comment or ask technical questions about this book, send email to:

bookquestions@oreilly.com

For more information about our books, conferences, Resource Centers, and the O'Reilly Network, see our web site at:

http://www.oreilly.com/

Safari® Books Online

 When you see a Safari® Books Online icon on the cover of your favorite technology book, that means the book is available online through the O'Reilly Network Safari Bookshelf.

Safari offers a solution that's better than e-books. It's a virtual library that lets you easily search thousands of top tech books, cut and paste code samples, download chapters, and find quick answers when you need the most accurate, current information. Try it for free at *http://safari.oreilly.com*.

Acknowledgments

The development of *Programming Visual Basic 2008* has been a labor of love for me, and I am blessed to have had so many others go through the labor with me. Joan Murray from Addison-Wesley was my editor on the first edition of the book. John Osborn at O'Reilly Media took up the task of guiding the second edition. I have been fortunate to have worked with John on three different book projects, and their success was possible thanks to his gallant efforts.

Several other authors and programmers took time out of their day jobs to review each chapter of the book and point out its deficiencies, which were numerous before their arrival. I especially wish to thank Glenn Berry, Alex Bierhaus, Harry Chen, Ken Getz, Lowell Mauer, and Dan Sullivan for their superb comments. When it came time to focus on Visual Basic's 2008 release, I also received fantastic input from Chris Williams, Daniel Seara, Ron Petrusha, and Sander Gerz.

Many thanks to Joe Binder, Jay Roxe, Prasadi de Silva, and Eric Knox, all members of the Visual Basic team at Microsoft. Each of them fielded a relentless onslaught of questions about esoteric Visual Basic and .NET features, and provided answers filled with knowledge, patience, and grace.

My agent, Claudette Moore, always deserves her own paragraph in any computer book I write. In fact, she would be a great subject for one of those literary-agent-focused biographies that the public is always clamoring for. Not only does she do a great job at all of the normal agency things, but she also shares personally in the joys and sorrows of the authors under her charge. Thank you for another fun year in books.

To Maki, my wife, and to Spencer, my son, I give a special wave of thanks. If you've ever spent time with authors, you know how cranky they can get. But Maki and Spencer combat crankiness with care and love, and it works. The words *thank you* seem so inadequate when I owe both of them so much. Thanks be to God because He provided such a tremendous family to me.

Introducing .NET

Welcome to .NET! I might as well have said, "Welcome to the universe," because like the universe, .NET is huge. And it's complex. And it's filled with black holes and other things that don't always make sense. Yet it (.NET, not the universe) turns out to be a fantastic system in which to develop software applications.

The .NET Framework was not developed in a vacuum (unlike the universe); Microsoft designed it and its related development languages—especially C# and Visual Basic—to address various issues that plagued Windows software developers and users. To fully understand why .NET was necessary, we need to take a short trip down computer memory lane.

Before .NET

Practical, general-purpose computers have been around since the mid-20th century. However, they were inaccessible to most people because (a) they cost millions of dollars; (b) they consumed gobs of electricity; (c) maintenance and programming could be done only by highly trained specialists; and (d) they tended to clash with the living room furniture.

Fast-forward about 30 years. IBM comes out with the "personal" computer. These "desktop" computers represented a great advance in technology, but only a minority of people ever used them. They continued to be expensive (thousands of dollars), and maintenance and programming still required significant investments in training. IBM PCs also looked hideous around the living room furniture.

Then came the Apple Macintosh. With its sleek design and its user-friendly functionality, it introduced the joy of computing to the masses. And while programming it was not always straightforward, it did give nice results. It's no wonder that Microsoft decided to copy—oops, I mean improve upon—its functionality.

Microsoft Windows 1.0 brought a greater level of usability to the IBM/Intel computing platform. But it wasn't a free ride for programmers. MS-DOS development was hard enough without the addition of the "message pumps" and the hundreds of Application Programming Interface (API) calls needed by Windows programs. Visual Basic 1.0, introduced in 1991, greatly simplified the development process, but with the advent of 32-bit systems, ActiveX and COM components, and the Web, even VB programmers soon felt overwhelmed.

Throughout the 1990s, the situation only seemed to worsen. Microsoft saw increased competition in the form of the Java™ language and the Linux operating system. Hackers were exploiting buffer overruns and other security issues present in the Windows platform. Users experienced myriad computer problems stemming from conflicting standards, competing data integration technologies, registry bloat, and "DLL hell." In frustration, an Excel user's group set fire to the entire Microsoft campus in Redmond.

Well, it didn't get that bad. But Microsoft did see that it needed to address the overall software development and usability issues on its beloved Windows platform. Its solution came in the form of the .NET Framework.

Back to Introducing .NET

When Microsoft announced its plans for .NET, it surprised many developers, especially Visual Basic developers, who saw it as a giant step backward for "Rapid Application Development." But the release of the .NET Framework version 1.0 in 2002 did bring many needed benefits:

.NET introduced a unified programming environment
> All .NET-enabled languages compile to "Microsoft Intermediate Language" before being assembled into platform-specific machine code. Visual Basic, C#, and other .NET languages are wrappers around this common .NET "language." Since all .NET-enabled compilers speak the same underlying language, they no longer suffer from the many data and language conflicts inherent in other cross-language component-based systems such as COM. The .NET version of Visual Studio also unified the standard user interface that lets programmers craft source code.

.NET committed developers to object-oriented technologies
> Not only does .NET fully embrace the object-oriented programming paradigm, but *everything* in .NET is contained in an object: all data values, all source code blocks, and the plumbing for all user-initiated events. Everything appears in the context of an object.

.NET simplified Windows programming

Programming in Visual Basic before .NET was easy enough, until it came time to interact with one of the API libraries, something that happened a lot in professional programming. With .NET, most of the regularly used APIs are replaced with a hierarchy of objects providing access to many commonly needed Windows features. Since the hierarchy is extensible, other vendors can add new functionality without disrupting the existing framework.

.NET enhanced security

Users and administrators can now establish security rules for different .NET features, to limit malicious programs from doing their damage. .NET's "managed" environment also resolves buffer overrun issues and memory leaks through features such as strong data typing and garbage collection.

.NET enhanced developer productivity through standards

The .NET Framework is built upon and uses many new and existing standards, such as XML and SOAP. This enhances data interchange not only on the Windows platform, but also in interactions with other platforms and systems.

.NET enhanced web-based development

Until .NET, a lot of web-based development was done using scripting languages. .NET brings the power of compiled, desktop development to the Internet.

.NET simplified the deployment of applications

If .NET is installed on a system, releasing a program can be as simple as copying its EXE file to the target system (although an install program is much more user-friendly). Features such as side-by-side deployment, ClickOnce deployment, and an end to file version conflicts and "DLL hell" (the presence of multiple versions of the same DLL on a system, or the inability to remove a version of a DLL) make desktop and web-based deployments a snap.

If you didn't understand some of the terms used in this section, that's all right. You will encounter them again, with explanations, in later chapters.

The .NET Object

To fully understand software development in .NET, you must understand what an *object* is. (If you are familiar with object-oriented programming—OOP—you can probably skip down to the next section, although you will miss some really great content.) While some of this section's information will also appear in Chapter 8, it is so important to the discussion of .NET that a portion appears here as well.

Objects and Data

From a programming standpoint, a computer performs four basic tasks:

- It stores *data* in the computer's memory area.
- It supports processing of this *data* through basic operations, including addition and subtraction, Boolean algebra, and text string manipulation.
- It allows the user to interact with the *data* stored in memory.
- It provides a way to bring the *data* in and out of memory, through input and output devices such as keyboards and printers, and through long-term storage media such as hard drives.

The core of these four activities is *data*. Computers exist to manipulate data. Operating systems provide the basic foundation for these activities, but it is software applications that make these features—the ability to manipulate data—real and meaningful to the user. High-level programming languages are the primary tools used to develop these applications, each of which uses some general methods to make data manipulation features available to the programmer. Back in the good old days of assembly language development, if you knew the memory address of a piece of data, you could access and manipulate it directly. In early flavors of BASIC and in most other "procedural" languages, data was accessed through *variables*.

As languages grew in complexity and purpose, so did their view of data. In the LISP (short for "<u>L</u>ist <u>P</u>rocessing" or "<u>L</u>ots of <u>I</u>rritating <u>S</u>illy <u>P</u>arentheses") language, any data value exists within a larger *list* or *set* of data. But in .NET languages, data is viewed through the *object*.

Objects are collections of data values and associated source code. While in older BASIC dialects, each data element was more or less independent through its named variable, related data values in OOP languages can be grouped into objects. Object implementations often include source code designed to manipulate the data values of that object.

Objects generally represent some *thing*, often a thing that has a real-world counterpart, whether physical or conceptual. For instance, your code may include a House object that has data *fields* or *properties* for the address, the exterior paint color, and the number of people living in the house. Associated source code could manage that data; a Paint *method* could alter the color value used for the exterior paint.

The data and code elements within an object are called *members*. Some members are hidden inside the object and can be accessed only by the object's source code. Other members are more public; any code in your application can use them, not just that subset of application code found inside the object. Consider a television as an object (see Figure 1-1).

Figure 1-1. A TV: it's an object, not just objectionable

The public members of a TV are generally easy to use: the power button, channel selector, volume control, and so on. They are the conduits through which the user controls the data values of the TV (its video and audio output). There are also hidden members inside the TV; you could use these members to impact the picture and sound quality, although this would be a bad idea for most users. You don't want me messing with the internal members of your TV set, trust me. In the same way, an object doesn't want code outside the object to mess with its internal members *except through the public members*. I don't care how a TV works internally, as long as I can get pictures and sound out of it by using the controls that are exposed (power, channel, volume).

Objects and Interfaces

The public members of an object represent its *interface*. If code outside the object wants to manipulate the data belonging to that object, it uses the members of the interface. It doesn't have to figure out the hidden members or how they work, and that's good. It's especially good if those internal members ever change for any reason, which happens more often than you think. Consider how the internals of TVs have changed just in the past 30 years. Here's a drawing of the TV my family had when I was a kid. Compare it to modern flat-panel TVs available today (see Figure 1-2).

My family's TV was cool. It had an AM/FM stereophonic hi-fi radio, a turntable that could play 33 1/3, 45, and 78 rpm records, and a large 19-inch screen with a vivid, black-and-white, crystal-clear display. Two kids could hide behind it when playing hide-and-seek. And my friend who had the same model said that you could draw these really cool permanent lines on the screen with a magnet. Who cares that the speaker panels looked like vertical shag carpet? Who cares that the unit took up 30% of the floor space in the room? Who cares that you could cook sausages on top of it from the heat generated by the vacuum tubes? It was more than a TV; it was an *entertainment center*.

The TV of my childhood   A newfangled thing

Figure 1-2. Are those really TVs?

Now compare it to the wimpy little flat-panel job on its right. If you look closely, you find that the interface to the TV hasn't really changed much in three decades. There are still controls for power, volume, and channel selection (although Horizontal Hold and Vertical Hold are gone, sniff). What has changed is the internal configuration. Gone are the humming vacuum tubes, all replaced with efficient transistors and solid-state components. But it doesn't really make much difference to the TV viewer, since the public interface remains the same.

Objects in OOP development work in the same way. As long as the public interface remains the same, the object's actual code and internal data storage system—also known as the object's *implementation*—can change with no impact to the overall application.

Objects and Instances

The interface and implementation of an object really represent only its design; these are the parts the programmer creates through the source code. They exist even before the program is compiled and installed on the user's computer. In fact, at this level, objects really aren't even known as objects. In most languages (including Visual Basic), the word *class* indicates the implementation of an object's interface.

Once your application is installed on a computer and starts up, the code creates *instances* of the class to store actual data in memory. These instances are the true objects of OOP development. Depending on how your code is written, a single class implementation might be used to create one or even hundreds of objects in memory at the same time.

In .NET, all of your code and data values appear inside objects. Pretty much everything you see in a running program is an object: a Windows form is an object; a listbox control on that form is an object; and a single item in that listbox is an object.

The Parts of the .NET Framework

So, now you know all about objects, and you are probably thinking it's time to toss this book into the pile and start programming. But there are a few more parts of the .NET Framework still to discuss. These parts show up ad nauseam in the .NET documentation, and they each have a three-letter acronym (TLA), or thereabouts.

The Common Language Runtime

At the center of the .NET Framework is the *Common Language Runtime* (CLR), so named not because it is *common* or ordinary, but because all .NET-enabled languages share it in *common*. Everything you do in a .NET program is *managed* by the CLR. When you create a variable, thank the CLR and its data *management* system. When you say goodbye to a piece of data, thank the CLR and how it *manages* the release of data through its garbage collection system. Did you notice how the word *manage* keeps showing up in those sentences? My editor sure did. But "manage" is the mot juste, since that is what the CLR does. In fact, software written for the .NET Framework is called *managed code*. Any code that falls outside the CLR's control, including COM (ActiveX) components used by your .NET application, is known as *unmanaged code*.

The CLR is a lot like Los Angeles International Airport. If you have ever been to LAX, you know that there is a whole lot of activity going on. Airplanes arrive and depart each minute. Cars by the thousands enter and leave the two-level roadway and the central parking structures. People and pickpockets move constantly among the eight main terminals and the massive international terminal. There's a lot happening, but so much of it is managed. Planes cannot take off or land without approval from the control tower. Access points and gates manage the roadways and parking garages. Friendly, courteous TSA agents manage the flow of passengers and pickpockets into and out of the secure areas of the terminals.

The control and management structures in place at LAX ensure an orderly and secure flow of people between their planes and the city of Los Angeles. The control and management structures of the CLR ensure an orderly and secure flow of data between .NET code and the rest of the computer or connected network.

You'd probably like to know the secret of how the CLR is able to process programs written in any .NET language, including Visual Basic, C#, and FORTRAN. So would Microsoft's competitors. Actually, they do know, because there is no secret.

All .NET-enabled languages convert (i.e., "compile") your source code into *Microsoft Intermediate Language* (or *MSIL*, pronounced "missile," and more commonly abbreviated as just *IL*). For those of you familiar with assembly language, it looks a lot like that. For those of you not familiar with assembly language, it looks a lot like gibberish. For example, here is some Visual Basic source code for a *console application* (a non-Windows text-based program, like the old MS-DOS programs) that simply outputs "Hello, World!" from a code procedure called Main:

```
Module Module1
  Sub Main( )
     Console.WriteLine("Hello, World!")
  End Sub
End Module
```

That's the whole .NET program. When the Visual Basic compiler converts it to MSIL, the Main procedure looks like this (slightly modified to fit on this page):

```
.method public static void  Main( ) cil managed
{
  .entrypoint
  .custom instance void [mscorlib]System.
     STAThreadAttribute::.ctor() = ( 01 00 00 00 )
  // Code size       11 (0xb)
  .maxstack  8
  IL_0000:  ldstr     "Hello, World!"
  IL_0005:  call
     void [mscorlib]System.Console::WriteLine(string)
  IL_000a:  ret
} // end of method Module1::Main
```

Yes, it is gibberish. But that's OK, because it fulfills the International Computer Book Association's requirement that every Chapter 1 include a "Hello, World" code sample. Also, the CLR understands it, and that's what really counts in .NET. As long as you can get your code into IL, .NET will process it. The Visual Basic compiler just happens to generate IL for you. Other .NET language compilers, including C#, target IL as well. You can even write your own IL code, but you're probably reading the wrong book for that. Just to put your mind at ease, this will be the last bit of IL you will see in this book.

The Common Language Specification

Languages that claim to support .NET cannot just say so for any old reason. They truly have to be compatible with .NET and its workings. This is done through the *Common Language Specification* (CLS). The CLS defines a minimum set of features that a language must implement before it is considered to be .NET-compliant, or more accurately, CLS-compliant.

A language can go beyond that minimum if it wants, and .NET includes many additional features upon which language-specific features may be built. A language that implements only the minimum CLS-specified features may not be able to fully interact with components from languages that exceed the minimum specification. Visual Basic is, of course, CLS-compliant, and in fact it goes way beyond that minimum.

The Common Type System

Since the CLR is controlling your source code anyway, Microsoft thought it would be good to have it control the source code's data as well. The .NET Framework does this through its *Common Type System* (CTS), which defines all of the core data types and data mechanisms used in .NET programs. This includes all numeric, string, and Boolean value types. It also defines the *object*, the core data storage unit in .NET.

The CTS divides all objects into two buckets. The first bucket, called *value types*, stores actual data right in the bucket. If you have a 32-bit integer value, it gets put right in the value type bucket, ready for your immediate use. The other bucket contains *reference types*. When you look in this bucket, you see a map that tells you where to find the actual data somewhere else in the computer's memory. It seems like value types are easier to use, and they are, but they come with a few restrictions not imposed on reference types.

Programs and components written using the CTS standard can exchange data with one another without any hindrances or limitations. (A few .NET data types fall outside the "core" CTS types, but you need to avoid them only when you want to specifically interact with components that can use only the core CTS types.)

When you write your applications in Visual Basic, most of your code will appear in *classes*. Classes are reference types that include both data values and associated code. The data values included in a class are most often the core CTS data types, but they can also contain objects that you design elsewhere in your application. Visual Basic also includes *structures*, the weaker yet quicker younger brother of classes. Structures implement value types, and also include both data and code.

Classes and structures are just two of the data/code types available in Visual Basic. *Interfaces* are class and structure skeletons; they include design details of what should appear in a related class or structure, but don't include any actual implementation or working code. *Delegates* define a procedure "signature" sans implementation, and are used to support *events*, those actions (initiated by the user, by the operating system, or by your code) that tell your code, "Get to work now!" *Sea otters* are aquatic mammals that are curiously related to the weasel, and like to eat sea urchins. *Modules* are blocks of code and data, but unlike classes and structures, you can't create independent objects from them. *Enumerations* group a set of related integer values, generally for use as a list of choices.

In .NET parlance, all of these terms (class, structure, interface, delegate, module, and enumeration, but not sea otter) are known collectively as *types*. You probably already knew that .NET had some confusing elements in it; you wouldn't have bought a book about it if it were easy. But despite all the complex technology, it is this simple word, *type*, which causes the most confusion. You will likely experience some angst throughout this book each time you read it. The problem: it's too general. Not only does it refer to these core elements of the CTS, but it is also used when talking about just the Visual Basic-specific value types (more often called the Visual Basic "data types"). The nickname for structures is "user-defined types," yet another confusing use of "type." Programmers who used Visual Basic before its .NET incarnation also remember "Type" as the language statement used to create user-defined types. Arrrgh! Microsoft should have used some word other than *type* for the world of classes, interfaces, enumerations, and so on. "Banana" would have been a better choice since it is only sometimes used to discuss software. But "type" *is* the word, so you better get used to seeing it. I will try to include as much context as possible when using the word throughout this volume.

The members of a type usually consist of simple data fields and code procedures, but you can also include other types as members. That is, a class can include a *nested* class if it needs to. Only certain types support nesting—see Chapter 8 for details. I also talk about *access levels* in that chapter. Each member has an access level that says what code can use that member. There are five access levels, ranging from *public* (anybody and their brother can use the member) to *private* (you have to be inside the type to even know it's there).

Chapter 6 discusses the .NET type system in greater detail, including the information you crave on classes, structures, and other bananas.

.NET Class Libraries

Computers are actually quite stupid. Whereas I can count all the way to 17, a computer tops out at 1; it only knows the digits 0 and 1. The CPU includes a set of simple operators used to manipulate the digits 0 and 1, and a few more operators that compare 1s and 0s in complex ways. The computer's last great trick is its ability to move 0s and 1s into and out of memory, but whoop-de-doo. Sure it does these things at nearly the speed of light, but can it calculate π to 3 million decimal places?

Well, actually it can. Computers don't know anything about the letters of the alphabet, and they really can handle only the digits 0 and 1, yet here I am using a computer to write an award-winning book. It is the ability to combine the simple 1-bit data values and operators into increasingly complex *libraries* of functionality that makes useful computers possible.*

The .NET Framework is built upon decades of increasingly complex functionality. When you install the .NET Framework, the CLR and its associated type system

---

* If you want to read a truly fascinating book on how complex software and hardware operations are formed from the most basic uses of 0 and 1, read Charles Petzold's *Code: The Hidden Language of Computer Hardware and Software* (Microsoft Press).

represent the core of the framework. By itself, the framework includes all the basic functionality needed to let you add 2 and 2 together and correctly get 4. And as a business application developer, you spend a lot of time doing just that. But what if you want to do something more complex, something that you know some other programmer has already done, like sorting a list of names or drawing a colored circle on a form? To get that answer, go to the *class libraries*, the .NET Class Libraries. These libraries, installed with the framework, include a lot of prewritten (increasingly complex) functionality that you don't have to write from scratch.

There are two class libraries in .NET: the *Base Class Library* (BCL) and the *Framework Class Library* (FCL). The BCL is smaller, and contains the most essential features that a program just couldn't do without. It includes only those classes that are an absolute must for supporting applications on the framework if Microsoft were to, say, port the framework to Linux.

The FCL is larger, and includes everything else Microsoft thought you would want to have in your programs, but was not absolutely essential to have in the BCL. Don't even ask how many classes there are in the FCL; you don't want to know. I bet that Microsoft doesn't even really know the full number. I am convinced that those wacky pranksters at Microsoft have included "gag" classes in the FCL, but they are so deeply buried that few programmers ever encounter them.

With thousands (yes, thousands!) of classes, enumerations, interfaces, and other types included in the BCL and FCL, you would think that it would be hard to find just the class you need. But it's not that difficult, at least not overwhelmingly difficult. The .NET Framework includes a feature called *namespaces*. All types in .NET appear in a hierarchy—a tree-like structure—with just a few minimal entries at the root. Each *node* in the hierarchy is a namespace. You uniquely identify any class or other type in the libraries by naming all the namespaces, from the root down to the local namespace that contains the class, separating each node with a period (.).

Unlike most hierarchies that have all branches starting from a single root node, the .NET namespace hierarchy has multiple root nodes. The largest root namespace is named System. It includes many classes, but it also includes several next-tier hierarchy nodes (namespaces). Since the framework includes features for both Windows-based and web-based application development, there are namespaces that contain the Windows-specific and web-specific development features. These namespaces appear just within the System namespace, and are called Windows and Web. All code related to on-screen forms in the Windows namespace appears in the Forms namespace, and within this namespace is the actual class that implements a form, named Form. Figure 1-3 presents an image of this namespace subset.

In Visual Basic, you identify a class by qualifying it with all its namespaces, starting from its root namespace. The Form class has the following fully qualified name:

```
System.Windows.Forms.Form
```

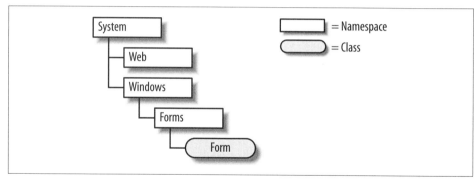

Figure 1-3. A hierarchy of namespaces and classes

All classes and types exist somewhere in the hierarchy, although not every class descends from System. Many of the supporting features specific to Visual Basic appear in the Microsoft.VisualBasic namespace, which has "Microsoft" as its root node instead of "System." When you create new projects in Visual Basic, the name of the project is, by default, a new top-level node in the hierarchy. If you create a new Windows application named WindowsApplication1, the default "Form1" form has the following fully qualified name:

    WindowsApplication1.Form1

This new application's namespace is not just a second-class appendage hanging off the System namespace. It is fully integrated into the full .NET namespace hierarchy; the WindowsApplication1 namespace is a root node, just like the System and Microsoft root nodes. Visual Basic includes features that let you alter the default namespace for your application, or place one of the application's classes in a specific namespace. You can even place your application's classes in the System namespace branch. Changing WindowsApplication1 to System.MySuperApp moves Form1 to:

    System.MySuperApp.Form1

If your application is actually a component or library destined for use in programs, your app's classes will appear in the namespace you specify when the other program loads your component into its application area. Your code will look like it is part of the Microsoft-supplied namespaces. Is that cool or what?

Although you can add your classes to the System namespace, you will incur the wrath of other .NET programmers. The System namespace is supposed to be for "system" (read: Microsoft-supplied) features, and that's it. Also, there's a chance that two vendors might use the same namespace path. So, to avoid potential namespace conflicts *and* dirty looks from other programmers, you should name your application's classes as:

    CompanyName.ApplicationName.ClassName

A single class or other type cannot be split across multiple namespaces, even within the same hierarchy branch. However, two classes or types may share a common name in different namespaces, even within the same branch.

All classes of the BCL and FCL appear intermingled throughout the entire namespace hierarchy. This means that you cannot necessarily tell whether a particular class is from the BCL or the FCL. Frankly, it doesn't really matter; your code won't care which library a class comes from, as long as it is available for use on the user's workstation.

Just before the release of Visual Studio 2008, Microsoft announced that it would make the source code for much of the Framework Class Library version 3.5 available for developers to review. This means that programmers who want to know how Microsoft sorts a list of names in memory or draws a colored circle on a form will get at least a partial glimpse of how it is done.

Assemblies and Manifests

An *assembly* is a "unit of deployment" for the parts of a .NET application or library. In 99.9% of cases, an assembly is simply a .NET executable file (an *.exe* file) or a .NET library of classes and other types (a *.dll* file). It is possible to split an assembly among multiple files, but usually it is one file for one assembly.

What makes an ordinary *.exe* or *.dll* file an assembly is the presence of a *manifest*. For single-file assemblies, the manifest appears right in the file; it can also appear in a file of its own. The manifest is a chunk of data that lists important details about the assembly, including its name, version information, default culture, information on referencing external assemblies and types, and a list of all the files contained in the assembly. The CLR will not recognize an assembly without its manifest, so don't lose it.

Assemblies can include an optional *strong name*. This helps to ensure the integrity and authenticity of an assembly through a digital signature attached to the manifest. The strong name uses public key cryptography to guarantee that the assembly is unique and has not been tampered with. Visual Studio and the .NET Framework include tools that let you add a strong name to an assembly.

When you deploy your application, you will normally place all assembly files, configuration files, and any related files specific to your application into the application's install directory, just like in the old Jurassic days before .NET. Shared assemblies designed to be used by more than one application on a single machine can be stored in the *Global Assembly Cache* (GAC). All assemblies placed in the GAC must have strong names. Some systems may allow only the system administrator to add assemblies to the GAC.

Metadata and Attributes

Assemblies are brought to you by the letter *m*. In addition to manifests and type members, assemblies also contain *metadata*. The application code and data elements stored in an assembly parallel the code and data items found in the related Visual

Basic source code; for each type and member in your source code, there is associated executable code in the deployed assembly. This makes sense, and is not much of a change from pre-.NET deployments. What is different is that the Visual Basic compiler now attaches additional information—metadata—to each type and member in the assembly. This metadata documents the name of the associated content, information about required data types, information on class inheritance for the element, and security permissions required before the element can be used by the user or other software.

Your Visual Basic source code can enhance the metadata for any element of your assembly through *attributes*. The metadata generated by an attribute is more than just some ID number. Attributes implement full .NET classes, with their own data values and associated logic. Any .NET code that knows how to process attributes can examine the attributes for a type or member and take action as needed. This includes Visual Studio, the Visual Basic compiler, and your own custom applications.

How's this for a mundane example: the .NET Framework includes an attribute named ObsoleteAttribute. This attribute lets you mark types or members of your assembly as obsolete or no longer supported. (Visual Studio uses this attribute to display a warning whenever you attempt to use an out-of-date BCL or FCL feature.) To use the attribute, add it to a member of your application using angle brackets:

```
Class MyClassWithOldMembers
    <ObsoleteAttribute> Sub DoSomeWork( )
    End Sub
End Class
```

This code defines a single class (MyClassWithOldMembers) with a single member procedure (DoSomeWork), a procedure that clearly does some work. The procedure is tagged with the ObsoleteAttribute attribute. By custom, all attribute names end in the word *Attribute*. You can leave off this portion of the word if you wish, as long as the resultant word does not conflict with any Visual Basic language keyword:

```
Class MyClassWithOldMembers
    <Obsolete> Sub DoSomeWork( )
    End Sub
End Class
```

When you compile the class and store it in an assembly, the <ObsoleteAttribute> attribute is stored as part of DoSomeWork's definition. You can now write a separate Visual Basic application that scans an assembly and outputs the name and status of every type and member it finds. When that analysis program encounters the obsolete member, it will detect ObsoleteAttribute in the metadata, and output the status:

```
DoSomeWork Procedure: Obsolete, don't use it!
```

Most attributes are designed with a specific purpose in mind. Some attributes instruct Visual Studio to display the members of a class in specific ways. You've probably already played with the form-editing features of Visual Studio to design a simple Windows desktop application. When you add a control (such as a button or a listbox) to a form and select that control, Visual Studio lets you edit details of that control through the Properties panel area (see Figure 1-4).

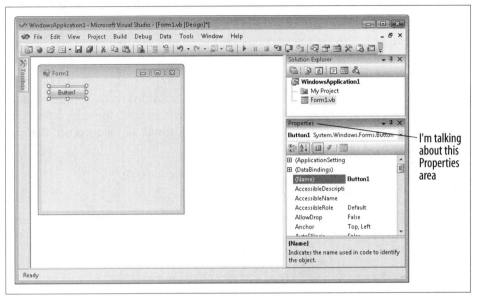

Figure 1-4. The Properties panel in Visual Studio

The Button control is implemented as a class, and many of its class members appear in the Properties panel, but not all of them. When the Button class was designed, attributes were added to its members that tell Visual Studio which members should appear in the Properties panel, and which should not. Visual Studio dutifully examines these attributes, and displays only the requested properties.

Versioning

Like yours, my applications are perfect from their initial release, and I never have a reason to modify them or add features. But there are software development organizations—including one large company that, so as not to cause embarrassment, I will refer to only by its initial letter of *M*—that feel the need to "one-up" their competition by coming out with "improved" versions of their previously released software offerings. Let's say that "M" happened to have a popular word processor that includes version 1.0 of a spellcheck component. "M" also happens to sell an email tool that depends specifically on version 1.0 of that same shared component. If, in a show of competitive machismo, "M" releases an update to the word processor *and* the spellcheck component (now version 2.0), what happens to the email tool's spellchecking ability?

Not that this ever happens in real life. But if it did, the replacement of a vital shared component with a newer but somewhat incompatible version could cause real problems. A related problem is the deployment of multiple versions of a single component on the same workstation, all in different directories. Can any of them be safely deleted?

.NET solves these problems through *versioning*. All assemblies that use shared components identify exactly which versions of the shared components they require. Although an application can be reconfigured to use a later version, it will use only the originally specified version of a shared component by default.

Multiple versions of a single shared component can be added to the GAC, a feature called *side-by-side deployment*. The CLR ensures that the right application links up with the right component. You can even run applications simultaneously that use different versions of the same component.

From Source Code to EXE

Now you know pretty much everything there is to know about .NET except for that pesky programming thing. Before delving into some actual code, let's take a little snack break and examine the lifetime of an application, from start to finish (see Figure 1-5).

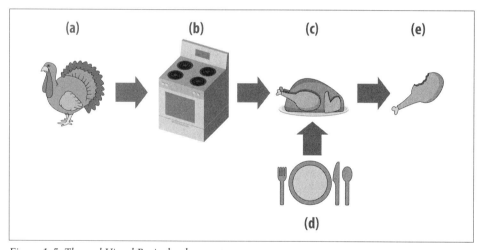

Figure 1-5. The real Visual Basic development process

So, here's what happens, step by step:

1. You, as the programmer, are responsible for preparing the basic ingredients (a) of the application. For Visual Basic programs, this means creating one or more source code files with a *.vb* extension. Your ingredients may also include other support files, such as resource files (text and graphics files, often used for multi-language support).

2. Your application is cooked by the Visual Basic compiler (b). The result is an assembly, complete with a manifest and metadata. The output is actually semi-compiled MSIL and includes ready-to-execute versions of the original source code's types and members, including all member and type names. All this content can be "decompiled" (returned back to full MSIL, although not to full Visual Basic) using a tool named *ildasm.exe* (the Microsoft Intermediate Language Disassembler), which is included with the .NET Framework. Since you probably don't want just anyone disassembling your application and looking at the code, Microsoft (and other third parties) also supplies an *obfuscator*, which sufficiently scrambles the content of your code to make it just difficult enough to discourage prying eyes.

3. The assembly (c) is deployed to the user's workstation. A few different methods are used to deploy the application, including (1) generating a standard Windows Installer setup package; (2) generating a ClickOnce deployment; or (3) performing an xcopy install, which involves nothing more than copying the EXE assembly itself to the destination machine. No matter which deployment method you choose, the .NET runtime (d) must also be installed on the user's workstation.

4. The user eats—I mean runs—the program (e). The CLR does a final *just-in-time* (JIT) compile of the MSIL assembly, to prepare it for use on the local platform. It then presents the application to the user, and manages all aspects of the application while it runs. The user experiences a level of joy and satisfaction rarely encountered when using other software applications.

As with the preparation of a Thanksgiving meal, the actual development process is somewhat more involved than just reading a paragraph (or a recipe book) about it. But it's not so difficult that it can't be put in a book like this one.

What About Visual Studio and Visual Basic?

Wait a minute, what about Visual Studio? That last section didn't even mention it. And it didn't need to, since *you do not need to use Visual Studio to develop, compile, deploy, or run Visual Basic applications*. The entire .NET Framework—including the Visual Basic compiler—is available for free from Microsoft's web site; download it and use it to develop and deploy applications that are every bit as powerful and complex as, well, Visual Studio.

The July 1983 issue of *Datamation* magazine includes an article from manly reader Ed Post, titled "Real Programmers Don't Use Pascal."* I highly recommend that you read this article, as it will help you quickly separate the real programmers from the "quiche eaters." And when you do, run away as fast as you can from the real programmers.

---

* *Datamation* 29 (7): July 1983, pp. 263–265. I also found the text of the article on the Internet by doing a search on the title. A similar version of the text, with only minor editorial changes, also exists under the title "Real Programmers Don't Write Pascal."

Oh, sure, they can reconstruct your source code from the obfuscated .NET assembly, but they will be useless on a team project using Visual Studio.

A "real programmer" could code any .NET application using Notepad, and it would run. Actually, real programmers would use Emacs or vi instead of Notepad (since Windows does not include a keypunch interface), but the results would be the same. They would growl as you blissfully type away in Visual Studio's elegant, well-designed, and fully customizable and extensible user interface. They would gripe and bare their cheese-cracker-with-peanut-butter-encrusted teeth at you while you use the IntelliSense and AutoCompletion features built into the Visual Studio code editor. They would consume another slice of quiche-shaped cold pizza while you drag-and-drop both Windows and web-based user interfaces.

Yes, the real programmer could generate full applications with just a text (or hex) editor and a .NET compiler, but you would get the glory, since you would be done in a fraction of the time it would take the FORTRAN lover to eek out his code.

Visual Studio 2008

Since this is a book on Visual Basic development and not on Visual Studio usage, I won't be delving too much into Visual Studio's features or its user interface elements. It is a great application, and its tight integration with the .NET Framework makes it the best tool for developing applications with .NET. But as the real programmer would tell you, it is really just a glorified text editor. Visual Studio hides a lot of the complexity of .NET code, and its automatic generation of the code needed to build your application's user interface is a must-have. Most of its features exist to simplify the process of adding code to your application.

Although I will not be including a 20-page review of Visual Studio right here, you will find images of Visual Studio throughout the text, placed so as to advance your understanding of the topics under discussion in each chapter. When you start up Visual Studio for the first time, it displays the Start Page. (See Figure 1-6. The screenshots in this book are taken from the Professional Edition of Visual Studio 2008.)

Visual Studio 2008 is the fourth major release of the product since .NET's initial introduction in 2002. Each release (in 2002, 2003, 2005, and 2008) corresponds to a related release of the .NET Framework (versions 1.0, 1.1, 2.0, and 3.5, respectively) and of the .NET implementation of Visual Basic. The 2008 release of Visual Studio is major. It is packed with new usability features, and comes in four delicious flavors:

Visual Studio 2008 Express Edition

> This entry-level product is geared toward the home hobbyist or weekend programmer who wants to learn .NET and one of its core programming languages, but won't be snuggling up to it on a daily basis. Visual Studio 2008 Express Edition is actually multiple Express Edition language products promoted together, including Visual Basic 2008 Express Edition. Microsoft's goal is to introduce as

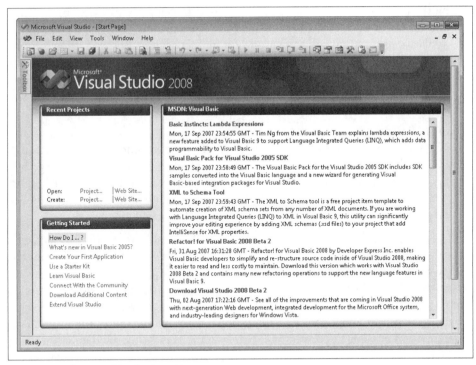

Figure 1-6. The Visual Studio Start Page

many people as possible to the joys of .NET programming, so it offers the Express Edition products at no cost. This edition includes a simplified Visual Studio-like user interface, but it does impose a few restrictions on your program-crafting ability. You can still edit the source code directly and craft applications of any complexity, but the Express UI won't always assist you with this. For instance, you cannot develop web applications with the Visual Basic Express product unless you install the separate Visual Web Developer 2008 product. Also, Express doesn't include much support for deployment; applications designed with the Express Edition are generally expected to be used on your own workstation only.

Visual Studio 2008 Standard Edition

Visual Studio's Standard Edition is just like the Express Edition, with a few extras thrown in, such as multiple-language support, web development tools, and deployment support through both ClickOnce and Windows Installer methods. SQL Server 2005 Express Edition is included.

Visual Studio 2008 Professional Edition

This is the minimum level required by programmers who will develop applications on a daily basis for money. It's the version that I use, and it includes all the "power" features needed by a single programmer for both desktop and web-based development. The straightjacketed Express user interface is out, replaced by the full Visual Studio "mighty" Integrated Development Environment (IDE) and all documentation. Also included are special tools that help you develop applications for Microsoft Office, and for mobile devices. But wait, there's more. You also get SQL Server 2005 Developer Edition. All instructions in this book that relate to using the development environment refer to the Professional Edition. But if you are following along using the Express or Standard Edition, you will be just fine since the interfaces are quite similar.

Visual Studio Team System 2008

The crème de la crème of the Visual Studio product line is Team System. It includes features needed by development teams that work on projects together, features such as project management tools and source code control. Visual Studio Team System 2008 Team Foundation Server, a separate product, can be installed on a shared server, and enhances the features of the Team System package.

SQL Server 2008, the latest edition of Microsoft's flagship database product, was officially launched on the same day as Visual Studio 2008. Unfortunately, "launch" had two different meanings depending on which of the products you were talking about. For Visual Studio 2008, "launch" meant you could download the product from Microsoft's web site several months before the launch event. For SQL Server, a mirror was used to allow access to the product a few months after the event. That difference was enough to prevent SQL Server 2008 from being the database version bundled with Visual Studio. But you do get SQL Server 2005 in your Visual Studio goodie bag, and you can always upgrade if needed.

Beyond the database support, Visual Studio 2008 has been endowed with several new usability and feature enhancements:

LINQ-specific features

We'll discuss the new LINQ feature in Chapter 17. Beyond the code changes added to .NET to support LINQ, Visual Studio includes special designers that assist you in programming with LINQ.

Support for Windows Presentation Foundation projects

Windows Presentation Foundation, formerly code-named Avalon, is a new XML-based user interface system supported by Windows for both desktop and web-based applications. Visual Studio 2008 lets you create WPF-based application or control projects. This book discusses Windows Presentation Foundation briefly in Chapter 18.

Improved HTML (web page) editor

The new HTML editor improves on the previous editions found in earlier releases of Visual Studio. The 2008 release includes a "split view" editor showing HTML and WYSIWYG views simultaneously (see Figure 1-7). Cascading Style Sheets (CSS) finally get their due with a new CSS style editor and IntelliSense support for CSS content.

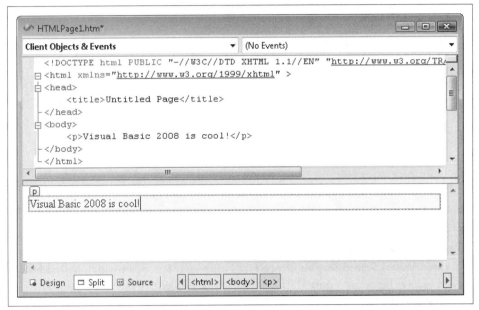

Figure 1-7. Have it both ways: HTML markup and display

Targeted library support

Earlier releases of Visual Studio were closely tied to the related release of .NET. Visual Studio 2008 continues that tradition through its association with version 3.5 of the .NET Framework. However, you can now target earlier versions of .NET (back through version 2.0) in Visual Studio 2008 with just the click of the mouse.

Enhanced debugging support

Visual Studio 2008 includes better support for remote debugging, especially on Windows Vista. But the most amazing of the new debugging features is the ability to step into the source code for the .NET Framework libraries, with Visual Studio dynamically obtaining the right version of the source code based on your project type and framework version.

Transparent IntelliSense

IntelliSense is a productivity tool that helps speed you along in your code-crafting frenzy. But sometimes the IntelliSense windows that popped up would obscure your source code. Visual Studio 2008 now lets you look through the IntelliSense list window just by holding down the Ctrl key (see Figure 1-8).

JavaScript IntelliSense and debugging support

Although Visual Studio once claimed amnesia concerning Java and JavaScript, it now fully embraces the latter. This enhanced JavaScript environment simplifies the creation of new Ajax applications. While not specifically needed for Visual Basic, this new support is a big plus for those who develop web-based applications.

```
Public Class Form1
    Private Sub Form1_Load(ByVal sender As Object, ByVal e As System.EventArgs)
        Me.|
    End Sub
End Class          AcceptButton
                   AccessibleDescription
                 ▾ ActivateMdiChild
                 ⚲ AddOwnedForm
                 ⚲ AllowTransparency
                 ⚲ Anchor
                 ⚲ AutoScaleFactor
                 ⚲ AutoScroll
                 ⚲ AutoScrollMargin
                 ⚲ AutoScrollMinSize
                    Common            All
```

Figure 1-8. Seeing right through Visual Studio's tricks

Despite all these great new features, Microsoft still refuses to implement the most requested Visual Studio feature, Procedure AutoCompletion, in which Visual Studio would create the entire content of a source code procedure based on your entry of its name and the use of the Ctrl-Space bar key combination. Instead, Microsoft fritters away its time on other so-called productivity features. With Procedure Auto-Completion, you could write entire applications in minutes. Until that feature becomes available, you and I will have to continue writing software, crafting the quality code that users have come to expect from our fingers.

Summary

Nearly two decades ago, Visual Basic transformed the Windows development landscape with its drag-and-drop programming model and its glitzy event-driven development structure. But Windows has changed a lot since those days of Windows 3.*x*. As Windows has changed, Visual Basic has changed right along with it. Visual Basic 2008, through its association with the .NET Framework, provides access to the programming tools needed to develop quality applications for the Windows desktop, the Internet, and the next generation of mobile devices.

And Microsoft is not halting this progress with the 2008 release. The next version of Visual Basic, code-named both VBx and Hawaii, promises to include even more advanced features. That release will be built on top of Microsoft's Dynamic Language Runtime (DLR), allowing it to freely interact with libraries from languages such as Ruby and Python.

Project

Welcome to the "Project" section, the part of each chapter where you have an opportunity to get "hands-on" with Visual Studio 2008 and Visual Basic. Development of the Library Project, the main project focus of this book, formally begins in Chapter 3, but there's still project work to do in the meantime. In this chapter, I'll introduce you to the sample source code provided with this book, and we'll take a stab at using it.

Since most "Project" sections, including this one, will involve Visual Studio, make sure you have it installed and ready to use. Also, since each "Project" section is designed for you to use interactively with the supplied source code, I will assume that you have downloaded and installed the source code (see Appendix A for instructions), and are viewing the source code with one eye while you read this section with the other. I will print sections of the source code in the book, but with tens of thousands of source code lines in the Library Project, I will not be able to print every line here. You will certainly get a lot out of each "Project" section by simply reading it, but you will get even more if you have access to the full source code.

In this chapter's project, we'll load a sample program into Visual Studio and run it. There are two ways to do this. The first way is just to open the existing project directly from the installation directory. Browse to the directory where you installed this book's source code, open the *Chapter 1* subdirectory, and double-click the *Chapter1.vbproj* file. This will open the project directly in Visual Studio, ready to use.

The second way is to use the chapter-specific project templates to create new projects in Visual Studio. The Setup program for this book's source code modifies your installation of Visual Studio, adding new entries in the New Project dialog window. Each of these new "project templates" can be used as the starting point for a new Visual Basic project. To load the Chapter 1 sample program using the template, start Visual Studio. The Start Page will appear, as shown way back in Figure 1-6. From the File menu, select New Project to display the New Project dialog window (see Figure 1-9).

Your New Project dialog window may differ slightly depending on the features you chose to install with Visual Studio. The available projects are grouped by the description in the "Project types" field. For instance, Figure 1-9 shows the various default project types you can create in Visual Basic, including Windows Forms Application (a standard desktop application for the Windows platform), Class Library (a DLL of class-defined features), and Console Application (command-line, text-based applications). To create a new application, first select the project type, select the template to use, and finally enter the name of the new project in the Name field. Clicking the OK button creates a new project.

Figure 1-9. The New Project dialog window: so many choices

To use the sample Chapter 1 project, select the Programming Visual Basic 2008 entry within the Visual Basic project type, and then select Chapter 1 Sample from the Templates field (see Figure 1-10). Finally, click OK to create the new sample project.

Figure 1-10. Selecting the Chapter 1 Sample project

Once the project loads, access the program's main form by double-clicking on the *Form1.vb* file in the Solution Explorer (see Figure 1-11).

This default presentation of Visual Studio Professional Edition includes three editing components: (1) the main editing area, where the view of "Form1" appears; (2) the Solution Explorer panel, which provides access to all files included in the project; and (3) the Properties panel, which lets you edit various aspects of the currently selected item in the main editor area or elsewhere in the user interface.

The sample project is pretty basic. It includes one form with a single action button. Clicking this button in the running application displays a simple message. Run the project by pressing the F5 key. When the main form appears, clicking on the "Go Ahead, Click Me!" button displays the message in Figure 1-12 (goal, sweet goal).

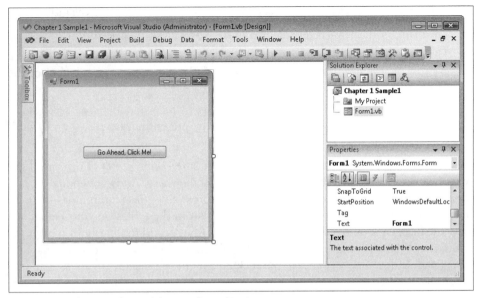

Figure 1-11. The main form of the sample application

Figure 1-12. Hello again, world!

So, what about all that complex code I had to write to develop this multifaceted application? It's all there for the viewing. From the Solution Explorer panel, right-click on the Form1.vb entry and select View Code from the shortcut menu. (As with most source code samples presented in this book, I have had to slightly adjust the code so that it displays properly on the printed page. Generally, this involves splitting a long logical line into two or more shorter ones.)

```vb
Public Class Form1
    Private Sub Button1_Click(ByVal sender As System.Object, _
        ByVal e As System.EventArgs) Handles Button1.Click
        MsgBox("Hello, World!")
    End Sub
End Class
```

We'll get into the intricacies of such code in later chapters, but here is the gist:

- The main form, Form1, is represented in code by a class, named "Form1."

- The form includes a command button named Button1 that exposes a Click event. This event is handled by the Button1_Click procedure, a member of the Form1 class.

- The "event handler," Button1_Click, includes a single statement, a MsgBox statement. This statement does the heavy lifting by presenting the ever-friendly message box to the world.

That's all the code that I wrote for *Form1.vb*. It sure seems pretty short for all the work it does. There has to be more code hiding somewhere. And sure enough, a half dozen or so additional files are included in the project. Visual Studio hides these by default, since it manages some or all of the content in these files on your behalf. To view the files, click on the Show All Files button (the second toolbar button from the left in the Solution Explorer panel). Look at all those files! To see the additional files associated with Form1, expand it by clicking on the plus sign (+) to its left (see Figure 1-13).

Figure 1-13. Viewing hidden files through the Solution Explorer

Double-click on the Form1.Designer.vb entry to see the code that Visual Studio automatically wrote for this form. (Dramatic pause.) Wow! Look at all that scary code. Actually, it's not that bad. By the end of this book, you will have a firm grasp on all of it. Here in Chapter 1, it's not really necessary to comprehend it all, but there are a few interesting lines to note. I'm including line numbers to make it easier to find the matching code in Visual Studio. If you want to view line numbers in Visual Studio (Professional Edition instructions listed here):

1. Select the Tools → Options menu item to display Visual Studio's options.

2. Select Text Editor → Basic → Editor from the tree view to the left. If the "Show all settings" field is checked, the last component you click in the tree view will be General, not Editor.

3. Select (check) the Line Numbers field on the right.

4. Click OK to apply the changes.

If you're new to Visual Basic or .NET programming, don't worry now if this code doesn't make sense; it will all become clear as you pass through the pages of this book.

```
01  <Global.Microsoft.VisualBasic.CompilerServices. _
        DesignerGenerated( )> _
02  Partial Public Class Form1

20  <System.Diagnostics.DebuggerNonUserCode( )> _
21  Protected Overloads Overrides Sub Dispose _
        (ByVal disposing As Boolean)
```

These lines show *attributes* in action. These two attributes (DesignerGenerated and DebuggerNonUserCode) are somewhat like the Obsolete attribute discussed earlier, in that they provide some informational identity to the related code. DesignerGenerated modifies the entire section of Form1's code, whereas DebuggerNonUserCode modifies only the Dispose member. For clarity, both attributes include their full namespace paths. The Global keyword at the beginning of the DesignerGenerated attribute is actually a Visual Basic keyword that says, "Start at the very tippy-top of the namespace hierarchy; this is not a relative path."

```
02  Partial Public Class Form1
```

Did you see the word *Partial* right there on line 02? I know I did. Hey, wait a minute; "Public Class Form1" also appeared in the *Form1.vb* file, but without the Partial keyword. Visual Basic 2008 includes a feature that lets you divide a single class (Form1 in this case) among multiple source code files by including the Partial keyword with at least one of the parts. Pretty cool, eh? It allows Visual Studio to add complex initialization code for your form (as found in this *Form1.Designer.vb* file) without it bothering your main source code file (*Form1.vb*).

```
03  Inherits System.Windows.Forms.Form
```

The Inherits keyword defines the inheritance relationship between this new Form1 class and the previously written System.Windows.Forms.Form class. Form is the "base" class and Form1 is the "derived" class; Form1 inherits all the functionality of the Form class, including its initial look and feel. I'll discuss these class relationships in more detail in Chapter 8.

```
44  Friend WithEvents Button1 As System.Windows.Forms.Button
```

Line 44 defines the "Go Ahead, Click Me!" button that appears in the center of the form. All controls that appear on your form are separate instances of classes. (Friend is a declaration statement described in Chapter 6.) The WithEvents keyword indicates that this instance of the Button class will respond to events, such as a user clicking on it with the mouse. This line doesn't actually create an instance of the Button class; that happens back on line 22.

```
22  Me.Button1 = New System.Windows.Forms.Button
```

The New keyword creates new instances of classes. In this case, that new instance is assigned to the Button1 class member defined on line 44. At this moment, Button1 is a default instance of the Button class; it doesn't have any of its custom settings, such as its size and position, or the "Go Ahead, Click Me!" display text. All of that is set in lines 27 to 31:

```
27  Me.Button1.Location = New System.Drawing.Point(64, 104)
28  Me.Button1.Name = "Button1"
29  Me.Button1.Size = New System.Drawing.Size(152, 23)
30  Me.Button1.TabIndex = 0
31  Me.Button1.Text = "Go Ahead, Click Me!"
```

Finally, the button is "glued" onto the form on line 38:

```
38  Me.Controls.Add(Me.Button1)
```

This adds the Button1 instance to the list of Controls managed by Form1. The Me keyword used throughout this code refers to the Form1 class itself, so Me.Button1 refers to the Button1 class member specifically in the current Form1 class.

Most of the code in this file appears in the InitializeComponent member procedure:

```
21  Private Sub InitializeComponent()
        ...
43  End Sub
```

When Visual Basic creates an instance of Form1 to display on the screen, it calls the InitializeComponent procedure to do the work of adding the controls to the form. Actually, Visual Basic calls the form's *constructor*, which in turn calls InitializeComponent. Constructors are special class members that perform any needed initialization on a class instance. They are called automatically by .NET each time a class instance is created. In Visual Basic, all constructors use the name *New*, as with the following code:

```
Friend Class ClassWithConstructor
    Public Sub New()
        ' ----- All initialization code goes here.
    End Sub
End Class
```

I'll talk much more about constructors in Chapter 8, but for now, locate the constructor in the code for Form1. (Very long pause.) What? There is no constructor? So, if there isn't a constructor, how is the InitializeComponent member ever called?

That's what I'd like to know. Actually, when the Visual Basic compiler generates the MSIL code for `Form1`, it adds a constructor silently, a constructor that calls `InitializeComponent`. How about that! Why didn't Microsoft simply include the constructor's code right in the source code? It's a simplicity-for-the-programmer thing. Microsoft needed to have a default constructor that would call `InitializeComponent`, but it didn't want a conflict to arise if you added your own default constructor in the non-Designer file. So it hid all the code until it came time to actually compile the form. Clearly, it's all rather hush-hush, so let's move on.

Well, that's pretty much the entire code, at least the part that matters to us now. Although we will rarely, if ever, examine the Visual Studio-generated code for the forms in the Library Project, it's good to see what's going on behind the scenes. If you were a Visual Basic 6 programmer, you probably looked at the source code for your forms through Notepad at one time or another. If you did, you noticed that the form and all its controls were defined with a hierarchy of special commands, and not with actual Visual Basic code. In .NET, that's all changed; the form and all its controls are created with ordinary Visual Basic code, so you can access it all and see what is really going on.

Now, turn to Chapter 2, where I delve into the Visual Basic language itself.

CHAPTER 2

Introducing Visual Basic

It was a dark and stormy night. Hector gazed wearily through his bloodshot eyes, through the black-rimmed corrective lenses, and through the haze of the fluorescent overhead lights at the phosphor-enriched display. Had it really been four months since he started the six-month project? Did his boss really threaten to fire him after seeing his progress? It seemed like all of those MS-DOS programs he had written for the company over the years meant nothing. Why did he promise to port the company's main internal system to Windows? In a moment of despair, tears streamed down his cheeks, diluting his last remaining can of Jolt Cola.

It's 8:00 a.m. A loud thump on Hector's desk brings him suddenly out of his slumber, the drool still trickling from the corner of his mouth. What's that? What's that box on his desk? "V-i-s-u-a-l B-a-s-i-c?" A note on the box says to rewrite his code in "this." Desperate to try anything, Hector installs the three floppy disks on his '386 powerhouse.

Six weeks later, Hector has completed the project, ahead of schedule, feature-complete, and with the accolades of his boss and department. And it's all due to Visual Basic. But VB didn't just improve his programming life. Overall, he's happier, has kicked the caffeine habit, is able to bench-press 300 pounds, no longer walks with a limp, has increased libido, and has whiter teeth. "Thank you, Visual Basic 1.0!"

The History of the Visual Basic Revolution

It's possible that I got a few of the details wrong in Hector's life. But for many business developers, Visual Basic 1.0 was a breath of fresh air. It's not that they could do more with Visual Basic; programs written in C were more powerful and had greater flexibility. But business programmers didn't always need that flexibility back in the transition from MS-DOS. They just wanted to manage data, and they didn't want to worry about how to present every little pixel on the screen. Visual Basic provided the tools to write applications quickly and with much less effort than that required by other Windows development tools and languages.

Visual Basic's simplicity was embraced by developers everywhere, but the honeymoon quickly wore off. Given the speed at which programs of reasonable quality could be cranked out with Visual Basic, programmers and businesses began demanding more. And Microsoft responded. Visual Basic 2.0 and 3.0 were released in quick succession in 1992 and 1993, providing enhanced database integration and additional visual development features. Version 4.0, released in 1996, introduced 32-bit programming to the language, and support for the already-popular Windows 95 platform. Two more quick releases—Visual Basic 5.0 in 1997 and Visual Basic 6.0 in 1998—added even more features and complexity to the otherwise "basic" language, features supporting some but not all object-oriented programming (OOP) techniques, ActiveX control development, and web-based logic coding. Microsoft had even integrated the core Visual Basic engine—christened Visual Basic for Applications, or VBA—into its suite of Office products, proclaiming it as the new official macro language and making the engine available to any third party that wanted to do the same.

Seven years after its initial introduction, Visual Basic had taken the programming world by storm. Millions of developers were using the language, including in-house developers at Fortune 500 companies, writing applications that supported core business functions. VB still retained some of the flavor of the original BASIC language—a "beginner's" programming language developed by John Kemeny and Thomas Kurtz at Dartmouth College back in 1963. This caused no end of snickering from C and C++ developers and other cola addicts. But VB programmers could see a powerful future for their language of choice.

Then the unthinkable happened. Microsoft announced that it would no longer enhance the core Visual Basic engine. Instead, it would rewrite and reimplement Visual Basic using its soon-to-be-released .NET development platform. Yes, Visual Basic would be endowed with all the power promised for Microsoft's new C- and Java-like language, C#. But for many hardcore VB developers, it was wrong, just wrong. Words were exchanged. Petitions were crafted. Letters to the editor sounded the call to the Visual Basic faithful, urging them to never write a single line of Visual Basic .NET code, ever. In frustration, a Visual Basic user's group set fire to the entire Microsoft campus in Redmond.

Well, that didn't happen. In fact, nothing bad happened at all. Visual Basic .NET turned out to be a software wunderkind, providing power and features that far surpassed anything available in Visual Basic 6.0. Its initial release in 2002 was proof that. Visual Basic .NET 2002 was powerful, but it was also a little hard to use, at least compared with version 6.0, and especially when compared with the original 1.0 product. Visual Basic .NET 2003, released just a year later (obviously), was a relatively minor update with not much in the way of new or easier functionality.

Visual Basic 2005 marked a return to the simpler days of Visual Basic development, days of harmony and peace between "newbies" and their general-purpose programming language. Not only did Microsoft remove the term ".NET" from the product name, but it also removed some of the barriers that kept entry-level programmers from approaching the language. Pre-.NET features, such as Edit and Continue and the display of forms through the simple use of the form's name, once again found their way into the language and into the hearts of software engineers. Visual Basic still retained all the power it gained with .NET, but with true improvements in usability. It was like when they add a label to your toothpaste that says, "New package, same great regular flavor!" Except that Visual Basic's flavor was improved, too. Visual Basic was once again accessible to first-time developers.

Since the 2005 release, Microsoft hasn't just been sitting on its laurels, as painful as that would be. It dug into its bag of tricks with both hands and came out with Visual Basic 2008, the latest VB offering. Formerly code-named Orcas, Visual Basic 2008 brings additional power and simplicity—yes, both of those—to the language. The biggest new feature, LINQ, makes data access easier by letting you tell the system what data you want instead of detailing how to obtain that data. The language also provides more direct access to new technologies such as Ajax and the Windows Presentation Foundation (WPF). But enough fawning. Let's start learning about the language.

Visual Basic from the Inside Out

As a general-purpose development language, Visual Basic includes gobs of features that allow you to develop just about any type of application supported by the Microsoft Windows platform. As such, all of its features could never be covered in a concise, 20- or 30-page chapter, and I won't try. What I will do in this chapter is to introduce you to the basics of the language, and its core features. Features not covered in this chapter are discussed throughout the rest of the book. It has to be that way, since I don't want you to finish this chapter and then say to yourself, "That Tim Patrick is so amazing. I learned all I needed to know about Visual Basic in one chapter; I didn't even have to read the rest of the book." My publisher would not be amused.

In the remainder of this chapter, I will take the "from the inside out" approach, starting the discussion with the core concepts of logic and data, and adding layer after layer of Visual Basic functionality as you turn the pages.

The Basics of Logic and Data

Lest you forget it, let me remind you again: computers are not really very smart. They know how to do only the simplest of tasks. If you want them to do anything remotely complex, you have to give precise, step-by-step instructions down to moving individual bits of data—only 1s and 0s, remember—around in memory.

Fortunately, most of the code you would ever need at that low level has already been written for you, and incorporated into the Windows operating system and the .NET Framework. Microsoft- and third-party-supplied code libraries give you a lot of pre-written functionality that's available for use in your own programs. And that's good, because you would rather be hurtled into space on a giant bungee cord than have to write business applications at the *machine code* level all day long.

Even though you have all this great prewritten code in your arsenal, you still have to tell the computer precisely what you want it to do, in fine detail, or it won't do it. And that's where *high-level languages* like Visual Basic come in. They provide the grammar you need to communicate with the computer. For any given tasks that the computer needs to perform, your job as a programmer is to determine the individual steps to accomplish that task—the *logic*—and translate those steps into computer-ese using the programming language.

As an example, let's say you receive a request from the sales department for a program that will reverse all the letters in any chunk of text provided to the program. "Our customers are clamoring for this; we need it by Tuesday," they say. OK, so first you figure out the logic, and then you implement it in Visual Basic. Using *pseudocode*, an artificial programming language that you make up yourself to help you write programs, you can sketch out the basics of this task (with leading line numbers):

```
01 Obtain the original text (or string) from the user.
02 If the user didn't supply any content, then quit now.
03 Prepare a destination for the reversed string, empty for now.
04 Repeat the following until the original string is empty:
05    Copy the last character from the remaining original string.
06    Put that character onto the end of the destination string.
07    Shorten the original string, dropping the last character.
08 [End of repeat section]
09 Show the user the destination string.
```

You could write this logic in many ways; this is just one example. You can now convert this pseudocode into your language of choice; in this case, Visual Basic (don't worry about the syntax details for now):

```
01 originalText = InputBox("Enter text to reverse.")
02 If (Len(originalText) = 0) Then Return
03 finalText = ""
04 Do While (originalText <> "")
05    oneCharacter = Right(originalText, 1)
06    finalText &= oneCharacter
07    originalText = Left(originalText, _
         Len(originalText) - 1)
08 Loop
09 MsgBox("The reverse is: " & finalText)
```

This *source code* is now ready to be used in a Visual Basic program. And it also demonstrates several essential aspects of coding:

- The individual steps of the step-by-step instructions are called *statements*. In Visual Basic, each statement appears on a line by itself. You can break long statements into multiple lines by connecting the lines with a space-underscore pair, as shown in line 07 of the code. When a single statement is spread across multiple lines in this manner, the entire statement is sometimes called a *logical line*. Since a single logical line often includes only a single primary Visual Basic action (such as the If or Do action, or the various assignment actions using the equals sign [=]), these actions are also referred to as statements.

- The statements of the code are processed one at a time, from top to bottom. However, certain statements alter the normal top-to-bottom flow of the program, as is done with the Do While...Loop block on lines 04 and 08 of the sample code. Such statements are called *flow control* statements, and include loops (repeating a block of code), conditions (optionally processing a block of code based on a comparison or calculated result), and jumps (moving immediately to some other section of the code).

- Data can be stored in *variables*, which are named containers for data values. The sample code block includes three variables: originalText, oneCharacter, and finalText, all of which store text (string) data. The .NET Common Type System (CTS) allows you to create variables for four primary types of basic data values: text (both single characters and longer strings), numbers (both integer and decimal values), dates (and times), and Booleans (true or false values). You can also build more complex types of data by grouping the basic types.

- Data is stored in a variable through an *assignment*. Generally, this involves placing a variable name on the left side of an = assignment operator, and putting the data or calculation to store in that variable on the right side of that same equals sign. The statement finalText = "" on line 03 stores an empty string ("") in the variable finalText. The &= assignment statement on line 06 shows a slightly different assignment syntax.

- Statements can include *function calls*, blocks of prewritten functionality, all squished down into a single name. Function calls do a bunch of work, and then *return* a final result, a data value. Function names are followed by a set of parentheses, which may include zero or more *arguments*, additional data values supplied by the calling code that the function uses to generate its result.

  The sample code includes many examples of function calls, including the Right function on line 05. This function returns a copy of the rightmost characters from another text string. It accepts two parameters: the original string from which to extract the rightmost characters, and an integer value indicating the number of characters to return. The code Right(originalText, 1) returns a copy of the rightmost single character (1) from originalText.

When you use a function in your source code, the function acts a little like a variable; all the text of the function call, from the start of its name to the end of its closing parenthesis, could be replaced by a variable that contained the same resulting data. Function calls cannot appear on the lefthand side of an assignment statement, but they can appear almost anywhere else that a variable can appear. For example, the following two lines could be used to replace line 02 in the sample:

```
' Replacing --> If (Len(originalText) = 0) Then Return
lengthOfText = Len(originalText)
If (lengthOfText = 0) Then Return
```

- In addition to functions, Visual Basic also includes procedures. *Procedures* bundle up prewritten code in a named package, just like functions, but they don't return a value. They must be used as standalone statements; you cannot use them where you would use a variable or a function call. The call to MsgBox on line 09 is a typical example of a procedure call in use. (MsgBox is actually a function, but in this code it is masquerading as a procedure; more on that later.)

The sample code listed previously could be made a little more efficient. In fact, it's entirely possible that Microsoft obtained an early draft of this book, since it included a string-reversal feature right in Visual Basic, and called it StrReverse:

```
originalText = InputBox("Enter text to reverse.")
If (Len(originalText) = 0) Then Return
finalText = StrReverse(originalText)
MsgBox("The reverse is: " & finalText)
```

That's right; Visual Basic already includes a string-reversal feature, some of that prewritten library code I keep talking about. Visual Basic includes many such *intrinsic functions* that are considered part of the language, and that bundle up useful prewritten functionality. Many of these functions appear in the Microsoft.VisualBasic namespace, which is automatically made available to your Visual Basic source code when you create a new VB project.

Data Types and Variables

Take my data...please! Ha, ha, that one always cracks me up. But it's actually what I ask my Visual Basic application to do: take data from some source (keyboard, hard disk, Internet, etc.) and present it in some useful way. All programs I write will actively manage at least some data in memory. Each data value is stored in a specific area of the computer's memory, as determined by the Common Language Runtime (CLR). The statements in Visual Basic exist primarily to manage and manipulate this data in useful and complex ways.

All data managed by the CLR is stored in the computer's memory, with each data value separated and protected from all others. It's as though each data value had its own individual teacup, as in Figure 2-1.

Figure 2-1. All types of teacups and data

All data values managed by the CLR have *content* and *type*. Content is the actual data: the text string "abc," the number 5, a sales invoice, orange pekoe. Whatever you put in the teacup, that's the content. In some cases, .NET allows you to store absolutely nothing in the teacup (for reference types as described shortly, or "nullable" value types as described in Chapter 6).

Type indicates the kind of content stored in the teacup. In Figure 2-1, this is shown by the shape of each teacup. Each teacup has limits on the type of data that can be poured into the teacup: a text string, an integer number, a customer invoice.

Literals

Some basic data values, such as numbers and text strings, can be entered into your source code and used just as they are. For instance, the MsgBox procedure displays a window with a supplied text message. The statement:

```
MsgBox("The answer is " & 42)
```

includes a *literal string*, "The answer is," and a *literal integer* value, 42. (The "&" symbol is an operator that connects two values together into a new string.) Literals are used once, and then they're gone. If I wanted to show the same "The answer is 42" message again, I would have to once again type the same literal values into a different part of the source code.

Visual Basic supports several types of basic literals. *String literals* are always surrounded by quote marks. If you want to include a quote mark itself in the middle of a string, include two instead of one:

```
"This is ""literally"" an example."
```

String literals can be really, really long, up to about 2 billion characters in length; if you were to type just one character per second, it would take more than 63 years to reach the maximum string length. Visual Basic also includes a *character literal* that is exactly one character in length; if you were to type just one character per second, well, never mind. These character literals are recognized by the "c" trailing after the string. The character literal "A" is entered as:

```
"A"c
```

Date and time literals are surrounded by number signs instead of quote marks. The date or time (or both) that you include can be in any format recognized by Microsoft Windows in your specific region. If you are using Visual Studio, it will reformat your date when you type in the literal:

```
#7/4/1776#
```

Eleven different kinds of numeric data values—both integers and floating-point values—make up the "core" set of numeric teacups. And who needs more than 11? With these 11 teacups, you can manage numbers from zero all the way to 1×10^{300} and beyond. To use a numeric literal, type the number right in your code, like **27**, or **3.1415926535**. Visual Basic also lets you specify which of the 11 numeric teacups to use for a number, by appending a special character to the end of the number. Normally, *27* is an integer 27. To make it a currency-focused "decimal," append an at sign (@):

```
27@
```

When I talk about data types in full detail in Chapter 6, I will list the different special characters, like @, that set the data type for literal numbers.

The fourth and final type of Visual Basic literal is the Boolean literal. Boolean values represent the simplest type of computer data: the bit. Boolean values are either true or false, on or off, yes or no, delicious or disgusting, cats or dogs, zero or nonzero. Booleans always represent any two opposite values or states. Back in the 1800s, George Boole invented *Boolean algebra*, a language he used to represent logic statements as mathematical equations. It just so happens that computers *love* Boolean algebra. All the basic operations of a computer, such as addition, are implemented using Boolean functionality.

Visual Basic includes the Boolean literals True and False. No quotes; no number signs—just the words *True* and *False*. Question: is Tim Patrick telling the truth about this? Answer:

```
True
```

In certain cases, you can treat numbers as Boolean values. I'll talk about it more later on, but for now just know that False equates to zero (0), and True equates to everything else (although generally, −1 is used for "everything else").

Variables

Literal data values are all well and good, but they are useful only once, and then they're gone. Each time you want to use a literal value, you must retype it. It's as though the data values are stored in disposable cups instead of fine china teacups. And besides, only programmers enter literal values, not users, so they are of limited use in managing user data.

Variables are not simply disposable cups; they are reusable. You can keep putting the same type of tea over and over into the teacup. A string variable teacup can hold a string for reuse over and over. For instance, in this block of code, response holds the various strings assigned to it:

```
01  response = "A"
02  MsgBox("Give me an 'A'!")
03  MsgBox(response)
04  MsgBox("Give me another 'A'!")
05  MsgBox(response)
06  MsgBox("What's that spell?")
07  response = StrDup(2, "A")
08  MsgBox(response)
```

The variable response is assigned twice with two different strings: an "A" (line 01) and then "AA" (line 07). It keeps whatever value was last assigned to it; both lines 03 and 05 display "A" in a message box window. And you don't have to assign just literal strings to it; anything that generates a string can assign its result to response. Line 07 uses a built-in Visual Basic function, StrDup, to return the two-character string "AA" and assign it to response.

Using variables is a two-step process. First you must *declare* the variable, and then you *assign* a value to it. The Dim statement takes care of the declaration part; it lets you indicate both the *name* and the *type* of a variable. Its basic syntax is pretty straightforward:

```
Dim response As String
```

where response is the name of the variable and String is its type. Assignment occurs using the = assignment operator:

```
response = "The answer"
```

A single variable can have new values assigned to it over and over again. For those times when you want your variable to have some specific value immediately upon declaration, you can combine declaration and assignment into a single statement:

```
Dim response As String = "The answer"
```

Of course, you're not limited to just a single declaration; you can create as many variables as you need in your code. Each one normally uses its own Dim statement:

```
Dim question As String
Dim answer As String
```

You also can combine these into a single statement, although I think it's just plain ugly:

```
Dim question As String, answer As String
```

See, I told you it was ugly. This is just the start of what's possible with the Dim statement. I'll get into more details as the chapter progresses.

Value Types and Reference Types

I talked about *value types* and *reference types* in Chapter 1. Value type variables store an actual value; the tea in a value type teacup is the content itself. All of the literal data values I mentioned previously, except for Strings, are value types.

Reference type variables store a "reference" to the actual data, data found somewhere else in memory. When you look into a reference type teacup, you have to read the tea leaves at the bottom to determine where the real data resides.

Either reference types have data or they don't. In the absence of data, a reference type has a value of Nothing, a Visual Basic keyword that indicates no data. Value types are never Nothing; they always contain some value, possibly the default value for that type (such as zero for numeric types). A special "nullable" type does let you assign Nothing to a value type, allowing you to implement the same "is there any data here at all" logic that exists with reference types. I'll talk about nullable types in Chapter 6.

Data Types

The String data type is useful, but it's only one of the teacup shapes at your disposal. The .NET Framework defines several core *data types*. Each data type is implemented as a specific class within the System namespace. The most basic data type, a large teacup that can hold any type of data, is called Object. More than just an object, this is object with a capital *O*. In the .NET Class Library namespace hierarchy, it's located at System.Object. It's the mother of all classes in .NET; all other classes, structures, enumerations, and delegates, no matter where they reside in the namespace hierarchy, whether they are written by Microsoft or by you, derive from System.Object. There's no getting around it; you cannot create a type that ultimately derives from anything else.

So, back to these "core" data types I've been hinting at. They match the four types of literal data values I listed before: strings, dates, numbers, and Boolean values. Table 2-1 lists these core data types. Each type also has a Visual Basic-specific name that you can (and should) use instead.

Table 2-1. Core .NET and Visual Basic data types

VB name	.NET name	Description
Boolean	Boolean	The Boolean data type supports only values of True and False. It's possible to convert numbers to Boolean values: 0 becomes False and everything else becomes True. When you convert a Boolean back to a number, False becomes 0 and True becomes −1.[a]
Byte	Byte	A numeric data type, Byte stores single-byte (8-bit) unsigned integers, ranging from 0 to 255. The Byte data type is pretty useful for working with nontext data, such as graphical images.

Table 2-1. Core .NET and Visual Basic data types (continued)

VB name	.NET name	Description
Char	Char	The Char data type holds exactly one text character. Each Char data value represents two bytes (16 bits) of storage, so it can manage *double-byte character sets*, providing support for languages such as Japanese that have a large number of characters. Although it is used to store single text characters, internally the Char data type maintains the characters as integer values, ranging from 0 to 65,535.
Date	DateTime	This date and time data type handles all dates between January 1, 1 AD and December 31, 9999 AD, in the Gregorian calendar. The time can be included as well; if no time is specified, midnight is used. Internally, the Date data type stores the date and time as the number of "ticks" since midnight on January 1, 1 AD. Each tick is 100 nanoseconds.
Decimal	Decimal	The Decimal data type is designed with currency in mind. It is very accurate in mathematical calculations, and has a pretty good range, supporting numbers just beyond 79-octillion, positive or negative. (Did he say 79-octillion?) That's 29 digits long, and that's important to remember, since you get only 29 digits total on both sides of the decimal point. That 79-octillion number comes with the limitation of no digits to the right of the decimal point. If you want one decimal position, you have to give up one to the left (the mantissa) and only keep numbers up to 7.9-octillion. If you want 29 digits after the decimal, you get a big fat zero for the mantissa. If you used to use Visual Basic 6.0, Decimal is similar to the Currency sub-data type.
Double	Double	The Double data type handles the largest possible numbers of all the core numeric data types. Its range is about 4.94×10^{-324} to $1.798 \times 10^{+308}$ for positive numbers, with a similar range for negative values. While you may think you are in giganto-number heaven, it's not all harps and wings. The Double data type is notoriously inaccurate in complex calculations. Sometimes a calculation that should result in zero will actually calculate as something like 0.00000000000005434, which is close. But comparisons of this number with zero will fail, since it is not zero.
Integer	Int32	The Integer data type is a 4-byte (32-bit) signed integer type. It handles numbers from −2,147,483,648 to 2,147,483,647. If you are a pre-.NET Visual Basic programmer, this new Integer data type is equivalent to the version 6.0 Long data type.
Long	Int64	The Long data type is even bigger than Integer; it's an 8-byte (64-bit) signed integer type. It handles numbers from −9,223,372,036,854,775,808 (wow!) to 9,223,372,036,854,775,807 (wow! wow!). It is not the same as the old Visual Basic 6.0 Long data type, as it has twice the storage capacity.
Object	Object	Object is the core type for all .NET types. It sits at the top of the class and type hierarchy; it is the ultimate base class for all other classes. It is a reference type, although value types eventually derive from it, too.
SByte	SByte	A numeric data type, SByte stores single-byte (8-bit) signed integers, ranging from −128 to 127. It is the signed version of the unsigned Byte data type.
Short	Int16	The Short data type is a 2-byte (16-bit) signed integer type. It stores numbers from −32,768 to 32,767. If you are a pre-.NET Visual Basic programmer, this new Short data type is equivalent to the version 6.0 Integer data type.
Single	Single	The Single data type is pretty much like the Double data type, only smaller. Its range for positive numbers is about 1.4×10^{-45} to $3.4 \times 10^{+38}$, with a similar range for negative numbers. Like the Double data type, the Single data type suffers from slight inaccuracies during calculations.

Table 2-1. Core .NET and Visual Basic data types (continued)

VB name	.NET name	Description
String	String	The String data type is a reference type that stores up to about 2 billion characters of text. It stores *Unicode* characters, which are 2-byte (16-bit) characters capable of storing characters from most languages in the world, including languages with large alphabets, such as Chinese.
UInteger	UInt32	UInteger stores 4-byte (32-bit) unsigned integers, ranging from 0 to 4,294,967,295. It is the unsigned version of the signed Integer data type.
ULong	UInt64	ULong stores 8-byte (64-bit) unsigned integers, ranging from 0 to 18,446,744,073,709,551,615. It is the unsigned version of the signed Long data type.
UShort	UInt16	UShort stores 2-byte (16-bit) unsigned integers, ranging from 0 to 65,535. It is the unsigned version of the signed Short data type.

[a] This is true only in Visual Basic. In other .NET languages, such as C#, False becomes 0, but True becomes 1, not −1. If you keep a Boolean value as Boolean, it is normally not an issue. But if you first convert your Booleans to numbers, and then start passing them around willy-nilly between code from different .NET languages, you may get surprising results.

The Microsoft developers in charge of Visual Basic data types lucked out on that job since all core Visual Basic data types are simply wrappers for specific data types implemented by .NET. The Visual Basic names given for each of these core data types are fully interchangeable with the .NET names. For example, Integer is fully equivalent to System.Int32. In fact, when writing Visual Basic code, it is better to use the Visual Basic synonyms, since most Visual Basic developers expect these data type names in the code they read and write.

Except for Object and String, all of these data types are value types. All value types are derived from System.ValueType (which in turn derives from System.Object).

The SByte, UInteger, ULong, and UShort data types were added to Visual Basic with its 2005 release, although their System namespace equivalents have been in .NET since its inception. Unlike the other core data types, these four types are not "CLS-compliant"; that is, they cannot be used to interact with .NET components and languages that limit themselves to just the very core required features of .NET. Generally this is not much of a limitation, but be on your guard when working with third-party components or languages.

Advanced Declaration

When I mentioned the need for *declaration* and *assignment* of variables, I was really focusing on value types. Reference types require one additional step: *instantiation*. Consider the following declaration statements:

```
Dim defaultValue As Integer
Dim nonDefaultValue As Integer = 5
Dim defaultReference As Object
```

These lines declare three separate variables: two value types (the Integers) and one reference type (the Object). Although only one variable has an explicit data assignment, all three have actually been assigned something, either explicitly or implicitly. Let's look at those statements again and see what is truly being assigned to each variable.

```
Dim defaultValue As Integer = 0
Dim nonDefaultValue As Integer = 5
Dim defaultReference As Object = Nothing
```

Both declaration and assignment already occurred for all the variables, just by using the Dim statement. The defaultValue variable, with its default assignment of 0, can be used immediately in equations. However, the reference type variable defaultReference is just an empty teacup, with no default data to manipulate. There are features in Visual Basic that let you compare a reference type with Nothing, and you could do this immediately, but it's not really data. And remember, variables live to manage data.

Reference data values need instantiation, and instantiation needs the New keyword:

```
Dim defaultReference As Object = New Object
```

Now defaultReference points to a real object; now the defaultReference teacup has something consumable inside it, although since it is just System.Object, it doesn't have much in the way of flavor. Strings are a little more interesting, and they also have more interesting *constructors*.

As you may recall from way back in Chapter 1, a constructor is a block of initialization code that runs when you create a new data value or object. Some objects allow you to supply extra information to a constructor, additional information that is used in the initialization process. A *default constructor* doesn't allow you to supply any extra information; it just works on its own, initializing data like it was nobody's business. There is no limit on the number of constructors in a class, but each one must vary in the type of extra information passed to it.

So, back to Strings. The default constructor for a string simply creates a blank, zero-length string:

```
Dim worldsMostBoringString As String = New String
```

Now, nobody ever does this, since the following statement works just as well:

```
Dim worldsMostBoringString As String = ""
```

That's because Strings are treated specially by Visual Basic. String literals are actually instantiations of String data values; it's as though you created a new String instance using the System.String class. At least that's true when using the String data type's default constructor. But String also has more interesting constructors. (I'll delve into the details of constructors in Chapter 8.) One of the constructors creates a new String instance initialized with a specific character repeated a number of times.

For instance, to create a `String` instance with a 25-character string of the letter *M*, use the following syntax:

```
Dim mmGood As String = New String("M"c, 25)
```

If you're going to use the same data type just after the `As` keyword that you use right after the `New` keyword, you can use a collapsed syntax:

```
Dim mmGood As New String("M"c, 25)
```

As with value types, you can also break the statement into distinct declaration and assignment statements:

```
Dim mmGood As String
mmGood = New String("M"c, 25)
```

Constants

Literals don't change, but you can use them only once in your code. *Constants* are a cross between a literal and a variable; they have a single, never-changing value just like data literals, but they also have a name that you can use over and over again, just like variables.

You declare constants using the `Const` keyword instead of the `Dim` keyword:

```
Const SpeedOfLight As Integer = 186000
```

Actual assignment of the value to the constant occurs in the statement itself, with the value following the = operator. Once your constant is declared and assigned, it's available for use in actual statements of your actual code:

```
MsgBox("Lightspeed in miles/second: " & SpeedOfLight)
```

Local Declaration and Fields

In the real world, you need to keep some data private, for your use only. Your neighbors have other juicy bits of data and information that they share among themselves. And then there is public data that isn't hidden from anyone. But it's not just this way in the real world; the fake world of Visual Basic has different levels of access and privacy for your data.

A little later in the chapter, we'll see that your application's logic code will always appear in procedures, named blocks of source code. You declare *local variables* (and constants) in these same procedures when you need a short-lived and personal variable that is only for use within a single procedure. Other variables (and constants) can appear outside procedures, but still within the context of a class or similar type. These *fields*, whether variable or constant, are immediately available to all the different procedures that also call the current class home.

You define all local variables using the `Dim` keyword. The `Dim` statement works for field definitions, but it's more common to use special *access modifier* keywords instead. These modifiers determine what code can access the fields, from `Private` (used only by code inside the class) to `Public` (also available outside the class):

```
Private ForInClassUseOnly As Integer
```

There are five access modifiers in all. I'll talk more about them and about fields in general in Chapter 6.

Intermission

That was a lot to take in. Getting your mind around data and variables is probably the most complex part of programming in Visual Basic. Once you have the data in variables, it's pretty easy to manipulate.

Although the thought of a cup of tea may cause you to run out of the room like a raving lunatic, you might want to take a few minutes, grab a cup, glass, saucer, or mug of your beverage of choice, and relax. I'll see you in about 20 or 30 minutes.

Comments

If you're an opera fan, you know how exciting a good opera can be, especially a classic work presented with the original foreign language libretto. If you're not an opera fan, you know how irritating it can be to listen to several hours of a foreign language libretto. With the advent of "supra titles" conveying the English-language interpretation of the content, those who until now have gotten little joy out of the opera experience will still find it repulsive, only this time in their native tongue. But at least now they will know why they don't enjoy the story.

That's really what comments do: tell you in your own language what is actually going on in a foreign language. In this book, the foreign language is Visual Basic, and English is the vernacular. You may find a particular block of Visual Basic code to be poorly written or even detestable, but if the accompanying comments are accurate, you can be disgusted in your own language, with a human-language understanding of the process.

Comments normally appear on lines by themselves, but you may also attach a comment to the end of an existing code line. If a logical line is broken into multiple physical lines using the "_" line continuation character, a trailing comment is valid only at the end of the final physical line:

```
' ----- This is a standalone comment, on a line by itself.
Dim counter As Integer   ' This is a trailing comment.
MsgBox("The counter starts at " & _   ' INVALID COMMENT HERE!
   counter)  ' But this one is valid.
```

Comments begin with the comment character, the standard single quote character (`'`). Any text following the comment character is a comment, and is ignored when your code is compiled into a usable application. Any single quote that appears within a literal string is not used as a comment marker.

```
MsgBox("No 'comments' in this text.")
```

Comments can also begin with the REM keyword (as in "REMark"), but most programmers use the single-quote variation instead.

Option Statements

A few code examples ago you saw that Visual Basic would supply a default *assignment* to a variable—at least for value types—if you neglected to include one. In certain cases, Visual Basic will also supply the *declaration* if you leave it out. In the statement:

```
brandNewValue = 5
```

if there is no related Dim statement that defines brandNewValue, Visual Basic will declare the variable on your behalf, assigning it to the Object data type. *Don't let this happen to you!* You don't know what kind of trouble you will have if you allow such practices in your code. You will quickly find your code filled with mysterious logic bugs, esoteric data issues, recurrent head lice, and so on.

The problem is that Visual Basic will not complain if you mistype the name of your auto-declared variable. Left unchecked, such practices could lead to code such as this:

```
brandNewValue = 5
MsgBox(brandNewVlaue)
```

My, my, my, look at that spelling mistake on the second line. What? Visual Basic compiled without any error? And now your message box displays nothing instead of 5? You could avoid such trauma by judicious use of the Option statements included in the Visual Basic language. There are four such statements:

Option Explicit On
> This statement forces you to declare all variables using Dim (or a similar statement) before use. It's possible to replace "On" with "Off" in the statement, but don't do it.

Option Strict On
> Visual Basic will do some simple data conversions for you when needed. For instance, if you assign a 64-bit Long data value to a 32-bit Integer variable, Visual Basic will normally convert this data to the smaller size for you, complaining only if the data doesn't fit. This type of conversion—a *narrowing conversion*—is not always safe since the source data will sometimes fail to fit in the destination.

(A *widening conversion*, as with storing Integer data in a Long, always works, since the destination can always hold the source value.) The Option Strict On statement turns off the automatic processing of narrowing conversions. You will be forced to use explicit conversion functions to perform narrowing conversions. This is good, since it forces you to think about the type of data your variables will hold. You can replace "On" with "Off" in this statement, but if I've warned you once, I've warned you twice: don't even try it.

Option Infer On

This new Visual Basic 2008 statement tells the compiler to make a guess at which data type you want a variable to use when you don't specifically tell it. I discuss type inference in Chapter 6, so I'll delay the details for now. Usually you will want to keep this option set to "On."

Option Compare Binary *and* Option Compare Text

These two variations of the Option Compare statement instruct your code to use specific sorting rules for certain string comparison features. In general, Binary comparisons are case-sensitive, whereas Text comparisons are not. It's up to you which method you want to use; the default is Binary.

These statements appear at the top of each source code file in your project, before any other code:

```
Option Explicit On
Option Strict On
```

Or, to save on precious disk space, set default values that apply to your entire project through the project's properties. In Visual Studio, select the Project → Properties menu command. On the project's properties window that appears, select the Compile tab, and set your default choices for the "Option explicit," "Option strict," "Option compare," and "Option infer" fields (see Figure 2-2).

Figure 2-2. Options, options everywhere

Basic Operators

Visual Basic includes several basic operators that let you do what your code really wants to do: manipulate data. To use them, just dial zero from your phone. No, wait; those operators let you place operator-assisted calls for only $2.73 for the first minute. The Visual Basic operators let you perform mathematical, logical, bitwise, and string management functions, all at no additional cost.

The most basic operator is the assignment operator, represented by the equals sign (=). You've already seen this operator in use in this chapter. Use it to assign some value to a variable (or constant); whatever appears to the right of the operator gets assigned to the reference type or value type variable on the left. The statement:

```
fiveSquared = 25
```

assigns a value of 25 to the variable fiveSquared.

Most operators are *binary operators*—they operate on two distinct values, one to the operator's left and one to the right; the result is a single calculated value. It's as though the calculation is fully replaced by the calculated result. For instance, the addition operation:

```
seven = 3 + 4
```

becomes:

```
seven = 7
```

before the final application of the assignment (=) operator. A *unary operator* appears just to the left of its operand. For instance, the unary negation operator turns a positive number into a negative number:

```
negativeSeven = -7
```

I'll comment on each operator in detail in Chapter 6. But we'll need a quick summary for now so that we can manipulate data before we get to that chapter. Table 2-2 lists the main Visual Basic operators and briefly describes the purpose of each one.

Table 2-2. Visual Basic operators

Operator	Description
+	The addition operator adds two numbers together.
+	The unary plus operator retains the sign of a numeric value. It's not very useful until you get into operator overloading, something covered in Chapter 12.
-	The subtraction operator subtracts the second operand from the first.
-	The unary negation operator reverses the sign of its associated numeric operand.

Table 2-2. Visual Basic operators (continued)

Operator	Description
*	The multiplication operator multiplies two numeric values together.
/	The division operator divides the first numeric operand by the second, returning the quotient including any decimal remainder.
\	The integer division operator divides the first numeric operand by the second, returning the quotient, but with the decimal remainder truncated.
Mod	The modulo operator divides the first numeric operand by the second, and returns only the remainder as an integer value.
^	The exponentiation operator raises the first operand (the base) to the power of the second (the exponent).
&	The string concatenation operator joins two string operands together, and returns a new string with the combined results.
And[a]	The conjunction operator returns True if both Boolean operands are also True.
AndAlso	This operator is just like the And operator, but it doesn't examine or process the second operand if the first one is False.
Or[a]	The disjunction operator returns True if either of the operands is also True.
OrElse	This operator is just like the Or operator, but it doesn't examine or process the second operand if the first one is True.
Not[a]	The negation operator returns the opposite of a Boolean operand.
Xor[a]	The exclusive or operator returns True if exactly one of the operands is also True.
<<	The shift left operator shifts the individual bits in an integer operand to the left by the number of bit positions in the second operand.
>>	The shift right operator shifts the individual bits of an integer operand to the right by the number of bit positions in the second operand.
=	The equal-to comparison operator returns True if the operands are "equal" to each other.
<	The less-than comparison operator returns True if the first operand is "less than" the second.
<=	The less-than-or-equal-to comparison operator returns True if the first operand is "less than or equal to" the second.
>	The greater-than comparison operator returns True if the first operand is "greater than" the second.
>=	The greater-than-or-equal-to comparison operator returns True if the first operand is "greater than or equal to" the second.
<>	The not-equal-to comparison operator returns True if the first operand is "not equal to" the second.
Like	The pattern comparison operator returns True if the first operand matches a string pattern specified by the second operand.
Is	The object equal-to comparison operator returns True if both operands truly represent the same instance of a data value in memory. Setting the second operand to Nothing lets you test a reference variable to see whether it contains data.
IsNot	The object not-equal-to comparison operator is the opposite of the Is operator.

[a] The And, Or, Not, and Xor operators also work as "bitwise" operators. I'll talk about that in "Operators" in Chapter 6.

As powerful as operators are, they possess even more power when you combine them. This works because any of the operands can be a complex *expression* that includes its own operands. Parentheses grouped around clauses in operands ensure that values are processed in the order you expect.

```
circleArea = pi * (radius ^ 2)
```

In this statement, the second operand of the * multiplication operator is another expression, which includes its own operator.

Using Functions and Subroutines

Years ago I worked for a software company that sometimes published software developed outside the organization, all for a non-Windows platform. While most of these programs were written in the C language, we also published software written in Pascal, assembly language, and good ol' BASIC. I inherited one such external application written entirely in BASIC, a program that assisted the user in 3D modeling and graphics rendering. It was a complex program, containing about 30,000 lines of source code. The problem was that it was one large block of 30,000 source code lines. No comments, no variable names longer than a few characters, no extra-strength buffered aspirin product. Just thousands of lines of code with flow control statements jumping this way and that. And, of course, it had a bug.

I was able to move past that event in my life without too much therapy, but at the time it was a shock to see code in that condition. And it was so unnecessary, since that flavor of BASIC was a *procedural language*, just like C and Pascal. Procedural languages allow you to break your code into named blocks of logic, called procedures. These procedures let you take a "divide and conquer" approach to programming; you write procedures that accomplish a specific logical portion of the code within your entire application, and then access these procedures from other procedures.

Visual Basic includes three types of procedures:

Subroutines
> These procedures, also called *subprocedures*, do a bunch of work and then return to the calling procedure. Data can be sent into the subroutine through its *argument list*, and some values may come back through that same list, but the procedure does not send an official final result back. A subroutine does its work, and once it is complete, the calling code continues on its merry way.

Functions
> Functions are just like subroutines, with one additional feature: you can return a single value or object instance from the function as its official result. Usually, the calling code takes this *return value* into consideration when it completes its own logic.

Properties

When used, properties actually look like variables. You assign and retrieve values to and from properties just like you would for a variable. However, properties include hidden code, often used to validate the data being assigned to the property.

Subroutines, functions, and properties are the code members of each class or similar type. I'll delay discussion of properties until a little later in the chapter. For now, let's enjoy functions and subroutines, which together are also known as *methods*. Let's start with subroutines. To call a subroutine, type its name as a statement, followed by a set of parentheses. Any data you need to send to the subroutine goes in the parentheses. For instance, the following subroutine call does some work, passing the ID number of a customer, and a starting date:

```
DoSomeWork(customerID, startDate)
```

Each subroutine defines the data type and order of the arguments you pass. This argument list may include one or more *optional arguments*, which are assigned default values if you don't include them. A subroutine might also be *overloaded*, defining different possible argument lists based on the number and data type of the arguments. We'll encounter a lot of these later.

Functions are a little more interesting since they return a usable value. Often, this value is assigned to a variable:

```
Dim balanceDue As Boolean
balanceDue = HasOutstandingBalance(customerID)
```

Then you can do something with this result. If you want, you can ignore the return value of a function, and we already have. The MsgBox function used earlier returns the identity of the on-screen button clicked by the user to close the message box. If you include only an OK button (the default), you probably don't care which button the user clicks.

```
MsgBox("Go ahead, click the OK button.")
```

But you can also capture the result of the button:

```
whichButton = MsgBox("Click Yes or No.", MsgBoxStyle.YesNo)
```

In this case, whichButton will be either MsgBoxResult.Yes or MsgBoxResult.No, two of the possible results defined by the MsgBox function.

Conditions

Sometimes you have to make some choices, and conditional expressions will help you do just that. Visual Basic includes support for *conditions*, which use data tests to determine which code should be processed next.

If Statements

The most common conditional statement is the `If` statement. It is equivalent to English questions in the form "If such-and-such is true, then do so-and-so." For instance, it can handle "If you have $20, then you can buy me dinner," but not "If a train departs Chicago at 45 miles per hour, when will it run out of coal?"

If statements have syntax that spans multiple source code lines:

```
01  If (hadAHammer = True) Then
02      DoHammer(inTheMorning, allOverThisLand)
03      DoHammer(inTheEvening, allOverThisLand)
04  ElseIf (hadAShovel = True) Then
05      DoShovel(inTheNoontime, allOverThisLand)
06  Else
07      TakeNap(allDayLong, onMySofa)
08  End If
```

The `If` statement lets you define *branches* in your code based on conditions. It is built from three main components:

Conditions

The expression found between the `If` (or `ElseIf`) keyword and the `Then` keyword is the condition. The sample includes two conditions, on lines 01 and 04. Conditions may be simple or complex, but they must always result in a Boolean `True` or `False` value. They can include calls to other functions and multiple logical and comparison operators.

```
If ((PlayersOnTeam(homeTeam) >= 9) And _
    (PlayersOnTeam(visitingTeam) >= 9)) Or _
    (justPracticing = True) Then
  PlayBall()
Else
  StadiumLights(turnOff)
End If
```

The original condition always follows the `If` keyword. If that conditions fails, you can specify additional conditions following an `ElseIf` keyword, as on line 04. You may include as many `ElseIf` clauses as you need. The optional `Else` condition doesn't let you specify a test expression. Instead, it matches everything not yet caught by the `If` or `ElseIf` clauses. Only one `Else` clause is allowed per `If` statement.

Branches

Each condition's `Then` keyword is followed by one or more Visual Basic statements that are processed if the associated condition evaluates to `True`. All statements up to the next `Else`, `ElseIf`, or `End If` are included in that branch's statement block. You may include any number of statements in a branch block, including additional subordinate `If` statements. In the sample code, branch lines

02 and 03 are processed if the original hadAHammer condition is true. Line 05 is processed instead if the original condition fails, but the second hadAShovel condition passes. If none of the conditions is True, the Else's branch, on line 07, executes.

Statement keywords

The If statement is one of several multiline statements in Visual Basic, all of which end with the keyword End followed by the original statement keyword (If in this case). The If statement's keywords, which give the statement its structure, include If, Then, ElseIf, Else, and End If. All ElseIf and Else clauses and related branches are optional. The simplest If statement includes only an If branch.

```
If (phoneNumberLength = 10) Then
    DialNumber(phoneNumber)
End If
```

For conditions with simple single-statement branches and no ElseIf clauses, a single-line alternative can keep your code looking clean.

```
If (SaveData() = True) Then MsgBox("Data saved.")
If (TimeOfDay >= #13:00#) _
    Then currentStatus = WorkStatus.GoHome _
    Else currentStatus = WorkStatus.BusyWorking
```

If statements are cool because they make your code more than just a boring set of linear step-by-step instructions that never deviate for any reason. Software is written to support some real-world process, and real-world processes are seldom linear. The If statement makes it possible for your code to react to different data conditions, taking the appropriate branch when necessary.

Once the entire If...End If block completes, processing continues with the next statement that follows the End If statement.

Select Case Statements

Sometimes you might write an If statement that tests a variable against one possible value, then another, then another, then another, and so on:

```
If (billValue = 1) Then
    presidentName = "Washington"
ElseIf (billValue = 2) Then
    presidentName = "Jefferson"
ElseIf (billValue = 5) Then
    presidentName = "Lincoln"
...
```

And on it goes, through many more ElseIf clauses. It's effective, but a little tedious, as your code must specifically test every case. The Select Case statement provides a cleaner alternative for simple value comparisons against a list:

```
01  Select Case billValue
02      Case 1
03          presidentName = "Washington"
04      Case 2
05          presidentName = "Jefferson"
06      Case 5
07          presidentName = "Lincoln"
08      Case 20
09          presidentName = "Jackson"
10      Case 50
11          presidentName = "Grant"
12      Case 10, 100
13          presidentName = "!! Non-president"
14      Case > 100
15          presidentName = "!! Value too large"
16      Case Else
17          presidentName = "!! Invalid value"
18  End Select
```

Unlike the If statement, which checks for a Boolean result, Select Case compares a single value against a set of test case values. In the example, the billValue variable is compared against the different values identified by each Case clause. All code that follows a Case clause (until the next Case clause) is the branch that is processed when a match is found. An optional Case Else condition (line 16) catches anything that is not matched by any other Case. Normally, Case clauses list single values for comparison. They can also include a list of comma-separated comparison values (line 12), or simple range comparison expressions (line 14).

IIf and If Functions

Visual Basic includes two variations of the If statement for "inline" use. Consider the following statement:

```
If (gender = "F") Then fullGender = "Female" _
    Else fullGender = "Male"
```

Using the IIf function, this statement compresses into a single assignment statement with an embedded condition:

```
fullGender = IIf(gender = "F", "Female", "Male")
```

The IIf function has three comma-delimited arguments. The first is the condition, which must result in a Boolean True or False value. The second argument is returned by the function if the condition is True; a condition result of False returns the third argument. For simple conditions that are destined to return single values to a common variable, it's really a useful function. But with anything really useful, there are caveats. The caveat with IIf is that *anything appearing inside the IIf statement will be processed, even if it is not returned as a result*. Here's a dangerous example:

```
purgeResult = IIf(level = 1, PurgeSet1( ), PurgeSet2( ))
```

The statement will correctly return the result of either PurgeSet1( ) or PurgeSet2( ) based on the value of level. The problem, or potential problem, is that both functions, PurgeSet1( ) and PurgeSet2( ), will be called; if level is 1, both PurgeSet1( ) and PurgeSet2( ) will be called, even though only the function result from PurgeSet1( ) will be returned.

To help avoid such side effects, Visual Basic 2008 added the new If operator. It looks just like the IIf function, except for the keyword If replacing the IIf keyword:

```
purgeResult = If(level = 1, PurgeSet1(), PurgeSet2())
```

Now only PurgeSet1( ) or PurgeSet2( ) will be called based on the condition, but not both. Although the If operator looks like a function, it is actually a true operator, known as the *ternary* operator. At compile time, Visual Basic treats it and its arguments as operator and operands and generates the appropriate logic.

A variation of the If operator takes just two arguments, excluding the initial Boolean argument.

```
realObject = If(object1, object2)
```

In this version of the If operator, if the first argument evaluates to Nothing, the operator returns the second argument. If the first argument is not Nothing—that is, if it really is something—the operator returns that first argument instead. The goal is to return non-Nothing, although that's a double negative.

Loops

Visual Basic includes three major types of loops: For...Next, For Each...Next, and Do...Loop. Just as conditions allow you to break up the sequential monotony of your code through branches, loops add to the usefulness of your code by letting you repeat a specific block of logic a fixed or variable number of times.

For...Next Loops

The For...Next loop uses a numeric counter that increments from a starting value to an ending value, processing the code within the loop once for each incremented value.

```
Dim whichMonth As Integer
For whichMonth = 1 To 12
    ProcessMonthlyData(whichMonth)
Next whichMonth
```

This sample loops 12 times (1 To 12), once for each month. You can specify any starting and ending values you wish; this range can also be specified using variables or functions that return numeric values. Once the starting and ending values are obtained, they are not recalculated each time through the loop, even if a function call is used to obtain one or both limits.

```
' ----- Month(Today) returns the numeric month
'        for the current date.
For whichMonth = 1 To Month(Today)
    ProcessMonthlyData(whichMonth)
Next whichMonth
```

Normally, the loop increments by one (1) each time through. You can alter this default by attaching a Step clause to the end of the For statement line:

```
For countDown = 60 To 0 Step -1
    ...
Next countDown
```

One additional syntax variation allows you to declare the loop counter variable within the statement itself. Such variables are available only within the loop, and cease to exist once the loop exits.

```
For whichMonth As Integer = 1 To 12
    ProcessMonthlyData(whichMonth)
Next whichMonth
```

For Each...Next Loops

A variation of the For loop, the For Each...Next loop scans through a set of ordered and related items, from the first item until the last. Arrays and collection objects also work, as does any object that supports the IEnumerable interface (all these topics are covered in Chapter 6). The syntax is quite similar to the standard For statement:

```
For Each oneRecord In setOfRecords
    ProcessRecord(oneRecord)
Next oneRecord
```

Do...Loop Loops

Sometimes you want to repeat a block of code as long as a certain condition is true, or only until a condition is true. The Do...Loop structure performs both of these tasks. The statement includes a While or Until clause that specifies the conditions for continued loop processing. For instance, the following statement does some processing for a set of dates, from a starting date to an ending date:

```
Dim processDate As Date = #1/1/2000#
Do While (processDate < #2/1/2000#)
    ' ----- Perform processing for the current date.
    ProcessContent(processDate)

    ' ----- Move ahead to the next date.
    processDate = processDate.AddDays(1)
Loop
```

Processing in this sample will continue until the processDate variable meets or exceeds 2/1/2000, which indicates the end of processing. The Until clause version is somewhat similar, although with a reversed condition result:

```
Do Until (processDate >= #2/1/2000#)
    ...
Loop
```

Make the included condition as simple or as complex as you need. Putting the `Until` or `While` clause at the bottom of the loop guarantees that the statements inside the loop will always be processed at least once:

```
Do
    ...
Loop Until (processDate >= #2/1/2000#)
```

If the loop condition is never met, the loop will continue forever. So, if you want your loop to exit at some point (and usually you do), make sure the condition can eventually be met.

There is another loop that is similar to `Do...Loop`, called the `While...End While` loop. However, it exists for backward compatibility only. Use the `Do...Loop` statement instead.

Exit Statements

Normally, when you enter a loop, you have every intention of looping for the full number of times specified by the initial conditions of the loop. For For loops, you expect to continue through the entire numeric range or collection of elements. In Do loops, you plan to keep the loop going as long as the exiting condition has not yet been met. But there may be loops that you want to exit early. You accomplish this using an `Exit` statement.

There are two loop-specific `Exit` statements:

Exit For
> Exits a `For...Next` or `For Each...Next` loop immediately

Exit Do
> Exits a `Do...Loop` statement immediately

Each `Exit` statement exits the loop that contains the statement; processing continues with the line immediately following the loop:

```
For whichMonth = 1 To 12
    If (ProcessMonthlyData(whichMonth) = False) Then Exit For
Next whichMonth
' ----- Code continues here no matter how the loop was exited.
```

The sample code is designed to loop through all 12 months. However, a processing failure for any of the 12 months will immediately exit the loop, abandoning all remaining month processing actions. The `Exit Do` statement similarly exits `Do...Loop` loops immediately.

In an Exit loop statement within *nested loops* (where one loop appears within another), only the matching loop that immediately contains the statement is exited:

```
For whichMonth = 1 To 12
   For whichDay = 1 to DaysInMonth(whichMonth)
      If (ProcessDailyData(whichMonth, whichDay) = False) _
         Then Exit For
   Next whichDay
   ' ----- The Exit For statement jumps to this line.
   '       Processing continues with the next month.
Next whichMonth
```

Continue Statements

Since exiting a loop abandons all remaining passes through the loop, you may miss out on important processing that would have happened in subsequent passes. Visual Basic includes a Continue statement that lets you abandon only the current pass through the loop.

There are different Continue statement variations for each loop type:

Continue For

Immediately jumps to the end of the For...Next or For Each...Next loop and prepares for the next pass. The loop variable is incremented and compared with the range or collection limits.

Continue Do

Immediately jumps to the end of the Do...Loop statement and prepares for the next pass. The Until or While condition is reevaluated.

Since the loop conditions are re-evaluated when using the Continue statements, there are times when Continue may cause the loop to exit, such as when it had been the final pass through the loop already.

In this example, the Continue For statement skips processing for months that have no data to process:

```
For whichMonth = 1 To 12
   If (DataAvailable(whichMonth) = False) Then Continue For
   RetrieveData(whichMonth)
   ProcessData(whichMonth)
   SaveData(whichMonth)
Next whichMonth
```

Creating Your Own Procedures

All logic statements in your code must appear within a procedure, whether in a subroutine, a function, or a property. Although there are thousands of prewritten procedures for you to choose from in the .NET Framework libraries, you can also add your own.

Subroutines

Subroutines begin with a Sub declaration statement and end with an End Sub statement. All of your subroutine's logic appears in between these two mighty jaws.

```
01  Sub ShowIngredients(ByVal gender As Char)
02      Dim theMessage As String = "Unknown."
03      If (gender = "M"c) Then
04          theMessage = "Snips and snails and puppy dog tails."
05      ElseIf (gender = "F"c) Then
06          theMessage = "Sugar and spice and everything nice."
07      End If
08      MsgBox(theMessage)
09  End Sub
```

Line 01 shows the subroutine's declaration line in its simplest form; throughout the book, you will find that there are additional keywords that decorate procedure declarations to change their behavior. The statement begins with the Sub keyword (for *sub*routine), followed by the name of the procedure, ShowIngredients.

The parentheses following this name contain the subroutine's *parameters*. Parameters allow another block of code that will use this procedure to pass data into the procedure, and optionally receive data back. You can include any number of parameters in the subroutine definition; simply separate them by commas. Each parameter specifies the name as it will be used in the procedure (gender in the sample) and its data type (Char). The arguments are treated as declared variables within the procedure, as is done with gender on lines 03 and 05.

The values supplied by the calling code are known as *arguments*. All arguments are passed *by value* or *by reference*. In the sample code, the argument passed into gender will be passed by value, as specified through the ByVal keyword. The related ByRef keyword indicates an argument to be passed by reference. If you don't include either keyword, ByVal is assumed. This passing method impacts whether changes made to the argument within the local procedure are propagated back to the calling code. However, the ability to update the original data is also influenced by whether the data is a *value type* or a *reference type*. Table 2-3 indicates the behavior for each combination of passing method and data type.

Table 2-3. Updating data, the .NET way

Passing method	Data type	Behavior
ByVal	Value type	Changes made to the local version of the argument have no impact on the original version.
ByVal	Reference type	Changes made to *members* of the data object immediately impact the original data object. However, the object itself cannot be changed or replaced with a completely new data object.

Table 2-3. Updating data, the .NET way (continued)

Passing method	Data type	Behavior
ByRef	Value type	Changes made to the local version are returned to the calling procedure, and permanently impact the original data value.
ByRef	Reference type	Changes made to either the data object or its members are also changed in the original. It is possible to fully replace the object sent into the procedure.

In most cases, if you are interested in modifying the value of a parameter and having the changes return to the caller, use ByRef; otherwise, use ByVal.

Lines 02 through 08 in the sample code comprise the *body* of the procedure, where all your logic appears. Any variables to be used solely in the routine are also defined here, as with the theMessage variable on line 02. The subroutine always concludes with an End Sub statement.

Functions

The syntax of a function differs only slightly from subroutines, to support a return value.

```
01  Function IsPrime(ByVal source As Long) As Boolean
02      ' ----- Determine whether source is a prime number.
03      Dim testValue As Long
04      If (source < 2) Then
05          Return False
06      ElseIf (source > 2) Then
07          For testValue = 2 To source \ 2&
08              If ((source Mod testValue) = 0) Then
09                  Return False
10              End If
11          Next testValue
12      End If
13      Return True
14  End Function
```

As with subroutines, the function's declaration line appears first (line 01), followed by the body (lines 02 through 13) and the closing End Function statement (line 14). The declaration line includes an extra data type definition after the parameter list. This is the data type of the final value to be returned to the calling code. Use this return value in the calling code just like any other value or variable. For example, the following line calls the IsPrime function and stores its Boolean result in a variable:

```
primeResult = IsPrime(23)
```

To indicate the value to return, use the Return statement (described later in the chapter). The sample code does this on lines 05, 09, and 13. (An older VB 6.0 syntax that lets you assign the return value to the name of the function still works.)

Properties

A little earlier I mentioned fields, which are variables or constants that appear within a class, but outside any procedure definition.

```
01  Class PercentRange
02      Public Percent As Integer
03  End Class
```

Properties are similar to fields; they are used like class-level variables or constants. But they are programmed like functions, accepting parameters, having return values, and including as much logic as you require.

Properties are often used to protect private class data with logic that weeds out inappropriate values. The following class defines a single property that provides access to the hidden related field:

```
01  Class PercentRange
02      ' ----- Stores a percent from 0 to 100 only.
03      Private savedPercent As Integer
04      Public Property Percent() As Integer
05         Get
06             Return savedPercent
07         End Get
08         Set(ByVal value As Integer)
09             If (value < 0) Then
10                 savedPercent = 0
11             ElseIf (value > 100) Then
12                 savedPercent = 100
13             Else
14                 savedPercent = value
15             End If
16         End Set
17      End Property
18  End Class
```

The Percent property (lines 04 to 17) protects access to the savedPercent field (line 03), correcting any caller-supplied values that exceed the 0 to 100 range. Properties include separate assignment and retrieval components, also called *accessors*. The Get accessor (lines 05 to 07) returns the property's monitored value to the caller. The Set accessor (lines 08 to 16) lets the caller modify the value of the property.

The property declaration statement (line 04) includes a data type that matches the data type passed into the Set accessor (line 08). This is the data type of the value set or retrieved by the caller. To use this sample Percent property, create an instance of the PercentRange class, and then use the property:

```
Dim activePercent As New PercentRange
activePercent.Percent = 107      ' An out-of-range Integer
MsgBox(activePercent.Percent)    ' Displays "100", not "107"
```

You can create read-only or write-only properties by including the ReadOnly or WriteOnly keyword just before the Property keyword in the declaration statement (line 04), and leaving out the unneeded accessor.

Properties do not need to be tied to fields. You can use properties to get and set any type of value, and store it or act upon it in any manner you wish.

Where to Put Your Procedures

Back in the good ol' days of Visual Basic 6.0, procedures could appear just about anywhere in your source code files. You would open a source file, type a function, and go; it was that easy. With the move to .NET, all Visual Basic procedures must now appear within a defined class (or a structure or module).

```
Class Employee
    Sub StartVacation()
        ...
    End Sub

    Function TotalVacationTaken() As Double
        ...
    End Function
End Class
```

When you create instances of your class later in code, the methods can be called directly through the object instance.

```
Dim executive As New Employee
...
executive.StartVacation()
```

Chapter 8 shows you how to use and build classes.

Other Flow Control Features

The loops and conditional statements available in Visual Basic let you reroute your code based on data. The language includes a few other statements that let you control the action in a more direct manner.

The GoTo Statement

The GoTo statement lets you jump immediately to some other location within the current procedure. The destination of a jump is always a *line label*, a named line position in the current procedure. All line labels appear at the start of a logical line, and end with a colon.

```
PromptUser:
    GetValuesFromUser(numerator, denominator)
    If (denominator = 0) Then GoTo PromptUser
    quotient = numerator / denominator
```

In this sample, the GoTo statement jumps back to the PromptUser label when the code detects invalid data. Processing continues with the line immediately following the PromptUser label. You can't use the same label name twice in the same procedure, although you can reuse label names in different procedures. If you want, include another logic statement on the same line as your label, right after the colon, although your code will be somewhat easier to read if you keep labels on their own lines.

```
LabelAlone:
    MsgBox("It's all alone.")
LabelAndCode: MsgBox("Together again.")
```

It's all right to include as many labels in your code as you need, but the GoTo statement is one of those elements of Visual Basic that is monitored closely by pesky international software agencies, such as the International Committee to Keep GoTo Always Gone (ICK-GAG). That group also scans computer books looking for derogatory references to its organization name—not that it would find anything like that in this book. But its core issue is that overuse of GoTo statements can lead to *spaghetti code*, such as the following:

```
Dim importantMessage As String = "Do"
GoTo Step2
Step6: importantMessage &= "AG!"
GoTo Step7
Step3: importantMessage &= "wit"
GoTo Step4
Step2: importantMessage &= "wn "
GoTo Step3
Step5: importantMessage &= "CK-G"
GoTo Step6
Step4: importantMessage &= "h I"
GoTo Step5
Step7: MsgBox(importantMessage)
```

Some people say that such code is hard to read. Others call it job security. No matter what you call it, it does make code very hard to maintain and review. You should probably keep an eye on your use of GoTo statements; if you don't, someone else might.

Visual Basic itself places some limits on the use of GoTo. You cannot jump into or out of certain multiline statements that would result in improperly initialized code or data values. For instance, you cannot jump into the middle of a For...Next statement from outside the statement, since the loop counter variable and the starting and ending ranges would not be properly initialized.

```
' ----- This GoTo statement will fail.
GoTo InsideTheLoop
For counter = 1 to 10
InsideTheLoop:
    MsgBox("Loop number: " & counter)
Next counter
```

However, once you are inside the loop, you can jump to line labels that also appear in the loop, and it's acceptable to jump out of the loop using GoTo. Some other multi-line structures impose similar restrictions.

The Return Statement

Not only can you jump around within a procedure using GoTo, but you can also jump right out of a procedure anytime you want using the Return statement. Normally, a procedure exits when processing reaches the last line of code in the procedure; processing then continues with the code that called the procedure. The Return statement provides a way to exit the procedure before reaching the end.

In subroutines, the Return statement appears by itself as a standalone statement:

```
Return
```

In functions, the statement must include the value to be returned to the calling code: a variable, a literal, or an expression that must match the specified return value data type of the function.

```
Return 25
```

Pre-.NET releases of Visual Basic used an Exit statement to immediately leave a procedure. These are still supported in .NET. There are three variations:

Exit Sub
Exits a subroutine

Exit Function
Exits a function

Exit Property
Exits a property

When exiting from a function, the Exit Function statement does not include a way to specify a return value. You must set the return value separately by assigning the return value to the name of the function.

```
Function SafeDivide(ByVal numerator As Double, _
    ByVal denominator As Double) As Double
  ' ----- The "#" sign makes a number a Double.
  If (denominator = 0#) Then
    ' ----- Return 0 on invalid division.
    SafeDivide = 0#
    Exit Function
  End If
  Return numerator / denominator
End Function
```

The End and Stop Statements

The End and Stop statements bring an immediate halt to your Visual Basic application. The End statement exits your program immediately, aborting all further code and data processing (although certain acquired resources are cleaned up).

The Stop statement suspends processing only when you are running your application within a debugger, such as the Visual Studio development environment. Stop returns control to the environment, allowing the developer to examine and possibly alter data and code before continuing on with the program. If a Stop is encountered in a standalone application running outside the debugger, it prompts the user to debug the application using any debugger installed on the workstation. Needless to say, the user will not be amused.

Events and Event Handlers

Visual Basic is an *event-driven language*. This is especially true of programs written to run on the Windows desktop. After some important initialization, the user is generally in control of all actions in the program. Who knows what the crazy user will do. He might click here. She might type there. It could be all mayhem and bedlam. But whatever the user does, your program will learn about it through *events*.

Since the first days of Windows, desktop programs have used a *message pump* to communicate user and system actions to your code. Mouse and keyboard input, system-generated actions, and other notifications from external sources flow into a program's common *message queue*. The message pump draws these messages out one by one, examines them, and feeds them to the appropriate areas of your code.

In traditional Windows programming, you craft the message pump yourself, including code that makes direct calls to event-handling procedures based on the message type. In a Visual Basic program (both in .NET and earlier), the language provides the message pump for you. It analyzes the messages as they are pumped out of the message queue, and directs them to the appropriate code. In .NET, this code appears within classes. Once a class has a chance to analyze the message, it can generate an event, which is ultimately processed by an *event handler*, a subroutine you write to respond to the action. This calling of the event handler is known as *firing an event*. So, there are two parts of an event: (1) some code that decides to fire the event; and (2) an event handler that responds to the fired event.

Events are really just indirect calls to a procedure. Instead of having the main code call another subroutine directly, it asks .NET to call the other subroutine for it, passing specific arguments that the calling code may wish to include. So, why would you want to do this instead of just making the subroutine call directly? For one thing, this indirect method lets you add event handlers long after the initial event-firing code was written. This is good, since the event-firing code may be in a third-party assembly that was written years ago. A second benefit is that one event can target multiple event handlers. When the event fires, each event handler will be called, and each can perform any custom logic found in the handler subroutine.

The code that fires the event passes event-specific data to the target event handler(s) through the handler's parameter list. For the indirect subroutine call to work, the event handler needs to contain the correct number of arguments, in the right order, each of a specific and expected data type. The Event statement defines this contract between the event and the handler.

```
Public Event SalaryChanged(ByVal NewSalary As Decimal)
```

This Event statement defines an event named SalaryChanged with a single argument, a Decimal value. Any event handler wishing to monitor the event must match this argument signature.

```
Sub EmployeePayChanged(ByVal updatedSalary As Decimal)...
```

Events can occur for any reason you deem necessary; they need not be tied to user or system actions. In this sample class, an event fires each time a change is made to the employee's salary. The RaiseEvent statement performs the actual firing of the event, specifying the name of the event to fire, and a set of arguments in parentheses.

```
Public Class Employee
    Public Name As String
    Private currentSalary As Decimal

    Public Property Salary() As Decimal
      Get
          Return currentSalary
      End Get
      Set(ByVal value As Decimal)
          currentSalary = value
          RaiseEvent SalaryChanged(currentSalary)
      End Set
    End Property

    Public Event SalaryChanged(ByVal NewSalary As Decimal)
End Class
```

The event handlers are not added directly to the class. Instead, they are attached to an instance of the class. The instance, declared as a class field, must be defined using the special WithEvents keyword, which tells Visual Basic that this instance will process events.

```
Public WithEvents MonitoredEmployee As Employee
```

Event handlers are ordinary subroutines, but they include the Handles keyword to indicate which event is being handled.

```
Private Sub EmployeePayChanged( _
    ByVal updatedSalary As Decimal) _
    Handles MonitoredEmployee.SalaryChanged
  MsgBox("The new salary for " & _
    MonitoredEmployee.Name & " is " & updatedSalary)
End Sub
```

All that is needed is something to kick off the action.

```
Public Sub HireFred()
    MonitoredEmployee = New Employee
    MonitoredEmployee.Name = "Fred"
    MonitoredEmployee.Salary = 50000    ' Triggers event
End Sub
```

When the salary is set, the Employee class's Salary property fires the SalaryChanged event using the Visual Basic RaiseEvent command. This generates a call to the EmployeePayChanged event handler, which finally displays the message.

The events built into the Windows Forms classes in .NET work just like this, but instead of watching with me for a salary increase, they are watching for mouse clicks and keyboard clacks. All of these system events use a common argument signature.

```
Event EventName(ByVal sender As System.Object, _
    ByVal e As System.EventArgs)
```

The sender argument identifies the instance of the object that is firing the event, in case the caller needs to examine its members. The e argument is an object that lets the caller send event-specific data to the handler through a single class instance. The System.EventArgs class doesn't have much in the way of members, but many events use a substitute class that is derived from System.EventArgs.

As we pass through the chapters of this book, there will be no end to the number of event examples you will see and experience. I will save the more involved and interesting samples until then.

Namespaces

Classes, structures, modules, enumerations, interfaces, and delegates—the major .NET types—don't just float around in the code of your application. They must all be grouped and managed into *namespaces*. As described in Chapter 1, namespaces provide a hierarchy for your types, sort of a tree-shaped condominium where each type has a home. Some of those homes (or nodes), such as System, get pretty crowded with all those type families living there. Others, such as System.Timers, may have only a few types dwelling in their ample abodes. But every type must live in the hierarchy; none of the types is adventurous enough to strike out on its own and build a ranch house.

At the very root of the hierarchy is Global, not a node itself, but a Visual Basic keyword that indicates the root of all roots. You can include Global when referencing your namespaces, but its use is required only when leaving it out would cause confusion between two namespace branches.

Directly under `Global` are the few top-level namespaces, including `System` and `Microsoft`. Each top-level namespace contains subordinate namespaces, and each of those can contain additional third-level namespaces, and so on. Namespace nodes are referenced relative to one another using a "dot" notation.

```
System.Windows.Forms
```

This specifies the third-level `Forms` namespace. You could also have typed:

```
Global.System.Windows.Forms
```

which means the same thing. Relative namespaces are also supported:

```
Forms
```

However, to use relative namespaces, you must tell your Visual Basic code to expect them. There are so many namespaces out there, and there may be several `Forms` namespaces somewhere in the hierarchy.

Referencing Namespaces

Before namespaces can be used in your code, they must be *referenced* and optionally *imported*. Referencing a namespace identifies the DLL assembly file that contains that namespace's types. Perform both of these actions through the References tab of each project's Properties form (see Figure 2-3).

Figure 2-3. References and imports for a project

Actually, you are not referencing the namespaces in the DLL, but rather the types, all of which happen to live in specific namespaces. However, for the core type DLLs supplied with the .NET Framework, it feels like the same thing. In fact, Microsoft even named many of the DLLs to match the namespaces they contain. *System.dll* contains types within the System namespace. *System.Windows.Forms.dll* includes types specific to Windows Forms applications, and all of these types appear in the System.Windows.Forms namespace or one of its subordinates.

If you don't reference a DLL in your project, none of its types will be available to you in your code. Visual Studio loads several references into your project automatically based on the type of project you create. Figure 2-3 shows the nine default references included within a Windows Forms application: System, System.Core, System.Data, System.Data.DataSetExtensions, System.Deployment, System.Drawing, System.Windows. Forms, System.Xml, and System.Xml.Linq.

Once you have referenced a library of classes (or other types) in your code, access any of its classes by specifying the full namespace to that class. For instance, the class for an on-screen form is referenced by System.Windows.Forms.Form. That's three levels down into the hierarchy, and some classes are even deeper. I hope that your health insurance plan covers carpal tunnel syndrome.

To avoid typing all those long namespaces over and over again, Visual Basic includes an *imports* feature. Imports are namespace-specific; once a namespace has been imported, you can access any of the types in that namespace without specifying the namespace name. If you import the System.Windows.Forms namespace, you only have to type "Form" to access the Form class. The bottom half of Figure 2-3 shows how to set these imports through the project's properties. The "Imported namespaces" list shows all available referenced namespaces. Simply check the ones you wish to import; System.Windows.Forms is already checked for you by default in Windows Forms applications.

You can also import a namespace directly in your source code. Use the Imports statement at the very start of a source code file:

```
Imports System.Windows.Forms
```

The Imports statement supports namespace abbreviations, short names that represent the full namespace in your code. Using the statement:

```
Imports Fred = System.Windows.Forms
```

lets you reference the Form class as "Fred.Form." Unlike the imports list in the project's properties, which impacts the entire project, the Imports statement affects only a single source code file.

Namespaces in Your Project

By default, all the classes and types in your project appear in a top-level namespace that takes on the name of your project. For a Windows Forms application, this default namespace is called WindowsApplication1. To specify a different top-level namespace, modify it through the Application tab of the project's properties, in the "Root namespace" field. All the types in your project appear in this namespace; if you specify an existing Microsoft-supplied namespace as your project's root namespace, all your types will appear in that specified namespace mixed in with the preexisting types. For standalone applications, this mixture will be visible only from your code.

From the root namespace, you can place types within subordinate namespaces by using the Namespace statement. Namespace is a block statement that ends with the End Namespace clause. Any types you create between the Namespace and End Namespace clauses will be contained in that subordinate namespace. For example, if your root namespace is WindowsApplication1, the following statements create a class whose full name is WindowsApplication1.WorkArea.BasicStuff.BusyData:

```
Namespace WorkArea.BasicStuff
    Class BusyData
        ...
    End Class
End Namespace
```

You can include as many Namespace statements in your code as needed. Nesting of namespaces is also supported:

```
Namespace WorkArea
    Namespace BasicStuff
        Class BusyData
            ...
        End Class
    End Namespace
End Namespace
```

The My Namespace

Visual Basic 2005 introduced a new "My" top-level namespace, designed to simplify common programming tasks. Microsoft added it to the language in part to draw holdout Visual Basic 6.0 stalwarts into the .NET fold. But most of it is really not that dramatic. My collects commonly used features that are currently sprinkled around the Framework Class Library (FCL), and puts them in a mini-hierarchy for convenient access. It's really not much more complicated than that. The hierarchy is nicely organized, with sections for user, application, and computer-specific information. It's used just like any other part of the framework, although you cannot use the Imports keyword to access its components by a relative path.

Overall, My is very easy to use. To display the version number of your application, for instance, use the following statement:

```
MsgBox(My.Application.Info.Version.ToString)
```

Some areas of the My namespace are dynamic; classes are added or removed as you modify your source code. In Windows Forms applications, the My.Forms branch includes entries for each one of the project's forms. As you add new forms, new entries are added automatically. The My.Forms object then makes a reference to each form available for use in your code.

```
My.Forms.Form1.Text = "Welcome"
```

Summary

Sadly, this chapter has reached its conclusion. You may feel that it went by all too fast; you may feel that you didn't really learn how to write Visual Basic programs; you may feel that a mild sedative would be right just about now. But don't fret. This chapter served as an introduction to the syntax and major features of Visual Basic. Now begins the deeper training. As we start this book's main focus—the Library Project—you will encounter specific examples of all features covered only briefly in this chapter.

Project

In this chapter, we will use the Code Snippets feature of Visual Studio to insert source code into a basic sample code framework. Code Snippets is essentially a hierarchical database of saved source code text. If you have installed the code for this book, you will find code snippets for most chapters included right in Visual Studio. In this chapter's project, I will show you how to use them to add chapter-specific code into your project.

Since we haven't officially started the Library Project, this chapter's project will simply extend the "Hello, World!" project we developed in Chapter 1, but with fun parts added. I will include some of the language features we discovered throughout this chapter.

PROJECT ACCESS

Load the Chapter 2 (Before) Code project, either through the New Project templates or by accessing the project directly from the installation directory. To see the code in its final form, load Chapter 2 (After) Code instead.

Each chapter's sample code includes a "Before" and "After" version. The "After" version represents the code as it will look when all the changes in that chapter's

"Project" section have been applied. The "Before" version doesn't have any of the chapter's project changes included, just placeholders where you will insert the code, one block at a time.

Like the project in Chapter 1, this chapter's project includes a basic Windows form with a single button on it. Clicking on the button displays the same "Hello, World!" message. However, this time, the message starts in an encoded form, and a separate class decodes the message and triggers an event that displays the form.

Once the project is open, view the source code attached to Form1. It should look somewhat like the following:

```
Public Class Form1
    ' *** Insert Code Snippet #2 here.

    Private Sub Button1_Click(ByVal sender As System.Object, _
            ByVal e As System.EventArgs) Handles Button1.Click
        ' *** Insert Code Snippet #3 here.
    End Sub

    ' *** Insert Code Snippet #4 here.
End Class

' *** Insert Code Snippet #1 here.
```

This sample uses a separate class to process the displayed message. The code for this class appears as snippet number 1. To insert the snippet, move the cursor *just after* the #1 snippet marker line, which reads:

```
' *** Insert Code Snippet #1 here.
```

To insert a snippet through the Visual Studio menus, select Edit → IntelliSense → Insert Snippet. The equivalent keyboard sequence is Ctrl-K, Ctrl-X. Or type a question mark (**?**) anywhere in the source code, followed by pressing the Tab key. Any of these methods displays the first level of snippets (see Figure 2-4).

Figure 2-4. Snip, snip, snip

From the snippet list, select Programming Visual Basic 2008, and then select Chapter 2. A list of the available snippet items for this chapter appears (see Figure 2-5).

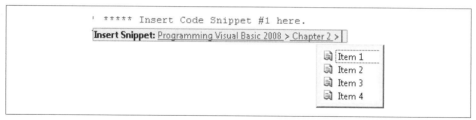

Figure 2-5. Item, item, item

Finally, select Item 1. The content magically appears within the source code. All insertions of code snippets throughout this book occur in exactly this way.

Snippet 1 inserts the SayHello class, part of the HelloStuff namespace, a portion of which appears here:

```
Namespace HelloStuff
    Friend Class SayHello
        Private secretMessage As String
        Private reverseFlag As Boolean
        Private decoded As Boolean

        Public Event MessageDecoded( _
            ByVal decodedMessage As String)

        Public Sub New(ByVal codedMessage As String, _
            ByVal reverseIt As Boolean)
            ...

        Public Sub DecodeMessage(ByVal rotationFactor As Integer)
            ...

        Public Sub ReportMessage( )
            ...
    End Class
End Namespace
```

The SayHello class includes three private fields (secretMessage, reverseFlag, and decoded), which monitor the current status of the display message. A constructor (New) allows the user to create a new instance of SayHello with an initial message text, and a flag that indicates whether the text should be reversed before display. The DecodeMessage subroutine converts each letter of the encoded message to its final form by shifting each letter a rotationFactor number of places. If the letter *E* appears and rotationFactor is 3, the letter *E* is shifted three spaces forward, to *H*. A negative rotation factor shifts the letters lower in the alphabet. The alphabet wraps at the A–Z boundary. Only letters are rotated, and upper- and lowercase are handled independently.

The ReportMessage method fires the MessageDecoded event, sending the previously decoded message to the event as an argument. So, where is this event handler? It's attached to an instance of SayHello that will be added to the Form1 class.

INSERT SNIPPET

Insert Chapter 2, Snippet Item 2.

```
Private WithEvents HelloDecoder As HelloStuff.SayHello
```

The HelloDecoder class is an instance of the HelloStuff.SayHello class that we just wrote, and the snippet makes it a member of the Form1 class. The WithEvents keyword says, "This instance will respond to events"; specifically, the MessageDecoded event from the SayHello class.

Let's add the code that triggers the message to display when the user clicks on the on-form button. This occurs in the button's click event.

INSERT SNIPPET

Insert Chapter 2, Snippet Item 3.

```
HelloDecoder = New HelloStuff.SayHello("!iqwtB ,tqqjM", True)
HelloDecoder.DecodeMessage(-5)
HelloDecoder.ReportMessage( )
```

These three lines create an instance of the SayHello class, storing it in the HelloDecoder class field. Can't read the first argument in the constructor? It's encoded! It's a secret! And the True flag says that it's been reversed to make it an even bigger secret (you don't know what it is!). The DecodeMessage removes the secrets by shifting each letter as needed, although the reversal doesn't happen until the call to ReportMessage.

The ReportMessage method doesn't actually display the message. Instead, it fires an event that makes the unscrambled message available to an event handler.

INSERT SNIPPET

Insert Chapter 2, Snippet Item 4.

```
Private Sub HelloDecoder_MessageDecoded( _
     ByVal decodedMessage As String) _
     Handles HelloDecoder.MessageDecoded
   ' ----- Show the decoded message.
   MsgBox(decodedMessage)
End Sub
```

The Handles keyword connects the subroutine with the fired event. The decoded message comes into the handler through the decodedMessage argument, and is splashed all over the screen with a simple yet powerful call to the MsgBox function.

That's it for the sample code. Now it's time to roll up your sleeves and embark on a full Visual Basic 2008 project.

Introducing the Project

You're sitting in your office, surfing the…I mean reading up on the latest technology issues most pressing to software developers. You're minding your own business, when *boom*, someone walks up to your desk and offers to pay you money to write a program. It happens every day, all over corporate America, and sometimes it just makes me sick.

But enough about my health problems. This desk-hovering somebody informs you that you must develop a software application, possibly a database application with a user-friendly interface. Although the feature set will be specified by the primary users, you, as the lead (or only) programmer, will design, document, develop, and deliver discs dripping with distinguished, dazzling, and dynamic digital…um…software. (Darn.)

Well, that's what happened to me. A client of mine had a large collection of books that they needed to organize as a traditional library. Seeing that I was a reasonably codependent software architect, the client asked me to develop some software to manage the books and such. Out of this request came the *Library Project*.

As you read through this chapter, you will have to keep my day job in mind. I write custom Visual Basic applications for small to medium-size organizations. Most of the projects are sized so that I can complete them by myself, including all design and documentation requirements, in less than a year. All my projects involve a "key user," one person—or sometimes a very small group—who speaks for the user community. These projects also involve someone who has "signature authority," a person authorized to pay for the project, or decide on its continued existence. This individual may be the same as the key user.

If you were developing, say, a replacement for Microsoft Word, you would likely lack a "key user." To obtain the specific requirements for the project, you may have to conduct general user interviews with dozens of user candidates. Or you might create a "persona," a fictional person who represents your intended target audience. (For Visual Studio, Microsoft used three personas named Einstein, Elvis, and Mort.)

Whichever method applies to you, the general discussion in this chapter should guide you to the happy conclusion: a design document that you will use to build the application.

The Library Project

My client needed a program that would manage a database of books and media items, and control how those items moved between bookshelves and patrons. The software needed to have both patron- and administrator-focused features. It would include various reports, including the printing of a receipt of checked-out items for the patron. And most of all, it needed to both print and read bar codes.

It sounds like a lot for one man to do, and it is a sizable project. But I don't have to do it alone; you will help me. Together, through the pages of this book, you and I will design that program, and develop that code, and bring joy to the users, and collect that paycheck. Actually, I will collect the paycheck, although it wouldn't hurt to ask your boss to pay you to read this fine book.

The remainder of this section documents the key features of the Library management application.

Library Item Features

The Library system will manage an inventory of books and other media items, locate them, and manage the details and status of each copy of an item. To make this a reality, the Library program will:

- Allow patrons or administrators to search for items currently in inventory. The program allows searches based on several different properties of each item.
- Support multiple search methods, including by title, by author name, by subject or topic, by a miscellaneous keyword, by the name of the related publisher, by the name of a series or group that contains the item, or by a bar code number attached to the actual item.
- Limit search results by the location of the item, or by the type of media (book, CD, DVD, etc.).
- Support the definition and use of distinct physical locations. The client has books and media stored at three different sites within their building, including a storage closet for seldom-accessed items.
- Display the details of a retrieved item in a familiar browser-style interface. For instance, when looking up a book by title, the user clicks on the author's name to access all other items by that same author.
- Allow access to each library item through a bar code scan. As is common in most libraries today, the items in this library's collection each have a bar code affixed, which serves as a unique identifier for the individual item copy.

Patron Features

In addition to books and other items, the program manages a list of patrons, the "customers" of the library who are permitted to check out items. To support interaction with patrons, the application will include these patron-specific features:

- Items can be checked out to patrons, and checked back into the library inventory.
- All patrons are assigned a "PIN" that acts as their password.
- Patrons can check out items without librarian and administrator assistance. They can use a bar code scanner to scan a patron library card and library items.
- The "media type" of an item determines its checkout (and subsequently its renewal) duration.
- Patrons can view their library record, including all books currently checked out, and a list of fines owed to the library.
- If permitted on a specific item, the patron can renew an item he has currently checked out.
- Patron-centric online help is available through the standard F1 key. This help file includes no information on administrative features, so as to reduce experimentation.
- Patrons can be divided into "patron groups" for the reporting and processing convenience of the administrative staff.

Administrative Features

Administrators include librarians, IT staff, and others who need advanced access to application features. They are the primary users of the system, not the patrons. The application includes the following administrator-specific features:

- A "login" feature provides access to the administrative features of the application. Only authorized users can log in through an assigned password. The login feature is normally hidden from view from ordinary patrons.
- Administrators can view patron details just like patrons can, but they also have access to additional patron details. Specifically, administrators can add new patrons and manage their identity and demographic details. Administrators can also disable a patron record to prevent further item checkouts.
- Administrators collect and manage patron fines, including the ability to add nonstandard fines or to dismiss unpaid fines.
- Administrators define the records for each item managed by the system's inventory database. This includes the basics of each item, such as title and authors. Each item includes one or more copies, which represent physical items that can be checked out. Bar codes are assigned to copies.

- Beyond the items and copies, administrators define all supporting values and lists, including author names and categories, the list of media types, publishers, book series names, status codes that identify the disposition of each item copy, and locations.

- Designated administrators can add, edit, and remove the accounts of other administrators. Each account includes feature-specific authorization settings (group rights).

- In addition to the scanning of bar codes, the program can assist administrators in the design and printing of both patron and item bar codes.

- A simple program-managed process allows the administrative staff to process overdue items and fines on a regular basis.

- The application allows holidays to be added and maintained. When a patron checks out a book, the program adjusts the due date of the item to avoid holidays.

- Administrator-centric online help provides assistance to the enhanced features of the application through the same F1 key available to patrons.

- The application includes some basic administrative reports, and the ability to "plug in" reports as needed in the future without the need to update the program itself.

The Application As a Whole

Beyond the basic features of the program as experienced by the patrons and administrators, there are a few other requirements:

- The program is "user-friendly" and easy to navigate, especially for patrons, without much training or assistance.

- The application stores its data in a SQL Server database.

- Distribution of the application is done by administrative staff that has local administrative privileges, so a standard Windows installation package is sufficient.

- Configuration of the application uses standard XML methods.

Except for these general and feature-specific requirements, I was given design freedom. But where did the listed requirements come from? They came from the users, the masters of the application. It was their *needs*—the needs of my customers and theirs, who would be using the product day in and day out—that determined the list of requirements.

The Needs of the Users

Back in the old days of computers, there were no users. Who needed users? The only ones manly enough to approach the hallowed inner sanctum of the computing systems were the programmers. Only they touched the vacuum tubes, connected the cables, toggled the front panels, and fondled the punch cards that provided access to the heart of the machine. These programmers were tough, and their programs, tougher. "We don't need no stinking users" was their mantra.

Then came the 1980s, with its *Greatest American Hero*-inspired attitude and its personal "personal" computers. Now there were users everywhere. They were like the Blob, only with fewer computing skills. But they were the masters because most programs were written for them. Programmers rarely used the programs they wrote; they were simply the interface between the user and the heart of the computer. Programmers provided the element of *control* needed by both the computer and the users. In fact, that is a programmer's job: to provide highly controlled access to the computer and the data it contains.

Users have a lot of needs, most of which can't be met by a computer. But for those that can, the needs come in five parts: data and information, process, usability, commonality, and project-specific needs. The design process involves an examination of these needs and the subsequent massaging of those needs into a software product. By examining the current data and procedures, conducting user interviews, and performing other need-extraction methods, you gather the details you require to craft the right solution.

Data and Information

Your ability to provide convenient and specific access to the data and information required by the user is what makes you, the programmer, so lovable. Most users got along just fine before computers. They kept their information on 3×5 index cards, or on legal pads, or on scrolls of parchment, or in hermetically sealed mayonnaise jars. But they had a reason to move to a computer-based storage medium: the convenience.

Data is the raw information stored by your program: names, numbers, images, or any other standalone values. *Information* is data in context: a customer record, an order, a slide show. When you provide a quality program that moves data up to the level of information, you are providing the level of convenience the user needs to move from mayonnaise jars to silicon chips.

Process

When the user demands her data back from the computer, you have three options:

- Dump every single byte of data to the screen, printer, or disk, and let the user sort it out. Actually, this is the system that some users had before they started using a computer.

- Protect the data from user access, insisting that the supplied password is invalid or expired, or that the data is unavailable. "Abort, Retry, Fail" anyone? Actually, this is the system that some other users had before they started using a computer.

- Present the data as information, in a format that is both usable and accessible.

Although the first two choices are indeed tempting, the third option is the best. And given the amount of data that your application will likely manage, you will have to dole out the interaction with it a bit at a time, and in an appropriate sequence. This is *process*.

Through the implementation of a valid process, you control not only the user's data, but also the orderly interaction with that data. Most users need to supply or retrieve only a small portion of their data at a time. But when they do, it will usually be in the context of some process. For instance, in an order-taking situation, the user (1) enters or confirms the customer's contact information; (2) enters or updates the order details; and (3) prints or electronically communicates the order information so that it can be fulfilled. Your application (surprise!) manages this three-step process.

Usability

If your program presents data and information to the user, and in a specific arrangement or order, but it is difficult to use, your users will hate you. They will loathe you. They will spread mean stories about you, true or not. And when they appear in groups, their vehemence can get downright ugly. I heard this story about an Excel user's group…but perhaps it was just a rumor.

As a programmer, it is your job to make the computer, and the software that runs on it, as usable as possible. And although you may not be able to control many of the basic system features, you are the king when it comes to your own software.

The more ease and usability you design into your programs, the happier your users will be. But I must warn you, ease of use for the user *always* means more work for the developer. *Always*. It's one of those unfair laws of the universe, and there is no way around it. But sometimes we try—to the user's peril.

Many, many years ago, I wrote some programs to demonstrate a hot new version of BASIC that ran on the Motorola 6809 processor. This release could handle programs that were twice the size of the previous version: a whopping 32 KB of source code. I was charged with testing the system, writing "big" programs that would show off the new functionality. I set to work in a fever of activity, but as my program approached about 27 KB, things started to happen, things that involved a shaking table and the smell of smoke. Seriously!

Since then, I have subconsciously feared the development of programs that I felt were too large for a particular system. So, when I went to work on Visual Basic, I brought to my projects some of this apprehension. I tried to make my programs easy to use, but I also held back on the number of forms I would add to my projects. It wasn't an irrational fear; the original versions of Visual Basic did impose limits on code size, the number of unique variable names, and the maximum number of forms. I once hit the limit on the number of unique variable names, but I never came close on the number of forms. Still, I held back. I was sure that if I added too many forms, my users would require medical attention for smoke inhalation.

Unfortunately, my users were still suffering. I had put too much data on each form, to the point where they were no longer communicating information. My phone would ring constantly with the same user-sponsored question: "How do I use the fields on such-and-such a form?" Of course, I always said, "Why don't you press the F1 key?" But it didn't make a bit of difference, since my online help pages were as long and complex as the forms they sought to simplify.

There did come a day when I escaped my phobia of form-laden applications. And on that day, I came up with the following rules for my own programs:

- Don't put too much information on a single form. When in doubt, move some information to another form.
- Present only the most necessary information and data to the user by default. Show additional information only if the user requests it.
- Make it easy for the user to access the enhanced data, but allow the program to run properly without it.
- Use text, graphics, and colors to the user's advantage.
- Simplify the application so that user documentation becomes unnecessary.
- Always provide user documentation. Make it simple enough so that calls to technical support become unnecessary.

These rules are generic enough to work with any type of application, and they are in-your-face enough to make them meaningful to us, the programmers, and to them, the users.

Commonality

Microsoft constantly touts *innovation*, and the ability to innovate has moved software products forward at a tremendous pace. But unfortunately, users can handle only so much innovation at a time. Consider the telephone. I inherited an old oak-boxed telephone from my grandparents (see Figure 3-1).

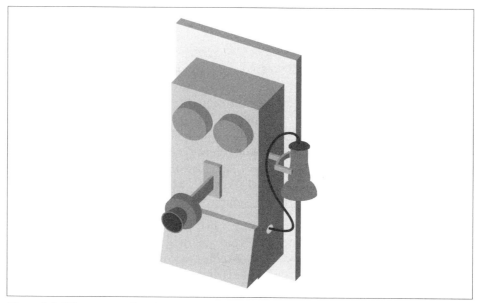

Figure 3-1. What a great phone!

It's a fun phone and so simple to use. When you want to make a call, you pick up the handset and crank the handle on the side of the unit for about three or four seconds. When the operator comes on the line, you tell her who you wish to call. What could be simpler? What could be more user-friendly? What could be more expensive than an operator-assisted call? But it was simple, and everyone instinctively knew how to use it.

Today's phones use buttons instead of cranks. Most of the buttons are simple digits that let you directly dial a specific phone number. But there are other buttons as well: Mute, Redial, Pause, Flash, #, and *. I'm afraid to push the Flash button, and what's with the SND and CLR buttons on cell phones? The problem is not the buttons themselves, but that every phone has a different selection of buttons. They have lost the *commonality* that made crank phones easy to use. Sure, they have many more features, but if the average person can't figure out how to use that functionality, what is the benefit?

Getting back to software: even new and innovative programs must retain some commonality with the operating system, and with other installed programs. As you speak to users about their needs and think about the great advancements in software technology you will provide, don't forget about commonality. Don't forget about one of the core needs of users: the need to not be overwhelmed by new ways of doing tasks they thought they already could do. Users need consistency.

Project-Specific Needs

Beyond the general user needs required of every project, there are needs specific to each project. As an application designer or software architect, this is where you spend most of your time. If you have a lot of programming experience, you may be able to fulfill the other needs without ever meeting with a user. But the project-specific needs require an understanding of the tasks that the user needs to accomplish with the proposed application.

Once the users discover that you have a real interest in their needs, they may dump on you. They might start listing off a whole wish list of features, more features than they could ever use. That's OK. When they hear how much time it will take or how much it will cost to implement, they may back off on a few requests. The important thing is to *document everything*. Write down what the user asks for, combine it with a reasonable time schedule (always) and cost estimate (if required), and return it to the key user for confirmation. If possible, have the user sign a document that says he agrees with the specific requirements listed in the document.

It is essential that there be *agreement* on the project design, at least for the initial phase or release. Since users' needs are so often a moving target, it is vital that an agreement on the project exist at some point in time. Later, after you have begun work on the project, the user will come to you, probably on a daily basis, and say, "Hey, that's not what I asked for." When that happens, point to the agreement and say, "Hey, yes it is." Changes will occur; I'll discuss how to handle those a little later in this chapter.

The Life of a Project

Projects have a lifetime all their own. Some are short-lived; I've written programs that were used for two weeks and then discarded when the business project was complete. Some programs go on forever, with continual improvements made over a series of version iterations. I'm typing into such a program right now.

As a developer, you should be aware of the lifetime of your project. Once you understand the lifetime, you can apply business processes to each major phase of the project's life. The skills needed to guide a project to its conclusion, or through each successive version of the project, are collectively called *project management*. Many organizations have dedicated project managers, especially for larger projects. For small projects, the programmer may have to carry the project management burden alone.

Fortunately, most project managers don't just make things up as they go (although I have met some who did). They work within a system, a *project methodology framework*, a management system that keeps the project plan on track. I will hit the highlights of a typical framework in the remainder of this chapter. If you go back to the bookstore where you received a discount on this book, you will find a full shelf of project methodology framework resources. Microsoft even has its own recommended framework, called the Microsoft Solutions Framework (MSF). Because most of the projects Microsoft develops are renewed through successive versions, the MSF is *cyclical* or *iterative*. For applications that, at least for now, will have only one major release, a *linear* approach works well. (See Figure 3-2 for both approaches.)

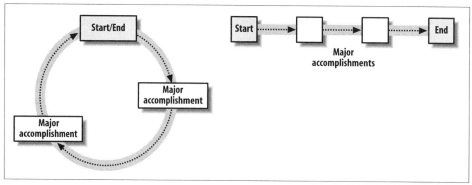

Figure 3-2. Two basic approaches to project management

Since this book will end with a completed project, and neither the next edition nor the movie rights have been arranged yet by my publisher, I will use the linear approach. Whichever approach you use, several major events happen between the start and end of the line or iteration, beginning with the project kickoff.

Project Kickoff

Once everyone agrees that there should be a project, they all come to a big meeting to get things started. Everyone who is considered to be in charge of any part of the project is there: the technical lead (you), the key user, the project manager, and the person with signature authority. If you're writing a program for yourself, only you will be in the room, but you can still provide bagels. This event, the *project kickoff*, marks the official start of the project. This meeting of the minds usually determines the initial schedule for information and resource gathering.

Documentation

It's important to document everything as you go through the entire project, especially in the early design stages. Not only will this help you recall essential aspects of the project later during the development phase, but it will also help you keep all involved parties informed about the status of the project. Imagine this conversation with your boss:

Boss: Management is asking about the status of the Hazel Project. Do you have anything up-to-date that I can give them?

You: Sure, I've got the project plan right here. I'll print you off a copy.

Boss: That'd be great. Hey, you see the new car Bernie in accounting just got?

You: I know! How does an accountant afford a car like that?

Boss: Beats me. It makes you wonder if he's cooking the books or something.

You: Hey author, weren't we talking about documentation?

Oh yeah, documentation. Proper and complete documentation is important in any project. Precise documentation will keep Bernie from accounting out of the big house. And it will keep you in step with the project from initial kickoff to final delivery.

Depending on the scope of the project and the requirements of your organization, your project may need just some basic documentation, or it may need several three-inch binders filled with design documents that examine every nook and cranny of the system. Some project management documents require a signature before the project can continue. Others are informational only. As a programmer, the two most important documents are the main *project design* document (from which you will build the application) and the *schedule* (that lets you gauge progress during the project).

Project Goals

The first important item you will document is the set of *project goals*. If a project (or iteration) has a definite end, it should be possible to identify the major accomplishments needed for that ending event. These goals should be broad, and concerned with the final project *deliverables*. Deliverables are those items that are produced as a result of a project. They generally include software, user and technical documentation, installation media, and related materials. They can also include contractual and project management items, such as a proposed schedule for the next phase or iteration of the project.

The project's goals help determine its *scope*, the extent of the features and supporting materials that will be produced during the project's lifetime. Determining scope is important because it sets the constraints, the limits that will keep the project from going out of control. Although some aspects of the project may change throughout its lifetime, if you allow a project to continue without restraint, you will end up with something like Windows Vista: a useful product that was over a year late and had some features delayed until post-release.

Design and Planning

My mother recently gave me a rather old piece of paper with a drawing of a house floor plan. As I examined this paper in more detail, I found that the design matched the house in which I grew up, a house that is, alas, no longer part of the vast Patrick family real estate holdings. Yet it is still part of the vast Patrick family memory cells, and the home I remembered from my childhood was remarkably similar to the simple sketch. Some forgotten builder was able to take that sketch, add wood and windows and doors and red shag carpeting and an avocado-green refrigerator, and turn it into a home.

Home builders don't work off rough sketches. Between the sketch and the builder was an *architect*, a designer who set down on paper precise details on how to build the house. An architect provides a lot of detail, although not everything. The builder still has the choice of basic materials and construction methodology. But without the project plan—the blueprints—the builder would just be hammering boards together at random, and applying red shag carpet where it didn't belong.

During the design phase, you play the role of an architect, crafting the user's dreams and wishes into a design that can then be turned into a software creation. The level of detail required in these *specifications* will vary by project and organization. For the Library Project, the bullet items listed at the start of this chapter comprise the bulk of the design detail. (It parallels the level of detail my clients have agreed to in similar projects.) Other organizations require excruciating detail, demanding flowcharts and functional specifications, diagrams, and pseudocode that is nearly as detailed as the final source code. For projects that include multiple programmers, you will likely have to specify the interfaces, the function or class member details that allow the code written by two different programmers to communicate accurately.

Whatever level of detail you include in your plan, you will also document certain key events that will happen throughout the entire project schedule. These *milestones* identify interim deliverables, results expected at specified moments throughout the timeline of the project. Comparing the milestone schedule against the actual results produced during development provides an overall view of how the project is progressing over time. Failing to meet several milestone deadlines may require an adjustment in the project schedule, cost, or scope.

Project Approval

A design document gives both the programmer and the user a point of agreement. Both sides can look at the design and say, "Yes, this is it; this is the plan." If the completed program is different from the proposed design, the user can say, "Hey, that wasn't what we agreed to." Sometimes the opposite happens; the programmer develops the application according to the plan, but the user claims that she requested something different. When this happens, the programmer can point to the design and say politely, "This is what we agreed to, and this is what was built."

To provide additional stability, the completed design usually includes a *project approval* document. This paper, signed by both the user representative and the development representative, says that (1) both sides have read the design document; (2) they agree with what it says; and (3) they commit to seeing the project through to completion as designed. As each representative *signs off* on the document, they pledge to give their support to the project.

The approval process also covers the *project cost and schedule*. A realistic estimate of the total time and costs needed to complete the project is as important as the project design itself. Any adjustments in the time and cost throughout the lifetime of the project can also provide valuable feedback on the progress being made.

Software and Other Development

Software development usually consumes most of a project's lifetime. Although the majority of work is done by the programmer or programming team, the user sometimes has a role in this step. By reviewing *prototypes* of specific portions of the application and testing *beta versions* of the nearly completed product, the user remains an active participant in this long project phase.

Changes to the Project

In general, developers always complete projects on time, under budget, and with all features included, and the satisfied user joyfully installs the software, using it daily to meet his demanding business challenges.

Ha, ha. Now that you've had a good laugh, let's continue with the chapter. Many projects do go well, and generally stick to the plan agreed to by the user and the developer. But other projects don't. Somewhere in the middle of the project's life, a change occurs. It may be due to difficulties in building the project, resulting in a *schedule change*. It may be due to new requirements in the user's needs (or desires), or in the related business process, resulting in a *scope change*.

Minor project changes may happen that neither the user nor the programmer is overly concerned about. But other changes can have a significant impact on cost or schedule, or both. Such changes can be documented and agreed to by both sides through a scope change document, sometimes called a *change order*. If the development team must adjust the schedule, or reduce or change the included features of the application, communicating this to the user through a scope change document keeps the user from being surprised at the ever-advancing end of the project.

Using scope change documents, and requiring sign-off from both sides, also helps prevent *scope creep*, the continual adjustment or expansion of software features included in the final product. As users see the progress you are making on the project, and what a great job you are doing, they may show their confidence in you by adding to the project, certain that you can complete the additional work well within the original timeline. Funneling all change requests through the scope change process provides a reality check to the user, giving him a sense of the effort (in terms of cost and schedule) required to develop software.

Acceptance Criteria Testing

There will come a day when you will say, "There, that's the last line of code I need to write for this project." Of course, you will be wrong, but it will feel good to say it. The real last day of coding won't be for several more weeks, after all of the testing is done.

Unit testing concentrates on the individual components, even down to the class and method levels. It ensures that each component or code block returns expected results when given specific input. Both good and bad inputs are sent into the components, and the results analyzed. Unit testing is actually the most cost-effective form of testing, since it is not concerned with the complex interactions of the various components that make up the entire system.

Interface testing is concerned with these interactions. Components that interact with one another are tested as a group, to make sure they work and play well together. Components that expose public interfaces are also tested for consistent results and secure access. *System testing* gives a chance for users to interact with the product, doing all they can to certify that the entire application works in a real-life setting. *Beta testing* is part of the system testing process. System testing may also involve *stress testing*, where the system is tested in extreme computing conditions to see whether it can support the load. Testing various installation scenarios ensures that the new software does not negatively impact other software or operating system components. *Regression testing* is a type of double testing. It involves retesting previously stable code to determine whether subsequent coding changes have introduced direct or indirect bugs into that code.

All of these testing phases are important, but there is one more type of testing that has a direct impact on the progression of the project: *acceptance criteria testing*. This involves a checklist of testable items that both the user and the programmer agree must pass successfully before the project is considered complete. This phase may cover items found in the other phases of testing, but it might also check for basic elements and features, such as the inclusion of quality documentation, or the delivery of the software on a certain medium, such as a CD-ROM. Once acceptance criteria testing is complete, the user signs off on that phase, and the project moves to final acceptance.

Project Acceptance

You've worked long and hard. It's been difficult at times, and perhaps you weren't sure whether you would ever finish. And I'm just talking about this chapter. Some projects take quite awhile to complete, and by the end everyone should be ready to see the fruits of his or her labor. The final step in the agreement portion of the project is the *project acceptance* document. This paper, signed by the user, says that the project was completed as requested (or as modified through change orders). Once this document is signed, the project is officially complete. The programmer is now handsomely paid, and takes a well-deserved three days off.

Deployment and Distribution

The project is now ready for installation on each user's workstation. The method of distribution and delivery depends on the project and target audience. Whether it's an internal network distribution, CD distribution to a small number of locations, web-based distribution to the general public, or boxed media product for sale in retail stores, the programming team usually has limited interaction with the target workstations. Of course, that can change quickly once the technical support phone line is plugged in.

Ongoing Support

After the product has been in use by the user population for a while, reports of application errors or desired enhancements may trickle in to the development team. These can be collected for consideration in a future versioned release, or acted on immediately in "service release" updates of the product. As you may have multiple versions of the product in use within the user community, it is essential that you are able to identify and test against any particular release. *Source code control* systems (including Microsoft Visual SourceSafe that ships with some editions of Visual Studio and Team Foundation Server) allow you to maintain version-specific images of the source code. You can also maintain an archive of release executables and other files for later testing.

If your application was written for a single customer or organization, there may be a *warranty period* during which some or all errors that are reported during the length of the warranty are fixed free of charge.

Summary

Projects are more than just source code. From design documents to project management tools to online help integration to web-based support functionality, a project encompasses resources that go way beyond the basic task of coding. If you are a lone developer, you will have to wear many hats to fully support the application. Those who are part of a larger product team don't have to worry about every possible component of the project, but they also lose out on some of the joy that comes with working on every aspect of a project.

Project

There are many tasks to complete before coding begins in a large project. The actual coding of the Library Project starts in Chapter 5. For this chapter, we will complete the project agreement document that describes the Library Project features.

This chapter does not include a Visual Studio project template that you can load and examine in Visual Studio. Instead, you must access the *Chapter 3* subdirectory from the book's installation directory. This subdirectory contains three files:

Project Agreement.doc
> This is the primary project document that identifies the features of the completed project. It is agreed upon by both the developer and user representatives. Deviation from this document occurs only through the "Change Order" process.

Change Order.doc
> This file is used to modify the original project through the "Change Order" process. When using this document, include a description of the change to be made to the project, and any schedule and cost impact.

Project Acceptance.doc
> This file is used when the project is complete, and the user is ready to accept the finished product. This document combines the "Acceptance Criteria Testing" and "Project Acceptance" elements described earlier in the chapter.

Please feel free to use these documents to support your own projects. However, the legal team at O'Reilly Media would like to remind you that if you choose to use these documents, you're on your own, bucko. These documents are meant as examples only. You should talk to a lawyer in your state if you wish to craft your own documents similar to these and have them be contractually binding.

The remainder of this section presents the *Project Agreement.doc* filled out with the details of the Library Project. Its primary content is a copy of the bullet items listed in the section "The Library Project" near the start of this chapter. It also documents some other project-specific requirements, and includes a typical estimate of project costs. For demonstration purposes, I have used an hourly rate of $25.00.

Project Agreement

Project Name: Library

User: The ACME Library

Date: February 27, 2008

~~~~~~

This project agreement defines a project to be performed by the developer for the user. By signing this agreement, the user representative acknowledges that he or she has read the agreement, and accepts the terms of the agreement identified in this document. The terms of this agreement, or the services provided, may be modified at a later time through a Change Order document.

_____   Date

Authorized User Representative

_____   Date

Authorized User Representative

~~~~~~

Project Objective

The ACME Company houses a small library for its employees, filled with business-specific documentation. The goal of this project is to develop a computer based "library system" that tracks the inventory of books and other available library items. Patrons (employees) may check items out from the library. Librarians (administrators) have access to additional application features, including the ability to manage inventory and patron fines.

Deliverables and Acceptance Criteria

Upon completion of the project tasks defined in this agreement, the developer will provide the following deliverables to the user. Also listed are any testable criteria that must be met for adequate project acceptance by the user.

Page 1

- **The library application**. This Visual Basic 2008 application will be installed on each workstation within the library, and will include both patron and administrative features.
- **The library database**. This database, stored in SQL Server 2005, will manage all inventory, patron, and transaction data for the library.
- **Documentation**. The developer will supply both user documentation (online help, distinct for patrons and administrators) and technical documentation (especially concerning the database).
- **Installation image**. The developer will supply all scripts and supporting documentation needed for the installation of the database. For the client portion, the developer will supply a standard Windows install package to be run on each workstation. ACME's IT department will install this product from a shared network drive or CD.
- **User training**. The developer will provide up to five hours of administrator and librarian training.

Project Tasks

The developer will accomplish the following tasks for the user.

Library Item Features

- Allow patrons or administrators to search for items currently in inventory. The program allows searches based on several different properties of each item.
- Support multiple search methods, including: by title, by author name, by subject or topic, by a miscellaneous keyword, by the name of the related publisher, by the name of a series or group that contains the item, or by a barcode number attached to the actual item.
- Limit search results by the location of the item, or by the type of media (book, CD, DVD, and so on).
- Support the definition and use of distinct physical locations. The client has books and media stored at three different sites within their building, including a storage closet for seldom-accessed items.
- Display the details of a retrieved item in a familiar browser-style interface. For instance, when looking up a book by title, the user clicks on the author's name to access all other items by that same author.
- Allow access to each library items through a barcode scan. As is common in most libraries today, the items in this library's collection each have a barcode affixed, which serves as a unique identifier for the individual item copy.

Page 2

Patron Features

- Items can be checked out to patrons, and checked back into the library inventory.
- All patrons are assigned a "PIN" that acts as their password.
- Patrons can check items out without librarian and administrator assistance. They can use a barcode scanner to scan a patron library card and library items.
- The "media type" of an item determines its checkout (and subsequently renewal) duration.
- Patrons can view their library record, including all books currently checked out, and a list of fines owed to the library.
- If permitted on a specific item, the patron can renew an item he or she has currently checked out.
- Patron-centric online help is available through the standard "F1" key. This help file includes no information on administrative features, so as to reduce experimentation.
- Patrons can be divided into "patron groups" for the reporting and processing convenience of the administrative staff.

Administrative Features

- A "login" feature provides access to the administrative features of the application. Only authorized users can login through an assigned password. The login feature is normally hidden from view from ordinary patrons.
- Administrators can view patron details just like patrons can, but they also have access to additional patron details. Specifically, administrators can add new patrons and manage their identity and demographic details. Administrators can also disable a patron record to prevent further item checkouts.
- Administrators collect and manage patron fines, including the ability to add non-standard fines, or dismiss unpaid fines.
- Administrators define the records for each item managed by the system's inventory database. This includes the basics of each item, such as title and authors. Each item includes one or more copies, which represent physical items that can be checked out. Barcodes are assigned to copies.
- Beyond the items and copies, administrators define all supporting values and lists, including author names and categories, the list of media types, publishers, book series names, status codes that identify the disposition of each item copy, and locations.
- Designated administrators can add, edit, and remove the accounts of other administrators. Each account includes feature-specific authorization settings (group rights).
- In addition to the scanning of barcodes, the program can assist administrators in the design and printing of both patron and item barcodes.

Page 3

- A simple program-managed process allows the administrative staff to process overdue items and fines on a regular basis.
- The application allows holidays to be added and maintained. When a patron checks out a book, the program adjusts the due date of the item to avoid holidays.
- Administrator-centric online help provides assistance to the enhanced features of the application through the same "F1" key available to patrons.
- The application includes some basic administrative reports, and the ability to "plug in" reports as needed in the future without the need to update the program itself.

The Application As a Whole

- The program is "user friendly" and easy to navigate, especially for patrons, without much training or assistance.
- The application stores its data in a SQL Server database.
- Distribution of the application is done by administrative staff that has local administrative privileges, so a standard Windows installation package is sufficient.
- Configuration of the application uses standard XML methods.

Project Estimate and Timetable

The following table summarizes the estimated costs and time to complete the project:

Task Description	Hourly Rate	Time Estimate	Price Estimate
1. Library Item Features	$25.00	30	$750.00
2. Patron Features	$25.00	35	$875.00
3. Administrative Features	$25.00	100	$2,500.00
4. Application As a Whole	$25.00	35	$875.00
Task Subtotal		**200**	**$5,000.00**
5. SQL Server 2005 (estimate only)			$5,000.00
Project Total			**$10,000.00**

Anticipated Project Start Date: March 1, 2008
Anticipated Project End Date: June 30, 2008

Page 4

Designing the Database

Data. Databases. It just kind of makes sense. If you have data, you need to put it somewhere. And what better place to put it than in a "data" base?

Just to make sure I had all the "bases" covered, I did a quick search on the Internet for a useful definition. What a shock. According to virtually every web site I found, a database is "a collection of data organized for easy retrieval by a computer." With a definition like that, pretty much everything I put on my system is stored in a database. All my disk files are organized for easy access. My saved emails can be sorted by subject or date received or sender, so they must be in a database, too. Even this document can be searched and sorted in any manner I wish. Is it a database?

Relational Databases

Perhaps that definition is too broad. These days, when we think of "database," it's generally a *relational database* system. Such databases are built on the "relational model" designed by Edgar Codd of IBM. In 1970, he issued "A Relational Model of Data for Large Shared Data Banks," the seminal paper on relational modeling, and later expanded on the basic concepts with C. J. Date, another "real programmer." Upon reading that 1970 paper—and if you have a free afternoon, you would really benefit from spending time with your family or friends rather than reading that paper—you will enter a world of n-tuples, domains, and expressible sets. Fortunately, you don't need to know anything about these terms to use relational database systems.

The relational databases that most programmers use collect data in *tables*, each of which stores a specific set of unordered *records*. For convenience, tables are presented as a grid of data values, with each *row* representing a single record and each *column* representing a consistent *field* that appears in each record. Table 4-1 presents a table of orders, with a separate record for each line item of the order.

Table 4-1. Boy, a lot of people drink coffee and tea

Record ID	Order ID	Customer ID	Customer Name	Product ID	Product	Price	Quantity
92231	10001	AA1	Al Albertson	BEV01COF	Coffee	3.99	3
92232	10001	AA1	Al Albertson	BRD05RYE	Rye bread	2.68	1
92233	10002	BW3	Bill Williams	BEV01COF	Coffee	3.99	1
92234	10003	BW3	Will Williams	BEV01COF	Tea	3.99	2
92235	10004	CC1	Chuck Charles	CHP34PTO	Potato chips	0.99	7

Putting all of your information in a table is really convenient. The important data appears at a glance in a nice and orderly arrangement, and it's easy to sort the results based on a particular column. Unfortunately, this table of orders has a lot of repetition. Customer names and product names repeat multiple times. Also, although the product ID "BEV01COF" indicates coffee, one of the lines lists it as "Tea." A few other problems are inherent in data that's placed in a single *flat file* database table.

Mr. Codd, the brilliant computer scientist that he was, saw these problems, too. But instead of just sitting around and complaining about them like I do, he came up with a solution: *normalization*. By breaking the data into separate tables with data subsets, assigning a unique identifier to each record/row in every table (a *primary key*), and making a few other adjustments, the data could be "normalized" for both processing efficiency and data integrity. For the sample orders in Table 4-1, the data could be normalized into three separate tables: one for order line items, one for customers, and one for products (see Tables 4-2, 4-3, and 4-4, respectively). In each table, I've put an asterisk next to the column title that acts as the primary key column.

Table 4-2. The table of customers

Customer ID *	Customer Name
AA1	Al Albertson
BW3	Bill Williams
CC1	Chuck Charles

Table 4-3. The table of products

Product ID *	Product Name	Unit Price
BEV01COF	Coffee	3.99
BRD05RYE	Rye bread	2.68
BEV01COF	Coffee	3.99
CHP34PTO	Potato chips	0.99

Table 4-4. The table of order line items

Record ID *	Order ID	Customer ID	Product ID	Quantity
92231	10001	AA1	BEV01COF	3
92232	10001	AA1	BRD05RYE	1
92233	10002	BW3	BEV01COF	1
92234	10003	BW3	BEV01COF	2
92235	10004	CC1	CHP34PTO	7

To get combined results from multiple tables at once, *join* (or link) their matching fields. For instance, you can link the Customer ID field in the table of line items with the matching Customer ID primary key field in the table of customers. Once joined, the details for a single combined line item record can be presented with the matching full customer name. It's the same for direct joins with any two tables that have linkable fields. Figure 4-1 shows the relationships between the customer, product, and order line tables.

Figure 4-1. Three tables, and yet they work as one

To join tables together, relational databases implement *query languages* that allow you to manipulate the data using *relational algebra* (from which the term *relational database* derives). The most popular of these languages, SQL, uses simple English-like sentences to join, order, summarize, and retrieve just the data values you need. The primary statement, SELECT, provides basic data selection and retrieval features. Three other common statements, INSERT, UPDATE, and DELETE, let you manipulate the records stored in each table. Together, these four statements make up the primary *data manipulation language* (DML) commands of SQL. SQL also includes *data definition language* (DDL) statements that let you design the tables used to hold the data, as well as other database features. I'll show examples of various SQL statements later in this chapter.

Vendor-specific systems such as Microsoft's SQL Server, Oracle's Oracle, Microsoft's Access, and IBM's DB2 extend these core DDL and DML features through additional data analysis and management tools. They also battle one another over important features such as data replication, crash-proof data integrity, the speed at which complex queries return the requested results, and who has the biggest private jet.

SQL Server 2005

Microsoft's primary business-level database tool is SQL Server. Although it began its life as a derivative of Sybase (another relational database), it has been given the Microsoft touch. Unlike Access (Microsoft's other relational database product), SQL Server includes advanced data management and analysis features, and a nifty price tag to go along with those features. Although Microsoft was somewhat late in joining the relational database game, it has done a pretty good job at playing catch-up. Oracle still gets high marks for at least its perception of being the most robust, the most stable, and the most platform-independent of the various players. But SQL Server scores big as well, especially with its somewhat lower costs and its more intuitive visual tools.

Originally, Microsoft touted SQL Server as a business-minded tool for business-minded people with their business-minded agendas and their business-minded three-piece poly-knit double-breasted suits, and it is still viewed in this way. But Microsoft is increasingly identifying the database as a development tool, especially with the 2005 release. It was no coincidence that Microsoft chose to debut that version of SQL Server November 7, 2005, the same day as the release of Visual Studio 2005. All flavors of Visual Studio now include some version of SQL Server—even the low-end Visual Studio Express Edition products have access to a SQL Server Express Edition complement. (As of this writing, it was available at no cost from Microsoft's web site.) And it's a two-way relationship between the products: you could always use SQL Server data in your .NET applications, but SQL Server 2005 now allows you to craft embedded stored procedures using .NET code, along with the native and more traditional T-SQL scripting language.

 Microsoft announced the release of SQL Server 2008, the latest version of its star database product, in tandem with Visual Studio 2008. However, although the two products share a common launch date, the actual availability dates of the two products are months apart, with SQL Server 2008 coming out after Visual Studio. Since I cannot be sure that you, as a reader, already have access to SQL Server 2008, I have opted to use SQL Server 2005 as this book's core database. Almost everything you read about SQL Server 2005 in this book will work identically in SQL Server 2008. If you choose to use the 2008 version of the product, you should have no difficulties in following the discussion in this book.

SQL Server, as the name implies, is a "server" product. It runs in the background on a system and communicates with you, the user, by having you first establish a standard network connection with the server engine. This is true even if the SQL Server engine runs on your own workstation. Watching a server product is about as exciting as reading some of those other Visual Basic 2008 tutorial books that you wisely avoided, so Microsoft provides various client tools that let you manage databases, tables, and other relational database properties. SQL Server Management Studio is the standard enterprise-level client tool for managing SQL Server databases. For SQL Server 2005 Express Edition, Microsoft supplies a reduced yet friendlier tool, SQL Server Management Studio Express (see Figure 4-2). This tool lets you manage databases and process DDL and DML statements. Management Studio Express is not included in SQL Server 2005 Express Edition; you must download or obtain it separately from Microsoft. As of this writing, it is available at no cost from Microsoft's web site.

Figure 4-2. SQL Server Management Studio Express

 Because some readers of *Programming Visual Basic 2008* may only have access to SQL Server 2005 Express Edition (and the related SQL Server 2005 Management Studio Express tool), all examples in this book are designed for use with that edition of the database engine. This only impacts the few times when I refer specifically to the client tools. All SQL statements (both DDL and DML) presented in this book and in the Library Project's source code will work with any edition of SQL Server 2005 or SQL Server 2008.

Although Microsoft continues to update and sell Microsoft Access, it is recommending more and more that professional developers use and distribute databases in SQL Server format. Microsoft will even permit you to redistribute SQL Server 2005 Express Edition with your application. To do this, you must first obtain a "SQL Server 2005 Express Edition redistribution license" from Microsoft. Fortunately, it's free and can be had for the asking from the SQL Server 2005 Express Edition web site, *http://www.microsoft.com/sql/express*.

SQL

Conducting business in Japan is pretty easy—once you know the language. The same is true of SQL Server: it's pretty easy to manipulate and access data, once you know the language. In this case, the language is SQL, or *Structured Query Language*. Originally developed by IBM, SQL has since become a standard across the database industry. Well, kind of. As with America and England, Microsoft's SQL Server and Oracle's Oracle are two relational databases that are divided by a common language. The core parts of the SQL language are pretty consistent between vendors, but each supplier adds a lot of extra features and syntax variations designed by Edgar Codd wannabes.

This section describes those DDL and DML statements that will be most useful in our development of the Library program. You'll be glad to know that SQL isn't too picky about the formatting of the various statements. Upper- and lowercase distinctions are ignored; SELECT is the same as select is the same as SeLeCt. (Traditional SQL code is mostly uppercase. I use uppercase for all keywords, and mixed case for tables, fields, and other custom items. Whatever you choose, consistency is important.) Also, employ whitespace as you see fit. You can put statements on one gigantic line, or put every word on a separate line. The only time whitespace and case matter is in the actual data text strings; whatever you type, that's how it stays.

SQL statements normally end with a semicolon, but some tools do not require you to include the semicolon, and other tools require that you exclude it. When using the SQL Server visual client tools (Management Studio and Management Studio Express), semicolons are optional, but it's a good idea to include them when you are using multiple statements together, one after another. SQL statements used in Visual Basic code never include semicolons.

Later, when you look at a SQL script I wrote, you will see the word GO from time to time. In SQL Server, this command says, "For all of the other statements that appeared so far, go ahead and process them now."

DDL Statements

This may come as a shock to you, but before you can store any data in a table, you have to create that table. SQL has just the tool to do this: the CREATE TABLE statement. It's one of the many DDL statements. The basic syntax is pretty straightforward:

```
CREATE TABLE tableName
(
    fieldName1    dataType    options,
    fieldName2    dataType    options,
    and so on...
)
```

Just fill in the parts and you're ready to populate (data, that is). *Table and field names* are built from letters and digits; you can include spaces and some other special characters, but it makes for difficult coding later on. Each vendor has its own collection of *data types*; I'll stick with the SQL Server versions here. The *options* let you specify things such as whether the field requires data, whether it represents the table's primary key, and other similar *constraints*. Extensions to the syntax let you set up constraints that apply to the entire table, *indexes* (which let you sort or search a specific column more quickly), and data storage specifics.

Here's a sample `CREATE TABLE` statement that could be used for the table of order line items (refer to Table 4-4):

```
CREATE TABLE LineItems
(
    RecordID    bigint      IDENTITY PRIMARY KEY,
    OrderID     bigint      NOT NULL,
    CustomerID  varchar(20) NOT NULL
            REFERENCES Customers (CustomerID),
    ProductID   varchar(20) NOT NULL,
    Quantity    smallint    NOT NULL
)
```

The `IDENTITY` keyword lets SQL Server take charge of filling the `RecordID` field with data; it will use a sequential counter to supply a unique `RecordID` value with each new record. The `PRIMARY KEY` clause identifies the `RecordID` field as the unique identifying value for each record in the table. The `bigint` and `smallint` data types indicate appropriately sized integer fields, and the `varchar` type provides space for text, up to the maximum length specified in the parentheses (20 characters). The `REFERENCES` option clause identifies a relationship between this `LineItems` table and another table named `Customers`; values in the `LineItems.CustomerID` field match the key values from the `Customers.CustomerID` field. (Note the "dot" syntax to separate table and field names. It shows up everywhere in SQL.) References between tables are also known as *foreign references*.

If you need to make structure or option changes to a table or its fields after it is created, SQL includes an `ALTER TABLE` statement that can change almost everything in the table. Additionally, there is a related `DROP TABLE` statement used to get rid of a table and all of its data. You might want to avoid this statement on live production data, as users tend to get a bit irritable when their data suddenly disappears off the surface of the earth.

Table 4-5 summarizes the available data types used in SQL Server.

Table 4-5. SQL Server data types

Data type	Description
bigint	An 8-byte (64-bit) integer field for values ranging from −9,223,372,036,854,775,808 to 9,223,372,036,854,775,807.
binary	Fixed-length binary data, up to 8,000 bytes in length. You specify the length through a parameter, as in binary(100).
bit	Supports three possible values: 1, 0, or NULL. Generally used for Boolean values. Internally, SQL Server stores multiple bit fields from a single record in a merged integer field.
char, nchar	Fixed-length standard (char) or Unicode (nchar) strings, up to 8,000 characters in length. You specify the length through a parameter, as in char(100).
cursor	This data type is used within stored procedures, and cannot be used to create a column.
datetime	A general date and time field for dates ranging from January 1, 1753 AD to December 31, 9999 AD. Time accuracy for any given value is within 3.33 milliseconds. SQL Server 2008 adds several new date-related data types: date (dates without times), time (times without dates), datetime2 (same as datetime, but with a larger range and accurate to 100 nanoseconds), and datetimeoffset (date and time ranges).
decimal, numeric	A fixed-precision and scale decimal field. You specify the maximum number of digits to appear on both sides of the decimal point (the precision) and the maximum number of those digits that can appear on the right side of the decimal point (the scale). For instance, a setting of decimal(10,4) creates a field with up to 10 total digits, four of which may appear after the decimal point. The maximum precision value is 38. numeric is a synonym for decimal, as is dec.
float	A floating-point decimal field with variable storage. You can specify the number of bits used to store the value, up to 53. By default, all 53 bits are used, so a setting of float is equivalent to float(53). The pseudodata type real is equivalent to float(24). The values stored are on the order of $\pm 1.0 \times 10^{\pm 38}$; the exact range and precision vary by the bits used for storage. This data type is susceptible to minor calculation errors.
hierarchyid	This data type, new with SQL Server 2008, supports querying of hierarchical and tree-shaped data. It is not available in SQL Server 2005.
image, text, ntext	Don't use these data types, as they will eventually be removed from SQL Server.
int	A 4-byte (32-bit) integer field for values ranging from −2,147,483,648 to 2,147,483,647.
money	An 8-byte (64-bit) high-accuracy field for storing currency values, with up to four digits after the decimal point. Stored data values range from −922,337,203,685,477.5808 to 922,337,203,685,477.5807.
rowversion, timestamp	This data type is used to record modification events on records. There are restrictions on its use, and it is not guaranteed to be unique within a table. timestamp is a deprecated synonym for rowversion; use rowversion instead.
smalldatetime	A general date and time field for dates ranging from January 1, 1900 AD to June 6, 2079 AD. Time accuracy for any given value is within one minute.
smallint	A 2-byte (16-bit) integer field for values ranging from −32,768 to 32,767.
smallmoney	A 4-byte (32-bit) high-accuracy field for storing currency values, with up to four digits after the decimal point. Stored data values range from −214,748.3648 to 214,748.3647.
sql_variant	A generic type that stores values from many other type-specific fields.
table	A special field that temporarily stores the results of a query in a compacted table format. Defining a table field is somewhat complex, and its use naturally carries with it certain restrictions.
tinyint	A 1-byte (8-bit) unsigned integer field for values ranging from 0 to 255.

Table 4-5. SQL Server data types (continued)

Data type	Description
uniqueidentifier	A 16-byte globally unique identifier (GUID). The related NEWID function generates values for this field.
varbinary	Variable-length binary data, up to 8,000 bytes in length. You specify the length through a parameter, as in varbinary(100). The field only consumes space for the actual content currently stored in the field. A special setting of varbinary(max) allows entry of up to about 2 billion bytes.
varchar, nvarchar	Variable-length standard (varchar) or Unicode (nvarchar) strings, up to 8,000 characters in length. You specify the length through a parameter, as in varchar(100). The field only consumes space for the actual content currently stored in the field. A special setting of varchar(max) allows entry of up to about 2 billion characters.
xml	Provides storage for typed and untyped XML data documents, up to 2 GB.

DML Statements

Although DDL statements are powerful, they aren't used that much. Once you create your database objects, there's not much call for tinkering. The DML statements are more useful for everyday data surfing.

The INSERT statement adds data records to a table. Data is added to a table one record at a time. (A variation of INSERT lets you insert multiple records, but those records must come from another existing table source.) To use the INSERT statement, specify the destination table and fields, and then the individual values to put into each field. One data value corresponds to each specified data column name.

```
INSERT INTO LineItems
    (OrderID, CustomerID, ProductID, Quantity)
    VALUES (10002, 'BW3', 'BEV01COF', 1)
```

Assuming this statement goes with the CREATE TABLE statement written earlier, this insert action will add a new record to the LineItems table with five new fields—four specified fields, plus the primary key automatically added to the RecordID field (since it was marked as IDENTITY). SQL Server also does a variety of data integrity checks on your behalf. Each data field you add must be of the right data type, but you already expected that. Since we designed the CustomerID field to be a reference to the Customer table, the insert will fail if customer BW3 does not already exist in the Customer table.

Numeric literals can be included in your SQL statements as needed without any additional qualification. String literals are always surrounded by single quotes, as is done for the customer and product IDs in this INSERT statement. If you need to include single quotes in the literal, enter them twice:

```
'John O''Sullivan'
```

Surround literal date and time values with single quotes:

```
'7-Nov-2005'
```

Such date and time values accept any recognized format, although you should use a format that is not easy for SQL Server to misinterpret.

Many field types support an "unassigned" value, a value that indicates that the field contains no data at all. Such a value is known as the "null" value, and is specified in SQL Server using the NULL keyword. You cannot assign NULL to primary key fields, or to any field marked with the NOT NULL option.

To remove a previously added record, use the DELETE statement:

```
DELETE FROM LineItems WHERE RecordID = 92231
```

The DELETE statement includes a WHERE clause (the WHERE RecordID = 92231 part). WHERE clauses let you indicate one or more records in a table by making comparisons with data fields. Your WHERE clauses can include AND and OR keywords to join multiple conditions, and parentheses for grouping.

```
DELETE FROM LineItems WHERE OrderID = 10001
    AND ProductID = 'BRD05RYE'
```

Such a DELETE statement may delete zero, one, or 1,000 records, so precision in the WHERE clause is important. To delete all records in the table, exclude the WHERE clause altogether.

```
DELETE FROM LineItems
```

The UPDATE statement also uses a WHERE clause to modify values in existing table records.

```
UPDATE LineItems SET Quantity = 4
    WHERE RecordID = 92231
```

Assignments are made to fields with the SET clause; put the field name (Quantity) on the left side of the equals sign, and the new value on the right (4). To assign multiple values at once, separate each assignment with a comma. You can also include formulas and calculations.

```
UPDATE LineItems SET Quantity = Quantity + 1,
    ProductID = 'BEV02POP'
    WHERE RecordID = 92231
```

As with the DELETE statement, the UPDATE statement may update zero, one, or many records based on which records match the WHERE clause.

The final DML statement, and the one most often used, is SELECT.

```
SELECT ProductID, Quantity FROM LineItems
    WHERE RecordID = 92231
```

SELECT scans a table (LineItems), looking for all records matching a given criterion (RecordID = 92231), and returns a smaller table that contains just the indicated fields (ProductID and Quantity) for the matching records. The most basic query returns all rows and columns.

```
SELECT * FROM LineItems
```

This query returns all records from the table in no particular order. The asterisk (*) means "include all fields."

The optional ORDER BY clause returns the results in a specific order.

```
SELECT * FROM LineItems
   WHERE Quantity > 5
   ORDER BY ProductID, Quantity DESC
```

This query returns all records that have a Quantity field value of more than five, and sorts the results first by the ProductID column (in ascending order) and then by the numeric quantity (in descending order, specified with DESC).

Aggregate functions and grouping features let you summarize results from the larger set of data. The following query documents the total ordered quantity for each product in the table:

```
SELECT ProductID, SUM(Quantity) FROM LineItems
   GROUP BY ProductID
```

You can use *joins* to link together the data from two or more distinct tables. The following query joins the LineItems and Customer tables on their matching CustomerID columns. This SELECT statement also demonstrates the use of table abbreviations (the "LI" and "CU" prefixes) added through the AS clauses; they aren't usually necessary, but they can help make a complex query more readable.

```
SELECT LI.OrderID, CU.CustomerName, LI.ProductID
   FROM LineItems AS LI INNER JOIN Customer AS CU
   ON LI.CustomerID = CU.CustomerID
   ORDER BY LI.OrderID, CU.CustomerName
```

This table uses an "inner join," one of the five main types of joins, each of which returns different sets of records based on the relationship between the first (left) and second (right) tables in the join:

Inner join
> Returns only those records where there is a match in the linked fields. This type of join uses the INNER JOIN keywords.

Left outer join
> Returns every record from the left table and only those records from the right table where there is a match in the linked fields. If a left table record doesn't have a match, it acts as though all the fields in the right table for that record contain NULL values. This type of join uses the LEFT JOIN keywords. One use might be to join the Product and LineItems tables. You could return a list of the full product name for all available products, plus the total quantity ordered for each one. By putting the Product table on the left of a left outer join, the query would return all product names, even if that product had never been ordered (and didn't appear in the LineItems table).

Right outer join

> This works just like a left outer join, but all records from the right table are returned, and just the left table records that have a match. This type of join uses the RIGHT JOIN keywords.

Full outer join

> Returns all records from the left and right tables, whether they have matches or not. When there is a match, it is reflected in the results. This type of join uses the FULL JOIN keywords.

Cross join

> Also called a *Cartesian join*. Returns every possible combination of left and right records. This type of join uses the CROSS JOIN keywords.

Joining focuses on the relationship that two tables have. (This use of "relationship," by the way, is not the basis for the term *relational database*.) Some tables exist in a "parent-child" relationship; one "parent" record has one or more dependent "child" records in another table. This is often true of orders; a single "order header" has multiple "line items." This type of relationship is known as *one-to-many*, since one record is tied to many records in the other table. And the relationship is unidirectional; a given child record does not tie to multiple parent records.

A *one-to-one* relationship ties a single record in one table to a single record in another table. It's pretty straightforward, and is often used to enhance the values found in the original record through a supplementary record in a second table.

In a *many-to-many* relationship, a single record in one table is associated with multiple records in a second table, *and* a single record in that second table is also associated with multiple records in the first table. A real-world example would be the relationship between teachers and students in a college setting. One teacher has multiple students in the classroom, but each student also has multiple teachers each semester. Practical implementations of many-to-many relationships actually require three tables: the two related tables, and a "go-between" table that links them together. I will show you a sample of such a table in the upcoming "Project" section of this chapter.

Beyond Basic SQL

The sample statements I listed here only scratch the surface of the data manipulation possibilities available through SQL. But by now you should have noticed that SQL is remarkably English-like in syntax, much more than even Visual Basic. In fact, the original name for the language—SEQUEL—was an acronym for "Structured *English* Query Language." As the SQL statements get more complex, they will look less and less like an eighth-grade essay and more like random collections of English words.

The goal here is to introduce you to the basic structure of SQL statements. Most of the statements we will encounter in the Library Project will be no more complex than the samples included here. If you're hungry for more, the "Books Online" component installed with SQL Server (a separate download for the Express Edition) has some pretty good usage documentation. Several good books on the ins and outs of SQL, including vendor-specific dialects, are also available.

Using Databases in Visual Basic

Visual Basic can interact with data stored in a database in a few different ways:

- Use ADO.NET, the primary data access technology included in the .NET Framework, to interact with database-stored content. This is the method used throughout the Library program to interact with its database. ADO.NET is discussed in Chapter 10, with examples of its use. I will also introduce ADO.NET-specific code into the Library Project in that chapter.

- Use the "data binding" features available in Visual Basic and Visual Studio. Binding establishes a connection between an on-screen data control or similar data-enabled object and content from a database. Code written for you by Microsoft takes care of all the communication work; you can even drag and drop these types of interactions. Although I will discuss data binding in Chapter 10 (since binding is based on ADO.NET), I tend to avoid it since it reduces the amount of control the programmer can exert on user data management. Data binding will not be used in the Library program.

- Extract the data from the database into a standard file, and use file manipulation features in Visual Basic to process the data. Hmm, that doesn't seem very useful, but I have actually had to do it, especially in the old days when some proprietary databases could not interact easily with Visual Basic code.

- Each time you need some of the data, tell the user that somehow the data has been lost, and that it must be reentered immediately. If you have ever been curious to know what the inside of an unemployment office looks like, this could be your chance.

If you are a former Visual Basic 6.0 (or earlier) programmer, you may think that your knowledge of ADO will translate directly into ADO.NET development. Ha! You couldn't be more wrong. Although the two data technologies share a partial name, the code written to use each method varies considerably. I will not discuss the older ADO technology at all in this book.

Documenting the Database

Technical content that describes the tables and fields in your application's database represents the most important piece of documentation generated during your application's lifetime. In fact, the need for good documentation is the basis for one of my core programming beliefs: project documentation is as important, and sometimes more important, than source code.

You may think I'm joking about this. Although you will (hopefully) find a lot of humor in the pages of this book, this is something I don't joke about. If you are developing an application that centers on database-stored user content, complete and accurate documentation of every table and field used in the database is a must. Any lack in this area will—not might, not perhaps, but will—lead to data integrity issues and a longer-than-necessary development timeline. Figure 4-3 puts it another way.

Figure 4-3. Any questions?

Why do I think that database documentation is even more important than user documentation or functional specifications? It's because of the impact the document will have on the user's data. If you have a documented database, you can make guesses about the functional specification, and probably come pretty close. If you lack user documentation, you can always write it when the program is done (as though there was any other way?). But if you lack database documentation, you are in for a world of hurt.

If you haven't worked on large database projects before, you might not believe me. But I have. I once inherited an existing enterprise-wide database system written in Visual Basic 3.0. The source code was bad enough, but the associated undocumented 100-table database was a mishmash of inconsistently stored data values. The confusing stored procedure code wasn't much better. Since there wasn't a clear set of documentation on each field, the six programmers who originally developed the system had each made their own decisions about what range of data would be allowed in each field, or about which fields were required or not.

Tracing back through the uncommented 100,000 lines of source code to determine what every field did was not fun, and it took a few months to complete it with accuracy. Since the customer had paid for and expected a stable and coherent system, most of the extra cost involved in replacing the documentation that should have been there in the first place was borne by my development group. Don't let this happen to you!

Summary

Most Visual Basic applications target the business world and are designed to interact with some sort of database. Understanding the database system used with your application is important; even more important is documenting the specific database features you incorporate into your application.

Because of the influence of relational databases and the SQL language on the database industry, it won't be hard to find a lot of resources to assist you in crafting SQL statements and complex data analysis queries. The Library Project in this book uses SQL Server 2005, but because of the generally consistent use of the core SQL language features, the application could just as easily have used Oracle, Microsoft Access, or any of a number of other relational databases.

Project

To assist in my development of Visual Basic database projects, I always write a "Technical Resource Kit" document before I begin the actual coding of the application. The bulk of this word processing document consists of the table- and field-level documentation for the application's associated database. Also included are the formats for all configuration and custom datafiles, a map of the online help pages, and information about third-party products used in the application. Depending on the type of application, my expectations for the user, and the terms of any contract, I may supply none, some, or all of the Resource Kit's content to the user community.

Let's begin the Technical Resource Kit for the Library Project by designing and documenting the database tables to be used by the application. This Resource Kit appears in the book's installation directory, in the *Chapter 4* subdirectory, and contains the following three files:

ACME Library Resource Kit.doc
　　A Microsoft Word version of the technical documentation for the project

ACME Library Resource Kit.pdf
　　A second copy of the Technical Resource Kit, this time in Adobe Acrobat (PDF) format

Database Creation Script.sql
　　A SQL Server database script used to build the actual tables and fields in the database

Technical Resource Kit Content

This section includes a listing of the tables included in the Library database. Each table includes a general description to assist you in your understanding of the database structure. You will encounter all of these tables in successive chapters, along with associated source code, so don't freak out if some table or field seems unknowable right now.

Security-related tables

Although patrons do not need to log in to the application to look up items in the database, administrators must log in before they can access enhanced features of the program. The following four tables manage the security credentials of each administrator. The application uses SQL Server or Windows-based security credentials only to access the database initially, not to restrict features.

> **Activity.** This table defines the features of the application that can be secured using group rights. These activities are linked with security groups (from the GroupName table) to establish the rights for a particular group.

Field	Type	Description
ID	bigint	Primary key. This key is not auto-generated; the value supplied matches internal values used within the Library application. Required.
FullName	varchar(50)	Descriptive name of this activity. Required.

The following activities are defined at this time:
- 1—Manage authors and names
- 2—Manage author and name types
- 3—Manage copy status codes
- 4—Manage media types
- 5—Manage series
- 6—Manage security groups
- 7—Manage library materials
- 8—Manage patrons
- 9—Manage publishers
- 10—Manage system values
- 11—Manage administrative users
- 12—Process and accept fees
- 13—Manage locations
- 14—Check out library items

- 15—Check in library items
- 16—Access administrative features
- 17—Perform daily processing
- 18—Run system reports
- 19—Access patrons without patron password
- 20—Manage bar codes
- 21—Manage holidays
- 22—Manage patron groups
- 23—View administrative patron messages

GroupName. Each record in this table defines a single security group. Librarians and other administrators each belong to a single security group.

Field	Type	Description
ID	bigint	Primary key; automatically assigned. Required.
FullName	varchar(50)	Name of this group. Required.

GroupActivity. This table connects records in the Activity table to records in the GroupName table (a many-to-many relationship) to establish the activities a security group can perform.

Field	Type	Description
GroupID	bigint	Primary key. The associated security group. Foreign reference to GroupName.ID. Required.
ActivityID	bigint	Primary key. The activity that members of the associated security group can perform. Foreign reference to Activity.ID. Required.

UserName. This table contains the actual records for each librarian or administrator. Each record includes the user's password and security group setting.

Field	Type	Description
ID	bigint	Primary key; automatically assigned. Required.
FullName	varchar(50)	Name of this user, administrator, or librarian. Required.
LoginID	varchar(20)	User ID that gives this user access to the system. It is entered into the Library program's "login" form, along with the password, to gain access to enhanced features. Required.
Password	varchar(20)	The password for this user, in an encrypted format. Optional.
Active	bit	Is this user allowed to access the system? 0 for False, 1 for True. Required.
GroupID	bigint	To which security group does this user belong? Foreign reference to GroupName.ID. Required.

Support code tables

Several tables exist simply to provide a list of values to other tables. In an application, these list tables often appear as the choices in a drop-down ("combo box") control.

CodeAuthorType. In the Library program, the word *author* is a generic term used for authors, illustrators, editors, and any other similar contributor to an item in the library's inventory. This table lets you define those roles.

Field	Type	Description
ID	bigint	Primary key; automatically assigned. Required.
FullName	varchar(50)	Name of this type of author or contributor. Required.

CodeCopyStatus. Copy status codes include things like "circulating," "being repaired," and any other primary status the library wishes to set. The checked-in or checked-out status is handled through other features, as is the flag that indicates whether an item is a reference item.

Field	Type	Description
ID	bigint	Primary key; automatically assigned. Required.
FullName	varchar(50)	Name of this status entry. Required.

CodeLocation. Physical locations where library items are stored. This could be separate sites, or rooms or areas within a common location.

Field	Type	Description
ID	bigint	Primary key; automatically assigned. Required.
FullName	varchar(50)	Name of this location. Required.
LastProcessing	datetime	The date when daily processing was last done for this location. If NULL, processing has not yet been done. Optional.

CodeMediaType. Types of media, such as books, magazines, videos, CDs, etc.

Field	Type	Description
ID	bigint	Primary key; automatically assigned. Required.
FullName	varchar(50)	Name of this media type. Required.
CheckoutDays	smallint	Number of days for which items in this type can be checked out, before renewal. Required.
RenewDays	smallint	Number of days to add to the original checkout period for a renewal of items within this type. Required.
RenewTimes	smallint	Maximum number of times the item can be renewed by a patron before it must be returned. Required.
DailyFine	money	Amount charged per day for an overdue item of this type. Required.

CodePatronGroup. Categories of groups into which patrons are placed. These are not security groups, but general groups for reporting purposes. This was added to support grouping of patrons by units within a company, or by class/grade within a school library setting.

Field	Type	Description
ID	bigint	Primary key; automatically assigned. Required.
FullName	varchar(50)	Name of this patron group. Required.

CodeSeries. Some items appear as part of a larger series or collection. This table defines the collection and series names.

Field	Type	Description
ID	bigint	Primary key; automatically assigned. Required.
FullName	varchar(50)	Name of this series or collection. Required.

Library items

The tables in this section manage the actual inventory of items. Since a library may own more than one copy of a single item, these tables manage the "named item" and its individual "copies" separately.

NamedItem. A library item, such as a book, CD, or magazine. This table represents a general item, and not the actual copy of the item.

Field	Type	Description
ID	bigint	Primary key; automatically assigned. Required.
Title	varchar(150)	Title of this item. Required.
Subtitle	varchar(150)	Subtitle of this item. Optional.
Description	varchar(max)	Full description of this item. Optional.
Edition	varchar(10)	Edition number for this item. Optional.
Publisher	bigint	This item's publisher. Foreign reference to Publisher.ID. Optional.
Dewey	varchar(20)	Dewey decimal number. Use / for line breaks. Optional.
LC	varchar(25)	Library of Congress number. Use / for line breaks. Optional.
ISxN	varchar(20)	ISBN, ISSN, or other standardized number of this item. Optional.
LCCN	varchar(12)	Library of Congress control number. Optional.
Copyright	smallint	Year of original copyright, or of believed original copyright. Optional.
Series	bigint	The series or collection in which this item appears. Foreign reference to CodeSeries.ID. Optional.
MediaType	bigint	The media classification of this item. Foreign reference to CodeMediaType.ID. Required.
OutOfPrint	bit	Is this title out of print? 0 for False, 1 for True. Required.

ItemCopy. A single copy of a named item. Separate copies of the same item will appear as separate records in this table.

Field	Type	Description
ID	bigint	Primary key; automatically assigned. Required.
ItemID	bigint	The related named item record. Foreign reference to NamedItem.ID. Required.
CopyNumber	smallint	Numbered position of this item within the set of copies for a named item. Required, and unique among items with the same ItemID field value.
Description	varchar(max)	Comments specific to this copy of the item. Optional.
Available	bit	Is this copy available for checkout or circulation? 0 for False, 1 for True. Required.
Missing	bit	Has this copy been reported missing? 0 for False, 1 for True. Required.
Reference	bit	Is this a reference copy? 0 for False, 1 for True. Required.
Condition	varchar(30)	Any comments relevant to the condition of this copy. Optional.
Acquired	datetime	Date this copy was acquired by the library. Optional.
Cost	money	Value of this item, either original or replacement value. Optional.
Status	bigint	The general status of this copy. Foreign reference to CodeCopyStatus.ID. Required.
Barcode	varchar(20)	Bar code found on the copy. At this time, only numeric bar codes are supported. Optional.
Location	bigint	The site or room location of this item. Foreign reference to CodeLocation.ID. Optional.

Publisher. An organization that publishes books or some other type of media.

Field	Type	Description
ID	bigint	Primary key; automatically assigned. Required.
FullName	varchar(100)	Name of the publisher. Required.
WebSite	varchar(255)	URL for this publisher's web site. Optional.

Author. Someone who writes, edits, illustrates, or in some other way contributes to a book or media item. In all cases, when the term *author* appears in this table, it refers to anyone who contributes to the item.

Field	Type	Description
ID	bigint	Primary key; automatically assigned. Required.
LastName	varchar(50)	Last name of this author. Required.
FirstName	varchar(30)	First name of this author. Optional.
MiddleName	varchar(30)	Middle name or initial of this author. Optional.

Field	Type	Description
Suffix	varchar(10)	Name suffix, such as "Jr." Optional.
BirthYear	smallint	Year of birth. Use negative numbers for BC. Optional.
DeathYear	smallint	Year of death. Use negative numbers for BC. Optional.
Comments	varchar(250)	Miscellaneous comments about this author. Optional.

ItemAuthor. An author, editor, and so on, for a specific named item. This table establishes a many-to-many relationship between the NamedItem and Author tables.

Field	Type	Description
ItemID	bigint	Primary key. The associated named item. Foreign reference to NamedItem.ID. Required.
AuthorID	bigint	Primary key. The author associated with the named item. Foreign reference to Author.ID. Required.
Sequence	smallint	Relative order of this author among the authors for this named item. Authors with smaller numbers appear first. Required.
AuthorType	bigint	The specific type of contribution given by this author for this named item. Foreign reference to CodeAuthorType.ID. Required.

Keyword. Custom words that can be applied to named items to make searching easier.

Field	Type	Description
ID	bigint	Primary key; automatically assigned. Required.
FullName	varchar(50)	Name of this keyword. Required.

ItemKeyword. Connects a keyword with a named item through a many-to-many relationship between the NamedItem and Keyword tables.

Field	Type	Description
ItemID	bigint	Primary key. The associated named item. Foreign reference to NamedItem.ID. Required.
KeywordID	bigint	Primary key. The keyword to associate with the named item. Foreign reference to Keyword.ID. Required.

Subject. Subject headings used to classify named items.

Field	Type	Description
ID	bigint	Primary key; automatically assigned. Required.
FullName	varchar(150)	Name of this subject. Required.

ItemSubject. Connects a subject with a named item through a many-to-many relationship between the `NamedItem` and `Subject` tables.

Field	Type	Description
ItemID	bigint	Primary key. The associated named item. Foreign reference to `NamedItem.ID`. Required.
SubjectID	bigint	Primary key. The subject to associate with the named item. Foreign reference to `Subject.ID`. Required.

Patron-related tables

The tables in this section define the actual patron records and their relationship to item copies (when such copies are checked out by the patron).

Patron. An identified library user. Patrons usually have checkout privileges.

Field	Type	Description
ID	bigint	Primary key; automatically assigned. Required.
LastName	varchar(30)	Last name of this patron. Required.
FirstName	varchar(30)	First name of this patron. Required.
LastActivity	datetime	Date of last checkout, renewal, or return. Optional.
Active	bit	Is this an active patron? 0 for False, 1 for True. Required.
Comments	varchar(max)	Any comments associated with this patron. Optional.
AdminMessage	varchar(500)	Comments that are displayed to administrative users when the patron's record is accessed. Optional.
Barcode	varchar(20)	Bar code found on this patron's library card. At this time, only numeric bar codes are supported. Optional.
Password	varchar(20)	Patron's password, in an encrypted format. Required.
Email	varchar(100)	Patron's email address. Optional.
Phone	varchar(20)	Patron's phone number. Optional.
Address	varchar(50)	Patron's street address. Optional.
City	varchar(20)	Patron's city. Optional.
State	varchar(2)	Patron's state abbreviation. Optional.
Postal	varchar(10)	Patron's postal code. Optional.
PatronGroup	bigint	The group in which this patron appears. Foreign reference to `CodePatronGroup.ID`. Optional.

PatronCopy. This table manages item copies currently checked out by a patron, or item copies that were previously checked out and have since been returned.

Field	Type	Description
ID	bigint	Primary key; automatically assigned. Required.
Patron	bigint	The associated patron. Foreign reference to Patron.ID. Required.
ItemCopy	bigint	The item copy currently or previously checked out by the patron. Foreign reference to ItemCopy.ID. Required.
CheckOut	datetime	The date when this item copy was initially checked out. Required.
Renewal	smallint	The number of times this item copy has been renewed. Set to 0 when the item copy is first checked out. Required.
DueDate	datetime	Current due date for this item copy. Required.
CheckIn	datetime	The date when this item copy was returned. Optional.
Returned	bit	Has the item copy been returned? 0 for False, 1 for True. Required.
Missing	bit	Is the item copy missing and considered lost? 0 for False, 1 for True. Required.
Fine	money	Total fine accumulated for this item copy. Defaults to 0.00. An administrator may reduce an accumulated fine. Required.
Paid	money	Total amount paid (in fees) for this item copy. Required.
ProcessDate	datetime	When an item copy is processed for overdue fines, this field contains the last date for which processing was done. Optional.

PatronPayment. Fines, payments, and dismissals on a patron copy record. Overdue fines are not recorded in this table, but administrator-initiated fines due to charges for missing items are recorded here.

Field	Type	Description
ID	bigint	Primary key; automatically assigned. Required.
PatronCopy	bigint	The associated item checked out by the patron. Foreign reference to PatronCopy.ID. Required.
EntryDate	datetime	Date and time when this entry was recorded. Required.
EntryType	varchar(1)	The type of payment entry. Required. The possible values are: • P = The patron made a payment. • F = A fine (other than a standard overdue fine) was imposed by an administrator. • D = A portion (or all) of the fine was dismissed. • R = A refund was given to the patron due to overpayment.
Amount	money	The amount associated with this entry. The value is always positive. Required.
Comment	varchar(50)	A short comment about this entry. Optional.
UserID	bigint	The user who added this payment event. Foreign reference to UserName.ID. Optional.

Bar code-related tables

There are three levels of definition to create a bar code: (1) the sheet on which a grid of labels prints; (2) a single label on the sheet; and (3) the individual items that appear on each label. The three tables in this section define those three levels.

BarcodeSheet. Describes the template for a single page of bar code labels.

Field	Type	Description
ID	bigint	Primary key; automatically assigned. Required.
FullName	varchar(50)	Name of this sheet template. Required.
UnitType	varchar(1)	Units used in the various measurements found in most fields in this record. Required. • I = Inches • C = Centimeters • P = Points • T = Twips
PageWidth	decimal(10,4)	Width of the entire page. Required.
PageHeight	decimal(10,4)	Height of the entire page. Required.
MarginLeft	decimal(10,4)	Left border, up to the edge of the printable label area. Required.
MarginRight	decimal(10,4)	Right border, up to the edge of the printable label area. Required.
MarginTop	decimal(10,4)	Top border, up to the edge of the printable label area. Required.
MarginBottom	decimal(10,4)	Bottom border, up to the edge of the printable label area. Required.
IntraColumn	decimal(10,4)	The width of the blank area between label columns. Required.
IntraRow	decimal(10,4)	The height of the blank area between label rows. Required.
ColumnsCount	smallint	The number of label columns on this template. Required.
RowsCount	smallint	The number of label rows on this template. Required.

BarcodeLabel. Describes the template for a single label on a bar code sheet. Any number of labels may be on a single sheet, but they all have the same shape and format.

Field	Type	Description
ID	bigint	Primary key; automatically assigned. Required.
FullName	varchar(50)	Name of this label template. Required.
BarcodeSheet	bigint	The sheet template on which this label template appears. Foreign reference to BarcodeSheet.ID. Required.
UnitType	varchar(1)	Units used in the various measurements found in most fields in this record. Required. • I = Inches • C = Centimeters • P = Points • T = Twips

BarcodeLabelItem. Describes a single item as found on a bar code label. Items include static and generated text, lines, rectangles, and generated bar codes.

Field	Type	Description
ID	bigint	Primary key; automatically assigned. Required.
Priority	smallint	Identifies the order in which items on the label are printed. Lower numbers are printed first. Required.
BarcodeLabel	bigint	The label template on which this item appears. Foreign reference to `BarcodeLabel.ID`. Required.
ItemType	varchar(1)	What type of item does this record represent? Required. • T = Static text • B = Bar code • N = Bar code number • L = Line • R = Rectangle
PosLeft	decimal(10,4)	Left edge of the item relative to the left edge of the label. Measured according to the related `BarcodeLabel.UnitType` field. Required.
PosTop	decimal(10,4)	Top edge of the item relative to the top edge of the label. Measured according to the related `BarcodeLabel.UnitType` field. Required.
PosWidth	decimal(10,4)	Width of the item, or of the box in which the item is drawn. For lines, this is the *x* coordinate of the endpoint. Measured according to the related `BarcodeLabel.UnitType` field. Required.
PosHeight	decimal(10,4)	Height of the item, or of the box in which the item is drawn. For lines, this is the *y* coordinate of the endpoint. Measured according to the related `BarcodeLabel.UnitType` field. Required.
Rotation	smallint	Rotation angle, in degrees, of the box in which the item is drawn. Zero (0) equals no angle, and increasing angles proceed clockwise. Ranges from 0 to 359. Only used when `ItemType` is T, B, N, or R. Optional.
FontName	varchar(50)	The name of the font used to write the text. Valid only when `ItemType` is T or N. Optional.
FontSize	decimal(10,4)	The size of the font used to write the text. Valid only when `ItemType` is T, B, or N. Optional.
StaticText	varchar(100)	The static text to display on the label. Valid only when `ItemType` is T. Optional.
FontStyle	varchar(4)	The style of the font text. May be any combination of the following four codes: • B = Bold • I = Italic • U = Underline • K = Strikeout Leave this field NULL to use the normal style. Valid only when `ItemType` is T or N. Optional.

Field	Type	Description
Color1	bigint	The main color of the text, bar code, or line. When printing a rectangle, this is the border color. If NULL, black is used. A standard Windows 32-bit RGB color value. Optional.
Color2	bigint	The fill color when printing a rectangle. If NULL, white is used. A standard Windows 32-bit RGB color value. Optional.
Alignment	smallint	The alignment of the text within the bounding box. Valid only when ItemType is T, B, or N. • 1 = Align in top-left corner of box • 2 = Align in top-center area of box • 4 = Align in top-right corner of box • 16 = Align in middle-left area of box • 32 = Align in middle-center area of box • 64 = Align in middle-right area of box • 256 = Align in bottom-left corner of box • 512 = Align in bottom-center area of box • 1024 = Align in bottom-right corner of box
PadDigits	smallint	The number of digits in which to pad the bar code number. Set to zero (0) to ignore padding. Ranges from 0 to 20. If the bar code length is less than the specified number of digits, it is padded on the left with zeros. Applies only to ItemTypes of B and N.

Other miscellaneous tables

Two additional tables provide support for features not handled through other tables.

Holiday. When checking out an item to a patron, the return date should not fall on a holiday (or any day that the library is closed) since the patron might not have a way to return the book on the day it's due. This table defines one-time and recurring holidays.

Field	Type	Description
ID	bigint	Primary key, automatically assigned. Required.
FullName	varchar(50)	Name of this holiday. Not necessarily unique. Required.
EntryType	varchar(1)	The type of entry. Required. From the following list: • A = Annual (as in "every December 25") • E = Weekly (as in "every Sunday") • O = One-time (as in "2/16/2004 is President's Day")
EntryDetail	varchar(10)	Entry-type-specific detail. Required. Differs for each entry type. **Entry type** **Detail value** A Month and day in "mm/dd" format E Single digit: 1 = Sunday through 7 = Saturday O Date in "yyyy/mm/dd" format

SystemValue. This table stores miscellaneous enterprise-wide settings that apply to every workstation. Local workstation-specific settings are stored on each machine, not in the database.

Field	Type	Description
ID	bigint	Primary key; automatically assigned. Required.
ValueName	varchar(50)	Name of this value. Required.
ValueData	varchar(100)	Information associated with this entry. Optional.

The following system values are defined at this time. The name of the code appears in the ValueName field. The corresponding value appears in the ValueData field.

BarcodeCode39

Is the specified bar code in "code 39" or "code 3 of 9" format? If so, an asterisk will be placed before and after the bar code number before it is printed on a label. Use a value of 0 for False or any nonzero value for True (-1 is preferred). If missing or NULL, False is assumed.

BarcodeFont

The name of the font used to print bar codes. This font must be installed on any workstation that displays or prints bar codes. It is not needed to scan bar codes.

DatabaseVersion

Which structural version of the database is currently in use? Right now, it is set to "1," and is reserved for future enhancement.

DefaultLocation

CodeLocation.ID value for the location that is set as the default.

FineGrace

Number of days that an item can be overdue without incurring a fine.

NextBarcodeItem

The next starting value to use when printing item bar codes.

NextBarcodeMisc

The next starting value to use when printing miscellaneous bar codes.

NextBarcodePatron

The next starting value to use when printing patron bar codes.

PatronCheckOut

Indicates whether patrons can check out items without being logged in as an administrative user. Use a value of 0 (zero) to indicate no checkout privileges, or any nonzero value to allow patron checkout (-1 is preferred). If this value is missing or empty, patrons will not be allowed to check out items without administrator assistance.

SearchLimit

> Indicates the maximum number of results returned in any search or lookup. If this value is missing or invalid, a default of 250 is used. The allowed range is between 25 and 5,000, inclusive.

TicketHeading

> Display text to be printed at the top of checkout tickets. All lines are centered on the ticket. Include the vertical bar character (|) to break the text into multiple lines.

TicketFooting

> Display text to be printed at the bottom of checkout tickets. All lines are centered on the ticket. Include the vertical bar character (|) to break the text into multiple lines.

UseLC

> Indicates whether books are categorized by Dewey or Library of Congress (LC) call numbers. Use a value of 0 (zero) to indicate Dewey, or any nonzero value for LC (-1 is preferred). If this value is missing or empty, Dewey is assumed.

Creating the Database

Adding the database to SQL Server is almost as easy as documenting it; in fact, it requires less typing. The CREATE TABLE statements are straightforward, and they all pretty much look the same. I'm going to show only a few of them here. The *Database Creation Script.sql* file in this book's installation directory includes the full script content.

The instructions listed here are for SQL Server 2005 Management Studio Express. You can perform all of these tasks using SQL Server 2005 Management Studio, or even the command-line tools supplied with SQL Server, but the details of each step will vary. The same CREATE TABLE statements work with whichever tool you choose.

If you haven't done so already, install SQL Server 2005 Express Edition (or whichever version of the database you will be using). SQL Server 2005 Management Studio Express is a separate product from SQL Server itself, so you must install that as well.

Most of the tables in the Library Project are simple data tables with a single primary key. Their code is straightforward. The Author table is a good example.

```
CREATE TABLE Author
(
   ID          bigint        IDENTITY PRIMARY KEY,
   LastName    varchar(50)   NOT NULL,
   FirstName   varchar(30)   NULL,
   MiddleName  varchar(30)   NULL,
   Suffix      varchar(10)   NULL,
   BirthYear   smallint      NULL,
   DeathYear   smallint      NULL,
   Comments    varchar(250)  NULL
);
```

The fields included in each CREATE TABLE statement appear as a comma-delimited list, all enclosed in parentheses. Each field includes either a NULL or a NOT NULL option that indicates whether NULL values may be used in that field. The PRIMARY KEY option automatically specifies NOT NULL.

Some statements create tables that link two other tables in a many-to-many relationship. One example is the GroupActivity table, which connects the GroupName table with the Activity table.

```
CREATE TABLE GroupActivity
(
   GroupID      bigint   NOT NULL,
   ActivityID   bigint   NOT NULL,
   PRIMARY KEY (GroupID, ActivityID)
);
```

The Author table had a single primary key, so the PRIMARY KEY option could be attached directly to its ID field. Since the GroupActivity table has a two-field primary key (which is common in relational databases), the PRIMARY KEY option is specified as an entry all its own, with the key fields specified as a parentheses-enclosed comma-delimited list.

Earlier in this chapter, I showed how you could establish a reference to a field in another table by using the REFERENCES constraint as part of the CREATE TABLE statement. You can also establish them after the tables are already in place, as I do in the script. Here is the statement that establishes the link between the GroupActivity and GroupName tables:

```
ALTER TABLE GroupActivity
   ADD FOREIGN KEY (GroupID)
   REFERENCES GroupName (ID);
```

Since I've already written the entire SQL script for you, I'll just have you process it directly using Microsoft SQL Server 2005 Management Studio Express. (If you will be using the full version of SQL Server or some other management tool, the provided script will still work, although the step-by-step instructions will differ.) Before adding the tables, we need to create a database specific to the Library Project. Start up Microsoft SQL Server 2005 Management Studio Express (see Figure 4-4).

To add a new database for the Library Project, right-click on the *Database* folder in the Object Explorer, and select New Database from the shortcut menu. On the New Database form that appears, enter **Library** in the Database Name field, and then click OK.

The Library database is a shell of a database; it doesn't contain any tables or data yet. Let's use the *Database Creation Script.sql* file from the book's installation directory to generate the tables and initial data. In Management Studio Express, select the File → Open → File menu command, and locate the *Database Creation Script.sql* file. (You may be prompted to log in to SQL Server again.) Opening this file places its content in a new panel within Management Studio Express.

Figure 4-4. SQL Server 2005 Management Studio Express main form

All that's left to do is to process the script. In the toolbar area, make sure that "Library" is the selected database (see Figure 4-5). Then click the Execute toolbar button, or press the F5 key. It's a small script with not a lot going on (at least from SQL Server's point of view), so it should finish in just a few seconds.

Figure 4-5. If you don't select "Library," your tables will go somewhere else

That's it! Close the script panel. Then, back in the Object Explorer, right-click on the *Library* database folder and select Refresh from the menu. If you then expand the Library database branch and its Tables sub-branch, you will see all the tables created by the script (see Figure 4-6).

With the database done, it's time to start programming.

Figure 4-6. Partial list of database tables

.NET Assemblies

The mere mention of the word *assembly* takes me back to my days as a high school freshman. The assembly was actually held in the school gym, with 2,000 screaming adolescents filling the bleachers around the basketball court. Since this was a school function, I naturally thought of an experience packed with fresh educational opportunities. School, education—the words just seem to go together. But then came the marching band, and the football players, and the cheerleaders, and the school mascot (a horse). For the next 30 minutes, the principal whipped the students into a controlled frenzy, attempting to prove the institution's place as the number-one school in the city. I still don't know what area we were supposed to be number one in, but it was all very exciting.

.NET assemblies are not that exciting. In fact, they're just files, EXE and DLL files, and without you to activate them, they just sit there taking up disk space. And as they are not doing anything else, let's take a moment to examine what they are and what they contain.

What Is an Assembly?

As I already mentioned in Chapter 1, an assembly is a "unit of deployment," which in most cases is just a file. An assembly is a repository for compiled .NET application code; any code you write will eventually be stored in some EXE file (if it is an application) or DLL file (for code libraries or extensions to an application). Everything that .NET needs to know to load and run your application is stored in the assembly.

Assemblies are either private or public. *Private assemblies* are designed for use in a single application only. If there aren't any DLLs, an EXE assembly *is* the application. Private assemblies appear in their own directory, the *installation directory* of the application or library. You can run two different private assemblies at the same time, and they won't bother each other. This is true even if each assembly uses the same combination of namespace and class names for its coded elements. If two application assemblies each implement a class named WindowsApplication1.Class1, they will not interfere with each other when running; they are private, and private means private.

Public assemblies are designed for shared use among multiple .NET applications. Public assemblies differ from private assemblies in two major ways:

- Public assemblies always have a *strong name*, an encrypted digital signature that is attached to an assembly to guarantee that it came from its named vendor or source. (Private assemblies can also include a strong name, but they don't have to.) The strong name is built from the assembly's name, version number, culture information, a "public key," and a digital signature generated from the assembly file that contains the manifest (described later). The .NET Framework includes a Strong Name generation tool (*sn.exe*) that assists in this process, and Visual Studio includes options that let you add a digital signature during the compilation process. (It's on the Signing tab of the project's properties.)

  The strong name of an assembly should be (and better be) unique; if two assemblies share a common strong name, they are copies of the same assembly.

- Public assemblies are stored in the Global Assembly Cache (GAC). Although you can put a copy of your shared component in your application's install directory, it will only truly be shared once it reaches the GAC directory. The GAC lives in a directory named *assembly* within the computer's Windows directory. (On my system, it's in *c:\windows\assembly*.) Once a .NET assembly has a strong name applied, you can add it to the GAC by either dragging the file into the *assembly* directory or using the Global Assembly Cache Tool (*gacutil.exe*). Don't worry about your file being lonely if it's not communing with your other installed files. On my freshly installed copy of .NET, I found nearly 400 files already in the GAC directory, including all the DLLs for the Framework Class Libraries (FCLs).

.NET lets you install multiple versions of an assembly on a system and use them at the same time (a process called *versioning*). This applies both to applications (EXE) and libraries (DLL), and to private assemblies and shared assemblies in the GAC. Don't believe me? Open up the GAC's *assembly* folder, set the Explorer folder to a Details view, and then sort by Assembly Name. If you scroll down, you'll see the same file show up multiple times. Figure 5-1 shows a part of the cache. Two copies of "Microsoft.VisualStudio.Windows.Forms" are listed (from the *Microsoft. VisualStudio.Windows.Forms.dll* file), one with a version number of 2.0 and one listing version 9.0.

Although there is usually a one-to-one relationship between files and assemblies, there may be cases when an assembly is made up of multiple files. For instance, an application might include an external graphics file in its assembly view. .NET keeps a close watch on these files. If any of the files are modified, deleted, or otherwise maimed, you will hear about it. For the purposes of discussion, the rest of this chapter considers only single-file assemblies.

Figure 5-1. The GAC has this duplication under control

What's Inside an Assembly?

An assembly's EXE or DLL file is a standard "Portable Execution" (PE) file, the same file format used for non-.NET executables and code libraries (pretty much any Windows EXE or DLL file). What makes .NET PE files different is all the extra stuff found inside. As a general word, *assembly* indicates a gathering together of various parts into a single unit. In a .NET assembly, these "various parts" are specifically designed for use with .NET.

A .NET PE file contains three main parts:

A PE header
> Required of all PE files, this section identifies the locations of the other sections of the file.

The MSIL code section
> The actual code associated with the assembly is stored as semicompiled Microsoft Intermediate Language (MSIL) code. Unfortunately, the Intel or AMD chip in your computer is apparently too brainless to process MSIL code directly (what were they thinking?), so the .NET Framework includes a *just-in-time* (JIT) compiler that can convert MSIL to native x86 code at a moment's notice.

The Metadata section
> All of the extra detail that .NET needs to rummage through to know about your assembly appears in this essential section. Some of these items, when taken together, make up the assembly's manifest, a type of document that completely describes the assembly to the world. In the following list of metadata elements, I've noted which items appear in the manifest:

The name of the assembly
> (Part of the manifest.) This is defined on the Application tab of the project's properties.

The version number of the assembly
> (Part of the manifest.) That's the four-part version number, as in 1.2.3.4. You've probably been wondering all day how you could set this number in your own projects. Your patience will be rewarded in this chapter's "Project" section, where I will demonstrate not just one, but two ways to set the assembly version number.

Strong name content
> (Part of the manifest.) This includes the publisher's public key.

Culture and language settings
> (Part of the manifest.) This is especially useful when you need to create language-specific resource files.

Assembly file listing
> (Part of the manifest.) Single-file assemblies will show only the EXE or DLL filename, but some assemblies may include several files in this section. All files in an assembly must appear within the same directory, or in a directory subordinate to the assembly file that contains the manifest.

Exported type information
> (Part of the manifest.) Some assemblies "export" some of their types for use outside the application. The details of those types appear here.

References
> (Part of the manifest, but in multifile assemblies, each file will contain its own list of references.) The metadata includes a listing of all external assemblies referenced by your application, whether they are private or appear in the GAC. This list indicates which specific version, culture, and platform-target of the external assembly your assembly expects.

Internal type information
> (Not part of the manifest.) All types crafted in your assembly are fully described within the metadata. Also, any additional metadata you added to your types through Visual Basic's attribute feature appear here.

In multifile assemblies, the manifest-specific elements appear only in the "main" file of the assembly.

The manifest is a subset of the metadata within your assembly. I hate to say that it's the most important part of the metadata—but it is. The manifest is the public expression of your assembly, and the only way that .NET knows whether it is legit. It's sort of like the "Nutrition Facts" label put on American food packaging (see Figure 5-2).

Assembly Facts

Serving Size   1 assembly
Files Per Assembly   1

Amount Per Assembly

Exported Types 12

	% Daily Value*
References 5	50%
Cultures 3	300%
Version 1.0.0.4	
Vitamin VB	100%
Vitamin C#	0%

* Percent Daily Values are based on a Pentium 4 with 1GB Memory. Your daily needs may be lower, but I doubt it.

Figure 5-2. Is that really good for me?

When you look at the food label, you know what the food package contains—although no one really knows what *riboflavin* is. When you look at the manifest for an assembly, you know at a glance what the assembly contains, and what requirements it has before it can be loaded and run.

Even before .NET burst onto the scene, executables and libraries already contained some "metadata," such as the version number of the file. But this data wasn't used to manage access between software components, nor was it organized in a generic and extensible way. The metadata in .NET embodies all of these attributes.

The presence of both the MSIL and metadata in each assembly makes these files very readable and understandable. With the right tools, even I seem to understand them. And if I can, anyone can, which leads to a big problem. Companies invest a lot of time and money in their software development efforts, and they don't want any rinky-dink two-bit startup reverse-engineering their code and getting all their algorithmic secrets. To prevent this casual reading of any .NET application, Microsoft and other third parties include *obfuscators*, software programs that scramble the contents of an assembly just enough so that it's hard for humans to understand, but not for the .NET Framework. I'll talk more about obfuscation in Chapter 22.

Reflection

It may be a bad thing for people to access the content of an assembly, but it's great when the code in an assembly can access itself. .NET includes a feature called *reflection* that lets you examine the contents of an assembly. You generally use this feature to access metadata in your own assembly, but it also works with any available assembly. Most reflection-related features appear in the System.Reflection namespace.

Through reflection, you can extract pretty much anything stored in the metadata of an assembly, including details on all types, their members, and even the parameters included with function members. This is why obfuscation is so important to vendors; between the compiled MSIL and the metadata, you can virtually regenerate the entire source code for an application from just its executable. The source code would be in MSIL, but it wouldn't be that tough for someone to massage much of it back into Visual Basic or C#.

Assemblies and Applications

.NET applications (EXE files) are an instance of an assembly. But a single application can include multiple assemblies; it fact, it almost always does. I wrote a little program that uses reflection to list all assemblies actively being used by the program itself. I gave the program the default name of *WindowsApplication1*. When I ran the program against itself, it generated the following list:

```
mscorlib
Microsoft.VisualStudio.HostingProcess.Utilities
System.Windows.Forms
System
System.Drawing
Microsoft.VisualStudio.HostingProcess.Utilities.Sync
Microsoft.VisualStudio.Debugger.Runtime
vshost
System.Data
System.Deployment
System.Xml
System.Core
System.Xml.Linq
System.Data.DataSetExtensions
Microsoft.VisualBasic
WindowsApplication1
System.Runtime.Remoting
```

Wow! Seventeen assemblies, including *WindowsApplication1*, the main program. Most of the assemblies are framework-supplied DLLs. For Microsoft.VisualBasic, it's the *Microsoft.VisualBasic.dll* assembly; for System, it's the *System.dll* assembly.

All of the assemblies (except the main program assembly) are shared libraries from the GAC. The application can also support private assemblies loaded from local DLL files.

The .NET Framework automatically loaded these assemblies for me when *WindowsApplication1* started up; it figured out which ones needed to be loaded by looking in the manifest for *WindowsApplication1*. When the framework loaded each assembly, it checked to see whether those assemblies in turn needed additional assemblies loaded, and so on. Pretty soon, your once-simple application becomes a dumping ground for assemblies all over the GAC. But that's OK, since the purpose of .NET is to manage it all.

The My Namespace and Assemblies

The .NET Framework, with its thousands of classes, contains a lot of packaged logic that I can use in my own programs. But I don't have all of the many assemblies and their classes memorized (yet), and it takes time to wander around the FCL documentation. With so many classes available, I sometimes shudder when I think of the effort it will take me to find just the right class or feature I need to accomplish some development task.

Fortunately, I'm not the only one who thinks this way; Microsoft agrees with me. Historically, Visual Basic programmers were sheltered from the complexities of Windows application development. Not that they needed to be; we all know that Visual Basic developers are generally a cut above the rest. But there was "the Visual Basic motto" to contend with: *Make Windows Development Fast and Easy*. And calling some esoteric method deep within the bowels of the System namespace just to get a minor piece of data is neither easy nor fast.

To bring back some semblance of the pleasant experience previously available in Visual Basic development, Microsoft introduced the My pretend namespace in its 2005 release of the language. The My pretend namespace collects a lot of useful features from all around the FCL, and organizes them in a much smaller hierarchy for simple and direct access. I briefly mentioned My in Chapter 1, but now is a good time to take a closer look at what it does.

The My pretend namespace looks a lot like other namespaces, such as System, System. Reflection, and System.Windows.Forms. But it's not really a namespace—it's pretend! For one thing, you can't use the Imports keyword to create a shortcut to branches within its hierarchy. Also, some sections of the hierarchy are dynamic; they change as your project changes. Table 5-1 lists the major nodes of the hierarchy.

Table 5-1. Major nodes in the My namespace hierarchy

Branch	Available features
My.Application	Provides information about the current application, including culture settings and the deployment method.
My.Application.Info	Gives further details about the application and its assembly, including the name and version.
My.Application.Log	Allows you to generate trace and logging output to registered logging destinations. Used only with client applications.
My.Computer	Provides access to general resources located on the local computer.
My.Computer.Audio	Plays named and system sounds through the computer's speakers.
My.Computer.Clipboard	Retrieves data from the system clipboard, and lets you add your own data to the clipboard in a variety of predefined and custom formats.
My.Computer.Clock	Gets the current system date and time dished up in a variety of ways.
My.Computer.FileSystem	Provides tools to examine and manipulate files and directories on local or networked filesystems.
My.Computer.FileSystem.SpecialDirectories	References special Windows folders such as *Documents*, *Desktop*, and *Temp*.
My.Computer.Info	Provides information about the installed operating system and other local system resources.
My.Computer.Keyboard	Exposes the current state of the keyboard and its keys.
My.Computer.Mouse	Makes available a few properties of the local computer's mouse.
My.Computer.Network	Reports on network availability, and provides features to interact with that network.
My.Computer.Ports	Lets you interact with the system's serial ports.
My.Computer.Registry	Reads and writes keys and values in the registry.
My.Forms	Presents a dynamic collection of all forms defined in the application. This node is available only in Windows Forms applications.
My.Log	Allows you to generate trace and logging output to registered logging destinations. Used only with ASP.NET applications.
My.Request	This object is similar to the older Active Server Pages Request object. It is available only in ASP.NET applications.
My.Resources	Provides dynamic access to application-specific or locale-specific resources included with the application.
My.Response	This object is similar to the older Active Server Pages Response object. It is available only in ASP.NET applications.
My.Settings	Provides dynamic access to the application settings system.
My.User	Identifies the current Windows user, including authentication information.
My.WebServices	Presents a collection of available web services for use in the application. This node is not available in ASP.NET applications.

The My namespace includes a lot of features you will use regularly, including access to the version number of the application. Instead of typing *System.Reflection.whatever* to get to the version number's "major" component, you can now just type:

```
My.Application.Info.Version.Major
```

Need a list of assemblies, but you're too lazy to type the word *Reflection*? Try:

```
My.Application.Info.LoadedAssemblies
```

Need to know the time right now in England?

```
My.Computer.Clock.GmtTime
```

Can you communicate over the local area network?

```
My.Computer.Network.IsAvailable
```

Who is running this computer anyway?

```
My.User.Name
```

There isn't much in the My namespace that you can't already do with standard FCLs. There are even a few parts of My that are repeats of features already included in the Visual Basic language, although with some enhancements. For instance, Visual Basic includes a Kill command that lets you delete files. The My.Computer.FileSystem. DeleteFile method also removes files, but it offers additional options, including one that lets you send the file to the Recycle Bin instead of just losing it forever.

Directives and Assemblies

Directives are Visual Basic statements—but then again, they're not. The two key directives—#Const and #If—provide instructions to the compiler on how to handle a block of Visual Basic source code. (A third directive, #Region, helps to visually present source code within Visual Studio, but it has no impact on the compiler or the final compiled application.) By using directives, you can tell the compiler to include or exclude specific chunks of source code from the final project. So, they aren't really Visual Basic source code statements, but they are available only in Visual Basic.

Why would you want to include or exclude code in an application? Well, I can think of several good reasons, some of which involve the CIA and former Federal Reserve chairman Alan Greenspan. But the most common use is when you want to produce two different versions of your application, based on some condition. For example, you may sell an "express" version and a "professional" version of a product. Much of the code is identical for the two versions, but the professional version would include features not available in the express version. Also, the express version may include a simplified presentation for a feature that has a more complex usage in the professional edition.

Some software products fulfill this need by using standard Visual Basic conditions.

```
If (professionalVersion = True) Then
    ShowWhizBangFeatures( )
Else
    ShowLaughableFeatures( )
End If
```

This, of course, works just fine. But the express application still contains all the enhanced features. Since it can't access any of that code, why even include it on the installation CD? If you use directives, you can mark down that problem as solved. Directives use conditional expressions, much like the professionalVersion = True condition in the preceding block of code. But they are defined with the #Const statement, and are called *compiler constants*.

```
#Const fullVersion = True
```

This statement defines a Boolean compiler constant. The constant can be used only with directives; if you try to use fullVersion in a standard Visual Basic statement, the compiler will complain. But it will work just fine in the #If directive.

```
#If (fullVersion = True) Then
    ShowWhizBangFeatures( )
#Else
    ShowLaughableFeatures( )
#End If
```

This code looks a lot like the previous code block, but with the added # signs. It looks the same but it's not. With the plain If statement, the following code gets compiled into the final application:

```
If (professionalVersion = True) Then
    ShowWhizBangFeatures( )
Else
    ShowLaughableFeatures( )
End If
```

Yeah, the whole block of code. But with the directives, what gets included in the compiled application depends on the value of fullVersion. If fullVersion is True, this gets compiled into the compiled application:

```
ShowWhizBangFeatures( )
```

The other four lines are gone; they've vanished…into thin air, as though they never existed. But in this case, it's a good thing. The goal was to have a version of the assembly completely devoid of the undesired code, and that's what happened.

To set the fullVersion compiler constant to generate the full version, you include this line at the top of each source code file that includes conditional #If code blocks:

```
#Const fullVersion = True
```

When you're ready to generate the "express" version, just change each of these lines to their False counterpart:

```
#Const fullVersion = False
```

Somehow, changing this line in every source code file that needs it seems like a lot of work, and it is. And what happens if I forget to set one of them to the right version? No good, I can tell you.

To keep Visual Basic developers from running down the halls screaming more than they normally would, Visual Studio provides a few different ways to set compiler constants once, and have them apply to every part of the application. The most common way to do this is through the project properties' Compile panel (see Figure 5-3). Click on the Advanced Compile Options button, and then add your global compiler constants to the "Custom constants" field.

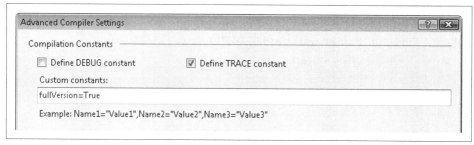

Figure 5-3. This is a whole lot easier than all that typing

Now, by adding either fullVersion = True or fullVersion = False to this field, you can build different versions of the application. The Visual Basic compiler also provides features that let you set up different compile scripts for your project. I won't talk about it in this book, but you can read up on the MSBuild tool in the Visual Studio documentation if you need this level of control.

Besides Booleans, compiler constants can be numbers and strings. The Visual Studio environment also defines some compiler constants for you. The DEBUG and TRACE constants are True or False based on the "Define DEBUG constant" and "Define TRACE constant" checkboxes that appear in Figure 5-3. The VBC_VER constant identifies the version of the Visual Basic compiler being used; it is set to 9.0 in Visual Basic 2008.

Summary

Assemblies aren't just souped-up EXE or DLL files; they contain gobs of metadata, including the manifest, that make .NET applications *self-describing*. The compiler uses this information to correctly configure and process the managed MSIL code in each assembly.

Although not actually parts of an assembly, this chapter also discussed the My namespace and directives, two Visual Basic features that impact what gets included in your assembly.

Project

This chapter's project officially kicks off the coding of the Library Project (muted applause). We'll start off with something simple: building the About form that provides basic information about the application, including its version number.

PROJECT ACCESS

Load the Chapter 5 (Before) Code project, either through the New Project templates or by accessing the project directly from the installation directory. To see the code in its final form, load Chapter 5 (After) Code instead.

Our goal is a pleasant form that conveys basic information about the program, a form that looks something like Figure 5-4.

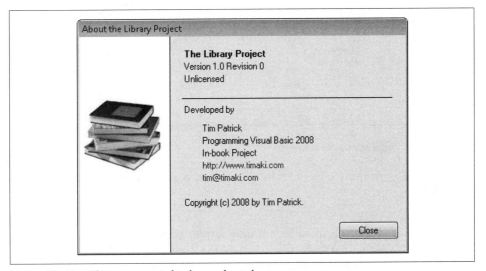

Figure 5-4. Everything you wanted to know about the program

Like any Visual Basic application for Windows, the creation of this form involves two steps: (1) adding controls to the form; and (2) writing the related code.

Adding Controls

If there is one area where Visual Basic excels, it is form creation. Programs can be created by the simple dragging and dropping of prebuilt controls onto the surface of a prebuilt form. It's all done from within the comfort and convenience of the Visual Studio Integrated Development Environment (IDE), as shown in Figure 5-5.

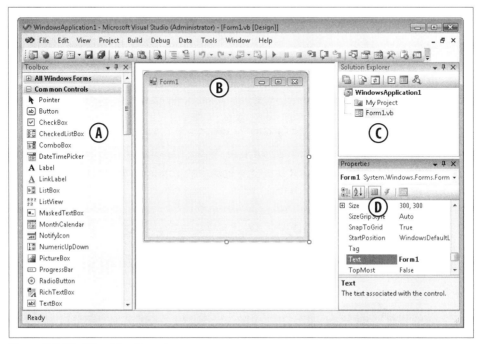

Figure 5-5. The Visual Studio environment

The displayed environment includes four key areas, which I've labeled with letters in Figure 5-5:

A. *The toolbox*

> This listing of controls includes not only display controls, but also controls that expose no specific user interface, such as the Timer. (If you don't see the toolbox, select the View → Toolbox menu command.) To add a control to a form, double-click the control in the toolbox, drag it from the toolbox to the form, or draw the control on the form after first selecting it from the toolbox.

B. *The form surface*

> Place any control that exposes a user interface here. The form is WYSIWYG, so you can see the final result as you design the form.

C. The Solution Explorer

All files related to your project appear here. For the current project, you will see only the My Project entry and an entry for the form, *Form1.vb*. There are actually more files. If you click the second button from the left at the top of the Solution Explorer, it will show you additional files, most of which are managed by Visual Studio on your behalf.

D. The Properties panel

When you select a control on your form surface, or the form surface itself, or an item in the Solution Explorer, the properties of the selected item appear in this area. You can alter the settings of many properties by typing in the new setting. Some properties include special tools to assist you in setting the property value.

If you haven't done so already, open the form *Form1.vb* in design view by double-clicking it in the Solution Explorer. We'll add eight text labels, three shape and line elements, two web-style hyperlinks, a command button, and a picture to the form's surface. I've already added the picture to the form for you, with an image of some books, naming it SideImage.

Set up the form by adjusting the following properties from their defaults. Click on the form surface, and then modify these property values using the Properties panel.

Property	Setting
(Name)	AboutProgram
ControlBox	False
FormBorderStyle	FixedDialog
Size	440, 311
StartPosition	CenterScreen
Text	About the Library Project

Next, add the eight basic text labels to the form's surface using the Label control. You'll find this control in the toolbox. As you add each Label control, use the following list of settings to set the properties for each label. The included text matches my situation, but feel free to modify the content as needed.

Label name	Property settings	
ProgramName	(Name):	ProgramName
	AutoSize:	True
	Font/Bold:	True
	Location:	136, 16
	Text:	The Library Project
ProgramVersion	(Name):	ProgramVersion
	AutoSize:	True
	Location:	136, 32
	Text:	Version X.Y Revision Z

Label name	Property settings	
LicenseInfo	(Name):	LicenseInfo
	AutoSize:	False
	Location:	136, 48
	Size:	280, 32
	Text:	Unlicensed
DevelopedBy	(Name):	DevelopedBy
	AutoSize:	True
	Location:	136, 88
	Text:	Developed By
DeveloperName	(Name):	DeveloperName
	AutoSize:	True
	Location:	160, 112
	Text:	Tim Patrick
DeveloperBook	(Name):	DeveloperBook
	AutoSize:	True
	Location:	160, 128
	Text:	Programming Visual Basic 2008
DeveloperProject	(Name):	DeveloperProject
	AutoSize:	True
	Location:	160, 144
	Text:	In-book Project
CompanyCopyright	(Name):	CompanyCopyright
	AutoSize:	True
	Location:	136, 208
	Text:	Copyright (c) 2008 by Tim Patrick.

Let's add some lines and colored sections to the form. Visual Basic 6.0 included distinct shape controls for lines, rectangles, and ellipses that you could apply directly to the form surface. .NET no longer includes these items; you have to add them by hand using source-code-specified drawing commands.[*] But we can simulate lines and rectangles using the standard Label control, sans the text.

Label name	Property settings	
VersionDivider	(Name):	VersionDivider
	AutoSize:	False
	BackColor:	Black
	Location:	136, 80
	Size:	280,1
	Text:	[Don't add any text]
BackgroundSide	(Name):	BackgroundSide
	AutoSize:	False
	BackColor:	White
	Location:	0, 0
	Size:	120, 296
	Text:	[Don't add any text]

---

[*] Microsoft does offer line and shape controls as part of its "Power Packs" for Visual Basic 2005. You'll find them in the download area of Microsoft's Visual Basic Development Center, located at *http://msdn.microsoft.com/vbasic*. As of this writing, 2008 editions of the Power Packs are not yet available, but the 2005 versions will probably work just fine with Visual Basic 2008.

Label name	Property settings	
BackgroundDivider	(Name):	BackgroundDivider
	AutoSize:	False
	BackColor:	Black
	Location:	120, 0
	Size:	1, 296
	Text:	[Don't add any text]

If the BackgroundSide label obscures the graphic, right-click on the label and select Send To Back from the shortcut menu that appears.

The LinkLabel control is similar to the more basic Label control, but you can include "links" in the text, clickable sections that are similar to the links on a web page. We'll use these to display the web site and email address. Add two LinkLabel controls to the form and use the following settings to configure each control's properties.

LinkLabel name	Property settings	
CompanyWeb	(Name):	CompanyWeb
	AutoSize:	True
	LinkBehavior:	HoverUnderline
	Location:	160, 160
	Text:	http://www.timaki.com
CompanyEmail	(Name):	CompanyEmail
	AutoSize:	True
	LinkBehavior:	HoverUnderline
	Location:	160, 176
	Text:	tim@timaki.com

The final control to add is a button that lets the user close the form. Add a Button control to the form with the following properties.

Button name	Property settings	
ActClose	(Name):	ActClose
	DialogResult:	Cancel
	Location:	344, 240
	Size:	80, 24
	Text:	Close

Forms can be configured so that a press of the Esc key triggers a Button control on the form, as though the user was clicking on the button instead of pressing the Esc key. To do this, click on the form surface, and then set its CancelButton property to ActClose. We had to delay this step until the button was actually added to the form; the CancelButton property would not have allowed a setting for a nonexistent button.

Well, the form should look pretty good by now. The last thing I like to do is to set up the *tab order*, the order in which the user accesses each field on the form when pressing the Tab key on the keyboard. To edit the tab order, select the form surface and then select the View → Tab Order menu command. Each control on the form that can be given a tab order value will suddenly have a tab order number next to it.

Click on each number or control in order until you get the arrangement you want. (See Figure 5-6 to view how I ordered the controls.) Finally, select the View → Tab Order menu command again, or press the Esc key, to leave the tab ordering process.

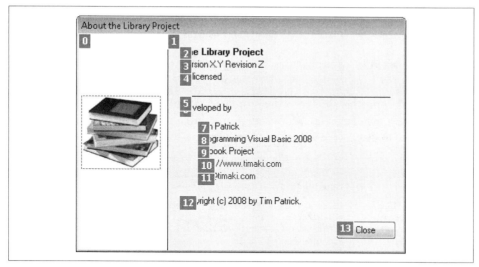

Figure 5-6. Nice and orderly

You can also set the tab order for each control by modifying its TabIndex property using a zero-based numbering system. However, it's usually faster to set these values by clicking on each control in order.

Adding the Code to the Form

Now it's time to add some real Visual Basic code. Not that we haven't added any until now. Everything we did on the form, although we didn't see it happen, was converted into Visual Basic source code. Let's take a quick look. In the Solution Explorer, click on the Show All Files button, the second button from the left. When all the files appear, click on the "plus sign" next to Form1.vb, and finally, double-click Form1.Designer.vb (see Figure 5-7).

Since it's more than 200 lines of source code bliss, I won't be printing it here. But look it over; it's all pretty interesting. As you dragged-and-dropped controls on the form and modified its properties, Visual Studio edited this file on your behalf. It's part of your form's class (all forms are classes that derive from System.Windows. Forms.Form). You can tell by the Partial keyword at the top.

```
Partial Public Class AboutProgram
    Inherits System.Windows.Forms.Form
```

Figure 5-7. Accessing the hidden, secret, forbidden code—yeah, it's out there

Most of the action happens in the InitializeComponent procedure. When you are finished looking it all over, close up the designer code and return to the form surface. To make our form a real and interesting form, we need it to do three things:

- Show the actual version number of the application. This should be determined and displayed right when the form first appears.

- Jump to the appropriate web site or email recipient when clicking on the link labels. These events get processed in response to a user action.

- Close the form when the user clicks the Close button. This is also a user-driven event.

Let's start with the easy one, closing the form. I'm sure you remember about *events* from Chapter 1. Events are blocks of code that are processed in response to something happening, most often a user action such as a mouse click. All of the actions we want to perform on this form will be in response to a triggered event (lucky us). The easiest way to get to the "default" event for a control is to double-click the control. Try it now; double-click the Close button. When you do, the IDE opens the source code view associated with the form, and adds an empty event handler (the ActClose_Click subroutine).

```
Public Class AboutProgram
    Private Sub ActClose_Click(ByVal sender As System.Object, _
        ByVal e As System.EventArgs) Handles ActClose.Click

    End Sub
End Class
```

Every forms-based event (and in fact, most other types of events) in .NET has pretty much the same arguments: (1) a sender argument that indicates which object triggered this event; and (2) the e argument, which allows sender to supply any additional information that may be useful in the event. In this case, the sender argument will be a reference to the ActClose button, since that's the object that will generate the Click event. A button's Click event doesn't have any more useful information available, so e is the default object type, System.EventArgs, which is pretty much just a place-holder, and the object from which all of the more interesting e argument types derive.

The name of this event handler is ActClose_Click, but if you want to change it to FredAndWilma, that's fine; it won't mess up anything. But you must keep the Handles ActClose.Click clause intact. This is the part that links the event handler to the actual event.

The code to close the form is extremely simple. Enter it now, either by using the first code snippet for this chapter or by typing it directly.

INSERT SNIPPET

Insert Chapter 5, Snippet Item 1.

```
' ----- Close the form.
Me.Close()
```

This statement says, "I'm the AboutProgram form/object, and I command myself to close." If you run the program right now (press the F5 key), you close the form by clicking on the Close button. Since the AboutProgram form was the only form in the application, closing it automatically ended the entire application, no questions asked.

OK, back up to the second item, the web-style links. You could go back to the form surface and double-click on each link label to create an event handler for each label's default event (in this case, the LinkClicked event). But you can also add the event handler subroutines right in the editor, either by typing the code yourself (which is no fun) or by using the two drop-down lists just above the editor window (see Figure 5-8).

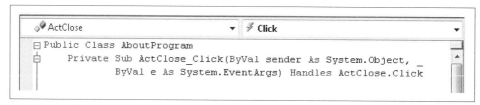

Figure 5-8. The Class Name and Method Name fields

The Class Name list appears on the left side. Selecting an entry from this list updates the righthand list, the Method Name list. To add an event handler template for the CompanyWeb's LinkClicked event, first select CompanyWeb from the Class Name list, and then select LinkClicked from the Method Name list. The following code block appears in the code window:

```
Private Sub CompanyWeb_LinkClicked(ByVal sender As Object, _
        ByVal e As System.Windows.Forms. _
        LinkLabelLinkClickedEventArgs) _
        Handles CompanyWeb.LinkClicked

End Sub
```

This template's argument list is a little more interesting, since its e argument is an object of type System.Windows.Forms.LinkLabelLinkClickedEventArgs. The LinkLabel control allows you to have multiple web-style links in a single control, interspersed among regular text. The e argument has a Link property that tells you which of the links in the control was clicked by the user. Since our labels have only a single link, we won't bother to check it. We'll just show the web page immediately anytime the link is clicked.

INSERT SNIPPET

Insert Chapter 5, Snippet Item 2.

```
' ----- Show the company web page.
Process.Start("http://www.timaki.com")
```

The Process object is part of the System.Diagnostics namespace, and Start is one of its shared members that lets you start up external applications and resources. You pass it any valid URL and it will run using the user's default browser or application for that URL. Let's try it again with the CompanyEmail's LinkClicked event. Add in the template any way you choose and then type or insert the code that starts a new message to an email address.

INSERT SNIPPET

Insert Chapter 5, Snippet Item 3.

```
' ----- Send email to the company.
Process.Start("mailto:tim@timaki.com")
```

The last event to design is one of the first events called in the lifetime of the form: the Load event. It's called just before the form appears on the screen. Double-clicking on the surface of the form creates an event handler template for the Load event. If you prefer to use the Class Name and Method Name drop-down lists instead, select (AboutProgram Events) from the Class Name list before using the Method Name list.

```
Private Sub AboutProgram_Load(ByVal sender As Object, _
        ByVal e As System.EventArgs) Handles Me.Load

End Sub
```

Let's add code to this event handler that displays the correct version number, using the version information found in `My.Application.Info.Version`, an instance of the `System.Version` class.

INSERT SNIPPET

Insert Chapter 5, Snippet Item 4.

```
' ----- Update the version number.
With My.Application.Info.Version
    ProgramVersion.Text = "Version " & .Major & "." & _
        .Minor & " Revision " & .Revision
End With
```

This code uses a `With` statement to reduce the amount of typing needed in the main assignment statement. Inside the `With...End With` statement, you aren't required to retype the object name that appears just after the `With` keyword—in this case, `My.Application.Info.Version`. You can just refer to that object's members by typing a dot (.) followed by the name of the member. You could forgo the `With` statement and type the full object name each time you wanted to use one of the version values, but this way keeps the code cleaner and less overwhelming.

Setting the Version Number

If you run the program, it will display the currently defined version number, "1.0 Revision 0," as shown in Figure 5-9.

The Library Project
Version 1.0 Revision 0
Unlicensed

Figure 5-9. The version number from the AboutProgram form

My question—and I hope I can answer it before the paragraph is finished—is, "Where is that version number defined, and how can it be changed?" It turns out that I do know the answer: the version values are stored as metadata within the assembly. Visual Studio includes a form that lets you modify the basic informational metadata stored in the assembly. To access the form, display the project's properties (double-click on My Project in the Solution Explorer), select the Application tab, and then click on the Assembly Information button (see Figure 5-10).

Our `AboutProgram` form displays the assembly's version number, which is set using the four text fields next to the Assembly Version label. Those four fields represent the Major, Minor, Build, and Revision numbers of the assembly. Go ahead, set them to some other values, click OK, and run the program again.

Figure 5-10. The Assembly Information form, filled out with some relevant values

Although this form is convenient, it's just another example of Visual Studio writing some of your project's code on your behalf. Every field on this form gets saved in a source code file included with your project. To view it, make sure you have the Show All Files button still selected in the Solution Explorer. Expand the My Project item using its "plus sign," and then double-click on the *AssemblyInfo.vb* item. This file defines several assembly-specific attributes (which we'll explore in Chapter 18), including the following informational entries:

```
<Assembly: AssemblyTitle("The Library Project")>
<Assembly: AssemblyDescription( _
    "ACME Library Database System")>
<Assembly: AssemblyCompany("ACME")>
<Assembly: AssemblyProduct("Library")>
<Assembly: AssemblyCopyright( _
    "Copyright © 2008 by Tim Patrick")>
<Assembly: AssemblyTrademark("")>
<Assembly: AssemblyVersion("1.0.0.0")>
```

As you can see, this file has been updated with the values I typed into the Assembly Information form. Thank you Visual Studio! You see the AssemblyVersion attribute defined here. If you modify these values, the changes will be reflected in the Assembly Information form, and also in your running application and final compiled assembly.

The last thing we will do for now to the AboutProgram form is to give it a meaningful filename. Currently, it is named *Form1.vb*, but *AboutProgram.vb* would be much more descriptive. To change the name, select Form1.vb in the Solution Explorer, and modify the File Name property to "AboutProgram.vb" in the Properties panel. If you still have all the files showing, you will see Visual Studio also update the names of the file's two subordinate files, the designer file (*AboutProgram.Designer.vb*) and the resource file (*AboutProgram.resx*).

Now would be a great time to save your work (File → Save All).

Adding the Main Form

As useful and full featured as the AboutProgram form is, such forms are seldom the core focus of an application. In the Library Project, this form will be displayed only when triggered from the "Main" form, so let's add a simple main form now. In Visual Studio, select the Project → Add Windows Form menu command. When the Add New Item form appears, select Windows Form from the list of available items, and give it a name of "MainForm.vb" before clicking the Add button.

When the new form appears, adjust the following properties as indicated.

Property	Setting
(Name)	MainForm
FormBorderStyle	FixedSingle
MaximizeBox	False
Size	576, 459
Text	The Library Project

From the toolbox, add a Button control to the form with the following properties.

Property	Setting
(Name)	ActHelpAbout
Size	80, 24
Text	&About...

If you're familiar with Visual Basic development from its pre-.NET days, you will recognize the "&" character in the button's text. This special character sets the "shortcut" for the button. When you press the Alt key and the letter that follows "&" (in this case, *A*), the program acts as though you clicked on the button with the mouse.

Double-click the button and add the following code to the click event procedure.

INSERT SNIPPET

Insert Chapter 5, Snippet Item 5.

```
' ----- Show the About form.
AboutProgram.ShowDialog( )
```

Here we specify a direct reference to the `AboutProgram` form. Before the 2005 version of Visual Basic, showing a new form required that you create an instance of the form class before showing it.

```
(New AboutProgram).ShowDialog( )
```

That syntax still works, and is the way to go if you need to display multiple copies of the same form on-screen at the same time. However, the `AboutProgram.ShowDialog( )` syntax is much cleaner for single-use forms, and more closely reflects how form presentation was done in Visual Basic since its initial release. Actually, this statement is using the `My` namespace. The full statement looks like this:

```
My.Forms.AboutProgram.ShowDialog( )
```

The `My.Forms` collection allows you to reference any form within it without having to say "My.Forms" first. The members of the `My.Forms` collection represent *default instances* of each form in the project.

That's all the code we need for now, but if you run the program, it will still show only the `AboutProgram` form. That's because the `AboutProgram` form is set as the "startup" form. To alter this, open the project's properties window, select the Application tab, and set the "Startup form" field to "MainForm."

Since the `AboutProgram` form is now being shown as a "dialog" form (through a call to its `ShowDialog` method), its behavior is somewhat different. Each form includes a `DialogResult` property whose value is returned by the `ShowDialog` method when the form closes. Each button on your form can be configured to automatically set this property and close the form. The Close button on the `AboutProgram` form does just that; its own `DialogResult` property is set to `Cancel`, which is assigned to the form's `DialogResult` property when the user clicks the Close button. As a side effect, anytime a value (other than `None`) gets assigned to the form's `DialogResult` property, the form closes.

The upshot of that drawn-out paragraph is that you can now delete the event handler for the Close button's `Click` event, and the button will still close the form. Delete the `ActClose_Click` procedure from the `AboutProgram`'s source code, run the program, and see what happens. The Close button still closes the form, even without the event handler.

You could also have left the procedure there, cleared the Close button's `DialogResult` property, and added the following statement to that button's event handler:

```
Me.DialogResult = Windows.Forms.DialogResult.Cancel
```

That brings to three the number of different ways we can close the `AboutProgram` form. It's the flexibility of .NET at work; there are many different ways to accomplish the same task. So, be creative!

Extra Credit: Adding an Icon

If you've still got a little energy left, we can make one more change before this chapter runs out of paper: adding a custom icon to the main form. Just follow these step-by-step instructions:

1. Display the main form by double-clicking on the MainForm.vb item in the Solution Explorer.

2. Select the form's surface.

3. Select the form's Icon property in the Properties panel.

4. Click the "…" button in this property, and search for the *Book.ico* file in the *Chapter 5 Before* subdirectory of the book's installation directory. You can also use any other *.ico* file.

Save Your Work

Make sure you always save changes. By default, Visual Studio is configured to save your changes every time you run your program, but I like to save often just in case.

This chapter included a lot of manual instruction because there were so many cool Visual Studio features to play with; I just couldn't help myself. We'll probably keep up this pace somewhat for a few chapters, but eventually there will be so much code that a lot of it will come from the code snippets.

Data and Data Types

Data is a funny word—although not as funny as *datum*. Our minds are filled with data: the useful and useless trivia that clogs thought; the millions of memories that keep superficial conversations going strong. But the word *data* rarely comes up in conversation. Unless you are a computer junkie, or you hang around the office all hours of the day or night waiting for reports of crunched numbers, you never have a need to use the term. I have never been asked to lend someone a cup of data. My friends never try to judge my health by asking, "How's your data going?" And you almost never hear it used as a character name in popular science fiction television shows.

Despite its lack of usage in everyday communication, data is extremely important. In the programming world, it is everything. In this chapter, we will discuss how Visual Basic uses and manipulates data within your applications, and how you can master the tools that make this manipulation possible.

The Nature of Computer Data

In Chapter 2, I mentioned how all data in a computer eventually breaks down to individual bits, electrical impulses that represent either 1 or 0, on or off, true or false. Since our decimal number system requires more than just those two values, computers work in the world of binary—a number system limited to only the numbers 0 and 1. Fortunately, it's pretty easy to represent basic decimal integer numbers using binary notation. You probably remember Mrs. Green back in second grade telling you about the different place values of multidigit numbers, shown in Figure 6-1.

The same type of diagram can be used for binary numbers; only the position names and values are changed. For convenience, we call these positions by their decimal names, or use the related powers of two. All of this is shown in Figure 6-2.

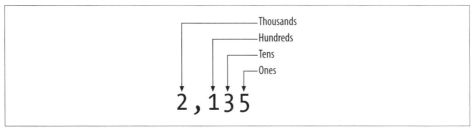

Figure 6-1. The fruits of Mrs. Green's labors

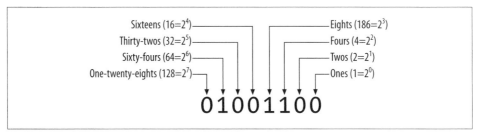

Figure 6-2. The positions of an "8-bit" (8-digit) binary number

To figure out what this number is in decimal, just add up the columns. Let's see, there's one each of fours, eights, and sixty-fours, and none of the rest; 4 + 8 + 64, that's 76. Since any binary digit can never be more than 1, the counting is pretty simple. I showed an 8-bit (8-digit) binary example here—which can handle the numbers 0 through 255— but you can represent larger decimal numbers by adding more binary digits.

That's just fine for integer values, but how do you represent decimal and fractional numbers? What about negative numbers; where do they fit in this binary system? And it's not just numbers. My computer can process text data, arrays of numbers, graphical images, and customer records. How are those stored in binary form?

To handle myriad data forms, every computer includes a small community of Lilliputians who are good at math, language, and art. No wait, I think that's from a story I'm reading my son at bedtime. Oh yes, now I remember. Computers implement *data types* to handle all the various forms of data to be managed. Each data type acts as an interpreter between a collection of bits and a piece of information that a computer user can better utilize and understand.

All data types ultimately store their content as individual bits of data, but they differ in how those bits get interpreted. Imagine a data type named `Vitamin` that indicated which vitamins were included in a food product. Figure 6-3 shows how the 8 bits used earlier could be assigned and interpreted as vitamins.

With such a data type, you could assign vitamin values to food items tracked in your application. (This is just a sampling of vitamins; you would require more bits to handle all of the vitamins. This example should not be construed as an offer of medical services. Consult your doctor.)

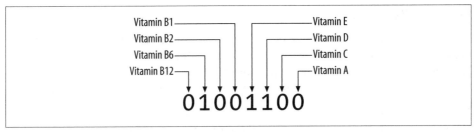

Figure 6-3. Loaded with vitamins B6, D, and E

For an example that is more in tune with Visual Basic, take that number 76 we were discussing earlier. It's easy enough to convert it to binary representation, as in 01001100. The .NET Framework includes a few data types that do this conversion automatically, varying only by the number of binary digits (bits) they can handle. In the computer world, 76 also represents a letter of the alphabet—the capital letter *L*. That's because there's a data type that establishes a dictionary between binary values and alphabetic (and other) characters. Windows programs have long used *ASCII* (American Standard Code for Information Interchange) as its number-to-character dictionary. This 8-bit system documents how to convert the numbers 0 through 255 into all the various characters used in English, including punctuation and other miscellaneous characters. Another dictionary, *Unicode*, uses 16 bits of data to handle around 65,000 different characters. .NET uses Unicode for its character and "string" data types.

Another rule-bearing data type is Boolean, which uses a single bit to represent either True (a bit value of 1) or False (0). Negative integers, floating-point and fixed-point decimal values, and dates and times round out the kinds of basic data most often managed by computers and their applications. More complex *data structures* can be built up from these basic types.

Data in .NET

All data types in .NET are implemented as classes within the System namespace. One such data type is System.Byte, which implements an 8-bit integer value, just like we discussed earlier. It holds integer values from 0 to 255. These values are always stored using 8 bits of binary data, but they magically appear in decimal form whenever you ask them to be presented.

The .NET Framework includes 15 core interpretive data types: 8 for integers, 3 for decimal numbers, 2 for character data, a combined data type for dates and times, and a Boolean data type.

Integer Data Types

Based on the number of available data types (8 out of the 15 core types), you would think that most programmers worked with integers all day long—and you'd be right. Whether it's actual user data or loop counters or status codes or the storage method for enumerated data types, integers show up everywhere in .NET code.

The range of values for an integer data type depends directly on the number of binary digits managed by that data type; the more digits, the bigger the range. Also, half of the integer data types store both positive and negative values (called "signed" integers), whereas the other half support only positive numbers ("unsigned"). Table 6-1 lists the eight integer data types included with .NET, and their associated ranges.

Table 6-1. Integer data types in .NET

.NET data type	Bits	Style	Range of values
System.Byte	8	Unsigned	0 to 255
System.SByte	8	Signed	−128 to 127
System.Int16	16	Signed	−32,768 to 32,767
System.UInt16	16	Unsigned	0 to 65,535
System.Int32	32	Signed	−2,147,483,648 to 2,147,483,647
System.UInt32	32	Unsigned	0 to 4,294,967,295
System.Int64	64	Signed	−9,223,372,036,854,775,808 to 9,223,372,036,854,775,807
System.UInt64	64	Unsigned	0 to 18,446,744,073,709,551,615

Looking at these types another way, Table 6-2 shows the relationship between the types and their number of bits and range style.

Table 6-2. Bits and signed status for integer .NET data types

	8-bits	16-bits	32-bits	64-bits
Signed	SByte	Int16	Int32	Int64
Unsigned	Byte	UInt16	UInt32	UInt64

Decimal Data Types

Once upon a time, life was happy. Strangers said hello when they met you on the street. Succulent fruit burst forth from the trees. In short, God was in His heaven, and everything was right with the world—and then along came fractions. At first, they didn't seem that bad, since so many of them could be easily converted into a plain numeric form by inserting a decimal point in the number: 1/2 became 0.5; 1/4 became the longer yet smaller 0.25; 1/3 became 0.333333333333333333333333333333333333 333333333333333333333333333333333333333333333333333333333333333333333333 3333333333333333333333333333333333333333333333333333333333333333333333333… hey, what's going on here? I can't write all those 3s. The book would be 2,000 pages, or more. Eventually people discovered that in many cases, it just wasn't worth the bother of writing out all the 3s, so they just stopped at some point, as in 0.33333333. It wasn't perfectly accurate, but it was good enough.

This is what life is like for computer-based decimal values. You can have perfect accuracy—up to a point. After that, you have to settle for good enough. The .NET Framework includes three decimal data types. Two of them accept limited accuracy in exchange for a large range of values. The third has perfect accuracy, but its range is more limited. Table 6-3 documents these three types.

Table 6-3. An accurate list of the inaccurate decimal data types

.NET data type	Accuracy	Range	Description
System.Decimal	Perfect	Limited	The Decimal data type provides around 28 combined digits on both sides of the decimal point. And although it may truncate after the last available digit position, it is accurate within those digits. Because of this, it is perfect for working with money.
			The more digits you have on the left of the decimal, the fewer you have available for the right of the decimal, and vice versa. For numbers with no decimal portion, the range is from −79,228,162,514,264,337,593,543,950,335 to 79,228,162,514,264,337,593,543,950,335. (That's 29 digits, but who's counting?) For numbers with only zero (0) to the left of the decimal, the range is −0.0000000000000000000000000001 to 0.0000000000000000000000000001.
System.Single	Imperfect	Big	The Single data type offers a much larger range than Decimal does, but it does have some accuracy problems. Sometimes when you do a complex calculation that you know should result in zero, the actual calculated result might be 0.0000000000023. It's close to zero, but not exactly zero. But you can use very large or very small numbers. For negative values, the range is $-3.402823E^{+38}$ to $-1.401298E^{-45}$; for positive values, its range is $1.401298E^{-45}$ to $3.402823E^{+38}$.
System.Double	Imperfect	Huge	The Double data type is just like the Single data type, but with a bigger attitude—I mean a larger range. For negative values, the range is $-1.79769313486231E^{+308}$ to $-4.94065645841247E^{-324}$; for positive values, the range is $4.94065645841247E^{-324}$ to $1.79769313486232E^{+308}$.

Character Data Types

Hey, check this out. *ktuefghbiokh*. Pretty cool, eh? That's the power of a computer in action managing text data. So efficient; so graceful; so *lskjdfljsdfjl*. Although computers are really number machines, they handle text just as well. Of course, it's really just you doing all the wordsmithing. In fact, the computer isn't even smart enough to tell the difference between numbers and letters; it's all bits to the CPU. Pretty mindless, if you ask me. I mean, what's the use of having all that computing power if you can't even think?

Despite all their speed and technology, computers are still just lumps of silicon wrapped up in a nice package. The computer I'm typing on doesn't even know that I'm insulting it; I can type these things on and on, and there's nutten that thiz komputre cann due about itt.

The framework includes two text-related data types: System.Char and System.String. The Char data type holds a single character, no more, no less. At 16 bits, it holds any of the thousands of Unicode characters.

The String data type allows up to about two billion Unicode characters to be "strung" together into one long text block. Strings in .NET are immutable; once you create a string, it cannot be changed in any way. If you want to add text to an existing string, .NET will instead create a brand-new string built from the original two immutable strings.

Although Char and String are different data types, you can easily move data back and forth between them, since they are both based on basic Unicode characters.

Date and Time Data Type

The System.DateTime data type lets you store either date or time values (or both) as data. Internally, DateTime is just a simple integer counter that displays a converted date or time format when needed. As a number, it counts the number of "ticks" since 12:00 a.m. on January 1, 1 AD. Each "tick" is exactly 100 nanoseconds, so it's pretty precise. The maximum allowed date is December 31, 9999 in the Gregorian calendar.

Boolean Data Type

The System.Boolean data type represents the true essence of computer data: the bit. It holds one of two possible values: True or False. Shockingly, the data type actually requires between 2 and 4 bytes of data space to keep track of that single bit of data.

It turns out that Boolean values are very important in programs. As a developer, you are always testing to see whether various conditions are met before you process a block of code. All of these conditions eventually boil down to Boolean values and operations. .NET even has ways to easily migrate data between integer values and the Boolean data type. In such conversions, 0 becomes False, and the world of all other possible values becomes True. When moving from Boolean to an integer equivalent, False becomes 0 and True becomes –1. (If you ever use the C# language, you'll find that it converts True to 1, not –1. Internally in .NET, True does convert to 1, but for historical reasons, Visual Basic uses –1. This difference normally isn't a problem unless you store Boolean values as integers in a disk file and expect both Visual Basic and C# programs to interpret the data correctly.)

The System.Object Class

You already knew that .NET is an object-oriented development environment. What you probably didn't know is that some pranksters at Microsoft placed a bet to see whether they could make the entire .NET system one big derived class. Well, the group that said it could be done won the bet. Everything in .NET—all code and all data—is derived from a single base class: System.Object. By itself, this class doesn't have too many features. It can tell you its name, its type, and whether two instances of an object are in fact one and the same object. Other than that, it isn't useful for much except to be used as a starting point for all other classes and types.

Because all classes in .NET—including all data types—derive from System.Object, you can treat an instance of any class (or data type) as Object. The data will remember what type it really is, so if you have a System.Int32 posing as System.Object, you can change it back to System.Int32 later.

Value Types and Reference Types

Back in Chapter 1, you read about the difference between *value types* and *reference types*: value types are buckets that contain actual data, and reference types contain instructions on where you can find the actual data. In general, value types contain simple and small data values, whereas reference types point to large and complex data blocks. This isn't always true, but for most data you work with, it will be true.

System.Object is a reference type from which all other types and classes derive. This includes all the core data types, so you would think that they would be reference types as well. But there is another class stuck in between System.Object and most of the Visual Basic data types. This class, System.ValueType, implements the basic definition and usage of a value type. Table 6-4 lists some of the differences between value and reference types.

Table 6-4. Value type and reference type usage

Value types	Reference types
Ultimately derive from System.ValueType, which in turn derives from System.Object.	Ultimately derive from System.Object.
Derived core data types: Boolean, Byte, Char, DateTime, Decimal, Double, Int16, Int32, Int64, SByte, Single, UInt16, UInt32, UInt64.	Derived core data type: String.

Table 6-4. Value type and reference type usage (continued)

Value types	Reference types
Provide support for Visual Basic "structures."	Provide support for Visual Basic "classes."
Enumerations are derived as follows: `System.Object←System.ValueType←System.Enum`.	Delegates, used as references to class methods, are derived as follows: `System.Object←System.Delegate`. One type of delegate, the "multicast delegate," is further derived through `System.MulticastDelegate`.
Value types cannot derive from other classes or structures, nor can further structures derive from them.	Reference types can be derived from other classes, and can be used as base classes.
Instances cannot be set to `Nothing`. (Using a nullable type overcomes this limitation.)	Instances can be set to `Nothing`.
Instances can only contain data of the specified type. For instance, `System.Int32` instances can only contain 32-bit signed integer data.	Instances usually refer to data of their defined type, but an instance can also point to a derived type. For example, an instance of `System.String` could refer to any data that used `System.String` as a base class.
Do not go through the full .NET garbage collection process.	Are destroyed through garbage collection.

(In addition to classes and structures, Visual Basic also defines "modules." The .NET documentation identifies modules as reference types, but you can't create instances of them.)

A value type can only contain data of its own type, but reference types can point to derived instances. This is important in .NET, since it was designed to allow a `System.Object` instance to refer to any data in an application. `System.Object` instances can refer to either value type or reference type data. For reference types, this is easy to understand since that instance will just point to some derived instance of itself. But if you assign a value type to a `System.Object` reference, .NET has to mark that instance in a special way to indicate that a reference type contains a value type. This process is called *boxing*, and the reverse process is called *unboxing*. Although boxing is useful, and sometimes essential, it comes with a substantial performance hit.

Visual Basic Data Types

All the data types implemented in the Visual Basic language are wrappers for the core .NET data types. Only some of the names have been changed to protect the innocent. Table 6-5 lists the Visual Basic data types and their .NET equivalents.

Table 6-5. Visual Basic data types and related .NET types

Visual Basic type	.NET type
`Boolean`	`System.Boolean`
`Byte`	`System.Byte`
`Char`	`System.Char`
`Date`	`System.DateTime`

Table 6-5. Visual Basic data types and related .NET types (continued)

Visual Basic type	.NET type
Decimal	System.Decimal
Double	System.Double
Integer	System.Int32
Long	System.Int64
Object	System.Object
SByte	System.SByte
Short	System.Int16
Single	System.Single
String	System.String
UInteger	System.UInt32
ULong	System.UInt64
UShort	System.UInt16

All the Visual Basic data types are fully interchangeable with their .NET equivalents. Any instance of System.Int32 can be treated as though it were an instance of Integer, and vice versa.

Literals

The quickest way to include values of a particular data type in your Visual Basic code is to use a *literal*. You've already seen literals in action in this book. Chapter 1 included a literal in its sample project.

```
MsgBox("Hello, World!")
```

This call to the MsgBox function includes a *String literal*. String literals always appear within a set of double quotes. Most numeric literals appear with a data-type-defining character on the end of the literal, but there are other variations. Table 6-6 lists the different literal values you can include in your code.

Table 6-6. Literals supported by Visual Basic

Literal type	Example	Description
Boolean	True	The Boolean data type supports two literal values: True and False.
Char	"Q"c	Single-character literals appear in double quotes with a trailing character c. A literal of type Char is not the same as a single-character literal of type String.
Date	#11/7/2005#	Date or time literals appear between a set of number signs. You can include dates, times, or a combination of both. The date or time values can be in any format recognized by Windows, although Visual Studio may reformat your date literal for conformity with its own standards.
Decimal	123.45D 123.45@	Floating-point values of type Decimal are followed by a capital *D*, or the character @.

Table 6-6. Literals supported by Visual Basic (continued)

Literal type	Example	Description
Double	123.45R 123.45#	Floating-point values of type Double are followed by a capital *R*, or the character *#*. Also, if you use a numeric literal with a decimal portion, but with no trailing data type character, that literal will be typed as a Double.
Hexadecimal	&HABCD	You can include hexadecimal literals in your code by starting the value with the "&H" character sequence, followed by the hex digits.
Integer	123.45I 123.45%	Integral values of type Integer are followed by a capital *I*, or the character *%*. Also, if you use a numeric literal that falls in the range of an Integer, but with no trailing data type character, that literal will be typed as an Integer.
Long	123.45L 123.45&	Integral values of type Long are followed by a capital *L*, or the character *&*. Also, if you use a numeric literal that falls in the range of a Long and outside the range of an Integer, but with no trailing data type character, that literal will be typed as a Long.
Octal	&O7654	You can include octal literals in your code by starting the value with the "&O" character sequence, followed by the octal digits.
Short	123.45S	Integral values of type Short are followed by a capital *S*.
Single	123.45F 123.45!	Floating-point values of type Single are followed by a capital *F*, or the character *!*.
String	"A ""B"" C"	String literals appear within a set of double quotes, with no special character following the closing quote. Use two quote characters within the string literal to embed a single quotation mark.

Constants

Literals are nice, but it isn't always clear what they mean. Encountering the number 12 in a formula, for instance, might cause the formula to generate correct results, but it would still be helpful to know what 12 means. Is it the number of months in a year, the number of hours in a day, the minimum number of teeth in a mouth to eat steak, or something even more sinister?

Constants provide a way to assign meaningful names to literal values. They are treated a lot like literal values, but once defined, they can be used over and over again in your code. Each use of a literal value, even if it has the same value, represents a distinct definition and instance of that value.

In Visual Basic, constants are defined using the Const keyword.

```
Const MonthsInYear As Short = 12
```

This constant definition has the following parts:

A name
   In this case, the name is MonthsInYear.

A data type

This example defines a Short constant. The data type always follows the As keyword. If you leave out this As clause, the constant's data type will be whatever the assigned literal would have been on its own. Only the following data types can be used for constants: Boolean, Byte, Char, Date, Decimal, Double, Integer, Long, Object, SByte, Short, Single, String, UInteger, ULong, UShort, or the name of an enumeration (discussed in the next section).

An initializer

The initializer assigned here is 12. Once assigned, this value cannot be altered while your code is running. Constants are always value types, not reference types. Initializers are usually simple literals, but you can also include simple calculations:

```
Const Seven As Integer = 3 + 4
```

An access level

The definition of MonthsInYear listed here represents the typical format of a constant definition included within a code procedure. You can also define constants outside procedures, but still within a class or other type. When you do this, you generally add an *access modifier* keyword just before the Const keyword. This keyword indicates how much code will be able to use the constant. I'll describe access modifiers a little later, in the section on variables. Constants defined within a procedure can only be used within that procedure.

Once you define a constant, you can use it anywhere you would use an equivalent literal.

```
Const GreatGreeting As String = "Hello, World!"
...Later...
MsgBox(GreatGreeting)
```

Enumerations

Enumerations, one of the core .NET types, allow you to group together named, related integer values as a set. Once bound together, the enumeration can be used like any other data type; you can create variables that are specific instances of an enumeration.

Enumerations are a multiline construct; the first line defines the name and underlying data type of the enumeration. Each enumeration member appears on a separate line, ending with a final closing End Enum line.

```
01  Enum CarType As Integer
02      Sedan = 1
03      StationWagon = 2
04      Truck = 3
05      SUV = 4
06      Other = 5
07  End Enum
```

The declaration line (line 01) includes the `Enum` keyword, the name of the enumeration (`CarType`), and the underlying data type (`Integer`). The `As` data type clause is optional; if you leave it off, the enumeration defaults to `Integer`. If you do supply a data type, it must be one of the following: `Byte`, `Integer`, `Long`, `SByte`, `Short`, `UInteger`, `ULong`, or `UShort`.

Each member of the enumeration (lines 02 to 06) must include at least a member name (such as `Sedan`). You can optionally assign a numeric value to some or all of the members, as I have done in the sample. If a member lacks an assignment, it is set to one more than the previous member. If none of the members have an assigned value, the first is assigned 0, the next 1, and so on.

Once defined, enumeration members act a lot like integer constants; you can use them anywhere you would normally use a literal or constant. When referencing the members of an enumeration in your code, include both the enumeration name and the member name.

```
CarType.Sedan
```

The `Enum` statement cannot be used within a method or procedure. Instead, you define an enumeration as a member of a type (class, structure, or module), or as its own standalone type, just like a class. The .NET Framework includes many useful predefined enumerations intended for use with framework features. For instance, the `System.DayOfWeek` enumeration includes members for each day of the week.

Variables

Literals are nice, and constants and enumerations are nicer, but none of them can be altered once your program starts. This tends to make your application rigid and inflexible. If all your customers are named "Fred" and they only place orders for $342.34, it probably won't be much of a limitation. But most users want more variety in their software. *Variables* are named containers for data, just like constants, but their contents can be modified throughout the run of an application. Also, they can contain both value types and reference types. Here's the basic syntax for defining a new variable:

```
Dim customerName As String
```

The `Dim` keyword—originally from the word *dimension*—defines a new variable; in this case, a variable named `customerName` with a data type of `String`. This named container is ready to hold any `String` value; assign to it string literals, other string variables, or the return value from functions that generate strings. Since it is a reference type, it can also be set to `Nothing`, a special Visual Basic value and keyword that means "this reference type is empty, really empty."

```
customerName = Nothing                       ' Nothing
customerName = "Fred"                         ' Literal
customerName = GetCustomerName(customerID)    ' Function result
```

All variables contain their default value until set to something else. For reference types and nullable types, the default is Nothing; for numeric values, the default is 0. Booleans default to False. You can include an initial assignment as part of the Dim statement to override the default assignment.

```
Dim countdownSeconds As Short = 60
Dim processingDate As Date = Today
Dim customerName As String = GetCustomerName(customerID)
```

The last line in that code block shows a reference type—String—being assigned the String result of a function. You can also assign a brand-new instance of a reference instance to a reference type variable. And it's new. That is, it uses the special New keyword, which says, "I'm creating a new instance of the specific data type." There are a few different variations, but they all produce the same results.

```
' ----- One-line variation.
Dim someEmployee As New Employee

' ----- Another one-line variation.
Dim someEmployee As Employee = New Employee

' ----- Two-line variation.
Dim someEmployee As Employee
someEmployee = New Employee
```

Remember that reference types are buckets that contain directions for locating the actual data. When a reference variable first springs into existence, it contains Nothing. That is, the bucket contains no instructions at all since there is no related data stored anywhere. When you assign a new instance to a reference type variable, that instance gets stored somewhere in memory, and instructions for locating that data are dumped into the bucket. In the previous code block, each use of the New keyword creates a new data instance somewhere in memory. This data's location is then assigned to the someString variable.

Many classes include one or more *constructors*, initialization routines that set up the initial values of the instance. You can call a specific constructor through the New clause. The String data type includes constructors that let you build an initial string. One of these special constructors lets you create a new string containing multiple copies of a specific character. The following statement assigns a string of 25 asterisks to the lotsOfStars variable:

```
Dim lotsOfStars As New String("*"c, 25)
```

Constructors are discussed in detail in Chapter 8.

Dim statements can appear anywhere in a procedure, but by tradition they appear right at the start of a procedure, before any other logic statements.

```
Sub MyProcedure()
    Dim myVariable As Integer
    ' ----- Additional code goes here...
End Sub
```

As with constants, variables can be defined either within a procedure, or outside a procedure but within a type. (Variables and constants declared outside a procedure are known as *fields*. Variables and constants declared inside a procedure are known as *local variables* and *local constants*, respectively.) The Dim keyword is always used with in-procedure variable declarations. At the type level, the Dim keyword is replaced by one of the following *access modifiers*:

Private

> Private variables can be used by any member or procedure within the type, but nowhere else. If you derive a new class from a base class that includes a private type variable, the code in that derived class will have no access at all to that Private variable; it won't even know it exists.

Friend

> Friend variables are private to an assembly. They can be used by any code in their related type, but also by any code anywhere in the same assembly. Now that's friendly.

Public

> Public variables are available everywhere. It is possible to write an application or component that exposes its types to code beyond itself. Anything marked Public can be exposed in this way.

Protected

> Protected variables are like Private type variables, but code in derived classes can also access them. You can use the Protected keyword only in a class definition; it doesn't work in a structure or module.

Protected Friend

> Protected Friend variables combine all the features of Friend and Protected. They can be used only in classes.

A single class or type may contain both fields and local variables and constants.

```
Class MyClass
    ' ----- Here's a field.
    Private InternalUseOnly As Boolean

    Sub MyProcedure()
        ' ----- Here's a local variable.
        Dim myVariable As Integer
    End Sub
End Class
```

There are other syntax variations to the Dim statement, some of which I will discuss later in this chapter and in other chapters.

Scope and Lifetime

When you define a variable within a procedure, it has *procedure-level scope*. This means you can use the variable anywhere within that procedure. Your procedure will likely have "block statements," those statements, such as For...Next and If...Then, that require more than one line of source code to complete. If you add a Dim statement between the starting and ending lines of one of these statements, that declared variable will have only *block-level scope*. It will be available only within that block of the procedure.

```
For counter = 1 To 10
    Dim processResult As Integer
    ' ----- More  code here.
Next counter
MsgBox(processResult)  ' This line will fail
```

This code declares processResult within the For...Next block. So, it's available only for use inside that block; any attempted use of processResult outside the For block generates an immediate error.

The *lifetime* of a procedure-level variable begins when the code first enters that procedure, and ends when the code exits the procedure. This is true for both procedure-level and block-level variables. This means that if you assign a block-level variable some value before exiting the block, it will still have that value if you reenter that block during the same procedure call.

For fields (class-level variables), the scope depends on the access level used when declaring the variable. The lifetime of a field begins when the class instance is created in code, and ends when the instance is destroyed or goes completely out of use.

Variable and Constant Naming Conventions

The names that you give to your variables will not have that much impact on how your application runs on the user's workstation, but they can affect the clarity of the source code. In the days before .NET, many Windows programming languages used a system called *Hungarian Notation* to craft variable names. Such names helped to communicate information about the data type and usage of a variable to anyone reading the source code. Unfortunately, the rules used to define Hungarian variable names were somewhat complex, and varied not only among programming languages, but also among programmers using the same language.

When Microsoft released .NET back in 2002, its documentation included various programming recommendations. One of those recommendations was "Stop using the Java programming language." Another recommendation encouraged programmers to cease from using Hungarian Notation, and instead embrace a new system that used casing rules to differentiate variables. The rules state that all variable names should employ mixed-case names (where each logical word in the variable name starts with a capital letter and continues with lowercase letters). The only differentiation comes in the capitalization of the initial letter:

- Set the first letter of all local variables and all method parameters to lowercase. This is known as *Camel Casing*.
- Set the first letter of all fields, methods, type members (including controls), and types to uppercase. This is known as *Pascal Casing*.

In the interest of full disclosure, I must tell you that I modified the original recommendations slightly from the documentation supplied with Visual Studio. The original rules were a little more complex when it came to field and method parameter names. Personally, I find the two rules listed here to be adequate for my needs.

You might give a local variable a name like `lookInThisVariable`, which capitalizes the first letter of each word, but not the initial letter. If you defined this variable as a field instead, you would change its name to `LookInThisVariable`, capitalizing the first letter.

Local Type Inference

Visual Basic is a *strongly typed language*. This means that all data values are either `Integer`, or `Short`, or `String`, or some other specific data type. Even the default `Object` data type is considered strong. To create a variable without a data type would be weak, and Visual Basic programmers are anything but weak.

Normally, you specifically tell Visual Basic what data type to use for a variable. But a new Visual Basic 2008 feature called *local type inference* lets the Visual Basic compiler join in the fun of assigning data types to variables. And what fun it is!

In standard variable declaration, you include the data type with an As clause.

```
Dim whatAmI As String
whatAmI = "You're a string, and nothing but a string."
```

But with local type inference, Visual Basic will figure out the data type all on its own when you leave off the As clause.

```
Dim thing1
Dim thing2
thing1 = "This is a string."
thing2 = 25
MsgBox(thing1.GetType.ToString)
MsgBox(thing2.GetType.ToString)
```

When you run this code, two messages appear to tell you the strong-type-name of each thing: `System.String` and `System.Int32`, respectively. (Don't worry about the "GetType" stuff for now. It just identifies the true type of the things.) Visual Basic acts as though the first two lines looked like this:

```
Dim thing1 As String
Dim thing2 As Integer
```

Once Visual Basic identifies the data type for one of the as-of-yet-untyped variables, that variable is glued to that type. The following code will fail:

```
Dim thing1
thing1 = "This is a string."
thing1 = 25  ' This fails, since thing1 is a string.
```

As the name implies, local type inference works only with local variables. Class fields must be declared with a specific data type. Other restrictions apply. See dealer for details.

You can turn the type inference system on and off using the Option Infer statement at the top of each source code file.

```
Option Infer On
```

You can also set this on a project-wide basis through the Compile tab of the project properties.

Type inference exists to support the new LINQ features discussed in Chapter 17. Although you can let Visual Basic infer most or all of the variables in your application, it is not a good thing to do in practice. As smart as the compiler is, it doesn't think deeply about the overall logic of your application, and it may make different data typing choices than you would. For instance, Visual Basic may infer a variable as Integer, even though you plan to stuff large Long values into it later. If you have the opportunity to include meaningful and accurate As clauses with your Dim statements, do it. Because I said so. Because it's the right thing to do.

Operators

Visual Basic includes a variety of *operators* that let you manipulate the values of your variables. You've already seen the *assignment operator* (=), which lets you assign a value directly to a variable. Most of the other operators let you build up *expressions* that combine multiple original values in formulaic ways for eventual assignment to a variable. Consider the following statement:

```
squareArea = length * width
```

This statement includes two operators: assignment and multiplication. The multiplication operator combines two values (length and width) using multiplication, and the assignment operator stores the product in the squareArea variable. Without operators, you would be hard-pressed to calculate an area or any complex formula.

There are two types of non-assignment operators: *unary* and *binary*. Unary operators work with only a single value, or *operand*. Binary operators require two operands, but result in a single processed value. Operands include literals, constants, variables, and function return values. Table 6-7 lists the different operators with usage details.

Table 6-7. Visual Basic non-assignment operators

Operator	Description
+	Addition. Adds two operands together, producing a sum. Some programmers also use this operator to perform string concatenation, but it's better to join strings using another operator (&) specifically designed for that purpose. Syntax: *operand1* + *operand2* Example: 2 + 3
+	Unary plus. Ensures that an operand retains its current sign, either positive or negative. Since all operands automatically retain their sign, this operator is usually redundant. It may come in handy when we discuss "operator overloading" in Chapter 12. Syntax: +*operand* Example: +5
-	Subtraction. Subtracts one operand (the second) from another (the first), and returns the difference. Syntax: *operand1* − *operand2* Example: 10 − 4
-	Unary negation. Reverses the sign of its operand. When used with a literal number, it results in a negative value. When used with a variable that contains a negative value, it produces a positive result. Syntax: −*operand2* Example: −34
*	Multiplication. Multiplies two operands together, and returns the product. Syntax: *operand1* * *operand2* Example: 8 * 3
/	Division. Divides one operand (the first) by another (the second), and returns the quotient. If the second operand contains zero, a divide-by-zero error occurs. (When working with `Single` and `Double` values, divide-by-zero actually returns special "infinity" or "not a number" indicators.) Syntax: *operand1* / *operand2* Example: 9 / 3
\	Integer division. Divides one operand (the first) by another (the second), and returns the quotient, first truncating any decimal portion from that result. If the second operand contains zero, a divide-by-zero error occurs. (See the caveat listed with the / operator.) Syntax: *operand1* \ *operand2* Example: 9 \ 4
Mod	Modulo. Divides one operand (the first) by another (the second), and returns the remainder as an integer value. If the second operand contains zero, a divide-by-zero error occurs. (See the caveat listed with the / operator.) Syntax: *operand1* Mod *operand2* Example: 10 Mod 3
^	Exponentiation. Raises one operand (the first) to the power of another (the second). Syntax: *operand1* ^ *operand2* Example: 2 ^ 8

Table 6-7. Visual Basic non-assignment operators (continued)

Operator	Description
&	String concatenation. Joins two operands together, and returns a combined string result. Both operands are converted to their String equivalent before being joined together.
	Syntax: *operand1* & *operand2*
	Example: "O" & "K"
And	Conjunction. Performs a logical or bitwise conjunction on two operands, and returns the result. For logical (Boolean) operations, the result will be True only if both operands evaluate to True. For bitwise (integer) operations, each specific bit in the result will be set to 1 only if the corresponding bits in both operands are 1.
	Syntax: *operand1* And *operand2*
	Example: isOfficer And isGentleman
Or	Disjunction. Performs a logical or bitwise disjunction on two operands, and returns the result. For logical (Boolean) operations, the result will be True if either operand evaluates to True. For bitwise (integer) operations, each specific bit in the result will be set to 1 if the corresponding bit in either operand is 1.
	Syntax: *operand1* Or *operand2*
	Example: enjoyMountains Or enjoySea
AndAlso	Short-circuited conjunction. This operator is equivalent to the logical version of the And operator, but if the first operand evaluates to False, the second operand will not be evaluated at all. This operator does not support bitwise operations.
	Syntax: *operand1* AndAlso *operand2*
	Example: isOfficer AndAlso isGentleman
OrElse	Short-circuited disjunction. This operator is equivalent to the logical version of the Or operator, but if the first operand evaluates to True, the second operand will not be evaluated at all. This operator does not support bitwise operations.
	Syntax: *operand1* OrElse *operand2*
	Example: enjoyMountains OrElse enjoySea
Not	Negation. Performs a logical or bitwise negation on a single operand. For logical (Boolean) operations, the result will be True if the operand evaluates to False, and False if the operand evaluates to True. For bitwise (integer) operations, each specific bit in the result will be set to 1 if the corresponding operand bit is 0, and set to 0 if the operand bit is 1.
	Syntax: Not *operand1*
	Example: Not readyToSend
Xor	Exclusion. Performs a logical or bitwise "exclusive or" on two operands, and returns the result. For logical (Boolean) operations, the result will be True only if the operands have different logical values (True or False). For bitwise (integer) operations, each specific bit in the result will be set to 1 only if the corresponding bits in the operands are different.
	Syntax: *operand1* Xor *operand2*
	Example: chickenDish Xor beefDish

Table 6-7. Visual Basic non-assignment operators (continued)

Operator	Description
<<	Shift left. The Shift Left operator shifts the bits of the first operand to the left by the number of positions specified in the second operand, and returns the result. Bits pushed off the left end of the result are lost; bits added to the right end are always 0. This operator works best if the first operand is an unsigned integer value.
	Syntax: *operand1* << *operand2*
	Example: &H25 << 3
>>	Shift right. The Shift Right operator shifts the bits of the first operand to the right by the number of positions specified in the second operand, and returns the result. Bits pushed off the right end of the result are lost; bits added to the left end are always the same as the bit originally in the leftmost position. This operator works best if the first operand is an unsigned integer value.
	Syntax: *operand1* >> *operand2*
	Example: &H25 >> 2
=	Equals (comparison). Compares two operands and returns True if they are equal in value.
	Syntax: *operand1* = *operand2*
	Example: expectedAmount = actualAmount
<>	Not equals. Compares two operands and returns True if they are not equal in value.
	Syntax: *operand1* <> *operand2*
	Example: startValue <> endValue
<	Less than. Compares two operands and returns True if the first is less in value than the second. When comparing string values, the return is True if the first operand appears first when sorting the two strings.
	Syntax: *operand1* < *operand2*
	Example: raiseRate < inflationRate
>	Greater than. Compares two operands and returns True if the first is greater in value than the second. When comparing string values, the return is True if the first operand appears last when sorting the two strings.
	Syntax: *operand1* > *operand2*
	Example: raiseRate > inflationRate
<=	Less than or equal to. Compares two operands and returns True if the first is less than or equal to the value of the second.
	Syntax: *operand1* <= *operand2*
	Example: raiseRate <= inflationRate
>=	Greater than or equal to. Compares two operands and returns True if the first is greater than or equal to the value of the second.
	Syntax: *operand1* >= *operand2*
	Example: raiseRate >= inflationRate
Like	Pattern comparison. Compares the first operand to the pattern specified in the second operand, and returns True if there is a match. The pattern operand supports some basic wildcard and selection options, and is fully described in the documentation supplied with Visual Studio. .NET also includes a feature called *regular expressions* that provides a much more comprehensive pattern matching solution.
	Syntax: *operand1* Like *operand2*
	Example: governmentID Like ssnPattern

Table 6-7. Visual Basic non-assignment operators (continued)

Operator	Description
Is	Type comparison. Compares the first operand to another object, a data type, or Nothing, and returns True if there is a match. I will document this operator in more detail later in the text, and in Chapter 8.
	Syntax: *operand1* Is *operand2*
	Example: someVariable Is Nothing
IsNot	Negated type comparison. This operator is a shortcut for using the Is and Not operators together. The following two expressions are equivalent:
	```first IsNot second``` ```Not (first Is second)```
	Syntax: *operand1* IsNot *operand2*
	Example: something IsNot somethingElse
TypeOf	Instance comparison. Returns the data type of a value or variable. The type of every class or data type in .NET is implemented as an object, based on System.Type. The TypeOf operator can be used only with the Is operator:
	Syntax: TypeOf *operand1* Is *typeOperand*
	Example: TypeOf someVariable Is Integer
AddressOf	Delegate retrieval. Returns a delegate (described in Chapter 8) that represents a specific instance of a procedure or method.
	Syntax: AddressOf *method1*
	Example: AddressOf one.SomeMethod
GetType	Type retrieval. Returns the data type of a value or variable, just like the TypeOf operator. However, GetType works like a function, and does not need to be used with the Is operator.
	Syntax: GetType(*operand1*)
	Example: GetType(one)

Non-assignment operators use their operands to produce a result, but they do not cause the operands themselves to be altered in any way. The assignment operator does update the operand that appears on its left side. In addition to the standard assignment operator, Visual Basic includes several operators that combine the assignment operator with some of the binary operators. Table 6-8 lists these assignment operators.

Table 6-8. Visual Basic assignment operators

Operator	Based on
=	Standard assignment operator
+=	+ (addition)
−=	− (subtraction)
*=	* (multiplication)
/=	/ (division)
\=	\ (integer division)
^=	^ (exponentiation)

Table 6-8. Visual Basic assignment operators (continued)

Operator	Based on
&=	& (concatenation)
<<=	<< (shift left)
>>=	>> (shift right)

These assignment operators are just shortcuts for the full-bodied operators. For instance, to add 1 to a numeric variable, you can use either of these two statements:

```
' ----- Increment totalSoFar by 1.
totalSoFar = totalSoFar + 1

' ----- Another way to increment totalSoFar by 1.
totalSoFar += 1
```

Static Variables

Normally, the lifetime of a local procedure-level variable ends when the procedure ends. But sometimes you might want a variable to retain its value between each call into the procedure. Sometimes you might also want a million dollars, but you can't always have it. But you can have variables that keep their values if you want. They're called *static variables*. To declare a static variable, use the Static keyword in place of the Dim keyword.

```
Static keepingTrack As Integer = 0
```

The assignment of 0 to keepingTrack is done only once, when creating the instance of the type that contains this statement. Thereafter, it keeps whatever value is assigned to it until the instance is destroyed. Static variables can only be created within procedures.

Arrays

Software applications often work with sets of related data, not just isolated data values. Visual Basic includes two primary ways of working with such sets of data: collections (discussed in Chapter 16) and arrays. An *array* assigns a numeric position to each item included in the set, starting with 0 and ending with one less than the number of items included. An array of five items has elements numbering from 0 to 4.

As an example, imagine that you were developing a zoo simulation application. You might include an array named animals that includes each animal name in your zoo:

- Animal #0: Aardvark
- Animal #1: Baboon
- Animal #2: Chimpanzee

- Animal #3: Donkey
- …and so on…

Visual Basic identifies array elements by a parenthesized number after the array name. For our animals, a simple assignment puts the String name of each animal in an array element.

```
animal(0) = "Aardvark"
animal(1) = "Baboon"
animal(2) = "Chimpanzee"
animal(3) = "Donkey"
```

Using each array element is just as easy.

```
MsgBox("The first animal is: " & animal(0))
```

Each element of an array is not so different from a standalone variable. In fact, you could just consider the set of animals in the example code to be distinct variables: a variable named animal(0), another variable named animal(1), and so on. But they are better than ordinary variables because you can process them as a set. For instance, you can scan through each element using a For...Next loop. Consider an Integer array named eachItem with elements numbered from 0 to 2. The following code block adds up the individual items of the array as though they were distinct variables:

```
Dim totalAmount As Integer
totalAmount = eachItem(0) + eachItem(1) + eachItem(2)
```

But since the items are in a numbered array, you can use a For...Next loop to scan through each element, one at a time.

```
Dim totalAmount As Integer = 0
For counter As Integer = 0 to 2
   ' ----- Keep a running total of the items.
   totalAmount += eachItem(counter)
Next counter
```

Before you assign values to array elements, or retrieve those elements, you must declare and size the array for your needs. The Dim statement creates an array just as it does ordinary variables; the ReDim statement resizes an array after it already exists.

```
Dim animal(0 To 25) As String   ' 26-element array
Dim moreAnimals() As String     ' An undefined String array
ReDim moreAnimals(0 To 25)      ' Now it has elements
```

Normally, the ReDim statement would wipe out any existing data stored in each array element. Adding the Preserve keyword retains all existing data.

```
ReDim Preserve moreAnimals(0 to 30)  ' Keeps elements 0 to 25
```

Each element of the array is an independent object that can be assigned data as needed. In this example, each element is a String, but you can use any value type or reference type you wish in the array declaration. If you create an array of Object elements, you can mix and match the data in the array; element 0 need not contain the same type of data as element 1.

The array itself is also an independent object—a class instance that manages its set of contained elements. If you need to specify the entire array, and not just one of its elements (and there are times when you need to do this), use its name without any parentheses or positional values.

Multidimensional Arrays

Visual Basic arrays support more than one *dimension* (or "rank"). The dimensions indicate the number of independent ranges supported by the array. A one-dimensional array, like the animal array earlier, includes a single range. A two-dimensional array includes two comma-delimited ranges, forming a grid arrangement of elements, with separate ranges for rows and columns.

```
Dim ticTacToeBoard(0 To 2, 0 To 2) As Char  ' 3 x 3 board
```

An array can have up to 60 different dimensions, although there are usually better ways to organize data than breaking it out into that many dimensions.

Array Boundaries

The *lower bound* of any array dimension is normally 0, as indicated by the 0 To *x* clause when defining or redimensioning the array. You can actually leave the "0 To" part out of the statement, and just include the upper bound.

```
' ----- These two lines are equivalent.
Dim animal(0 To 25) As String
Dim animal(25) As String
```

These two statements both create an array with 26 elements, numbered 0 through 25.

There are a few special cases where nonzero lower bounds are allowed, such as when working with older COM-generated arrays. But the standard Visual Basic declaration syntax does not allow you to create arrays with nonzero lower bounds.

To determine the current lower or upper bound of an array dimension, use the LBound and UBound functions.

```
MsgBox("The board is " & (UBound(ticTacToeBoard, 1) + 1) & _
    " by " & (UBound(ticTacToeBoard, 2) + 1))
```

If your array includes only a single dimension, you don't have to tell LBound or UBound which dimension you want to check.

```
MsgBox("The upper element is numbered " & UBound(animal))
```

Each array also includes GetLowerBound and GetUpperBound methods that return the same results as LBound and UBound. (I discuss methods in detail in Chapter 8.) However, the dimension number you pass to the GetLowerBound and GetUpperBound methods starts from 0, whereas LBound and UBound dimension values start the counting at 1.

```
MsgBox("The board is " & _
    (ticTacToeBoard.GetUpperBound(0) + 1) & _
    " by " & (ticTacToeBoard.GetUpperBound(1) + 1))
```

Initializing Arrays

Once you've declared your array elements, you can store and retrieve elements whenever you need. It's also possible to store elements in your array right at declaration time. The list of new array elements appears in a set of curly braces.

```
Dim squares() As Integer = {0, 1, 4, 9, 16, 25}
```

You must leave out the lower and upper bound specifications when creating an array in this way. The squares array shown here will have elements numbered 0 to 5.

Nullable Types

Value types are hard-working variables, maintaining their data values throughout their lives. Reference types work hard, too, but they can be filled with Nothing and get a little rest time. This difference has long been a thorn in the side of value types. Is it too much to ask to give these working-class variables a little down time?

Well, Microsoft has heard this plea, and starting with Visual Basic 2008, value types can now be assigned with Nothing. These new *nullable types* are essential when you want to have an undefined state for a standard value type (especially useful when working with database fields). Consider this class that manages employee information:

```
Public Class Employee
    Public Name As String
    Public HireDate As Date
    Public FireDate As Date

    Public Sub New(ByVal employeeName As String, _
            ByVal dateHired As Date)
        Me.Name = employeeName
        Me.HireDate = dateHired
    End Sub
End Class
```

This class works well, except that FireDate is not really correct. By default, FireDate will be set to January 1, 1, at midnight, and you can use that date as your "never fired" date. But what happens if your company really did fire someone just at that moment, two thousand years ago?

To resolve this issue, nullable types let you assign and retrieve Nothing from value type variables. These vitamin-enriched value types are declared using a special question-mark syntax.

```
' ----- Either of these two statements will work.
Public FireDate As Date?
Public FireDate2? As Date
```

I prefer the first syntax, with the question mark added to the data type. But either statement will work. Once it's declared, a value type can take either standard data or Nothing.

```
FireDate = Nothing
FireDate = #7/18/2008#
If (FireDate Is Nothing) Then...
```

There is a special syntax when defining your own custom value types as nullable, but since it uses the "generics" Visual Basic feature, I'll wait to introduce it until Chapter 16.

Common Visual Basic Functions

This final section includes a brief listing of the functions built into the Visual Basic language, many of which you will use regularly in your applications. Also listed here are some members of the Framework Class Library (FCL) that replicate features that were part of the Visual Basic language before .NET, but were moved into the framework for more general access. For the exact syntax required to use these functions, access the Visual Studio online help.

Conversion Functions

The conversion functions allow you to convert data of one Visual Basic data type to another. It's not a free-for-all, so don't go converting the string "hello" to an integer and expect it to work. But converting numbers from one numeric type to another, or converting numbers between string and numeric types, generally works just fine.

All of these statements (except CType) have the same basic syntax:

dest = C*Xxxx*(*source*)

where *source* is the value to be converted by C*Xxxx*. You don't have to assign the result to a variable; you can use the result anywhere you would use a similar literal or variable value. Table 6-9 lists the built-in conversion functions.

Table 6-9. Visual Basic conversion functions

Function	Description
CBool	Converts a value to a Boolean.
CByte	Converts a value to a Byte.
CChar	Converts a value to a Char. If the source value is a string, only the first character is converted.
CDate	Converts a value to a Date. If the source value is a string, it must be in a valid date or time format.
CDbl	Converts a value to a Double.
CDec	Converts a value to a Decimal.

Table 6-9. Visual Basic conversion functions (continued)

Function	Description
CInt	Converts a value to an Integer.
CLng	Converts a value to a Long.
CObj	Converts a value to an Object. This is useful when you want to store a value type as an Object instance.
CSByte	Converts a value to an SByte.
CShort	Converts a value to a Short.
CSng	Converts a value to a Single.

CType	Converts a value to any defined type, class, or interface, either in your application or in the FCL. The syntax is:
	
	 `CType(sourceData, newType)`
	
	 where *newType* is a data type. For instance:
	
	 `CType(5, String)`
	
	 converts the Integer 5 to a String. As with other conversion functions, you can't convert data from one type to another if the types are incompatible, or if there is no conversion available that knows how to generate the target type from the source type. Operator overloading, discussed in Chapter 12, provides a way to let the CType function convert between types that would otherwise be incompatible.

CUInt	Converts a value to a UInteger.
CULng	Converts a value to a ULong.
CUShort	Converts a value to a UShort.

Date-Related Functions

Visual Basic includes several functions designed to manage date and time values. Table 6-10 lists these functions. Most of these functions accept one or more source arguments, and return either Date, String, or a numeric result.

Table 6-10. Visual Basic date-related functions and properties

Function	Description
DateAdd	Adds or subtracts a time or date value to a starting date. For instance, you can add 12 minutes, or subtract three years, from a given date.
DateDiff	Returns the difference between two date or time values. You can specify the interval, such as months or seconds.
DatePart	Returns one component of a date or time, such as the hour or the year.
DateSerial	Returns a Date built from specific month, day, and year values.
DateString	Returns the current date as a string. You can also set the date on the local computer using this keyword.
DateValue	Returns the date portion of a combined date and time value; the time portion is discarded.

Table 6-10. Visual Basic date-related functions and properties (continued)

Function	Description
Day	Returns the day from a given date value.
FormatDateTime	Formats a given date or time as a string, using a small set of predefined formats. This function is included for backward compatibility with older VBScript code.
Hour	Returns the hour from a given time value.
IsDate	Indicates whether the data supplied to this function is a valid date.
Minute	Returns the minute from a given time value.
Month	Returns the month from a given date value.
MonthName	Returns the name of a month for a numeric month value, 1 through 12.
Now	Returns the current date and time. Equivalent to TimeOfDay.
Second	Returns the seconds from a given time value.
TimeOfDay	Returns the current date and time. Equivalent to Now.
Timer	Returns the number of seconds that have elapsed since midnight of the current day. This function is reset to 0 each midnight.
TimeSerial	Returns a Date built from specific hour, minute, and second values.
TimeString	Returns the current time as a string. You can also set the time on the local computer using this keyword.
TimeValue	Returns the time portion of a combined date and time value; the date portion is discarded.
Today	Returns the current date.
Weekday	Returns an integer that indicates the day of the week.
WeekdayName	Returns the name of a weekday for an integer day of the week.
Year	Returns the year from a given date value.

Variables created as System.DateTime (or Visual Basic Date) each include several properties and methods that provide features similar to the functions listed in Table 6-10. For instance, the Second property returns the number of seconds.

```
Dim meetingTime As Date
meetingTime = #11/7/2005 8:00:03am#
MsgBox(meetingTime.Second)    ' Displays '3'
MsgBox(Second(meetingTime))   ' Also displays '3'
```

You can use either the intrinsic Visual Basic functions or the equivalent System. DateTime methods and properties in your code. Each technique provides the same result.

Numeric Functions

Visual Basic programmers just love working with numbers; it's in their blood. Fortunately, Visual Basic includes lots of features for working wonders with numbers. In addition to the standard data manipulation operators, Table 6-11 lists several number-related functions.

Table 6-11. Visual Basic number-related functions

Function	Description
Fix	Truncates the decimal portion of a number, returning only the whole portion. Similar to the Int function.
FormatCurrency	Formats a given number as a currency value, using a small set of predefined formats. This function is included for backward compatibility with older VBScript code.
FormatNumber	Formats a given number as a general number, using a small set of predefined formats. This function is included for backward compatibility with older VBScript code.
FormatPercent	Formats a given number as a percentage, using a small set of predefined formats. This function is included for backward compatibility with older VBScript code.
Hex	Formats a number as hexadecimal, and returns its string representation.
Int	Returns the whole number that is less than or equal to the supplied value. Similar to the Fix function.
IsNumeric	Indicates whether the data supplied to this function is a valid number.
Oct	Formats a number as octal, and returns its string representation.
Val	Extracts the first valid number from a string and returns it.

The .NET Framework includes the System.Math class, which contains several math-related function members. Some of these, such as Round, Sin, and Log, were implemented as intrinsic functions in Visual Basic 6.0, but have been moved from the language to the Math class in .NET.

Visual Basic also includes several functions used for financial and accounting calculations. These functions were also included in Visual Basic 6.0. As they are not relevant to the project discussed in this book, I will only list their names here: DDB, FV, IPmt, IRR, MIRR, NPer, NPV, Pmt, PPmt, PV, Rate, SLN, and SYD.

String Functions

String manipulation is a core part of Windows programming. The new XML features included with .NET are really just fancy string-manipulation routines, although with the complexities hidden from view. Visual Basic includes many functions designed to manipulate strings and characters. They are listed in Table 6-12.

As with most functions, these functions return a new string or value, leaving the original string or source values intact. The lone exception is the Mid statement, which modifies the source variable's value.

Table 6-12. Visual Basic string-related functions

Function	Description
Asc, AscW	Returns the numeric ASCII or Unicode value for a character.
Chr, ChrW	Given a number, these functions return the matching ASCII or Unicode character.
Filter	Returns an array that is a subset of a source array, but including only those elements that matched a pattern.
Format	Formats number, date, and time values using predefined or custom formatting codes.
GetChar	Extracts a single character from a larger string.
InStr	Returns the position of a substring within a larger string.
InStrRev	Returns the position of a substring within a larger string, searching from the end of the string until the beginning.
Join	Returns a string built from a concatenation of an array of strings.
LCase	Converts a string to its lowercase equivalent.
Left	Returns the leftmost portion of a string.
Len	Returns the length of a string.
LSet	Left-aligns a string within a larger string of spaces.
LTrim	Removes spaces from the start of a string.
Mid	Extracts a substring from the middle of a larger string.
Mid statement	Modifies a range of characters in an existing string with new content. This is not a function, but a special Visual Basic statement. Its syntax varies considerably from that of most other Visual Basic features.
Replace	Replaces occurrences of a substring with another substring, all within a larger string.
Right	Returns the rightmost portion of a string.
RSet	Right-aligns a string within a larger string of spaces.
RTrim	Removes spaces from the end of a string.
Space	Generates a string containing a specified number of space characters. Similar to the StrDup function.
Split	Splits a string into an array of substrings based on a delimiter.
Str	Converts a number to its string representation.
StrComp	Compares two strings, and returns an integer indicating their sort order.
StrConv	Converts a string to a new format based on a conversion code. Some of the conversions involve changing the case of the content.
StrDup	Generates a string containing a specified number of a given character. Similar to the Space function, but works with any character.
StrReverse	Reverses the characters in a string.
Trim	Removes spaces from the start and end of a string.
UCase	Converts a string to its uppercase equivalent.

Variables created as System.String (or Visual Basic String) each include several properties and methods that provide features similar to the functions listed in Table 6-12. For instance, the Length property returns the number of characters in the string.

```
Dim simpleString As String = "abcde"
MsgBox(simpleString.Length)    ' Displays '5'
MsgBox(Len(simpleString))      ' Also displays '5'
```

You can use either the intrinsic Visual Basic functions or the equivalent System. String methods and properties in your code. Each technique provides the same result, although the syntax details and options may vary.

Other Functions

Visual Basic includes several functions that refuse to be squeezed into any of the other categories. Table 6-13 documents these functions.

Table 6-13. Visual Basic miscellaneous functions

Function	Description
DirectCast	Converts a value from one data type to another, although the starting and ending data types must be related. Similar to the TryCast and CType functions.
ErrorToString	Returns the string representation of an error code. This works only with the system error codes previously available in Visual Basic 6.0, although these codes are still available in .NET.
IsArray	Indicates whether the data supplied to this function is a valid array.
IsDBNull	Indicates whether the data supplied to this function is a NULL database value.
IsError	Indicates whether the data supplied to this function is an error condition.
IsNothing	Indicates whether the data supplied to this function is undefined, or set to Nothing.
IsReference	Indicates whether the data supplied to this function is a reference type or a value type.
QBColor	Returns a color code from a small set of predefined colors.
RGB	Returns a color code built from the individual red, green, and blue components.
SystemTypeName	Given a Visual Basic data type name, this function returns the equivalent .NET data type name.
TryCast	Converts a value from one data type to another, although the starting and ending data types must be related. Similar to the DirectCast and CType functions.
TypeName	Returns a data type name that summarizes the data type of the supplied content. The returned string is a generalized summary, and not necessarily the "true" data type name.
VarType	Returns a code indicating the general data type of the supplied content.

Summary

When you're working with Visual Basic, you're working with data. The data types included with Visual Basic are simply wrappers for the core data types in .NET, but Visual Basic also adds many functions and features that enhance your ability to manage and organize data.

Project

You look tired. Why don't you take a five-minute break, and then we'll dive into the project code.

Welcome back! In this chapter, we'll use the data type and function features we read about to design some general support routines that will be used throughout the program. All of this code will appear in a Visual Basic module named General, all stored in a project file named *General.vb*.

PROJECT ACCESS

Load the Chapter 6 (Before) Code project, either through the New Project templates or by accessing the project directly from the installation directory. To see the code in its final form, load Chapter 6 (After) Code instead.

I've already added the *General.vb* file with its module starting and ending blocks.

```
Friend Module General

End Module
```

All the code we add in this chapter will appear between these two lines. Remember, modules are a lot like classes and structures, but you can't create instances of them; all their members are shared with all parts of your source code. This allows them to be used anywhere in the application. We don't need to do anything special to make them available to the entire program, other than to set the access level of each member as needed.

First, we'll add some general constants used throughout the program. Back in Visual Basic 6.0, I would have called these "global constants." But now they are simply shared members of the General module. Add the following code just below the Module General statement.

INSERT SNIPPET

Insert Chapter 6, Snippet Item 1.

```
' ----- Public constants.
Public Const ProgramTitle As String = "The Library Project"
Public Const NotAuthorizedMessage As String = _
   "You are not authorized to perform this task."
Public Const UseDBVersion As Integer = 1

' ----- Constants for the MatchingImages image list.
Public Const MatchPresent As Integer = 0
Public Const MatchNone As Integer = 1
```

```
Public Enum LookupMethods As Integer
    ByTitle = 1
    ByAuthor = 2
    ...remaining items excluded for brevity...
End Enum

Public Enum LibrarySecurity As Integer
    ManageAuthors = 1
    ...remaining items excluded for brevity...
    ViewAdminPatronMessages = 23
End Enum
Public Const MaxLibrarySecurity As LibrarySecurity = _
    LibrarySecurity.ViewAdminPatronMessages
```

These constants and enumerations are pretty self-explanatory based on their Pascal-cased names. UseDBVersion will be used to ensure that the application matches the database being used when multiple versions of each are available. The MatchPresent and MatchNone constants will be used for library item lookups.

The two enumerations define codes that specify the type of library item lookup to perform (LookupMethods), and the security codes used to limit the features that a specific administrator will be able to perform in the application (LibrarySecurity).

It's time to add some methods. The first method, CenterText, centers a line of text within a specific width. For instance, if you had the string "Hello, World" (12 characters in length) and you wanted to center it on a line that could be up to 40 characters long, you would need to add 14 spaces to the start of the line (determined by subtracting 12 from 40, and then dividing the result by 2). The routine uses a couple of the string-specific Visual Basic functions (such as Trim, Left, and Len) to manipulate and test the data, and the integer division \ operator to help calculate the number of spaces to insert.

INSERT SNIPPET

Insert Chapter 6, Snippet Item 2.

```
Public Function CenterText(ByVal origText As String, _
        ByVal textWidth As Integer) As String
    ' ----- Center a piece of text in a field width. If the
    '       text is too wide, truncate it.
    Dim resultText As String

    resultText = Trim(origText)
    If (Len(resultText) >= textWidth) Then
        ' ----- Truncate as needed.
        Return Trim(Left(origText, textWidth))
    Else
        ' ----- Start with extra spaces.
        Return Space((textWidth - Len(origText)) \ 2) & _
            resultText
    End If
End Function
```

The function starts by making a copy of the original string (origText), removing any extra spaces with the Trim function. It then tests that result to see whether it will even fit on the line. If not, it chops off the trailing characters that won't fit, and returns that result. For strings that do fit on a line textWidth characters wide, the function adds the appropriate number of spaces to the start of the string, and returns the result.

Code snippet #2 also added a function named LeftAndRightText. It works just like CenterText, but it puts two distinct text strings at the extreme left and right ends of a text line. Any questions? Great. Let's move on.

Code snippet #3 adds a routine named DigitsOnly. It builds a new string made of just the digits found in a source string, origText. It does this by calling the IsNumeric function for each character in origText, one at a time. Each found digit is then concatenated to the end of destText.

INSERT SNIPPET

Insert Chapter 6, Snippet Item 3.

```
Public Function DigitsOnly(ByVal origText As String) As String
   ' ----- Return only the digits found in a string.
   Dim destText As String
   Dim counter As Integer

   ' ----- Examine each character.
   destText = ""
   For counter = 1 To Len(origText)
      If (IsNumeric(Mid(origText, counter, 1))) Then _
         destText &= Mid(origText, counter, 1)
   Next counter
   Return destText
End Function
```

The last two functions, CountSubStr and GetSubStr, count and extract substrings from larger strings, based on a delimiter. Visual Basic includes two functions, Mid and GetChar, that also extract substrings from larger strings, but these are based on the position of the substring. The CountSubStr and GetSubStr functions examine substrings by first using a delimiter to break the larger string into pieces.

INSERT SNIPPET

Insert Chapter 6, Snippet Item 4.

The CountSubStr function counts how many times a given substring appears in a larger string. It uses Visual Basic's InStr function to find the location of a substring (subText) in a larger string (mainText). It keeps doing this until it reaches the end of mainText, maintaining a running count (totalTimes) of the number of matches.

```
Public Function CountSubStr(ByVal mainText As String, _
      ByVal subText As String) As Integer
   ' ----- Return a count of the number of times that
   '       a subText occurs in a string (mainText).
   Dim totalTimes As Integer
   Dim startPos As Integer
   Dim foundPos As Integer

   totalTimes = 0
   startPos = 1

   ' ----- Keep searching until we don't find it no more!
   Do
      ' ----- Search for the subText.
      foundPos = InStr(startPos, mainText, subText)
      If (foundPos = 0) Then Exit Do
      totalTimes += 1

      ' ----- Move to just after the occurrence.
      startPos = foundPos + Len(subText)
   Loop

   ' ----- Return the count.
   Return totalTimes
End Function
```

Just to be more interesting than I already am, I used a different approach to implement the GetSubStr function. This function returns a delimited section of a string. For instance, the following statement gets the third comma-delimited portion of bigString:

```
bigString = "abc,def,ghi,jkl,mno"
MsgBox(GetSubStr(bigString, ",", 3))  ' Displays: ghi
```

I used Visual Basic's Split function to break the original string (origString) into an array of smaller strings (stringParts), using delim as the breaking point. Then I return element number whichField from the result. Since whichField starts with 1 and the array starts at 0, I must adjust the position to return the correct element.

```
Public Function GetSubStr(ByVal origString As String, _
      ByVal delim As String, ByVal whichField As Integer) _
      As String
   ' ----- Extracts a delimited string from another
   '       larger string.
   Dim stringParts() As String

   ' ----- Handle some errors.
   If (whichField < 0) Then Return ""
   If (Len(origString) < 1) Then Return ""
   If (Len(delim) = 0) Then Return ""

   ' ----- Break the string up into delimited parts.
   stringParts = Split(origString, delim)
```

```
    ' ----- See whether the part we want exists and return it.
    If (whichField > UBound(stringParts) + 1) Then Return "" _
        Else Return stringParts(whichField - 1)
End Function
```

If these functions seem simple to you, great! Most Visual Basic code is no more difficult than these examples. Sure, you might use some unfamiliar parts of the FCL, or
interact with things more complicated than strings and numbers. But the overall
structure will be similar. Most source code is made up of assignment statements,
tests using the If statement, loops through data using a For...Next or similar statement, and function calls. And that's just what we did in these short methods.

Windows Forms

William Shakespeare wrote, "All the world's a form, and all the controls and labels merely players: they have their exit events and their entrance events; and one control in its time exposes many properties" (from "As You Code It," Act 2.7.0). Although .NET was still in beta when he penned these words, they apply perfectly to any Windows Forms application you write, even today.

The .NET technology known as *Windows Forms* includes all the classes and features needed to develop standard "desktop" applications for Microsoft Windows. In the early days of Windows, this was pretty much the only type of program you could write for the platform. But now it is just one of many application types, along with console applications, web ("Web Forms") applications, and services.

Inside a Windows Application

If you're new to development on the Windows system, writing applications in the .NET Framework may keep you from a full appreciation of what really happens inside a Windows application, and from being involuntarily committed to an asylum. That's because the internals of Windows applications are no fun.

Windows was originally developed as an application running within MS-DOS, and this had a major impact on the design of Windows and of any applications running within its pseudo-operation-system environment. The latest releases of Windows are true operating systems, no longer dependent on MS-DOS. But the programming methodology was left unchanged for backward compatibility. Applications written in Visual Basic for .NET still use this Windows 1.0 technology internally, but it is mostly hidden by the many well-designed classes of the Windows Forms package.

Everything Is a Window

Rumors abound about why Microsoft attached the name "Windows" to its flagship product. Some say it represented the "Windows of Usability and Opportunity" that users would gain by using the enhanced graphical user interface. Some believe it represents the building cavity through which Microsoft executives promised to toss several key developers and managers if the product bombed. But the name actually refers to the different elements that appear on-screen when using Windows and its included applications. In short, everything you see on the screen either is a window or appears within a window: all forms, all controls, all scroll bars, and all display elements. Figure 7-1 points out some of the windows within a typical Microsoft Windows 2.0 display.

Figure 7-1. Some of the many windows of Windows 2.0

Every main application window was clearly a "window," as were all push buttons, text entry fields, checkbox and radio selection buttons, listboxes, and "combo" boxes (with a separate window for the "drop-down" portion). Static text and graphical images were drawn on a window's surface, and did not embody windows by themselves. But certainly hundreds of windows could be on display at any one time.

Although the original developers on the Windows project team suffered from a deplorable lack of originality in the area of feature naming, Microsoft compensated for this somewhat with its release of Visual Basic. Though everything was still a window internally, Microsoft divided the public world of windows into two hemispheres: *forms* and *controls*. There were always some internal differences between these two types of windows, and the new names did a lot to bring normalcy to the Windows application development situation. Microsoft elected to keep these useful monikers when it implemented the .NET Windows Forms package.

Messages and the Message Pump

When you interact with Windows, it's pretty easy for you (as a human) to detect the different forms and controls on the screen. The image of Windows 2.0 I showed you in Figure 7-1 looks like a typical Windows screen, with its ability to interact with the keyboard and mouse, but it isn't. Go ahead; try to tap Figure 7-1 with your finger. You can tap all day long, but except for putting a hole in the page and not being able to get your money back on the book, nothing else will happen. But while you're tapping, you could shout out, "I just tapped on the OK button" or "I just tapped on the 4 button of the Calculator window."

This is what Microsoft Windows does for you. Windows keeps a list of all windows displayed on the screen, how they overlap and obscure each other, and which application each window belongs to. (Some applications are broken into multiple "threads" that all run at the same time. In such programs, Windows keeps track of all windows on a per-thread basis, not just on a per-application basis.) Each user input action (such as mouse clicks and key presses) gets placed in the *system message queue* by the related device driver. As you click on the screen with your mouse, Windows extracts the system message from this queue, determines where you clicked, tries to figure out which window the mouse-click occurred on, and then informs that window's application about the mouse click by adding a *message* to the application's *message queue*. It does the same thing for keyboard input and other actions that a window might need to know about.

To function within the Windows environment, your application (or a specific thread within your application) includes a *message pump*, a block of code that monitors the message queue. Each incoming message includes the ID number of the intended window. The code extracts the message from the queue, and routes it to the *window procedure* (also called a *WndProc*) of the appropriate window for final processing. In the C language, this message pump looks somewhat like this:

```
while (!done)
{
    /* ----- Extract and examine the next message. */
    MSG msg;
```

```
    if (GetMessage(&msg, NULL, 0, 0))
    {
        /* ----- WM_QUIT means it's time to exit the program. */
        if (msg.message == WM_QUIT)
            done = true;

        /* ----- Send the message to the right window. */
        TranslateMessage(&msg);
        DispatchMessage(&msg);
    }
}
```

I know, I know. It makes you glad that you write in Visual Basic.

So, each application (actually, each thread within an application) has one message pump, but multiple window procedures. The message pump exists to route incoming messages to the correct window procedure.

Window Procedures

Just as the message pump dispatches messages to distinct window procedures, the WndProc routine directs processing to individual code blocks or procedures based on the type of incoming message. Here's a general logic outline (pseudocode) that shows the structure of a typical window procedure:

```
If (message type is a mouse click)
    Do mouse-click related code
Else If (message type is a key press)
    Do key-press related code
Else If (message type is a window resize)
    Do window-resizing-related code
Else...
```

(The pseudocode uses successive If statements, but an actual window procedure would more commonly use a Select Case type of statement to process the incoming message.) So, the window procedure is like a vending machine. If the customer pushes the cola button, do the processing that returns a can of cola. If the customer presses the chewing gum button, do the processing that returns chewing gum. If the customer presses the coin return button, keep the money.

For each type of message (at least those that the program wants to handle), some related code gets processed when a message arrives. Boy, that really sounds familiar, but I just can't seem to recall what...*events*! This sounds just like events in Visual Basic. And so it does. Even way back in Visual Basic 1.0, all generated applications included a message pump and WndProc procedures for each window, all hidden from view. The primary task of these WndProc procedures was to call the code in your Visual Basic event handlers.

Windows in .NET

Take it from someone who used to write Windows applications in the C language: writing message pumps and window procedures isn't a lot of fun. Microsoft did try to mask some of the tedium with a variety of technologies, including "Message Crackers" and "MFC." It was Visual Basic that finally succeeded in burying the complexity under a programmer-friendly logical system.

The .NET Framework uses a system that is quite similar to that of older Visual Basic implementations, having the WndProc call custom event handlers written by you. It bundles up all this power and simplicity in a technology called Windows Forms. All of its classes appear in the System.Windows.Forms namespace. Many of these classes implement specific types of windows, such as ordinary main windows, buttons, text boxes, drop-down combo box lists, and so on.

If you really want to, you can still access the message pump and the various WndProc routines. Each window-specific class includes a WndProc method that you can override and craft yourself. The message pump is found in the System.Windows.Forms.Application.Run method. You could commandeer any of these components and control the whole ball of wax yourself, but you'll soon find out that the Windows Forms development process is so pleasant, you will work hard to forget what "message pump" even means.

Forms and Controls

In .NET, as in older versions of Visual Basic, windows are grouped into "forms" and "controls." But they are still all windows, built from the same core components. If you don't believe me, check out the classes for the various forms and controls in .NET. Both forms and controls derive from the common System.Windows.Forms.Control class, which abstracts the core Windows "window" functionality.

Some of the controls supplied with .NET (and also with the older Visual Basic) don't actually implement on-screen window elements. These controls—such as the "Timer" control—include no user interface experience, but do provide a programming experience that is similar to that of the visible controls. I'll list the specific controls a little later in this chapter, and indicate which ones are not user interface controls.

Designing Windows Forms Applications

Creating a Windows Forms application in Visual Basic is easy. Let's try it. Start Visual Studio and select New Project from the File menu. The New Project form appears, as shown in Figure 7-2.

Figure 7-2. Visual Studio's New Project form

Select the Windows Project type, and then the Windows Forms Application Template. Give the project any name you want in the Name field, and then click OK. The new project has a single form (Form1) already for you to use. At this point, Visual Studio has already added about 250 lines of source code to your application. If you click on the Show All Files button in the Solution Explorer panel (described way back in Chapter 1, Figure 1-13) and open the various files in the project, you can see the code for yourself. Some of the most interesting code is in the *Form1.Designer.vb* file, slightly edited here:

```vb
Partial Class Form1
    Inherits System.Windows.Forms.Form

    'Form overrides dispose to clean up the component list.
    <System.Diagnostics.DebuggerNonUserCode()> _
    Protected Overrides Sub Dispose(ByVal disposing As Boolean)
        Try
            If disposing AndAlso components IsNot Nothing Then
                components.Dispose()
            End If
        Finally
            MyBase.Dispose(disposing)
        End Try
    End Sub

    'Required by the Windows Form Designer
    Private components As System.ComponentModel.IContainer

    'NOTE: The following procedure is required by
    'the Windows Form Designer
```

```
'It can be modified using the Windows Form Designer.
'Do not modify it using the code editor.
<System.Diagnostics.DebuggerStepThrough()> _
Private Sub InitializeComponent()
    components = New System.ComponentModel.Container()
    Me.AutoScaleMode = _
        System.Windows.Forms.AutoScaleMode.Font
    Me.Text = "Form1"
End Sub
End Class
```

All the code that implements a form's behavior appears in the Form class in the System.Windows.Forms namespace. This project's initial form, Form1, inherits from that base form, receiving all of Form's functionality and default settings. Any custom design-time changes made to Form1's user interface, such as adding child controls, are added to the InitializeComponent procedure automatically as you use Visual Studio. Check out the routine periodically to see how it changes.

Most programs will have multiple forms. I suppose that .NET could select one of the forms at random to display when a program first runs. That would be fun and unpredictable. But it doesn't work that way. Instead, you indicate the starting form through the project's properties, via the "Startup form" field on the Application tab (see Figure 7-3). (The project properties window appears when you select the Project → Properties menu command in Visual Studio, or when you double-click on the My Project item in the Solution Explorer.)

Figure 7-3. The startup options for a Windows Forms application

When a .NET application begins, the framework calls a method named Main somewhere in your code. You indicate which form's Main routine is used through the "Startup form" field. It includes a list of all forms; just choose the one you want. But wait, you haven't added a Main method to any of your forms? No problem. Visual Basic will write a simple Main routine on your behalf that will display the indicated form. This ad hoc Main routine, added at compile time, performs just the minimum processing needed to display the form.

If you want to add a custom Main routine to your form, or to some other non-Form class in your application, that's no problem. If you uncheck the "Enable application framework" field on that same properties form, the "Startup form" list changes to include any class in your application with a compatible Main routine. But the application framework enables a lot of cool functionality, and all without any work on your part. Disable it only when you need precise control over the application's early lifetime.

Using Custom Main Methods

If you do decide to write your own Main routine in a non-Form class, you'll eventually want to display your application's main form. Back in Visual Basic 6.0, whenever you wanted to display a form, you called its Show method:

```
Form1.Show
```

This simple syntax disappeared when the first .NET version of Visual Basic appeared in 2002, but it returned with the 2005 release. Say that you wanted to start your application from a Sub Main procedure in a module separate from your main form. First, you need to add a new module to the project. Select the Project → Add Module menu command. Modify the new Module1 code module so that it looks like the following block of code:

```
Module Module1
    Public Sub Main( )
        Form1.Show( )
    End Sub
End Module
```

In the project's properties, uncheck the "Enable application framework" field, and select either Module1 or Sub Main from the "Startup form" list. That's pretty simple: call Module1's Main method, show the Form1 form, and you're done. And in truth, if you run this program, you will be done pretty quickly. In fact, Form1 will appear for only the briefest moment before exiting the program. Why didn't Form1 stick around?

The program exited immediately because of that bothersome message pump, or more correctly, the lack of a message pump. Each window (or form or control) has a distinct WndProc procedure, but there is only one message pump for each application or thread. In this simple program, Form1 has its own WndProc procedure, but it doesn't control the message pump by itself. You have to specifically tell the program to start running the message pump. Since the standard message pump for Windows Forms applications appears in the System.Windows.Forms.Application.Run method, altering the Sub Main code to include it will enable the pump and keep Form1 displayed until the user closes the form or accidentally kicks the power cord out of the outlet.

```
Module Module1
    Public Sub Main( )
        System.Windows.Forms.Application.Run(Form1)
    End Sub
End Module
```

You can add all sorts of initialization code to your Sub Main procedure, and show the main form only when your code is ready to interact with the user.

If you need to add a new form to your application, use the Project → Add Windows Form menu command.

Working with Forms

In .NET, all forms are simply classes, variations of the `System.Windows.Forms.Form` class. Each time you create a new form, you are creating a derived class based on that common `Form` class. And your new class is loaded with functionality; it includes all the fields, methods, bugs, properties, and events that make up the `Form` class. Visual Studio takes these elements and presents them in a way that makes it easy to program a form, both through source code and through the drag-and-drop interface of the Visual Studio Forms Designer.

When you first add a form to your application, it's kind of plain and boring. Use the Properties panel (see Figure 7-4) to adjust the form to your liking. This panel shows the principle properties for the currently selected item within the Visual Studio environment. It includes a separate entry for each property setting, most of which can be updated through simple text entry. For instance, you can alter the caption displayed at the top of the form by changing the content of the `Text` property from `Form1` to `Cool Form`.

Figure 7-4. The properties of your form

Table 7-1 lists some of the more interesting form properties and their uses.

Table 7-1. Form properties

Property	Description
(Name)	This is the name of the form, or more correctly, of the class that is the form. By default, it is named `Form`x, where x is some number. It needs to be changed to something informative.
AcceptButton	Indicates which `Button` control already placed on the form should be triggered when the user presses the Enter key.
AutoScroll	If you set this field to `True`, the form automatically adds scroll bars that move around the contents of the form if the form is sized too small to show everything.

Table 7-1. Form properties (continued)

Property	Description
BackColor	The background color. Uses a specific or general system color.
BackgroundImage	Use this property, along with the BackgroundImageLayout property, to place a graphic on the background of the form.
CancelButton	This is just like the AcceptButton property, but the assigned button is triggered by the Esc key, not the Enter key.
ContextMenuStrip	This property lets you create a custom shortcut menu that appears when the user right-clicks on the background of the form. ContextMenuStrip refers to a separate control that you add to the form.
ControlBox	You hide or show the control box in the upper-left corner of the form through this property setting.
Cursor	Indicates the style of mouse cursor that appears when the mouse is over the form. This property demonstrates one of the many editors that appear within the properties window. If you click the "down arrow" at the right of the property setting, it displays a graphical list of all included mouse cursors. Click an image to get the one you want. (Other properties include custom editors designed for their type of content.) This list includes only the built-in cursors. You can also modify this property in the form's source code if you need to set the cursor to a custom graphic.
FormBorderStyle	This property indicates the type of form to display. The default is Sizable, which lets the user resize the form by dragging the bottom-right corner. If you set this property to None, the form's title bar and borders disappear. You could use this setting for an application's "Splash" welcome form, which normally has no form border.
Icon	Sets the graphic displayed in the upper-left corner of the form's border.
IsMdiContainer	Enables "multiple document interface" support on this form. This allows a master form to "contain" multiple child document forms. Visual Studio itself can display forms and source code windows in the MDI style.
KeyPreview	If you set this property to True, the form's KeyDown and KeyPress events will get to process any keys entered by the user, even if those keys were destined for a control contained on the form. This is useful when you need to capture keys that apply to the entire form, such as using the F1 key to trigger online help.
Location	Sets the top and left positions of the form on the screen. The StartPosition property also impacts the location of the form.
MainMenuStrip	Identifies the MenuStrip control to use for the form's main menu. The referenced MenuStrip control is added separately to the form.
MaximizeBox	Indicates whether the "maximum box" appears in the upper-right corner of the form. This button lets the user show a form in "full-screen" mode.
MinimizeBox	Indicates whether the "minimize box" appears in the upper-right corner of the form. This button lets the user send the form to the system task bar.
MinimumSize	On forms that can be resized, this property indicates the minimum allowed size of the form. The user will not be able to size the form any smaller than this. This property, like some of the others, is a *composite property*, built by merging two or more other properties. In this case, it is built from distinct Width and Height subproperties.
Opacity	Allows you to specify the level of transparency for a distinct color that appears on the form (set via the TransparencyKey field). Setting this field to 100% means that that color is fully displayed with no transparency; setting it to 0% makes that color fully transparent. You can set this property anywhere from 0% to 100%. Anything that appears behind the form will be partially or completely visible through the transparent portions of this form.

Table 7-1. Form properties (continued)

Property	Description
ShowInTaskbar	Specifies whether this form should appear as an item in the system task bar.
Size	Indicates the current size of the form through distinct Width and Height subproperties.
StartPosition	Specifies how the form should be placed on the screen when it first appears. It is set through a list of predefined values, which actually link to an enumeration.
Tag	You can put any type of data you want in this property; it's there for your use.
Text	The form's display caption is set through this field.
TopMost	If set to True, this form will appear on top of all others, even when it is not the active form.
TransparencyKey	Indicates the color to use for transparency when the Opacity field is other than 100%.
WindowState	Identifies the current state of the window: normal, maximized, or minimized.

I listed only about half of the available properties; clearly you have a lot of control over the form and how it is presented to the user. What's really interesting is that many of these properties are not limited to just forms. Some of these properties come from the mutual System.Windows.Forms.Control class, and also appear in all other controls that use that same base class. This includes properties such as Location, BackColor, and Text. Although the text displayed in a form's caption and the text displayed on a command button differ significantly in their presentation, the usage through code is identical.

```
Form1.Text = "This is a form caption."
Button1.Text = "This is a button caption."
```

Although you can set all of the properties in Table 7-1 through the Properties panel, you can also update and view them through code. In fact, if you've modified any of the properties through the Properties panel, you've already updated them through source code, since Visual Studio is just updating your code for you. Try it out! Set the form's TopMost property to True, and then view the InitializeComponent routine in the *Form1.Designer.vb* file. You'll find the following new statement near the bottom of the method:

```
Me.TopMost = True
```

I know what you're thinking: "I'm a programmer, but my text editor is having all the programming fun. When do I get a chance to modify properties through code?" That's a fair question. Properties are pretty easy to modify. You just name the object to be modified along with the property name and its new value, as Visual Studio did with the TopMost property.

```
Me.Text = "The Library Project"
```

You can also retrieve the property values by naming them.

```
MsgBox("The form's caption is: " & Me.Text)
```

You access the form's various methods in much the same way. For instance, the Close method closes the form:

```
Me.Close()
```

Of course, these statements need to appear within some valid procedure, such as an event handler. Let's add some code to the form's Click event so that when the user clicks on the form, the new code will alter the form's caption, remind us what that caption is, and close the form, causing the program to exit. What a great program! Access the form's source code by selecting Form1.vb in the Solution Explorer, and then clicking on the View Code button at the top of the Solution Explorer. The form's default code block appears.

```
Public Class Form1

End Class
```

As you remember from earlier in the chapter, this is the tourist portion of the Form1 class, the part that Visual Studio shows to the public (you), and not the more interesting hidden parts (the part in *Form1.Designer.vb*). But we'll be able to make this section interesting in no time. Add a Click event to the form's surface by selecting (Form1 Events) from the Class Name list (above and to the left of the code text editor), and then selecting Click from the Method Name drop-down list to its right, as shown in Figure 7-5.

Figure 7-5. Adding a Click event to the form

Modify the event handler so that it displays the code listed here:

```
Private Sub Form1_Click(ByVal sender As Object, _
    ByVal e As System.EventArgs) Handles Me.Click
  Me.Text = "The Library Project"
  MsgBox("The form's caption is: " & Me.Text)
  Me.Close( )
End Sub
```

If you run this code and click on the form's surface, a message box appears with the form's caption just before the application exits (see Figure 7-6).

Adding Controls

New forms are like blank canvases, and like the great painters before us, we have available a large palette of colorful tools at our disposal. In Visual Studio, these tools are in the form of *controls*, .NET classes designed specifically for use on form surfaces. Visual Basic and .NET include dozens of Windows Forms controls, and even more are available from third parties. You can even build your own controls, either by deriving them from existing control classes or by implementing them completely from scratch.

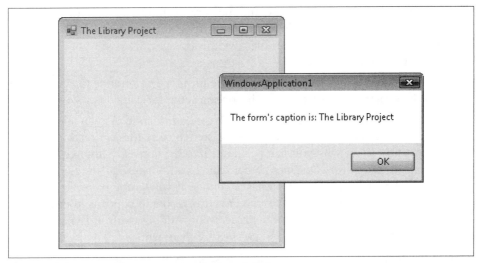

Figure 7-6. A program that communicates when clicked

Visual Studio's Toolbox includes all the basic controls you need to build high-quality, or even pathetic low-quality, software applications. Access the Toolbox, part of which appears in Figure 7-7, through the View → Toolbox menu command.

Figure 7-7. Visual Studio's Toolbox with Windows Forms controls

There are five ways to add a control to a form:

- Double-click on a control in the Toolbox. An instance of the control appears on the form in its default location with all of its default settings.
- Drag-and-drop a control from the Toolbox to the form.

- Click on a control in the Toolbox, and then use the mouse to draw the rectangular area on the form where the control will appear. Some controls, such as the ComboBox control, have limits on their width or height; they will not necessarily size themselves as you intend.

- Ask someone else to add the control to the form. This option is for the faint of heart. If you are reading this book, this option is not for you.

- Add the control to the form using Visual Basic source code. As you add controls to the form in Visual Studio, it is writing source code for you on your behalf. There is no reason why you can't add such code yourself. Although there are warnings in the *Form1.Designer.vb* file telling you not to edit the file, you can hand-modify the InitializeComponents routine if you properly conform to the code style generated by Visual Studio. You can also add controls in other areas of your code, such as in the form's Load event. Adding controls dynamically is beyond the scope of this book, but go ahead, experiment.

Some controls have no true user-interface presence in a running application. These controls, when added to your form, appear in a panel just below the form's surface. You can still interact with them just like form-based controls.

Once a control appears on the form, use the mouse to move the control, or resize it using the resizing anchors that appear when the control is selected. A few of the controls are limited in their resizing options. The ComboBox control, for instance, can only be resized horizontally; its vertical size is determined by things such as the font used in the control. Other controls let you resize them, but only sometimes. The Label control can be manually resized only when its AutoSize property is set to False.

Some controls include a small arrow button, often near the upper-right corner of the control. These are Smart Tags, similar to the Smart Tags feature included in Microsoft Office. Clicking the Smart Tag provides access to useful features associated with the control, as shown in Figure 7-8.

Figure 7-8. The Smart Tag for a ComboBox control

Table 7-2 lists some of the more commonly used controls, all included in the Toolbox by default with a new Windows Forms application. If you create a Web Forms application in Visual Studio—used to design web-based applications with ASP.NET— the available controls will differ from this list. See Chapter 23 for a discussion of ASP.NET applications.

Table 7-2. Windows Forms controls available in Visual Studio

Icon	Control	Description
	BackgroundWorker	.NET includes support for multithreaded applications. The `BackgroundWorker` control lets you initiate a background task right from the comfort of your own form. It's especially useful when you wish to update form-based display elements interactively with another "worker" thread. You kick off the new work task through this control's `RunWorkerAsync` method, and perform the actual work in its `DoWork` event.
	Button	A standard push button. A button's `Click` event is its most common programmatic feature, although you can also use its `DialogResult` property to trigger a dialog-specific action.
	CheckBox	This control implements a two-way (on, off) or three-way (on, off, other) "checked" selection field. The `ThreeState` property indicates the total number of choices. Use the `Checked` Boolean property for two-way checkboxes, or the `CheckState` property for three-way checkboxes.
	CheckedListBox	The `CheckedListBox` control combines the best of the `ListBox` and `CheckBox` worlds, giving you a list where each item can be checked in a two-way or three-way manner. The `GetItemChecked` and `GetItemCheckState` methods (and their "Set" counterparts) provide one of the many ways to examine the status of items in the list. Be aware of a similar control named `CheckBoxList`; it is for use in ASP.NET applications only.
	ColorDialog	Displays the standard Windows form used for color selection by the user. Display the color dialog using this control's `ShowDialog` method, getting the result via the `Color` property.
	ComboBox	This control implements the standard Windows drop-down `ComboBox` control, in all its various styles. The list of items can include any objects you wish; it is not just limited to strings. You can also provide custom "owner-draw" code that lets you draw each list item yourself.
	ContextMenuStrip	This control lets you design a shortcut or "context" menu, to be displayed when the user right-clicks on the form or the control of your choice. It is designed and used in much the same way as the standard `MenuStrip` control.
	DataGridView	The `DataGridView` control implements a standard table-like grid used to display or edit data in individual cells. It is loaded with more display options than you can shake a stick at. The displayed data can be bound to some external data source, or you can make it up on the fly. A "virtual data" mode also lets you load data only as needed.
	DateTimePicker	The `DateTimePicker` control lets the user enter a date, a time, or both, through either basic text entry or mouse-based controls. Although not as free-form as a simple text field, it does enforce the selection of a date or time. You can set minimum and maximum boundaries on the user's selection. The `MonthCalendar` control provides an alternative interface for date-specific selection.
	DomainUpDown	Through this control, the user selects one from among a list of choices that you define, choices that have a specific inherent order. Use this control as an alternative to a `ComboBox` or `TrackBar` control when warranted.

Icon	Control	Description
	FolderBrowserDialog	Displays the standard Windows form used for directory or folder selection by the user. Display the selection dialog using this control's ShowDialog method, getting the result via the SelectedPath property.
	FontDialog	Displays the standard Windows form used for font selection by the user. Display the selection dialog using this control's ShowDialog method, getting the result via the Font property. Other properties provide access to components of the selected font.
	GroupBox	The GroupBox control provides a simple way to visibly group controls on a form. Subordinate controls are drawn or pasted directly onto the GroupBox control. To access similar functionality without the visible border or caption, use the Panel control.
	HelpProvider	The HelpProvider control lets you indicate online help details for other controls on the form. When used, it adds several extra "Help" pseudoproperties to each of the other form controls through which you can supply the help context details. When implemented properly, the indicated online help content will display when the user presses the F1 key in the context of the active control.
	HScrollBar	This control implements a horizontal scroll bar, allowing the user to scroll among a display region or list of choices. For a vertical implementation of this control, use the VScrollBar control. Several other controls include their own copy of these scroll bars.
	ImageList	The ImageList control encapsulates a set of small graphics or icons for use by other controls that support image lists. Image lists are commonly used by ListView, Toolbar, and TreeView controls.
A	Label	This control displays static text on a form. By using the various border and background properties, you can display simple lines and rectangles on a form. Visual Basic 6.0 included specific line and rectangle drawing controls, but they are not available in .NET. You must either simulate them using a Label control, or draw them yourself using the drawing commands (which isn't that difficult—see Chapter 18).
A	LinkLabel	The LinkLabel control implements a static label that includes one or more "links" within the text content. These links are similar to the standard text links that appear in web browser content. The control calls its LinkClicked event handler when the user clicks on any of the embedded links.
	ListBox	This control implements the standard Windows listbox control, displaying a list of items from which the user can select zero or more. The list of items can include any objects you wish; it is not just limited to strings. You can also provide custom "ownerdraw" code that lets you draw each list item yourself.
	ListView	The ListView control presents a set of items with optional display properties. It is quite similar to the (pre-Vista) Windows File Explorer with all its various display modes. You can add column-specific data for the "details" view. The items in the control appear as a set of ListViewItem class objects.

Icon	Control	Description
	MaskedTextBox	This variation of the standard text field helps the user enter formatted numeric or text data by displaying an entry template or mask. For instance, you can force the user to enter a telephone number in "xxx-xxx-xxxx" format by using a numeric mask with embedded hyphen characters.
	MenuStrip	This control lets you design standard form menus, which are displayed along the top of the user area of the form. Menus within the menu strip are implemented through ToolStripMenuItem class instances. The menu strip is a toolbar-like implementation of a standard Windows menu. You can add other types of controls to the menu, including toolbar-specific ComboBox controls. Context-sensitive menus, displayed when the user right-clicks on the form or a control, are implemented through the ContextMenuStrip control.
	MonthCalendar	The MonthCalendar control displays a subset of a calendar, focusing on a month-specific view. More than one month can be displayed at a time, in vertical, horizontal, or grid configuration. The DateTimePicker control provides an alternative interface for date-specific selection.
	NotifyIcon	The NotifyIcon control lets you place an icon in the "system tray" area of the Windows task bar, and communicate important messages to the user through this interface. Since this control has no form-specific user interface, it is possible to use it without having a standard form displayed.
	NumericUpDown	Allows the user to select a numeric value using a scrollable up/down section method. Use this control as an alternative to HScrollBar, TextBox, TrackBar, or VScrollBar controls when warranted.
	OpenFileDialog	Displays the standard Windows form used for "open" file selection by the user. The user can select one or more existing files from local or remote filesystems. Display the selection dialog using this control's ShowDialog method, getting the result via the FileName or FileNames property. The OpenFile method provides a quick way to open the selected file.
	PageSetupDialog	Displays the standard Windows form used for printed page configuration by the user. Display the selection dialog using this control's ShowDialog method, getting the result via the PageSettings and PrinterSettings properties.
	Panel	The Panel control logically groups controls on a form. Subordinate controls are drawn or pasted directly onto the Panel control. To access similar functionality with a visible border and user-displayed caption, use the GroupBox control.
	PictureBox	This control displays an image in a variety of formats. It should not be confused with the Visual Basic 6.0 PictureBox control, which is more closely related to the Windows Forms Panel control.
	PrintDialog	Displays the standard Windows form used for document printing and print property selection by the user. Display the selection dialog using this control's ShowDialog method. This control is used in conjunction with an instance of the System.Drawing.Printing.PrintDocument class, which is created through code or via the PrintDocument control.

Icon	Control	Description
	PrintDocument	This control is used as part of the print and print preview process. It adds a wrapper around your custom print implementation, providing a consistent method of selecting and printing document pages.
	PrintPreviewDialog	This control provides a standardized interface for print preview, implementing all elements of the entire print preview dialog. When used with a PrintDocument class or control, it displays on-screen precisely what will appear on the final printed page. In fact, your printing code doesn't necessarily know whether it is printing to the printer or to the print preview display.
	ProgressBar	The ProgressBar provides graphical feedback to the user for a task completion range. Normally, the range goes from 0% to 100%, but you can supply a custom range. The Value property indicates the current setting between the Minimum and Maximum range limits.
	PropertyGrid	The PropertyGrid control allows the user to graphically edit specific members of an attached class instance. The Properties panel within the Visual Studio environment is an instance of this control. This control makes heavy use of class-based attributes to control the display and edit features of properties. Chapter 18 uses this control to support bar code label management in the Library Project.
	RadioButton	This control implements the standard Windows radio selection button. Although the circular "point" display is most common, the control can also appear as a toggle button by setting the Appearance property appropriately. The Checked property indicates the current value of a control. All RadioButton controls that appear within the same "group context" act in a mutually exclusive manner. Use the Panel and GroupBox controls to create specific group contexts.
	ReportViewer	The ReportViewer control allows you to design and display custom banded reports tied to collections or ADO.NET data sources. It also works with SQL Server Reporting Services generated reports. Using this control to design a report will add an *.rdlc* file to your project that contains the actual report design.
	SaveFileDialog	Displays the standard Windows form used for "save" file selection by the user. The user can select a new or existing file from local or remote filesystems. The control optionally prompts the user to overwrite existing files. Display the selection dialog using this control's ShowDialog method, getting the result via the FileName property. The OpenFile method provides a quick way to open the selected file.
	SplitContainer	This control adds a "split bar" by which you can divide your form into multiple sizable regions, each of which contains a Panel control. Use the Orientation property to alter the direction of the split. The order in which you add SplitContainer controls to a form will impact the usability of the splits; experimentation is recommended.
	StatusStrip	This control displays a "status bar," usually along the bottom edge of a form, through which you can display status and other context-sensitive information to the user. The strip can contain multiple ProgressBar, StatusStripPanel, and ToolStripLabel controls.

Icon	Control	Description
	TabControl	The TabControl control lets you divide the controls of your form into multiple "tabbed" regions. Each named tab has an associated TabPage control, which works a lot like the Panel control. Add or paste subordinate controls directly to each TabPage control.
[abl]	TextBox	This control implements the standard Windows text box, in both its single-line and multiline styles. The main body content is set through the Text property. The PasswordChar and UseSystemPasswordChar properties allow you to mask the input when accepting a user-supplied password.
	Timer	This control triggers a timed event at an interval you specify. The size of the interval, in milliseconds, is set through the Interval property. If the Enabled property is set to True, the Tick event handler will be called at each met interval. Although you can set the interval as small as one millisecond, it is unlikely that you will achieve this frequency with today's hardware.
	ToolStrip	The ToolStrip control implements a toolbar on which other controls appear. It comes with a set of associated controls and classes that provide advanced rendering and user interaction features.
	ToolStripContainer	The ToolStripContainer control provides a convenient way to add MenuStrip, StatusStrip, and ToolStrip controls to the edges of a form.
	ToolTip	The ToolTip control lets you indicate a "tool tip" for other controls on the form. When used, it adds a "ToolTip" pseudoproperty to each of the other form controls, through which you can supply the associated tool tip text. When the mouse hovers over a control with an assigned tool tip text, a small text window appears temporarily over the control to provide useful information to the user.
	TrackBar	The TrackBar control allows the user to make a selection among a small number of related and ordered values. Its real-world counterpart is the volume control on a radio. Use this control as an alternative to an HScrollBar, NumericUpDown, or VScrollBar control when warranted.
	TreeView	The TreeView control presents a set of items in a hierarchical arrangement. It is quite similar to the "directory tree" portion of the (pre-Vista) Windows File Explorer. Each item in the tree is a "node" that can have zero or more child nodes.
	VScrollBar	This control implements a vertical scroll bar, allowing the user to scroll among a display region or list of choices. For a horizontal implementation of this control, use the HScrollBar control. Several other controls include their own copy of these scroll bars.
	WebBrowser	Implements a web browser within your application. You can use the standard web-based navigation features available within Internet Explorer for URL-based access, or provide your own custom HTML content through the DocumentText property or related properties.

Although there is no reasonable limit on the number of controls you can add to a form, there is a limit on how much information the user can experience on a single form without a direct wired connection to the brain. Don't go too wild.

Events and Delegates

Each form and control in a .NET application contains its own WndProc window procedure, and as it processes each incoming message from the message pump, it translates those messages into events. *Events* are the standard .NET technique that controls—and all other classes—use to say, "Hey, something is happening, and you might want to do something about it." When you include a form or control in your application, you can monitor one, some, or all of these events, and write custom code that responds appropriately. All the custom code you write for each event appears in an *event handler*. But what actually happens between the finger of the user on the mouse and the logic in your custom event handler? Figure 7-9 shows you graphically what actually happens between action and custom logic.

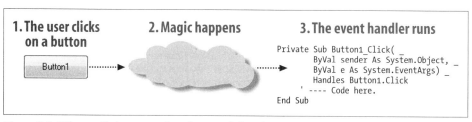

Figure 7-9. What really happens when the user clicks a button

Clearly, there is still some mystery surrounding event processing.

Controls—and all classes—determine which events they will make available. For controls, many of the events parallel user-initiated actions: Click, MouseDown, KeyPress, and SizeChanged. But there are also many events that could be triggered only by modifications to the control through your source code: TabIndexChanged (when the tab-key order of the controls changes), BackgroundImageChanged, and CursorChanged are just three of the many events that the user cannot affect directly. A few final events tie to system-level changes, such as the SystemColorsChanged event, which fires when the user modifies the system-wide color scheme through the control panel.

Each event has not only a name (such as Click), but also a set of parameters that the event handler will receive when called. Here's a typical event handler for a Button control:

```
Private Sub Button1_Click(ByVal sender As System.Object, _
    ByVal e As System.EventArgs) Handles Button1.Click

End Sub
```

This event handler receives two arguments from the triggering event: a System.Object instance (sender) and a System.EventArgs instance (e). Other event handlers may use a slightly different set of arguments, so how do you know what to use? Any events defined within a control class must also indicate the number and type of arguments it will send to the event handler. Visual Basic includes an `Event` statement that defines events. Although the `Button` control was likely written in C#, here is a possible look at what the event definition for the `Button`'s `Click` event might look like in Visual Basic:

```
Public Event Click(ByVal sender As System.Object, _
    ByVal e As System.EventArgs)
```

This definition sure looks a lot like the event handler, and it should. The `Event` statement establishes a parameter-passing contract between the control and any code that wants to receive event notifications. In this case, the `Click` event promises to send two arguments to the event handler. The first, `sender`, is a reference to the object that the event refers to. For `Button` controls, this parameter receives a reference to the `Button` instance itself. The second argument, `e`, provides a method for passing an entire object of additional information. The `System.EventArgs` class doesn't have much information, but some events use a variation of the second argument that uses `System.EventArgs` as its base class.

It turns out that the arguments used for the `Click` event are pretty common among the different controls and events. Instead of retyping the argument list in each `Event` statement, the designer of a control can define a *delegate*, a .NET type that defines an argument list and, for functions, a return value.

```
Public Delegate Sub StandardEventDelegate( _
    ByVal sender As System.Object, _
    ByVal e As System.EventArgs)
```

Event statements can then use the defined delegate as a shortcut for typing out the entire parameter list.

```
Public Event Click As StandardEventDelegate
```

Whether the `Event` statement uses a delegate or a full argument list, it has a firm grasp on what data it needs to send to any listening event handlers. And it sends those arguments using the Visual Basic `RaiseEvent` statement. Let's trace this process down for the `Button` control. When the user clicks on the button, the message pump finds a way to get a message to the WndProc procedure for the `Button` control. That control examines the message, sees it is a mouse click, and decides to tell event handlers about it. Then, from within the WndProc code, it raises the event.

```
RaiseEvent Click(Me, New System.EventArgs)
```

The Visual Basic `Me` keyword refers to the `Button` control instance itself. The `e` argument for a `Button` control contains no information beyond the default fields included in a `System.EventArgs` instance, so WndProc just sends a new empty instance. Controls with other event arguments would have created an instance first, filled it in with the relevant data, and passed that instance to the event handler.

If an event fires in an application, and there is no event handler to hear it, does it make a sound? Perhaps not. There is no requirement that an event have any active handlers listening. But when we do want to listen for an event, how do we do it? The standard way to do this in a Windows Forms application is a two-step process. First, the user of the control (your form class) needs to announce to the control, "I want to monitor your events." Then it attaches event handlers to specific events.

Earlier in the chapter, we saw that adding a control to the Form1's user interface actually triggers Visual Studio to write source code in the *Form1.designer.vb* file. Here's the code added for a Button control named Button1 (with line numbers):

```
01  Partial Class Form1
02      Inherits System.Windows.Forms.Form
03
04      Friend WithEvents Button1 As System.Windows.Forms.Button
05
06      Private Sub InitializeComponent()
07          Me.Button1 = New System.Windows.Forms.Button
08
09          Me.Button1.Location = New System.Drawing.Point(48, 16)
10          Me.Button1.Name = "Button1"
11          Me.Button1.Size = New System.Drawing.Size(75, 23)
12          Me.Button1.TabIndex = 0
13          Me.Button1.Text = "Button1"
14          Me.Button1.UseVisualStyleBackColor = True
15
16          Me.Controls.Add(Me.Button1)
17      End Sub
18  End Class
```

The code in the InitializeComponent method creates the Button control instance (line 07), modifies its properties to get just the look we want (lines 09 to 14), and attaches it to the form (line 16). But there is one additional line that defines the actual Button1 reference type variable (line 04):

```
Friend WithEvents Button1 As System.Windows.Forms.Button
```

I talked about class-level fields in Chapter 6, and Button1 is just a typical class-level field. But the WithEvents keyword included in the statement is what lets the control know that someone wants to monitor event notifications. Now, whenever a Button1 event fires, it knows that Form1 may contain event handlers that are watching and listening.

The second part of our two-step event-to-handler connection process involves the actual connection of the handler. Let's look at the Click event handler definition again for the Button1 instance:

```
Private Sub Button1_Click(ByVal sender As System.Object, _
    ByVal e As System.EventArgs) Handles Button1.Click

End Sub
```

It's just an ordinary class method, but with a Handles clause hanging off the end of the definition. This clause is what links the event handler with the Button1.Click event itself. You can follow the Handles keyword with multiple event names.

```
Private Sub ManyButtons_Click(ByVal sender As System.Object, _
    ByVal e As System.EventArgs) Handles Button1.Click, _
    Button2.Click, Button3.Click

End Sub
```

Now the single ManyButtons_Click event handler will listen for Click events from three different controls. You can even mix up the monitored events; one event handler can listen for different named events.

```
Private Sub ManyEvents(ByVal sender As System.Object, _
    ByVal e As System.EventArgs) Handles Button1.MouseDown, _
    Button2.MouseUp

End Sub
```

Another variation is to have multiple event handlers monitor a single event, although Visual Basic gets to decide which handler to call first.

```
Private Sub FirstHandler(ByVal sender As System.Object, _
    ByVal e As System.EventArgs) Handles Button1.Click

End Sub

Private Sub SecondHandler(ByVal sender As System.Object, _
    ByVal e As System.EventArgs) Handles Button1.Click

End Sub
```

There is another way to connect events to event handlers that does not involve either the WithEvents keyword or the Handles keyword, and that lets you control the processing order for multiple handlers. Once you have an instance of an event-exposing class, you attach a handler to one of its events using the AddHandler statement. The following statement links Button1's Click event to an event handler named MyHandler. The MyHandler method must have the correct argument list for the defined event.

```
AddHandler Button1.Click, AddressOf MyHandler
```

A related RemoveHandler statement detaches a handler from an event.

A lot of complicated steps take you from an initial user or system action to the code in an event handler. I've spent a lot of chapter space discussing exactly how events work, but with good reason. Events and event processing are core features of .NET application development. Eventually, you will spend so much time writing event handlers that it will all become second nature to you. But I also went into all of this detail so that you could take full advantage of this technology. Not only does Visual Basic let you monitor controls for events, it also lets you design new events into your own classes. You can use the Delegate, Event, RaiseEvent, WithEvents, Handles, AddHandler, and RemoveHandler keywords for your own custom events, triggered by whatever conditions you choose. If you have a class that represents an employee, you can have it trigger a Fired event whenever the employee loses his job. By adding custom events, you make it possible for custom code to be attached to your class logic, even if a programmer doesn't have access to your class's source code.

Making Forms Useful

Any form identified as your project's startup object appears automatically when the program begins. All other forms need to be displayed manually, using either the `Show` or the `ShowDialog` method of that form. For instance, if you have a form called `Form2`, you can display it using its `Show` method:

```
Form2.Show( )
```

The `Show` method displays a *modeless form*. Modeless forms can be accessed independently from all other forms in the running application. All modeless forms can be activated at any time just by clicking on them; the form you click on will come to the front of the others and receive the input focus. A program might have one, two, or dozens of modeless forms open at once, and the user can move between them freely.

Modal forms take control of all input in the application for as long as they appear onscreen. Modal forms are commonly called "dialogs"; the user must complete a modal form and close it before any other open forms in the application can be accessed. The message box window that appears when you use the `MsgBox` function is a common modal dialog window. The `ShowDialog` method displays forms modally, and lets you return a value from that form. The values returned are the members of the `System.Windows.Forms.DialogResult` enumeration.

If you think of forms as works of literature by Alexandre Dumas, modeless forms would be a lot like *The Three Musketeers*: "All for one and one for all." They work with one another in support of the entire application. Modal forms are akin to *The Count of Monte Cristo*. Yes, there are other forms/characters in the application/story, but they are nothing when the Count is in view.

To display the Count—that is, a modal form—use the form's `ShowDialog` method, and optionally capture its return value.

```
Dim theResult As DialogResult
theResult = Form2.ShowDialog( )
```

Modal dialogs are useful for editing some record that requires a click on the OK button when changes are complete. Let's say you were writing an application that displayed a list of books by Alexandre Dumas. It might include two forms: (1) a "parent" form that displays the list of books; and (2) a "child" form that lets you type the name of a single book. Wouldn't it be great if you could return the name of the book (or, perhaps, an ID number of a record for the book as stored in a database) instead of a `DialogResult` value?

If the `ShowDialog` method, a public method of the underlying `Form` class, can return a result code, perhaps we can add another public method to a form that will return a result code that has actual meaning. Indeed, we can. Consider the child form (named `BookEntry`) with a data entry field (`BookTitle`), and OK (`ActOK`) and Cancel (`ActCancel`) buttons, as shown in Figure 7-10.

Figure 7-10. Book title entry form

When empowered with the following code, this simple form returns whatever is typed in the field when the user clicks OK (first rejecting blank values), or returns a blank string on Cancel:

```
Public Class BookEntry
    Public Function EditTitle() As String
        ' ----- Show the form, and return what the user enters.
        If (Me.ShowDialog() = DialogResult.OK) Then
            Return BookTitle.Text.Trim
        Else
            Return ""
        End If
    End Function

    Private Sub ActCancel_Click(ByVal sender As System.Object, _
            ByVal e As System.EventArgs) Handles ActCancel.Click
        ' ----- Return a blank title for "Cancel."
        Me.DialogResult = DialogResult.Cancel
        ' ----- Continue with EditTitle()
    End Sub

    Private Sub ActOK_Click(ByVal sender As System.Object, _
            ByVal e As System.EventArgs) Handles ActOK.Click
        ' ----- Only accept valid titles.
        If (Len(BookTitle.Text.Trim) = 0) Then
            MsgBox("Please supply a valid title.")
        Else
            Me.DialogResult = DialogResult.OK
            ' ----- Continue with EditTitle()
        End If
    End Sub
End Class
```

To use this form, the parent form calls the `EditTitle` method, which returns the book title entered by the user.

```
Dim newTitle As String = BookEntry.EditTitle()
```

The `EditTitle` routine shows the form modally with the `ShowDialog` method, and just sits there until the user closes the form. Closing the form is done through the OK or Cancel button event; setting the form's `DialogResult` property has the side effect of closing the form. Great!

Once the form closes, execution returns to `EditTitle`, which does a quick status-check before returning the final value. And there we have it: a new public interface for a form's most important return value. We'll use this method a lot in the Library Project application.

Summary

Windows programming really hasn't changed much since Windows 1.0. It still does everything through messages, message queues, and window procedures. What has changed is the way the code is abstracted for the benefit of the programmer. The .NET Framework's package for Windows development, Windows Forms, makes Windows desktop development easy and—dare I say it—fun!

Project

This chapter's project code implements the Library Project's basic "Main" form, as well as the "Splash" form that appears when the project first starts up. Microsoft, knowing that this was a common need, included support for both main and splash forms in Visual Basic's Application Framework system. By default, this system is enabled through the project properties' Application panel (see Figure 7-11).

Figure 7-11. Main and splash fields identified through the project properties

The "Startup form" and "Splash screen" fields indicate the main and splash forms, respectively. It's quick, it's easy, and it's just the thing for us. So, let's get to work. Now would be a great time to load the starter project for Chapter 7.

PROJECT ACCESS

Load the Chapter 7 (Before) Code project, either through the New Project templates or by accessing the project directly from the installation directory. To see the code in its final form, load Chapter 7 (After) Code instead.

Configuring the Splash Screen

I've already added a new form file to the project, named *Splash.vb* (the form itself is named Splash), including some simple display elements to gussy it up somewhat. Check out the graphic on the form. It's presented through a PictureBox control, but it's stored in the application as a *resource*, a collection of strings and images attached to your source code. The *Resources* folder in the Solution Explorer includes this graphics file. It's linked into the picture box through that control's Image property. And it sure makes the form look pretty. Your job will be to attach this form into the startup sequence of the application.

Access the project properties' Application panel (which you just saw in Figure 7-11), and set the "Splash screen" field to Splash. This has the side effect of setting My.Application.SplashScreen to the Splash form. Now run the program. You should see the splash screen appear for about 1/100 of a second, quickly replaced by the main form. Hey, what was that?

Altering the "Splash screen" field does cause the splash screen to briefly appear, but the application will keep it up only until it thinks the program has done enough preparation for the main form. Since we aren't doing any preparation, it shows the main form right away.

Eventually, we will add a bunch of database-related startup code that will consume a little more time. But for now we'll have to fake it. In the Application Framework model, any code you want to process when the program first begins appears in the application's Startup event. This event is one of a small collection of events included with the My hierarchy. The source code for these events appears in the *ApplicationEvents.vb* file, a file that Visual Studio automatically adds to your project when needed. Use the View Application Events button on the project properties' Application panel to open that file's source code.

```
Namespace My
    Class MyApplication

    End Class
End Namespace
```

Let's pretend that the initialization required for the Library Project takes about three seconds. .NET includes a Sleep method that delays the code for a specific number of milliseconds. Code snippet 1 adds the Startup event handler for the application. Add it between MyApplication's Class and End Class keywords.

INSERT SNIPPET

Insert Chapter 7, Snippet Item 1.

```
Private Sub MyApplication_Startup(ByVal sender As Object, _
     ByVal e As Microsoft.VisualBasic.ApplicationServices. _
     StartupEventArgs) Handles Me.Startup
   ' ----- Take a three-second nap.
   System.Threading.Thread.Sleep(3000)
End Sub
```

Now run the program, and you will see the splash screen stick around for about three seconds (3,000 milliseconds). As gratifying as it is to see the splash screen for that long, there's a good chance that the actual database and application initialization code will take much less than three seconds. I mean, we're talking about SQL Server here. It's supposed to be blazing fast.

So, it's clear that we still need to delay the removal of the splash screen. The My. Application object just happens to include the very property we need to enforce a delay. The MinimumSplashScreenDisplayTime property indicates the minimum number of milliseconds that the splash screen must be displayed. The bad part is that you have to assign it in a really strange place, at least when compared to how much Visual Basic programming we've learned so far.

Delete all the code that you added from snippet 1, which would be the entire MyApplication_Startup method. Then fill in that empty space with the following code.

INSERT SNIPPET

Insert Chapter 7, Snippet Item 2.

```
Protected Overrides Function OnInitialize _
     (ByVal commandLineArgs As System.Collections. _
     ObjectModel.ReadOnlyCollection(Of String)) As Boolean
   ' ----- Display the splash form for at least 3 seconds.
   My.Application.MinimumSplashScreenDisplayTime = 3000
   Return MyBase.OnInitialize(commandLineArgs)
End Function
```

That code block contains a lot of things we just haven't talked about yet, and won't talk about for a few more chapters. Suffice it to say that the OnInitialize method is one of the first things that happens in the lifetime of the program, and that is the place where MinimumSplashScreenDisplayTime must be assigned.

The last thing to do for the splash screen is to include some code that displays the version number. We already did this for the About form back in Chapter 5, so we'll just add similar code to the Splash form's Load event. We'll update the copyright message, too. Open the source code for the Splash form and add the following code.

INSERT SNIPPET

Insert Chapter 7, Snippet Item 3.

```
Private Sub Splash_Load(ByVal sender As Object, _
      ByVal e As System.EventArgs) Handles Me.Load
   ' ----- Update the version number.
   With My.Application.Info.Version
      ProgramVersion.Text = "Version " & .Major & "." & _
         .Minor & " Revision " & .Revision
   End With
   ProgramCopyright.Text = My.Application.Info.Copyright
End Sub
```

Run the program again and sit in awe as you witness a fully functional splash screen.

Configuring the Main Form

Although we designed a main form in an earlier chapter, it was pretty sparse, including only an About button. This chapter's project adds all the user interface elements to the form. In fact, I've already added that form's controls to its surface for you (see Figure 7-12). But you can add some of the event handlers that will give some of its display pizzazz.

All the general event code for the form appears as code snippet 4.

INSERT SNIPPET

Insert Chapter 7, Snippet Item 4.

Most of this code exists to move things around on the display. For example, the user can access different features of the form by clicking on the icons or related text labels along the left side of the form. Each icon and label triggers one of seven common routines that exist to rearrange the furniture. The upper-left icon, PicLibraryItem, calls the common TaskLibraryItem routine when clicked.

```
Private Sub PicLibraryItem_Click( _
      ByVal sender As System.Object, _
      ByVal e As System.EventArgs) _
      Handles PicLibraryItem.Click
   ' ----- Library Item mode.
   TaskLibraryItem( )
End Sub
```

Figure 7-12. The basic look of the main form

The `TaskLibraryItem` procedure adjusts the various panels and fields on the display so that the user sees those fields needed to look up library items.

```
Private Sub TaskLibraryItem( )
    ' ----- Update the display.
    AllPanelsInvisible( )
    PanelLibraryItem.Visible = True
    ActLibraryItem.BackColor = SystemColors.Control
    LabelSelected.Location = New System.Drawing.Point( _
        LabelSelected.Left, PicLibraryItem.Top)
    Me.AcceptButton = ActSearch
End Sub
```

The `AllPanelsInvisible` routine also does some on-screen adjustment.

I like to have the existing text in a TextBox field selected when it becomes the active control. Each text control includes a `SelectAll` method that accomplishes this feat. We'll call that method during each TextBox control's Enter event, an event that occurs when a control receives the keyboard input focus.

```
Private Sub SearchText_Enter(ByVal sender As Object, _
        ByVal e As System.EventArgs) Handles SearchText.Enter
    ' ----- Highlight the entire text.
    SearchText.SelectAll( )
End Sub
```

Using the mouse to access the different features of the form is good, but I'm a keyboard person. To deal with keyboard users like me, the code adds support for feature access using the F2 through F9 keys.

```
Private Sub MainForm_KeyDown(ByVal sender As Object, _
      ByVal e As System.Windows.Forms.KeyEventArgs) _
      Handles MyBase.KeyDown
   ' ----- The keys F2 through F9 access the different
   '       sections of the form.
   Select Case (e.KeyCode)
      Case Keys.F2
         TaskLibraryItem( )
         e.Handled = True
      Case Keys.F3
         TaskPatronRecord( )
         e.Handled = True
      Case Keys.F4
         ' ----- Allow form to handle Alt+F4.
         If (e.Alt = True) Then
            Me.Close( )
         Else
            TaskHelp( )
         End If
         e.Handled = True
      Case Keys.F5
         TaskCheckOut( )
         e.Handled = True
      Case Keys.F6
         TaskCheckIn( )
         e.Handled = True
      Case Keys.F7
         TaskAdmin( )
         e.Handled = True
      Case Keys.F8
         TaskProcess( )
         e.Handled = True
      Case Keys.F9
         TaskReports( )
         e.Handled = True
   End Select
End Sub
```

As each keystroke comes into the KeyDown event handler, the Select Case statement examines it. When a matching Case entry is found, the code within the Case block executes. Pressing the F2 key triggers the code in the Case Keys.F2 block. Keys is one of the many built-in enumerations that you can use in your .NET applications. Notice the special code for the F4 key. It allows the Alt-F4 key combination to exit the application, which is the standard key combination for exiting Windows programs.

Normally, all keystrokes go to the active control, not to the form. To enable the MainForm.KeyDown event handler, the form's KeyPreview property must be set to True. Set this property back in the form designer.

Making the Program Single-Instance

The Library Project is designed for use only within a small library; it will run on only a few workstations at a time, perhaps up to 10 at most. And there's no need to run more than one copy on a single workstation, since each copy includes all the available application features. One of the cool features included with Visual Basic is the ability to create a "single-instance application," one that enforces the one-at-a-time run policy on each workstation. Although you could create such applications before, it is now enabled with a single mouse click.

To make the Library Project a single-instance application, display the project properties' Application panel, and then select the "Make single instance application" field. When the user tries to start up a second instance, .NET will refuse to carry out the request. Instead, it will trigger the application's StartupNextInstance event. Any special handling you wish to perform on a second instance startup will be done in this handler. Like the Startup event handler, the StartupNextInstance handler appears in the *ApplicationEvents.vb* file.

For the Library Project, the only thing we really need to do when the user tries to start a second instance is to make sure the application is displayed front and center, where the user can readily view it. Open the *ApplicationEvents.vb* file, and add the StartupNextInstance event handler.

INSERT SNIPPET

Insert Chapter 7, Snippet Item 5.

```
Private Sub MyApplication_StartupNextInstance( _
      ByVal sender As Object, _
      ByVal e As Microsoft.VisualBasic.ApplicationServices. _
      StartupNextInstanceEventArgs) _
      Handles Me.StartupNextInstance
   ' ----- Force the main form to the front.
   My.Application.MainForm.Activate( )
End Sub
```

That's all the changes for this chapter. See you on the next page.

Classes and Inheritance

How many .NET programmers does it take to change a light bulb? None—they call a method on the light bulb object, and it changes itself. Ha, ha, ha! That's funny, but only if you understand the *object-oriented programming* (OOP) concepts that are the basic foundation of the .NET system. (Actually, it's not even that funny if you do understand OOP.) Without OOP, it would be difficult to support core features of .NET, such as the central System.Object object, which is the basic foundation of the .NET system. Also, productivity would go way down among Windows developers, who are the basic foundation of the .NET system.

Although I briefly mentioned OOP development concepts in Chapter 1 and Chapter 2, it was only to provide some context for other topics of discussion. But in this chapter, I hold back no longer. After a vigorous discussion of general OOP concepts, I'll discuss how you can use these concepts in your .NET code.

Object-Oriented Programming Concepts

If you've read this far into the book, it's probably OK to let you in on the secret of object-oriented computing. The secret is: it's all a sham, a hoax, a coverup. That's right, your computer does not really perform any processing with objects, no matter what their orientation. The CPU in your computer processes data and logic statements the old-fashioned way: one step at a time, moving through specific areas in memory as directed by the logic, manipulating individual values and bits according to those same logic statements. It doesn't see data as collective objects; it sees only bits and bytes.

One moment, I've just been handed this important news bulletin. It reads, "Don't be such a geek, Tim. It's not the computer doing the object-oriented stuff, it's the programmer." Oh, sorry about that. But what I said before still stands: the final code as executed by your CPU isn't any more object-oriented than old MS-DOS code. But *object-oriented language compilers* provide the illusion that OOP is built into the computer. You design your code and data in the form of objects, and the compiler takes it from there. It reorganizes your code and data, adds some extra code to do the simulated-OOP magic, and bundles it all up in an EXE file. You could write any OOP program using ordinary procedural languages, or even assembly language. But applications that focus on data can often be written much more efficiently using OOP development practices.

The Object

The core of object-oriented programming is, of course, the *object*. An object is a person, place, or thing. Wait a minute, that's a noun. An object is *like* a noun. Objects are computer data-and-logic constructs that symbolize real-world entities, such as people, places, or things. You can have objects that represent people, employees, dogs, sea otters, houses, file cabinets, computers, strands of DNA, galaxies, pictures, word processing documents, calculators, office supplies, books, soap opera characters, space invaders, pizza slices, majestic self-amortizing canals, plantations of ripening tea, a few of my favorite things, and sand.

Objects provide a convenient software means to describe and manage the data associated with one of these real-world objects. For instance, if you had a set of objects representing DVDs in your home video collection, the object could manage features of the DVD, such as its title, the actors performing in the content, the length of the video in minutes, whether the DVD was damaged or scratched, its cost, and so on. If you connected your application to the DVD-ROM player in your system, your object could even include a "play" feature that (assuming the DVD was in the drive) would begin to play the movie, possibly from a timed starting position or DVD "chapter."

Objects work well because of their ability to simulate the features of real-world counterparts through software development means. They do this through the four key attributes of objects: *abstraction*, *encapsulation*, *inheritance*, and *polymorphism*.

Throughout this chapter, the term *object* usually refers to an *instance* of something, a specific in-memory use of the defined element, an instance with its own set of data, not just its definition or design. *Class* refers to the design and source code of the object, comprising the *implementation*.

Abstraction

An abstraction indicates an object's limited view of a real-world object. Like an abstract painting, an abstracted object shows just the basic essentials of the real-world equivalent (see Figure 8-1).

Objects can't perfectly represent real-world counterparts. Instead, they implement data storage and processes on just those elements of the real-world counterpart that are important for the application. Software isn't the only thing that requires abstraction. Your medical chart at your doctor's office is an abstraction of your total physical health. When you buy a new house, the house inspector's report is an abstraction

Original   **Abstract**

Figure 8-1. Actually, the one on the left is kind of abstract, too

of the actual condition of the building. Even the thermometer in your back yard is an abstraction; it cannot accurately communicate all of the minor temperature variations that exist just around the flask of mercury. Instead, it gathers all the information it can, and communicates a single numeric result.

All of these abstract tools record, act on, or communicate just the essential information they were designed to manage. A software object, in a similar way, only stores, acts on, or communicates essential information about its real-world counterpart. For instance, if you were designing an object that monitored the condition of a building, you might record the following:

- Building location and address
- Primary construction material (wood, concrete, steel-beam, etc.)
- Age (in years)
- General condition (from a list of choices)
- Inspector notes

Although a building would also have color, a number of doors and windows, and a height, these elements may not be important for the application, and therefore would not be part of the abstraction. Those values that are contained within the object are called *properties*. Any processing rules or calculations contained within the object that act on the properties (or other supplied internal or external data) are known as *methods*. Taken together, methods and properties make up the *members* of the object.

Encapsulation

The great advantage of software is that a user can perform a lot of complex and time-consuming work quickly and easily. Actually, the software takes care of the speed and the complexity on behalf of the user, and in many cases, the user doesn't even care how the work is being done. "Those computers are just so baffling; I don't know and I don't care how they work as long as they give me the results I need" is a common statement heard in management meetings. And it's a realistic statement too, since the computer has *encapsulated* the necessary data and processing logic to accomplish the desired tasks.

Encapsulation carries with it the idea of *interfaces*. Although a computer may contain a lot of useful logic and data, if there was no way to interact with that logic or data, the computer would basically be a useless lump of plastic and silicon. Interfaces provide the means to interact with the internals of an object. An interface provides highly controlled entries and exits into the data and processing routines contained within the object. As a consumer of the object, it's really irrelevant how the object does its work internally, as long as it produces the results you expect through its publicly exposed interfaces.

Using the computer as an example, the various interfaces include (among other things) the keyboard, display, mouse, power connector, USB and 1394 ports, speakers, microphone jack, and power button. Often, the things I connect to these interfaces are also *black boxes*, encapsulations with well-defined public interfaces. A printer is a mystery to me. How the printer driver can send commands down the USB cable and eventually squirt ink onto 24-pound paper is just inexplicable, but I don't know and I don't care how it really works, as long as it does work.

Inheritance

Inheritance in .NET isn't like inheritance in real life; no one has to die before it works. But as in real life, *inheritance* defines a relationship between two different objects. Specifically, it defines how one object is descended from another.

The original class in the object relationship is called the *base class*. It includes various and sundry interface members, as well as internal implementation details. A *derived class* is defined using the base class as the starting point. Derived classes *inherit* the features of the base class. By default, any publicly exposed members of the base class automatically become publicly exposed members of the derived class, including the implementation. A derived class may choose to *override* one, some, or all of these members, providing its own distinct or supplementary implementation details.

Derived classes often provide additional details specific to a subset of the base class. For instance, a base class that defines *animals* would include interfaces for the common name, Latin species name, number of legs, and other typical properties belonging to all animals. Derived classes would then enhance the features of the base class, but only for a subset of animals. A *mammal* class might define gestation time for birthing young, whereas a parallel *avian*-derived class could define the diameter of an egg. Both *mammal* and *avian* would still retain the name, species name, and leg count properties from the base *animal* class. An instance of *avian* would be an *animal*; an instance of *mammal* would be an *animal*. However, an instance of *avian* would not be a *mammal*. Also, a generic instance of *animal* could be considered as an *avian* only if it was originally defined as an *avian*.

Even though a base and derived class have a relationship, implementation details that are *private* to the base class are not made available to the derived class. The derived class doesn't even know that those private members exist. A base class may include *protected* members that, although hidden from users of the class, are visible to the derived class. Any member defined as *public* in the base class is available to the derived class, and also to all users of the base class. (Visual Basic defines another level named *friend*. Members marked as friend are available to all code in the same assembly, but not to code outside the assembly. Public members can be used by code outside the defining assembly.)

Examples of inheritance do exist in the real world. A clock is a base object from which an alarm clock derives. The alarm clock exposes the public interfaces of a clock, and adds its own implementation-specific properties and methods. Other examples include a knife and its derived Swiss Army knife, a chair and its derived recliner, and a table and its derived Periodic Table of the Chemical Elements.

Polymorphism

The concepts introduced so far could be implemented using standard procedural programming languages. Although you can't do true inheritance in a non-OOP language such as C, you can simulate it using flag fields: if a flag field named "type" in a non-OOP class-like structure was set to "mammal," you could enable use of certain mammal-specific fields. There are other ways to simulate these features, and it wouldn't be too difficult.

Polymorphism is a different avian altogether. Polymorphism means "many forms." Because a derived class can have its own (overridden) version of a base class's member, if you treat a *mammal* object like a generic *animal*, there could be some confusion as to which version of the members should be used, the *animal* version or the *mammal* version. Polymorphism takes care of figuring all this out, on an ad hoc basis, while your program is running. Polymorphism makes it possible for any code in your program to treat a derived instance as though it were its base instance. This makes for great coding. If you have a routine that deals with *animal* objects, you can pass it objects of type *animal*, *mammal*, or *avian*, and it will still work. This type of polymorphism is known as *subtyping polymorphism*, but who cares what its name is.

Another variation of polymorphism is *overloading*. Overloading allows a single class method (forget about derived classes for now) to have multiple forms, but still be considered as a single method. For instance, if you had a house object with a paint method (that would change the color of the house), you could have one paint method that accepted a single color (paint the house all one color) and another paint method that accepted two colors (the main color plus a trim color). When these methods are overloaded in a single class, the compiler determines which version to call based on the data you include in the call to the method.

Interfaces and Implementation

OOP development differentiates between the public definition of a class, the code written to implement that class, and the resultant in-memory use of that class as an object. It's similar to how, at a restaurant, you differentiate between a menu, the cooking of your selection, and the actual food that appears at your table:

- The description of an item on the menu is (to some extent) its *interface*; it describes what the real object will expose publicly in terms of taste, smell, and so on.

- The method used by the kitchen staff to make the food is the *implementation*; it's how the meal is prepared. There may be different implementations by different restaurants for the same menu item. In objects, the implementation is hidden from public view; in a restaurant, food preparation is thankfully hidden from view or no one would ever eat there.

- The food you receive from the kitchen is—ta-da!—the object, the actual *instance* of what the menu described. Many hungry customers may each order the same menu item, and each would receive a distinct instance of the food.

OOP in Visual Basic and .NET

Conceptually, OOP really isn't that complex. Since both humans and programmers interact with real-world objects and instances every day, it's pretty easy to wrap their minds around the idea of programming with objects. But how easy is it to communicate these object concepts to the computer through the Visual Basic compiler and the .NET Framework? Can it be done without weekly sessions on a shrink's comfy sofa? Duh! It's Visual Basic; of course it's easy.

One reason objects are so easy in .NET is that they have to be. Everything in your .NET program is part of an object, and if everything about .NET was hard, you'd be reading a book on Macintosh development right about now. But it's not too hard because the Visual Basic implementation of objects parallels the conceptual ideas of objects.

Classes

Visual Basic uses *classes* and *structures* to define objects. I'll talk about structures a little later in the chapter. The Class keyword starts the definition of a class.

```
Class Superhero
    ' ----- Class-related code goes here.
End Class
```

That's most of it: the Class keyword, and a name for the class ("Superhero," in this case). All classes reside in a namespace (discussed way back in Chapter 1). By default, your classes appear in a namespace that is named after your project. You can alter this in the project properties (to set the top-level namespace for your assembly) and with the Namespace statement (to indicate relative namespaces from your assembly's top-level namespace).

```
Namespace GoodGuys
    Class Superhero
    End Class
End Namespace
```

If your application's default namespace is WindowsApplication1, the class in this sample code would be identified as WindowsApplication1.GoodGuys.Superhero. You can add any number of classes to a namespace. Classes that use the same name, but that appear in different namespaces, are unrelated.

The members of a class appear between the Class and End Class clauses. You can also split a class's definition into multiple source code files. If you do split up a class like this, at least one of the parts must include the keyword Partial in the definition.

```
Partial Class Superhero
```

As with variable definitions, classes are defined using one of the access modifier keywords: Public, Private, Protected, Friend, or Protected Friend. Flip back to Chapter 6, in the "Variables" section, if you need a refresher course.

The .NET Framework Class Libraries (FCLs) are simply loaded with classes and objects, and they are all pretty much defined with this simple keyword: Class.

Class Members

Calling your class Superhero won't endow it with any special powers if you don't add any *members* to the class. All class members must appear between the Class and End Class boundaries, although if you use the Partial feature to break up your class, you can sprinkle the members among the different class parts in any way you wish.

You can include 11 different kinds of members in your Visual Basic classes. Other books or documents may give you a different number, but they're wrong, at least if they organize things the way I do here:

Variable fields

Value type and reference type variables can be added directly to your class as top-level members. As full class members, they are accessible by any code defined in the same class, and possibly by code that uses your class. Variables are defined using one of the access modifiers.

```
Class Superhero
    Public Name As String
    Protected TrueIdentity As String
End Class
```

Variable fields are quick and convenient to add to classes, but sometimes they are a little too freewheeling. Public fields can be modified at will, without any limitations, even if you desire to limit the allowed range of a field. Also, fields don't work directly with all Visual Basic features, including some LINQ-specific features. When problems such as these arise, you can use property members instead of variable field members. I'll introduce properties in just a few paragraphs.

Constant fields

You define constants just like variable fields, but include the Const keyword. As with local procedure-level constants, you must assign a value to the constant immediately in source code, using literals or simple nonvariable calculations.

```
Private Const BaseStrengthFactor As Integer = 1
```

Enumerations

Enumerations define related integral values. Once defined, you can use them in your code just like other integer values.

```
Private Enum GeneralSuperPower
    Flight
    Strength
    Speed
    VisionRelated
    HearingRelated
    WaterRelated
    TemperatureRelated
    ToolsAndGadgets
    GreatCostume
End Enum
```

Enumerations can also be defined at the namespace level, outside any specific class.

Sub methods

Classes include two types of methods: subs and functions. All logic code in your application appears in one of these method types or in properties, so don't bother looking for such code in an enumeration. Sub methods perform some defined logic, optionally working on data passed in as *arguments*.

```
Public Sub DemonstrateMainPower( _
        ByVal strengthFactor As Integer)
    ' ----- Logic code appears here.
End Sub
```

The `DemonstrateMainPower` method, as a public member of your class, can be called either by code within the class, or by any code referencing an instance of your class. This method includes a single parameter, `strengthFactor`, through which calls to the method send in data arguments.

You can jump out of a sub method at any time using the `Return` statement, or the older pre-.NET `Exit Sub` statement.

Function methods

Function methods are just like sub methods, but they support a return value. You define the data type of the return value with an `As` clause at the end of the function definition. You can assign the return value using the `Return` statement, or by assigning the function name directly within the code.

```
Public Function GetSecretIdentity( _
      ByVal secretPassword As String) As String
   If (secretPassword = "Krypton") Then
      ' ----- I created a class field named
      '        TrueIdentity earlier.
      Return TrueIdentity
   Else
      GetSecretIdentity = "FORGET IT BAD GUY"
   End If
End Function
```

If you use the assignment-to-function-name style of return value assignment, use the `Exit Function` statement to return to the calling code at any time.

Properties

Properties combine the ideas of fields and methods. You can create read-write, read-only, or write-only properties through the `Get` and `Set` accessors. The following code defines a write-only property:

```
Public WriteOnly Property SecretIdentity() As String
   Set(ByVal value As String)
      TrueIdentity = value
   End Set
End Property
```

Delegates

Delegates define arguments and return values for a method, and encase them in a single object all their own. They are generally used to support the event process, callback procedures, and indirect calls to class methods.

```
Public Delegate Sub GenericPowerCall( _
   ByVal strengthFactor As Integer)
```

Since delegates are pretty generic, they are often defined at the namespace level, outside any class definition.

Events

Adding events to your class allows consumers of your class to react to changes and actions occurring within a class instance. The syntax used to define events looks a lot like a method definition, but an alternative syntax uses previously defined delegates to indicate the signature of the event.

```
' ----- Non-delegate definition.
Public Event PerformPower( _
   ByVal strengthFactor) As Integer

' ----- Delegate definition.
Public Event PerformPower As GenericPowerCall
```

Declares

The Declare statement lets you call code defined in external DLL files, although it works only with pre-.NET Windows DLL calls. The syntax for declares closely resembles the syntax used to define methods.

```
Public Declare Function TalkToBadGuy Lib "evil.dll" ( _
   ByVal message As String) As String
```

Once defined, an externally declared sub or function can be used in your code as though it were a built-in .NET sub or function definition. The .NET Framework does a lot of work behind the scenes to shuttle data between your program and the DLL. Still, care must be taken when interacting with such external "unmanaged" code, especially if the DLL is named *evil.dll*.

Interfaces

Interfaces allow you to define abstract classes and, in a way, class templates. A section near the end of this chapter discusses interfaces. Interfaces can also be defined at the namespace level, and usually are.

Nested types

Classes can include other subordinate classes (or structures) for their own internal or public use. If you make such a "child" class public, you can return instances of these classes to code that uses the larger "parent" class.

```
Class Superhero
   Class Superpower
   End Class
End Class
```

You can nest classes to any depth, but don't go overboard. Creating multiple classes within the same namespace will likely meet your needs without making the code overly complex. But that's just my idea; do what you want. It's your code after all. If you want to throw your life away on a career in the movies, that's fine with me.

Adding a nice variety of members to a class is a lot of fun. You can add class members in any variety, in any order, and in any quantity. If you add a lot of members, you might even get a quantity discount on Visual Studio from Microsoft, but don't hold your breath.

Shared Class Members

Normally, objects (class instances) are greedy and selfish; they want to keep everything to themselves and not share with others. That's why each instance of a class you create has its own version of the data elements defined as class members. Even class methods and properties give the appearance of being distinct for each class instance. It's as though each object was saying, "I've got mine; get your own." It's this attitude that has led to what is now commonly called "class warfare."

In an attempt to promote affability among software components and push for "kinder and gentler" classes, Microsoft included the Shared keyword in its class design. The Shared keyword can be applied to variable field, sub method, function method, and property members of your class. When defined, a *shared member* can be used *without the need to create an instance of that class*. You reference these shared members using just the class name and the member name.

```
Class ClassWithSharedValue
    Public Shared TheSharedValue As Integer
End Class
...later, in some other code...
ClassWithSharedValue.TheSharedValue = 10
```

Shared members are literally "shared" by all instances of your class, and if public, by code outside the class as well. Since they don't require an object instance, they are also limited to just those resources that don't require an object instance. This means that a shared method cannot access a nonshared variable field of the same class. Any class members that are not marked Shared are known as *instance members*.

Overloaded Members and Optional Arguments

Overloading of a method occurs by attaching the Overloads keyword to each overloaded member.

```
Class House
    Public Overloads Sub PaintHouse()
        ' ----- Use the same color(s) as before.
    End Sub

    Public Overloads Sub PaintHouse(ByVal baseColor As Color)
        ' ----- Paint the house a solid color.
    End Sub

    Public Overloads Sub PaintHouse(ByVal baseColor As Color, _
            ByVal trimColor As Color)
        ' ----- Paint using a main and a trim color.
    End Sub

    Public Overloads Sub PaintHouse(ByVal baseColor As Color, _
            ByVal coats As Integer)
        ' ----- Possibly paint with many coats, of paint
        '          that is, not of fabric.
    End Sub
End Class
```

When you call the PaintHouse method, you must pass arguments that match one of the overloaded versions. Visual Basic determines which version to use based on the argument signature. If you pass the wrong type or number of arguments, the program will refuse to compile.

Two of the overloaded members in this class look alike, except for the second coats argument.

```
Public Overloads Sub PaintHouse(ByVal whichColor As Color)

Public Overloads Sub PaintHouse(ByVal baseColor As Color, _
    ByVal coats As Integer)
```

Instead of defining two distinct methods, I could have combined them into a single method, and defined an *optional argument* for the coats parameter.

```
Public Overloads Sub PaintHouse(ByVal baseColor As Color, _
    Optional ByVal coats As Integer = 1)
```

The Optional keyword can be used on any number of parameters, but no nonoptional parameters can appear after them; the optional arguments must always be last in the list. Although the calling code might not pass a value for coats, .NET still requires that every parameter receive an argument. Therefore, each optional argument includes a *default value* using a simple assignment within the parameter definition. The optional argument coats uses a default value of 1 through the = 1 clause.

Inheritance

Visual Basic supports inheritance, the joining of two classes in an ancestor-descendant relationship. To implement inheritance, define the base class, and then add the derived class using the keyword Inherits. What a surprise!

```
Class Animal
    ' ----- Animal class members go here.
End Class

Class Mammal
    Inherits Animal

    ' ----- All members of Animal are automatically
    '       part of Mammal. Add additional Mammal
    '       features here.
End Class
```

The Inherits statement must appear at the start of the class definition, before the definition for any class members. It must include the name of exactly one other class, the base class. If you split up your derived class using the Partial keyword, you need to use the Inherits statement in only one of the parts. And since a derived class can use only a single base class, you're pretty much limited to using the Inherits statement only once per class. (The base class can be used in several different derived classes, and the derived class can further be used as a base class for other derived classes.)

Derived classes automatically inherit all defined members of the base class. If a derived class needs to provide special functionality for a member defined in the base class, it overrides that member. This is a two-step process: (1) the base class must allow its member to be overridden with the Overridable keyword; and (2) the derived class must supply the overriding code using the Overrides keyword.

```
Class Animal
    Public Overridable Sub Speak()
        MsgBox("Grrrr.")
    End Sub
End Class

Class Canine
    Inherits Animal
    Public Overrides Sub Speak()
        MsgBox("Bark.")
    End Sub
End Class
```

Any class that derives from Animal can now supply its own custom code for the Speak method. But the same is true for classes derived from Canine; the Overridable keyword is passed down to each generation. If you need to stop this attribute at a specific generation, use the NotOverridable keyword. This keyword is valid only when used in a derived class since base class members are nonoverridable by default.

```
Class Canine
    Inherits Animal
    Public NotOverridable Overrides Sub Speak()
        MsgBox("Bark.")
    End Sub
End Class
```

There are times when it is not possible to write a truly general method in the base class, and you want to require that every derived class define its own version of the method. Using the MustOverride keyword in the base member definition enables this requirement.

```
Class Animal
    Public MustOverride Sub DefenseTactic()
End Class
```

Members marked as MustOverride include no implementation code of their own, since it would go unused. (Also notice that DefenseTactic has no closing End Sub statement.) Because there is no code associated with this member, the entire Animal class has a deficiency. If you created an instance of Animal and called its DefenseTactic method, panic would ensue within the application. Therefore, it is not possible to create instances of classes that contain MustOverride members. To note this limitation, the class is also decorated with the MustInherit keyword.

```
MustInherit Class Animal
    Public MustOverride Sub DefenseTactic()
End Class
```

It won't be possible to create an instance of Animal directly, although you can derive classes from it, and create instances of those classes. Also, you can create an Animal variable (a reference type) and assign an instance of an Animal-derived class to it.

```
Dim zooMember As Animal
Dim monkey As New Simian    ' Simian is derived from Animal
zooMember = monkey
```

Such code doesn't really seem fair to the base class. I mean, it defined all the core requirements for derived classes, but it doesn't get any of the credit since it can't be directly instantiated. But there is a way for a base class to control its own destiny, to take all the glory for itself. It does this with the NotInheritable keyword.

```
NotInheritable Class Animal
End Class
```

The only way to use a NotInheritable class is to create an instance of it; you cannot use it as the base class of another derived class. (If your noninheritable class contains shared members, they can be accessed without the need to create an instance.)

Inherits, MustInherit, NotInheritable, Overrides, Overridable, NotOverridable—this certainly isn't your grandmother's Visual Basic anymore. And there's still one more of these inimitable keywords: Shadows. When you override a base class member, the new code must use a definition that is identical to the one provided in the base class. That is, if you override a function method with two String arguments and an Integer return code, the overriding code must use that same signature. Shadowed members have no such requirements. A shadowed member matches an item in the base class "in name only"; everything else is up for grabs. You can even change the member type. If you have a sub method named PeanutButter in a base class, you can shadow it in the derived class with a variable field (or constant, or enumeration, or nested class) also named PeanutButter.

```
Class Food
    Public Sub PeanutButter()
    End Sub
End Class
Class Snack
    Inherits Food
    Public Shadows PeanutButter As String
        ' Hey, it's not even a "Sub"
End Class
```

Without the Shadows keyword in the Snack class, a compile-time error would occur.

Creating Instances of Classes

Step one: designing classes. Step two: deriving classes. Step three: creating class instances. Step four: cha-cha-cha. Visual Basic uses the New keyword to create instances of your custom classes.

```
Dim myPet As Animal = New Animal
' ----- Or...
Dim myPet As New Animal
' ----- Or...
Dim myPet As Animal
myPet = New Animal
```

The instance can then be used like any other .NET instance variable. Member access occurs using "dot" notation.

```
myPet.Name = "Fido"
```

You can also (within reason) pass instance variables between their base and derived variations.

```
Dim myPet As Animal
Dim myDog As Canine
myDog = New Canine
myDog.Name = "Fido"
myPet = myDog          ' Since Canine derives from Animal
MsgBox(myPet.Name)     ' Displays "Fido"
```

If you have Option Strict set to On, there will be limits on your ability to convert between types, especially narrowing conversions (where the source data type will not always "fit" in the target variable). In such cases, you must use the CType function (or one of a few similar .NET and Visual Basic supplied functions) to enable the conversion.

```
myDog = CType(myPet, Canine)
```

Referring to class instances is simply a matter of referring to the variable or object that contains the instance. That is true for code that uses an instance from outside the class itself. For the code within your class (such as in one of its methods), you refer to members of your instance as though they were local variables (with no qualification), or use the special Me keyword.

```
Class Animal
    Public Name As String
    Public Sub DisplayName( )
        ' ----- Either of these lines will work.
        MsgBox(Name)
        MsgBox(Me.Name)
    End Sub
End Class
```

A similar keyword, MyClass, usually acts like the Me keyword, but it has some different functionality when a class instance is stored in a variable from a different (base or derived) class type. If you create an instance of Canine, but store it in an Animal variable, references using Me will focus on the Canine code, whereas references to MyClass will focus on the Animal code. I won't be using MyClass in the Library Project, and for most simple uses of class instances, you will never use it either. But there are times when it is important to differentiate between base and derived code, and this is the way to do it.

The MyBase keyword references elements of the base class from which the current class derives. It references only the closest base class; if you have a class named Class5 that derives from Class4, which in turn derives from Class3, which derives from Class2, which derives from Class1, which eventually derives from System.Object, references to MyBase in the code of Class5 refer to Class4. Well, that's almost true. If you try to use MyBase.MemberName, and MemberName doesn't exist in Class4, MyBase will search back through the stack of classes until it finds the closest definition of MemberName.

```
Class Animal
    Public Overridable Sub ObtainLicense()
        ' ----- Perform Animal-specific licensing code.
    End Sub
End Class

Class Canine
    Inherits Animal
    Public Overrides Sub ObtainLicense()
        ' ----- Perform Canine-specific licensing code, then...
        MyBase.ObtainLicense()  ' Calls code from Animal class
    End Sub
End Class
```

Constructors and Destructors

Class instances have a lifetime: a beginning, a time of activity, and finally, thankfully, an end. The beginning of an object's lifetime occurs through a *constructor*; its final moments are dictated by a *destructor* before passing into the infinity of the .NET garbage collection process.

Each class includes at least one constructor, whether explicit or implicit. If you don't supply one, .NET will at least perform minimal constructor-level activities, such as reserving memory space for each instance variable field of your class. If you want a class to have any other startup-time logic, you must supply it through an explicit constructor.

Constructors in Visual Basic are sub methods with the name New. A New constructor with no arguments acts as the *default constructor*, called by default whenever a new instance of a class is needed.

```
Class Animal
    Public Name As String
    Public Sub New()
        ' ----- Every animal must have some name.
        Name = "John Doe of the Jungle"
    End Sub
End Class
```

Without this constructor, new instances of Animal wouldn't have any name assigned to the Name field. And since String variables are reference types, Name would have an initial value of Nothing. Not very user-friendly. A default constructor gives you a chance to provide at least the minimum needed data and logic for a new instance.

You can provide additional custom constructors by adding more New methods, each with a different argument signature.

```
Class Animal
    Public Name As String
    Public Sub New()
        ' ----- Every animal must have some name.
        Name = "John Doe of the Jungle"
    End Sub
    Public Sub New(ByVal startingName As String)
        ' ----- Use the caller-supplied name.
        Name = startingName
    End Sub
    Public Sub New(ByVal startingCode As Integer)
        ' ----- Build a name from a numeric code.
        Name = "Animal Number " & CStr(startingCode)
    End Sub
End Class
```

The following code demonstrates each constructor:

```
MsgBox((New Animal).Name)
    ' Displays "John Doe of the Jungle"

MsgBox((New Animal("Fido")).Name)
    ' Displays "Fido"

MsgBox((New Animal(5)).Name)
    ' Displays "Animal Number 5"
```

You can force the consumer of your class to use a custom constructor by excluding a default constructor from the class definition. Also, if you're deriving your class from anything other than System.Object, it's usually a good idea to call the base class's constructor as the first line of your derived constructor, although the default constructor in the base class will be called…by default.

```
Class Canine
    Inherits Animal
    Public Sub New()
        MyBase.New()  ' Calls Animal.New()
        ' ----- Now add other code.
    End Sub
End Class
```

Killing a class instance is not as easy as it might seem. When you create local class instances in your methods, they are automatically *destroyed* when that method exits *if you haven't assigned the instance to a variable outside the method.* If you create an instance in a method and assign it to a class member, it will live on in the class member for the lifetime of the class, even though the method that created it has exited.

But let's think only about local instances for now. An instance is destroyed when the routine exits. You can also destroy an instance immediately by setting its variable to Nothing.

```
myDog = Nothing
```

Setting the variable to a new instance will destroy any previous instance stored in that variable.

```
myDog = New Canine
myDog.Name = "Fido"
myDog = New Canine   ' Sorry Fido, you're gone
```

When an object is destroyed, .NET calls a special method named Finalize, if present, to perform any final cleanup before removing the instance from memory. Finalize is implemented as a Protected method of the base System.Object class; you must override this method in your class to use it.

```
Class Animal
   Protected Overrides Sub Finalize()
      ' ----- Cleanup code goes here. Be sure to call the
      '       base class's Finalize method.
      MyBase.Finalize()
   End Sub
End Class
```

So, what's with that crack about killing instances being so hard? The problem is that .NET controls the calling of the Finalize method; it's part of the garbage collection process. The framework doesn't continually clean up its garbage. It's like the service at your house; it gets picked up by the garbage truck only once in a while. Until then, it just sits there, rotting, decaying, decomposing, and not having its Finalize method called. For most objects, this isn't much of a problem; who cares if the memory for a string gets released now or 30 seconds from now. But there are times when it is important to release acquired resources as quickly as possible. For instance, if you acquire a lock on an external hardware resource and release it only in the destructor, you could be holding that lock long after the application has exited. Talk about a slow death.

There are two ways around this problem. One way is to add a separate cleanup method to your class that you expect any code using your class to call. This will work—until some code forgets to call the method. (You should therefore also call this routine from the Finalize destructor.) The second method is similar, but it uses a framework-supplied interface called IDisposable. (I'll talk about interfaces in a minute, so don't get too worried about all the code shown here.)

```
Class Animal
   Implements IDisposable

   Protected Overrides Sub Finalize()
      ' ----- Cleanup code goes here. Be sure to call the
      '       base class's Finalize method.
```

```
        MyBase.Finalize()
    End Sub

    Public Overloads Sub Dispose() _
          Implements IDisposable.Dispose
        ' ----- Put cleanup code here. Also make these calls.
        MyBase.Dispose()    ' Only if base class is disposable.
        System.GC.SuppressFinalize(Me)
    End Sub
End Class
```

The `SuppressFinalize` method tells the garbage collector, "Don't call `Finalize`; I've already cleaned up everything." Any code that uses your class will need to call its `Dispose` method to perform the immediate cleanup of resources. So, it's not too different from the first way I talked about, but it does standardize things a bit. Also, it enables the use of the Visual Basic `Using` statement. This block statement provides a structured method of cleaning up resources:

```
Using myPet As New Animal
    ' ----- Code here uses myPet.
End Using
' ----- At this point, myPet is destroyed, and Dispose is
'        called automatically by the End Using statement.
```

Interfaces

The `MustOverride` and `MustInherit` keywords force derived classes to implement specific members of the base class. But what if you want the derived class to implement *all* members of the base class? You could use `MustOverride` next to each method and property, but a better way is to use an *interface*. Interfaces define *abstract classes*, classes consisting only of definitions, no implementation. (OOP purists will point out that a class with even just one `MustOverride` flag is also an abstract class. Fine.) Interfaces create a *contract*, an agreement that the implementing class or structure agrees to carry out.

The `Interface` statement begins the interface definition process. By convention, all interface names begin with the capital letter *I*.

```
Interface IBuilding
    Function FloorArea() As Double
    Sub AlterExterior()
End Interface
```

As you see here, the syntax is a somewhat simplified version of the class definition syntax. All interface members are automatically public, so access modifiers aren't included. Only the definition line of each member is needed since there is no implementation. In addition to function and sub methods, interface members also include properties, events, other interfaces, classes, and structures. Interfaces can also derive from other interfaces (using the `Inherits` keyword), and automatically include all the members of the base interface.

You attach interfaces to a class using the `Implements` keyword. This same keyword is used later to indicate which class member defines which interface member.

```
Class House
    Implements IBuilding

    Public Function FloorArea() As Double _
            Implements IBuilding.FloorArea
        ' ----- Add implementation here.
    End Function

    Public Sub PaintHouse() Implements IBuilding.AlterExterior
        ' ----- Add implementation here.
    End Sub
End Class
```

Class implementations of interface members are not required to maintain the original interface member name (although the argument signature must match the one in the interface). In the sample code, `FloorArea` kept the name of the equivalent interface member, but the `AlterExterior` member was implemented using the `PaintHouse` method. This makes possible some interesting code.

```
Dim someHouse As New House
Dim someBuilding As IBuilding
someBuilding = someHouse
someBuilding.AlterExterior()  ' Calls someHouse.PaintHouse()
```

Classes can only inherit from a single base class, but there is no limit on the number of interfaces that a class can implement.

```
Class House
    Implements IBuilding, IDisposable
```

Also, a single class member can implement multiple interface members.

```
Public Sub PaintHouse() Implements _
    IBuilding.AlterExterior, IContractor.DoWork
```

So, why use interfaces? Interfaces provide a generic way to access common functionality, even among objects that have nothing in common. Classes named `Animal`, `House`, and `Superhero` probably have nothing in common in terms of logic, but they may all need a consistent way to clean up their resources. If they each implement the `IDisposable` interface, they gain that ability without the need to derive from some common base class.

Modules and Structures

In addition to classes, Visual Basic provides two related object definition features: structures and modules. Although they have different names than "class," they still act a lot like classes, but with different features enabled or disabled.

Modules provide a place to include general global code and data values in your application or assembly. All members of a module are Shared. In fact, a module acts just like a class with the Shared keyword added to each member, yet with one major difference: no inheritance relationship is allowed with modules. You cannot create a derived module from a base class or module, nor can you use a module as a base for any other type. Modules are a carryover from pre-.NET versions of Visual Basic, which included "Modules" for all non-Form code.

```
Friend Module GenericDataAndCode
    ' ----- Application-global constant.
    Public Const AllDigits As String = "0123456789"

    ' ----- Application-global function.
    Public Function GetEmbeddedDigits( _
            ByVal sourceString As String) As String
    End Sub
End Module
```

You cannot create an instance of a module. As with classes, modules appear in the context of a namespace. Unlike a class with shared members, you do not need to specify the module name to use the module member. All module members act as global variables and methods, and can be used immediately in any other code in your application without further qualification. (You can restrict a module member's use to just the module by declaring the member as Private.)

Structures are much more like classes than are modules. Classes implement reference types, but structures implement value types. All structures derive from System.ValueType (which in turn derives from System.Object). As such, they act like the core Visual Basic data types, such as Integer. You can create instances of a structure using the same syntax used to create class instances. However, you cannot use a structure as the base for another derived structure. And although you can include a constructor in your structure, destructors are not supported.

Because of the way that structures are stored and used in a .NET application, they are well suited to simple data types. You can include any number of members in your structure, but it is best to keep things simple.

Partial Methods

Earlier in the chapter I wrote about partial classes, the ability to divide a class into multiple files. Partial classes are especially common in code created by code generators. Visual Studio is, in part, a code generator; as you drag-and-drop controls on your form, it generates code for you in a partial Form class. In such cases, partial classes have two authors: the automated generator and you.

Partial methods, new in Visual Basic 2008, are also used by code generators, although you are free to employ them yourself. They are particularly useful when some automatically generated class wants to give its second author (you) the ability to supply some optional logic that will enhance the automatically generated logic. Partial methods might be more accurately called "optional methods," since you have the option to implement them or not.

Partial methods have two parts: (1) an unimplemented half; and (2) an optional implemented half. The two halves appear in different parts of a partial class. A partial method is never split between a base and derived class; they have nothing to do with inheritance.

The unimplemented half of a partial method looks like an empty sub method definition, but with the `Partial` keyword added.

```
Partial Private Sub ImplementIfYouDare( )
End Sub
```

Partial methods must always be sub methods, never functions, and they must always be declared as `Private`. If you supply any parameters, they must always be decorated with the `ByVal` keyword, not `ByRef`. Boy, that's a lot of restrictions.

The implemented half looks really familiar, except for the lack of a "Partial" prefix. But it sure looks good with real code between its jaws.

```
Private Sub ImplementIfYouDare( )
    MsgBox("I did it, so there.")
End Sub
```

So, what's the big deal with these partial methods? Perhaps not much, but looking at an example might help. Let's return to our living, breathing `Animal` class, this time with a partial method included. Let's start with the auto-generated side of the world.

```
Partial Class Animal
    Public Sub Move( )
        ' ----- Interesting movement code, then...
        MoveSideEffects( )
    End Sub

    Partial Private Sub MoveSideEffects( )
    End Sub
End Class
```

Sometimes when an animal moves, it has side effects, such as scaring other animals. As the second half of the implementation team, you could program these side effects by completing the other half of the partial method. But if there were no side effects for this particular implementation, you could just leave the partial method unfinished. It's optional.

Yawn, yawn, snore, snore. "Get to the point, Tim," you say. The point is that if you never write the second half of a partial method, the Visual Basic compiler will leave out both halves, generating code as though the unimplemented half was never auto-generated in the first place. So, that earlier `Animal` class becomes:

```
Partial Class Animal
    Public Sub Move()
        ' ----- Interesting movement code, then...
    End Sub
End Class
```

Not only did the partial method definition disappear, but the call to that method inside the Move routine disappeared as well.

As a lone programmer writing lonely code, you will probably never craft a partial method; the event system is a much better way to generically respond to actions within a class. But you might have a chance to write the implementation side of a partial method. Partial methods will be used in some LINQ-specific code, especially when designing LINQ code that communicates with SQL Server. But more on that in Chapter 17.

Related Issues

Let me take a few moments here before getting into the project code to discuss some issues that don't really fit into any particular chapter discussion, but that you might end up using a lot in your own applications.

The MsgBox Method

Although I've used it on practically every page of this book so far, I have never formally introduced you to the MsgBox method. Part of the Microsoft.VisualBasic namespace, MsgBox is a carryover from the MsgBox function in the original release of Visual Basic. It displays a simple message window, including a selection of response buttons and an optional icon. As a function, it returns a code indicating which button the user clicked to close the form, one of the MsgBoxResult enumeration values. The syntax is:

```
Public Function MsgBox(ByVal Prompt As Object, _
    Optional ByVal Buttons As MsgBoxStyle = MsgBoxStyle.OKOnly, _
    Optional ByVal Title As Object = Nothing) As MsgBoxResult
```

The Prompt parameter accepts a string for display in the main body of the dialog; Buttons indicates which buttons, icons, and other settings to use when displaying the dialog; and Title accepts a custom window title if you want something other than the application title to appear. The following statement displays the window in Figure 8-2:

```
Dim result As MsgBoxResult = MsgBox( _
    "It's safe to click; the computer won't explode.", _
    MsgBoxStyle.YesNoCancel Or MsgBoxStyle.Question, _
    "Click Something")
```

Figure 8-2. Communicating an important message

The MsgBox function is considered to be an intrinsic part of the language. But as a member of the Microsoft.VisualBasic namespace, it's generally used only within the Visual Basic language. If you were to do some .NET coding in C#, you would normally opt instead for the MessageBox.Show method. It works pretty much like the MsgBox function, but its second and third arguments are reversed. Some .NET conformists insist that MsgBox—and anything that appears in the Microsoft.VisualBasic namespace—must be spurned in favor of class library alternatives. I find it to be a preference choice, but you may encounter just such a person insisting that your code is substandard. You can read my views about such tactics in Chapter 26.

If you plan to develop Visual Basic code that targets Microsoft's Silverlight platform, avoiding Microsoft.VisualBasic can bring about improved performance when downloading your assembly to the client workstation. Silverlight applications benefit greatly from reductions in compiled code size, at least for download purposes. Anything you can do to eliminate dependencies on external assemblies such as Microsoft.VisualBasic will help speed your program along.

Using DoEvents

Programs are designed to do a lot of thinking, and sometimes they think so much, they pretty much lock up the computer. This is especially true of Visual Basic methods that perform a lot of database-heavy transactions, one right after another. The system defers less important screen updates so that more important data processing code can occur first. That's great, but sometimes the user thinks, "This stupid computer's dead again," and pulls the plug. If the screen would simply provide better updates, the user might be more patient.

Each control on your form (and the form itself) includes a Refresh method, but it can be a bother to constantly refresh everything. And refreshing the display wouldn't do much to enable the "Cancel" button that you want your user to click to abort all that lovely data processing. To make life easier, Visual Basic includes a DoEvents method.

When this method is called, the current method's code pauses temporarily, and messages in the thread's incoming message queue are processed, including "paint" (screen update) messages. DoEvents is part of the My namespace, and is used as a standalone statement:

```
My.Application.DoEvents( )
```

Be warned that overuse of DoEvents can slow down your application, and can lead to problems related to an event being called too many times. In general, it should be used only in a processing-intensive block of code, and then it should be spread out so that it is called only a few times per second at the most.

ParamArray Arguments

Any method can enable optional arguments, and the calling code can choose to include or exclude those arguments. But what if you wanted to add an unlimited number of optional arguments to a method? How could you write, for instance, a function that would return the average of all supplied arguments, with no limits on the number of arguments? Although you could accept an array variable with the source data values, you could also use a *parameter array argument*, also called a ParamArray argument.

As with optional arguments, ParamArray arguments must appear at the end of a method's argument list, and there can be only one, because one is more than enough for any method. Parameter array arguments use the ParamArray keyword just before the argument name.

```
Public Function CalculateAverage( _
      ParamArray sourceData( ) As Decimal) As Decimal
    ' ----- Calculate the average for a set of numbers.
    Dim singleValue As Decimal
    Dim runningTotal As Decimal = 0@

    If (sourceData.GetLength(0) = 0) Then
       Return 0@
    Else
       For Each singleValue In sourceData
          runningTotal += singleValue
       Next singleValue
       Return runningTotal / sourceData.GetLength(0)
    End If
End Function
```

Calls to the CalculateAverage function now accept any number of decimal values.

```
MsgBox(CalculateAverage(1, 2, 3, 4, 5)) ' Displays: 3
```

Summary

The ability to extend classes through inheritance is truly the foundation on which complex yet manageable programs are built in .NET. And they are not overly complex, either. Classes are simple containers for their members, and the variety and complexity of the available members are not that great. So, it's really amazing that you can write almost any type of program, and implement any number of features, using these simple foundational tools. Oh yeah, the Visual Basic language helps, too.

As we add code to the Library Project throughout this book, you will become more and more familiar with classes, structures, modules, and their members. And although you'll never remember whether ByRef or ByVal is the default parameter-passing mechanism for methods, you will add properties, methods, events, fields, and other types to classes like you were born with the ability.

Project

This chapter's code implements two features of the Library Project: (1) a simple helper class used with ListBox and ComboBox controls to manage text and data; and (2) a set of generic forms used to edit lookup tables in the Library, such as tables of status codes.

Supporting List and Combo Boxes

In Visual Basic 6.0 and earlier, ListBox and ComboBox controls included two primary array-like collections: List (used to store the display text for each item) and ItemData (used to store a 32-bit numeric value for each item). The List array was important to the user since it presented the text for each item. But many programmers depended more on the ItemData array, which allowed a unique identifier to be attached to each list item.

```
cboMonth.AddItem "January"
cboMonth.ItemData(cboMonth.NewIndex) = 1
cboMonth.AddItem "February"
cboMonth.ItemData(cboMonth.NewIndex) = 2
...
cboMonth.AddItem "December"
cboMonth.ItemData(cboMonth.NewIndex) = 12
```

Later, after the user selected a value from the list, the numeric ID could be used for database lookup or any other designated purpose.

```
nMonth = cboMonth.ItemData(cboMonth.ListIndex)
```

The bad news is that neither List nor ItemData exists in the .NET variation of ListBox or ComboBox controls. The good news is that both are replaced with a much more flexible collection: Items. The Items collection stores any type of object you want: instances of Integer, String, Date, Animal, or even Superhero, and you can mix them within a single ListBox. Since Items is just a collection of System.Object instances, you can put any type of object you wish in the collection. The ListBox (or ComboBox) uses this collection to display items in the list.

So, how does a ListBox control know how to display text for any mixture of objects? By default, the control calls the ToString method of the object. ToString is defined in System.Object, and you can override it in your own class. The ListBox control also includes a DisplayMember property that you can set to the field or property of your class that generates the proper text.

Let's see a ListBox in action. Add a new ListBox to a form, and then add the following code to the form's Load event handler.

```
Public Class Form1
    Private Sub Form1_Load(ByVal sender As System.Object, _
        ByVal e As System.EventArgs) Handles MyBase.Load
        ListBox1.Items.Add(1)
        ListBox1.Items.Add("Easy")
        ListBox1.Items.Add(#5/3/2006#)
    End Sub
End Class
```

Running this code displays the form in Figure 8-3.

Figure 8-3. A simple ListBox with three different items

For the old ItemData value, the ListBox control includes a ValueMember property that identifies the identifier field or property for the objects in the Items collection. But you don't have to use ValueMember. Instead, you can simply extract the object in question from the Items collection, and examine its members with your own custom code to determine its identity. In reality, it's a little more work than the old Visual Basic 6.0 method. But then again, since you can store objects of any size in the Items collection, you could opt to store entire database records, something you could never do before .NET.

Still, storing entire records in a `ListBox` or `ComboBox` control is pretty wasteful. It's usually much better to store just an ID number, and use it as a lookup into a database. That's what we'll do in the Library Project. To support this, we'll need to create a simple class that will expose a text and data value. First, let's go back into the Library code.

PROJECT ACCESS

Load the Chapter 8 (Before) Code project, either through the New Project templates or by accessing the project directly from the installation directory. To see the code in its final form, load Chapter 8 (After) Code instead.

Let's put the class in a source code file all its own. Add a new class file through the Project → Add Class menu command. Name the file *ListItemData.vb* and click the Add button. The following code appears automatically:

```
Public Class ListItemData

End Class
```

This class will be pretty simple. It will include only members for text and item display. In case we forget to connect the text field to the `ListBox` or `ComboBox`'s `DisplayMember` property, we'll also include an override to the `ToString` function, plus a custom constructor that makes initialization of the members easier. Add the following code to the body of the class.

INSERT SNIPPET

Insert Chapter 8, Snippet Item 1.

```
Public ItemText As String
Public ItemData As Integer

Public Sub New(ByVal displayText As String, _
      itemID As Integer)
   ' ----- Initialize the record.
   ItemText = displayText
   ItemData = itemID
End Sub

Public Overrides Function ToString() As String
   ' ----- Display the basic item text.
   Return ItemText
End Function

Public Overrides Function Equals(ByVal obj As Object) _
      As Boolean
```

```
' ----- Allow IndexOf( ) and Contains( ) searches by ItemData.
If (TypeOf obj Is Integer) Then
    Return CBool(CInt(obj) = ItemData)
Else
    Return MyBase.Equals(obj)
End If
End Function
```

Later, when it's time to populate a ListBox, we can use this object to add the display and identification values.

```
ListBox1.Items.Add(New ListItemData("Item Text", 25))
```

The override of the Equals method allows us to quickly look up items already added to a ListBox (or similar) control using features already included in the control. The ListBox control's Items collection includes an IndexOf method that returns the position of a matching item. Normally, this method will match only the object itself; if you pass it a ListItemData instance, it will report whether that item is already in the ListBox. The updated Equals code will also return True if we pass an Integer value that matches a ListItemData.ItemData member for an item already in the list.

```
Dim itemPosition As Integer = SomeListBox.Items.IndexOf(5)
```

Editing Code Tables

Back in Chapter 4, when we crafted the database for the Library Project, several of the tables were created to fill simple ComboBox lists in the application. All of these tables begin with the prefix "Code," and contain records that rarely, if ever, change in the lifetime of the application. One such table is CodeCopyStatus, which identifies the current general condition of an item in the library's collections.

Field	Type	Description
ID	Long - Auto	Primary key; automatically assigned. Required.
FullName	Text(50)	Name of this status entry. Required.

Since all of these tables have basically the same format—an ID field and one or more content fields—it should be possible to design a generic template to use for editing these tables. A base (class) form would provide the basic editing features, to be developed in full through derived versions of the base form.

For the project, we will add two forms: a "summary" form (that displays a list of all currently defined codes) and a "detail" form (that allows editing of a single new or existing code). To make things even simpler, we will include only the most basic record-management functionality in the summary form. Most of the code needed to edit, display, and remove codes will appear in the detail forms.

The Generic Detail Form

Add a new form to the project (Project → New Windows Form), naming it *BaseCodeForm.vb*. Alter the following properties as indicated.

Property	Setting
(Name)	BaseCodeForm
ControlBox	False
FormBorderStyle	FixedDialog
ShowInTaskbar	False
Size	406, 173
StartPosition	CenterScreen
Text	Code Form

Now access the source code for this class (View → Code). The code will never create instances of this generic form directly, so let's disallow all direct instantiation by including the MustInherit keyword.

```
Public MustInherit Class BaseCodeForm

End Class
```

The main features of the form will be the adding of new code records, the editing of existing code records, and the removal of existing records. Add three function skeletons that support these features. We could have made them MustOverride, but as you'll see later, we will want the option to keep the default functionality from the base generic form.

INSERT SNIPPET

Insert Chapter 8, Snippet Item 2.

```
Public Overridable Function AddRecord() As Integer
   ' ----- Prompt to add a new record. Return the ID
   '        when added, or -1 if cancelled.
   Return -1
End Function

Public Overridable Function DeleteRecord( _
      ByVal recordID As Integer) As Boolean
   ' ----- Prompt the user to delete a record.
   '        Return True on delete.
   Return False
End Function

Public Overridable Function EditRecord( _
      ByVal recordID As Integer) As Integer
```

```
' ----- Prompt the user to edit the record. Return the
'       record's ID if saved, or -1 on cancel.
    Return -1
End Function
```

The detail form will take responsibility for filling the ListBox control on the summary form with its items. Two methods will handle this: one that adds all items, and one that updates a single item. The derived class will be required to supply these features.

INSERT SNIPPET

Insert Chapter 8, Snippet Item 3.

```
' ----- Fill a ListBox control with existing records.
Public MustOverride Sub FillListWithRecords( _
    ByRef destList As ListBox, ByRef exceededMatches As Boolean)

' ----- Return the formatted name of a single record.
Public MustOverride Function FormatRecordName( _
    ByVal recordID As Integer) As String
```

The detail form must also display the proper titles and usage information on the summary form.

INSERT SNIPPET

Insert Chapter 8, Snippet Item 4.

```
' ----- Return a description of this editor.
Public MustOverride Function GetEditDescription() As String

' ----- Return the title-bar text for this editor.
Public MustOverride Function GetEditTitle() As String
```

Although most of the tables will supply a short list of alphabetized codes, some tables will include a large number (possibly thousands) of codes. The summary form will support a search method, to locate an existing code quickly. Since only certain derived forms will use this feature, we won't include MustOverride.

INSERT SNIPPET

Insert Chapter 8, Snippet Item 5.

```
Public Overridable Sub SearchForRecord( _
        ByRef destList As ListBox, _
        ByRef exceededMatches As Boolean)
    ' ----- Prompt the user to search for a record.
    Return
End Sub
```

Finally, the detail form will indicate which of the available features can be used from the summary form. The summary form will call each of the following functions, and then enable or disable features as requested.

INSERT SNIPPET

Insert Chapter 8, Snippet Item 6.

```
Public Overridable Function CanUserAdd() As Boolean
   ' ----- Check the security of current user to see
   '       if adding is allowed.
   Return False
End Function

Public Overridable Function CanUserEdit() As Boolean
   ' ----- Check the security of the user to see
   '       if editing is allowed.
   Return False
End Function

Public Overridable Function CanUserDelete() As Boolean
   ' ----- Check the security of the user to see
   '       if deleting is allowed.
   Return False
End Function

Public Overridable Function UsesSearch() As Boolean
   ' ----- Does this editor support searching?
   Return False
End Function
```

That's it for the generic detail form. Later on in the book, we'll create derived versions for each of the code tables.

The Generic Summary Form

The summary form is a little more straightforward, since it is just a plain form. When it starts up, it uses an instance of one of the derived detail forms to control the experience presented to the user. I've already added the form to the project; it's called *ListEditRecords.vb*, and it looks like Figure 8-4.

A large ListBox control fills most of the form, a control that will hold all existing items. There are also buttons to add, edit, delete, and search for items in the list. There's a lot of code to manage these items; I've already written it in a code snippet.

Figure 8-4. The Generic Summary form

Switch to the form's source code view, and add the source code just after the `Public Class ListEditRecords` line.

INSERT SNIPPET

Insert Chapter 8, Snippet Item 7.

The first line of the added code defines a private instance of the generic detail form we just designed.

```
Private DetailEditor As Library.BaseCodeForm
```

This field holds an instance of a class derived from `BaseCodeForm`. That assignment appears in the public method `ManageRecords`.

```
Public Sub ManageRecords(ByRef UseDetail _
      As Library.BaseCodeForm)
   ' ----- Set up the form for use with this code set.
   Dim exceededMatches As Boolean
```

```
    DetailEditor = UseDetail
    RecordsTitle.Text = DetailEditor.GetEditTitle( )
    RecordsInfo.Text = DetailEditor.GetEditDescription( )
    Me.Text = DetailEditor.GetEditTitle( )
    ActAdd.Visible = DetailEditor.CanUserAdd( )
    ActEdit.Visible = DetailEditor.CanUserEdit( )
    ActDelete.Visible = DetailEditor.CanUserDelete( )
    ActLookup.Visible = DetailEditor.UsesSearch( )
    DetailEditor.FillListWithRecords(RecordsList, _
        exceededMatches)
    RefreshItemCount(exceededMatches)
    Me.ShowDialog( )
End Sub
```

The code that calls ManageRecords passes in a form instance, one of the forms derived from BaseCodeForm. Once assigned to the internal DetailEditor field, the code uses the public features of that instance to configure the display elements on the summary form. For instance, the detail form's CanUserAdd function, which sports a Boolean return value, sets the Visible property of the ActAdd button. The FillListWithRecords method call populates the summary ListBox control with any existing code values. After some more display adjustments, the Me.ShowDialog method displays the summary form to the user.

Although the user will interact with the controls on the summary form, most of these controls defer their processing to the detail form, DetailEditor. For example, a click on the Add button defers most of the logic to the detail form's AddRecord method. The code in the summary form doesn't do much more than update its own display fields.

```
Private Sub ActAdd_Click(ByVal sender As System.Object, _
        ByVal e As System.EventArgs) Handles ActAdd.Click
    ' ----- Let the user add a record.
    Dim newID As Integer
    Dim newPosition As Integer

    ' ----- Prompt the user.
    newID = DetailEditor.AddRecord( )
    If (newID = -1) Then Return

    ' ----- Add this record to the list.
    newPosition = RecordsList.Items.Add( _
        (New Library.ListItemData( _
        DetailEditor.FormatRecordName(newID), newID)))
    RecordsList.SelectedIndex = newPosition
    RefreshButtons( )
    RefreshItemCount(False)
End Sub
```

Most of the remaining code in the summary form either is just like this (for edit, delete, and search features), or is used to refresh the display based on user interaction with the form. Be sure to examine the code to get a good understanding of how the code works. In later chapters, when we add actual detail forms, we'll see this code in action.

Functional Programming

In this chapter, we'll cover two major Visual Basic programming topics: *lambda expressions* and *error handling*. Both are mysterious, one because it uses a Greek letter in its name and the other because it might as well be in Greek for all the difficulty programmers have with it. Lambda expressions in particular have to do with the broader concept of *functional programming*, the idea that every computing task can be expressed as a function and that functions can be passed around willy-nilly within the source code. Visual Basic is not a true functional programming language, but the introduction of lambda expressions in Visual Basic 2008 brings some of those functional ways and means to the language.

Lambda Expressions

Lambda expressions are named for *lambda calculus* (or λ-calculus), a mathematical system designed in the 1930s by Alonzo Church, certainly a household name between the wars. Although his work was highly theoretical, it led to features and structures that benefit most programming languages today. Specifically, lambda calculus provides the rationale for the Visual Basic functions, arguments, and return values that we've already learned about. So, why add a new feature to Visual Basic and call it "lambda" when there are lambda things already in the language? Great question. No answer.

Lambda expressions let you define an object that contains an entire function. Although this is something new in Visual Basic, a similar feature has existed in the BASIC language for a long time. I found an old manual from the very first programming language I used, BASIC PLUS on the RSTS/E timeshare computer. It provided a sample of the DEF statement, which let you define simple functions. Here is some sample code from that language that prints a list of the first five squares:

```
100   DEF SQR(X)=X*X
110   FOR I=1 TO 5
120     PRINT I, SQR(I)
130   NEXT I
140   END
```

The function definition for SQR( ) appears on line 100, returning the square of any argument passed to it. It's used in the second half of line 120, generating the following output:

```
1       1
2       4
3       9
4       16
5       25
```

Lambda expressions in Visual Basic work in a similar way, letting you define a variable as a simple function. Here's the Visual Basic equivalent for the preceding code:

```
Dim sqr As Func(Of Integer, Integer) = _
    Function(x As Integer) x * x
For i As Integer = 1 To 5
    Console.WriteLine("{0}{1}{2}", i, vbTab, sqr(i))
Next i
```

The actual lambda expression is on the second line:

```
Function(x As Integer) x * x
```

Lambda expressions begin with the Function keyword, followed by a list of passed-in arguments in parentheses. After that comes the definition of the function itself, an expression that uses the passed-in arguments to generate some final result. In this case, the result is the value of x multiplied by itself.

One thing you won't see in a lambda expression is the Return statement. Instead, the return value just seems to fall out of the expression naturally. That's why you need some sort of variable to hold the definition and return the result in a function-like syntax.

```
Dim sqr As Func(Of Integer, Integer)
```

Lambda expression variables are defined using the Func keyword—so original. The data type argument list matches the argument list of the actual lambda expression, but with an extra data type thrown in at the end that represents the return value's data type. Here's a lambda expression that checks whether an Integer argument is even or not, returning a Boolean result:

```
Public Sub TestNumber( )
    Dim IsEven As Func(Of Integer, Boolean) = _
        Function(x As Integer) (x Mod 2) = 0
    MsgBox("Is 5 Even? " & IsEven(5))
End Sub
```

This code displays a message that says, "Is 5 Even? False." Behind the scenes, Visual Basic is generating an actual function, and linking it up to the variable using a delegate. (A delegate, as you probably remember, is a way to identify a method generically through a distinct variable.) The following code is along the lines of what the compiler is actually generating for the previous code sample:

```
Private Function HiddenFunction1( _
    ByVal x As Integer) As Boolean
  Return (x Mod 2) = 0
End Function

Private Delegate Function HiddenDelegate1( _
  ByVal x As Integer) As Boolean

Public Sub TestNumber( )
  Dim IsEven As HiddenDelegate1 = _
    AddressOf HiddenFunction1
  MsgBox("Is 5 Even? " & IsEven(5))
End Sub
```

In this code, the lambda expression and related IsEven variable have been replaced with a true function (HiddenFunction1) and a go-between delegate (HiddenDelegate1). Although lambdas are new in Visual Basic 2008, this type of equivalent functionality has been available since the first release of Visual Basic for .NET. Lambda expressions provide a simpler syntax when the delegate-referenced function is just returning a result from an expression.

Lambda expressions were added to Visual Basic 2008 primarily to support the new LINQ functionality (see Chapter 17). They are especially useful when you need to supply an expression as a processing rule for some other code, especially code written by a third party. And in your own applications, Microsoft is a third party. Coincidence? I think not!

Implying Lambdas

Lambda expressions are good and all, but it's clear that equivalent functionality was already available in the language. And by themselves, lambda expressions are just a simplification of some messy function-delegate syntax. But when you combine lambda expressions with the *type inference* features discussed back in Chapter 6, you get something even better: pizza!

Perhaps I should have written this chapter after lunch. What you get is *lambda expressions with inferred types*. It's not a very romantic name, but it is a great new tool.

Let's say that you wanted to write a lambda expression that multiplies two numbers together.

```
Dim mult As Func(Of Integer, Integer, Integer) = _
  Function(x As Integer, y As Integer) x * y

MsgBox(mult(5, 6))  ' Displays 30
```

This is the Big Cheese version of the code: I tell Visual Basic everything, and it obeys me without wavering. But there's also a more laissez faire version of the code that brings type inference into play.

```
Dim mult = Function(x As Integer, y As Integer) x * y
```

Hey, that's a lot less code. I was getting pretty tired of typing *Integer* over and over again anyway. The code works because Visual Basic looked at what you assigned to mult and correctly identified its strong data type. In this case, mult is of type Function(Integer, Integer) As Integer (see Figure 9-1). It even correctly guessed the return type.

```
Dim mult = Function(x As Integer, y As Integer) x * y
    Dim mult As <Function(Integer, Integer) As Integer>
```

Figure 9-1. Visual Basic is also good at playing 20 questions

This code assumes that you have Option Infer set to On in your source code, or through the Project properties (it's the default). Chapter 6 discusses this option.

We could have shortened the mult definition up even more.

```
Dim mult = Function(x, y) x * y
```

In this line, Visual Basic would infer the same function, but it would use the Object data type throughout instead of Integer. Also, if you have Option Strict set to On (which you should), this line will not compile until you add the appropriate As clauses.

Expression Trees

Internally, the Visual Basic compiler changes a lambda expression into an "expression tree," a hierarchical structure that associates operands with their operators. Consider this semicomplex lambda expression that raises a multiplied expression to a power:

```
Dim calculateIt = Function(x, y, z) (x * y) ^ z
```

Visual Basic generates an expression tree for calculateIt that looks like Figure 9-2.

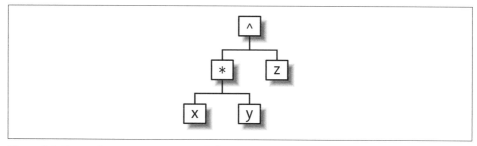

Figure 9-2. Expression trees group operands by operator

When it comes time to use a lambda expression, Visual Basic traverses the tree, calculating values from the lower levels up to the top. These expression trees are stored as objects based on classes in the System.Linq.Expressions namespace. If you don't like typing lambda expressions, you can build up your own expression trees using these objects. However, my stomach is rumbling even more, so I'm going to leave that out of the book.

Complex Lambdas

Although lambda expressions can't contain Visual Basic statements such as For... Next loops, you can still build up some pretty complex calculations using standard operators. Calls out to other functions can also appear in lambdas. In this code sample, mult defers its work to the MultiplyIt function:

```
Private Sub DoSomeMultiplication( )
   Dim mult = Function(x As Integer, y As Integer) _
      MultiplyIt(x, y) + 10

   MsgBox(mult(5, 6))  ' Displays 40
End Sub

Public Function MultiplyIt(ByVal x As Integer, _
      ByVal y As Integer) As Integer
   Return x * y
End Function
```

That's pretty straightforward. But things get more interesting when you have lambda expressions that return other lambda expressions. Lambda calculus was invented partially to see how any complex function could be broken down into the most basic of functions. Even literal values can be defined as lambdas. Here's the lambda expression that always returns the value 3:

```
Dim three = Function( ) 3
```

You've already seen lambda expressions that accept more than one argument:

```
Dim mult1 = Function(x As Integer, y As Integer) x * y
```

In lambda calculus, this can be broken down into smaller functionettes, where each includes only a single argument:

```
Dim mult2 = Function(x As Integer) Function(y As Integer) x * y
```

The data type of mult2 is not exactly the same as mult1's data type, but they both generate the same answer from the same x and y values. When you use mult1, it calculates the product of x and y and returns it. When you use mult2, it first runs the Function(x As Integer) part, which returns another lambda calculated by passing the value of x into its definition. If you pass in "5" as the value for x, the returned lambda is:

```
Function(y As Integer) 5 * y
```

This lambda is then calculated, and the product of 5 and y is returned. Calling mult2 in code is also slightly different. You don't pass in both arguments at once. Instead, you pass in the argument for x, and then pass y to the returned initial lambda.

```
MsgBox(mult2(5)(6))
```

When run, the mult2(5) part gets replaced with the first returned lambda. Then that first returned lambda is processed using (6) as its *y* argument. Isn't that simple? Well, no, it isn't. And that's OK, since the two-argument mult1 works just fine. The important part to remember is that it's possible to build complex lambda expressions up from more basic lambda expressions. Visual Basic will use this fact when it generates the code for your LINQ-related expressions. We'll talk more about it in Chapter 17, but even then, Visual Basic will manage a lot of the LINQ-focused lambda expressions for you behind the scenes.

Variable Lifting

Although you can pass arguments into a lambda expression, you may also use other variables that are within the scope of the lambda expression.

```
Private Sub NameMyChild()
    Dim nameLogic = GetChildNamingLogic()
    MsgBox(nameLogic("John"))  ' Displays: Johnson
End Sub

Private Function GetChildNamingLogic() As _
        Func(Of String, String)
    Dim nameSuffix As String = "son"
    Dim newLogic = Function(baseName As String) _
                        baseName & nameSuffix
    Return newLogic
End Function
```

The GetChildNamingLogic function returns a lambda expression. That lambda expression is used in the NameMyChild method, passing John as an argument to the lambda. And it works. The question is how. The problem is that nameSuffix, used in the lambda expression's logic, is a local variable within the GetChildNamingLogic method. All local variables are destroyed whenever a method exits. By the time the MsgBox function is called, nameSuffix will be long gone. Yet the code works as though nameSuffix lived on.

To make this code work, Visual Basic uses a new feature called *variable lifting*. Seeing that nameSuffix will be accessed outside the scope of GetChildNamingLogic, Visual Basic rewrites your source code, changing nameSuffix from a local variable to a variable that has a wider scope.

In the new version of the source code, Visual Basic adds a *closure class*, a dynamically generated class that contains both the lambda expression and the local variables used by the expression. When you combine these together, any code that gets access to the lambda expression will also have access to the "local" variable.

```
Private Sub NameMyChild()
    Dim nameLogic = GetChildNamingLogic()
    MsgBox(nameLogic("John"))  ' Displays: Johnson
End Sub
```

```
Public Class GeneratedClosureClass
   Public nameSuffix As String = "son"
   Public newLogic As Func(Of String, String) = _
      Function(baseName As String) baseName & Me.nameSuffix
End Class

Private Function GetChildNamingLogic() As  _
      Func(Of String, String)
   Dim localClosure As New GeneratedClosureClass
   localClosure.nameSuffix = "son"
   Return localClosure.newLogic
End Function
```

The actual code generated by Visual Basic is more complex than this, and it would include all of that function-delegate converted code I wrote about earlier. But this is the basic idea. Closure classes and variable lifting are essential features for lambda expressions since you can never really know where your lambda expressions are at all hours of the night.

Object Initializers

To initialize object properties not managed by constructors, you need to assign those properties separately just after you create the class instance.

```
Dim newHire As New Employee
newHire.Name = "John Doe"
newHire.HireDate = #2/27/2008#
newHire.Salary = 50000@
```

The With...End With statement provides a little more structure.

```
Dim newHire As New Employee
With newHire
   .Name = "John Doe"
   .HireDate = #2/27/2008#
   .Salary = 50000@
End With
```

A new syntax included in Visual Basic 2008 lets you combine declaration (with the New keyword) and member assignment. The syntax includes a new variation of the With statement.

```
Dim newHire As New Employee With { _
   .Name = "John Doe", _
   .HireDate = #2/27/2008#, _
   .Salary = 50000@}
```

Well, as far as new features go, it's not glitzy like lambda expressions or variable lifting. But it gets the job done.

Error Handling in Visual Basic

Debugging and error processing are two of the most essential programming activities you will ever perform. There are three absolutes in life: death, taxes, and software bugs. Even in a relatively bug-free application, there is every reason to believe that a user will just mess things up royally. As a programmer, your job is to be the guardian of the user's data as managed by the application, and to keep it safe, even from the user's own negligence (or malfeasance), and also from your own source code.

I recently spoke with a developer from a large software company headquartered in Redmond, Washington; you might know the company. This developer told me that in any given application developed by this company, more than 50% of the code is dedicated to dealing with errors, bad data, system exceptions, and failures. Certainly, all this additional code slows down each application and adds a lot of overhead to what is already called "bloatware." But in an age of hackers and data entry mistakes, such error management is an absolute must.

Testing—although not a topic covered in this book—goes hand in hand with error management. Often, the report of an error will lead to a bout of testing, but it should really be the other way around: testing should lead to the discovery of errors. A few years ago, NASA's *Mars Global Surveyor*, in orbit around the red planet, captured images of the *Beagle 2*, a land-based research craft that crashed into the Martian surface in 2003. An assessment of the *Beagle 2*'s failure pinpointed many areas of concern, with a major issue being inadequate testing:

> This led to an attenuated testing programme to meet the cost and schedule constraints, thus inevitably increasing technical risk. (From Beagle 2 ESA/UK Commission of Inquiry Report, April 5, 2004, Page 4)

Look at all those big words. Boy, the Europeans sure have a way with language. Perhaps a direct word-for-word translation into American English will make it clear what the commission was trying to convey:

> They didn't test it enough, and probably goofed it all up.

The Nature of Errors in Visual Basic

You will deal with three major categories of errors in your Visual Basic applications:

Compile-time errors
Some errors are so blatant that Visual Basic will refuse to compile your application. Generally, such errors are due to simple syntax issues that can be corrected with a few keystrokes. But you can also enable features in your program that will increase the number of errors recognized by the compiler. For instance, if you set `Option Strict` to `On` in your application or source code files, implicit narrowing conversions will generate compile-time errors.

```
' ----- Assume: Option Strict On
Dim bigData As Long = 5&
Dim smallData As Integer
' ----- The next line will not compile.
smallData = bigData
```

Visual Studio 2008 includes features that help you locate and resolve compile-time errors. Such errors are marked with a "blue squiggle" below the offending syntax. Some errors also prompt Visual Studio to display corrective options through a pop-up window, as shown in Figure 9-3.

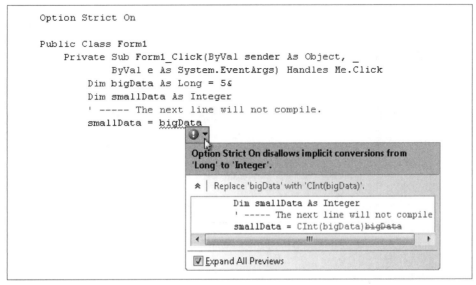

Figure 9-3. Error correction options for a narrowing conversion

Runtime errors

Runtime errors occur when a combination of data and code causes an invalid condition in what otherwise appears to be valid code. Such errors frequently occur when a user enters incorrect data into the application, but your own code can also generate runtime errors. Adequate checking of all incoming data will greatly reduce this class of errors. Consider the following block of code:

```
Public Function GetNumber( ) As Integer
    ' ----- Prompt the user for a number.
    '        Return zero if the user clicks Cancel.
    Dim useAmount As String

    ' ----- InputBox returns a string with whatever
    '        the user types in.
    useAmount = InputBox("Enter number.")
    If (IsNumeric(useAmount) = True) Then
        ' ----- Convert to an integer and return it.
        Return CInt(useAmount)
    Else
```

```
        ' ----- Invalid data. Return zero.
           Return 0
        End If
     End Function
```

This code looks pretty reasonable, and in most cases, it is. It prompts the user for a number, converts valid numbers to integer format, and returns the result. The IsNumeric function will weed out any invalid non-numeric entries. Calling this function will, in fact, return valid integers for entered numeric values, and 0 for invalid entries.

But what happens when a fascist dictator tries to use this code? As history has shown, a fascist dictator will enter a value such as "342304923940234." Because it's a valid number, it will pass the IsNumeric test with flying colors, but since it exceeds the size of the Integer data type, it will generate the dreaded runtime error shown in Figure 9-4.

Figure 9-4. An error message only a fascist dictator could love

Without additional error-handling code or checks for valid data limits, the GetNumber routine generates this runtime error, and then causes the entire program to abort. Between committing war crimes and entering invalid numeric values, there seems to be no end to the evil that fascist dictators will do.

Logic errors

Logic errors are the third, and the most insidious, type of error. They are caused by you, the programmer; you can't blame the user on this one. From process-flow issues to incorrect calculations, logic errors are the bane of software development, and they result in more required debugging time than the other two types of errors combined.

Logic errors are too personal and too varied to directly address in this book. You can force many logic errors out of your code by adding sufficient checks for invalid data, and by adequately testing your application under a variety of conditions and circumstances.

You won't have that much difficulty dealing with compile-time errors. A general understanding of Visual Basic and .NET programming concepts, and regular use of the tools included with Visual Studio 2008, will help you quickly locate and eliminate them.

The bigger issue is: what do you do with runtime errors? Even if you check all possible data and external resource conditions, it's impossible to prevent all runtime errors. You never know when a network connection will suddenly go down, or the user will trip over the printer cable, or a scratch on a DVD will generate data corruption. Anytime you deal with resources that exist outside your source code, you are taking a chance that runtime errors will occur.

Figure 9-4 showed you what Visual Basic does when it encounters a runtime error: it displays to the user a generic error dialog, and offers a chance to ignore the error (possible corruption of any unsaved data) or exit the program immediately (complete loss of any unsaved data).

Although both of these user actions leave much to the imagination, they don't instill consumer confidence in your coding skills. Trust me on this: the user will blame you for any errors generated by your application, even if the true problem was far removed from your code.

Fortunately, Visual Basic includes three tools to help you deal completely with runtime errors, if and when they occur. These three Visual Basic features—unstructured error handling, structured error handling, and unhandled error handling—can all be used in any Visual Basic application to protect the user's data—and the user—from unwanted errors.

Unstructured Error Handling

Unstructured error handling has been a part of Visual Basic since it first debuted in the early 1990s. It's simple to use, catches all possible errors in a block of code, and can be enabled or disabled as needed. By default, methods and property procedures include no error handling at all, so you must add error-handling code—unstructured or structured—to every routine where you feel it is needed.

The idea behind unstructured error handling is pretty basic. You simply add a line in your code that says, "If any errors occur at all, temporarily jump down to this other section of my procedure where I have special code to deal with it." This "other section" is called the *error handler*.

```
Public Sub ErrorProneRoutine( )
    ' ----- Any code you put here before enabling the
    '       error handler should be pretty resistant to
    '       runtime errors.

    ' ----- Turn on the error handler.
    On Error GoTo ErrorHandler

    ' ----- More code here with the risk of runtime errors.
    '       When all logic is complete, exit the routine.
    Return
```

```
ErrorHandler:
    ' ----- When an error occurs, the code temporarily jumps
    '       down here, where you can deal with it. When you're
    '       finished, call this statement:
    Resume
    ' ----- which will jump back to the code that caused
    '       the error. The "Resume" statement has a few
    '       variations available. If you don't want to go
    '       back to main code, but just want to get out of
    '       this routine as quickly as possible, call:
    Return
End Sub
```

The On Error statement enables or disables error handling in the routine. When an error occurs, Visual Basic places the details of that error in a global Err object. This object stores a text description of the error, the numeric error code of the error (if available), related online help details, and other error-specific values. I'll list the details a little later.

You can include as many On Error statements in your code as you want, and each one could direct errant code to a different label. You could have one error handler for network errors, one for file errors, one for calculation errors, and so on. Or you could have one big error handler that uses If...Then...Else statements to examine the error condition stored in the global Err object.

```
ErrorHandler:
    If (Err.Number = 5) Then
        ' ----- Handle error-code-5 issues here.
```

You can find specific error numbers for common errors in the online documentation for Visual Studio, but it is this dependence on hardcoded numbers that makes unstructured error handling less popular today than it was before .NET. Still, you are under no obligation to treat errors differently based on the type of error. As long as you can recover from error conditions reliably, it doesn't always matter what the cause of the error was. Many times, if I have enabled error handling where it's not the end of the world if the procedure reaches the end in an error-free matter, I simply report the error details to the user, and skip the errant line.

```
Public Sub DoSomeWork()
    On Error GoTo ErrorHandler
    ' ----- Logic code goes here.
    Return

ErrorHandler:
    MsgBox("An error occurred in 'DoTheWork':" & _
        Err.Description)
    Resume Next
End Sub
```

This block of code reports the error, and then uses the `Resume Next` statement (a variation of the standard `Resume` statement) to return to the code line immediately following the one that caused the error. Another option uses `Resume some_other_label`, which returns control to some specific named area of the code.

Disabling Error Handling

Using `On Error GoTo` enables a specific error handler. Although you can use a second `On Error GoTo` statement to redirect errors to another error handler in your procedure, a maximum of one error handler can be in effect at any moment. Once you have enabled an error handler, it stays in effect until the procedure ends, you redirect errors to another handler, or you specifically turn off error handling in the routine. To take this last route, issue the following statement:

```
On Error GoTo 0
```

Ignoring Errors

Your error handler doesn't have to do anything special. Consider this error-handling block:

```
ErrorHandler:
    Resume Next
```

When an error occurs, this handler immediately returns control to the line just following the one that generated the error. Visual Basic includes a shortcut for this action.

```
On Error Resume Next
```

By issuing the `On Error Resume Next` statement, all errors will populate the `Err` object (as is done for all errors, no matter how they are handled), and then skip the line generating the error. The user will not be informed of the error, and will continue to use the application in an ignorance-is-bliss stupor.

Structured Error Handling

Unstructured error handling was the only method of error handling available in Visual Basic before .NET. Although it was simple to use, it didn't fulfill the hype that surrounded the announcement that the 2002 release of Visual Basic .NET would be an object-oriented programming (OOP) system. Therefore, Microsoft also added *structured error handling* to the language, a method that uses standard objects to communicate errors, and error-handling code that is more tightly integrated with the code it monitors.

This form of error processing uses a multiline `Try...Catch...Finally` statement to catch and handle errors.

```
Try
    ' ----- Add error-prone code here.
Catch ex As Exception
    ' ----- Error-handling code here.
Finally
    ' ----- Cleanup code goes here.
End Try
```

The Try Clause

Try statements are designed to monitor smaller chunks of code. Although you could put all the source code for your procedure within the Try block, it's more common to put within that section only the statements that are likely to generate errors.

```
Try
    My.Computer.FileSystem.RenameFile(existingFile, newName)
Catch...
```

"Safe" statements can remain outside the Try portion of the `Try...End Try` statement. Exactly what constitutes a "safe" programming statement is a topic of much debate, but two types of statements are generally unsafe: (1) those statements that interact with external systems, such as disk files, network or hardware resources, or even large blocks of memory; and (2) those statements that could cause a variable or expression to exceed the designed limits of the data type for that variable or expression.

The Catch Clause

The `Catch` clause defines an error handler. As with unstructured error handling, you can include one global error handler in a `Try` statement, or you can include multiple handlers for different types of errors. Each handler includes its own `Catch` keyword.

```
Catch ex As ErrorClass
```

The ex identifier provides a variable name for the active error object that you can use within the Catch section. You can give it any name you wish; it can vary from Catch clause to Catch clause, but it doesn't have to.

ErrorClass identifies an exception class, a special class specifically designed to convey error information. The most generic exception class is `System.Exception`; other, more specific exception classes derive from `System.Exception`. Since `Try...End Try` implements "object-oriented error processing," all the errors must be stored as objects. The .NET Framework includes many predefined exception classes already derived from `System.Exception` that you can use in your application. For instance, `System.DivideByZeroException` catches any errors that (obviously) stem from dividing a number by zero.

```
Try
    result = firstNumber / secondNumber
Catch ex As System.DivideByZeroException
    MsgBox("Divide by zero error.")
Catch ex As System.OverflowException
    MsgBox("Divide resulting in an overflow.")
Catch ex As System.Exception
    MsgBox("Some other error occurred.")
End Try
```

When an error occurs, your code tests the exception against each Catch clause until it finds a matching class. The Catch clauses are examined in order from top to bottom, so make sure you put the most general one last; if you put System.Exception first, no other Catch clauses in that Try block will ever trigger because every exception matches System.Exception. How many Catch clauses you include, or which exceptions they monitor, is up to you. If you leave out all Catch clauses completely, it will act somewhat like an On Error Resume Next statement, although if an error does occur, all remaining statements in the Try block will be skipped. Execution continues with the Finally block, and then with the code following the entire Try statement.

The Finally Clause

The Finally clause represents the "do this or die" part of your Try block. If an error occurs in your Try statement, the code in the Finally section will always be processed after the relevant Catch clause is complete. If no error occurs, the Finally block will still be processed before leaving the Try statement. If you issue a Return statement somewhere in your Try statement, the Finally block will still be processed before leaving the routine. (This is getting monotonous.) If you use the Exit Try statement to exit the Try block early, the Finally block is still executed. If, while your Try block is being processed, your boss announces that a free catered lunch is starting immediately in the big meeting room and everyone is welcome, the Finally code will also be processed, but you might not be there to see it.

Finally clauses are optional, so you include one only when you need it. The only time that Finally clauses are required is when you omit all Catch clauses in a Try statement.

Unhandled Errors

I showed you earlier in the chapter how unhandled errors can lead to data corruption, crashed applications, and spiraling, out-of-control congressional spending. All good programmers understand how important error-handling code is, and they make the extra effort of including either structured or unstructured error-handling code.

Yet there are times when I, even I, as a programmer, think, "Oh, this procedure isn't doing anything that could generate errors. I'll just leave out the error-handling code and save some typing time." And then it strikes, seemingly without warning: an unhandled error. Crash! Burn! Another chunk of user data confined to the bit bucket of life.

Normally, all unhandled errors "bubble up" the call stack, looking for a procedure that includes error-handling code. For instance, consider this code:

```
Private Sub Level1( )
    On Error GoTo ErrorHandler
    Level2( )
    Return

ErrorHandler:
    MsgBox("Error Handled.")
    Resume Next
End Sub

Private Sub Level2( )
    Level3( )
End Sub

Private Sub Level3( )
    ' ----- The Err.Raise method forces an
    '          unstructured-style error.
    Err.Raise(1)
End Sub
```

When the error occurs in Level3, the application looks for an active error handler in that procedure, but finds nothing. So, it immediately exits Level3 and returns to Level2, where it looks again for an active error handler. Such a search will, sadly, be fruitless. Heartbroken, the code leaves Level2 and moves back to Level1, continuing its search for a reasonable error handler. This time it finds one. Processing immediately jumps down to the ErrorHandler block and executes the code in that section.

If Level1 didn't have an error handler, and no code farther up the stack included an error handler, the user would see the Error Message Window of Misery (refer to Figure 9-4), followed by the Dead Program of Disappointment.

Fortunately, Visual Basic does support a "catchall" error handler that traps such unmanaged exceptions and lets you do something about them. This feature works only if you have the "Enable application framework" field selected on the Application tab of the project properties. To access the code template for the global error handler, click the View Application Events button on that same project properties tab. Select "(MyApplication Events)" from the Class Name drop-down list above the source code window, and then select UnhandledException from the Method Name list. The following procedure appears in the code window:

```
Private Sub MyApplication_UnhandledException( _
     ByVal sender As Object, _
     ByVal e As Microsoft.VisualBasic. _
     ApplicationServices.UnhandledExceptionEventArgs) _
     Handles Me.UnhandledException

End Sub
```

Add your special global error-handling code to this routine. The e event argument includes an Exception member that provides access to the details of the error via a System.Exception object. The e.ExitApplication member is a Boolean property that you can modify either to continue or to exit the application. By default, it's set to True, so modify it if you want to keep the program running.

Even when the program does stay running, you will lose the active event path that triggered the error. If the error stemmed from a click on some button by the user, that entire Click event, and all of its called methods, will be abandoned immediately, and the program will wait for new input from the user.

Managing Errors

In addition to simply watching for them and screaming "Error!" there are a few other things you should know about error management in Visual Basic programs.

Generating Errors

Believe it or not, there are times when you might want to generate runtime errors in your code. In fact, many of the runtime errors you encounter in your code occur because Microsoft wrote code in the Framework Class Libraries (FCLs) that specifically generates errors. This is by design.

Let's say that you had a class property that was to accept only percentage values from 0 to 100, but as an Integer data type.

```
Private StoredPercent As Integer
Public Property InEffectPercent() As Integer
   Get
      Return StoredPercent
   End Get
   Set(ByVal value As Integer)
      StoredPercent = value
   End Set
End Property
```

Nothing is grammatically wrong with this code, but it will not stop anyone from setting the stored percent value to either 847 or –847, both outside the desired range. You can add an If statement to the Set accessor to reject invalid data, but properties don't provide a way to return a failed status code. The only way to inform the calling code of a problem is to generate an exception.

```
Set(ByVal value As Integer)
    If (value < 0) Or (value > 100) Then
        Throw New ArgumentOutOfRangeException("value", _
            value, "The allowed range is from 0 to 100.")
    Else
        StoredPercent = value
    End If
End Set
```

Now, attempts to set the InEffectPercent property to a value outside the 0-to-100 range will generate an error, an error that can be caught by On Error or Try...Catch error handlers. The Throw statement accepts a System.Exception (or derived) object as its argument, and sends that exception object up the call stack on a quest for an error handler.

Similar to the Throw statement is the Err.Raise method. It lets you generate errors using a number-based error system more familiar to Visual Basic 6.0 and earlier environments. I recommend that you use the Throw statement, even if you employ unstructured error handling elsewhere in your code.

Mixing Error-Handling Methods

You are free to mix both unstructured and structured error-handling methods broadly in your application, but a single procedure or method may use only one of these methods. That is, you may not use both On Error and Try...Catch...Finally in the same routine. A routine that uses On Error may call another routine that uses Try...Catch...Finally with no problems.

Now you may be thinking to yourself, "Self, I can easily see times when I would want to use unstructured error handling, and other times when I would opt for the more structured approach." It all sounds very reasonable, but let me warn you in advance that there are error-handling zealots out there who will ridicule you for decades if you ever use an On Error statement in your code. For these programmers, "object-oriented purity" is essential, and any code that uses nonobject methods to achieve what could be done through an OOP approach must be destroyed.

 I'm about to use a word that I forbid my elementary-school-aged son to use. If you have tender ears, cover them now, though it won't protect you from seeing the word on the printed page.

Rejecting the On Error statement like this is just plain *stupid*. As you may remember from earlier chapters, everything in your .NET application is object-oriented, since all the code appears in the context of an object. If you are using unstructured error handling, you can still get to the relevant exception object through the Err.GetException( ) method, so it's not really an issue of objects.

Determining when to use structured or unstructured error handling is no different from deciding to use C# or Visual Basic to write your applications. For most applications, the choice is irrelevant. One language may have some esoteric features that may steer you in that direction (such as optional method arguments in Visual Basic), but the other 99.9% of the features are pretty much identical.

The same is true of error-handling methods. There may be times when one is just plain better than the other. For instance, consider the following code that calls three methods, none of which includes its own error handler:

```
On Error Resume Next
RefreshPart1( )
RefreshPart2( )
RefreshPart3( )
```

Clearly, I don't care whether an error occurs in one of the routines or not. If an error causes an early exit from RefreshPart1, the next routine, RefreshPart2, will still be called, and so on. I often need more diligent error-checking code than this, but in low-impact code, this is sufficient. To accomplish the same thing using structured error handling would be a little more involved.

```
Try
    RefreshPart1( )
Catch
End Try
Try
    RefreshPart2( )
Catch
End Try
Try
    RefreshPart3( )
Catch
End Try
```

That's a lot of extra code for the same functionality. If you're an On Error statement hater, by all means use the second block of code. But if you are a more reasonable programmer, the type of programmer who would read a book such as this, use each method as it fits into your coding design.

The System.Exception Class

The System.Exception class is the base class for all structured exceptions. When an error occurs, you can examine its members to determine the exact nature of the error. You also use this class (or one of its derived classes) to build your own custom exception in anticipation of using the Throw statement. Table 9-1 lists the members of this object.

Table 9-1. Members of the System.Exception class

Object member	Description
Data property	Provides access to a collection of key-value pairs, each providing additional exception-specific information.
HelpLink property	Identifies online help location information relevant to this exception.
InnerException property	If an exception is a side effect of another error, the original error appears here.
Message property	A textual description of the error.
Source property	Identifies the name of the application or object that caused the error.
StackTrace property	Returns a string that fully documents the current stack trace, the list of all active procedure calls that led to the statement causing the error.
TargetSite property	Identifies the name of the method that triggered the error.

Classes derived from System.Exception may include additional properties that provide additional detail for a specific error type.

The Err Object

The Err object provides access to the most recent error through its various members. Anytime an error occurs, Visual Basic documents the details of the error in this object's members. It's often accessed within an unstructured error handler to reference or display the details of the error. Table 9-2 lists the members of this object.

Table 9-2. Members of the Err object

Object member	Description
Clear method	Clear all the properties in the Err object, setting them to their default values. Normally, you use the Err object only to determine the details of a triggered error. But you can also use it to initiate an error with your own error details. See the description of the Raise method later in the table.
Description property	A textual description of the error.
Erl property	The line number label nearest to where the error occurred. In modern Visual Basic applications, numeric line labels are almost never used, so this field is generally 0.
HelpContext property	The location within an online help file relevant to the error. If this property and the HelpFile property are set, the user can access relevant online help information.
HelpFile property	The online help file related to the active error.
LastDLLError property	The numeric return value from the most recent call to a pre-.NET DLL, whether it is an error or not.
Number property	The numeric code for the active error.
Raise method	Use this method to generate a runtime error. Although this method does include some arguments for setting other properties in the Err object, you can also set the properties yourself before calling the Raise method. Any properties you set will be retained in the object for examination by the error-handler code that receives the error.
Source property	The name of the application, class, or object that generated the active error.

The Debug Object

Visual Basic 6.0 (and earlier) included a handy tool that would quickly output debug information from your program, displaying such output in the "Immediate Window" of the Visual Basic development environment.

```
Debug.Print "Reached point G in code"
```

The .NET version of Visual Basic enhances the Debug object with more features, and a slight change in syntax. The Print method is replaced with WriteLine; a separate Write method outputs text without a final carriage return.

```
Debug.WriteLine("Reached point G in code")
```

Everything you output using the WriteLine (or similar) method goes to a series of "listeners" attached to the Debug object. You can add your own listeners, including output to a work file. But the Debug object is really used only when debugging your program. Once you compile a final release, none of the Debug-related features works anymore, by design.

If you wish to log status data from a released application, consider using the My.Application.Log object instead (or My.Log in ASP.NET programs). Similar to the Debug object, the Log object sends its output to any number of registered listeners. By default, all output goes to the standard debug output (just like the Debug object) and to a logfile created specifically for your application's assembly. See the online help for the My.Application.Log object for information on configuring this object to meet your needs.

Other Visual Basic Error Features

The Visual Basic language includes a few other error-specific statements and features that you may find useful:

ErrorToString *function*
> This method returns the error message associated with a numeric system error code. For instance, ErrorToString(10) returns "This array is fixed or temporarily locked." It is useful only with older unstructured error codes.

IsError *function*
> When you supply an object argument to this function, it returns True if the object is a System.Exception (or derived) object.

Summary

The best program in the world would never generate errors, I guess. But come on, it's not reality. If a multimillion-dollar Mars probe is going to crash on a planet millions of miles away, even after years of advanced engineering, my customer-tracking application for a local video rental shop is certainly going to have a bug or two. But you can mitigate the impact of these bugs using the error-management features included with Visual Basic.

Project

This chapter's project code will be somewhat brief. Error-handling code will appear throughout the entire application, but we'll add it in little by little as we craft the project. For now, let's just focus on the central error-handling routines that will take some basic action when an error occurs anywhere in the program. As for lambda expressions, we'll hold off on such code until a later chapter.

General Error Handler

As important and precise as error handling needs to be, the typical business application will not encounter a large variety of error types. Applications such as the Library Project are mainly vulnerable to three types of errors: (1) data entry errors; (2) errors that occur when reading data from, or writing data to, a database table; and (3) errors related to printing. Sure, there may be numeric overflow errors or other errors related to in-use data, but it's mostly interactions with external resources, such as the database, that concern us.

Because of the limited types of errors occurring in the application, it's possible to write a generic routine that informs the user of the error in a consistent manner. Each time a runtime error occurs, we will call this central routine, just to let the user know what's going on. The code block where the error occurred can then decide whether to take any special compensating action, or continue on as though no error occurred.

PROJECT ACCESS

Load the Chapter 9 (Before) Code project, either through the New Project templates or by accessing the project directly from the installation directory. To see the code in its final form, load Chapter 9 (After) Code instead.

In the project, open the *General.vb* class file, and add the following code as a new method to Module General.

INSERT SNIPPET

Insert Chapter 9, Snippet Item 1.

```
Public Sub GeneralError(ByVal routineName As String, _
    ByVal theError As System.Exception)
    ' ----- Report an error to the user.
    MsgBox("The following error occurred at location '" & _
        routineName & "':" & vbCrLf & vbCrLf & _
        theError.Message, _
```

```
        MsgBoxStyle.OKOnly Or MsgBoxStyle.Exclamation, _
        ProgramTitle)
   End Sub
```

Not much to that code, is there? So, here's how it works. When you encounter an error in some routine, the in-effect error handler calls the central GeneralError method.

```
Public Sub SomeRoutine( )
   On Error GoTo ErrorHandler

   ' ----- Lots of code here.
   Return

ErrorHandler:
   GeneralError("SomeRoutine", Err.GetException( ))
   Resume Next
End Sub
```

You can use it with structured errors as well.

```
Try
   ' ----- Troubling code here.
Catch ex As System.Exception
   GeneralError("SomeRoutine", ex)
End Try
```

The purpose of the GeneralError global method is simple: communicate to the user that an error occurred, and then move on. It's meant to be simple, and it is simple. You could enhance the routine with some additional features. Logging of the error out to a file (or any other active log listener) might assist you later if you needed to examine application-generated errors. Add the following code to the routine, just after the MsgBox command, to record the exception.

INSERT SNIPPET

Insert Chapter 9, Snippet Item 2.

```
My.Application.Log.WriteException(theError)
```

Of course, if an error occurs while writing to the log, that would be a big problem, so add one more line to the start of the GeneralError routine.

INSERT SNIPPET

Insert Chapter 9, Snippet Item 3.

```
On Error Resume Next
```

Unhandled Error Capture

As I mentioned earlier, it's a good idea to include a global error handler in your code, in case some error gets past your defenses. To include this code, display all files in the Solution Explorer using the Show All Files button, open the *ApplicationEvents.vb* file, and add the following code to the MyApplication class.

INSERT SNIPPET

Insert Chapter 9, Snippet Item 4.

```
Private Sub MyApplication_UnhandledException( _
      ByVal sender As Object, ByVal e As Microsoft. _
      VisualBasic.ApplicationServices. _
      UnhandledExceptionEventArgs) Handles _
      Me.UnhandledException
   ' ----- Record the error, and keep running.
   e.ExitApplication = False
   GeneralError("Unhandled Exception", e.Exception)
End Sub
```

Since we already have the global GeneralError routine to log our errors, we might as well take advantage of it here.

That's it for functional and error-free programming. In the next chapter, which covers database interactions, we'll make frequent use of this error-handling code.

ADO.NET

If you have ever read any programming books related to Microsoft development technologies, you have already read a chapter just like this one. It seems that every Windows programming book has an obligatory chapter on database interaction. The reason for this widespread coverage comes as no surprise: Microsoft comes out with a new database technology every two years or so.

If you are new to Windows development, you haven't yet been briefed on the following sometimes conflicting, sometimes complementary database interaction tools:

- ODBC—Open DataBase Connectivity
- ISAM—Indexed Sequential Access Method
- DAO—Data Access Objects
- RDO—Remote Data Objects
- OLE DB—Object Linking and Embedding for Databases
- ADO—ActiveX Data Objects

When you look at this list, you might think, "Wow, that's great. There are so many options to choose from." You would be foolish to think this. This list isn't great; it's terrible. Imagine, just for a moment, that we weren't talking about database interfaces, but about other, more practical issues. What if you had to replace the engine in your car every two years? What if the steering column had to be replaced annually? What if you had to replace the oil every 3,500 miles or three months, whichever came first? Could you imagine life in such a world?

Whenever Microsoft introduced a new database object technology into the mix, it was quickly followed by a flurry of reprogramming to bring older "legacy" Visual Basic (and other) applications up to the latest database technology. This wasn't always possible, as time and budget constraints kept organizations on older platforms. For nearly a decade I maintained a quarter-million-line application using DAO, only recently updating it to .NET technologies. Although ADO, a more powerful and flexible technology than DAO, was available for many years during that interim, the cost at the time to move from DAO to ADO was prohibitive.

So far, it seems that *ADO.NET*, Microsoft's database library for .NET, is different. It's been out for about seven years (as of this writing), and Microsoft hasn't yet teased programmers with a replacement. ADO.NET is quite flexible, and that flexibility will hopefully allow it to stretch itself over new advances in technology for the foreseeable future.

If you are familiar with the ADO technology, prepare to forget it. ADO.NET is not the natural successor to ADO. It's a completely new technology that is unrelated to ADO, and although it shares some terminology with ADO and other older tools, ADO.NET does this only to play with your mind.

What Is ADO.NET?

ADO.NET is a set of classes, included with the .NET Framework, that represent the primary method by which .NET applications interact with relational databases and other open and proprietary data management systems. But it's not just for interaction; ADO.NET is, in reality, a partial in-memory relational database all by itself. You can create tables and relationships (joins) with ADO.NET objects, add and remove records, query tables based on selection criteria, and do other simple tasks that are typical of standalone relational database systems.

All classes included with ADO.NET appear in the System.Data namespace; other subordinate namespaces provide derived classes geared toward specific database platforms. For instance, the System.Data.SqlClient namespace targets SQL Server databases, and System.Data.OracleClient focuses on Oracle RDBMS systems. Other database providers can develop streamlined implementations of the various ADO.NET classes for use with their own systems, and supply them as a separate namespace.

ADO.NET implements a *disconnected* data experience. In traditional database programming, especially in desktop applications, the connection between an application and its database was fixed and long-term. When the program started up, the connection started up. When the program exited many hours later, the connection finally ended. But in a world of massively scalable web sites, keeping a database connected for hours on end is sometimes wasteful and often impossible.

ADO.NET encourages you to open data connections just long enough to get the data that fulfills your immediate needs. Once you have the data, you drop the connection until the next time you need to retrieve, insert, or update database content. If you issue the following SQL statement:

```
SELECT * FROM Customer WHERE BalanceDue > 0
```

you have a choice of (1) scanning through all the records once in a quick and simple manner; or (2) loading the data into an in-memory table-like object, closing the connection, and working with the loaded records as though they were the originals.

If you use the first method, you can take your sweet time waltzing through the records, taking many minutes to process each one. But ADO.NET frowns upon this type of selfish behavior. The goal is to get in and get out as quickly as you can.

Because of the disconnected nature of ADO.NET, some techniques common in database applications need to change. For instance, the long-term locking of database records during a user modification ("pessimistic concurrency") is difficult to accomplish in ADO.NET's disconnected environment. You will have to use other methods, such as transactions or atomic stored procedure features, to accomplish the same goals.

Overview of ADO.NET

ADO.NET divides its world into two hemispheres: *providers* and the *data set*. Imagine your kitchen as the world of ADO.NET, with your refrigerator representing the provider, and the oven/stove as the data set. The provider "provides" access to some content, such as food, or an Oracle database (which normally appears in the meat-and-cheese drawer). It's a long-term storage facility, and content that goes in there usually stays in there for quite a while. If something is removed, it's because it is no longer valid, or has become corrupted.

A data set, like an oven, prepares (cooks) and presents content originally obtained from the long-term storage. Once presented, it will either be consumed, or be returned to the refrigerator for more long-term storage. This analogy isn't perfect; in fact, something just doesn't smell right about it. But it conveys the basic idea: providers give you access to stored data, some of which can be moved into and processed through an application and its data set on a short-term basis.

Providers

Large database systems, such as SQL Server and Oracle, are standalone "servers" (hence the "SQL *Server*" name) that interact with client tools and applications only indirectly. These systems generally accept network connections from clients through a TCP/IP port or similar connection. Once authenticated, the client makes all its requests through this connection before disconnecting from the system.

Back in the early 1990s, Microsoft implemented *ODBC* (based on other existing standards) as a common system through which clients would connect to database servers, as well as other simpler data sources. Clients no longer had to worry about all the networking protocols needed to talk with a database; all that code was included in the ODBC driver.

Microsoft later released a similar data connection system called *OLE DB*, based on ActiveX technology. OLE DB drivers for common systems soon appeared, although you could still get to ODBC resources through a generic ODBC driver built into OLE DB.

In .NET, both ODBC and OLE DB are replaced by *providers*, libraries of code that provide all the communication between the database and your application. Providers are an integral part of ADO.NET, and you will have to use them to get to your databases. Fortunately, providers exist for the main database systems, and an "OLE DB provider" exists for systems without their own providers.

Four primary objects make up the programmer's view of the provider:

The Connection *object*

> This object directs communication between your program and the data source. It includes properties and methods that let you indicate the location or connection parameters for the data source. Multicommand transactions are managed at this object level.

The Command *object*

> This object takes the SQL statement you provide, and prepares it for transport through the Connection object. You can include parameters in your command for stored procedure and complex statement support.

The DataReader *object*

> The DataReader provides a simple and efficient way to retrieve results from a data query. Other objects in ADO.NET use it to receive and redirect data for use within your program, but your code can use it directly to process the results of a SELECT statement or other data retrieval action.

The DataAdapter *object*

> This object is what makes communication between a data set and the rest of a provider possible. One of its primary jobs is to modify data manipulation statements (the SELECT, INSERT, UPDATE, and DELETE statements) generated by a data set into a format that can be used by the related data source.

Using these objects is a little involved, but not hard to understand. To connect to a typical relational database, such as SQL Server, and process data, follow these steps:

1. Establish a connection to your data source using a Connection object.
2. Wrap a SQL statement in a Command object.
3. Execute that Command object in the context of the established Connection.
4. If any results are to be returned, use either a DataReader to scan through the records, or a combination of a DataAdapter and DataSet (or DataTable) to retrieve or store the results.
5. Close all objects that you opened to process the data.

Although the .NET Framework includes data providers for a few different data systems, the remainder of this chapter's discussion focuses only on the SQL Server provider, exposed through the System.Data.SqlClient namespace.

SQL Server 2005 includes support for a feature called "User Instances," for use with SQL Server 2005 Express Edition databases. This feature allows a low-privilege user to access a specific SQL Server Express database file without the need for an administrator to establish SQL Server security settings for that user. This feature is useful in environments where the related software was installed through the *ClickOnce* deployment method (discussed in Chapter 25) without administrator involvement. It also requires specific reconfiguration of the SQL Server Express installation before use. For more information on this feature, reference the "Working with User Instances" article in the ADO.NET portion of the MSDN documentation supplied with your Visual Studio installation.

Data Sets

If you are going to do more than just quickly scan the data that comes back from a DataReader query, you will probably use a data set to store, manage, and optionally update your data. Each data set provides a generic disconnected view of data, whether it is data from a provider, or data that you build through code. Although each provider is tied to a specific database platform (such as Oracle) or communication standard (such as OLE DB), the objects in the data set realm are generic, and can interact with any of the platform-specific providers.

Three main objects make up the world of data sets:

The DataSet *object*
> Each DataSet object acts like a mini database. You can add as many tables to a DataSet as you like, and establish foreign-key relationships between the fields of these tables. The internals of each DataSet are an unfathomable mystery, but you can export an entire DataSet to XML, and load it back in again later if you must.

The DataTable *object*
> Each table in your DataSet uses a separate DataTable object, accessible through the DataSet's Tables collection. DataTables are also useful as standalone objects. If you plan to add only a single table to your DataSet, you might opt to just use a DataTable object alone without a DataSet. Within each DataTable object, separate DataColumn and DataRow objects establish the field definitions and the actual data values, respectively.

The DataRelation *object*
> Use the DataRelation objects, stored within a DataSet's Relations collection, to establish field-level relationships and constraints between columns in your DataTable objects.

Although data sets are most often used with providers, you can use them independently to build your own in-memory collection of tables and relationships. This is similar to the "client-side record sets" that you could build with pre-.NET ADO objects, although the features included with ADO.NET make data sets much more powerful than the older record sets.

 Visual Basic 2008 includes "Typed DataSets," a feature used to integrate a DataSet with a specific data or record format. You may find them useful in your applications, but I won't be discussing them in this book. The new LINQ technology uses a similar feature to help establish relationships between LINQ and database tables.

Data Sets Versus No Data Sets

When used together, providers and data sets give an end-to-end interface to individual data values, from the fields in your database tables to the in-memory items of a DataRow record. Figure 10-1 shows this object interaction.

When you interact with data from an external database, you always use the provider classes, but it's up to you whether you want to also use data sets. There are pros and cons of both methods, some of which appear in Table 10-1.

Table 10-1. The pros and cons of using data sets

Without data sets	With data sets
You must supply all SQL statements, in the format the provider expects. This is true for all SELECT, INSERT, UPDATE, and DELETE requests.	The DataSet and DataAdapter work together to craft many of the SQL statements on your behalf.
Data retrieved through the DataReader is read-only. You must issue separate commands to update data.	Data read from the database can be modified in-memory, and updated as a batch with a single method call.
Data transfers are very efficient, since no overhead is needed to move data into a complex data set structure.	There may be a performance hit as the data set builds the necessary objects required for each transferred record.
Memory allocation is limited to a single record's worth of data fields, plus some minimal overhead.	Memory allocation is required for the entire result set, plus overhead for every table, field, column, and row in the result set.
Only a single DataReader can be open at a time (unless the provider supports MARS, which I'll discuss in just a bit).	Any number of data sets can be in use at once.
A live connection to the database exists as long as a DataReader is in use. If it takes you five minutes to scan a result set because you are doing a lot of per-record analysis, the connection will be active for the full five minutes.	Data connections are maintained only long enough to transfer data from or to the database.
DataReaders present one record at a time. The records must be processed in the order they arrive.	You can jump around the records in a data set, and reorganize them to meet your needs.
You spend a lot of time working with strings (for SQL statements) and raw data fields.	All data fields are organized logically, just like they are in the actual database. You can interact with them directly.

Table 10-1. The pros and cons of using data sets (continued)

Without data sets	With data sets
Each `Command` and `Connection` works with a single provider-supported data source.	Different `DataTables` within your `DataSet` can connect to distinct data sources. Also, you can hand-craft data so that each `DataRow` contains data from different sources.
Because you manage all SQL statements, you have a (relatively) high level of control over the entire data interaction process.	Because the view of the data is abstracted, you have a (relatively) limited level of control over the entire data interaction process (although advanced use of data sets does give you some additional control).

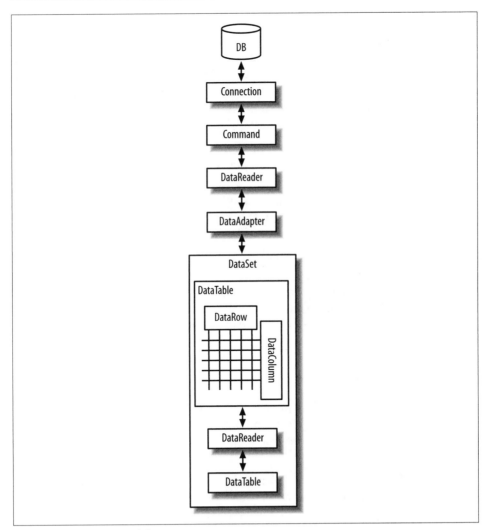

Figure 10-1. Providers and data sets in action

For me, the last entry in Table 10-1 is the clincher. The job of a programmer is to control the software experience of the user, and the more control, the better. That's why I generally hate "wizards" and "code generators" that take control away from me, the developer. There are limits to my paranoia, though; I put up with the basic template code supplied by Visual Studio when creating new projects. Still, you'll see my code-controlling personality in the Library Project, with my heavy dependence on `DataReaders` over `DataSets`. When I do store data long-term, I usually just stick the data in a `DataTable` without a containing `DataSet`.

MARS Support

I mentioned something called MARS in Table 10-1. MARS stands for "Multiple Active Result Sets." Normally, a single `Connection` object allows only a single `DataReader` to be in use at any given moment. This limitation is bidirectional. If you are scanning a `DataReader` via a `SELECT` statement, you cannot issue `INSERT`, `UPDATE`, or `DELETE` statements on that same connection until you close the `DataReader`.

With the introduction of MARS, a single connection can now handle multiple data transmission activities in either direction. SQL Server added MARS support with its 2005 release; Oracle has supported MARS-like features since the initial .NET release.

MARS connections seem like a feature you would always want to enable. But they do add additional overhead to your application that can slow it down. Also, MARS does not always mix well with multithreaded applications.

Connecting to SQL Server with Visual Studio

Visual Studio has many built-in tools that make working with data as simple as drag-and-drop. Well, it's not really that quick. But by answering a few questions and dragging and dropping one item, you can build an entire application that lets you edit data in your database. Let's try it together.

Creating a Data Source

Start up a new Windows Forms project in Visual Studio—just a plain Windows Forms project, not one of the Library-specific projects. Selecting the Data → Show Data Sources menu command brings up the Data Sources panel, as shown in Figure 10-2.

New projects don't include any data sources by default, so we need to add one. Click on the Add New Data Source link in the Data Sources panel. The Data Source Configuration Wizard guides you through the data source creation process:

1. The first step asks, "Where will the application get data from?" Select Database and click the Next button.

Figure 10-2. Where are the data sources?

2. The second step asks, "Which data connection should your application use to connect to the database?" We'll have to create a new connection for the Library database we designed way back in Chapter 4. Click the New Connection button.

3. The Choose Data Source dialog appears. Select Microsoft SQL Server from the "Data source" list, and then click the Continue button. If you have accessed this dialog before and checked the "Always use this selection" field, it's possible that this dialog will not appear at all.

4. The Add Connection dialog appears to collect the details of the new connection. If the "Data source" field contains something other than "Microsoft SQL Server," click the Change button to alter the connection type using the dialog mentioned in step 3.

5. Back on the Add Connection form fill in the "Server name" field with the name of your SQL Server instance. Hopefully, this drop-down list already has the instances listed, but if not, you'll have to enter it yourself. The default for SQL Server Express is the name of your computer, with "\SQLEXPRESS" attached. If your computer name is "MYSYSTEM," the instance name would be "MYSYS-TEM\SQLEXPRESS."

6. Configure your authentication settings in the "Log on to the server" section. I used standard Windows authentication, but it depends on how you set up the database in Chapter 4.

7. In the "Connect to a database" section, either select or type in **Library** for the database name.

8. Click the Test Connection button to make sure it all works. When you're finished, click the OK button to create the new connection.

9. OK, we're back on the Data Source Configuration Wizard form. The connection we just created should now appear in the list, as shown in Figure 10-3. Click Next.

Figure 10-3. The new database connection, ready to use

10. The next panel asks whether this data source should become part of the configurable settings for this project. We'll get into the settings features of Visual Basic in Chapter 14. For now, just accept the default and click Next.

11. We're almost there. Only 27 more steps to go! Just kidding. This is the last step in creating the data source. The final panel shows a list of the data-generating features in the Library database. Open the Tables branch and select Activity, as shown in Figure 10-4. Then click Finish.

Check out the Data Sources panel shown in Figure 10-5. It includes the new LibraryDataSet data source with its link to the Activity table.

Using a Data Source

So, what is this data source anyway? It is simply a link to some portion of your database, wrapped up in a typical .NET object. Now that it's part of your project, you can use it to access the data in the Activity table through your project's code, or by drag-and-drop. In the Data Sources panel, you will find that the "Activity" entry is actually a drop-down list. Select Details from the list, as I've done in Figure 10-6. (The surface of Form1 must be displayed for this to work.)

Finally, drag-and-drop the "Activity" entry onto the surface of Form1. When you let go, Visual Studio will add a set of controls to the form, plus a few more non-user-interface controls just below the form (see Figure 10-7).

Figure 10-4. The final step is to select the Activity table

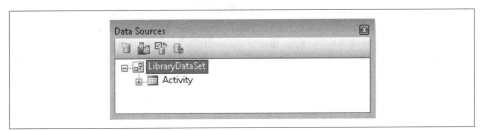

Figure 10-5. Finally, a real data source

Figure 10-6. Select the Details view instead of DataGrid

Figure 10-7. A complete program without writing a single line of code

By just dragging-and-dropping, Visual Studio added all the necessary controls and links to turn your form into a turbo-charged Activity table editor. Try it now by pressing the F5 key. In the running program, you can use the Microsoft Access-style record access "VCR" control to move between the records in the Activity table. You can also modify the values of each record, add new records, or delete existing records (but please restore things back to their original state when you are done; we'll need all the original records later). Talk about power! Talk about simplicity! Talk about unemployment lines! Who needs highly paid programmers like us when Visual Studio can do this for you?

Data Binding

In reality, Visual Studio isn't doing all that much. It's using a feature called "data binding" to link the on-form fields with the data source, the Library database's Activity table. *Data binding* is a feature built into Windows Forms controls that allows them to automatically display and edit values in an associated data source, such as a database. It's all sorted out through the properties of the control.

Select the FullNameTextBox control added to this project's form, and then examine its properties. Right at the top is a property section named "(DataBindings)." Its Text subproperty contains "ActivityBindingSource – FullName," a reference to the ActivityBindingSource non-user-interface control also added by Visual Studio. ActivityBindingSource, in turn, contains a reference to the LibraryDataSet object, the data source we created earlier. That data source links to SQL Server, to the Library database, and finally to the Activity table and its FullName field. Piece of cake!

If you count up all the objects involved in this data-binding relationship, you come up with something like 5,283 distinct objects. It's no wonder that Visual Studio did so much of the work for you. Data binding provides a lot of convenience, but it also takes away a lot of your *control* as a developer. Although there are properties and events that let you manage aspects of the data binding and its update process, most of the essential code is hidden away inside the data-binding portions of .NET. You may not touch, taste, fold, spindle, or mutilate it, and that's just bad. A quick look at one of my core programming beliefs says it all: *good software includes maximum control for the developer, and minimum control for the user.*

Part of your job as a developer is to provide a highly scripted environment for the user to access important data. This requires that you have control over the user's experience through your source code. Certainly, you will defer much of that control to others when you use any third-party supplied tools. As long as those tools allow you to control the user experience to your level of satisfaction, that's great. But I've always been disappointed with data binding, except when implementing a read-only display of data from the database. Similar features were in Visual Basic long before .NET arrived, and they have always made it difficult for the developer to control the various data interactions on the form.

Fortunately, if you eschew the data-binding features, Visual Basic will pass to you the responsibility of managing all interactions between the database and the user.

Interacting with SQL Server in Code

Communicating with a database yourself is definitely more work than dragging-and-dropping data sources, but whoever said programming was a cakewalk?

Building the Connection String

The first step on the road to the data-controlling lifestyle is to connect to the database using a connection string. If you have used ADO, you are already familiar with the connection strings used in ADO.NET, for they are generally the same. You probably also know that it is through connection strings that Microsoft keeps a tight rein on Windows developers. It's not that they are complex; they are nothing more than strings of semicolon-separated parameters. But the parameters to include, and their exact format, are the stuff of legend. The MSDN documentation included with Visual Studio does provide some examples of connection strings, but not much detail. A third-party resource, *http://www.connectionstrings.com*, also provides numerous examples of valid connection string formats.

The connection string we will use to connect to the Library database, fortunately, isn't overly complex. If you use your Microsoft Windows login to connect to the database, the following string will meet your needs (as one unbroken line):

```
Data Source=instance_name;Initial Catalog=Library;
   ↳Integrated Security=true
```

where *instance_name* is replaced by the name of your SQL Server instance or data source. The connection string we built visually earlier used "MYSYSTEM\SQLEX-PRESS" for its data source name.

To use SQL Server user IDs and passwords, try this format:

```
Data Source=instance_name;Initial Catalog=Library;
   ↳User ID=sa;Password=xyz
```

Of course, replace the user ID (*sa*) and password (*xyz*) with your own settings. If you want to include MARS support in your connection, add another semicolon-delimited component:

```
MultipleActiveResultSets=true
```

 Other connection string options let you connect to a SQL Server Express (SSE) database file directly, alter the "user instancing" method (often used with ClickOnce-deployed databases), and make other adjustments. Although they are somewhat scattered about, you can find these options documented in the MSDN documentation that comes with Visual Studio.

Establishing the Connection

Use the connection string to create a SqlConnection object, and then open the connection. Create a brand-new Windows Forms application in Visual Studio. Add a Button control to the surface of Form1. Double-click the button to access its Click event handler. Then add the following code to that handler:

```
' ----- Assumes:
'        Imports System.Data
Dim libraryDB As New SqlClient.SqlConnection( _
    "Data Source=MYSYSTEM\SQLEXPRESS;" & _
    "Initial Catalog=Library;Integrated Security=true")
libraryDB.Open( )
```

Make sure you replace "MYSYSTEM" with your own system's name. This entire block of code sure seems a lot easier to me than those 10 or 15 steps you had to follow earlier when setting up the connection through Visual Studio.

Using SQL Statements

Once the connection is open, you can issue SELECT, INSERT, UPDATE, DELETE, or any other data manipulation language (DML) or data definition language (DDL) statement accepted by the database. A SqlCommand object prepares your SQL statement for use by the open connection. Here's a statement that returns the description for entry number 1 in the Activity table:

```
SELECT FullName FROM Activity WHERE ID = 1
```

Creating a `SqlCommand` object that wraps around this statement is easy. The constructor for the `SqlCommand` object takes a SQL statement, plus a `SqlConnection` object. Add the following code to the end of your `Button1_Click` event handler:

```
Dim sqlStatement As New SqlClient.SqlCommand( _
    "SELECT FullName FROM Activity WHERE ID = 1", libraryDB)
```

Processing the Results

The only thing left to do is to pass the SQL statement to the database, via the connection, and retrieve the results as a `SqlDataReader` object. Once we get the data, process each record using that object's `Read` method. You access individual fields by name through the default `Item` collection. Add this additional code to the end of your `Button1_Click` event handler:

```
Dim sqlResults As SqlClient.SqlDataReader = _
    sqlStatement.ExecuteReader( )
sqlResults.Read( )
MsgBox(CStr(sqlResults.Item("FullName")))

' ----- Since Item is the default property, this works too...
' MsgBox(CStr(sqlResults("FullName")))

' ----- This shortened syntax also works...
' MsgBox(CStr(sqlResults!FullName))
```

Taking all these blocks of code together displays the message shown in Figure 10-8.

Figure 10-8. Basic data retrieved from a database

When you're finished, make sure you close all the connections you opened. Add this last bit of code to the end of your `Button1_Click` event handler:

```
sqlResults.Close( )
libraryDB.Close( )
```

Modifying Data

Making changes to database tables is coded just like data retrieval, but no `SqlDataReader` is needed. Instead of using the `ExecuteReader` method, use the `ExecuteNonQuery` method, which returns no results.

```
Dim sqlStatement As New SqlClient.SqlCommand( _
    "UPDATE Activity SET FullName = 'Sleeps all day'" & _
    " WHERE ID = 1", libraryDB)
sqlStatement.ExecuteNonQuery()
```

SQL Server 2005 has a convenient feature that will return a single field from a new record created via an INSERT statement. If you look back at the Library Project's database design, you will see that the ID fields in many of the tables are generated automatically. Traditionally, if you wanted to immediately retrieve the ID field for a new record, you first had to INSERT the record, and then perform a separate SELECT statement, returning the new record's ID field.

```
INSERT INTO CodeSeries (FullName)
    VALUES ('Children''s Books')

SELECT ID FROM CodeSeries
  WHERE FullName = 'Children''s Books'
```

SQL Server's OUTPUT INSERTED clause combines both of these statements into a single action.

```
INSERT INTO CodeSeries (FullName)
    OUTPUT INSERTED.ID
    VALUES ('Children''s Books')
```

When the INSERT is complete, SQL Server returns the ID field as a result set, just as though you had issued a separate SELECT statement. The SqlCommand's ExecuteScalar method is a simple way to retrieve a single value from a SQL query.

```
sqlStatement = New SqlClient.SqlCommand( _
    "INSERT INTO CodeSeries (FullName) " & _
    "OUTPUT INSERTED.ID VALUES ('Children''s Books')", _
    libraryDB)
Dim newID As Integer = CInt(sqlStatement.ExecuteScalar())
```

Database Transactions

Transactions enable "all or nothing" actions across multiple SQL statements. Once started, either all the SQL statements issued within the context of the transaction complete, or none of them complete. If you have 10 data updates to perform, but the database fails after only 5 of them, you can *roll back* the transaction. The database reverses the earlier statements, restoring the data to what it was before the transaction began. (Updates from other users are not affected by the rollback.) If all statements succeed, you can *commit* the entire transaction, making all of its changes permanent.

For SQL Server databases, transactions are managed through the provider's SqlTransaction object. Like the other ADO.NET features, it's easy to use. A transaction begins with a BeginTransaction method call on the connection.

```
Public atomicSet As SqlClient.SqlTransaction = _
    libraryDB.BeginTransaction()
```

To include a SQL statement in a transaction, assign the SqlTransaction object to the SqlCommand object's Transaction property.

```
sqlStatement.Transaction = atomicSet
```

Then call the appropriate Execute method on the command. When all commands complete, use the transaction's Commit method to make the changes permanent.

```
atomicSet.Commit( )
```

If, instead, you need to abort the transaction, use the Rollback method.

```
atomicSet.Rollback( )
```

ADO.NET Entity Framework

The release of ADO.NET included with Version 3.5 of the .NET Framework (that's the version that comes with Visual Studio 2008) includes a new component: the ADO.NET Entity Framework. Part entity-relationship modeling tool, part code generator, this new technology helps you craft logical data views of the data stored in your relational database or other data source.

The Entity Framework lets you design three types of objects based on your stored data: *entities* (similar to tables), *relationships* (database joins), and *entity sets* (related entities). Each type is represented by objects that expose the members of your core database in a more programmable fashion. For instance, you can design an entity object representing a table in your database, and the object's members can represent the fields in a single record.

"So what," you say? It sounds like the same features built into ADO.NET's DataTable object? But wait, there's more. What makes the Entity Framework so useful is (1) its mapping of physical data to logical views; (2) its support for entity inheritance; and (3) its ability to act as an ADO.NET provider.

Data mapping

The mapping of data is similar to creating a "view" in a traditional relational database; you can create entities that are built up from multiple source records spread across multiple database tables. This includes parent-child views of data; you can create an Order entity that refers to both the main order record and the multiple order line items included in the order. Logically, this new entity is treated as a single queryable element. When you request data through the new entity, you don't have to teach it each time how to join and relate the various source pieces of data.

Entity inheritance

Once you have an entity defined, you can extend the structure of the entity through inheritance. For instance, you might want to create an entity called InternalOrder based on your original Order entity, adding members that track data specific to internal orders. These new fields might be in a specialized table, triggered by a Boolean flag on the main table of orders. But that doesn't matter: it can all be hidden by the logic of the entity itself. When you request an instance of InternalOrder, it will just know that you mean only the special internally flagged type of order, and not standard orders.

ADO.NET provider support

Once you've created your entities and related mapping logic, you can "connect" to the entities as though they were stored in their own database. Instead of connecting up to SQL Server and querying tables directly, you connect to the mapping context and query against the new logical view of your data.

Some of the technology that I will discuss in Chapter 17 has the flavor of the ADO.NET Entity Framework-focused code, but will specifically target SQL Server. The ADO.NET Entity Framework is the primary way to connect .NET's new LINQ technology to non-Microsoft databases such as Oracle and DB2. Unfortunately, a few months before the release of Visual Studio 2008, Microsoft announced that the Entity Framework would not be ready in time for the main product release (sorry, IBM and Oracle). It was slated to come out as a separate release a few months after Visual Studio. The final product may or may not be available as you read this.

Summary

There are programmers in this world who never have to access a database, who never worry about connections or transactions or record locking or INSERT statements or referential integrity. Yes, there are such programmers in the world—five, maybe six at last count. All other programmers must include code that manages external data of some sort, whether in a relational database, or an XML file, or a configuration file. ADO.NET is one of the .NET tools that make such data management easy. It's a lot different from the old ADO system, and I am still not convinced that having disconnected data 100% of the time is the way to go. But when I consider the power and flexibility of ADO.NET, I can't help feeling sorry for those six programmers who never use databases.

Project

It's likely that more than 50% of the code in the Library Project will directly involve database access, or manipulation of the data retrieved through ADO.NET. Constantly creating new Command and DataReader objects, although simple, is pretty hard on the fingers. Since so much of the code is repetitive, the code in this chapter's project will try to centralize some of that basic, boilerplate code.

Reference the Data Namespaces

The Library Project code has references to several of the important .NET namespaces, such as System, System.Windows.Forms, and Microsoft.VisualBasic. However, it doesn't yet reference any of the ADO.NET namespaces. (Recall that "referencing" means accessing a .NET DLL in a project and using its types in your code.) Before using them in code, we need to create references to them. This is done through the project properties window, on the References tab. You'll see a list of those assemblies already referenced by the application (see Figure 10-9).

Figure 10-9. References included in the Library Project

To add new references, click the Add button just below the list, and select Reference if prompted for the type of reference to add. On the Add Reference form, the .NET tab should already be active. It's pretty amazing to see just how many .NET assemblies are installed on your system already. But don't just sit there gawking: select both System.Data and System.Xml from the component list, and then click the OK button. The list of references in the project properties should now include both of the selected namespace libraries.

We can now refer to classes in the System.Data namespace directly. But typing "System. Data" before each use of a data-related class will get tedious. We could sprinkle "Imports System.Data" statements throughout the files in the project, but Visual Studio provides a more centralized solution. Since you still have the References tab open, look down to the "Imported namespaces" section. The large checklist indicates which namespaces should be automatically imported throughout your application. These namespaces don't require separate Imports statements in your code, but your source code acts as though you had added them anyway. Go ahead and select the checkbox next to the System.Data entry in this list. Then close the project properties window.

Most of the new code for this chapter appears in the *General.vb* file, so open it now. We will use two project-level (global) variables to manage the primary database connection to the Library database. The first variable, LibraryDB, is a SqlConnection object that uses our connection string for the Library database. A related object, HoldTransaction, will hold a SqlTransaction object when a transaction is in effect. Add these two lines to the General module. I put them just before the existing CenterText method.

INSERT SNIPPET

Insert Chapter 10, Snippet Item 1.

```
Public LibraryDB As System.Data.SqlClient.SqlConnection
Public HoldTransaction As System.Data.SqlClient.SqlTransaction
```

Connecting to the Database

Since the Library Project will depend so much on the database, we will build the SqlConnection object when first starting up the application.

 Maintaining the connection throughout the application goes against the advice I provided earlier that database connections should be short-lived. However, to keep the code as simple as possible for purposes of tutorial demonstration, I have chosen this approach. Also, because the Library Project is designed for a small installation base, it does not have the requirement of being highly scalable.

The ConnectDatabase procedure contains all the code needed to create this object. For now, I've just hardcoded the connection string into the routine. In a later chapter, we'll include that connection information as part of a configuration system. Add the following routine to your General module. Make sure you change the reference to "MYSYSTEM" to whatever is needed on your own system.

INSERT SNIPPET

Insert Chapter 10, Snippet Item 2.

```
Public Function ConnectDatabase() As Boolean
    ' ----- Connect to the database. Return True on success.
    Dim connectionString As String

    ' ----- Initialize.
    HoldTransaction = Nothing
```

```
' ----- Build the connection string.
' !!! WARNING: Hardcoded for now.
connectionString = "Data Source=MYSYSTEM\SQLEXPRESS;" & _
   "Initial Catalog=Library;Integrated Security=true"

' ----- Attempt to open the database.
Try
   LibraryDB = New SqlClient.SqlConnection(connectionString)
   LibraryDB.Open( )
Catch ex As Exception
   GeneralError("ConnectDatabase", ex)
   Return False
End Try

' ----- Success.
Return True
End Function
```

This project's "main" routine is actually the `MyApplication_Startup` application event, from the *ApplicationEvents.vb* source code file. (That's one that you will have to use the Show All Files button to see.) To build the connection object at startup, add the following code to the end of that event handler.

INSERT SNIPPET

Insert Chapter 10, Snippet Item 3.

```
' ----- Connect to the database.
If (ConnectDatabase( ) = False) Then
   Me.HideSplashScreen( )
   e.Cancel = True
   Return
End If
```

When the user exits the Library application, the code will call the `CleanUpProgram` method to properly dispose of the connection object. Return to the *General.vb* module, and add that method.

INSERT SNIPPET

Insert Chapter 10, Snippet Item 4.

```
Public Sub CleanUpProgram( )
   ' ----- Prepare to exit the program.
   On Error Resume Next
   LibraryDB.Close( )
End Sub
```

To simplify things, we'll call this routine from the application's MyApplication_ Shutdown event handler, back in the *ApplicationEvents.vb* file.

INSERT SNIPPET

Insert Chapter 10, Snippet Item 5.

```
CleanUpProgram( )
```

Interacting with the Database

Now that the database connection is established, it's time to do something with it. The first four centralized routines implement much of the code we discussed earlier: the creation of data readers and tables, and the processing of general SQL code. Add them to the General module.

INSERT SNIPPET

Insert Chapter 10, Snippet Item 6.

This snippet adds the following seven routines:

Function CreateDataTable
> Given a SQL statement, retrieve its results from the database, and put it all in a DataTable object. A SqlDataAdapter connects the SqlDataReader with the DataTable.

Function CreateReader
> Given a SQL statement, retrieve its results from the database, returning the associated SqlDataReader object.

Sub ExecuteSQL
> Send a SQL statement to the database for processing.

Function ExecuteSQLReturn
> Send a SQL statement to the database for processing, returning a single result value.

Sub TransactionBegin
> Begin a new transaction.

Sub TransactionCommit
> Commit the transaction, making all changes permanent.

Sub TransactionRollback
> Roll back the transaction, undoing any changes that were part of the transaction.

None of these routines include their own error-processing code; they either suppress errors with an "On Error Resume Next" statement, or rely on the calling routine to trap errors. This lets the calling routine take specific action based on the type of error generated. All of these routines are pretty similar to one another. Here is the code for CreateReader; one interesting part is the use of the HoldTransaction object when a transaction is in effect.

```
Public Function CreateReader(ByVal sqlText As String) _
      As SqlClient.SqlDataReader
   ' ----- Given a SQL statement, return a data reader.
   Dim dbCommand As SqlClient.SqlCommand
   Dim dbScan As SqlClient.SqlDataReader

   ' ----- Try to run the statement. Note that no error
   '       trapping is done here. It is up to the calling
   '       routine to set up error checking.
   dbCommand = New SqlClient.SqlCommand(sqlText, LibraryDB)
   If Not (HoldTransaction Is Nothing) Then _
      dbCommand.Transaction = HoldTransaction
   dbScan = dbCommand.ExecuteReader()
   dbCommand = Nothing
   Return dbScan
End Function
```

Processing Data Values

Building SQL statements by hand involves a lot of string manipulation, plus conditional processing for those times when data may be missing. For instance, if you want to store a text value in the database, you have to prepare it for use by a SQL statement (special processing for single quote marks), but if the text value is zero-length, you pass the word *NULL* in the statement instead. All of this data preparation can clog up your code, so why not centralize it? The eight routines in this section either prepare data for use in SQL statements, or adjust retrieved data for use in the application.

INSERT SNIPPET

Insert Chapter 10, Snippet Item 7.

DBCombo
: Takes the numeric code associated with a selected item in a ComboBox control and returns it as a string. If no item is selected or the value is -1, the routine returns NULL.

DBDate(String)
: Given a string containing a formatted date, returns a date ready for use in a SQL statement.

DBDate(Date)
: Given a true date value, returns a string date ready for use in a SQL statement.

DBGetDecimal

Returns a decimal number from a result set, even if the field contains a NULL value.

DBGetInteger

Returns an integer number from a result set, even if the field contains a NULL value.

DBGetText

Returns a string from a result set, even if the field contains a NULL value.

DBNum

Prepares a number for use in a SQL statement.

DBText

Prepares a string for use in a SQL statement.

Here is the code for the DBText routine. Strings in SQL statements must be surrounded by single quotes, and any embedded single quotes must be doubled.

```
Public Function DBText(ByVal origText As String) As String
   ' ----- Prepare a string for insertion in a SQL statement.
   If (Trim(origText) = "") Then
      Return "NULL"
   Else
      Return "'" & Replace(origText, "'", "''") & "'"
   End If
End Function
```

System-Level Configuration

The last blocks of code support the quick update and retrieval of system-wide configuration values stored in the SystemValue table of the Library database. The GetSystemValue routine returns the current setting of a configuration value when supplied with the value name. SetSystemValue updates (or adds, if needed) a named configuration value. Both of these routines appear in the General module.

INSERT SNIPPET

Insert Chapter 10, Snippet Item 8.

```
Public Function GetSystemValue( _
      ByVal valueName As String) As String
   ' ----- Return the data portion of a system value
   '       name-data pair.
   Dim sqlText As String
   Dim returnValue As String

   ' ----- Retrieve the value.
   returnValue = ""
```

```
    sqlText = "SELECT ValueData FROM SystemValue WHERE " & _
        "UPPER(ValueName) = " & DBText(UCase(valueName))
    Try
        returnValue = DBGetText(ExecuteSQLReturn(sqlText))
    Catch ex As Exception
        GeneralError("GetSystemValue", ex)
    End Try
    Return returnValue
End Function

Public Sub SetSystemValue(ByVal valueName As String, _
        ByVal valueData As String)
    ' ----- Update a record in the SystemValue table.
    Dim sqlText As String

    Try
        ' ----- See if the entry already exists.
        sqlText = "SELECT COUNT(*) FROM SystemValue WHERE " & _
            "UPPER(ValueName) = " & DBText(UCase(valueName))
        If (CInt(ExecuteSQLReturn(sqlText)) > 0) Then
            ' ----- Value already exists.
            sqlText = "UPDATE SystemValue " & _
                "SET ValueData = " & DBText(valueData) & _
                " WHERE UPPER(ValueName) = " & _
                DBText(UCase(valueName))
        Else
            ' ----- Need to create value.
            sqlText = "INSERT INTO SystemValue " & _
                (ValueName, ValueData) VALUES (" & _
                DBText(valueName) & ", " & _
                DBText(valueData) & ")"
        End If

        ' ----- Update the value.
        ExecuteSQL(sqlText)
    Catch ex As System.Exception
        GeneralError("SetSystemValue", ex)
    End Try
End Sub
```

The GetSystemValue routine is clear. It simply retrieves a single value from the database. SetSystemValue has to first check whether the configuration value to update already exists in the database. If it does, it modifies the records. Otherwise, it adds a full new record. To determine whether the record exists, it requests a count of records matching the system value name. It queries the database through our new ExecuteSqlReturn method, which returns a single value from a query. In this case, the value is the count of the matching records.

```
sqlText = "SELECT COUNT(*) FROM SystemValue WHERE " & _
    "UPPER(ValueName) = " & DBText(UCase(valueName))
If (CInt(ExecuteSQLReturn(sqlText)) > 0) Then
```

Using the GetSystemValue routine is easy, so let's use it right now. Go back to the MyApplication_Startup event handler in *ApplicationEvents.vb*, and add the following code to the end of the routine.

INSERT SNIPPET

Insert Chapter 10, Snippet Item 9.

```
' ----- Check the database version.
Dim productionDBVersion As String
productionDBVersion = Trim(GetSystemValue("DatabaseVersion"))
If (CInt(Val(productionDBVersion)) <> UseDBVersion) Then
   MsgBox("The program cannot continue due to an " & _
      "incompatible database. The current database " & _
      "version is '" & productionDBVersion & _
      "'. The application version is '" & _
      UseDBVersion & "'.", _
      MsgBoxStyle.OkOnly Or MsgBoxStyle.Critical, ProgramTitle)
   CleanUpProgram()
   Me.HideSplashScreen()
   e.Cancel = True
   Return
End If
```

Once in a while, I found it necessary to modify the structure of a database to such an extent that older versions of an application either crashed, or would cause major data headaches. To prevent this, I added a database version setting, DatabaseVersion, and use this code block to test against it. If the program doesn't match the expected database version, it will refuse to run.

Now that we have some basic database access tools, we're ready to start adding some real data interaction code to the Library application.

Security

Secrets are funny things. With billions of people on the planet, there is no shortage of really interesting events and stories, but none of them will hold our interest if there is a secret to be discovered somewhere else. For instance, former associate director of the FBI, W. Mark Felt, revealed himself to be the famous "Deep Throat" of Watergate fame, but not before 30 years of speculation and whispering about this secret identity had passed by. Other secrets are just as intriguing, even if we are in on the secret. Superman is fascinating in part due to his secret alter ego, Clark Kent. Many books include the word *Secret* in their titles to make them and their topics more interesting, titles such as *Japanese Cooking Secrets*.

In this era of information overload and increasingly permissive moral standards on television, secrets seem to be scarce. But everyone has important information that he needs to keep protected from others, and that includes the users of your programs. Fortunately, .NET programs and related data can be as secure as you need, if you use the security features available to you in the .NET Framework.

Here's a secret that I'll tell right now: I really don't know that much about computer security issues. Back in the early 1980s, I worked for a computer vendor that was coming out with its own Unix System V implementation. The company needed to confirm that its product would be sufficiently secure for governmental sales, and I was tasked with building a bibliography of computer security resources, including the famous "Orange Book," a government security standards document whose title has no rhyme.

Although I don't recall many of the security details, I do remember that it would take several city garbage trucks to haul away all the available materials on computer security. The bibliography I developed was more than 40 pages long! And that was just the table of contents. One article that I do recall was quite interesting. It discussed how passwords are generated in Unix systems, at least back when AT&T was in charge. The interesting part was that the entire algorithm was printed in a publicly available book. Anyone could examine the book and see how the passwords were generated. And if you were familiar with Unix, you knew that each user's encrypted password was stored in plain text in the file */etc/passwd*. But it wasn't a big deal.

Although the method for deriving the password was public knowledge, and although you could see everyone's encrypted password, Unix was still considered secure enough for use even in the military.

Security Features in .NET

Security in .NET involves many features, but they fall generally into three major areas:

Internal security

Classes and class members in .NET can be protected via user-based or role-based security. This *Code Access Security* (CAS) exists to keep unauthorized users from accessing powerful libraries of .NET features. Only those users meeting a minimum or specific set of rights can use those protected features.

External security

Since anyone can develop and distribute a .NET application, it's important to protect system resources from malicious code. This is a big issue, especially with the ongoing reports of hackers taking advantage of "buffer overrun" problems in released software from Microsoft and other vendors. Just as CAS keeps code from accessing certain features of a class, it interacts with the operating system to keep rogue code from accessing some or all files and directories, registry entries, network resources, hardware peripherals, or other .NET assemblies based on in-effect security policies.

Data security

Programs and computer resources aren't the only things that need to be protected. Some highfalutin users think their precious data is so important that it deserves to be protected through "special" software means. Encryption, digital signatures, and other cryptographic features provide the "special" support needed for such data.

Because the Library Project interacts with a major external resource—a SQL Server database—it does deal with external security issues, although indirectly through ADO.NET and system security policies. Still, because of this book's focus on typical business application development, this chapter will not discuss either internal security or external security issues. Instead, it will focus on data security topics, especially the encryption of data.

Cryptography and Encryption

Knowing a secret is one thing. Keeping it safe and protected from others is another. Making sure an enemy doesn't alter it while we're blabbing—I mean, confiding—it to someone else is still another issue. Confirming that a secret coming from someone else is reliable is yet another issue. Making sure that I get the best deal on car insurance is again another issue entirely.

Clearly, data security is about more than just keeping a piece of data protected from prying eyes. And it's not only prying eyes that concern us. Recently I experienced the Windows "blue screen of death" when I tried to synchronize the data on my desktop system with my electronic handheld scheduler. The potential for data corruption through the normal everyday use of technology is vast. Fortunately, the word processor I am using to type this chapter is frëë fℜôm su©h ¢θr®μptioñ¡

Keeping Secrets

When people think about encryption and data security, they generally focus on the "keeping secrets" aspect. The ability to cryptographically encode content, keep it from an adversary, and still have it decoded by you or an associate at some later time is important. Encryption techniques range from simple language aberrations (such as pig Latin) and replacement ciphers (letter substitutions, used in cryptogram puzzles) to complex enigma-machine-quality encoding systems.

Software-enabled encryption is now a part of our everyday experience. When you make credit card purchases from web sites, the chance is pretty good that your credit card information is encrypted and transferred in 128-bit secret fidelity.

Typical encryption methods make use of one or more *keys*, plus a combination of *hashing functions* and *encryption algorithms*, to convert sensitive content into a form that is not easily accessible without the original or related key. *Symmetric cryptography* is the name used for encryption methods using a single secret key.

Public-key encryption—also known as *asymmetric cryptography*—uses a pair of keys to encrypt and decrypt data. One of the keys, a *public key*, can be given to anyone who cares about communicating with you securely. You can even give it to your enemies; it's public. The related *private key* is kept safe for your use; you never show it to anyone, not even your mother. Content encrypted using one of the keys (and an encryption algorithm) can only be decrypted later using the other key. If your friend encrypts some information using the public key, nobody except you will be able to decrypt it, and it will require your private key. You can also encrypt data with your private key, but anyone would be able to decrypt it with the public key. We'll see uses for this seemingly insecure action a little bit later.

Data Stability

Data encryption helps to ensure the integrity of a block of data, even if that data is not encrypted. If you send someone an email during a lightning storm, there is certainly the chance that some or all of the email content could be electronically altered before it reaches the recipient. Let's say that some static in the transmission line just happens to cause one sentence of the content to be duplicated. Let's say that some static in the transmission line just happens to cause one sentence of the content to be duplicated. How would you know whether it was the author trying to make some clever point, or simply a computer glitch?

Including a *checksum* with the content can help to identify data problems during transmission. A checksum—sometimes called a *hash value*—takes the original content and passes it through a function that generates a short value that "represents" the original data. Checksum functions (or *hashing algorithms*) are very sensitive to even single-byte changes on the content, whether that single byte was altered, repositioned, added, or removed from the original data. By generating a checksum both before and after data transmission, you can confirm whether the content changed at all during the transfer.

Checksums represent a *unidirectional encryption* of the original data. It is impossible to use the checksum to obtain the original data content. That's all right, though, since the purpose of a checksum is not to deliver content secretly, but to deliver it unchanged. *Bidirectional encryption* is what I talked about in the "Keeping Secrets" section. If you have the right key and the right algorithm, bidirectional encryption restores original content from encrypted content.

Identity Verification

Let's say that you receive an email from your boss that says, "Order 50 copies of Tim Patrick's newest book, and hurry." How do you know this message is reliable, or really from your boss? In this case, the content alone should prove that it is trustworthy. But if you really wanted to verify the source, and your boss was unavailable, you could employ *digital signatures* to confirm the identity of the sender.

One method of using digital signatures employs public-key encryption to transmit an agreed-upon password or message, and passes that encrypted content along with the larger email. For instance, your boss could encrypt the text "I'm the boss" using his private key. When you receive the email, you could decrypt the digital signature using your boss's public key. If the decryption resulted in the "I'm the boss" message, you would know that the message did, in fact, come from your boss.

Encryption in .NET

The data encryption and security features included with .NET appear in the `System.Security.Cryptography` namespace. Most of the classes in this namespace implement various well-known encryption algorithms that have been accepted by organizations and governments as dependable encryption standards. For instance, the `DESCryptoServiceProvider` class provides features based on the Data Encryption Standard (DES) algorithm, an algorithm originally developed by IBM in the mid-1970s.

Symmetric Cryptography

Symmetric cryptography uses a single secret key to both encrypt and decrypt a block of data. Although these algorithms are often quite fast (when compared to asymmetric cryptography), the need to provide the full secret key to others to share data may make them inherently less secure. Still, for many applications, "secret key encryption" is sufficient.

The .NET Framework includes support for four symmetric encryption algorithms:

- *Data Encryption Standard* (*DES*), a 56-bit block cipher with primary support through the DESCryptoServiceProvider class. This algorithm is generally secure, but due to its small key size (smaller keys are more easily compromised), it is inappropriate for highly sensitive data.

- *RC2* (*Rivest Cipher number 2*), a 56-bit block cipher with primary support through the RC2CryptoServiceProvider class. Lotus originally developed the cipher for use in its Lotus Notes product. It is not excitingly secure, but for this reason, it was given more favorable export freedoms by the U.S. government.

- *Rijndael* (derived from the names of its two designers, Daemen and Rijmen), a variable bit (between 128 to 256 bits) block cipher with primary support through the RijndaelManaged class. It is related to a similar algorithm named Advanced Encryption Standard (AES), and is the most secure of the secret key algorithms provided with .NET.

- *Triple DES*, a block cipher that uses the underlying DES algorithm three times to generate a more secure result, with primary support through the TripleDESCryptoServiceProvider class. Although more secure than plain DES, it is still much more vulnerable than the Rijndael or AES standard.

The various "provider" classes are tools that must be used together with other cryptography classes to work properly. For instance, this sample code (based on code found in the MSDN documentation) uses the DESCryptoServiceProvider and CryptoStream classes, both members of System.Security.Cryptography, to jointly encrypt and decrypt a block of text:

```
Imports System
Imports System.IO
Imports System.Text
Imports System.Security.Cryptography

Class CryptoMemoryStream
    Public Shared Sub Main( )
        ' ----- Encrypt then decrypt some text.
        Dim key As New DESCryptoServiceProvider
        Dim encryptedVersion( ) As Byte
        Dim decryptedVersion As String
```

```vbnet
      ' ----- First, encrypt some text.
      encryptedVersion = Encrypt("This is a secret.", key)

      ' ----- Then, decrypt it to get the original.
      decryptedVersion = Decrypt(encryptedVersion, key)
   End Sub

Public Shared Function Encrypt(origText As String, _
      key As SymmetricAlgorithm) As Byte()
      ' ----- Uses a crytographic memory stream and a
      '       secret key provider (DES in this case)
      '       to encrypt some text.
      Dim baseStream As New MemoryStream
      Dim secretStream As CryptoStream
      Dim streamOut As StreamWriter
      Dim encryptedText() As Byte

      ' ----- A memory stream just shuffles data from
      '       end to end. Adding a CryptoStream to it
      '       will encrypt the data as it moves through
      '       the stream.
      secretStream = New CryptoStream(baseStream, _
         key.CreateEncryptor(), CryptoStreamMode.Write)
      streamOut = New StreamWriter(secretStream)
      streamOut.WriteLine(origText)
      streamOut.Close()
      secretStream.Close()

      ' ----- Move the encrypted content into a useful
      '       byte array.
      encryptedText = baseStream.ToArray()
      baseStream.Close()
      Return encryptedText
End Function

Public Shared Function Decrypt(encryptedText() As Byte, _
      key As SymmetricAlgorithm) As String
      ' ----- Clearly, this is the opposite of the
      '       Encrypt() function, using a stream reader
      '       instead of a writer, and the key's
      '       "decryptor" instead of its "encryptor."
      Dim baseStream As MemoryStream
      Dim secretStream As CryptoStream
      Dim streamIn As StreamReader
      Dim origText As String

      ' ----- Build a stream that automatically decrypts
      '       as data is passed through it.
      baseStream = New MemoryStream(encryptedText)
      secretStream = New CryptoStream(baseStream, _
         key.CreateDecryptor(), CryptoStreamMode.Read)
      streamIn = New StreamReader(secretStream)

      ' ----- Move the decrypted content back to a string.
      origText = streamIn.ReadLine()
```

```
        streamIn.Close( )
        secretStream.Close( )
        baseStream.Close( )
        Return origText
    End Function
End Class
```

This code combines a DES encryption class with a *stream*, a common tool in .NET applications for transferring data from one state or location to another. (Streams are a primary method used to read and write files.) Streams are not too hard to use, but the code still seems a little convoluted. Why doesn't the DESCryptoServiceProvider class simply include Encrypt and Decrypt methods? That's my question, at least. I'm sure it has something to do with keeping the class generic for use in many data environments. Still, as chunky as this code is, it's sure a lot easier than writing the encryption code myself. And it's general enough that I could swap in one of the other secret key algorithms without very much change in the code.

Asymmetric Cryptography

In secret key cryptography, you can use any old key you wish to support the encryption and decryption process. As long as you keep it a secret, the content of the key itself isn't really too important. The same cannot be said, though, of asymmetric (public key) cryptography. Because separate keys are used to encrypt and decrypt the data, specific private and public keys must be crafted specifically as a pair. You can't just select random public and private keys and hope that they work together.

The components used to support asymmetric cryptography include "generators" that emit public and private key pairs. Once generated, these keys can be used in your code to mask sensitive data. And due to the large key size, it's very difficult for anyone to hack into your encrypted data.

Public key encryption is notoriously slow; it takes forever and a day to encode large amounts of data using the source key. This is one of the reasons that the founding fathers didn't use public key encryption on the *Declaration of Independence*. Because of the sluggish performance of asymmetric encryption, many secure data systems use a combination of public-key and secret-key encryption to protect data. The initial authorization occurs with public-key processes, but once the secure channel opens, the data passed between the systems gets encrypted using faster secret-key methods.

.NET includes two public key cryptography classes for your encrypting and decrypting pleasure:

- *The Digital Signature Algorithm* (*DSA*), an algorithm designed by the U.S. government for use in digital signatures, with primary support through the DSACryptoServiceProvider class
- *The RSA algorithm* (named after its founders, Ron Rivest, Adi Shamir, and Len Adleman), an older though generally secure asymmetric algorithm, with primary support through the RSACryptoServiceProvider class

We will be using asymmetric encryption in the Library Project, but not until a later chapter. Even then, I won't be getting into too much detail about how asymmetric encryption works. Although the background information on prime number generation and large number factorization is fascinating, such discussions are beyond the scope of this book.

Hashing

Although hashing algorithms do not give you the ability to encrypt and decrypt data at will, they are useful in supporting systems that secure and verify data content. We will perform some hashing of data in the project code for this chapter, so stay alert.

Coming up with a hashing algorithm is easy. It took the best minds of the National Security Agency and the Massachusetts Institute of Technology to come up with reliable secret-key and public-key encryption systems, but you can develop a hashing algorithm in just a few minutes. A few years ago, I wrote my own hashing algorithm that I used for years in business applications. That fact alone should prove how simple and basic they can be. Here's a hashing algorithm I just made up while I was sitting here:

```
Public Function HashSomeText(ByVal origText As String) As Long
   ' ----- Create a hash value from some data.
   Dim hashValue As Long = 0&
   Dim counter As Long

   For counter = 1 To Len(origText)
      hashValue += Asc(Mid(origText, counter, 1))
      If (hashValue > (Long.MaxValue * 0.9)) Then _
         hashValue /= 2
   Next counter
   Return hashValue
End Function
```

In the code, I just add up the ASCII values of each character in the text string, and return the result. I do a check in the loop to make sure I don't exceed 90% of the maximum Long value; I don't want to overflow the hashValue variable and generate an error. Although HashSomeText does generate a hashed representation of the input data, it also has some deficiencies:

- It's pretty easy to guess from the hash value whether the incoming content was short or long. Shorter content will usually generate small numbers, and larger output values tend to indicate longer input content.

- It's not very sensitive to some types of content changes. For instance, if you rearrange several characters in the content, it probably won't impact the hash value. Changing a character will impact the value, but if you change one character from *A* to *B* and another nearby letter from *T* to *S*, the hash value will remain unchanged.

- The shorter the content, the greater the chance that two inputs will generate the same hash value.

Perhaps you want something a little more robust. If so, .NET includes several hashing tools:

- *Hash-based Message Authentication Code* (HMAC) is calculated using the Secure Hash Algorithm number 1 (SHA-1) hash function, made available through the HMACSHA1 class. It uses a 160-bit hash code. There are no specific restrictions on the length of the secret key used in the calculation. Although suitable for low-risk situations, the SHA-1 algorithm is susceptible to attack.

- *Message Authentication Code* (MAC) is calculated using the Triple-DES secret key algorithms (described earlier), made available through the MACTripleDES class. The secret key used in the calculation is either 16 or 24 bytes long, and the generated value is 8 bytes in length.

- *Message-Digest algorithm number 5* (MD5) hash calculation, made available through the MD5CryptoServiceProvider class. MD5 is yet another super-secret algorithm designed by Ron Rivest (that guy is amazing), but it has been shown to contain some flaws that could make it an encoding security risk. The resultant hash value is 128 bits long.

- Like the HMACSHA1 class, the SHA1Managed class computes a hash value using the SHA-1 hash function. However, it is written using .NET managed code only. HMACSHA1 and some of the other cryptographic features in .NET are simply wrappers around the older *Cryptography API* (CAPI), a pre-.NET DLL. SHA1Managed uses a 160-bit hash code.

- Three other classes—SHA256Managed, SHA384Managed, and SHA512Managed—are similar to the SHA1Managed class, but use 256-bit, 384-bit, and 512-bit hash codes, respectively.

Each of these algorithms uses a secret key that must be included each time the hash is generated against the same set of input data. As long as the input data is unchanged, and the secret key is the same, the resultant hash value will also remain unchanged. By design, even the smallest change in the input data generates major changes in the output hash value.

Other Security Features

That about sums up the major cryptography-related security features in .NET. There are a few other interesting security features that I won't discuss in detail, but they deserve at least a passing mention.

User Authentication and My.User

The Visual Basic My.User object includes several authentication features that can help you design security-enabled code. One useful member is the Name property, which supplies the name of the current authenticated user. The IsInRole method tells you whether the active user is included in, say, the Administrators security group.

For Windows Forms applications, the members of My.User will typically refer to the logged-in Windows user. However, you can use other authentication systems that meet your special development needs. Options include using the Internet-based "Windows Live ID" system from Microsoft, other third-party authentication systems, or your own custom-designed user management system.

The SecureString Class

It's amazing that with all of these advanced tools, programmers still spend much of their time building and parsing string data. Fortunately, .NET includes a plethora of useful string manipulation tools. Unfortunately, they aren't very secure. You may recall that .NET strings are immutable; once created, they are never changed. Eventually, they will be destroyed by the garbage collection process. But until then, they sit around in memory, just waiting to be scanned by some hacker-designed code. Internally, string data is stored as plain text, so if someone can get to the memory, he can copy the content for nefarious purposes.

SecureString to the rescue! The System.Security.SecureString class lets you store strings and get them back, but internally, the content of the string is encrypted. If anyone obtained the internal content of a class instance, it would look like gibberish.

Summary

When you write a business application for some organization or department, you might not care all that much about the security and integrity of the data managed by the software tool. As long as the data gets from the user's fingertips to the database and back, it's all hunky-dory.

Although such views may work for many applications, there are systems and users that expect much more in the way of security. Sometimes you need to ensure the security and integrity of the data managed by the application, especially if it will leave the confines of your software or associated database. The security features found in the System.Security.Cryptography namespace provide a fun variety of data hiding and restoration options.

Project

This chapter will see the following security-focused features added to the Library Project:

- The "login" form, which authenticates librarians and other administrative users
- Security group and user management forms
- A function that encrypts a user-supplied password
- Activation of some application features that depend on user authentication

Authentication Support

Since all of the library's data is stored in a SQL Server database, we already use either Windows or SQL Server security to restrict access to the data itself. But once we connect to the database, we will use a custom authentication system to enable and disable features in the application. It's there that we'll put some of the .NET cryptography features into use.

Before adding the interesting code, we need to add some global variables that support security throughout the application. All of the global elements appear in the *General.vb* file, within the GeneralCode module.

INSERT SNIPPET

Insert Chapter 11, Snippet Item 1.

```
Public LoggedInUserID As Integer
Public LoggedInUserName As String
Public LoggedInGroupID As Integer
Public SecurityProfile(MaxLibrarySecurity) As Boolean
```

Although we added it in a previous step, the LibrarySecurity enumeration is an important part of the security system. Its elements match those found in the Activity table in the Library database. Each enumeration value matches one element in the SecurityProfile array that we just added to the code.

```
Public Enum LibrarySecurity As Integer
   ManageAuthors = 1
   ManageAuthorTypes = 2
   ...more here...
   ManagePatronGroups = 22
   ViewAdminPatronMessages = 23
End Enum
Public Const MaxLibrarySecurity As LibrarySecurity = _
   LibrarySecurity.ViewAdminPatronMessages
```

All of the newly added global variables store identity information for the active administrator. When a patron is the active user, the program sets all of these values to their default states. Since this should be done when the program first begins, we'll add an InitializeSystem routine that is called on startup. It also appears in the General module.

```
Public Sub InitializeSystem( )
    ' ----- Initialize global variables here.
    Dim counter As Integer

    ' ----- Clear security-related values.
    LoggedInUserID = -1
    LoggedInUserName = ""
    LoggedInGroupID = -1
    For counter = 1 To MaxLibrarySecurity
        SecurityProfile(counter) = False
    Next counter
End Sub
```

(The SecurityProfile array has items that range from 0 to MaxLibrarySecurity, but the loop at the end of this code starts from element 1. Because the Activity table starts its counting at 1, I decided to just skip element 0.) The InitializeSystem method is called from the MyApplication_Startup event in the *ApplicationEvents.vb* file, just before establishing a connection to the database. Let's add that code now.

```
' ----- Perform general initialization.
InitializeSystem( )
```

Each time an administrator tries to use the system, and each time the administrator logs off and returns the program to patron mode, all of the security-related global variables must be reset. This is done in the ReprocessSecuritySet method, added to the General module.

```
Public Sub ReprocessSecuritySet( )
    ' ----- Reload in the security set for the current
    '       user. If no user is logged in, clear all settings.
    Dim counter As Integer
    Dim sqlText As String
    Dim dbInfo As SqlClient.SqlDataReader = Nothing
```

```
' ----- Clear out the existing items.
For counter = 1 To MaxLibrarySecurity
    SecurityProfile(counter) = False
Next counter

' ----- Exit if there is no user logged in.
If (LoggedInUserID = -1) Or _
    (LoggedInGroupID = -1) Then Return

Try
    ' ----- Load in the security elements for this user.
    sqlText = "SELECT ActivityID FROM GroupActivity " & _
        "WHERE GroupID = " & LoggedInGroupID
    dbInfo = CreateReader(sqlText)
    Do While (dbInfo.Read)
        SecurityProfile(CInt(dbInfo!ActivityID)) = True
    Loop
    dbInfo.Close()
Catch ex As Exception
    ' ----- Some database-related error.
    GeneralError("ReprocessSecuritySet", ex)
    If (dbInfo IsNot Nothing) Then dbInfo.Close()

    ' ----- Un-log in the administrator through recursion.
    LoggedInUserID = -1
    LoggedInGroupID = -1
    ReprocessSecuritySet()
Finally
    dbInfo = Nothing
End Try
End Sub
```

This routine uses code built in Chapter 10 and other earlier chapters. When it detects an authorized user (the LoggedInUserID variable), it creates a SqlDataReader object with that user's allowed security features, and stores those settings in the SecurityProfile array. Once it is loaded, any array element that is True represents an application feature that the administrator is authorized to use. I'll discuss the GroupActivity table a little later in this chapter.

If a database error occurs during processing, the code resets everything to patron mode, making a *recursive* call to ReprocessSecuritySet to clear the SecurityProfile array. (Recursion occurs when a routine directly or indirectly calls itself.)

Encrypting Passwords

The entire content of this chapter has been building to this very moment, the section where I reveal the winner of the next presidential election. Wait! Even better than that, I will use one of the .NET hashing methods to encrypt an administrator-supplied password before storing it in the database. One of the tables in the Library database, the

UserName table, stores the basic security profile for each librarian or other administrative user, including a password. Since anyone who can get into the database will be able to see the passwords stored in this table, we will encrypt them to make them a little less tempting. (For patrons simply using the program, there shouldn't be any direct access to the database apart from the application, but you never know about those frisky patrons.)

To keep things secure, we'll scramble the user-entered password, using it to generate a hash value, and store the hash value in the database's password field for the user. Later, when an administrative user wants to gain access to enhanced features, the program will again convert the entered password into a hash value, and compare that value to the on-record hashed password.

Each .NET hashing function depends on a secret code. Since the Library Project will only perform a unidirectional encryption, and it will never ask any other program to re-encrypt the password, we'll just use the user's login name as the "secret" key. I decided to use the HMACSHA1 hashing class, mostly for its ability to accept a variable-size key. Although it is reported to have security issues, that shouldn't be a problem for the way that we're using it. I mean, if someone actually got into the database trying to decrypt the passwords stored in the UserName table, she would already have full access to everything in the Library system.

Of course, the encryption code requires references to the System.Security. Cryptography namespace. We'll also need a reference to System.Text for some of the support code. Add the relevant Import statements to the top of the *General.vb* code file.

INSERT SNIPPET

Insert Chapter 11, Snippet Item 5.

```
Imports System.Text
Imports System.Security.Cryptography
```

The actual jumbling of the password occurs in the EncryptPassword routine, making its entrance in the General module.

INSERT SNIPPET

Insert Chapter 11, Snippet Item 6.

```
Public Function EncryptPassword(ByVal loginID As String, _
      ByVal passwordText As String) As String
   ' ----- Given a username and a password, encrypt the
   '       password so that it is not easy to decrypt. There
   '       is no limit on password length since it is going
   '       to be hashed anyway.
```

```
Dim hashingFunction As HMACSHA1
Dim secretKey() As Byte
Dim hashValue() As Byte
Dim counter As Integer
Dim result As String = ""

' ----- Prepare the secret key. Force it to uppercase for
'       consistency, and then stuff it in a byte array.
secretKey = (New UnicodeEncoding).GetBytes(UCase(loginID))

' ----- Create the hashing component using Managed SHA-1.
hashingFunction = New HMACSHA1(secretKey, True)

' ----- Calculate the hash value. One simple line of code.
hashValue = hashingFunction.ComputeHash( _
   (New UnicodeEncoding).GetBytes(passwordText))

' ----- The hash value is ready, but I like things in
'       plain text when possible. Let's convert it to a
'       long hex string.
For counter = 0 To hashValue.Length - 1
   result &= Hex(hashValue(counter))
Next counter

' ----- Stored passwords are limited to 20 characters.
Return Left(result, 20)
End Function
```

The primary methods of interacting with the security providers in .NET are via a byte array or a stream. I opted to use the byte array method, converting the incoming string values through the UnicodeEncoding object's GetBytes method. Once stored as a byte array, I pass the login ID and password as arguments to the HMACSHA1 class's features.

Although I could store the output of the ComputeHash method directly in a database field, I decided to convert the result into readable ASCII characters so that things wouldn't look all weird when I issued SQL statements against the UserName table. My conversion is basic: convert each byte into its printable hexadecimal equivalent using Visual Basic's Hex function. Then just string the results together. The UserName. Password field holds only 20 characters, so I chop off anything longer.

Just to make sure that this algorithm generates reasonable output, I called EncryptPassword with a few different inputs.

```
MsgBox("Alice/none:     " & _
    EncryptPassword("Alice", "") & vbCrLf & _
    "Alice/password: " & _
    EncryptPassword("Alice", "password") & vbCrLf & _
    "Bob/none:       " & _
    EncryptPassword("Bob", "") & vbCrLf & _
    "Bob/password:   " & _
    EncryptPassword("Bob", "password"))
```

This code generated the following message:

```
Alice/none:     6570FC214A797C023F40
Alice/password: 4AEC6C914C65D88BD082
Bob/none:       7F544120E3AB9FB48C32
Bob/password:   274A56F047293EA0B97E
```

Undoing Some Previous Changes

The UserName, GroupName, and GroupActivity tables in the database define the security profiles for each administrative user. Every user (a record in UserName) is part of one security group (a GroupName record). Each group includes access to zero or more enhanced application features; the GroupActivity table identifies which features match up to each security group record.

To manage these tables, we need to add property forms that edit the fields of a single database record. We already wrote some of the code awhile back. Chapter 8 defined the *BaseCodeForm.vb* file, a template for forms that edit single database records. That same chapter introduced the *ListEditRecords.vb* file, the "parent" form that displays a listing of already-defined database records. Our record editor for both users and security groups will use the features in these two existing forms.

 Your friendly author, Tim Patrick, is about to rant on and on about something that really bugs him. Why not join him in this rant?

When we designed the code for *BaseCodeForm.vb* in Chapter 8, my goal was to show you the MustInherit and MustOverride class features included with Visual Basic. They are pretty useful features. Unfortunately, they just don't mix well with user interface elements, and here's why: Visual Studio actually creates instances of your forms at design time so that you can interact with them inside the editor. If you were to delve into the source code for, say, a TextBox control, you would find special code that deals with design-time presentation of the control. Interesting? Yes. Flexible? Yes. Perfect in all cases? No.

The problem—and *problem* is putting it mildly—is that Visual Studio won't (actually, can't) create an instance of a class defined as MustInherit. That's because you *must inherit it through another class first before you create instances*. What does this mean to you? It means that if you try to design a form that inherits from a MustInherit form template, Visual Studio will not present the user interface portion of the form for your editing enjoyment. You can still access the source code of the form, and if this is how you want to design the inherited form, that's fine. But you and I are looking for simplicity in programming, and we plunked down good money for Visual Studio, so we're certainly going to use its visual tools to edit our visual forms.

The upshot of all this ranting—and I'm almost at the end of my rant, but you can keep going on if you want—is that we must change the *BaseCodeForm.vb* file, removing the MustInherit and MustOverride keywords, and making other appropriate adjustments. I've already made the changes to both the before and after templates of the Chapter 11 code.

This is part of the reality of programming in a complex system such as Visual Studio. Sometimes, even after you have done all your research and carefully mapped out the application features and structure, you run into some designer- or compiler-specific behavior that forces you to make some change. Once you learn to avoid the major issues, you find that it doesn't happen too often. But when it does occur, it can be a great time to rant.

Managing Security Groups

So, back to our GroupName record editor. I haven't added it to the project yet, so let's add it now. Because it will inherit from another form in the project, we have to allow Visual Studio to instantiate the base form by first compiling the application. This is easily done through the Build → Build Library menu command.

To create the new form, select the Project → Add Windows Form menu command. When the Add New Item window appears, select Windows Forms from the Categories list, followed by Inherited Form from the Templates list. Enter **GroupName.vb** in the Name field, and then click the Add button. When the Inheritance Picker form appears (see Figure 11-1), select BaseCodeForm from the list, and click OK. The new GroupName form appears, but it look remarkably like the BaseCodeForm form.

Figure 11-1. Who says you can't pick your own relatives?

Add two Label controls, two TextBox controls, two Button controls, and a CheckedListBox control from the toolbox, and set their properties using the following settings.

Control type	Property settings	
Label	(Name):	LabelFullName
	AutoSize:	True
	Location:	8, 10
	Text:	&Security Group Name:
TextBox	(Name):	RecordFullName
	Location:	128, 8
	MaxLength:	50
	Size:	248, 20
Label	(Name):	LabelActivity
	AutoSize:	True
	Location:	8, 34
	Text:	&Allowed Activities:
CheckedListBox	(Name):	ActivityList
	Location:	128, 32
	Size:	248, 244
Button	(Name):	ActOK
	Location:	208, 288
	Size:	80, 24
	Text:	OK
Button	(Name):	ActCancel
	DialogResult:	Cancel
	Location:	296, 288
	Size:	80, 24
	Text:	Cancel
Form (GroupName)	(Name):	GroupName
	AcceptButton:	ActOK
	CancelButton:	ActCancel
	Size:	392, 351
	Text:	Edit Security Group

Don't forget to adjust the tab order of the controls on the form.

Let's add the code all at once. Add the next code snippet to the class source code body.

INSERT SNIPPET

Insert Chapter 11, Snippet Item 7.

Hey, that's nearly 300 lines of source code. Good typing. The class includes two private members. ActiveID holds the ID number of the currently displayed GroupName database record, or –1 when editing new records. The StartingOver flag is a little more interesting. Remember that we are using a shared summary form to display all of the already-entered GroupName records. To allow this generic form, *ListEditRecords.vb*, to work with the different record editors, we pass an instance of the detail form (*GroupName.vb* in this case) to the summary form:

```
ListEditRecords.ManageRecords(New Library.GroupName)
```

Within the ListEditRecords form's code, the instance of GroupName is used over and over, each time the user wants to add or edit a GroupName database record. If the user edits one record, and then tries to edit another, the leftovers from the first record will still be in the detail form's fields. Therefore, we will have to clear them each time we add or edit a different record. The StartingOver flag helps with that process by resetting the focus to the first detail form field in the form's Activated event.

```
Private Sub GroupName_Activated(ByVal sender As Object, _
      ByVal e As System.EventArgs) Handles Me.Activated
   ' ----- Return the focus to the main field.
   If (StartingOver) Then RecordFullName.Focus( )
   StartingOver = False
End Sub
```

The related PrepareFormFields private method does the actual clearing and storing of data with each new Add or Edit call. For new records, it simply clears all entered data on the form. When editing an existing record, it retrieves the relevant data from the database, and stores saved values in the various on-form fields. The following statements display the stored group name in the RecordFullName field, a TextBox control:

```
' ----- Load in the values stored in the database.
sqlText = "SELECT FullName FROM GroupName WHERE ID = " & _
   ActiveID
RecordFullName.Text = CStr(ExecuteSQLReturn(sqlText))
```

Most of the routines in the GroupName form provide simple overrides for base members of the BaseCodeForm class. The CanUserAdd method, which simply returns False in the base class, includes actual logic in the inherited class. It uses the SecurityProfile array we added earlier to determine whether the current user is allowed to add group records.

```
Public Overrides Function CanUserAdd( ) As Boolean
   ' ----- Check the user for security access: add.
   Return SecurityProfile(LibrarySecurity.ManageGroups)
End Function
```

If you look through the added code, you'll find overrides for all of the BaseCodeForm members except for the UsesSearch and SearchForRecord methods. The derived class accepts the default action for these two members.

The user adds, edits, and deletes group name records through the AddRecord, EditRecord, and DeleteRecord overrides, respectively, each called by code in the ListEditRecords form. Here's the code for EditRecord:

```
Public Overrides Function EditRecord( _
    ByVal recordID As Integer) As Integer
  ' ----- Edit an existing record.
  ActiveID = recordID
  PrepareFormFields()
  Me.ShowDialog()
  If (Me.DialogResult = Windows.Forms.DialogResult.OK) Then _
    Return ActiveID Else Return -1
End Function
```

After storing the ID of the record to edit in the ActiveID private field, the code loads the data through the PrepareFormFields method, and prompts the user to edit the record with the Me.ShowDialog call. The form sticks around until some code or control sets the form's DialogResult property. This is done in the ActOK_Click event, and also through the ActCancel button's DialogResult property, which Visual Basic will assign to the form automatically when the user clicks the ActCancel button.

The AddRecord routine is just like EditRecord, but it assigns −1 to the ActiveID member to flag a new record. The DeleteRecord routine is more involved, and uses some of the database code we wrote in the last chapter.

```
Public Overrides Function DeleteRecord( _
    ByVal recordID As Integer) As Boolean
  ' ----- The user wants to delete the record.
  Dim sqlText As String

  On Error GoTo ErrorHandler

  ' ----- Confirm with the user.
  If (MsgBox("Do you really wish to delete the " & _
    "security group?", MsgBoxStyle.YesNo Or _
    MsgBoxStyle.Question, ProgramTitle) <> _
    MsgBoxResult.Yes) Then Return False

  ' ----- Make sure this record is not in use.
  sqlText = "SELECT COUNT(*) FROM UserName " & _
    "WHERE GroupID = " & recordID
  If (CInt(ExecuteSQLReturn(sqlText)) > 0) Then
    MsgBox("You cannot delete this record because " & _
      "it is in use.", MsgBoxStyle.OkOnly Or _
      MsgBoxStyle.Exclamation, ProgramTitle)
    Return False
  End If

  ' ----- Delete the record.
  TransactionBegin()
  sqlText = "DELETE FROM GroupActivity " & _
    "WHERE GroupID = " & recordID
  ExecuteSQL(sqlText)
  sqlText = "DELETE FROM GroupName WHERE ID = " & recordID
  ExecuteSQL(sqlText)
  TransactionCommit()
  Return True
```

```
ErrorHandler:
    GeneralError("GroupName.DeleteRecord", Err.GetException())
    TransactionRollback()
    Return False
End Function
```

After confirming the delete with the user, a quick check determines whether the group is still being used somewhere in the UserName table. If everything checks out fine, the record is deleted using a SQL DELETE statement. Since we need to delete data in two tables, I wrapped it all up in a transaction. If an error does occur, the error handler at the end of the routine will roll back the transaction through TransactionRollback.

Database Integrity Warning

If you have a background in database development, you have already seen the flaw in the delete code. Although I take the time to verify that the record is not in use before deleting it, it's possible that some other user will use it between the time I check the record's use and the time when I actually delete it. Based on the code and database configuration I've presented so far, it would indeed be an issue. When I designed this system, I expected that a single librarian would manage administrative tasks such as this, so I didn't worry about such conflicts and "race conditions."

If you are concerned about the potential for deleting in-use records through code like this, you can enable *referential integrity* on the relationships in the database. I established a relationship between the GroupName.ID and UserName.GroupID fields, but it was for informational purposes only. You can reconfigure this relationship to have SQL Server enforce the relationship between the tables. If you do this, it will not be possible to delete an in-use record; an error will occur in the program when you attempt it. That sounds good, and it is, but an overuse of referential integrity can slow down your data access. I will leave this configuration choice up to you.

When the user is done making changes to the record, a click on the OK button pushes the data back out to the database. The ActOK_Click event handler verifies the data, and then saves it.

```
If (ValidateFormData() = False) Then Return
If (SaveFormData() = False) Then Return
Me.DialogResult = Windows.Forms.DialogResult.OK
```

The ValidateFormData method does some simple checks for valid data, such as requiring that the user enter the security group name, and that it is unique. If everything looks good, the SaveFormData routine builds SQL statements that save the data.

```
Private Function SaveFormData() As Boolean
    ' ----- The user wants to save changes.
    '          Return True on success.
```

```
Dim sqlText As String
Dim newID As Integer = -1

On Error GoTo ErrorHandler

' ----- Prepare to save the data.
Me.Cursor = Windows.Forms.Cursors.WaitCursor
TransactionBegin()

' ----- Save the data.
If (ActiveID = -1) Then
   ' ----- Create a new entry.
   sqlText = "INSERT INTO GroupName (FullName) " & _
      "OUTPUT INSERTED.ID VALUES (" & _
      DBText(Trim(RecordFullName.Text)) & ")"
   newID = CInt(ExecuteSQLReturn(sqlText))
Else
   ' ----- Update the existing entry.
   newID = ActiveID
   sqlText = "UPDATE GroupName SET FullName = " & _
      DBText(Trim(RecordFullName.Text)) & _
      " WHERE ID = " & ActiveID
   ExecuteSQL(sqlText)
End If

' ----- Clear any existing security settings.
sqlText = "DELETE FROM GroupActivity " & _
   "WHERE GroupID = " & newID
ExecuteSQL(sqlText)

' ----- Save the selected security settings.
For Each itemChecked As ListItemData In _
      ActivityList.CheckedItems
   sqlText = "INSERT INTO GroupActivity (GroupID, " & _
      "ActivityID) VALUES (" & newID & ", " & _
      itemChecked.ItemData & ")"
   ExecuteSQL(sqlText)
Next itemChecked

' ----- Complete all changes.
TransactionCommit()
ActiveID = newID

' ----- This change may affect this user.
If (LoggedInGroupID = ActiveID) Then _
   ReprocessSecuritySet()

' ----- Success.
ActiveID = newID
Me.Cursor = Windows.Forms.Cursors.Default
Return True
```

```
ErrorHandler:
    Me.Cursor = Windows.Forms.Cursors.Default
    GeneralError("GroupName.SaveFormData", Err.GetException())
    TransactionRollback()
    Return False
End Function
```

Be sure to check out the other routines in the GroupName form; they exist to support and enhance the user experience.

Managing Users

We also need a form to manage records in the UserName table. Since the code for that form generally follows what we've already seen in the GroupName form, I won't bore you with the details. I've already added *UserName.vb* to your project, but to prevent bugs in your code while you were in the middle of development, I disabled it (at least in the "Before" version of the code). To enable it, select the file in the Solution Explorer window. Then in the Properties panel, change the Build Action property from None to Compile.

The only interesting code in this form that is somewhat different from the GroupName form is the handling of the password. To keep things as secure as possible, I don't actually load the saved password into the on-form Password field. It wouldn't do any good anyway since I've stored a hashed version in the database.

Since I use the user's Login ID as the secret key when encrypting the password, I must regenerate the password if the user ever changes the Login ID. The private OrigLoginID field keeps a copy of the Login ID when the form first opens, and checks for any changes when resaving the record. If changes occur, it regenerates the password.

```
passwordResult = EncryptPassword(Trim(RecordLoginID.Text), _
    Trim(RecordPassword.Text))
```

Using the UserName and GroupName editing forms requires some additional code in the main form. Add it to the body of the General module.

INSERT SNIPPET

Insert Chapter 11, Snippet Item 8.

The AdminLinkGroups and AdminLinkUsers controls are web-style link labels that we added to the program a few chapters back. The LinkClicked event—not the Clicked event—triggers the display of the code editor. Here's the code to edit the GroupName table:

```
Private Sub AdminLinkGroups_LinkClicked( _
        ByVal sender As Object, ByVal e As System.Windows. _
        Forms.LinkLabelLinkClickedEventArgs) _
        Handles AdminLinkGroups.LinkClicked
```

```
' ----- Let the user edit the list of security groups.
If (SecurityProfile(LibrarySecurity.ManageGroups) _
      = False) Then
   MsgBox(NotAuthorizedMessage, MsgBoxStyle.OkOnly Or _
      MsgBoxStyle.Exclamation, ProgramTitle)
   Return
End If

' ----- Edit the records.
ListEditRecords.ManageRecords(New Library.GroupName)
ListEditRecords = Nothing
End Sub
```

Per-User Experience

Now that we have all of the security support code added to the project, we can start using those features to change the application experience for patrons and administrators. It's not polite to tempt people with immense power, so it's best to hide those features that are not accessible to the lowly and inherently less powerful patron users.

First, let's provide the power of differentiation by adding the administrative login form, shown in Figure 11-2.

Figure 11-2. The official Library Project administrative login form

I've already added the *ChangeUser.vb* form to the project. If you're using the "Before" version of this chapter's code, select ChangeUser.vb in the Solution Explorer. Then change its Build Action property (in the Properties panel) from None to Compile, just as you did with the *UserName.vb* form.

All of the hard work occurs in the form's ActOK_Click event handler. If the user selects the Return to Patron Mode option, all security values are cleared, and the main form hides most features (through code added later).

```
LoggedInUserID = -1
LoggedInUserName = ""
LoggedInGroupID = -1
ReprocessSecuritySet( )
```

This form gets connected into the application through the main form's ActLogin_
Click event. Open up the *MainForm.vb* file, double-click on the Login button in the
upper-right corner, and add the following code to the Click event template that
appears.

INSERT SNIPPET

Insert Chapter 11, Snippet Item 9.

```
' ----- Prompt the user for patron or administrative mode.
ShowLoginForm( )
```

That wasn't much code. Add the ShowLoginForm method's code to the form as well.

INSERT SNIPPET

Insert Chapter 11, Snippet Item 10.

```
Private Sub ShowLoginForm( )
    ' ----- Prompt the user for patron or administrative mode.
    Dim userChoice As Windows.Forms.DialogResult
    userChoice = ChangeUser.ShowDialog( )
    ChangeUser = Nothing
    If (userChoice = Windows.Forms.DialogResult.OK) Then _
        UpdateDisplayForUser( )
End Sub
```

Let's also enable the F12 key to act as a login trigger. Add the following code to the
Select Case statement in the MainForm_KeyDown event handler.

INSERT SNIPPET

Insert Chapter 11, Snippet Item 11.

```
Case Keys.F12
    ' ----- Prompt the user for patron or administrative mode.
    ShowLoginForm( )
    e.Handled = True
```

The ShowLoginForm routine calls another method, UpdateDisplayForUser, which hides
and shows various display elements on the main form based on the security profile of
the current user. Add it to the MainForm class code. I won't show the code here, but
basically it looks at the LoggedInUserID variable, and if it is set to −1, it hides all the
controls for advanced features.

INSERT SNIPPET

Insert Chapter 11, Snippet Item 12.

Currently, when you run the application, all the advanced features appear, even though no administrator has supplied an ID or password. Calling `UpdateDisplayForUser` when the main form first appears solves that problem. Add the following code to the end of the `MainForm_Load` method.

INSERT SNIPPET

Insert Chapter 11, Snippet Item 13.

```
' ----- Prepare for a patron user.
UpdateDisplayForUser()
```

The last update (five updates, actually) involves limiting the major sections of the form to just authorized administrators. For instance, only administrators who are authorized to run reports should be able to access the reporting panel on the main form. Locate the `TaskReports` method in the main form, and find the line that displays the panel.

```
PanelReports.Visible = True
```

Replace this line with the following code.

INSERT SNIPPET

Insert Chapter 11, Snippet Item 14.

```
If (SecurityProfile(LibrarySecurity.RunReports)) Then _
    PanelReports.Visible = True
```

We need to do the same thing in the `TaskCheckOut`, `TaskCheckIn`, `TaskAdmin`, and `TaskProcess` methods. In each case, replace the line that reads:

```
Panel???.Visible = True
```

with code that checks the security settings before showing the panel.

INSERT SNIPPET

Insert Chapter 11, Snippet Items 15 through 18.

- Use Snippet 15 for `TaskCheckOut`.
- Use Snippet 16 for `TaskCheckIn`.
- Use Snippet 17 for `TaskAdmin`.
- Use Snippet 18 for `TaskProcess`.

Run the program and you'll see that it's starting to look like a real application. If you want access to the enhanced features, try a Login ID of "admin" with no password. You can change that through the UserName form if you want!

Since we have a way to secure access to the data and features of the Library Project, let's move to the next chapter and start focusing on the data, the focal point of any business application.

Overloads and Extensions

Do you ever wish you could do things beyond what people were designed to do? Like flying? We all dream about it, but we can't do it without several hundred pounds of jet fuel. Or what about bending steel in our bare hands? Does that sound like anyone you know? Then there's breathing underwater, doing long division in your head, speaking a foreign language fluently without much study, and having a successful career as an author of popular computer books. Ah, one can dream.

It's not that we want to do all of these things, but once in a while it would be nice to be *slightly enhanced* with the ability to do one or two of the things that are beyond our natural abilities. Unfortunately, it doesn't work for humans very often, but could it work for .NET operators?

You probably didn't even know that the humble Visual Basic addition operator (+) had dreams of flying, or of speaking Hungarian, or of bending steel. Well, operators are people, too. And now their dreams can be fulfilled because Visual Basic supports *operator overloading*.

This chapter will show how you can direct the body-building enhancement process for the various Visual Basic operators. I'll also introduce *extension methods*, which let you similarly enhance classes, even if you don't have access to the original source code for those classes.

What Is Operator Overloading?

Operator overloading allows your code to enhance the basic Visual Basic operators, and endow them with abilities not previously granted to them by the compiler. Overloading doesn't change the syntax used when employing operators, but it does change the types of objects that each operator can manage. For instance, the multiplication operator (*) normally interacts only with numbers, but you can augment it to work with your own custom Bumblebee class.

```
Dim swarm As Bumblebee
Dim oneBumblebee As New Bumblebee
```

```
Dim twoBumblebee As New Bumblebee
swarm = oneBumblebee * twoBumblebee
```

The meaning you apply to the overloaded operator is up to you. Although you would normally want to retain the additive nature of the addition operator when overloading it, you don't have to. In fact, you could overload the addition operator so that it subtracts one value from another. But I'd fire you if you did that working for me. Just so you know.

All operator overloading features tie directly to one or more of your classes. Overloaded features look curiously like standard function members, and appear as members of your classes.

Visual Basic includes two types of operators: *unary* and *binary*, defined based on the number of operands recognized by the operator. Unary operators accept a single operand, which always appears to the right of the operator name or symbol. The logical Not operator is a unary operator:

```
oppositeValue = Not originalValue
```

Binary operators accept two operands, one on each side of the operator. The multiplication operator is a binary operator:

```
ten = two * five
```

The nature of an operator is that once it has done its work, the operator and its input operand(s) are, in effect, fully replaced by the calculated result. The expression "10/5" is replaced by the calculated "2" result, and this result is used to complete whatever statement or expression the original operation appeared in. It works just like a function.

```
' ----- These two lines (probably) place the same
'       calculated result in theAnswer.
theAnswer = 2 * 5
theAnswer = DoubleIt(5)
```

To get ready for operator overloading, alter your mind to see operators as functions. Look past the confines of your operator universe, and open yourself to the truth that operators and functions are one. If you've ever programmed in LISP, I truly feel sorry for you. But you also already understand operators as functions. In LISP, everything is a function. To multiply two numbers together in LISP, you use "prefix" syntax, where the operator name comes first. The expression "seven times three" uses this syntax:

```
(* 7 3)
```

Once complete, the entire parenthesized expression is replaced, function-like, by its answer. The LISP expression:

```
(+ 2 (* 7 3))
```

becomes:

```
(+ 2 21)
```

becomes:

23

Defining overloaded operators in Visual Basic 2008 is somewhat similar. If you were to translate the definition of multiplication into Visual Basic function-ese, it might look like this:

```
Public Shared Function *( _
    ByVal firstOperand As Integer, _
    ByVal secondOperand As Integer) _
    As Integer
```

The operator (*) becomes a function name, with operands playing the role of function parameters, ultimately generating a value exposed through the function's return value. Although operators aren't defined as functions in this way in Visual Basic, overloads of those operators are.

To overload the multiplication operator in our imaginary Bumblebee class, we use the Operator keyword to define a "multiplication function" for operands of the Bumblebee class.

```
Partial Class Bumblebee
    Public Shared Operator *(ByVal operand1 As Bumblebee, _
        ByVal operand2 As Bumblebee) As Bumblebee
        ' ----- Multiply two bumblebees together.
        Dim finalResult As New Bumblebee

        ' ----- Add special "multiplication" code here, then...
        Return finalResult
    End Operator
End Class
```

Now, when you multiply two Bumblebee instances together with the multiplication operator, Visual Basic recognizes the "operand1 * operand2" pattern as matching a multiplication operator overload with two Bumblebee arguments, and calls this class-based Operator function to get the result.

All Operator declarations must include the Public and Shared keywords. If they weren't shared, Visual Basic would be required to create an extra instance of the class just to access the operator overload code, and that wouldn't be very efficient.

What Can You Overload?

You can overload pretty much any of Visual Basic's standard operators (except for Is and IsNot), plus a few other features. This section describes each overloadable operator, grouped by general type. Each section includes a table of operators. To overload an operator in a class, use the name in the Operator column as the function name. If there were an operator named XX, the matching Operator statement would be as follows:

```
Public Shared Operator XX(...)
```

Mathematical Operators

Visual Basic defines 10 mathematical or pseudo-mathematical operators. All but one of these exists to manipulate numbers. The leftover operator is the string concatenation operator (&), which works with strings, but kind of looks like the other mathematical operators in its syntax and use.

Two of the operators, plus (+) and minus (-), are both unary and binary operators. The minus sign (-) works as a unary "negation" operator (as in "−5") and as a binary "subtraction" operator (the common "5 − 2" syntax). When overloading these operators, the difference lies in the number of arguments included in the argument signature.

```
Public Shared Operator -(ByVal operand1 As SomeClass, _
    ByVal operand2 As SomeClass) As SomeClass
    ' ----- This is the binary "subtraction" version.
End Operator

Public Shared Operator -(ByVal operand1 As SomeClass) _
    As SomeClass
    ' ----- This is the unary "negation" version.
End Operator
```

Table 12-1 lists the mathematical operators that support overloading.

Table 12-1. The overloadable mathematical operators

Operator	Type	Comments

+	Unary	The unary "plus" operator. You can already use this operator with numbers, as in "+5." But if you enter this value in Visual Studio, the plus operator gets stripped out since it is considered redundant. However, if you overload this operator on a class of your own, Visual Studio will retain the unary form of this operator when used in code.
		
		`' ----- Assuming the unary + operator is overloaded...`
		`Dim oneBuzz As New Bumblebee`
		`Dim moreBuzz As Bumblebee = +oneBuzz`
		
		Since this is a unary operator, include only a single argument when defining the Operator method.

+	Binary	The standard addition operator. Remember, just because the operator is called the "addition" operator doesn't mean that you have to retain that connotation. However, you should attempt to overload the operators as close to their original meaning as possible. Visual Basic itself overloads this operator to let it act a little like the string concatenation operator.
-	Unary	This is the unary "negation" operator that comes just before a value or expression.
-	Binary	The subtraction operator, although if you can figure out how to subtract one bumblebee from another, you're a better programmer than I am.
*	Binary	The multiplication operator.
/	Binary	The standard division operator.
\	Binary	The integer division operator. Remember, you are not required to retain any sense of "integer" in this operator if it doesn't meet your class's needs.

Table 12-1. The overloadable mathematical operators (continued)

Operator	Type	Comments
^	Binary	The exponentiation ("to the power of") operator.
Mod	Binary	The modulo operator, sometimes called the remainder operator since it returns the remainder of a division action.
&	Binary	The string concatenation operator.

Comparison Operators

Visual Basic includes seven basic comparison operators, most often used in If statements and similar expressions that require a *Boolean* conditional calculation. The Operator methods for these comparison operators have the same syntax as is used for mathematical operators, but most of them must be implemented in pairs. For example, if you overload the less than (<) operator, Visual Basic requires you to overload the greater than (>) operator within the same class, and for the same argument signature.

All comparison operators are Boolean operators. Although you can alter the data types of the arguments passed to the operator, they must all return a Boolean value.

```
Public Shared Operator <=(ByVal operand1 As SomeClass, _
    ByVal operand2 As SomeClass) As Boolean
    ' ----- The <= operator returns a Boolean result.
End Operator
```

Table 12-2 lists six of the seven basic comparison operators that you can overload. Each entry includes a "buddy" value that identifies the matching operator that must also be overloaded.

Table 12-2. The overloadable comparison operators

Operator	Buddy	Comments
=	<>	The equal to operator compares two operands for equivalence, returning True if they are equal.
<>	=	The not equal to operator compares two operands for non-equivalence, and returns True if they do not match.
<	>	The less than operator returns True if the first operand is "less than" the second.
>	<	The greater than operator returns True if the first operand is "greater than" the second.
<=	>=	The less than or equal to operator returns True if the first operand is "less than or equal to" the second. Aren't you getting tired of reading basically the same sentence over and over again?
>=	<=	The greater than or equal to operator returns True if the first operand is "greater than or equal to" the second.

The seventh comparison operator is Like. In standard Visual Basic, it compares the first operand to a string "pattern," which is a set of matching characters and wildcards:

```
If (someValue Like somePattern) Then
```

You don't have to use the same pattern rules when overloading the Like operator and you can accept any data type for the pattern operand, but you must still return a Boolean result.

```
Public Shared Operator Like(ByVal operand1 As Bumblebee, _
    ByVal operand2 As Integer) As Boolean
  ' ----- See if Bumblebee matches an Integer pattern.
End Operator
```

There is no "buddy" operator that you must implement when overloading the Like operator.

Bitwise and Logical Operators

Among the logical and bitwise operators included in Visual Basic, four already perform double duty as overloaded operators. The bitwise And, Or, Xor, and Not operators accept integer operands, generating numeric results with values transformed at the individual bit level. They also work as logical operators, accepting and returning Boolean values, most often in conditional statements. But they can handle the stress of being overridden a little more.

When you do override these four operators, you are overriding the bitwise versions, not the logical versions. Basically, this means that you have control over the return value, and aren't required to make it Boolean.

Table 12-3 lists the eight overloadable bitwise and logical operators.

Table 12-3. The overloadable bitwise and logical operators

Operator	Comments
<<	The shift left operator performs bit shifting on a source integer value, moving the bits to the left by a specified number of positions. Although you do not have to use this operator to perform true bit shifting, you must accept a shift amount (an Integer) as the second operand. ```Public Shared Operator <<(ByVal operand1 As Bumblebee, _ ByVal operand2 As Integer) As Bumblebee ' ----- Add shifting code here.End Operator```
>>	The shift right operator performs bit shifting just like the shift left operator, but it moves the bits in the "right" direction. I guess that would make those bits more conservative. Your code can make the return value more liberal if you want, but as with the shift left operator, you must accept an Integer as the second operand.
Not	The bitwise negation operator is unary, accepting only a single operand argument.
And	The bitwise conjunction operator sets a bit in the return value if both equally positioned bits in the source operands are also set.
Or	The bitwise disjunction operator sets a bit in the return value if either of the equally positioned bits in the source operands is set.
Xor	The bitwise exclusion operator sets a bit in the return value if only one of the equally positioned bits in the source operands is set.

Table 12-3. The overloadable bitwise and logical operators (continued)

Operator	Comments
IsTrue	Overloading the Or operator does not automatically overload the related OrElse operator. To use OrElse, you must also overload the special IsTrue operator. It's not a real Visual Basic operator, and you can't call it directly even when overloaded. But when you use the OrElse operator in place of an overloaded Or operator, Visual Basic calls the IsTrue operator when needed. There are a few rules you must follow to use the IsTrue overload: • The overloaded Or operator must return the class type of the class in which it is defined. If you want to use OrElse on the Bumblebee class, the overload of the Or operator in that class must return a value of type Bumblebee. • The overloaded IsTrue operator must accept a single operand of the containing class's type (Bumblebee), and return a Boolean. • You must also overload the IsFalse operator. How you determine the truth or falsity of a Bumblebee is up to you.
IsFalse	The IsFalse overload works just like IsTrue, and has similar rules, but it applies to the And and AndAlso operators.

The CType Operator

The Visual Basic CType feature looks more like a function than an operator:

```
result = CType(source, type)
```

But looks are deceiving. It is not a true function, and as with the other conversion functions (such as CInt), it is actually processed at compile time, long before the program even runs. By allowing you to overload it as an operator, Visual Basic enables you to create custom and special conversions between data types that don't seem compatible. The following method template converts a value of type Bumblebee to an Integer:

```
Public Shared Operator CType(ByVal operand1 As Bumblebee) _
      As Integer
   ' ----- Perform conversion here, returning an Integer.
End Operator
```

If you try to type that last block of code into Visual Basic, it will complain that you are missing either the Widening or the Narrowing keyword (see Figure 12-1).

```
Public Class Bumblebee        Conversion operators must be declared either 'Widening' or 'Narrowing'.
    Public Shared Operator CType(ByVal operand1 As Bumblebee) _
          As Integer
        ' ----- Perform conversion here, returning an Integer.
    End Operator
```

Figure 12-1. Visual Basic complains about all things wide and narrow

I mentioned widening and narrowing conversions in passing in Chapter 2, but let's examine them in more depth. When you convert between some core data types in Visual Basic, there is a chance that it will sometimes fail because the source value cannot fit into the destination value. This is true when converting a Short value to a Byte.

```
Dim quiteBig As Short = 5000
Dim quiteSmall As Byte
' ----- These next two lines will fail.
quiteSmall = quiteBig
quiteSmall = CByte(quiteBig)
```

And it's obvious why it fails: A Byte variable cannot hold the value 5000. But what about this code?

```
Dim quiteBig As Short = 5
Dim quiteSmall As Byte
' ----- These next two lines will succeed.
quiteSmall = quiteBig
quiteSmall = CByte(quiteBig)
```

It will run just fine, since 5 fits into a Byte variable with room to spare. (If Option Strict is set to On, the first assignment will still fail to compile.) Still, there is nothing to stop me from reassigning a value of 5000 to quiteBig and trying the assignment again. It's this *potential* for failure during conversion that is the issue.

When a conversion has the potential to fail due to the source data not being able to fully fit in the target variable, it's called a *narrowing conversion*. Narrowing conversions are a reality, and as long as you have checked the data before the conversion, there shouldn't be any reason to permanently restrict such conversions.

Widening conversions go in the opposite direction. They occur when any source value in the original data type will always fit easily in the target type. A widening conversion will always succeed as long as the source data is valid.

Visual Basic allows widening conversions to occur automatically, implicitly. You don't have to explicitly use CType to force the conversion. If you had a widening conversion from Bumblebee to Integer, and you had set Option Strict to On, the following code would work just fine:

```
Dim sourceValue As New Bumblebee
Dim destValue As Integer = sourceValue
```

If the conversion from Bumblebee to Integer was narrowing, you would have to force the conversion using CType just so that Visual Basic was sure you really wanted to do this.

```
Dim sourceValue As New Bumblebee
Dim destValue As Integer = CType(sourceValue, Integer)
```

When you create custom conversions with the overloaded CType operator, you must inform Visual Basic whether the conversion is widening or narrowing by inserting either the Widening or Narrowing keyword between the Shared and Operator keywords.

```
Public Shared Narrowing Operator CType( _
      ByVal operand1 As Bumblebee) As Integer
   ' ----- Perform narrowing conversion here.
End Operator
```

Other Operator Overloading Issues

There are a few other rules you must follow when overloading operators, but first let's look at a semi-useful Bumblebee class.

```
Class Bumblebee
   Public Bees As Integer

   Public Sub New( )
      ' ----- Default constructor.
      Bees = 0
   End Sub

   Public Sub New(ByVal startingBees As Integer)
      ' ----- Assign an initial number of bees.
      Bees = startingBees
   End Sub

   Public Shared Operator +(ByVal operand1 As Bumblebee, _
         ByVal operand2 As Bumblebee) As Bumblebee
      ' ----- Join bumblebee groups.
      Dim newGroup As New Bumblebee
      newGroup.Bees = operand1.Bees + operand2.Bees
      Return newGroup
   End Operator

   Public Shared Operator -(ByVal operand1 As Bumblebee, _
         ByVal operand2 As Bumblebee) As Bumblebee
      ' ----- Separate bumblebee groups.
      Dim newGroup As New Bumblebee
      newGroup.Bees = operand1.Bees - operand2.Bees
      If (newGroup.Bees < 0) Then newGroup.Bees = 0
      Return newGroup
   End Operator

   Public Shared Operator *(ByVal operand1 As Bumblebee, _
         ByVal operand2 As Bumblebee) As Bumblebee
      ' ----- Create a swarm.
      Dim newGroup As New Bumblebee
      newGroup.Bees = operand1.Bees * operand2.Bees
      Return newGroup
   End Operator
```

```
   Public Shared Widening Operator CType( _
        ByVal operand1 As Bumblebee) As Integer
      ' ----- Perform conversion here.
      Return operand1.Bees
   End Operator
End Class
```

The class is pretty simple; it exists to maintain a simple count of bees. But by over-loading the addition, subtraction, multiplication, and CType operators, we can use instances of bees with a more natural syntax.

```
Dim studyGroup1 As New Bumblebee(20)
Dim studyGroup2 As New Bumblebee(15)
Dim swarmGroup As Bumblebee = studyGroup1 * studyGroup2
MsgBox("The swarm contains " & CInt(swarmGroup) & " bees.")
```

Running this code correctly generates a 300-bee swarm and the message in Figure 12-2.

Figure 12-2. Bees sure know how to multiply

Including a CType overload that generates an Integer allowed me to convert a Bumblebee using the CInt operator. I could also have changed the last line to use the true CType operator.

```
MsgBox("The swarm contains " & _
    CType(swarmGroup, Integer) & " bees.")
```

Declaration Requirements

As mentioned earlier, you must always make Operator methods Public Shared. And because the overloaded operators need some sort of intimate connection to their containing class, at least one of the operands or the return value must match the type of the containing class. (In some overloads, Visual Basic requires that it be one of the operands that match.) Either of the two following overloads will work just fine, since Bumblebee is used for one of the operands:

```
Public Shared Operator <=(ByVal operand1 As Bumblebee, _
      ByVal operand2 As Integer) As Boolean
   ' ----- Compare a bumblebee to a value.
End Operator
```

```
Public Shared Operator <=(ByVal operand1 As Date, _
    ByVal operand2 As Bumblebee) As Boolean
  ' ----- Compare a date to a bumblebee.
End Operator
```

However, you cannot set both operands to a non-Bumblebee type at the same time and still keep the overload in the Bumblebee class.

```
Class Bumblebee
   Public Shared Operator <=(ByVal operand1 As Date, _
       ByVal operand2 As Integer) As Boolean
     ' ----- This will not compile.
   End Operator
End Class
```

Overloading Overloads

You can overload overloaded operators. No, dear editor, I didn't type the same word twice by mistake. You can add multiple argument-and-return-value signature variations of an overloaded operator to a single class.

```
Public Shared Widening Operator CType( _
     ByVal operand1 As Bumblebee) As Integer
   ' ----- Perform conversion to Integer here.
End Operator

Public Shared Widening Operator CType( _
     ByVal operand1 As Bumblebee) As Date
   ' ----- Perform conversion to Date here, somehow.
End Operator
```

As long as the argument signatures or return values differ, you can add as many overloads of an operator as you want. You don't need to use the Overloads keyword either.

Be Nice

That's right. Be nice. Just because you have the power to redefine addition to be division, you don't have to be so shocking. Don't make the maintenance programmers who have to modify your code later work harder because of your mischievous operator overloads. When you add overloads, let the meaning of the new feature at least have the feeling of the original operator. My fellow maintenance programmers and I will thank you.

Extension Methods

What if you want to modify the behavior of a class, but you don't have access to the source code? You could derive from it and build a new class, but that's not always convenient. You could call up the original developer and beg for the code, but some of those programmers are tight-fisted when it comes to their software.

Another option is to use a new Visual Basic 2008 feature: *extension methods*. Here's how it works:

1. You decide which class you want to extend with new methods.

2. You write those methods within a standard Module in your source code.

3. You start using the new methods as though they were included in the class definition.

The String data type includes several built-in methods that return a modified version of a string instance. For example, in this code:

```
Dim bossyString As String = "are you talking to me?"
MsgBox(bossyString.ToUpper())
```

the text that appears in the message box will be all uppercase because the ToUpper method returns a new uppercase version of the original string instance. A matching ToLower method works the other way, but what I really want is a ToTitle method that capitalizes just the first letter of each word.

```
MsgBox(bossyString.ToTitle())
```

The String class doesn't include a ToTitle method, but we can add it thanks to extension methods. To create an extension method, create a method within a standard module that accepts the target data type as its first parameter.

```
Module MyExtensions
    <System.Runtime.CompilerServices.Extension()> _
    Public Function ToTitle(ByVal sourceText As String) As String
        Return StrConv(sourceText, VbStrConv.ProperCase)
    End Function
End Module
```

Normally, you would call this function as is, passing in the original string.

```
MsgBox(ToTitle(bossyString))
```

And that code does work, but the addition of the Extension attribute (from the System.Runtime.CompilerServices namespace) turns ToTitle into an extension method, extending the String data type. Your code isn't really modifying String. Behind the scenes, the Visual Basic compiler is converting the new method-like syntax into the old function-like syntax on each use of ToTitle.

By themselves, extension methods don't do much. Calling ToTitle(bossyString) is not that different from bossyString.ToTitle(). But as with so many new features in Visual Basic 2008, extension methods were added just to raise the price of the product. Just kidding! Actually, the new extension methods feature is an important support for the new LINQ technology.

Summary

Operator overloading is a pretty neat feature, but you don't really need it. Anything you can do by overloading the addition operator you can also do by adding an Append method to a class. But operator overloading does allow you to bring your classes more into the mainstream of Visual Basic syntax usage.

Extension methods can also be replicated using standard method code, but there are some features of LINQ that specifically take advantage of extension methods.

When you do overload your operators or use extension methods, make sure you include sufficient documentation or comments to make it clear what it means to left-shift a customer, Normalize( ) a String, or multiply a bank account. Hey, I'd like to know about that last one.

Project

This chapter's project will add a lot of code to the Library application, as much as 25% of the full code base. Most of it is identical to code we added in earlier chapters, so I won't print it all here. There's a lot to read here, too, so I won't overload you with pasting code snippets right and left. But as you add each new form to the project, be sure to look over its code to become familiar with its inner workings.

PROJECT ACCESS

Load the Chapter 12 (Before) Code project, either through the New Project templates or by accessing the project directly from the installation directory. To see the code in its final form, load Chapter 12 (After) Code instead.

Overloading a Conversion

Operator overloading is a useful tool, and I have grown especially fond of the CType overload. Let's add a CType overload to a class we first designed back in Chapter 8: ListItemData. This class exposes both ItemText and ItemData properties, providing access to the textual and numeric aspects of the class content. Its primary purpose is to support the tracking of ID numbers in ListBox and ComboBox controls. If we need to know the ID number of a selected item in a ListBox control (let's name it SomeList), we use code similar to the following:

```
Dim recordID As Integer = _
    CType(SomeList.SelectedItem, ListItemData).ItemData
```

There's nothing wrong with that code. But I thought, "Wouldn't it be nice to convert the ListItemData instance to an Integer using the CInt function, and not have to mess with member variables like ItemData?"

```
Dim recordID As Integer = _
    CInt(CType(SomeList.SelectedItem, ListItemData))
```

Hmm. The code's not that different. But hey, why not? Let's do it. To support this conversion, we need to add a CType overload to the ListItemData class. Open that class's file, and add the following code as a member of the class.

INSERT SNIPPET

Insert Chapter 12, Snippet Item 1.

```
Public Shared Widening Operator CType( _
        ByVal sourceItem As ListItemData) As Integer
    ' ----- To convert to integer, simply extract the
    '       integer element.
    Return sourceItem.ItemData
End Operator
```

That's pretty simple. This widening conversion from ListItemData to Integer just returns the Integer portion of the instance. There are only about four or five places in the current Library Project that directly access the ItemData member, and it's not that important to go back and change them. But we'll use this conversion overload frequently in the new code added in this chapter.

Global Support Features

We need to add a few more global variables and common global routines to support various features used throughout the application. Two new global variables will track settings stored in the database's SystemValue table. Add them as members to the General module (in *General.vb*).

INSERT SNIPPET

Insert Chapter 12, Snippet Item 2.

```
Public DefaultItemLocation As Integer
Public SearchMatchLimit As Integer
```

The Library program identifies books and other items as stored in multiple locations, such as multiple branches or storage rooms. DefaultItemLocation indicates which one of these locations, from the CodeLocation table, is the default. The DefaultLocation entry of the SystemValue database table stores this value permanently.

When searching for books, authors, or other things that could result in thousands of matches, the SearchMatchLimit indicates the maximum number of matches returned by such searches. It's stored as the SearchLimit system value.

Since we're already in the General module, add two more helper functions.

ConfirmDefaultLocation

This routine verifies that a valid DefaultLocation entry exists in the SystemValue table. It returns True on success.

GetCopyDisposition

This routine provides a short description for the current status of a specific library item copy. It analyzes the item's and patron's records, and returns one of the following status code strings: New Item Copy, Checked In, Checked Out, Overdue, Missing, or Reference.

Extending a Framework-Supplied Class

What's in a name? Well, if it's the author names in the Library Project, they might include first and last names, prefixes (such as "Dr.") and suffixes ("Jr."), and dates for birth and death. Some of those parts are optional, so formatting the author name is a multistep process. Since the application will need to format author names in several places throughout the code, let's add a central routine, FormatAuthorName, that does the work for us.

```vb
<System.Runtime.CompilerServices.Extension()> _
Public Function FormatAuthorName( _
      ByRef dbInfo As SqlClient.SqlDataReader) As String
   ' ----- Given an author record, return the formatted name.
   Dim authorName As String

   On Error Resume Next

   ' ----- Format the name.
   authorName = CStr(dbInfo!LastName)
   If (IsDBNull(dbInfo!FirstName) = False) Then
      authorName &= ", " & CStr(dbInfo!FirstName)
      If (IsDBNull(dbInfo!MiddleName) = False) Then _
         authorName &= " " & CStr(dbInfo!MiddleName)
   End If
   If (IsDBNull(dbInfo!Suffix) = False) Then _
      authorName &= ", " & CStr(dbInfo!Suffix)

   ' ----- Add in the birth and death years.
   If (IsDBNull(dbInfo!BirthYear) = False) Or _
         (IsDBNull(dbInfo!DeathYear) = False) Then
```

```
        authorName &= " ("
        If (IsDBNull(dbInfo!BirthYear) = True) Then
            authorName &= "????"
        Else
            authorName &= CStr(Math.Abs(CInt(dbInfo!BirthYear)))
            If (CInt(dbInfo!BirthYear) < 0) Then _
                authorName &= "BC"
        End If
        authorName &= "-"
        If (IsDBNull(dbInfo!DeathYear) = False) Then
            authorName &= CStr(Math.Abs(CInt(dbInfo!DeathYear)))
            If (CInt(dbInfo!DeathYear) < 0) Then _
                authorName &= "BC"
        End If
        authorName &= ")"
    End If

    ' ----- Finished.
    Return authorName
End Function
```

This routine is an extension method that extends the `SqlClient.SqlDataReader` class. The fully qualified `Extension` attribute makes the connection between our custom extension and the framework-defined `SqlDataReader` class. Given a `SqlDataReader` built from records in the Author table, the function formats and returns a friendly author name in the format "Public, John Q, Jr. (1900–1999)." Elsewhere in the application, it's called as though it were a member of the data reader instance.

```
dbInfo.FormatAuthorName( )
```

We could have left out the extension method features altogether by simply omitting the `Extension` attribute. Then, calls for author formatting would look like this:

```
FormatAuthorName(dbInfo)
```

Record Editors and Supporting Forms

Now things really start to hop. We'll add 23 new forms to the application in this chapter. Most of them implement basic code editors, similar to the *UserName.vb* and *GroupName.vb* files we built in Chapter 11. Other forms exist to provide additional support for these record editors. I won't reprint anything I've gone over before, but I'll point out some interesting new code on our way through each of these 23 forms.

If you're following along in the "Before" version of this chapter's project, you will need to enable each form as you encounter it. To do this, select the file in the Solution Explorer window, and change the file's Build Action property (in the Properties panel) from None to Compile.

Search-limiting forms

The first four forms allow the librarian to limit the information overload that comes through using a database with thousands of books, publishers, and authors. You probably remember that the generic ListEditRecords form displays all existing records from a table of records by default. This works fine for the security groups stored in the GroupName table since you probably won't have even a dozen of those. But listing all books in even a small library can generate quite an imposing list. And depending on the speed of your workstation, it can take awhile to load all book titles into the list.

The four "search-limiting" forms help to reduce the number of records appearing in the list at once. When the librarian accesses the list of books and other library items, the ItemLimit form (see Figure 12-3) provides a quick search prompt that reduces the listed results.

Figure 12-3. The ItemLimit form acts like a bar-room bouncer for items

The form lets the user retrieve all records, or specific items based on item name (with wildcard support). Once the matches are loaded, the user can access this form again by clicking on the Lookup button on the ListEditRecords form for those types of code editors that support lookups (authors, items, patrons, and publishers).

We are ready to include these four search-limiting forms in the project:

AuthorLimit.vb
> This form limits author records as loaded from the Author table.

ItemLimit.vb
> This is the form we just talked about. It limits the display of library items from the NamedItem table.

PatronLimit.vb
> Just in case patrons are flocking to your library, this form lets you limit the records loaded from the Patron table.

PublisherLimit.vb
> This form limits records from the Publisher table.

Keyword and subject editors

Although most record editors provide a full editing experience through the ListEditRecords form, some are subordinate to other editor forms. Keywords and subjects are a good example. Though each has its own independent tables (Keyword and Subject), I chose to allow editing of them through the form that edits individual library items, the NamedItem form (added later). That form manages all interactions between the Keyword and Subject records and the NamedItem table, all through the intermediate many-to-many tables ItemKeyword and ItemSubject.

The KeywordAdd and SubjectAdd forms provide a simple text entry form for a single keyword or subject. Include each of these forms now in the project:

- *KeywordAdd.vb*
- *SubjectAdd.vb*

More named item support forms

As we'll see later, the NamedItem form is one of the most complex forms added to the Library Project so far. It manages everything about a generalized library item (such as a book). Each item can have multiple copies, authors, keywords, subjects, and so on. It's simply too much editing power to include on a single form. We already added two of the subordinate forms: KeywordAdd and SubjectAdd. Let's add five additional support forms:

AuthorAddLocate.vb

This form presents a wizard-like interface that lets the user add a new or existing author record to an item. *Authors* in the Library program is a generic term that refers to authors, editors, illustrators, performers, and so on. This form's three wizard steps let the user (1) indicate the type of author via the CodeAuthorType table; (2) perform a search for an existing author by name; and (3) select from a list of matching author names. If the desired author isn't yet in the database, the last step allows a new author to be added. Figure 12-4 shows the first two of these steps.

Figure 12-4. The first two of three author wizard steps

Most of the logic is controlled through the Next button's event handler. The code in this routine varies based on the current wizard panel in view (as indicated by the ActivePanel class-level variable). Here's the code that runs when the user clicks Next after selecting the author type:

```
' ----- Make sure a name type is selected.
If (CInt(CType(NameType.SelectedItem, _
    ListItemData)) = -1) Then
  MsgBox("Please select a name type from the list.", _
    MsgBoxStyle.OkOnly Or MsgBoxStyle.Exclamation, _
    ProgramTitle)
  NameType.Focus()
  Return
End If

' ----- Move to the search panel.
ActivePanel = PanelCriteria
SecondPanel.Visible = True
FirstPanel.Visible = False
ActBack.Enabled = True
LastName.Focus()
```

Did you see the first logic line in that code? We used the CInt conversion function to get an ItemData value from a list item. This calls our overloaded CType operator in the ListItemData class.

PublisherAddLocate.vb

This form is just like the AuthorAddLocate form, but focuses on publishers. Its wizard has only two steps since publishers are not grouped by type. It locates or adds records in the Publisher table. When it's time to add a publisher to an item, the item editor form calls the public PublisherAddLocate.PromptUser function. This function returns the ID of the selected publisher record, or –1 to abort the adding of a publisher. A return value of –2 clears any previously selected publisher ID.

SeriesAddLocate.vb

This form is similar to the PublisherAddLocate form, but it prompts for records from the CodeSeries table.

ItemAuthorEdit.vb

Once an author has been added to an item, the only way to change it to a different author is to remove the incorrect author, and add the correct author separately through the AuthorAddLocate form. But if the user simply selected the wrong author type (such as "Editor" instead of "Illustrator"), it's kind of a burden to search for the author name again just to change the type. The ItemAuthorEdit form lets the user modify the type for an author already added to an item. It modifies the ItemAuthor.AuthorType database field.

ItemCopy.vb

A library will likely have multiple copies of a particular book, CD, or other item. In the Library program, this means that each `NamedItem` record can have more than one `ItemCopy` record attached to it. Each copy is edited through the `ItemCopy` form (see Figure 12-5).

Figure 12-5. Details only a librarian could love

Although this code does not inherit from `BaseCodeForm` as other record editors do, it still has many of the features of those forms, including a `SaveFormData` routine that writes records to the database.

One interesting thing that this form does have is support for reading bar codes. Many bar code readers act as a "wedge," inserting the text of a scanned bar code into the keyboard input stream of the computer. Any program monitoring for bar codes simply has to monitor normal text input.

Bar code wedge scanners append a carriage return (the Enter key) to the end of the transmitted bar code. This lets a program detect the end of the bar code number. But in most of the Library program's forms, the Enter key triggers the OK button and closes the form. We don't want that to happen here. To prevent this, we'll add some code to this form that disables the auto-click on the OK button whenever the insertion point is in the Barcode text entry field.

Insert Chapter 12, Snippet Item 5.

```
Private Sub RecordBarcode_Enter( _
      ByVal sender As Object, ByVal e As System.EventArgs) _
      Handles RecordBarcode.Enter
   ' ----- Highlight the entire text.
   RecordBarcode.SelectAll( )

   ' ----- Don't allow Enter to close the form.
   Me.AcceptButton = Nothing
End Sub

Private Sub RecordBarcode_Leave( _
      ByVal sender As Object, ByVal e As System.EventArgs) _
      Handles RecordBarcode.Leave
   ' ----- Allow Enter to close the form again.
   Me.AcceptButton = ActOK
End Sub

Private Sub RecordBarcode_KeyPress(ByVal sender As Object, _
      ByVal e As System.Windows.Forms.KeyPressEventArgs) _
      Handles RecordBarcode.KeyPress
   ' ----- Ignore the enter key.
   If (e.KeyChar = ChrW(Keys.Return)) Then e.Handled = True
End Sub
```

With this code, when the user presses the Enter key in the Barcode field manually, the form will not close. But it's a small price to pay for bar code support.

Inherited code editors

Twelve of the forms added in this chapter inherit directly from the `BaseCodeForm` class. Add them to the project as I review each one.

Author.vb

The `Author` form edits records in the `Author` database table. As a typical derived class of `BaseCodeForm`, it overrides many of the public elements of its base class. Two overrides that we haven't yet used in earlier chapters are the `UsesSearch` and `SearchForRecord` methods. These allow the user of the `ListEditRecords` form to limit the displayed authors through the prompting of the `AuthorLimit` form described earlier in this chapter. (The `FillListWithRecords` override also calls `SearchForRecord` to prompt the user for the initial list of authors to display.)

In `SearchForLimit`, the call to `AuthorLimit.PromptUser` returns a comma-separated string in "Last, First" format.

```
' ----- Prompt the user for the limited author name.
exceededMatches = False
userLimit = (New AuthorLimit).PromptUser( )
If (userLimit = "") Then Return
```

The user can include the asterisk (*) character as a wildcard in the first or last name parts. The asterisk has become a common character to use in all types of wildcard searches. Unfortunately, it is not supported in SQL Server SELECT statements. SQL Server uses the percent (%) character for a wildcard instead (as do many other SQL-compliant database platforms). As SearchForLimit extracts the first and last names, it ensures that the right wildcard character is used.

```
' ----- Use the limits to help prepare the search text.
limitLast = Trim(GetSubStr(userLimit, ",", 1))
limitFirst = Trim(GetSubStr(userLimit, ",", 2))
If ((limitLast & limitFirst) = "") Then Return
If (InStr(limitLast, "*") = 0) Then limitLast &= "*"
If (InStr(limitFirst, "*") = 0) Then limitFirst &= "*"
limitLast = Replace(limitLast, "*", "%")
limitFirst = Replace(limitFirst, "*", "%")
```

This code uses our custom GetSubStr routine already added to the General module. Once the name parts are extracted, the Visual Basic Replace function replaces all instances of * with %. You'll find similar code in the other record editors that allow limits on the list of records, such as the Publisher form added later.

While you have the source code open for this form, zoom up to the top. There, you'll find an interesting Imports statement:

```
Imports MVB = Microsoft.VisualBasic
```

Normally, Imports is followed immediately by a namespace. This variation includes the MVB = prefix, which defines a shortcut for the Microsoft.VisualBasic namespace for code in this file. With Visual Basic importing so many namespaces into an existing class that also defines a lot of public members, there are bound to be member name conflicts. In this case, the conflict is the Left form member. Since this source code for the Author form sees everything through the prism of that form, when you include the keyword Left in your logic, the code naturally assumes that you mean the form's Left property, which sets the left position of the form. The problem is that Left is also a common string manipulation function that extracts the leftmost characters from a larger string:

```
smallerString = Left(largerString, 5)
```

In a form, this code generates an error since it thinks Left means Me.Left. To use the string version of Left, you have to prefix it with its namespace:

```
smallerString = Microsoft.VisualBasic.Left( _
    largerString, 5)
```

The special Imports statement lets us substitute a shorter name for the rather long Microsoft.VisualBasic namespace:

```
smallerString = MVB.Left(largerString, 5)
```

You will find a few instances of such code in this and other forms that include the MVB shortcut.

The `Author` form has one more notable element. A Name Matches label appears near the bottom of the form, as shown in Figure 12-6.

Figure 12-6. The bottom of the Author form showing Name Matches

This field helps the user avoid adding the same author to the database twice. As changes are made to the Last Name and First Name fields, the Name Matches field gets refreshed with matching author names found in the `Author` table. The `RefreshMatchingAuthors` routine counts the number of matching authors through the following code:

```
sqlText = "SELECT COUNT(*) AS TheCount " & _
    "FROM Author WHERE LastName LIKE " & _
    DBText(Trim(RecordLastName.Text))
If (Trim(RecordFirstName.Text) <> "") Then
    sqlText &= " AND FirstName LIKE " & _
        DBText(MVB.Left(Trim( _
        RecordFirstName.Text), 1) & "%")
End If
matchCount = CInt(ExecuteSQLReturn(sqlText))
```

This is similar to the lookup code in the `SearchForLimit` routine, but it only adds a wildcard to the first name before doing the search.

CodeAuthorType.vb

The `CodeAuthorType` form edits records in the related `CodeAuthorType` table. Who knew?

CodeCopyStatus.vb

This form edits records in the `CodeCopyStatus` database table.

CodeLocation.vb

As expected, this form edits records in the `CodeLocation` table. Once you've added at least one record to that table, you'll be able to set the default location for the database. I'll discuss this again a little later in this chapter.

CodeMediaType.vb

The `CodeMediaType` form, which edits records in the `CodeMediaType` table, includes a few more fields than the other "Code" table editors. Most of the fields accept numeric input. Although I do a final check for valid numeric data just before writing the record to the database, I try to prevent any non-numeric data from showing up in the first place by restricting the acceptable keystrokes. For instance, the `RecordCheckoutDays` text field's `KeyPress` event includes this code:

```
' ----- Only allow digits and backspaces.
If (e.KeyChar = vbBack) Or _
   (IsNumeric(e.KeyChar)) Then Return
e.Handled = True
```

Setting the e.Handled property to True stops Visual Basic from doing anything else (pretty much) with the entered key. It's a quick and easy way to dispose of a user-entered keystroke.

CodePatronGroup.vb

This form edits records in the CodePatronGroup table.

CodeSeries.vb

This editor manages records in the CodeSeries table. Earlier I mentioned how series names and keywords are subordinate to named items. But it made sense to me to also provide direct management for series names, in case you wanted to build up a common list before adding individual library items. So, this form performs double duty: you can access it as a standard record editor through the ListEditRecords form, and it's also used for a specific named item through the not-yet-added NamedItem form.

When editing item-specific series names, the user first gets to search for a series name by typing it. Since I don't want the user to have to retype the series name again in this editor form, I wanted to pass the typed series name into the CodeSeries form, but none of the overridden public methods supported this. So, we'll need to add a new method that will accept the typed name. The AddRecord member already overrides the base function of the same name.

```
Public Overrides Function AddRecord() As Integer
    ' ----- Add a new record.
    ActiveID = -1
    PrepareFormFields()
    Me.ShowDialog()
    If (Me.DialogResult = Windows.Forms. _
       DialogResult.OK) Then _
       Return ActiveID Else Return -1
End Function
```

Let's add an overload to this function that includes a string argument. The caller will pass the originally typed text to this argument. We'll assign it to the RecordFullName control's Text property so that it shows up automatically when the form opens.

INSERT SNIPPET

Insert Chapter 12, Snippet Item 6.

```
Public Overloads Function AddRecord( _
    ByVal seriesText As String) As Integer
  ' ----- Add a new record, but use a starting value
  '       previously entered by the user.
  ActiveID = -1
  PrepareFormFields()
  RecordFullName.Text = seriesText
  Me.ShowDialog()
  If (Me.DialogResult = Windows.Forms.DialogResult.OK) Then _
    Return ActiveID Else Return -1
End Function
```

Yes, we could have used some name other than AddRecord for this function and avoided adding an overload. But it's nice to keep things consistent.

Holiday.vb

This form manages the records in the Holiday table. In a later chapter, we'll add a cache of holidays within the program for quick access.

Patron.vb

The Patron form provides editing services for records in the Patron table, and appears in Figure 12-7.

Figure 12-7. Most of the Patron form (Messages tab details are hidden)

This form includes a `TabControl` to help break up the number of fields the user has to experience at once. If you have ever used the tab control included with Visual Basic 6.0, you'll quickly appreciate the .NET replacement. It manages all of the panel-switching logic automatically when the user selects a different tab. Each panel is a separate `TabPage` class instance. In your code, forcing the tab control to display a different tab is as easy as assigning the appropriate `TabPage` instance to the `TabControl` object's `SelectedTab` property, as with this code line from the `ValidateFormData` function:

```
TabPatron.SelectedTab = TabGeneral
```

Although this form looks quite complex, it's made up almost entirely of code we've seen in other forms. Beyond the standard overrides of `BaseCodeForm` members, this form includes bar code scanning support borrowed from the `ItemCopy` form, password logic stolen from the `UserName` form, and name-matching code similar to that used in the `Author` form.

I included a Manage Patron's Items button on the form, but we won't add its logic until a later chapter. An extra public function, `EditRecordLimited`, becomes important at that time.

Publisher.vb

The `Publisher` form lets the user edit the records in the `Publisher` table. It's a pretty simple form with only two data entry fields. A Status field indicates how many `NamedItem` records link to this publisher. A small button appears to the right of the text entry field for the publisher's web site. This is the "show me the web site" button, and when clicked, it brings up the supplied web page in the user's default browser. To enable this button, add the following code to the `ShowWeb` button's `Click` event handler.

INSERT SNIPPET

Insert Chapter 12, Snippet Item 7.

```
' ----- Show the web site displayed in the field.
Dim newProcess As ProcessStartInfo

On Error Resume Next
If (Trim(RecordWeb.Text) = "") Then Return
newProcess = New ProcessStartInfo(Trim(RecordWeb.Text))
Process.Start(newProcess)
```

SystemValue.vb

This code editor handles items in the `SystemValue` table. Although we will connect it to a link on the main Library form in this chapter, we will change this access method in a future chapter.

Well, that's 11 of the 12 derived forms. The last one is the `NamedItem` form, shown in Figure 12-8.

Figure 12-8. The NamedItem form with the General tab active

The NamedItem form is the largest and most complex of the forms that derive from BaseCodeForm. It edits primary library items recorded in the NamedItem database table. It's complex because it also directly or indirectly manages records in other subordinate tables: ItemAuthor, ItemCopy, ItemKeyword, ItemSubject, and indirectly, Author, Keyword, Publisher, and Subject.

All of the fields on the General and Classification tabs are basic data entry fields that flow directly into the NamedItem table, just as is done with the other record-editing forms. The Publisher and Series fields use separate selection forms (PublisherAddLocate and SeriesAddLocate) to obtain the ID values stored in NamedItem. Here's the code that looks up the publisher:

```
' ----- Prompt the user.
newPublisher = (New PublisherAddLocate).PromptUser()
If (newPublisher = -1) Then Return

' ----- Check to clear the publisher.
If (newPublisher = -2) Then
   RecordPublisher.Text = "Not Available"
   PublisherID = -1
   Return
End If
```

The other four tabs—Authors/Names, Subjects, Keywords, and Copies—manage subordinate records. The code is pretty consistent among the four different tabs, so I'll limit my comments to the Authors/Names tab (see Figure 12-9).

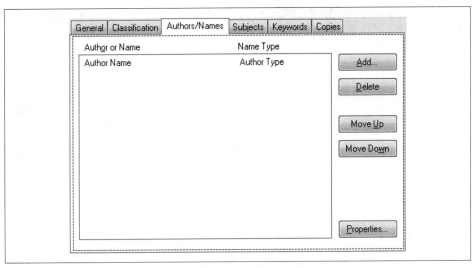

Figure 12-9. The NamedItem form with the Authors/Names tab active

The controls on this tab are quite similar to those on the ListEditRecords form; they exist to manage a set of records in a table. In this case, it's the ItemAuthor table. For the presentation list, I chose to use a ListView control instead of a standard ListBox control. By setting a ListView control's View property to Details, setting its FullRowSelect field to True, and modifying its Columns collection (see Figure 12-10), you can quickly turn it into a multicolumn listbox.

When you add an item to this list, you also have to add "subitems" to have anything appear in all but the first column.

```
Dim newItem As Windows.Forms.ListViewItem = _
    AuthorsList.Items.Add("John Smith")
newItem.SubItems.Add("Illustrator")
```

The Add button brings up the AuthorAddLocate form, whereas the Properties button displays the ItemAuthorEdit form instead.

Before any of the subordinate records can be added, the "parent" record must exist in the database. That is because the "child" records include the ID number of the parent record, and without a parent record, there is no parent ID number.

Figure 12-10. The ColumnHeader editor for a ListView control

If you look in each of the Add button routines on this form, you will find code such as the following:

```
' ----- The record must be saved first.
If (ActiveID = -1) Then
   ' ----- Confirm with the user.
   If (MsgBox("The item must be saved to the database " & _
      "before authors or names can be added. Would you " & _
      "like to save the record now?", _
      MsgBoxStyle.YesNo Or MsgBoxStyle.Question, _
      ProgramTitle) <> MsgBoxResult.Yes) Then Return

   ' ----- Verify and save the data.
   If (ValidateFormData() = False) Then Return
   If (SaveFormData() = False) Then Return
End If
```

If this is a brand-new NamedItem record (ActiveID = -1), this code will save it before allowing the user to add the subordinate record. Any invalid data that prevents the record from being saved will be caught in the call to ValidateFormData.

Actually, the calls to both ValidateFormData and SaveFormData are the same ones that occur when the user clicks on the OK button. Normally, that triggers a return of the new record's ID number to the calling form. But what if SaveFormData gets called by adding an author, but then the user clicks the Cancel button (which normally returns a –1 value to indicate "no record added")? To avoid that, the SaveFormData function sets a class-level variable named SessionSaved:

```
SessionSaved = True
```

This flag is cleared when the form first opens, but is set to True pretty much anytime a subordinate record changes. The NamedItem form's overridden AddRecord and EditRecord functions check for this flag before returning to the calling form.

```
If (Me.DialogResult = Windows.Forms.DialogResult.OK) Or _
    (SessionSaved = True) Then Return ActiveID Else Return -1
```

There's lots of other interesting code in the NamedItem form. But at nearly 1,400 lines (not counting the related designer code), I'll have to let you investigate it on your own.

Connecting the Editors to the Main Form

OK, take a breath. That was a lot of code to go through. But if you run the program now, you won't see any difference at all. We still need to connect all of the record editors to the main form. They all connect through the LinkLabel controls on the main form's Administration panel (PanelAdmin). We need to add 12 LinkClicked event handlers to access all of the new and various forms. Go ahead and add them now to the MainForm class.

INSERT SNIPPET

Insert Chapter 12, Snippet Item 8.

Each of the LinkClicked event handlers is almost a mirror image of the other, except for a few object instance names here and there. Here's the code that handles a click on the Publisher link label:

```
Private Sub AdminLinkPublishers_LinkClicked( _
        ByVal sender As System.Object, ByVal e As _
        System.Windows.Forms.LinkLabelLinkClickedEventArgs) _
        Handles AdminLinkPublishers.LinkClicked
    ' ----- Make sure the user is allowed to do this.
    If (SecurityProfile(LibrarySecurity.ManagePublishers) = _
            False) Then
        MsgBox(NotAuthorizedMessage, MsgBoxStyle.OkOnly Or _
            MsgBoxStyle.Exclamation, ProgramTitle)
        Return
    End If

    ' ----- Let the user edit the list of publishers.
    ListEditRecords.ManageRecords(New Library.Publisher)
    ListEditRecords = Nothing
End Sub
```

After doing a quick security check, the code calls up the standard ListEditRecords form, passing it an instance of the record editor it is to use.

There are still a few inactive links on the Administration panel that we'll enable in later chapters.

Setting the Default Location

The program is now ready to run with all of its new features in place. Since we added only administrative features, you must click the Login button in the upper-right corner of the main form before gaining access to the Administration panel and its features. Unless you changed it, your login username is "admin" with no password.

Although you can now run the program and access all of the record editors, you won't be able to add new item copies until you set a default location. To set the location:

1. Add at least one location through the Locations link on the Administration panel.

2. Obtain the ID number of the CodeLocation record you want to be the default. You can use SQL Server Management Studio Express's query features to access the records in this table. If this is the first time you've added records to the CodeLocation table, the first item you add will have an ID value of 1.

3. Back in the Library program, edit the SystemValue table through the System Values link on the Administration panel.

4. Add or modify the "DefaultLocation" system value, setting its value to the ID number of the default location record.

Alternatively, you can update the DefaultLocation record in the SystemValue table directly using SQL Server Management Studio Express. If the ID of the location to use is 1, use this SQL statement to make the change:

```
UPDATE SystemValue
   SET ValueData = '1'
   WHERE ValueName = 'DefaultLocation'
```

In a future chapter, we'll add a more user-friendly method to update this default location.

Speaking of user-friendly, we're about to enter the not-user-friendly but logic-friendly world of text structured data: XML.

XML

Because computers are computers and people are people, they generally have different requirements when it comes to getting their data into a usable format. XML is an attempt to arrange data in a structure that is usable for both people and software.

XML has really come into vogue in recent years, but its roots are quite old. It's derived from SGML (Standard Generalized Markup Language), as is HTML (cousins!). SGML in turn came from GML (Generalized Markup Language), a "metalanguage" (a language that describes another language) designed by IBM back in the 1960s. So, blame IBM if you want to, but either way, you will come in regular contact with XML as you develop .NET applications.

I might as well tell you right from the start: either you will love XML, or you will hate it, but probably both. It's a strange beast, this XML, as you would expect from any acronym that takes letters from the middle of the words it represents ("eXtensible Markup Language"). XML represents an alphabet of data manipulation technologies, an alphabet which strangely has seven Xs. But enough of the teasing; let's *extend* our understanding of this basic .NET technology.

What Is XML?

XML is nothing more than a data format that is both human-readable and machine-readable. Have you ever tried to open a Microsoft Word document with Notepad? Good luck (see Figure 13-1). Although you can usually sift out the main text of the document, most of what you see is gobbledygook. That's because it is in a *proprietary binary* format. It's *proprietary* because, frankly, you shouldn't be poking your fingers in there. That's what Microsoft Word is for. And it's *binary* because you can store a lot of information conveniently in a little bit of disk space. With such a file, I can store my data any way I choose. If fact, I can write my data out willy-nilly, and not have to get permission from anyone, because it's mine, mine, all mine.

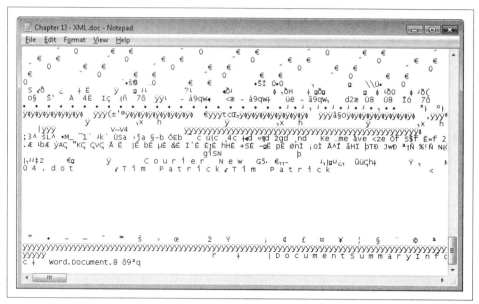

Figure 13-1. This chapter in Notepad

Binary files are great for storing any kind of data: numbers, strings, base-64 encrypted images, streams of networking data chatter, anything. The problem is that unless you know the exact structure you used to write it out, there is little chance of ever getting the data back. This is good if your goal is secrecy, but if you ever need to share that data with another person or program, or worse yet, debug the output from your errant program, you're in for a tough time. If one little byte gets messed up, the whole file might be useless.

There are, of course, other ways to store your data. For files that store records of data, tab-delimited and CSV (comma-separated value) files provide a convenient transfer medium, in a more human-friendly format. For instance, consider this data from Microsoft's sample "Northwind Traders" database, stored as comma-separated values:

```
ProductID,ProductName,SupplierID,Category,UnitPrice,Available
"1","Chai","652","Beverages","$18.00","Yes"
"2","Chang","9874","Beverages","$19.00","No"
"3","Aniseed Syrup","9874","Condiments","On Sale","Yes"
```

Now that's better. This data is pretty easy to understand. Each piece of data is grouped by commas, and the first row indicates what each column contains. And the best part is that many programs already know how to read files in this format. If you save this data in a text file with a *.csv* extension, and open it in Microsoft Excel, the data automatically appears in columns.

But it could be better. For instance, what do those "652" and "9874" values refer to anyway? And is it correct that the unit price of Aniseed Syrup is "On Sale?"

Sure, I can load this data into my program, but can I do anything with it? At least it's an easy read for both people and computer programs, and isn't that what I said XML was all about?

Well, yes. Although XML includes rules and features that make it more flexible than your average text datafile, it's not that different. For all the hype, XML is just a way of storing data. Any of the fancy-schmancy XML traits discussed in this chapter could be performed easily with data stored in simpler text or binary proprietary formats. In fact, it is often quicker and more convenient to develop using a proprietary format, because your data will contain exactly and only what you need, without any fluff.

That being said, XML does include many aspects that make it a strong contender when considering a data format:

It's straightforward to read
Each data element includes a type of title. Good titles make for good reading.

It's easy to process
All data includes starting and ending tags, so a program can process the data without much effort. And one bad element won't necessarily ruin the whole file.

It's flexible
You can store any type of data in XML. It is just a text file, after all. If you have a certain XML file format used in version 1 of your program, and you add features to it in version 2, you can do it in a way that still allows version 1 programs to use version 2 files without breaking.

It's self-describing
XML includes several features that let you describe the content of a given XML file. Two of the most popular are DTD (Document Type Definition) and XSD (XML Schema Definition). You use these tools to indicate exactly what you expect your datafile to contain. Additionally, XML allows you to embed comments in the content without impacting the actual data.

It's self-verifying
Tools are available, including tools in .NET, which can confirm the integrity and format of an XML file by comparing the content to the associated DTD or XSD. This lets you verify a file before you even process it.

It's an open standard
XML has gained widespread acceptance, even across divergent computer platforms.

It's built into .NET
This is going to be the biggest reason for using it. In fact, you won't be able to get away from XML in .NET, even if you try. It's everywhere.

But there's bad news, too:

It's bulky

XML content contains a lot of repetitive structural information, and generally lots of whitespace. You could abbreviate many of the structure elements, and remove all the whitespace (XML doesn't require it), but that would remove the human-readable aspects of the data. Some platforms, such as cell phone browsers, like to keep data small. XML is anything but small.

It's text

Wait a minute, this is a good thing—most of the time. Sometimes you just need to store binary data, such as pictures. You can't really store true binary data in an XML file without breaking one of the basic rules about XML: text only! Often, binary data is encoded in a text-like format, such as base-64 (which uses readable characters to store binary data).

It's inefficient

This comes from having data in a verbose semi-human-readable format, rather than in a terse, compact binary form. It simply takes longer for a computer to scan text looking for matching angle brackets than it does to move a few bytes directly from a lump of binary data into a location in memory.

It's human-readable

There are not many secrets in an XML file. And although you could encrypt the data elements in the file, or the entire file for that matter, that would kind of defeat the purpose of using XML.

It's machine-readable

If you are expecting the average Joe to pick up an XML printout and read it in his easy chair, think again. XML is not appropriate for every type of datafile.

It's not immune to errors

As I keep repeating, XML is just a text file. If you open it in Notepad and let your five-year-old pound on the keyboard, the content will have problems. XML is not a panacea; it's just a useful file format.

The XML Rule

Before we look at some actual XML, you need to know *The Rule*. You must obey *The Rule* with every piece of XML text you write.

THE RULE

If you open it, close it.

That's it. Don't forget it. Obey it. Live it. I'll explain what it means later.

XML Content

There's no better way to learn about XML than to start looking at it. If you've never used XML, but you've written some HTML, this should look somewhat familiar.

Some Basic XML

Here's a simple chunk of XML for you to enjoy:

```
<?xml version="1.0"?>
<hello>
   <there>
      <!-- Finally, real data here. -->
      <world target="everyone">think XML</world>
      <totalCount>694.34</totalCount>
      <goodbye />
   </there>
</hello>
```

Hey, I didn't say it was going to be interesting. As I mentioned before, it's just data, but it is useful data, and here's why:

It's obviously XML

This is clear from the first line, which always starts with <?xml.... This line also indicates the XML version number, which tells XML processing routines (parsers) to adjust behavior if needed. That's foresight.

It's structured

XML is a hierarchical data structure. That is, you can have data *elements* embedded inside other data elements to any depth you want. Every element is bounded by a set of *tags*. In this sample, the tags are hello, there, world, totalCount, and goodbye. Tags always appear inside <angle brackets>, and always appear in pairs, as in <hello>...</hello>. (This is where *The Rule*, "If you open it, close it," comes in.) Don't forget the / just before the tag name in the closing bracket. This syntax lets you organize your data into specifically arranged named units. For tag pairs that have nothing in between them, you can use the shortened syntax <*tagname* />, as I did with the goodbye tag. By the way, XML tags are case-sensitive, so type carefully.

It's readable

It's human-readable, thanks to all the whitespace, although you could remove it all and still have XML. It's also computer-readable because of the consistent use of tags.

It's a single unit of data

All XML files have a single *root element* in which all other elements must appear. In the sample, <hello> is the root element. Once that element is closed (through its ending tag) you can't add any additional elements. Nope. Nada.

It's got comments

See that <!--...--> line? That's a comment. You can stick comments here and there just like they were free-floating tags.

It's got attributes

XML supports two varieties of data: real data and attributes. Real data values come between the innermost tag pairs, as with think XML and 694.34 in the sample. Attributes provide extended information about the tags themselves. I included an attribute named target in the world element. The content of all attributes must be in quotes. I could have made this attribute a subelement instead, and a lot of people do. There is disagreement among programmers as to when data should be an element or an attribute. Let your conscience be your guide.

So, there you have it—some clean, clear XML data.

Some Basic—and Meaningful—XML

Let's see what that comma-delimited data from Northwind Traders that I listed previously could look like in XML.

```
<?xml version="1.0"?>
<productList>
   <supplier ID="652" fullName="Beverages R Us">
      <product ID="1" available="Yes">
         <productName>Chai</productName>
         <category>Beverages</category>
         <unitPrice>18.00</unitPrice>
      </product>
   </supplier>
   <supplier ID="9874" fullName="We Sell Food">
      <product ID="2" available="No">
         <productName>Chang</productName>
         <category>Beverages</category>
         <unitPrice>19.00</unitPrice>
      </product>
      <product ID="3" available="Yes" onSale="true">
         <productName>Aniseed Syrup</productName>
         <category>Condiments</category>
         <unitPrice>12.00</unitPrice>
      </product>
   </supplier>
</productList>
```

Moving the data to XML has greatly increased the size of the content. But with an increase in size comes an increase in processing value. I was immediately able to get some benefit from the hierarchical structure of XML. In the original data, supplier was just another column. But in the XML version, all the data is now grouped into supplier sections, which makes sense (at least, if that is how I was planning to use the data).

You can also see that I followed *The Rule*. Every opening tag has a matching closing tag. Whatever you do, don't forget *The Rule*.

Now, you're saying to yourself, "Tim, I could have grouped the data by supplier once I loaded the comma-delimited data into my program." And to that I say, "You're right." I told you that XML was just another data format. By itself, the XML content is not all that sexy. It's really the tools that you use with your XML data that make it zoom. Because XML uses a consistent yet generic structure to manage data, it was a snap to develop tools that could process consistent yet generic data in ways that look interesting and specific.

What About the Human-Readable Part?

One of the tools used with XML is *XSLT*, which stands for XSL Transformations (XSL stands for eXtensible Stylesheet Language). XSLT is a hard-to-use scripting language that lets you transform some XML data into whatever other data or output format you want. It's just one of a handful of XSL-related languages created to manipulate XML data in complex ways. Ready for some hands-on XSL fun? Take the useful chunk of XML listed previously (the <productList> sample), and replace the first ?xml line with the following two lines:

```
<?xml version="1.0"?>
<?xml-stylesheet type="text/xsl" href="hello.xsl"?>
```

Save all of that beautiful XML text to a file on your desktop as *hello.xml*. Next, put the following XSLT script into another file on your desktop named *hello.xsl*. (Notice that I broke one line with a special marker so that the content could fit in this book. Please don't really break the comma-separated list on that line in the file.)

```
<?xml version="1.0"?>
<xsl:stylesheet
      xmlns:xsl="http://www.w3.org/1999/XSL/Transform"
      version="1.0">
  <xsl:template match="/">
    <xsl:text>
    ProductID,ProductName,SupplierID,Category,
    ↳UnitPrice,Available
    </xsl:text>
    <BR/>
    <xsl:apply-templates/>
  </xsl:template>
  <xsl:template match="supplier">
    <xsl:variable name="supID" select="@ID"/>
    <xsl:for-each select="product">
      "<xsl:value-of select="@ID"/>",
      "<xsl:value-of select="productName"/>",
      "<xsl:value-of select="$supID"/>",
      "<xsl:value-of select="category"/>",
      "<xsl:choose>
        <xsl:when test="@onSale='true'">On Sale</xsl:when>
```

```
      <xsl:otherwise>
        $<xsl:value-of select="unitPrice"/>
      </xsl:otherwise>
    </xsl:choose>",
    "<xsl:value-of select="@available"/>"
    <BR/>
  </xsl:for-each>
</xsl:template>
</xsl:stylesheet>
```

I told you it was hard to use, and even harder to look at. OK, now for the show. I have Internet Explorer installed on my system, but this should work with most current browsers. Open the *hello.xml* file in your browser, and *voilà*, the following beautifully formatted text should appear:

```
ProductID,ProductName,SupplierID,Category,UnitPrice,Available
"1","Chai","652","Beverages","$18.00","Yes"
"2","Chang","9874","Beverages","$19.00","No"
"3","Aniseed Syrup","9874","Condiments","On Sale","Yes"
```

Now that's more like it. XML and XSLT together have made this advance in data technology possible. (I did cheat a little in this example. You will notice the `<BR/>` entries in the XSLT script that don't appear in the final output. I added these just to make it look right in your browser.) But seriously, although I was able to generate a comma-separated data set with XSLT, more common tasks for XSLT include generating nicely formatted HTML based on XML data, or generating a new XML document with a specific alternative view of the original data. How does it work? Basically, the `<xsl:template>` elements tell the parser to look for tags in the XML document that match some pattern (such as "supplier"). When it finds a match, it applies everything inside the `<xsl:template>` tags to that matching XML tag and its contents. The pattern specified in the "match" attributes uses an XML technology called *XPath*, a system to generically search for matching tags within your XML document.

Sounds confusing? Well, it is, and don't get me started on how long it took to write that short little XSLT script. XSLT scripting is, blissfully, beyond the scope of this book. Of course, tools are available to make the job easier. But XSLT is useful only if the XML data it manipulates is correct. You could write an XSL Transformation to report on data inconsistencies found in an XML document, but it won't work if some of the tags in your document are misspelled or arranged in an inconsistent manner. For that, you need another advancement in XML technology: XSD.

XML Schemas

XSD (XML Structure Definitions) lets you define the *schema*—the "language" or "vocabulary"—of your particular XML document. Remember, XML is a wide-open generic standard; you can define the tags any way you want and nobody will care, at least until you have to process the tags with your software. If they aren't correct, your processing will likely fail. XSD lets you define the rules that your XML document *must* follow if it is to be considered a valid document for your purposes.

(DTD, or Document Type Definition, is a similar, though older, technology. It's widely support by XML tools, but it is not as flexible as XSD. There are also other schema definition languages similar to XSD, but since XSD is built right into .NET, we'll focus on that.)

XSD schemas are every bit as endearing as XSLT scripts. Let's create an XSD for our original sample <productList> XML listed previously. First, we need to change the top of the XML to let it know that an XSD schema file is available. Change this:

```
<?xml version="1.0"?>
<productList>
```

to this:

```
<?xml version="1.0"?>
<productList xmlns="SimpleProductList"
     xmlns:xsi="http://www.w3.org/2001/XMLSchema-instance"
     xsi:noNamespaceSchemaLocation="hello.xsd">
```

These directives tell the XML parser to look in *hello.xsd* for the schema. They also define a namespace; more on that later. The *hello.xsd* file contains the following schema:

```
<xs:schema xmlns:xs="http://www.w3.org/2001/XMLSchema"
     targetNamespace="SimpleProductList">
  <xs:element name="productList" type="ProductListType"/>

  <xs:complexType name="ProductListType">
    <xs:sequence>
      <xs:element name="supplier" type="SupplierType"
        maxOccurs="unbounded"/>
    </xs:sequence>
  </xs:complexType>

  <xs:complexType name="SupplierType">
    <xs:sequence>
      <xs:element name="product" type="ProductType"
        maxOccurs="unbounded"/>
    </xs:sequence>
    <xs:attribute name="ID" type="xs:integer"/>
    <xs:attribute name="fullName" type="xs:string"/>
  </xs:complexType>

  <xs:complexType name="ProductType">
    <xs:sequence>
      <xs:element name="productName" type="xs:string"/>
      <xs:element name="category" type="xs:string"/>
      <xs:element name="unitPrice" type="xs:decimal"/>
    </xs:sequence>
    <xs:attribute name="ID" type="xs:integer"/>
    <xs:attribute name="available" type="YesOrNoType"/>
    <xs:attribute name="onSale" type="xs:boolean"/>
  </xs:complexType>
```

```
<xs:simpleType name="YesOrNoType">
  <xs:restriction base="xs:string">
    <xs:enumeration value="Yes"/>
    <xs:enumeration value="No"/>
  </xs:restriction>
</xs:simpleType>
</xs:schema>
```

It looks nasty, doesn't it? Actually, it's more straightforward than XSLT. Basically, the schema says that for each element (or "tag" or "node") in my XML document, here are the subelements and attributes they contain, and the data type of each of them. You can even create your own pseudodata types (actually, limiting factors on existing data types), as I did with the YesOrNoType data type, which limits the related value to the strings Yes and No.

You can look at the XML file with the attached XSD schema in your browser, but it wouldn't be all that interesting. It just shows you the XML. But schemas will be useful when you need to assess the quality of XML data coming into your software applications from external sources.

XML Namespaces

The product list XML shown earlier is nice, but someone else could come up with a product list document that is just as nice, but with different naming and formatting rules. For instance, someone might create a document that looks like this:

```
<?xml version="1.0"?>
<allProducts>
    <vendor ID="652" vendorName="Beverages R Us">
        <item ID="1" available="Yes">
            <itemName>Chai</itemName>
            <group>Beverages</group>
            <priceEach>18.00</priceEach>
        </item>
    </vendor>
</allProducts>
```

All of the data is the same, but the tags are different. Such a document would be incompatible with software written to work with our original document. Running the document through our XSD would quickly tell us that we have a bogus data set, but it would be nicer if something told us that from the start. Enter *namespaces*. Namespaces provide a convenient method to say, "This particular tag in the XML document uses this XSD-defined language." Notice the start of the XSD schema shown previously:

```
<xs:schema xmlns:xs="http://www.w3.org/2001/XMLSchema">
```

This line sets up a namespace named xs by using the xmlns attribute. (The :xs part tells XML what you want to call your namespace.) The value of the attribute is a Uniform Resource Identifier (URI), just a unique value that you are sure no one else is going to use. Typically, you use a web site address for your own company; the web site doesn't have to exist. You could even put your phone number there, just as long as it is unique.

The most common way to use a namespace is to prefix the relevant tags in your XML document with the new namespace name, as in "xs:schema" instead of just "schema." This tells the parser, "If you are checking my syntax against an XSD schema, use the one that I defined for the xs namespace." You can also use a "default" namespace for a given element and all its descendants by including the xmlns attribute in the outermost element. Then all elements within that outermost element will use the specified namespace. I used this method in one of the preceding examples:

```
<productList xmlns="SimpleProductList"...
```

For basic XML files that will only be used by your program, you may not need to bother with namespaces. They really come in handy when you are creating XML data that uses some publicly published standard. There are also instances where a single XML file might contain data related to two or more distinct uses of XML. In this case, different parts of your XML file could refer to different namespaces.

As with other parts of the XML world, XSD and namespaces are not all that easy to use, but they are flexible and powerful. As usual, there are tools, including tools in Visual Studio, which let you build all of this without having to think about the details.

As I keep saying, XML is just data, and if your program and data don't understand each other, you might as well go back to chisel and stone. XML and its related technologies provide a method to help ensure that your data is ready to use in your application.

Using XML in .NET: The Old Way

Visual Basic includes two primary methods for working with XML content: the old way and the new way. The old way uses classes from the System.Xml namespace, and provides traditional object-based access to XML tags, attributes, and data. The new way, introduced in the 2008 release, uses classes in the System.Xml.Linq namespace, and provides access to XML content directly within the syntax of Visual Basic source code. I'll discuss both methods in this chapter, starting with the old way.

Since XML is no fun to manage as a big chunk of text, .NET includes several classes that manage XML data. All of these tools appear in the System.Xml namespace and its subordinate namespaces:

System.Xml
> The main collection of old-way XML-related classes.

System.Xml.Linq
> Classes that integrate XML with LINQ technologies. This is the new way that I'm going to talk about later.

```
System.Xml.Schema
```
Classes that create and use XSD schemas.

```
System.Xml.Serialization
```
Classes that read and write XML documents via a standard .NET stream.

```
System.Xml.XPath
```
Classes that implement the XPath technology used to search XML documents.

```
System.Xml.Xsl
```
Classes that enable XSL Transformations.

The features included in each class tie pretty closely to the structure of XML and related technologies such as XSD and XSLT.

The Basic XML Classes, Basically

The System.Xml namespace includes the most basic classes you will use to manage XML data. An XmlDocument object is the in-memory view of your actual XML document:

```
Dim myData As New System.Xml.XmlDocument
```

Your document is made up of declarations (that <?xml...?> thing at the top), data elements (all the specific tags in your document), attributes (inside each starting element tag), and comments. These are represented by the XmlDeclaration, XmlElement, XmlAttribute, and XmlComment classes, respectively. Together, these four main units of your document are called *nodes*, represented generically by the XmlNode class. (The four specific classes all inherit from the more basic XmlNode class.) When you build an XML document by hand in memory, you use the individual classes such as XmlElement. Later on, when you need to scan through an existing document, it is easier to use the generic XmlNode class.

Let's build a subset of our sample XML product data.

```
<?xml version="1.0"?>
<productList>
   <!-- We currently sell these items. -->
   <supplier ID="652" fullName="Beverages R Us">
      <product ID="1" available="Yes">
         <productName>Chai</productName>
         <category>Beverages</category>
         <unitPrice>18.00</unitPrice>
      </product>
   </supplier>
</productList>
```

Declare all the variables you will use, and then use them.

```
Dim products As XmlDocument
Dim prodDeclare As XmlDeclaration
Dim rootSet As XmlElement
Dim supplier As XmlElement
Dim product As XmlElement
```

```
Dim productValue As XmlElement
Dim comment As XmlComment

' ----- Create the document with a valid declaration.
products = New XmlDocument
prodDeclare = products.CreateXmlDeclaration("1.0", _
    Nothing, String.Empty)
products.InsertBefore(prodDeclare, products.DocumentElement)

' ----- Create the root element, <productList>.
rootSet = products.CreateElement("productList")
products.InsertAfter(rootSet, prodDeclare)

' ----- Add a nice comment.
comment = products.CreateComment( _
    " We currently sell these items. ")
rootSet.AppendChild(comment)

' ------ Create the supplier element, <supplier>.
'           Include the attributes.
supplier = products.CreateElement("supplier")
supplier.SetAttribute("ID", "652")
supplier.SetAttribute("fullName", "Beverages R Us")
rootSet.AppendChild(supplier)

' ----- Create the product element, <product>, with the
'           subordinate data values.
product = products.CreateElement("product")
product.SetAttribute("ID", "1")
product.SetAttribute("available", "yes")
supplier.AppendChild(product)

productValue = products.CreateElement("productName")
productValue.InnerText = "Chai"
product.AppendChild(productValue)

productValue = products.CreateElement("category")
productValue.InnerText = "Beverages"
product.AppendChild(productValue)

productValue = products.CreateElement("unitPrice")
productValue.InnerText = "18.00"
product.AppendChild(productValue)
```

It really works, too. To prove it, put this code in the Click event of a button, and end it with the following line:

```
products.Save("c:\products.xml")
```

Run the program and view the *c:\products.xml* file to see the XML product data. There are many different ways to use the XML classes to create an XML document in memory. For instance, although I used the SetAttribute method to add attributes to the supplier and product nodes, I could have created separate attribute objects, and appended them onto these nodes, just like I did for the main elements.

```
Dim attrData As XmlAttribute
attrData = products.CreateAttribute("ID")
attrData.Value = "652"
supplier.SetAttributeNode(attrData)
```

So, this is nice and all, but what if you already have some XML in a file, and you just want to load it into an XmlDocument object? Simply use the XmlDocument object's Load method.

```
Dim products As XmlDocument
products = New XmlDocument
products.Load("c:\products.xml")
```

For those instances where you just want to read or write some XML from or to a file, and you don't care much about manipulating it in memory, the XmlTextReader and XmlTextWriter classes let you quickly read and write XML data via a text stream. But if you are going to do things with the XML data in your program, the Load and Save methods of the XmlDocument object are a better choice.

Finding Needles and Haystacks

In our sample data, all of the products appear in supplier groups. If we just want a list of products, regardless of supplier, we ask the XmlDocument object to supply that data via an XmlNodeList object.

```
Dim justProducts As XmlNodeList
Dim oneProduct As XmlNode

' ----- First, get the list.
justProducts = products.GetElementsByTagName("product")

' ----- Then do something with them.
For Each oneProduct In justProducts
    ' ----- Put interesting code here.
Next oneProduct
MsgBox("Processed " & justProducts.Count.ToString() & _
    " product(s).")
```

For a more complex selection of nodes within the document, the System.Xml.XPath namespace implements the XPath searching language, which gives you increased flexibility in locating items. The Visual Studio documentation describes the methods and searching syntax used with these classes.

Schema Verification

An XmlDocument object can hold any type of random yet valid XML content, but you can also verify the document against an XSD schema. If your XML document refers to an XSD schema, includes a DTD, or uses XDR (XML Data Reduced schemas, similar to XSD), an XmlReader, when configured with the appropriate XmlReaderSettings, will properly compare your XML data against the defined rules, and throw an exception if there's a problem.

```
Dim products As New XmlDocument
Dim xmlRead As XmlTextReader
Dim withVerify As New XmlReaderSettings
Dim xmlReadGood As XmlReader

' ----- Open the XML file and process schemas
'       referenced within the content.
withVerify.ValidationType = ValidationType.Schema
xmlRead = New XmlTextReader("c:\temp\products.xml")
xmlReadGood = XmlReader.Create(xmlRead, withVerify)

' ----- Load content, or throw exception on
'       validation failure.
products.Load(xmlReadGood)

' ----- Clean up.
xmlReadGood.Close( )
xmlRead.Close( )
```

XML Transformations

XSL Transformations are no more difficult than any of the other manipulations of
XML. Just as there are many ways to get XML source data (from a file, building it by
hand with XmlDocument, etc.), there are many ways to transform the data. If you just
want to go from input file to output file, the following code provides a quick and efficient method. It uses a System.Xml.Xsl.XslCompiledTransform instance to perform the
magic.

```
' ----- Above: Imports System.Xml.Xsl
Dim xslTrans As XslCompiledTransform

' ----- Open the XSL file as a transformation.
xslTrans = New XslCompiledTransform( )
xslTrans.Load("c:\convert.xsl")

' ----- Convert and save the output.
xslTrans.Transform("c:\input.xml", "c:\output.txt")
```

Using XML in .NET: The New Way

When Visual Basic first came out, no one had even heard of XML. But now it's
everywhere. It's like that black oozing stuff that bonds with Peter Parker in *Spider-
man 3*, but without all the creepy special effects. And now in Visual Basic 2008, XML
is part of the language syntax itself. When will it end?

It turns out that making XML part of the language is pretty cool. In the old-way section a few pages ago, I showed you some code that created the XML product list for
"Chai." The XML content was 11 lines long, but it took nearly 50 lines of source
code to produce it. But you can build that same XML content using the new way in
pretty close to the final 11 lines.

```
Dim chaiItem As System.Xml.Linq.XDocument = _
    <?xml version="1.0"?>
    <productList>
        <!-- We currently sell these items. -->
        <supplier ID="652" fullName="Beverages R Us">
            <product ID="1" available="Yes">
                <productName>Chai</productName>
                <category>Beverages</category>
                <unitPrice>18.00</unitPrice>
            </product>
        </supplier>
    </productList>
```

How about that! Except for the first declaration line, the content is identical to the
final XML. The new *XML Literals* feature makes building XML documents a snap.
The content gets stored in the new XDocument object, part of the System.Xml.Linq
namespace. If you want to store just a section of XML instead of the entire document, use the XElement class instead.

```
Dim productSection As System.Xml.Linq.XElement = _
    <product ID="1" available="Yes">
        <productName>Chai</productName>
        <category>Beverages</category>
        <unitPrice>18.00</unitPrice>
    </product>
```

If you have type inference enabled in your program (Option Infer On), you don't even
need to tell Visual Basic whether it's an XElement or an XDocument.

```
Dim productSection = _
    <product ID="1" available="Yes">
        <productName>Chai</productName>
        <category>Beverages</category>
        <unitPrice>18.00</unitPrice>
    </product>
```

Just like the XmlDocument class, the XDocument class includes Load and Save methods to
manage file-based XML.

Embedded XML Expressions

Including XML in your source code is amazing stuff, but it will stay amazing only if
you always sell Chai for $18.00 per unit. Real XML content is usually going to come
from variable data. And despite the XML "Literal" name, XML Literals can include
nonliteral variable content through *embedded XML expressions*. Whenever you want
to add data from a variable or expression to your XML text, you use the special <%=
and %> symbols to offset your custom data.

```
Dim productID As Integer = 1
Dim productName As String = "Chai"
Dim productCategory As String = "Beverage"
Dim productPrice As Decimal = 18@
Dim isAvailable As Boolean = True
```

```
Dim productSection = _
   <product ID=<%= productID %>
      available=<%= Format(isAvailable, "Yes/No") %>>
      <productName><%= productName %></productName>
      <category><%= productCategory %></category>
      <unitPrice><%= productPrice %></unitPrice>
   </product>
```

Of course, to generate an entire catalog of products, you're going to be doing a lot of typing. In Chapter 17, I'll introduce some additional ways to embed XML expressions with entire tables of data.

XML Axis Properties

Earlier in the chapter, in "Finding Needles and Haystacks," I showed you how you could access specific sections of old-style XML documents. The new-style XML objects also include ways to scan and access portions of the XML tree. These are called *XML axis properties*, and they come bundled up in three syntax-friendly varieties:

Child-member axis
> You can access an immediate child tag of any XElement by using the child's name as a member of the parent object, enclosing the child's name in a set of angle brackets:
>
> ```
> childElement = parentElement.<childName>
> ```

Descendent-member axis
> A variation of the child-member axis syntax lets you access named members at any depth within a parent element. Instead of using just a single dot (.) between the parent and child names, use three dots:
>
> ```
> setOfElements = parentElement...<descendentName>
> ```

Attribute axis
> Access any attribute of an element by treating the attribute name as a member name, prefixing the attribute name with the @ character:
>
> ```
> attributeValue = parentElement.@attributeName
> ```

The following block of code scans through the product list we designed early in the chapter, displaying the ID number and name of each product on the console:

```
For Each oneProduct In allProducts...<product>
   Console.WriteLine(oneProduct.@ID & ": " & _
      oneProduct.<productName>.Value)
Next oneProduct
```

This code uses all three axis styles. The For Each...Next loop scans through all matching <product> entries by using a descendent-member axis. In each matching product element, the code accesses the ID attribute using an attribute axis, and gets the name of the product using a child-member axis, along with the Value property of the returned child element. The output looks like this:

```
1: Chai
2: Chang
3: Aniseed Syrup
```

For more advanced ways of scanning through XML content and selecting child elements based on complex criteria, see Chapter 17.

Namespaces and Schemas for XML Literals

As with the old way of managing XML, the new way lets you include namespaces in your XML content. To add an XML namespace prefix, simply include it in the content as you would in any other XML scenario.

```
Dim foodItems = _
    <?xml version="1.0"?>
    <menu:items xmlns:menu="http://www.timaki.com/menu">
        <menu:item>
          <menu:name>Pizza</menu:name>
          <menu:price>12.99</menu:price>
        </menu:item>
        <menu:item>
          <menu:name>Breadsticks</menu:name>
          <menu:price>1.99</menu:price>
        </menu:item>
    </menu:items>
```

You can also define the namespace, the xmlns part, by using a variation of the Visual Basic Imports statement.

```
Imports <xmlns:menu="http://www.timaki.com/menu">
...later...
Dim foodItems = _
    <?xml version="1.0"?>
    <menu:items>
    ...and so on...
```

Visual Basic will still insert the xmlns definition at the right place in the XML content. It's actually stored as a distinct XNamespace object within the XDocument or XElement. To generate an XNamespace object for your own use, Visual Basic includes a new GetXmlNamespace function.

```
Dim justTheNamespace = GetXmlNamespace(menu)
```

Summary

There are a lot of useful features in the various System.Xml namespaces, and you can manage complex data in very effective ways. It's not always the most efficient way to manage data, but if you have structured hierarchical data, it may be the most direct and clearest method.

Although XML lurks everywhere in the .NET Framework, and in all applications written using .NET, you could actually write large and interesting applications without looking at a single line of XML content. Even if your application needs to interact with XML content, the new XML features included in Visual Basic make managing XML as easy as typing the content directly into Notepad. Wait a minute, that's not easy or fun. But it's a lot better than piecing the content together through string concatenation.

XML is a very useful and flexible data format that is here to stay. Although it will always lack the speed of more compact data standards, its benefits are numerous. There has been talk of introducing a "binary XML" format as a standard, although nothing concrete has come of it yet. If binary XML does become a standard, you will likely continue to use the same classes and methods introduced in this chapter, with the possible addition of an `OutputFormat` ("Text" or "Binary") property.

Project

The administrator of the Library system will want to see statistics and information at a glance, or run various reports that provide meaningful summary or detail views of system data. Although as a programmer I could try to add every conceivable type of report that the user may need, I have learned from experience that this is not possible. Users always want the moon, usually in the form of some weird esoteric report that I know they will use once and never look at again (although they will call once a year asking for the same report to be written again). I don't like recompiling and rereleasing the entire application every time a user needs a new report. Instead, I keep the reports outside the application, stored as separate programs. Then, from one form in the main application, I make all of those external reports available in a nice convenient list.

To implement this generic feature, I use a report configuration file, a simple XML file that contains information on the available reports, and how to run them. I want my selection list to have indented items so that I can visibly group reports for convenience. To do this, I will make my XML file into an unlimited depth hierarchy, with each level representing a further level of displayed indent. For instance, let's say I wanted the following outline of reports (with report group titles in bold):

Detail Reports

    Daily Report

    Monthly Reports

        Monthly Value

        Monthly Inventory

Summary Reports

    Inventory Summary

The XML configuration would follow this structure:

```
<Group name="Detail Reports">
    <Item name="Daily Report"/>
    <Group name="Monthly Reports">
        <Item name="Monthly Value"/>
        <Item name="Monthly Inventory"/>
    </Group>
</Group>
<Group name="SummaryReports">
    <Item name="Inventory Summary"/>
</Group>
```

Of course, this is greatly simplified (not to mention noncompliant) XML. In addition to the hierarchy, I also want to include support for a variety of reporting methods. To keep things simple, the Library Project will include three types of reports:

Built-in reports

The application includes a limited number of reports that are permanently built into the main application (assembly). The reports are numbered, starting from 1, and at this time I have five reports in mind. The designer of the XML configuration file can choose to include these in the display of reports or not by simply including or not including them in the file. In the absence of a configuration file, these reports will appear in the list by default. In addition to the report number (1 to 5), each entry has a display text and a long description.

Application reports

These reports are separate and distinct EXE files, and are started via standard application initiation methods. Each entry includes a display text, the full path to the application, optional arguments, a flag to pass the identity of the user initiating the report, and a long description.

URL reports

These reports are simple calls to web pages, or any other valid URL. For instance, you could include a report entry that does a "mailto:" to the local organization's help desk. Each entry includes the display text, the URL itself, and a long description.

The project activities in this chapter involve both coding and documentation of the new external resource (the XML file format).

PROJECT ACCESS

Load the Chapter 13 (Before) Code project, either through the New Project templates or by accessing the project directly from the installation directory. To see the code in its final form, load Chapter 13 (After) Code instead.

Update Technical Documentation

First, let's add clear documentation on the structure of the XML configuration file. There is no easy way to communicate the structure of an XML file to an ordinary user. Although such documentation is a requirement, hopefully the application will also include a tool to let an administrator build the configuration file. Such a program, sadly, is not included in this book's project. It is left as an exercise for the reader. (I always wanted to say that.)

Report Configuration File

The library application can be configured to run any number of reports through the Reports form. The list of available reports is managed through an XML report configuration file, a file containing "groups" and "items." All items are reports, and appear within a group. You can nest groups within groups to any depth, and the list of reports displayed in the Library program will indent each subordinate group to help the user see the organization of the reports. There is no limit to the nesting of groups.

The root element of the XML file must be named <reportList>, and it may contain any number of <reportGroup> and <reportItem> data elements:

- <reportItem>: Represents a single report entry. This entry has one required attribute, and up to five subordinate data elements depending on the setting of the attribute:

  — type (attribute): Set to one of the following values:

    • built-in: Run one of the built-in programs. This type of report uses the <displayText>, <reportPath>, and <description> data elements.

    • program: Runs a separate EXE program. This type of report uses the <displayText>, <reportPath>, <reportArgs>, <reportFlags>, and <description> data elements.

    • url: Starts a URL, such as a web page or a "mailto" email to a recipient address. This type of report uses the <displayText>, <reportPath>, and <description> data elements.

  — <displayText>: A short name or description for this report, as it will appear in the list of report choices. This element is required for all types of reports.

  — <reportPath>: The full path, URL, or number of the report, depending on the type of report. For program (EXE) reports, this is the full UNC or driver letter-based path to the report, without additional arguments. For built-in reports, this is a report number, from 1 to 5 (values and their meanings are listed later in this section). For URL reports, this is the actual URL, as in *"http://mysite.com/myreport.aspx"* or *"mailto:helpdesk@mysite.com."* This element is required for all types of reports.

— `<reportArgs>`: For program (EXE) reports, this entry includes any command-line arguments to be included when running the program. This element is valid only for program (EXE) reports, and is always optional.

— `<reportFlags>`: For program (EXE) reports, this entry indicates the optional flags that should be appended to the application command as arguments. At this time, the only flag is the U flag. When this element is set to U, the argument -u *userid* is appended to the command string (where *userid* is the user's login ID, from the database field `UserName.LoginID`). This element is valid only for program (EXE) reports, and is always optional.

— `<description>`: This is a longer, verbose description of the report, up to about 200 characters, which will appear on the Report form when the user selects the report from the list. This description should assist the user in selecting the right report. This element is valid for all types of reports, but is always optional.

- `<reportGroup>`: Represents a category group, used to visibly group and indent reports in the display list. This element must contain exactly one `<displayText>` element, but may contain any number of `<reportItem>` or `<reportGroup>` elements:

— `<displayText>`: A short name or description for this group, as it will appear in the list of report choices. This element is required.

When using the "built-in" report type, the `<reportPath>` element is set to one of the following integer values:

- 1—Items Checked Out Report
- 2—Items Overdue Report
- 3—Items Missing Report
- 4—Fines Owed by Patrons Report
- 5—Library Database Statistics Report

This technical description appears in the Technical Resource Kit document, originally developed in Chapter 4.

Create Report Entry Class

With .NET's ability to store whole objects as `ListBox` items, we can create a custom class that contains all the information needed to select and run a report from the list of reports. This class is fairly simple, with nothing but basic public fields, plus an overridden `ToString` function, used by the `ListBox` control to properly display each list item.

In the Library Project, add a new class file named *ReportItem.vb* through the Project → Add Class menu command. Add the following enumeration to the file, but add it outside the Class...End Class boundaries. This enumeration indicates what type of entry each list item represents.

INSERT SNIPPET

Insert Chapter 13, Snippet Item 1.

```
Public Enum ReportItemEnum
    ' ----- The type of item in the report select list.
    GroupLabel = 0
    BuiltInCheckedOut = 1
    BuiltInOverdue = 2
    BuiltInMissing = 3
    BuiltInFinesOwed = 4
    BuiltInStatistics = 5
    ExeProgram = 6
    UrlProgram = 7
End Enum
```

To this same file, add the members of the ReportItem class. This class contains all the information we need to run reports loaded from the configuration file.

INSERT SNIPPET

Insert Chapter 13, Snippet Item 2.

```
' ----- Instance of report selection items used
'       in the ReportSelect form.
Public ItemType As ReportItemEnum
Public Indent As Integer      ' Indent level. Starts with 0.
Public DisplayText As String
Public ReportPath As String  ' ExeProgram / UrlProgram only
Public ReportArgs As String  ' ExeProgram only
Public Description As String

Public Overrides Function ToString() As String
    ' ----- Display an indented string. Prepend with spaces.
    Return StrDup(Indent * 5, " ") & DisplayText
End Function
```

Design the Report Form

Librarians and administrators use the Select Report form (see Figure 13-2) to view reports. The form includes a ListBox control that displays all reports and report groups, a Run button that starts a report, and a Close button that returns the user to the main form. A label displays the full description of a report, when available, just below the ListBox.

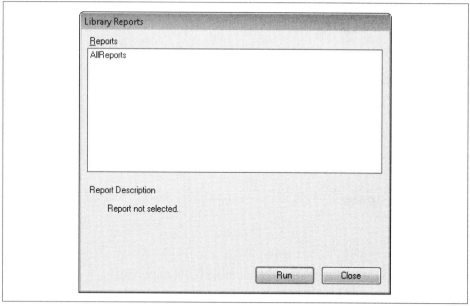

Figure 13-2. The Select Report form

Add a new form file named *ReportSelect.vb* through the Project → Add Windows Form menu command. Add the controls and settings as listed in Table 13-1.

Table 13-1. Controls and settings for the Report form

Control/form	Type	Settings	
LabelReports	Label	(Name):	LabelReports
		Location:	8, 8
		Text:	&Reports
AllReports	ListBox	(Name):	AllReports
		Location:	8, 24
		Size:	392, 160
LabelDescription	Label	(Name):	LabelDescription
		Location:	8, 200
		Text:	Report Description
FullDescription	Label	(Name):	FullDescription
		AutoSize:	False
		Location:	32, 224
		Size:	368, 64
		Text:	Report not selected.
		UseMnemonic:	False
ActRun	Button	(Name):	ActRun
		DialogResult:	None
		Location:	232, 304
		Size:	80, 24
		Text:	Run

Table 13-1. Controls and settings for the Report form (continued)

Control/form	Type	Settings	
ActClose	Button	(Name):	ActClose
		DialogResult:	Cancel
		Location:	320, 304
		Size:	80, 24
		Text:	Close
ReportSelect	Form	(Name):	ReportSelect
		AcceptButton:	ActRun
		CancelButton:	ActClose
		ControlBox:	False
		FormBorderStyle:	FixedDialog
		StartPosition:	CenterScreen
		Text:	Library Reports

Adjust the tab order of the new controls by selecting the form, and then using the View → Tab Order menu command.

Although the administrator has probably given useful names to each report, the terseness of each report name may still confuse the user. Each report includes an optional full description. As the user selects reports from the list, an event handler updates the FullDescription label just below the main list. Add this event handler member to the class.

INSERT SNIPPET

Insert Chapter 13, Snippet Item 3.

```
Private Sub AllReports_SelectedIndexChanged( _
      ByVal sender As Object, ByVal e As System.EventArgs) _
      Handles AllReports.SelectedIndexChanged
   ' ----- Display a description of the report, if available.
   Dim reportEntry As Library.ReportItem

   ' ----- Clear any previous description.
   FullDescription.Text = "No report selected."
   If (AllReports.SelectedIndex <> -1) Then
      ' ----- Locate the content and display it.
      reportEntry = CType(AllReports.SelectedItem, _
         Library.ReportItem)
      FullDescription.Text = reportEntry.Description
   End If
End Sub
```

Populate Reports from Configuration File

The RefreshReportList method loads the data from the report configuration file and processes the results. Eventually, the location of this file will be recorded in the application's configuration file, but we won't be adding that until a later chapter.

For now, let's put in a hardcoded test file location, and mark it for later update. I opted to use the old-style XML objects for this code because the new-style XML features we need to make the code easy to write won't be introduced until a later chapter.

INSERT SNIPPET

Insert Chapter 13, Snippet Item 4.

```
Private Sub RefreshReportList()
    ' ----- Load in the list of available reports.
    Dim configFile As String
    Dim configData As Xml.XmlDocument
    Dim reportEntry As ReportItem
    Dim counter As Integer

    On Error GoTo ErrorHandler

    ' ----- Clear the existing list.
    AllReports.Items.Clear()

    ' ----- Get the location of the configuration file.
    ' TODO: Load this from the application's configuration.
    '       For now, just hardcode the value.
    configFile = "c:\ReportConfig.txt"

    ' ----- Load the configuration file.
    If (configFile <> "") Then
        If (System.IO.File.Exists(configFile)) Then
            ' ----- Load in the file.
            configData = New Xml.XmlDocument
            configData.Load(configFile)

            ' ----- Process the configuration file.
            LoadReportGroup(configData.DocumentElement, 0)
        End If
    End If

    ' ----- If the configuration file resulted in no reports
    '       appearing in the list, add the default reports.
    If (AllReports.Items.Count = 0) Then
        For counter = 1 To _
            CInt(ReportItemEnum.BuiltInStatistics)
            ' ----- Build the report entry.
            reportEntry = New ReportItem
            reportEntry.Indent = 0
            reportEntry.ItemType = CType(counter, ReportItemEnum)
            Select Case reportEntry.ItemType
                Case ReportItemEnum.BuiltInCheckedOut
                    reportEntry.DisplayText = "Items Checked Out"
                Case ReportItemEnum.BuiltInOverdue
                    reportEntry.DisplayText = "Items Overdue"
```

```
                Case ReportItemEnum.BuiltInMissing
                    reportEntry.DisplayText = "Items Missing"
                Case ReportItemEnum.BuiltInFinesOwed
                    reportEntry.DisplayText = "Patron Fines Owed"
                Case ReportItemEnum.BuiltInStatistics
                    reportEntry.DisplayText = "Database Statistics"
            End Select

            ' ----- Add the report entry to the list.
            AllReports.Items.Add(reportEntry)
        Next counter
    End If
    Return

ErrorHandler:
    GeneralError("ReportSelect.RefreshReportList", _
        Err.GetException())
    Resume Next
End Sub
```

Because the report configuration file allows nested report groups to any level, we need to use a recursive routine to repeatedly descend to each successive level. The LoadReportGroup routine, called by RefreshReportList, adds all report items and report groups within a starting report group. It's initially called from the reference point of the root <reportList> element. Each time it finds a child <reportGroup> element, it calls itself again, but this time starting from the reference point of the child <reportGroup> element.

INSERT SNIPPET

Insert Chapter 13, Snippet Item 5.

```
Private Sub LoadReportGroup(ByVal groupNode As Xml.XmlNode, _
        ByVal indentLevel As Integer)
    ' ----- Add the groups and items at this level,
    '       and recurse as needed.
    Dim scanNode As Xml.XmlNode
    Dim detailNode As Xml.XmlNode
    Dim reportEntry As ReportItem

    ' ----- Process each item or group.
    For Each scanNode In groupNode.ChildNodes
        ' ----- Build a content item for the list.
        reportEntry = New ReportItem
        reportEntry.Indent = indentLevel

        ' ----- Get the display name.
        detailNode = scanNode.SelectSingleNode("displayText")
        If (detailNode Is Nothing) Then Continue For
        reportEntry.DisplayText = Trim(detailNode.InnerText)
```

```
If (scanNode.Name = "reportGroup") Then
   ' ----- Start a new display group.
   reportEntry.ItemType = ReportItemEnum.GroupLabel
   AllReports.Items.Add(reportEntry)

   ' ----- Recurse to child items.
   LoadReportGroup(scanNode, indentLevel + 1)
ElseIf (scanNode.Name = "reportItem") Then
   ' ----- This is an item. Record its location.
   detailNode = scanNode.SelectSingleNode("reportPath")
   If Not (detailNode Is Nothing) Then _
      reportEntry.ReportPath = _
      Trim(detailNode.InnerText)

   ' ----- Get any command-line arguments.
   detailNode = scanNode.SelectSingleNode("reportArgs")
   If Not (detailNode Is Nothing) Then _
      reportEntry.ReportArgs = _
      Trim(detailNode.InnerText)

   ' ----- Get any item-specific flags.
   detailNode = scanNode.SelectSingleNode("reportFlags")
   If Not (detailNode Is Nothing) Then
      ' ---- "U" adds "-u loginid" to the command.
      If (InStr(UCase(detailNode.InnerText), "U") > 0) _
         And (LoggedInUserName <> "") Then _
         reportEntry.ReportArgs = _
         Trim(reportEntry.ReportArgs & " -u " & _
         LoggedInUserName)
   End If

   ' ----- Store the full description.
   detailNode = scanNode.SelectSingleNode("description")
   If Not (detailNode Is Nothing) Then _
      reportEntry.Description = _
      Trim(detailNode.InnerText)

   ' ----- So, what type of entry is it?
   If (scanNode.Attributes("type").Value = _
         "built-in") Then
      ' ----- Built-in program. Check for valid ID.
      If (IsNumeric(reportEntry.ReportPath) = False) Or _
         (Val(reportEntry.ReportPath) < 1) Or _
         (Val(reportEntry.ReportPath) > _
         CInt(ReportItemEnum.BuiltInStatistics)) Then _
         Continue For
      reportEntry.ItemType = CType(CInt( _
         reportEntry.ReportPath), ReportItemEnum)
      AllReports.Items.Add(reportEntry)
   ElseIf (scanNode.Attributes("type").Value = _
         "program") Then
      ' ----- EXE program-based report.
      If (reportEntry.ReportPath = "") Then Continue For
      reportEntry.ItemType = ReportItemEnum.ExeProgram
```

```
            AllReports.Items.Add(reportEntry)
        ElseIf (scanNode.Attributes("type").Value = _
            "url") Then
            ' ----- URL-based report.
            If (reportEntry.ReportPath = "") Then Continue For
            reportEntry.ItemType = ReportItemEnum.UrlProgram
            AllReports.Items.Add(reportEntry)
        End If
    End If
Next scanNode
Return

ErrorHandler:
    GeneralError("ReportSelect.LoadReportGroup", _
        Err.GetException())
    Resume Next
End Sub
```

Add the form's Load event, which loads in the content from the configuration file.

INSERT SNIPPET

Insert Chapter 13, Snippet Item 6.

```
Private Sub ReportSelect_Load(ByVal sender As Object, _
    ByVal e As System.EventArgs) Handles MyBase.Load
    ' ----- Display the list of reports.
    RefreshReportList()
End Sub
```

Running the Reports

Now that all of the groups and items appear in the list, we have to run the actual reports. The ActRun button's Click event handles this duty. For now, we will just add the framework to support the calling of each report. The built-in reports will be added in Chapter 21.

INSERT SNIPPET

Insert Chapter 13, Snippet Item 7.

```
Private Sub ActRun_Click(ByVal sender As System.Object, _
    ByVal e As System.EventArgs) Handles ActRun.Click
    ' ----- Run the selected report.
    Dim reportEntry As Library.ReportItem

    On Error GoTo ErrorHandler

    ' ----- Make sure a report is selected.
    If (AllReports.SelectedIndex = -1) Then
```

```
      MsgBox("Please select a report from the list.", _
         MsgBoxStyle.OKOnly Or MsgBoxStyle.Exclamation, _
         ProgramTitle)
      Return
   End If

   ' ----- Different code for each type of entry.
   reportEntry = CType(AllReports.SelectedItem, _
      Library.ReportItem)
   Me.Cursor = Windows.Forms.Cursors.WaitCursor
   Select Case reportEntry.ItemType
      Case ReportItemEnum.GroupLabel
         ' ----- No report for group entries.
         MsgBox("Please select a report from the list.", _
            MsgBoxStyle.OKOnly Or MsgBoxStyle.Exclamation, _
            ProgramTitle)
      Case ReportItemEnum.BuiltInCheckedOut
         ' ----- Items Checked Out
         ' TODO: Write BasicReportCheckedOut()
      Case ReportItemEnum.BuiltInOverdue
         ' ----- Items Overdue
         ' TODO: Write BasicReportOverdue()
      Case ReportItemEnum.BuiltInMissing
         ' ----- Items Missing
         ' TODO: Write BasicReportMissing()
      Case ReportItemEnum.BuiltInFinesOwed
         ' ----- Fines Owed by Patrons
         ' TODO: Write BasicReportFines()
      Case ReportItemEnum.BuiltInStatistics
         ' ----- Library Database Statistics
         ' TODO: Write BasicReportStatistics()
      Case ReportItemEnum.ExeProgram
         ' ----- Start a program.
         Process.Start("""" & reportEntry.ReportPath & _
            """ " & reportEntry.ReportArgs)
      Case ReportItemEnum.UrlProgram
         ' ----- Start a URL.
         Process.Start(reportEntry.ReportPath)
   End Select
   Me.Cursor = Windows.Forms.Cursors.Default
   Return

ErrorHandler:
   GeneralError("ReportSelect.ActRun_Click", _
      Err.GetException())
   Resume Next
End Sub
```

For external reports, the event handler calls the Process.Start method. This amazing method accepts either a standard command-line expression, or any valid URL or web page address.

Connecting the Select Report Form

To make the reports available to the user, we must enable a link to the report form from the main form. We included a distinct panel on that form just for printing reports. The ActDoReports button on that panel triggers a call to the new report selection form. Create a new event handler for the ActDoReports button and add the following code.

INSERT SNIPPET

Insert Chapter 13, Snippet Item 8.

```
' ----- Show the reports form.
ReportSelect.ShowDialog()
```

Now that we have a firm grasp on the world of XML, we'll let Visual Basic do all the hard work of manipulating it for application configuration purposes.

Application Settings

More than seven score years ago, President Abraham Lincoln began his famous Gettysburg Address with "Four score and seven years ago…". Why this poetic reference to the founding of America 87 years earlier? He could have started the speech with "Last week, I was talking with members of my cabinet" or even "These three confederate soldiers walked into a bar…". But he stuck with the decades-old anecdote.

Lincoln understood that his listeners, as humans, had a tie with the past, a fondness for the familiar, a love of fast sports cars, and a desire to see the stability of a former era restored. This is how people are. They like peace, not war. They like the status quo, not change. They like dinner on the table when they return home from a hard day at the office. They like short lines at the amusement park. They like seeing their favorite football team win once again.

People like to know that things are configured in a way that makes sense to them, set up in a way that is familiar and known. They expect this in life, and they expect this in their software. That's why Visual Basic includes features that let you maintain user-specific and application-specific settings, to give the people what they want.

A Short History of Settings

Since that short yet dynamic speech by Lincoln, programmers have sought a convenient way to maintain configurable values in their applications. In the early days of MS-DOS development, it was a configuration free-for-all; each program provided its own settings system. Many applications needed no specialized configuration, but those that did often stored configuration settings together with the application's managed data, all in proprietary *.dat* files.

With the advent of mainstream Windows development, Microsoft introduced file-based settings management through its *application programming interface* (API). The "private profile" API calls (`GetPrivateProfileInt`, `GetPrivateProfileString`, `SetPrivateProfileString`, and a few others) supplied a standard way to store short configuration values in an open and easy-to-understand text file format. Microsoft used these "INI" files (named for their *.ini* file extension) for its own configuration. A few of these files still reside in your system's *Windows* folder. Here's the content I found in my system's *win.ini* file:

```
; for 16-bit app support
[fonts]
[extensions]
[mci extensions]
[files]
[Mail]
MAPI=1
[CDWINSETUP]
AUTOUNLOAD=No
[MSUCE]
Advanced=0
CodePage=Unicode
Font=Arial
```

The format of an INI file was simple to understand. Each file included named sections defined within square brackets, as in [fonts]. Each section maintained a set of key-value pairs in the form "key=value." The format was simple enough that anyone could use Notepad to make changes. It wasn't even that hard for a program to write its own INI-file management routines, but having them included in the Windows API made them that much more attractive.

But then came the clutter. With so many programs opting to store their configuration files in a known central location, the *Windows* folder quickly became the file equivalent of Grand Central Station at 5:00 p.m. on a Friday. Speed was an issue, too, since the constant parsing and rewriting of INI files consumed precious CPU resources.

Microsoft came up with a solution: the *registry*. This hierarchical database of key-value pairs cleaned up the filesystem and brought speed improvements to configuration management. It also added new administrator-defined security settings for access to the registry, and provided support for some limited strongly typed data. But the new API features weren't the most intuitive (although Visual Basic did include simple commands, such as GetSetting, that provided limited access to registry keys and values).

The registry threw technology at the configuration values problem, but it wasn't a full triumph. With so many vendors stuffing gobs of data in the registry, bloat once again became an issue. And with the system managing all access to the registry, the larger the registry, the worse the performance.

.NET's initial release included application-specific configuration files, a sort-of return to those days of INI-file yesteryear. In some ways, "app.config" and "web.config" files were better than INI files since they contained structured XML content. But big whoop. INI files had structure, and you could update them in Notepad. .NET config files were notoriously difficult to update, either within a .NET application or externally in Notepad (due to some weird caching issues). Also, *.config* files had neither the security nor the strong data typing available in the registry.

Configuration settings have been giving programmers at least some level of angst since Windows first appeared. But a new and improved settings system, first added to Visual Basic in 2005, seeks to change all that.

Settings in Visual Basic 2008

The settings system in Visual Basic 2008 is a multifile, XML-based, strongly typed, and easy-to-manage configuration approach. Its file-focused methodology includes these features and benefits:

- Data is stored in XML format for efficient processing by .NET libraries. Although it is not free-form text, XML is not overwhelmingly difficult when manual updates need to be made by mere mortals.

- The data stored in each settings-specific file is strongly typed, reducing errors from the processing of invalid data.

- Settings are managed on a per-application, per-user, and even per-assembly-version basis to promote security and reduce conflicts. You can also store multiple sets of settings per application as you require, such as one set of settings per document opened by your application. (I won't discuss it in this chapter, but you can search for "SettingsKey property" in the online help for additional information on this feature.)

- Visual Studio includes a user-friendly management tool used to configure settings within an application.

- Visual Basic has its own simple interface to make the use and update of settings at runtime easier.

But it's not all fun and games. As a developer, you have to do some of the heavy lifting, such as coming up with meaningful names for each setting ("MainFormLocation," "DatabaseConnection," etc.), and altering the behavior of your program as needed based on the stored settings.

The actual settings appear in XML files scattered throughout the filesystem:

- At design time, all the settings you create get stored in a *Settings.settings* file, stored in the *My Project* subdirectory of your source code folder. Here's the *Settings.settings* file as it exists so far in the Library Project:

```
<?xml version='1.0' encoding='utf-8'?>
<SettingsFile xmlns="http://schemas.microsoft.com/
↳VisualStudio/2004/01/settings"
    CurrentProfile="(Default)">
  <Profiles>
    <Profile Name="(Default)" />
  </Profiles>
  <Settings />
</SettingsFile>
```

- At runtime, all user-specific settings appear in a *user.config* file, typically stored in *C:\Documents and Settings\<user>\Local Settings\Application Data\<company>\ <appdata>\<version>*, where *<user>* is the Windows username, *<company>* is the company name recorded in the assembly, *<appdata>* is a combination of values that help to differentiate the settings based on use, and *<version>* is the four-part version number of the assembly. It seems like a difficult place to store settings, but it keeps things nice and ordered. (The location of the *user.config* file is a little different if you deploy an application using ClickOnce, a method described in Chapter 25.)

  You're probably wondering whether this contributes to disk bloat. Yes! Each time you bump up the version number of your application, .NET creates a new settings file to go with it. There's a way to mitigate this somewhat, but with 120 GB hard drives, no one's really complaining about disk space usage anymore.

- Some settings are application-focused, and apply to all users of the application on a particular workstation. These are stored in the *app.config* file that appears in the same folder as your assembly's executable. The settings appear in an XML branch named <applicationSettings> within this file. Application-focused settings cannot be modified by the application; you must manually update the *app.config* file to force a change.

The settings system is a great place to store *state*, things that you want the program to remember from the last time it was run, but that shouldn't be hardcoded into the source code.

Adding Settings to a Project

The Project Properties window within Visual Studio 2008 provides centralized control of the settings for an application. The Settings panel of this window, shown in Figure 14-1, provides access to the application's custom settings.

To add a setting, type in its Name, select its data Type from the drop-down list, choose the Scope (User or Application), and enter its Value using whatever value editor is available for the selected type. The Type list includes many default selections, including the basic Visual Basic data types, fonts, colors, and drawing-related sizes. Also included is a "(Connection string)" type that, when selected, enables a Connection Properties string builder in the Value column.

It's important that you select the correct type for each stored setting; otherwise, your workstation will explode. Actually, I think they fixed that in a later beta. It's really because all settings are strongly typed. If you set the type to Integer, you won't be able to stuff the word *None* in there as a special flag as you could have done with an INI file. You can choose any valid .NET type for the data type, although complex types without their own custom editors will require that you set their value through code.

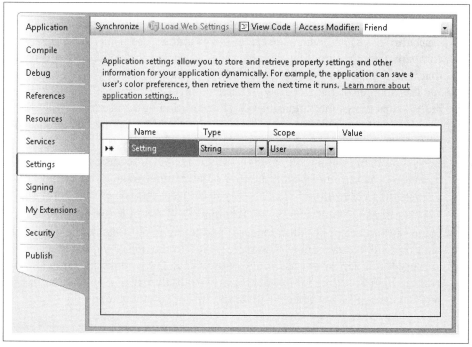

Figure 14-1. The Settings panel with no defined settings

What happens when you add a new setting to your Visual Basic project? Let's find out. I'll add two settings to a new Windows Forms project: an Integer named WarningLimit, and a System.Drawing.Font named NoticeFont (see Figure 14-2).

	Name	Type	Scope	Value
	WarningLimit	Integer	User	25
	NoticeFont	System.Drawing.Font	User	Arial, 14.25pt, style=Bold

Figure 14-2. The Settings panel with two new settings

As you already know, Visual Studio is just a user-friendly wrapper around .NET code, and the Settings panel is no different. So, the real changes occur somewhere in the code, or more correctly, in both code and the related *Settings.settings* file. If you "Show All Files" in the Solution Explorer panel, and expand My Project followed by *Settings.settings*, you will find that this XML file has its own Visual Basic source code file, *Settings.Designer.vb*.

If you open the *Settings.Designer.vb* file, you find the following partial code:

```
Namespace My
    Partial Friend NotInheritable Class MySettings
        Inherits Global.System.Configuration. _
            ApplicationSettingsBase
```

```
        <Global.System.Configuration. _
           UserScopedSettingAttribute( ), _
           Global.System.Diagnostics. _
           DebuggerNonUserCodeAttribute( ), _
           Global.System.Configuration. _
           DefaultSettingValueAttribute("25")> _
        Public Property WarningLimit( ) As Integer
            Get
                Return CType(Me("WarningLimit"),Integer)
            End Get
            Set
                Me("WarningLimit") = value
            End Set
        End Property

        <Global.System.Configuration. _
           UserScopedSettingAttribute( ), _
           Global.System.Diagnostics. _
           DebuggerNonUserCodeAttribute( ), _
           Global.System.Configuration. _
           DefaultSettingValueAttribute( _
           "Arial, 14.25pt, style=Bold")> _
        Public Property NoticeFont( ) _
              As Global.System.Drawing.Font
            Get
                Return CType(Me("NoticeFont"), _
                   Global.System.Drawing.Font)
            End Get
            Set
                Me("NoticeFont") = value
            End Set
        End Property
    End Class
End Namespace
```

I excluded a lot of the extra code. It's amazing how much code Microsoft loads up in prewritten attributes, and it's not really possible to know what goes on inside. I can guess what the DefaultSettingValueAttribute attribute does for each setting (assigns the initial default value of the setting), but some of the others are mysteries. Oh well. Even the ancients didn't have answers for everything.

But the code that remains is quite clear. Visual Studio generates two properties within the My.MySettings class, properties named—amazingly enough—WarningLimit and NoticeFont. Here's the property entry for NoticeFont:

```
Public Property NoticeFont( ) As Global.System.Drawing.Font
    Get
        Return CType(Me("NoticeFont"), _
           Global.System.Drawing.Font)
    End Get
    Set
        Me("NoticeFont") = value
    End Set
End Property
```

You won't find any private class members that store the hidden `WarningLimit` and `NoticeFont` values. Instead, somewhere else in this partial class is a default property (named `Item`) that gets and sets each defined property value, accessed through `Me("something")`.

The settings available through this default property are loaded directly from the XML stored in the *Settings.settings* file. (This file is compiled into the application; you don't have to distribute *Settings.settings* with the application.) Here's the content from that file with our two new configuration values:

```
<?xml version='1.0' encoding='utf-8'?>
<SettingsFile xmlns="http://schemas.microsoft.com/
↳VisualStudio/2004/01/settings"
  CurrentProfile="(Default)"
  GeneratedClassNamespace="My"
  GeneratedClassName="MySettings"
  UseMySettingsClassName="true">
  <Profiles />
  <Settings>
    <Setting Name="WarningLimit"
        Type="System.Int32" Scope="User">
      <Value Profile="(Default)">25</Value>
    </Setting>
    <Setting Name="NoticeFont"
        Type="System.Drawing.Font" Scope="User">
      <Value Profile="(Default)">
        Arial, 14.25pt, style=Bold</Value>
    </Setting>
  </Settings>
</SettingsFile>
```

Each setting contains distinct `Name`, `Type`, `Scope`, and `Value` attributes or entries, matching the four columns that appeared in the Visual Studio settings editor.

My.Settings

Visual Basic creates an instance of the `My.MySettings` class we just saw previously, and makes it available as `My.Settings`. As you add settings to your project, they become strongly typed class members of `My.Settings`. To access one, simply reference it directly in your code.

```
MsgBox("The font for notices is: " & _
    My.Settings.NoticeFont.ToString())
```

(The output for this code appears in Figure 14-3.) The `My.Settings.NoticeFont` is an actual instance of `System.Drawing.Font` that you can use like any other `Font` instance.

You can modify the value of any setting scoped as "User," and have the new value preserved for your next use of the application (i.e., for the current user's next use of the application).

```
My.Settings.WarningLimit = 30
```

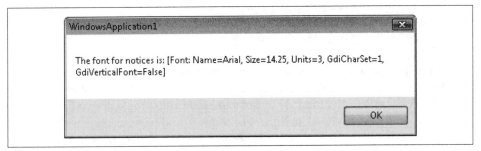

Figure 14-3. Be sure to take "notice" of this font

All changes made to these settings are saved automatically to the user-specific setting files by default. If you don't want the updates saved automatically, set the My. Application.SaveMySettingsOnExit flag to False. Then, when you are ready to save the new settings, use the My.Settings.Save method.

Settings come in three delicious flavors: default, persisted, and current. *Default settings* are those values defined by the programmer through the Visual Studio settings editor. *Persisted settings* include the saved changes to specific settings, and the default settings for those that have never been altered by the user. *Current settings* include any changes made to the settings during the current session, but not yet saved. You can play with these states using members of the My.Settings object:

- The Save method, as mentioned previously, saves all current settings to a persisted state.
- The Reload method restores any current values with the persisted versions.
- The Reset method wipes out all current and persisted settings, and returns all configuration entries to their default values.

One of the strangest aspects of settings is that they are version-specific. If you release your application as version 1.0.0.0, and then later release version 1.1.0.0, each user will lose all of the previously persisted settings. Actually, they won't be lost, but they will be stuck in 1.0.0.0-land. If you always want to have the most up-to-date settings as modified by the user, you will have to make sure that older settings are "upgraded" when installing a new version. My.Settings includes an Upgrade method that does the work for you. But if the user installs a newer version and upgrades the settings, makes changes to those settings, and then calls Upgrade again, any changes made since the last upgrade will be lost.

To get around this problem, the code should upgrade settings only when a new version appears. The easiest way to do this is to include a setting called something like SettingsUpgraded and set it to False. Check this flag before calling Upgrade. If it is still False, it is safe to call Upgrade. Once the code upgrades the settings, change SettingsUpgraded to True.

```
If (My.Settings.SettingsUpgraded = False) Then
    My.Settings.Upgrade()
    My.Setttings.SettingsUpgraded = True
End If
```

This need to upgrade settings whenever even minor version number changes are made to an assembly seems a bit over the top. But it's necessary to support .NET's goal of side-by-side installation. The user should be able to install two different versions of your application on the same workstation, and use each one without interference from the other. Storing version-specific settings helps to achieve this goal.

Bound Settings

Although using and updating your own custom configuration values can be exciting, even more exciting is that the fields in your Windows Forms and related controls can interact with the persisted settings automatically. By *binding* form- and control-specific properties to the settings system, Visual Basic automatically saves and restores user-controlled preferences within the user interface.

A typical use for bound settings is to have the application remember where a particular form appeared on the screen when the program was last run. The form's Location property maintains its on-screen position. Recording this value to the settings requires two steps. First, create a setting of type System.Drawing.Point to hold the persisted location value. Second, indicate in the form's properties that its Location value should persist to the new settings entry.

Perform the first step by adding a new user-scoped System.Drawing.Point setting in the project properties' Settings panel. Let's name it "MainFormPosition," and leave the Value field blank for now.

Back in the form editor, select the form object itself, and then access the Properties panel. Expand the "(ApplicationSettings)" property to locate the "(PropertyBinding)" subproperty. Clicking the "…" button for this entry displays the Application Settings dialog. This selection process appears in Figure 14-4.

Find the Location entry in the list, and choose "MainFormPosition" for its value. Now, each time you run the application containing this bound setting, the modified form will "remember" its previous location.

Summary

As with XML, the .NET settings system is one of those internal, behind-the-scenes, don't-let-the-boss-know features that makes your program great to use, but without all of the whiz-bang showing-off stuff. Personally, I found it a little hard to part with my precious INI files and all of their simplicity. But the automation attached to the settings system makes the migration painless.

Figure 14-4. Bringing up the application settings dialog for a form

Project

Of course, we will add settings to the Library Project in this chapter, but we'll also go back and start to use some of those settings in code that we previously entered as hardcoded values.

I really struggled over whether to use application-scoped or user-scoped configuration values for some of the rarely changing settings, such as the database connection string. I finally decided on the user area so that they could be modified through the features of the program. Application-scoped settings are read-only and can only be updated outside the program, so that idea is out. The expectation with application-scoped settings is that the system administrator will manage them, either by using Notepad on the XML file, or through some custom administrative tool. Since we aren't going to take the time in this book's project to write a separate administration tool, we'll keep everything at the user level and allow modification through the main Library program.

PROJECT ACCESS

Load the Chapter 14 (Before) Code project, either through the New Project templates or by accessing the project directly from the installation directory. To see the code in its final form, load Chapter 14 (After) Code instead.

Update Technical Documentation

Let's document the settings used by the application in the project's Resource Kit. Add the following content to the Resource Kit word processing file.

User settings

The Library Project uses Visual Basic's *settings* system to track user-specific state values maintained between uses of the application. All of these settings are stored in an XML file in the user's portion of the *C:\Documents and Settings* (or equivalent) directory in a format dictated by .NET. The following is a list of the settings recognized by the Library program:

DBConnection (String)

> A properly formatted connection string that identifies the SQL Server database used by the application. If missing, the application will prompt for the location of the database on startup.

HelpFile (String)

> Indicates the UNC or drive letter-based location of the basic application online help file, with a *.chm* extension.

HelpFileAdmin (String)

> Indicates the UNC or drive letter-based location of the administrative application online help file, with a *.chm* extension.

HideLogin (Boolean)

> Indicates whether the Login button in the upper-right corner of the main Library form should be hidden from view when in patron (nonadministrative) mode. Use True to hide the button or False to show the button. If this field is missing, False is assumed.

MainFormPosition (System.Drawing.Point)

> The position of the upper-left corner of the main Library form. This value is updated each time the application closes.

ReceiptPostlude (String)

> Any raw character data to send to the receipt printer at the end of each ticket. This text may include the following special characters:

> \n

> > A newline character (ASCII 10)

> \r

> > A carriage return character (ASCII 13)

> \e

> > An escape character (ASCII 27)

> \x??

> > Any ASCII value, where ?? is a two-character hexadecimal code

> \\

> > The backslash character ("\")

ReceiptPrinter (String)

> The UNC pathname to the receipt printer used by this workstation to print out patron checkout receipts and payment receipts.

ReceiptWidth (Integer)

> The width, in characters, of each line on the receipt printer. If missing or empty, the program uses a default width of 40 characters.

ReportConfig (String)

> Indicates the UNC or drive letter-based location of the XML report configuration file. This file has the XML format described in the "Report Configuration File" section of this document. This file indicates the reports available in the application.

SettingsUpgraded (Boolean)

> When upgrading the application from an older release, this flag indicates whether the settings associated with that older release have already been upgraded into this new version. It defaults to False for all new releases.

UseReceipts (Boolean)

> Indicates whether printed receipts are to be used at this workstation. If this field is missing, False is assumed.

This technical description appears in the Technical Resource Kit document, originally developed in Chapter 4 and updated in subsequent chapters. Some of the content added here refers to features and technical content that won't be added until later chapters, so don't spend too much time thinking about features that you thought you already forgot.

Add the Settings

Since we know all of the settings we will add to the application, let's add them now. Open the project properties window and select the Settings tab. Add each setting to the application using Table 14-1 as a guide. If a setting in Table 14-1 has no listed value, leave the Value field blank as well in the settings editor.

Table 14-1. Default settings for the Library Project

Name	Type	Scope	Value
DBConnection	String	User	
HelpFile	String	User	
HelpFileAdmin	String	User	
HideLogin	Boolean	User	False
MainFormPosition	System.Drawing.Point	User	
ReceiptPostlude	String	User	
ReceiptPrinter	String	User	

Table 14-1. Default settings for the Library Project (continued)

Name	Type	Scope	Value
ReceiptWidth	Integer	User	40
ReportConfig	String	User	
SettingsUpgraded	Boolean	User	False
UseReceipts	Boolean	User	False

Make sure you type the settings names as listed. The application will not be able to match up incorrectly spelled names.

Positioning the Main Form

I showed you how to link a form's or control's property value to one of the settings earlier in this chapter, so let's do it for real in the project. We'll link the main form's Location property to the MainFormPosition setting. Just to refresh your memory, follow these steps to enable the link:

1. Open *MainForm.vb* in Design view.
2. Make sure the form itself is selected, not one of its subordinate controls.
3. In the Properties panel, expand the "(ApplicationSettings)" property.
4. Select the "(PropertyBinding)" subproperty, and click on the "…" button in its value area.
5. Locate the Location property in the binding list.
6. Select the MainFormPosition setting for the Location property's value. It should be the only setting available since it is the only one we defined as type System.Drawing.Point.
7. Click the OK button to enable the link.

Caching and Using Settings

Although all the settings are as close as typing "My.Settings.*something*" in the code, some settings may initially be undefined, and using them could involve a lot of repetitive code that checks for valid settings. To reduce overall code and CPU cycles, we will cache some of the settings for easy use throughout the application.

Let's add three more global variables to cache some of the settings. Open the *General.vb* module, and add these three new class members.

INSERT SNIPPET

Insert Chapter 14, Snippet Item 1.

```
Public MainHelpFile As String
Public MainAdminHelpFile As String
Public FineGraceDays As Integer
```

Let's give these variables initial values in the InitializeSystem method, where the code already initializes some other values. Add the following statements to that routine in the General module.

INSERT SNIPPET

Insert Chapter 14, Snippet Item 2.

```
FineGraceDays = -1

' ----- Locate the online help files.
MainHelpFile = My.Settings.HelpFile & ""
MainAdminHelpFile = My.Settings.HelpFileAdmin & ""
```

In an earlier chapter, we stored some settings in the SystemValue table that apply to all workstations that connect to the database. Since we're caching settings anyway, we should add some code to cache these database-stored values so that we don't have to keep opening and closing the database. Add the LoadDatabaseSettings method to the General module.

INSERT SNIPPET

Insert Chapter 14, Snippet Item 3.

```
Public Sub LoadDatabaseSettings()
    ' ----- Get some system-level values from
    '       database storage.
    Dim holdText As String

    On Error Resume Next

    ' ----- Get the default location.
    holdText = GetSystemValue("DefaultLocation")
    If (holdText = "") Then holdText = "-1"
    DefaultItemLocation = CInt(holdText)

    ' ----- Get the maximum number of search matches.
    holdText = GetSystemValue("SearchLimit")
    If (holdText = "") Then holdText = "-1"
    SearchMatchLimit = CInt(holdText)

    ' ----- Get the number of days to wait before
    '       charging fines.
    holdText = GetSystemValue("FineGrace")
    If (holdText = "") Then holdText = "-1"
    FineGraceDays = CInt(holdText)
End Sub
```

We will call this routine during application startup, just after we open and confirm the database. Add the following code to the end of the MyApplication_Startup event handler. If it's been awhile, remember that this handler is in the *ApplicationEvents.vb* file, one of the files normally hidden from view in the Solution Explorer.

INSERT SNIPPET

Insert Chapter 14, Snippet Item 4.

```
' ----- Load some settings that reside in the database.
LoadDatabaseSettings()
```

It's time to actually use a setting. The My.Settings.HideLogin setting indicates whether the Login button (ActLogin) on the main Library application form should appear when running in nonadministrator (nonlibrarian) mode. The administrator can still bring up the login form through the F12 key, even if the button is hidden. In an environment where the patrons may be unknown, the system will be slightly more secure if the temptation of a Login button is removed.

The UpdateDisplayForUser routine in the MainForm class includes code for user mode (LoggedInUserID = -1) and administrator mode (LoggedInUserID <> -1). In the user mode block (the first block), replace this line:

```
ActLogin.Visible = True
```

with the following code:

INSERT SNIPPET

Insert Chapter 14, Snippet Item 5.

```
' ----- Show or hide the Login button per the settings.
ActLogin.Visible = Not My.Settings.HideLogin
```

Adding Configuration Forms

It's time to add the forms that will manage all of the various application settings, both those stored locally in the user-focused settings file, and the system-wide settings stored in the database. Most of the settings are pretty simple—just basic strings, numbers, and Boolean flags—so it shouldn't overwhelm the administrator to have them all appear on a single form. But before we get to that form, we'll add a form that lets us manage the database connection.

I thought about calling up the connection properties dialog that Visual Studio uses to establish connection strings. I'm sure it's possible, but it provides way more flexibility than we need in this project. For instance, it supports the configuration of non-SQL Server databases, which is of no interest to the Library Project.

Instead, we'll design a simpler form that collects only those data values that we need to build the Library connection string. The LocateDatabase form appears in Figure 14-5.

Locate Database

Identify the server (machine) on which the Library database resides.
The Library Project supports SQL Server databases.

Server / Host:

Database Name:

Authentication:

User ID:

Password:

OK   Cancel

Figure 14-5. The new "Locate Database" form

I've already added the form and its controls to the project. Open the *LocateDatabase.vb* file to see the form. Four of the fields on this form are basic text entry fields (one with a password mask character). The fifth entry field, Authentication, lets the user select between Microsoft Windows authentication and SQL Server authentication.

Most of the form's code parallels what we've seen in many of the other forms already in the application. Go ahead and add in all of the form's code now.

INSERT SNIPPET

Insert Chapter 14, Snippet Item 6.

The significant work in this form occurs in the Load event when the existing connection string is parsed out into distinct data entry fields, and in the PromptUser routine where the parts are put back together.

There are many different ways you could chop up the connection string into its base parts. I took the basic divide-and-conquer approach, extracting out each semicolon- and equals sign-separated component. Here's the main block of code from the Load event handler that does the chopping and extracting:

```
' ----- Load in the existing data.
connectionString = My.Settings.DBConnection & ""
For counter = 1 To CountSubStr(connectionString, ";") + 1
    ' ----- Each comma-delimited part has the format
    '       "key=value".
    oneKey = GetSubStr(connectionString, ";", counter)
    oneValue = Trim(GetSubStr(oneKey, "=", 2))
    oneKey = Replace(UCase(Trim(GetSubStr( _
        oneKey, "=", 1))), " ", "")
```

```
            ' ----- Process each part.
        Select Case oneKey
            Case "DATASOURCE"
                ' ----- Show the server host.
                RecordServer.Text = oneValue
            Case "INITIALCATALOG"
                ' ----- Show the default database name.
                RecordDatabase.Text = oneValue
            Case "INTEGRATEDSECURITY"
                ' ----- Only check for "true". False is assumed.
                If (UCase(oneValue) = "TRUE") Then _
                    RecordAuthentication.SelectedIndex = _
                    RecordAuthentication.Items.IndexOf( _
                    AuthenticationTypeWindows)
            Case "USERID"
                ' ----- A user ID forces SQL authentication.
                RecordAuthentication.SelectedIndex = _
                    RecordAuthentication.Items.IndexOf( _
                    AuthenticationTypeSQL)
                RecordUser.Text = oneValue
            Case "PASSWORD"
                ' ----- A password forces SQL authentication.
                RecordAuthentication.SelectedIndex = _
                    RecordAuthentication.Items.IndexOf( _
                    AuthenticationTypeSQL)
                RecordPassword.Text = oneValue
        End Select
    Next counter
```

Putting the parts together is less complicated. Here's the needed string concatenation code found in the PromptUser routine:

```
newConnection = "Data Source=" & Trim(RecordServer.Text) & _
    ";Initial Catalog=" & Trim(RecordDatabase.Text)
If (CInt(CType(RecordAuthentication.SelectedItem, _
        ListItemData)) = AuthenticationTypeWindows) Then
    ' ----- Use Windows security.
    newConnection &= ";Integrated Security=true"
Else
    ' ----- Use SQL Server security.
    newConnection &= ";User ID=" & Trim(RecordUser.Text) & _
        ";Password=" & Trim(RecordPassword.Text)
End If
```

Although the LocateDatabase form does all of the parsing and building of the connection string, it doesn't actually update the saved setting. Instead, it returns the newly built connection string, and depends on the calling code to save it.

Now, back to our single-form configuration editor, *Maintenance.vb*. This form does all of the direct modification of the values in both the database and the local My.Settings items. Figures 14-6 and 14-7 show the two main panels of the Maintenance form. The centralized settings stored in the database are "system-wide," and the "workstation-specific" values are those accessed through My.Settings.

Figure 14-6. The new "Maintenance" form showing the "System-Wide" panel

This form begins its work in its Load event handler, Maintenance_Load. This routine sets up the choices in some drop-down fields, including a list of fonts. The code loops through the collection of installed fonts made available through the GDI+ object System.Drawing.Text.InstalledFontCollection.

```
Dim allFonts As New _
    System.Drawing.Text.InstalledFontCollection
RecordFontName.Items.Add(New ListItemData( _
    "<Not Selected>", -1))
For counter = 0 To allFonts.Families.Length - 1
    RecordFontName.Items.Add(New ListItemData( _
        allFonts.Families(counter).Name, counter))
Next counter
```

The routine also includes similar code to load a list of installed printers.

```
For Each installedPrinter As String In _
        PrinterSettings.InstalledPrinters
    RecordPrinterLocation.Items.Add(installedPrinter)
Next installedPrinter
```

Once everything is set up, the PopulateCurrentValues procedure completes the initialization. Its code retrieves all the current values from both the database and the

Figure 14-7. The new "Maintenance" form showing the "Workstation-Specific" panel

My.Settings object, and stores those values in the various on-screen data entry fields. I've already added the database-specific code. Go ahead and add in the settings-specific code.

INSERT SNIPPET

Insert Chapter 14, Snippet Item 7.

```
LibraryConnection = My.Settings.DBConnection & ""
RecordDBLocation.Text = GetDBDisplayText(LibraryConnection)
RecordConfigLocation.Text = My.Settings.ReportConfig & ""
RecordBasicHelp.Text = My.Settings.HelpFile & ""
RecordAdminHelp.Text = My.Settings.HelpFileAdmin & ""
EnableReceipts.Checked = My.Settings.UseReceipts
RecordPrinterLocation.Text = My.Settings.ReceiptPrinter & ""
RecordPrinterWidth.Text = CStr(My.Settings.ReceiptWidth)
RecordPostlude.Text = My.Settings.ReceiptPostlude & ""
HideLogin.Checked = My.Settings.HideLogin
```

Most of the code in this form deals with basic user interaction while the form is in use. For example, the ActDBLocation_Click event handler displays the LocateDatabase form we added earlier. Add the relevant source code to that event handler.

INSERT SNIPPET

Insert Chapter 14, Snippet Item 8.

```
' ----- Prompt for the database connection details.
Dim newConnection As String

' ----- Prompt the user for the new setting.
newConnection = LocateDatabase.PromptUser()
If (newConnection = "") Then Return

' ----- Store the new value.
LibraryConnection = newConnection
RecordDBLocation.Text = GetDBDisplayText(LibraryConnection)
```

Several of the settings specify the locations of files used by the application, such as the online help files. The user can type in the path to the file directly, or use the Open File dialog to locate the file visually. To display this dialog, I've added an OpenFileDialog control named LocateFile. Using it is a matter of setting the various file-specific properties and calling the ShowDialog method. Here's some of the code already included in the ActBasicHelp_Click event handler used to locate the non-administrative online help file:

```
' ----- Set up the file structure.
LocateFile.DefaultExt = "chm"
LocateFile.FileName = RecordBasicHelp.Text
LocateFile.Filter = "Help Files (*.chm)|*.chm|" & _
    "All Files (*.*)|*.*"
LocateFile.FilterIndex = 1
LocateFile.Title = "Locate Help"

' ----- Prompt the user.
If (LocateFile.ShowDialog() <> _
    Windows.Forms.DialogResult.OK) Then Return

' ----- Save the file path.
RecordBasicHelp.Text = LocateFile.FileName
```

Once the user has made the various setting changes, a click on the OK button saves each new setting to its storage area. I've included the database-focused saving code in the SaveFormData routine. I'll let you add the settings-focused code, near the end of that routine.

Insert Chapter 14, Snippet Item 9.

```
My.Settings.DBConnection = LibraryConnection
My.Settings.ReportConfig = Trim(RecordConfigLocation.Text)
My.Settings.HelpFile = Trim(RecordBasicHelp.Text)
My.Settings.HelpFileAdmin = Trim(RecordAdminHelp.Text)
My.Settings.HideLogin = HideLogin.Checked
My.Settings.UseReceipts = EnableReceipts.Checked
My.Settings.ReceiptPrinter = Trim(RecordPrinterLocation.Text)
My.Settings.ReceiptPostlude = RecordPostlude.Text

' ----- Save the receipt printer width.
If (Trim(RecordPrinterWidth.Text) = "") Then
   My.Settings.ReceiptWidth = DefaultReceiptPrinterWidth
Else
   My.Settings.ReceiptWidth = CInt(RecordPrinterWidth.Text)
End If
```

Although the Maintenance form provides a user-friendly interface to the database-stored settings, you probably remember that we already wrote code to update SystemValue table records through the *SystemValue.vb* file. In Chapter 12, we connected that form to the main form, but we're going to alter that logic. First, we'll add the call to the SystemValue form to the Maintenance form's `ActAllValues_Click` event handler.

Insert Chapter 14, Snippet Item 10.

```
' ----- Let the user edit the list of system values.
Dim RecordsForm As Library.ListEditRecords

' ----- Edit the records.
RecordsForm = New Library.ListEditRecords
RecordsForm.ManageRecords(New Library.SystemValue)
RecordsForm = Nothing

' ----- Refresh the display elements.
PopulateCurrentValues()
```

Then we'll change the `AdminLinkValues_LinkClicked` event handler back in *MainForm.vb*. Currently, it calls the SystemValue editor directly. Replace that part of the `LinkClicked` handler's code with code that calls the Maintenance form instead.

```
' ----- Access the maintenance portion of the program.
Maintenance.ShowDialog( )
```

Connecting to the Configured Database

The last change in this chapter uses the configured connection string to establish the connection to the database. When we originally wrote the `ConnectDatabase` routine in the `General` module, we added a hardcoded connection string just to get the program working.

```
' ----- Build the connection string.
' !!! WARNING: Hardcoded for now.
connectionString = "Data Source=MYSYSTEM\SQLEXPRESS;" & _
    "Initial Catalog=Library;Integrated Security=true"
```

Now that we have a user-configured connection string available, we will use that instead. The changes we must make to this routine are somewhat extensive, so just replace the function's existing content with the updated code.

```
' ----- Connect to the database. Return True on success.
Dim connectionString As String
Dim configChanged As Boolean

' ----- Initialize.
HoldTransaction = Nothing
configChanged = False

' ----- Obtain the connection string.
If (Trim(My.Settings.DBConnection & "") = "") Then
    ' ----- Inform the user about the need to configure
    '       the database.
    If (MsgBox("This copy of the application has not " & _
        "been configured to connect to the library " & _
        "database. If you know the database settings, " & _
        "you can configure it now. Would you like to " & _
        "proceed?", MsgBoxStyle.YesNo Or _
        MsgBoxStyle.Question, ProgramTitle) _
        <> MsgBoxResult.Yes) Then Return False
```

```
      ' ----- Prompt for the new connection details.
      connectionString = LocateDatabase.PromptUser( )
      If (connectionString = "") Then Return False
      configChanged = True
   Else
      connectionString = My.Settings.DBConnection
   End If

TryConnectingAgain:

   ' ----- Attempt to open the database.
   Try
      LibraryDB = New SqlClient.SqlConnection(connectionString)
      LibraryDB.Open( )
   Catch ex As Exception
      ' ----- Some database failure.
      GeneralError("ConnectDatabase", ex)

      ' ----- Perhaps it is just a configuration issue.
      If (MsgBox("The connection to the database may " & _
         "have failed due to invalid configuration " & _
         "settings. Would you like to change the " & _
         "database configuration at this time?", _
         MsgBoxStyle.YesNo Or MsgBoxStyle.Question, _
         ProgramTitle) <> MsgBoxResult.Yes) Then Return False

      ' ----- Prompt for new details.
      connectionString = LocateDatabase.PromptUser( )
      If (connectionString = "") Then Return False
         configChanged = True
      GoTo TryConnectingAgain
   End Try

   ' ----- Save the udpated configuration if needed.
   If (configChanged = True) Then _
      My.Settings.DBConnection = connectionString

   ' ----- Success.
   Return True
```

The basic gist of the code involves setting the connectionString variable to the persisted connection string, and using that to open the LibraryDB object. The new code obtains the connection string from My.Settings.DBConnection. If for any reason the connection string is missing or fails to generate an open database connection, the user is prompted to supply or correct the connection string through our new LocateDatabase form.

The program is back to a condition where you can run it. The first time you run the program, it will prompt you to supply the database connection information. The values you supply will match the hardcoded version that used to be in the ConnectDatabase routine:

- Set Server/Host to "MYSERVER\SQLEXPRESS" or to the name of your actual SQL Server host.
- Set Database Name to "Library" or any other name you previously assigned to your library database.
- Set Authentication to "Microsoft Windows" if you use Windows integrated security. If you need to connect using SQL Server's security system, set this field to "SQL Server," and enter a valid user ID and password.

In the next chapter, we'll focus on file manipulation techniques. Although we did update the settings file in this chapter, it was done indirectly through features provided by the framework. Chapter 15 will discuss more direct approaches to file manipulation.

CHAPTER 15

Files and Directories

Software development in the 21st century has really turned programmers into a bunch of softies (no pun intended). In the old days of computers, developers had to solder programs into the computer by hand. Complex calculations could take days to set up, and one misplaced wire meant lead poisoning or worse. The suffering was real, and older issues of *Popular Electronics* are riddled with articles by former programmers who went crazy in their attempt to craft one more ballistics calculation algorithm.

Life improved tremendously for programmers when John von Neumann and others suggested that a computer could store internally the logic for an algorithm, and process it directly from memory instead of through hard-wired configurations. Engineers were soon putting their programs onto punch cards and paper tapes. The danger of lead poisoning was quickly replaced by the larger evil of paper cuts.

Punch cards were great—until you dropped your stack that took you hours or days to assemble. Some programmer somewhere dropped one too many card stacks and proclaimed, "That's it! I'm going to invent the hard disk and related technologies such as IDE and SCSI. Sure I'll become fabulously wealthy, but at least I won't have to deal with these stupid cards anymore."

And thus was born the filesystem, the structured storage of programs and information on a disk surface. Filesystems have been a part of Microsoft technologies since Bill Gates first wooed IBM. It's no coincidence that the "DOS" in "MS-DOS" stands for *Disk Operating System*. Bill knew how essential filesystems were, and so do you.

In this chapter, we'll talk about interactions with files and directories, the main units of storage and organization in the Windows filesystem. We'll also see some of the technologies and features .NET provides to manipulate files and their content. Just make sure you turn the pages carefully; I wouldn't want you to get a paper cut.

Traditional Visual Basic File Management

Visual Basic has included significant file management features since its first release. In fact, more features in Visual Basic deal with file and directory manipulation than with pretty much anything else.

Most of the functions that allow you to read and modify file content use a *file handle*, a numeric identifier that refers to a specific open file. This file handle is generated with the FreeFile function, and must be obtained before calling any of the traditional Visual Basic file features.

```
Dim fileID As Integer
fileID = FreeFile()
FileOpen(fileID, "C:\TestData.txt", OpenMode.Append)
PrintLine(fileID, "Important output to file.")
FileClose(fileID)
```

File handle-based file manipulation works just fine, but it is so early-'90s. It's not really a .NET technology, and is not object-based at all (unless you consider that an Integer is an object). Therefore, I won't be covering it in this book, or using it in the Library Project. Table 15-1 lists the major Visual Basic features that use file handles. If you need to know about the handle-based features in Visual Basic, or if your work involves migrating pre-.NET Visual Basic applications, use this table to help you locate full feature details in the technical documentation supplied with Visual Basic.

Table 15-1. Visual Basic features that use file handles

Feature	Description
EOF	Returns a Boolean indicating whether the current position in the file is at or past the end of the file. Use this function to determine when to stop reading existing data from a file.
FileAttr	Accesses the file attributes currently set on an open file handle.
FileClose	Closes a specific file opened using a file handle.
FileGet	Retrieves structured data from a file and stores it in a matching object.
FileGetObject	Same as FileGet, but with slightly different data typing support.
FileOpen	Opens a file for input or output.
FilePut	Writes an object to a file in a structured manner.
FilePutObject	Same as FilePut, but with slightly different data typing support.
FileWidth	Sets the default line width for formatted text output files.
FreeFile	Returns the next available file handle.
Input	Retrieves a value previously written to a file using Write or WriteLine.
InputString	Retrieves a specific number of characters from an input file.
LineInput	Returns a complete line of input from a file.
Loc	Returns the current byte or record location in the file.

Table 15-1. *Visual Basic features that use file handles (continued)*

Feature	Description
Lock	Locks a file or specific records in a file so that others cannot make changes.
LOF	Returns the length of an open file, in bytes.
Print	Sends text output to a file.
PrintLine	Sends text output to a file, ending it with a line terminator.
Reset	Closes all files currently opened with file handles.
Seek	Gets or sets the current position in a file.
SPC	This function helps format text for output to columnar text files.
TAB	This function helps format text for output to columnar text files.
Unlock	Removes locks previously set with Lock.
Write	Writes data to a file using a consistent format that can be easily read later.
WriteLine	Same as Write, but ends the output with a line terminator.

Manipulating Files Through Streams

The .NET Framework includes a new object-oriented approach to reading and writing files: *streams*. The abstract Stream object, found at System.IO.Stream, defines a generic interface to a chunk of data. It doesn't matter where that data is: in a file, in a block of memory, in a String variable—if you have a block of data that can be read or written one byte at a time, you can design a derived stream class to interact with it.

Stream Features

The basic features of a Stream object include the Read and Write methods that let you read or write bytes. As data is read from or written to a stream, the Stream object maintains a "current position" within the stream that you can adjust using the Seek method, or examine using the Position property. The Length property indicates the size of the readable data. The class also exposes variations of these basic features to allow as much flexibility as possible.

Not every stream supports all features. Some streams are read-only, forward-only constructs that don't support writing or seeking. Other streams support all possible features. The features available to you depend on the type of stream you use. Since Stream itself is abstract, you must create an instance of one of its derived classes. .NET defines several useful streams ready for your use:

FileStream

> The FileStream object lets you access the content of a file using the basic methods of the generic Stream class. FileStream objects support reading, writing, and seeking, although if you open a read-only file, you won't be able to write to it.

MemoryStream

A stream based on a block of raw memory. You can create a memory stream of any size, and use it to temporarily store and retrieve any data.

NetworkStream

This class abstracts data coming over a network socket. Whereas most of the derived stream classes reside in System.IO, this class sits in System.Net.Sockets.

BufferedStream

Adds buffering support to a stream to improve performance on streams with latency issues. You wrap a BufferedStream object around another stream to use it.

CryptoStream

This stream allows you to attach a cryptographic service provider to it, resulting in encrypted output from plain input, or vice versa. Chapter 11 includes examples that use this type of stream.

DeflateStream *and* GZipStream

Let you use a stream to compress or decompress data as it is processed, all using standard compression algorithms.

Streams are useful on their own, but you can also combine streams so that an incoming network stream can be immediately encrypted, compressed, and stored in a block of stream memory.

Using a Stream

Using a stream is simple; first you create it, and then you start reading and writing bytes left and right. Here's some sample code I wrote that moves data into and out of a memory stream. It's loosely based on the code you'll find in the MSDN documentation for the MemoryStream class.

```
' ----- The Stream, or There and Back Again.
Dim position As Integer
Dim memStream As IO.MemoryStream
Dim sourceChars() As Byte
Dim destBytes() As Byte
Dim destChars() As Char
Dim asUnicode As New System.Text.UnicodeEncoding()

' ----- Create a memory stream with room for 100 bytes.
memStream = New IO.MemoryStream(100)

' ----- Convert the text data to a byte array.
sourceChars = asUnicode.GetBytes( _
   "This is a test of the emergency programming system.")

Try
   ' ----- Store the byte-converted data in the stream.
   memStream.Write(sourceChars, 0, sourceChars.Length)
```

```
' ----- The position is at the end of the written data.
'       To read it back, we must move the pointer to
'       the start again.
memStream.Seek(0, IO.SeekOrigin.Begin)

' ----- Read a chunk of the text/bytes at once.
destBytes = New Byte(CInt(memStream.Length)) {}
position = memStream.Read(destBytes, 0, 25)

' ----- Get the remaining data one byte at a time,
'       just for fun.
While (position < memStream.Length)
   destBytes(position) = CByte(memStream.ReadByte())
   position += 1
End While

' ----- Convert the byte array back to a set of characters.
destChars = New Char(asUnicode.GetCharCount( _
   destBytes, 0, position)) {}
asUnicode.GetDecoder().GetChars(destBytes, 0, _
   position, destChars, 0)

' ----- Prove that the text is back.
MsgBox(destChars)
Finally
   memStream.Close()
End Try
```

The comments hopefully make the code clear. After creating a memory stream, I push a block of text into it, and then read it back out. (The text stays in the stream; reading it did not remove it.) Actually, the stream code is pretty simple. Most of the code deals with conversions between bytes and characters. If it looks overly involved, that's because it is.

Beyond Stream Bytes

For me, all that converting between bytes and characters is for the birds. When I write business applications, I typically deal in dates, numbers, and strings: customer names, order dates, payment amounts, and so on. I rarely have a need to work at the byte level. I sure wish there was a way to send this byte stuff down a programming stream of its own so that I wouldn't have to see it anymore.

Lucky me! .NET makes some wishes come true. Although you can manipulate streams directly if you really want to or need to, the System.IO namespace also includes several classes that provide a more programmer-friendly buffer between you and the stream. These classes—implemented as distinct readers and writers of stream data—provide simplified methods of storing specific data types, and retrieving them back again.

The readers and writers are designed for single-direction start-to-finish processing of data. After creating or accessing a stream, you wrap that stream with either a reader or a writer, and begin traversing the extent of the stream from the beginning. You always have access to the underlying stream if you need more fine-tuned control at any point.

There are three main pairs of readers and writers:

BinaryReader *and* BinaryWriter

These classes make it easy to write and later read the core Visual Basic data types to and from a (generally) nontext stream. The BinaryWriter.Write method includes overloads for writing Bytes, Chars, signed and unsigned integers of various sizes, Booleans, Decimals and Doubles, Strings, and arrays and blocks of Bytes and Chars. Curiously missing is an overload for Date values.

The BinaryReader counterpart includes separate Read methods for each of the writable data types. The ReadDouble method returns a Double value from the stream, and there are similar methods for the other data types.

StreamReader *and* StreamWriter

These classes are typically used to process line-based text files. The StreamReader class includes a ReadLine method that returns the next text line in the incoming stream as a standard String. The related StreamWriter.Write method includes all the overloads of BinaryWriter.Write, and also has a version that lets you format a string for output. The reader includes features that let you read data one character at a time, one block at a time, or one entire file at a time.

StringReader *and* StringWriter

This pair of classes provides the same features as the StreamReader and StreamWriter pair, but uses a standard String instance for data storage instead of a file.

One additional pair—TextReader and TextWriter—provides the base class for the other nonbinary readers and writers. You can't create instances of them directly, but they do let you treat the stream and string versions of the readers and writers generically.

With these new tools, it's easier to process non-Byte data through streams. Here's a rewrite of the simple memory stream code I wrote earlier, adjusted to use a StreamReader and StreamWriter:

```
' ----- The Stream, or There and Back Again.
Dim memStream As IO.MemoryStream
Dim forWriting As IO.StreamWriter
Dim forReading As IO.StreamReader
Dim finalMessage As String
Dim asUnicode As New System.Text.UnicodeEncoding()

' ----- Create a memory stream with room for 100 bytes.
memStream = New IO.MemoryStream(100)
```

```
Try
    ' ----- Wrap the stream with a writer.
    forWriting = New IO.StreamWriter(memStream, asUnicode)

    ' ----- Store the original data in the stream.
    forWriting.WriteLine( _
        "This is a test of the emergency programming system.")
    forWriting.Flush( )

    ' ----- The position is at the end of the written data.
    '       To read it back, we must move the pointer to
    '       the start again.
    memStream.Seek(0, IO.SeekOrigin.Begin)

    ' ----- Create a reader to get the data back again.
    forReading = New IO.StreamReader(memStream, asUnicode)

    ' ----- Get the original string.
    finalMessage = forReading.ReadToEnd( )

    ' ----- Prove that the text is back.
    MsgBox(finalMessage)
Finally
    memStream.Close( )
End Try
```

That code sure is a lot nicer without all of that conversion code cluttering up the works. (We could simplify it even more by leaving out all of the optional Unicode encoding stuff.) Of course, everything is still being converted to bytes under the surface; the memory stream only knows about bytes. But `StreamWriter` and `StreamReader` take that burden away from us, performing all of the messy conversions on our behalf.

Reading a File Via a Stream

Most `Stream` processing involves files, so let's use a `StreamReader` to process a text file. Although we already decided in Chapter 14 that INI files are a thing of the past, it might be fun to write a routine that extracts a value from a legacy INI file. Consider a file containing this text:

```
[Section0]
Key1=abc
Key2=def

[Section1]
Key1=ghi
Key2=jkl

[Section2]
Key1=mno
Key2=pqr
```

Now there's something you don't see everyday, and with good reason! Still, if we wanted to get the value for Key2 in section Section1 (the "jkl" value), we would have to fall back on the GetPrivateProfileString API call from those bad old pre-.NET programming days. Or, we could implement a StreamReader in a custom function all our own.

```
Public Function GetINIValue(ByVal sectionName As String, _
    ByVal keyName As String, ByVal iniFile As String) _
    As String
' ----- Given a section and key name for an INI file,
'       return the matching value entry.
Dim readINI As IO.StreamReader
Dim oneLine As String
Dim compare As String
Dim found As Boolean

On Error GoTo ErrorHandler

' ----- Open the file.
If (My.Computer.FileSystem.FileExists(iniFile) = False) _
    Then Return ""
readINI = New IO.StreamReader(iniFile)

' ----- Look for the matching section.
found = False
compare = "[" & Trim(UCase(sectionName)) & "]"
Do While (readINI.EndOfStream = False)
    oneLine = readINI.ReadLine()
    If (Trim(UCase(oneLine)) = compare) Then
        ' ----- Found the matching section.
        found = True
        Exit Do
    End If
Loop

' ----- Exit early if the section name was not found.
If (found = False) Then
    readINI.Close()
    Return ""
End If

' ----- Look for the matching key.
compare = Trim(UCase(keyName))
Do While (readINI.EndOfStream = False)
    ' ----- If we reach another section, then the
    '       key wasn't there.
    oneLine = Trim(readINI.ReadLine())
    If (Len(oneLine) = 0) Then Continue Do
    If (oneLine.Substring(0, 1) = "[") Then Exit Do

    ' ----- Ignore lines without an "=" sign.
    If (InStr(oneLine, "=") = 0) Then Continue Do
```

```
' ----- See if we found the key. By the way, I'm
'       using Substring( ) instead of Left( ) so
'       I don't have to worry about conflicts with
'       Form.Left in case I drop this routine into
'       a Form class.
If (Trim(UCase(oneLine.Substring(0, _
        InStr(oneLine, "=") - 1))) = compare) Then
    ' ----- Found the matching key.
    readINI.Close( )
    Return Trim(Mid(oneLine, InStr(oneLine, "=") + 1))
End If
Loop

' ----- If we got this far, then the key was missing.
readINI.Close( )
Return ""

ErrorHandler:
    ' ----- Return an empty string on any error.
    On Error Resume Next
    If (readINI IsNot Nothing) Then readINI.Close( )
    readINI = Nothing
    Return ""
End Function
```

This routine isn't an exact replacement for GetPrivateProfileString; it doesn't support a default return value, or perform file caching for speed. You could improve the routine with better error handling. But it does retrieve the value we seek, and it does it by reading the INI file one line at a time through a StreamReader.

```
MsgBox(GetINIValue("Section1", "Key2", iniFilePath))
    ' ----- Displays 'jkl'
```

File Management with the My Namespace

The My namespace includes several file management features in its My.Computer. FileSystem branch, including features that create streams for reading and writing.

My Namespace Versus Visual Basic Commands

Most of the My.Computer.FileSystem object's members exist to replace or supplement file management features already present in Visual Basic. Table 15-2 lists some of the long-standing file and directory interaction features in Visual Basic, and their equivalents in My.Computer.FileSystem.

Table 15-2. Two ways to do the same thing

Visual Basic feature	Purpose	My.Computer.FileSystem equivalent
ChDir	Change the current "working" directory on a specified or default drive.	The `FileSystem.CurrentDirectory` property gets and sets the current "working" directory as understood by the application. You set the active directory through an absolute or relative path string.
ChDrive	Change the current "working" drive.	The `FileSystem.CurrentDirectory` property not only reports or changes the active directory, it also modifies the active drive.
CurDir	Identify the current "working" directory and drive as a full path string.	Once again, `FileSystem.CurrentDirectory` is the substitute for this Visual Basic directory feature. `CurDir` does have a little more flexibility: it allows you to determine the current directory on a drive other than the current drive. This can't be done with `FileSystem.CurrentDirectory`.
Dir	Retrieve files and directories in a parent directory that match a specific name pattern.	The `FileSystem.GetDirectories` and `FileSystem.GetFiles` methods both support wildcard patterns when retrieving matching directory and file names. `Dir` requires that you call it once for each entry to return, and it doesn't work well when processing nested directories. The `FileSystem` equivalents return collections of matching items, and can optionally descend the entire subdirectory tree of a base path.
FileCopy	Make a copy of a file.	The `FileSystem.CopyFile` provides a few additional user-friendly features beyond `FileCopy`. But what's the deal with the reversal of "File" and "Copy"?
FileDateTime	Retrieve the creation or modification date and time of a file.	Use the `FileSystem.GetFileInfo` method to retrieve a `FileInfo` object replete with details about a file. You'll probably focus on the `FileInfo.LastWriteTime` property, but you can also get the original creation time and the last access time, features not available through the lowly and now disgraced `FileDateTime` function.
FileLen	Retrieve the length, in bytes, of a file.	Obtain a `FileInfo` object through the `FileSystem.GetFileInfo` method, and access that object's `Length` property to get the file size in bytes.
GetAttr	Retrieve the attributes of a file as a bit field.	Get details on a file through the `FileSystem.GetFileInfo` method, and use the returned `FileInfo` object's `Attributes` property to examine your attribute of choice. This object also exposes an `IsReadOnly` Boolean value.
Kill	Delete a file or empty directory.	The `FileSystem.DeleteFile` and `FileSystem.DeleteDirectory` methods replace the `Kill` procedure, and provide additional options not available with `Kill`. Plus, you won't have the police knocking at your door asking why you constantly type *Kill, Kill, Kill*.

Table 15-2. Two ways to do the same thing (continued)

Visual Basic feature	Purpose	My.Computer.FileSystem equivalent
MkDir	Create a new directory.	The `FileSystem.CreateDirectory` method is a gentle replacement for `MkDir`. Anyway, "mkdir" is an old Unix command, and you're not programming on Unix, are you?
Rename	Change the name of a file or directory.	Rename is replaced by distinct `FileSystem.RenameFile` and `FileSystem.RenameDirectory` methods.
RmDir	Delete a directory, even if it contains files.	The `FileSystem.DeleteDirectory` deletes directories that still contain other files, an action that `RmDir` rejected. There's also an option to send the files to the Recycle Bin.
SetAttr	Modify the attributes of a file using a bit field.	Same process listed for `GetAttr` earlier in this table. The `FileInfo` object's `Attributes` and `IsReadOnly` properties are read/write values, assuming you have the necessary security rights to change attributes.

Why would Microsoft introduce so many new My features that duplicate existing Visual Basic features? Perhaps it's a way to bring consistency to file-based programming practices through a more object-oriented approach. Or maybe it's yet another move by Microsoft, the U.S. government, the Knights Templar, Burger King, and other groups set on world domination by controlling you, your family, and your community through the "hidden hand" of extra-long source code statements.

Reading and Writing Files Through My

The `My.Computer.FileSystem.OpenTextFileReader` and parallel `OpenTextFileWriter` methods provide shortcuts to the filename-based constructor for `StreamReader` and `StreamWriter` objects. The statement:

```
Dim inputStream As IO.StreamReader = _
    My.Computer.FileSystem.OpenTextFileReader( _
    fileNamePath)
```

is identical to:

```
Dim inputStream As New IO.StreamReader(fileNamePath)
```

For me, the second version is better due to its terse nature, but it's between you and your source code review team as to which one you will use.

If you want to load the entire contents of a file into either a `String` or a `Byte` array, there's no need to open up a stream now that My includes the `My.Computer.FileSystem.ReadAllText` and related `ReadAllBytes` methods. This statement dumps the entire contents of a file into a `String`:

```
Dim wholeFile As String = _
    My.Computer.FileSystem.ReadAllText( _
    fileNamePath)
```

The My.Computer.FileSystem.WriteAllText and WriteAllBytes methods do the same thing, but in the opposite direction. There's an append Boolean argument that lets you either append or replace the new content relative to any existing content in the file.

```
My.Computer.FileSystem.WriteAllText( _
    fileNamePath, dataToWrite, True)  ' True=append
```

One feature that has always been missing from Visual Basic is the ability to conveniently scan a delimited file (such as tab-delimited or comma-delimited) or a fixed-width-field file, and extract the fields on each line without a lot of extra parsing code. Visual Basic now includes the Microsoft.VisualBasic.FileIO.TextFieldParser object that simplifies this process. This object lets you indicate either a field delimiter (such as the tab character) or an array of column sizes. Once you associate it with a file path, it reads each data line, breaking up the distinct fields for you into a string array. The My.Computer.FileSystem.OpenTextFieldParser method opens the file and defines the parsing method in one fell swoop.

```
Dim dataFields( ) As String
Dim sourceFile As FileIO.TextFieldParser

' ----- Open the file with tab-delimited fields.
sourceFile = My.Computer.FileSystem.OpenTextFieldParser( _
    sourceFilePath, vbTab)

' ----- Process each line.
Do While Not sourceFile.EndOfData
    dataFields = sourceFile.ReadFields( )
    ' ----- dataFields is a simple string array,
    '       so you can examine each field directly.
    If (dataFields(0) = "NEW") Then
    ' ----- and so on...
Loop
sourceFile.Close( )
```

The TextFieldParser object can also detect comment lines and ignore them silently. I am sure that it's using a StreamReader secretly hidden inside the object's black box. Although the internals are hidden from view, the exposed features of this object make it a snap to process field-based text files.

Summary

Managing and manipulating files isn't brain surgery. But with the filesystem as a major focus of any operating system, tools and methods for reading and updating files just seem to multiply like rabbits. The .NET Framework uses the Stream as its primary file interaction method, so this should help make things simpler. Of course, it piles dozens of wrapper classes on top of the basic stream, but that's another issue.

As for the management of files and directories, .NET is going in the opposite direction, giving you more and more language and object features to perform the same basic tasks. Beyond the traditional Visual Basic and My namespace features I introduced in this chapter, there are additional duplicate features in the .NET class libraries. Use the methods that meet your needs, and "file" the others away for future reference.

Project

I have some good news and some bad news. The bad news is that the Library Project does not make direct reads or writes of standard files, and has no need for file streams. That means we won't be adding any code to the project in this chapter at all. The good news is that we still have interesting things to talk about. Besides, I figured that since you had finished more than half of the book, you could use a break.

PROJECT ACCESS

Chapter 15 does not include any project templates, so don't bother looking in Visual Studio for them.

Configuring Log Output

Whenever an error occurs in the Library application, the GeneralError routine first shows the error message to the user, and then logs it to any configured "log listeners."

```
Public Sub GeneralError(ByVal routineName As String, _
    ByVal theError As System.Exception)
    ' ----- Report an error to the user.
    On Error Resume Next

    MsgBox("The following error occurred at location '" & _
        routineName & "':" & vbCrLf & vbCrLf & _
        theError.Message, MsgBoxStyle.OkOnly Or _
        MsgBoxStyle.Exclamation, ProgramTitle)
    My.Application.Log.WriteException(theError)
End Sub
```

So, who's listening? If you are running the program within Visual Studio, Visual Basic always configures a log listener that displays the text in the Immediate Window panel. But that doesn't do much good in a compiled and deployed application.

You can design your own log listeners, but .NET also includes several predefined listeners, all of which can be enabled and configured through the application's *app.config* file. If you access the "After" version of Chapter 14's project, you will find content in its *app.config* file that sets up one such listener. Here's a portion of that file, showing just the relevant sections:

```
<system.diagnostics>
  <sources>
    <!-- This section defines the logging configuration
         for My.Application.Log -->
    <source name="DefaultSource" switchName="DefaultSwitch">
      <listeners>
        <add name="FileLog"/>
      </listeners>
    </source>
  </sources>

  <switches>
    <add name="DefaultSwitch" value="Information" />
  </switches>

  <sharedListeners>
    <add name="FileLog" type=
    ↳"Microsoft.VisualBasic.Logging.FileLogTraceListener,
    ↳Microsoft.VisualBasic, Version=8.0.0.0, Culture=neutral,
    ↳PublicKeyToken=b03f5f7f11d50a3a,
    ↳processorArchitecture=MSIL"
    ↳initializeData="FileLogWriter"/>
  </sharedListeners>
</system.diagnostics>
```

The `<sharedListeners>` section defines the details for a particular log listener. In this case, it's the `FileLogTraceListener` listener, a class in the `Microsoft.VisualBasic.Logging` namespace. It's enabled in the `<source>/<listeners>` section, where it's included through an `<add>` tag. There's a lot of stuff here that seems bizarre or extremely picky (such as the public key token). Fortunately, it's all documented in MSDN if you ever need the details.

The `FileLogTraceListener` listener sends relevant logging data to an application-specific logfile. By default in Windows Vista, the file resides in the following:

```
C:\Users\username\Application Data\
↳Company\Product\Version\AppName.log
```

The *username* part is replaced by the name of the currently logged-in user. The *Company*, *Product*, and *Version* parts represent the company name, product name, and version number of your assembly as defined in its assembly attributes. *AppName* is the name of your application with the *.exe* extension stripped off. On my Windows Vista system, the logfile for the Library Project appears here:

```
C:\Users\username\Application Data\
↳ACME\Library\1.0.0.0\Library.log
```

If you don't like that location, you can change the output to any location you choose. To do it, you'll need to alter the `<add>` tag in the `<sharedListeners>` section, adding two additional attributes to that tag.

```
<sharedListeners>
  <add name="FileLog" type=
```

```
          ∟ "Microsoft.VisualBasic.Logging.FileLogTraceListener,
          ∟ Microsoft.VisualBasic, Version=8.0.0.0, Culture=neutral,
          ∟ PublicKeyToken=b03f5f7f11d50a3a,
          ∟ processorArchitecture=MSIL"
          ∟ initializeData="FileLogWriter"
          ∟ location="Custom"
          ∟ customLocation="c:\temp\" />
    </sharedListeners>
```

The new `location` and `customLocation` attributes do the trick. Set the `customLocation` attribute to the directory where the logfile should go. These attributes link to properties of the same name in the `FileLogTraceListener` class. Visual Studio's documentation describes these properties and attributes, plus others that are available for you to configure through *app.config*.

This *app.config* change is based on an MSDN article titled "How to: Write Event Information to a Text File" that you can search for in your online help. (Use the Search feature, not the Index feature.)

Other Log Output Options

Another MSDN article, "Walkthrough: Changing Where My.Application.Log Writes Information," describes how to send log output to more than just a simple text file. It discusses ways to log application information to the system Event Log, to a delimited file, to an XML-formatted file, and to the console display.

Some of the changes you need to make to the *app.config* file are, again, mysterious, so I'll just list them here for your examination. Add the following content to the *app.config* file to define the available listeners:

```
<add name="EventLog"
  type="System.Diagnostics.EventLogTraceListener,
      System, Version=2.0.0.0,
      Culture=neutral, PublicKeyToken=b77a5c561934e089"
      initializeData="sample application"/>

<add name="Delimited"
  type="System.Diagnostics.DelimitedListTraceListener,
  ∟ System, Version=2.0.0.0,
  ∟ Culture=neutral, PublicKeyToken=b77a5c561934e089"
  ∟ initializeData="c:\temp\SomeFile.txt"
  ∟ delimiter=";;;"
  ∟ traceOutputOptions="DateTime" />

<add name="XmlWriter"
  type="System.Diagnostics.XmlWriterTraceListener,
  ∟ System, Version=2.0.0.0,
  ∟ Culture=neutral, PublicKeyToken=b77a5c561934e089"
  ∟ initializeData="c:\temp\SomeFile.xml" />
```

```
<add name="Console"
  type="System.Diagnostics.ConsoleTraceListener,
  ┕ System, Version=2.0.0.0,
  ┕ Culture=neutral, PublicKeyToken=b77a5c561934e089"
  ┕ initializeData="true" />
```

The `initializeData` attribute in each entry contains the values sent to the arguments of the relevant class constructor. Other attributes (except for type) modify the properties of the same name in the class specified through the type attribute. For all the options available to you for each listener, look up its class entry in the Visual Studio documentation.

To enable any of these listeners, use an `<add>` tag in the `<source>`/`<listeners>` section. The following XML block enables all the listeners defined in this chapter's project:

```
<sources>
  <!-- This section defines the logging configuration
       for My.Application.Log -->
  <source name="DefaultSource" switchName="DefaultSwitch">
    <listeners>
      <add name="FileLog"/>
      <add name="EventLog" />
      <add name="Delimited" />
      <add name="XmlWriter" />
      <add name="Console" />
    </listeners>
  </source>
</sources>
```

Obtaining a Bar Code Font

Since we have a little time left, let's talk about obtaining a bar code font. The Library Project will include bar code printing support, but only if you have a bar code font installed on your system. It's no emergency, but you should obtain one before you reach Chapter 18, where we develop the bar code configuration code.

When you downloaded the code for this book, it didn't include a bar code font. It's all due to licensing issues and the like, you understand. But bar code fonts are easy to get. You can purchase a professional bar code font if you want to, and if you plan to deploy this project into an actual library setting, you probably should. But if you're only reading this book for the great humor, you can download one of the many free bar code fonts available on the Internet. I've included some links to bar code font providers on the web site where you obtained the source code for this book. Even if you don't plan to use the bar code printing features, I recommend that you download a free bar code font just so that you can try out some of the Chapter 18 features.

Once you've installed the font, you will need to tell the Library program to use it. The settings form we designed in the previous chapter included a selection field for this font. It's the Barcode Font Name field on the System-Wide tab of the Maintenance form. You can see it in the middle of Figure 14-6. I made it a system-wide setting because it seemed best to have all administrators in a single library using a common font.

If your font is a "Code 3 of 9" bar code font (also called "Code 39"), make sure you select the Barcode is "Code 39" or "Code 3 of 9" field on that same form. (The provider of the font will let you know whether it is a Code 3 of 9 font or not.) These fonts require an asterisk before and after the bar code number. Selecting this field will cause the Library program to add the asterisk characters automatically.

Well, I'm getting tired of talking about files, be they fonts or config files. In the next chapter, we'll go back into the world of code and its fraternal twin, data.

CHAPTER 16

Generics

When I was in high school, my family sometimes shopped at a local grocery warehouse named Fedmart. Signs on the window clearly stated that there was "no connection between Fedmart and the federal government," but people continued to shop there anyway. They had these small $1 frozen cheese pizzas that my mom would buy in bulk for me and my friends, teenage boys who didn't care much about what went down the esophagus.

Most of the store stocked the typical grocery products, but there was one aisle near the south border of the store that sold only "generic" products. Walking into this section was like walking into a black-and-white television; all of the product labels were plain clear or white, with simple black lettering. And they were cheap. They did the job, but just barely. You would never want to run out of name-brand ketchup in the middle of a celebratory barbeque with your friends, and offer up a bottle of generic ketchup as a replacement. Somehow I remember clearly reading the black lettering on the white label of that watery ketchup substitute, about how it met the federal ketchup standards. At that moment I had an epiphany, a sudden realization that would change the way I thought about life in these United States forever: the government has a federal ketchup standard!

Sadly, Fedmart closed down before I finished my senior year, leaving a vacuum in the generic ketchup and aluminum foil marketplace. But as a Visual Basic programmer, you can still gain access to generics, through .NET's generics technology. *Generics*— the ability to use placeholders for data types—first appeared in Visual Basic 2005 and the related .NET Framework 2.0. This chapter provides you with the "specifics" on generics.

What Are Generics?

In .NET, "generics" is a technology that lets you define data type placeholders within types or methods. Let's say you needed to define a class to track customer data, but you didn't want to enforce a specific format on the customer "ID" value. Part of your code needs to interact with customer objects using an Integer ID value, while another part of the code will use an alphanumeric key for the customer. You might ask, "Why don't you just include both types of identifiers as distinct fields in your customer record?" That wouldn't work because I am trying to come up with a reasonably simple example and answering that question would just distract me. So, here's the numeric version of the class:

```
Class CustomerWithNumberID
    Public ID As Integer
    Public FullName As String
End Class
```

Here's the variation that uses a string ID:

```
Class CustomerWithStringID
    Public ID As String
    Public FullName As String
End Class
```

Of course, you could define ID as System.Object, and stick anything you wanted in that field. But System.Object is considered "weakly typed," and there is nothing to stop you from mixing in Integer and String ID values for different instances in an array of customer objects.

What you want is a system that lets you define the class generically, and hold off on specifying the data type of ID until you actually create an instance of the class, or a complete collection of related class instances. With such a system, you could define a general-purpose version of the customer class.

```
Class CustomerWithSomeID
    Public ID As <DatatypePlaceholder>
    Public FullName As String
End Class
```

Later, when it was time to create an instance, you could tell the language which data type to use for the placeholder.

```
Dim oneCustomer As CustomerWithSomeID(replacing _
    <DatatypePlaceholder> with Integer)
```

This is what generics let you do. Here's the actual Visual Basic syntax that defines the nonspecific customer class:

```
Class CustomerWithSomeID(Of T)
    Public ID As T
    Public FullName As String
End Class
```

The general placeholder, T, appears in a special Of clause, just after the class name. (You don't have to name the placeholder *T*, but it's become a tradition when presenting sample code using generics.) As a data type, T can be used anywhere within the class definition where you don't want to define the data type upfront. The class, and its ID member, are now ready for instantiation with an actual replacement data type for T. To create a new instance, try this code:

```
Dim numberCustomer As CustomerWithSomeID(Of Integer)
```

When (Of Integer) is attached to the end of the class definition, Visual Basic acts as though you actually declared a variable for a class that had an Integer member named ID. In fact, you did. When you create an instance of a generic class, the compiler defines a separate class that looks like a non-generic class with all of the placeholders replaced.

```
Dim customer1 As New CustomerWithSomeID(Of Integer)
Dim customer2 As New CustomerWithSomeID(Of Integer)
Dim customer3 As New CustomerWithSomeID(Of String)
```

These lines define two instances of CustomerWithSomeID(Of Integer), and one instance of CustomerWithSomeID(Of String). customer1 and customer2 are truly instances of the same data type, but customer3 is an instance of a completely different data type. Assignments between customer1 and customer2 will work, but you can't mix either of them with customer3 without performing an explicit conversion.

```
' ----- This works just fine.
customer1 = customer2

' ----- This will not compile.
customer3 = customer1
```

As true compile-time data types generated automatically by the compiler, they exhibit all of the personality of other non-generic classes. Even Visual Studio's IntelliSense properly detects the substituted data type. Figure 16-1 includes a tool tip, just to the right of the instance member selection list, that properly identifies the customer1.ID member as Integer.

Figure 16-1. Congratulations, Mr. and Mrs. Generic: it's an Integer

Within the class definition, the T placeholder can appear anywhere, even within argument lists and local variable declarations.

```
Class SomeClass(Of T)
    Public Function TransformData(ByVal sourceData As T) As T
        ' ----- Add generic transormation code here.
        Dim workData As T
        ...
    End Function
End Class
```

Generics work with structures and interfaces as well.

```
Structure SomeStructure(Of T)
    Public GenericMember As T
End Structure

Interface ISomeInterface(Of T)
    Sub DoWorkWithData(ByVal theData As T)
End Interface
```

Variations of Generic Declaration

If there were a minimum federal government data type placeholder requirement, the implementation of generics just described would certainly meet it. It's kind of nice to postpone the definition of data types until the last minute. But .NET generics don't stop there.

Multiple Placeholders

Generic placeholders—also known as *type parameters*—are like those knives you buy on late-night TV. You don't get one; you get more! As many as you need, it turns out. Each generic class can include multiple placeholders by adding them to the initial Of clause.

```
Class MultiTypes(Of T1, T2)
    Public Member1 As T1
    Public Member2 As T2
End Class
```

As before, you aren't required to use the boring names *T1* and *T2*. Whatever names you choose, include them as a comma-separated list just after the Of keyword. When you're ready to create an instance, replicate the comma-delimited list in the same order, but using actual types. In this statement, Integer replaces T1, and String replaces T2:

```
Dim useInstance As MultiTypes(Of Integer, String)
```

Data Type and Interface Constraints

The type parameters you include in a generic, such as T, accept any valid data type, including Integer, String, System.Windows.Forms.Form, or your own custom types. That is, T can be replaced by anything that derives from System.Object, which is everything. You can even imagine the statement:

```
Class SomeClass(Of T)
```

being replaced by:

```
Class SomeClass(Of T As System.Object)
```

adding the As clause to make it look like other Visual Basic declarations. Well, you can stop imagining and start acting: placeholders support the As clause. If you don't include an As clause, Visual Basic assumes you mean As System.Object, but you can follow As with any type you want.

```
Class FormOnlyClass(Of T As System.Windows.Forms.Form)
```

By adding a specific class with the As clause, you enforce a *constraint* on the generic type, a limitation that must be met to use the type. In this case, the constraint says, "You may supply any class value for *T* as long as *it is or it derives from* System.Windows.Forms.Form." This means you can create an instance of FormOnlyClass using one of your application's forms, but not using non-Form classes.

```
' ----- This works.
Dim usingForm As FormOnlyClass(Of Form1)

' ----- This doesn't work.
Dim usingForm As FormOnlyClass(Of Integer)
```

When you add a constraint to a type parameter, it impacts the features you can use with that type parameter. Consider this generic class destined to work with forms, but not declared that way:

```
Class WorkWithForms(Of T)
    Public Sub ChangeCaption(ByVal whichForm As T, _
        ByVal newCaption As String)
        ' ----- The following line will not compile.
        whichForm.Text = newCaption
    End Sub
End Class
```

In this class, the assignment to whichForm.Text will fail because the WorkWithForms class does not know that you plan to use it with forms. It only knows that you plan to use T, and T is, by default, of type System.Object. There's no Text property in the System.Object class; I checked.

If we change the definition of WorkWithForms to accept Form objects, the outlook for compiling this code changes dramatically.

```
Class WorkWithForms(Of T As Windows.Forms.Form)
    Public Sub ChangeCaption(ByVal whichForm As T, _
        ByVal newCaption As String)
        ' ----- Yes! It now compiles.
        whichForm.Text = newCaption
    End Sub
End Class
```

Since T has to be a Form type or something derived from Form, Visual Basic knows that all the members of the Form class, including Text, are available to all things T. Therefore, the assignment to whichForm.Text works.

In addition to classes, you can also use interfaces to constrain your generic types.

```
Class ThrowAwayClass(Of T As IDisposable)
```

Instances of ThrowAwayClass can be created as needed, but only if the type supplied with the declaration implements the IDisposable interface.

```
' ----- This works. Pens use IDisposable.
Dim disposablePen As ThrowAwayClass(Of System.Drawing.Pen)

' ----- This doesn't work, since the Integer data type
'       doesn't implement IDisposable.
Dim disposableNumber As ThrowAwayClass(Of Integer)
```

But wait, there's more! See, I told you it was like shopping for knives on TV. Besides your run-of-the-mill types and interfaces, you can also follow the As clause on the generic placeholder with the New keyword.

```
Class SomeClass(Of T As New)
```

The As New clause says to the generic type, "Accept any type for T, but only if that type includes a constructor that requires no arguments." That is, T must include a default constructor. Once defined, you'll be able to create new instances of T—whatever type it actually turns out to be—in your generic type.

```
Class SomeClass(Of T As New)
    Public Sub SomeSub( )
        Dim someVariable As New T
    End Sub
End Class
```

If your generic class includes multiple type parameters, each parameter can include its own As class with a distinct type or interface constraint.

Simultaneous Constraints

It's nice that each of those knives you purchased can slice a watermelon, but what if you want to chop wood with that same knife, or use it to upgrade that electrical work you've been postponing? You're looking for a multifunctional tool, just like you find in each generic placeholder. If you need one placeholder to include a constraint for a specific class, an interface, and "New" all at once, you can do it. After the As keyword, include the multiple constraints in curly braces.

```
Class SomeClass(Of T As {Windows.Forms.Form, _
    IDisposable, New})
```

Now, any type you supply in the Of clause when creating an instance of this class *must meet all of the constraints*, not just one of them. And here's something new: you can include more than one interface constraint at a time.

```
Class SomeClass(Of T As {ISerializable, IDisposable})
```

And you can still include a class constraint and the New constraint, even with those multiple interfaces. (You can't include more than one class constraint for a single placeholder.) If your generic type includes multiple type parameters, each of them can have its own multiple constraints set.

Nesting Generic Types

Generic types can include their own nested types.

```
Class Level1(Of T1)
    Public Level1Member As T1
    Class Level2(Of T2)
        Public Level2Member1 As T1
        Public Level2Member2 As T2
    End Class
End Class
```

You can nest the generics as deeply as you need.

Non-Generic Types with Generic Members

If generic types seem a little scary or overwhelming, don't fret. You don't have to create a full generic type to use the new generic features. You can add generic support to just a single method within an otherwise normal class.

```
Class SomeClass
    ' ----- The class itself does not have the generic
    '       Of clause, so it's not generic. But...

    Public Shared Sub ReverseValues(Of T) _
        (ByRef first As T, ByRef second As T)
        ' ----- This method is generic with its own Of clause.

        ' ----- Reverse the contents of two variables.
        Dim holdFirst As T

        holdFirst = first
        first = second
        second = holdFirst
    End Sub
End Class
```

Generic methods are useful when you need to have a local variable of the placeholder's type within the method (as is done with holdFirst here), but you don't know the type in advance. Using this shared ReverseValues method works like any other method, with the extra Of clause stuck in.

```
Dim x As Integer = 5
Dim y As Integer = 10
SomeClass.ReverseValues(Of Integer)(x, y)
MsgBox(x)  ' Displays 10
```

If you will be using the placeholder for one or more of the method arguments, Visual Basic will infer the type based on the passed value. If Visual Basic is able to guess the type in this way, you don't even need the Of clause when calling the generic method.

```
SomeClass.ReverseValues(x, y)
```

As with generic types, generic methods allow you to add constraints to the placeholders.

Overloading Generic Types and Members

Earlier I mentioned how the compiler essentially creates separate classes for each instance variation of a generic class that you create. This means that these two instances actually use completely different and generally unrelated classes:

```
Dim numberVersion As SomeClass(Of Integer)
Dim textVersion As SomeClass(Of String)
```

So, SomeClass(Of Integer) and SomeClass(Of String) are completely different classes, even though they have the same base name. In a way, Visual Basic is *overloading* the class name for you, letting you use it in two (or more) different ways.

Generics also let you get involved in the class-overloading game. Normally, you can only create a single class with a given name—inside a particular namespace, that is. But with generics, you can reuse a class name, as long as the placeholders used among the classes are different enough, either in their number or in their applied constraints.

```
Class SomeClass(Of T1)
   ' ----- This is a generic class with one placeholder.
End Class

Class SomeClass(Of T1, T2)
   ' ----- This is a completely different generic
   '       class with two placeholders.
End Class
```

Visual Basic will figure out which version to use based on the Of clause you include with the instance declaration.

```
Dim simpleVersion As SomeClass(Integer)
Dim complexVersion As SomeClass(Integer, String)
```

Generics and Collections

Generics really shine in the area of collections. The initial release of .NET had, among the thousands of possibly useful classes, a set of "collection" classes, all in the System.Collections namespace. Each collection lets you stuff as many other object instances as you want inside that collection, and retrieve them later. The collections differ in how you stuff and retrieve, but they all allow you to stick any type of object in the collection.

One of the collection classes is the System.Collections.Stack class. Stacks let you store objects like pancakes: the first object you add to the stack goes on the bottom, and each one you add goes on top of the previous object. When you're ready to eat a pancake—I mean, remove an item—it comes off the top. (This "last in, first out" system is sometimes called "LIFO.") The Push and Pop methods manage the addition and removal of objects.

```
Dim numberStack As New Collections.Stack
numberStack.Push(10)
numberStack.Push(20)
numberStack.Push(30)
MsgBox(numberStack.Pop())    ' Displays 30
MsgBox(numberStack.Pop())    ' Displays 20
MsgBox(numberStack.Pop())    ' Displays 10
```

There is also a Peek method that looks at the topmost item, but doesn't remove it from the stack. The thing with stacks (and other similar collections) is that you don't have to put just one type of object into the stack. You can mix any ol' types of objects you want.

```
Dim numberStack As New Collections.Stack
numberStack.Push(10)                   ' Integer
numberStack.Push("I'm sneaking in.")   ' String
numberStack.Push(Me.Button1)           ' Control
```

The stack doesn't care, since it's just treating everything as System.Object. But what if you needed to ensure that *only integers* were put into the stack? What if you wanted to limit a stack to any specific data type, but didn't want to write separate stack classes for each possible type?

This sure sounds like a job for generics to me. It sounded that way to Microsoft, too. So, it added a bunch of new generic collections to the framework. They appear in the System.Collections.Generic namespace. There are a few different classes in this namespace, including classes for linked lists, queues, chocolate chip cookies, and dictionaries. And hey, there's a class called Stack(Of T). That's just what we need.

```
Dim numberStack As New Collections.Generic.Stack(Of Integer)
numberStack.Push(10)
numberStack.Push(20)
numberStack.Push(30)
```

Now, if we try to add anything other than an Integer to numberStack, an error occurs.

```
' ----- This won't work.
numberStack.Push("I'll try again.")
```

Generic Nullable Types

Back in Chapter 6, I introduced nullable types, a way to allow Nothing to be used with value types.

```
Dim numberOrNothing As Integer?
```

Although you can't tell from that source code line, nullable types are actually implemented using generics. The full version of numberOrNothing's declaration is:

```
Dim numberOrNothing As Nullable(Of Integer)
```

Visual Basic simply provided a shortcut for this syntax through the ? suffix. You can use either syntax to declare your nullable instances.

Summary

Having generics available for .NET development really makes Visual Basic even more flexible and useful than all the hype you heard about it. You always had the ability to use placeholders for data—they're called *variables*. Generics provide that same placeholder functionality, but with data types instead of just plain data.

When you control all development aspects of an application, you might think that generics aren't for you. After all, you're not going to let an Integer variable slip into a collection of dates. But they are quite handy for enforcing standards within your code, which is always good.

Project

When a patron checks out a book or other library item, the due date is automatically calculated based on a number of days stored in the CodeMediaType.CheckoutDays database field. But what happens if that calculated date is a holiday, and the library is closed? The patron might not be able to return the book until the next day, and would incur a fine. This fine, though small, could start a chain reaction in the patron's life that would lead to poverty, despair, and an addiction to soap operas. Fortunately, this can all be avoided by adding a list of holidays to the project. If an item's return date falls on a documented holiday, the program adjusts the date forward until it finds a non-holiday date.

PROJECT ACCESS

Load the Chapter 16 (Before) Code project, either through the New Project templates or by accessing the project directly from the installation directory. To see the code in its final form, load Chapter 16 (After) Code instead.

Managing Holidays

As a small, standalone application that fully manages its own data, there isn't necessarily a pressing need for generics in the Library application. However, generics provide more advantages than just limiting the types of data stored in a class or collection. They also enhance data conversion and IntelliSense support, since Visual Basic can tell immediately, for instance, what type of data will appear in a collection.

We'll store all holidays managed by the Library Project in the Holiday database table. The contents of this table will seldom change, and will be frequently accessed during the checkout process. To speed things up, we'll cache the data inside the application. And to simplify management of that cache, we'll store the holidays in a generic collection.

First, let's create the class that holds a single holiday entry. Add a new class to the project through the Project → Add Class menu command, and give it the name *HolidaySet.vb*. The familiar structure of an empty class appears.

```
Public Class HolidaySet

End Class
```

The Holiday database table includes two main fields used in calculating holidays: EntryType and EntryDetail. Let's store these as members of the class, and add a flag that ensures the entry is valid.

INSERT SNIPPET

Insert Chapter 16, Snippet Item 1.

```
Private HolidayType As String
Private HolidayDetail As String
Private IsValid As Boolean
```

We'll populate these private members through the class constructor.

INSERT SNIPPET

Insert Chapter 16, Snippet Item 2.

```
Public Sub New(ByVal entryType As String, _
      ByVal entryDetail As String)
   ' ----- Create a new holiday entry instance.
   HolidayType = Left(Trim(UCase(entryType)), 1)
   HolidayDetail = entryDetail

   ' ----- See if the details are valid.
   IsValid = True
   Select Case HolidayType
      Case "A"
         ' ----- The detail should be in mm/dd format.
         IsValid = IsDate(entryDetail & "/2004")
      Case "E"
         ' ----- The detail is a number from 1 to 7.
         If (Val(entryDetail) < 1) Or _
            (Val(entryDetail) > 7) Then IsValid = False
      Case "O"
         ' ----- The detail should be a valid date.
         IsValid = IsDate(entryDetail)
      Case Else
         ' ---- Invalid. This should never happen.
         IsValid = False
   End Select
End Sub
```

Clearly, the holiday entries have a coding system all their own, and it wouldn't be fair to force code elsewhere in the application to deal with all the complexities of holiday date comparisons. So, let's add a public method to the class that indicates whether a given date matches the holiday stored in an instance.

INSERT SNIPPET

Insert Chapter 16, Snippet Item 3.

```
Public Function IsHoliday(ByVal whatDate As Date) As Boolean
   ' ----- Given a date, see if it matches the entry
   '       type in this instance.
   Dim buildDate As String

   ' ----- If this record is invalid, then it is never a
   '       holiday match.
   If (IsValid = False) Then Return False

   Select Case HolidayType
      Case "A"
         ' ----- Annual.
         buildDate = HolidayDetail & "/" & Year(whatDate)
         If (IsDate(buildDate)) Then
            Return CBool(CDate(buildDate) = whatDate)
         Else
            ' ----- Must be 2/29 on a non-leap-year.
            Return False
         End If
      Case "E"
         ' ----- Day of the week.
         Return CBool(Val(HolidayDetail) = _
            Weekday(whatDate, FirstDayOfWeek.Sunday))
      Case "O"
         ' ----- See if this is an exact one-time match.
         Return CBool(CDate(HolidayDetail) = whatDate)
   End Select
End Function
```

We're done with that class. Now we just need a place to keep our cached holiday records. The System.Collections.Generic namespace includes a few different collection classes that we could use. Since the only thing we really need to do with the holidays once they are in the collection is scan through them, looking for matches, the standard no-frills list seems best. Its class name is List(Of T), and its primary feature, according to the .NET documentation, is that it lets you access members by index. That's fine.

Open the *General.vb* file and find where the global variables appear, somewhere near the top. Then add a definition for the global collection that will store all the holidays.

INSERT SNIPPET

Insert Chapter 16, Snippet Item 4.

```
Public AllHolidays As Collections.Generic.List( _
    Of Library.HolidaySet)
```

There it is! There it is! The `Of` clause. This is a generic collection. Yeah! OK, party's over; let's move on.

Locate the `InitializeSystem` method, still in the *General.vb* file, and add the code that will initialize the global holiday cache.

INSERT SNIPPET

Insert Chapter 16, Snippet Item 5.

```
AllHolidays = New Collections.Generic.List(Of HolidaySet)
```

That's it for infrastructure. Let's add some routines that access this generic list. We need a routine that will tell us, `True` or `False`, whether a given date (the planned due date of a library item) matches any of the holidays or not. Add the function `IsHolidayDate` to *General.vb*.

INSERT SNIPPET

Insert Chapter 16, Snippet Item 6.

```
Public Function IsHolidayDate(ByVal whatDate As Date) _
        As Boolean
    ' ----- See if the given date is a holiday.
    Dim oneHoliday As Library.HolidaySet

    ' ----- Scan through the holidays, looking for a match.
    For Each oneHoliday In AllHolidays
        If (oneHoliday.IsHoliday(whatDate)) Then Return True
    Next oneHoliday

    ' ----- Not a holiday.
    Return False
End Function
```

This routine, IsHolidayDate, shows where generics really come in handy. It's all in the For Each statement that the magic occurs. In a normal collection, we wouldn't be sure what type of items were stored in the collection, be they HolidaySet or String or Integer. Well, *we* would know since *we* are the developer, but Visual Basic plays dumb in this area, and assumes you mixed up the data types in one collection.

But because we tied the AllHolidays collection to the HolidaySet class using the Of HolidaySet clause, Visual Basic now understands that we are only going to store items of HolidaySet in the AllHolidays collection. That means we don't have to explicitly convert items retrieved from the collection to the HolidaySet data type. If we weren't using a generic class, the code would look something like this:

```
Dim scanHoliday As System.Object
Dim oneHoliday As Library.HolidaySet

For Each scanHoliday In AllHolidays
   oneHoliday = CType(scanHoliday, Library.HolidaySet)
   If (oneHoliday.IsHoliday(whatDate)) Then Return True
Loop
```

Since non-generic collections boil everything down to System.Object, we would have to explicitly convert each collection object to HolidaySet using CType or a similar conversion function. But with a generic collection, Visual Basic takes care of it for us.

We still need to cache the holidays from the database, so add a RefreshHolidays method to *General.vb* that does this.

INSERT SNIPPET

Insert Chapter 16, Snippet Item 7.

```
Public Sub RefreshHolidays()
   ' ----- Load in the list of holidays.
   Dim sqlText As String
   Dim dbInfo As SqlClient.SqlDataReader
   Dim newHoliday As Library.HolidaySet

   On Error GoTo ErrorHandler

   ' ----- Clear the current list of holidays.
   AllHolidays.Clear()

   ' ----- Get the holidays from the database.
   sqlText = "SELECT * FROM Holiday"
   dbInfo = CreateReader(sqlText)
   Do While dbInfo.Read
      newHoliday = New Library.HolidaySet( _
         CStr(dbInfo!EntryType), CStr(dbInfo!EntryDetail))
      AllHolidays.Add(newHoliday)
```

```
   Loop
   dbInfo.Close( )
   Return

ErrorHandler:
   GeneralError("RefreshHolidays", Err.GetException( ))
   On Error Resume Next
   If Not (dbInfo Is Nothing) Then _
      dbInfo.Close( ) : dbInfo = Nothing
   Return
End Sub
```

You've seen a lot of code like this already, code that loads records from a database table into the program. I won't sport with your intelligence by explaining it to you line by line.

There are two places where we need to call RefreshHolidays: when the program first starts up, and later whenever changes are made to the list of holidays. We won't worry about other users changing the list; we'll just focus on when the local application updates the list. First, open the sometimes-hidden *ApplicationEvents.vb* file, and add this code to the MyApplication_Startup event handler, just after the existing call to LoadDatabaseSettings( ).

INSERT SNIPPET

Insert Chapter 16, Snippet Item 8.

```
RefreshHolidays( )
```

One down, and one to go. Open the *MainForm.vb* file, and locate the AdminLinkHolidays_LinkClicked event handler. This is the handler that lets the user edit the list of holidays. Add the same RefreshHolidays( ) line to the end of this routine.

INSERT SNIPPET

Insert Chapter 16, Snippet Item 9.

```
' ----- Reload the holidays if they changed.
RefreshHolidays( )
```

As you can see right in this routine, we already added the editor to manage the list of holidays. The only thing left to do is to actually access the holiday list when checking out items. We'll do that in a future chapter.

LINQ

Many years ago my TV's remote control died. I had received this TV secondhand from a college-student friend of mine—that should tell you about the quality of the set—and it was already a few years old. But I could still watch *Gilligan's Island*, so why complain? But when I contacted the manufacturer to get a replacement remote, they told me it was going to cost 75 bucks! The TV didn't cost anywhere near that, and I'm sure *Gilligan's Island* cost even less to produce.

The TV was pretty much useless without a remote control, so I went out and bought a *universal remote control*. These handy devices have the infrared codes for most common television manufacturers built right into the circuitry. Simply scan through all of the codes to find your TV set, and in a matter of minutes—and this demonstrates the modern miracle that is electronics—you will still not have the functionality you had with your original remote. I did lose all use of the closed-captioning system, but the power, channel, and volume buttons seemed to work.

Despite its deficiencies, the universal remote could control a TV, a VCR, and a DVD player, all through a common set of buttons. Imagine a universal remote control for your Visual Basic development. Well, stop imagining and start grabbing that *TV Guide*: Visual Basic is now empowered with LINQ, a new feature in Visual Basic 2008 that lets you query unrelated data sources using a common syntax.

What Is LINQ?

LINQ, short for <u>L</u>anguage <u>In</u>tegrated Query, is not just one, but somewhere around a million new Visual Basic and .NET technologies all working in tandem to make your programming life easier. Well, not easier in every case. As with any new whizbang technology, there's good and bad.

The Good

LINQ exists because some weary programmers at Microsoft were tired of accessing data in their databases differently than they did their file-based data, or their in-memory object data, or their XML data. With LINQ, a single syntax lets you access all of these flavors of data, and more. The syntax itself is similar to SQL, the database query language already familiar to you, your programming associates, and a team of hackers at the FBI.

Visual Basic 2008 includes LINQ support for SQL Server database tables and objects ("LINQ to SQL"), ADO.NET data sets ("LINQ to ADO.NET" and "LINQ to DataSet"), in-memory object collections such as arrays or Generic collections ("LINQ to Objects"), and XML ("LINQ to XML"). Soon after the official Visual Studio 2008 release, Microsoft released the ADO.NET Entity Framework ("LINQ to Entities"), which provides enhanced LINQ support to SQL Server, Oracle, DB2, and other database platforms. That's a great start, but the good news doesn't end there.

LINQ is extensible. That means you can enhance LINQ so that it can query any type of data you specify. LINQ to Spreadsheet, LINQ to Tab-Delimited-File, and LINQ to DVD-Chapter-Content are all possible. Is that a universal remote control I see in your programming language? As exciting as those possibilities are, I don't have space in this book to show you how to develop them, and that's where the bad news comes in.

The Bad

LINQ is a swell system for querying data—once you have established the connection between the query statements and the data. For some of the LINQ flavors, especially LINQ to Objects, there's not much to connect, so the querying is a snap. For other LINQ varieties, especially of the database sort, you must create go-between classes that join your requests to the data. LINQ is a generic technology that can interact with any data once you provide the glue. And that glue can sometimes get very sticky.

As an example, consider LINQ to SQL. This LINQ implementation needs a class that represents the tables and records that you will query through LINQ. These classes aren't hard to create, and they look a lot like the original database tables. However, if you modify the structure of your table, you will need to modify the go-between class to take advantage of the table changes. It's a task that you would have needed to do anyway, even without LINQ, but it's something to keep in mind when considering the way that some programmers go gaga over LINQ.

The go-between nature of LINQ also means that some data processing may be slower when compared to accomplishing the same task without LINQ. Extra layers of data and code mean extra things for your computer to do. But that's already life in the world of the .NET Framework, so I wouldn't avoid LINQ because of it.

Supporting Technologies

LINQ is a big deal for Microsoft and for the .NET Framework. Most of the new features added to Visual Basic's 2008 edition were introduced primarily to support LINQ. Before we get into using LINQ, let's take a quick look at the technologies involved in making LINQ possible.

- Query expressions, the heart of data access through LINQ. This chapter discusses query expressions in detail.

- Lambda expressions, discussed in Chapter 9.

- Extension methods, covered in Chapter 12.

- Local type inference, discussed in Chapter 6.

- Anonymous types, something that is new to Visual Basic in 2008, but also something that I haven't discussed yet. I'll give you the details just after this list.

- Relaxed delegates, a feature that lets Visual Basic make educated guesses as to whether a method and a delegate are a match or not. It's similar to type inference, but for delegates instead of plain types.

- XML Literals, XML axis properties, embedded XML expressions, and XML namespace support within your source code. You probably remember all about these features from the discussion in Chapter 13.

- Nullable types, discussed in Chapter 6, with some extended discussion appearing in the Generics chapter, Chapter 16.

- Partial methods, first appearing in Chapter 8.

- Object initializers, demonstrated in Chapter 9.

- Other new language and compiler features that must not have been important enough since they didn't get their own new cool-sounding names.

Anonymous Types

Anonymous types are a new feature included in Visual Basic to support LINQ, but you can use them in your own code as well. They are exactly what the name states: types without names. Well, that's not fully accurate. The types do have names, but they are generated automatically by the Visual Basic compiler, and they never show up directly in your source code.

Consider a typical class designed to hold information on sushi selections.

```
Class Sushi
   Public FishName As String
   Public ServingCost As Decimal
End Class
```

Creating an instance of this class is straightforward.

```
Dim tastyFood As New Sushi
tastyFood.FishName = "maguro"
tastyFood.ServingCost = 3.5@
```

Or, using the *object initializer* syntax I talked about back in Chapter 9, you can create the instance and fill in its fields, all in one statement.

```
Dim tastyFood As New Sushi With { _
    .FishName = "maguro", .ServingCost = 3.5@}
```

Anonymous types take this terse syntax one step further by leaving out the class name altogether.

```
Dim tastyFood = New With { _
    .FishName = "maguro", .ServingCost = 3.5@}
```

The tastyFood instance is now an instance of a class with two members, a string named FishName and a decimal value named ServingCost. The only thing it doesn't have is a class name that is known to you. But Visual Basic knows what it is.

Just for fun I compiled that last block of code and looked up the name of the generated type. Here it is:

```
VB$AnonymousType_0`2<T0,T1>
```

Hmm. I still think sushi tastes better. What's really interesting is that Visual Basic created a generic type with two type parameter placeholders: T0 (probably linked to the FishName string member) and T1 (probably the decimal ServingCost).

Anonymous types are major users of type inference. Visual Basic is guessing the data type of each member based on the data you supply with each name. In the sushi instances, the ServingCost member is of type Decimal based on the decimal literal supplied with the instance definition.

LINQ to Objects

LINQ lets you query data from many different sources of data, and each LINQ-to-data interaction is managed by a *LINQ provider*. I listed the providers included with Visual Basic 2008 a little earlier; they all have the name "LINQ to *something*." For me, the most straightforward of the providers is LINQ to Objects, designed to interact with sets of in-memory objects. LINQ to Objects lets you process queries based on object collections, Visual Basic arrays, and any object that supports .NET's IEnumerable or IEnumerable(Of T) interfaces, including your own custom collections. (Various objects within the world of ADO.NET support these interfaces, but those types fall under the LINQ to DataSet provider, discussed a little later.)

When you run LINQ to Objects queries, the output of the query is a new set of objects that contains a subset of the original source object data. This lets you run queries by saying things like, "Hey LINQ, from this list of employees and their properties, give me just the names of those employees who were hired in the past 90 days." This results set, a collection based on IEnumerable, can be further queried or used as you would any other collection in your Visual Basic code.

 Although LINQ has a finite number of operators and keywords, they can be used in a rich variety of combinations, only some of which I will introduce in this chapter. For additional examples and syntax descriptions, see the LINQ section of the MSDN documentation included with your copy of Visual Studio.

Before we get into some of the more complex LINQ providers, let's discover the syntax of LINQ queries using LINQ to Objects. In the next few sections, I'll use two small in-memory collections of books as my query source data. Here's the class definition for each book that includes a few reasonable members:

```
Class Book
    Public Title As String
    Public AuthorID As String
    Public Pages As Integer
End Class
```

Authors appear in a separate class. Book and Author instances match up through the common AuthorID field.

```
Class Author
    Public AuthorID As String
    Public FullName As String
End Class
```

I'll create two small collections to manage the authors and books.

```
Dim Writers As New Generic.List(Of Author)
Dim Library As New Generic.List(Of Book)

Writers.Add(New Author With _
    {.AuthorID = "LT", .FullName = "Tolstoy, Leo"})
Writers.Add(New Author With _
    {.AuthorID = "LW", .FullName = "Wallace, Lew"})
Writers.Add(New Author With _
    {.AuthorID = "JB", .FullName = "Barrie, J. M."})

Library.Add(New Book With _
    {.Title = "War and Peace", _
     .AuthorID = "LT", .Pages = 1424})
Library.Add(New Book With _
    {.Title = "Anna Karenina", _
     .AuthorID = "LT", .Pages = 976})
```

```
Library.Add(New Book With _
    {.Title = "Ben-Hur", _
    .AuthorID = "LW", .Pages = 544})
Library.Add(New Book With _
    {.Title = "Peter Pan", _
    .AuthorID = "JB", .Pages = 192})
```

To make our understanding of the output for each query easier, let's pretend that I've written a method that displays the results of any query in table form. I'll call the routine ShowResults.

Basic Query Expressions

LINQ expressions are built from *query clauses* that have the same feel as clauses in SQL statements at the database level. With the exception of the From clause, which must appear first, the other clauses can generally appear in any order within the query.

The From Clause

Every basic LINQ query begins with the From keyword.

```
Dim bookBag = From bk In Library
ShowResults(bookBag)
' Results --> War and Peace   LT   1424
'             Anna Karenina   LT   976
'             Ben-Hur         LW   544
'             Peter Pan       JB   192
```

This four-word query is pretty much the shortest LINQ query you can write. I stored the results of the query in the bookBag variable (with its data type inferred by the query), but the query can also be used directly as an expression.

```
ShowResults(From bk In Library)
```

The bk variable included in the query is known as a *range variable* or *iteration variable*. (You don't have to use "bk"; I just chose that name at random. It's a variable, so give it any name you wish.) This variable provides a way to identify objects and object members from the source data within the query. Since Library is a collection, it wouldn't make sense to say Library.Title when referring to the title of just one book. Instead, you refer to bk.Title.

Personally, I find this *variable* In *source* syntax a little indirect. I much prefer the table-alias syntax used in SQL queries.

```
SELECT * FROM Library AS bk
```

The SQL AS keyword performs much the same function as the LINQ In keyword. Yet despite my internal tension, the In syntax prevails; you cannot use the AS syntax in LINQ since the As keyword in Visual Basic is used for data type assignment.

The Select Clause

If you use only the From clause in your query, it returns all data from the original object set, including all object members. If you want to limit the results so that only some of the members are included, use the Select clause to identify the fields to include.

```
Dim bookBag = From bk In Library _
            Select bk.AuthorID, bk.Title
ShowResults(bookBag)
' Results --> LT   War and Peace
'             LT   Anna Karenina
'             LW   Ben-Hur
'             JB   Peter Pan
```

The results set of this new query omits the page count found in the original data. That's because the LINQ query requested only the AuthorID and Title fields; the Pages member did not make it through the Select clause. Also, notice that I reversed the order of the AuthorID and Title fields from the original class definition. This reversal is reflected in the printed results.

Behind the scenes, LINQ is creating a new anonymous type that includes two members: a string AuthorID field and a string Title field. One instance of this anonymous type is created for each resultant query record. These instances are then bundled up in a new collection that is based on IEnumerable(Of T). This lets you use the query results in a new query, or in any code that would normally interact with a collection of results, such as a For Each statement.

```
Dim bookBag = From bk In Library _
            Select bk.AuthorID, bk.Title
For Each oneResult In bookBag
   MsgBox(oneResult.Title)
Next oneResult
' The Loop Displays --> War and Peace
'                       Anna Karenina
'                       Ben-Hur
'                       Peter Pan
```

In addition to migrating fields from the original objects over to the results set, you can use operators and functions to modify the results. This next example uses the StrReverse function to alter the title name before compiling the results:

```
Dim backward = From bk In Library _
            Select StrReverse(bk.Title)
ShowResults(backward)
' Results --> ecaeP dna raW
'             aninerak annA
'             ruH-neB
'             naP reteP
```

Although we're still pretty early into our discussion of LINQ, you should know now that working with LINQ requires lots of experimentation. Despite its goal of consistency, LINQ is full of surprises. For instance, the previous example didn't create the anonymous type collection that I expected. Instead, it discerned that the results set contained only strings, and created a simple string set instead of a collection of types with a string member. Be on your guard against little shocks like this when writing LINQ queries.

The Distinct Clause

By default, the Select clause returns all records from the source. Getting complete information is a good thing, but sometimes it's too much of a good thing, especially when the information contains duplicates. For instance, this query returns just the author IDs for each available book:

```
Dim justIDs = From bk In Library _
              Select bk.AuthorID
ShowResults(justIDs)
' Results --> LT
'             LT
'             LW
'             JB
```

The results are complete, but "LT" appeared twice. Depending on your needs, that might be a bad thing. By adding the Distinct clause, you can weed out the unneeded duplication.

```
Dim justIDs = From bk In Library _
              Select bk.AuthorID _
              Distinct
ShowResults(justIDs)
' Results --> LT
'             LW
'             JB
```

The Distinct keyword looks at entire records for duplicates. A record is excluded only if *all fields* in that record exactly match *all fields* in another record.

The Where Clause

Whereas the Select clause lets you weed out unwanted fields, the Where clause lets you eliminate entire objects based on criteria you specify.

```
Dim bigBooks = From bk In Library _
               Where bk.Pages >= 1000
ShowResults(bigBooks)
' Results --> War and Peace   LT   1424
```

This query examines all incoming source records in the `Library` collection and includes a source object in the results only if it has a page count of 1,000 or more. `Where` clauses can be complex, with multiple criteria joined with `And` and `Or` keywords, and grouped with parentheses.

```
Dim choices = From bk In Library _
              Where bk.Pages >= 1000 _
              Or (bk.Pages < 1000 _
              And InStr(bk.Title, "-") > 0) _
              Select bk.Title
ShowResults(bigBooks)
' Results --> War and Peace
'             Ben-Hur
```

That last query also showed how you can include non-LINQ features, such as the `InStr` function, in your criteria, allowing you to restrict the results based on calculated results.

The Order By Clause

LINQ results, depending on the source of the data, are not guaranteed to appear in any particular order. To generate query results in a specific order, use the `Order By` clause. The `Order By` keywords precede one or more source fields or calculated values, delimited by commas, and you can optionally include the `Ascending` or `Descending` keyword to reverse the sort order of each sorting field. (`Ascending` is the default for each field.)

```
Dim bookBag = From bk In Library _
              Select bk.Pages, bk.Title _
              Order By Pages Descending
ShowResults(bookBag)
' Results --> 1424   War and Peace
'              976   Anna Karenina
'              544   Ben-Hur
'              192   Peter Pan
```

Fields included in the `Order By` clause must be present in the `Select` clause; leave off the range variable prefix (`bk` in this case). If you use a `From` clause without a `Select` clause, you must include the range variable prefix in your `Order By` fields.

Joining Sources

If you were only ever going to query data from a single data collection or source, you probably would not have needed something like LINQ in the first place. When it does come time for you to merge results from different tables, LINQ again provides a SQL-like syntax for joining the tables. Actually, it provides two variations, paralleling the syntax variations supported by different SQL vendors.

The first syntax uses the Join keyword to specify a field-specific link. The following query "inner joins" the Library and Writers tables at the expected AuthorID connection point.

```
Dim bookBag = From bk In Library _
              Join au In Writers _
              On bk.AuthorID Equals au.AuthorID _
              Select bk.Title, au.FullName _
              Order By bk.Title
ShowResults(bookBag)
' Results --> Anna Karenina    Tolstoy, Leo
'             Ben-Hur          Wallace, Lew
'             Peter Pan        Barrie, J. M.
'             War and Peace    Tolstoy, Leo
```

The special On and Equals keywords assist in the join syntax. If your join involves multiple keys, you can use the And keyword to specify the different key links.

```
Dim results = From t1 In Table1 _
              Join t2 In Table2 _
              On t1.Key1 Equals t2.Key1 _
              And t1.Key2 Equals t2.Key2
```

The second join syntax lets you use the Where clause to indicate the field links.

```
Dim bookBag = From bk In Library, _
              au In Writers _
              Where bk.AuthorID = au.AuthorID _
              Select bk.Title, au.FullName _
              Order By bk.Title
' Same results as before
```

LINQ includes another join variation that generates *hierarchical query results*. In such queries, one of the fields in each resultant record will be a collection that contains multiple results. This syntax allows LINQ to return a list of all authors, one author per row, where each author record includes a "books" field, possibly with multiple values.

```
Dim authorBooks = From au In Writers _
                  Group Join bk In Library _
                  On au.AuthorID Equals bk.AuthorID _
                  Into Published = Group _
                  Select au.FullName, Published _
                  Order By FullName
ShowResults(authorBooks)
' Results --> Barrie, J. M.    Peter Pan
'             Tolstoy, Leo     War and Peace
'                              Anna Karenina
'             Wallace, Lew     Ben-Hur
```

This query has a somewhat strange syntax, but it successfully creates a results set with two columns: FullName (for the author name) and Published (for the collection of books published by a specific author). For each returned record, the Published member is a subordinate collection that can be processed like any other collection.

Skip and Take

The Skip clause lets you skip over the first *x* records in the results set, effectively throwing them in the trash, like unwanted banana peels. The Take clause does just the opposite, keeping only the first few records in the generated results. The following query skips over the first two records in the original data collection, returning just those records following the ignored values:

```
Dim someBooks = From bk In Library _
                Select bk.AuthorID, bk.Title _
                Skip 2
ShowResults(someBooks)
' Results --> LW   Ben-Hur
'             JB   Peter Pan
```

Related Skip While and Take While clauses let you use a Boolean expression instead of a number to indicate when to continue skipping or taking records.

Skip and Take are useful for paging results, as when showing just one "page" of results at a time from a larger set of queried results. Logic similar to the following could be used to show just the records destined for CurrentPage:

```
Dim onePageWorth = From bk In Library _
                   Select bk.AuthorID, bk.Title _
                   Skip ItemsPerPage * CurrentPage _
                   Take ItemsPerPage
```

One word of warning about Skip and Take: it does make a difference where you put them in your query. (I'll explain the technical reason why this is in the "Deferred Execution" section, later in this chapter.) For instance, consider this query based on our original book data:

```
Dim someBooks = From bk In Library _
                Order By bk.Title _
                Take 2
```

This query returns Anna Karenina followed by Ben-Hur, as you would expect. But if you move the Take clause earlier, you get a different result.

```
Dim someBooks = From bk In Library _
                Take 2 _
                Order By bk.Title
```

This time, the query returns Anna Karenina followed by War and Peace. In the first query, the contents of Library were sorted by Title *before* the two records were taken. In the second query, the two records were taken first, before any sorting had been applied.

It's not just Take and Skip that are impacted by this ordering. All clauses in your query are affected. Thinking through the logic of your query is essential, since a misplaced clause can give you unexpected results.

Converting Results to Other Forms

Because the results of any LINQ query conform to the IEnumerable(Of T) interface, they are immediately ready to be used in other queries or in enumerable scans. If you need to access the records in a more traditional form for other purposes, LINQ provides a few conversion features that quickly move the results into either an array or a generic collection.

Each query result includes three methods that perform these conversions: ToArray, ToDictionary, and ToList. ToArray converts the results into a standard Visual Basic array, with one result record stored in each array element.

```
Dim queryResults = From ...
Dim arrayVersion = queryResults.ToArray()
```

ToList performs a similar operation, creating a new Generic.List collection based on the results of the query. ToDictionary creates a Generic.Dictionary collection, but you must provide a function to ToDictionary that extracts the key. In most cases, a lambda expression that identifies the key field will suffice.

```
Dim authors = From au In Writers _
              Order By au.FullName
Dim authorDict = authors.ToDictionary(Function(x) x.AuthorID)
MsgBox(authorDict("LW").FullName)
' Results --> Wallace, Lew
```

Aggregate Queries

Aggregate queries let you "sum up" information from a larger query into a condensed or single result. Instead of starting with the From keyword, pure aggregate queries begin with the Aggregate keyword. Each aggregate query uses one or more of the *aggregate functions*, such as the Sum function in the following query:

```
Dim numBooks = Aggregate bk In Library _
               Into Sum(bk.Pages)
MsgBox(numBooks)  ' Displays: 3136
```

LINQ includes eight standard aggregate functions, shown in Table 17-1. Each function accepts an expression that indicates what should be aggregated during the query.

Table 17-1. Standard aggregate functions

Function	Description
All	Returns a Boolean value indicating whether the expression passed to it is true for all records. The clause All(bk.Pages > 1000) would return False since only one book has more than 1,000 pages.
Any	Similar to All, but returns True if just one of the records matches the supplied criteria expression.

Table 17-1. Standard aggregate functions (continued)

Function	Description
Average	Returns the average of whatever expression is passed to it.
Count	Returns a count of records with True expression results. To return a count of all records in a query, use Count(True).
LongCount	Same as Count, but returns a Long instead of an Integer.
Max	Returns the maximum numeric expression from the set of records.
Min	Returns the minimum numeric expression from the set of records.
Sum	Returns the sum of the numeric expressions from the set of records.

If you include more than one aggregate function in the query, the results set is a single record that includes multiple named fields. Use an alias before the aggregate function to give it a name. (Aliases are allowed in all query types, not just aggregates.)

```
Dim numBooks = Aggregate bk In Library _
               Into TotalPages = Sum(bk.Pages), _
               AvgPages = Average(bk.Pages)
MsgBox(numBooks.AvgPages)  ' Displays: 784
```

You can also include aggregate expressions in standard non-aggregate queries. The following query returns a count of books written by each author, using the Count aggregate function to add up the results for each author:

```
Dim authorBooks = From au In Writers _
                  Group Join bk In Library _
                  On au.AuthorID Equals bk.AuthorID _
                  Into NumBooks = Count(True) _
                  Select au.FullName, NumBooks _
                  Order By FullName
ShowResults(authorBooks)
' Results --> Barrie, J. M.   1
'             Tolstoy, Leo    2
'             Wallace, Lew    1
```

Advanced Query Expressions

You've probably been wondering when some of the new technology features such as lambda expressions and extension methods will show up in my examples. Well, in a way, they already did. When you create LINQ queries using query expressions, the Visual Basic compiler converts what you type into code that uses extension methods and lambda expressions. You might remember from Chapter 9 that lambda expressions are themselves updated by the compiler into something simpler. Once your queries are broken down into subatomic particles, the CPU is ready to act.

But you don't have to start with full queries. You can create your own queries using extension methods and lambda expressions. The extended methods in question are attached to the IEnumerable interface. This means that anything that looks like a collection or array can be involved in extension-method-based queries, using lambda expressions as the arguments.

Let's convert one of our earlier queries into its extension method counterpart.

```
Dim bigBooks = From bk In Library _
               Where bk.Pages >= 1000
```

It's the query that returns only big books. The same query using extension methods looks like this:

```
Dim bigBooks = Library.Where(Function(bk) bk.Pages >= 1000)
```

In this example, the Where method is actually an extension method of the IEnumerable interface, which also includes Select, OrderBy, Join, GroupJoin, Count, Max, Min, and other methods that correspond to operators within the LINQ query language. As I discussed in Chapter 12, you can add your own extension methods to the IEnumerable interface, giving you even more ways to customize your LINQ queries.

LINQ to XML

In Chapter 13, I introduced *XML Literals*, XML content that is embedded right into your Visual Basic source code. When you bring LINQ into the picture, you suddenly have a way to generate large XML documents by merging a set of records with an XML Literal template.

The following block of code creates an XML document using our Library and Writers collections, intermixing LINQ and XML in a way that actually makes my head hurt:

```
Dim bookXML As XDocument = _
    <?xml version="1.0"?>
    <booklist>
        <%= From bk In Library _
            Join au In Writers _
            On bk.AuthorID Equals au.AuthorID _
            Order By bk.Title _
            Select _
            <book>
                <title><%= bk.Title %></title>
                <author><%= au.FullName %></author>
                <pages><%= bk.Pages %></pages>
            </book> _
        %>
    </booklist>

bookXML.Save("books.xml")
```

Notice how you must put line continuation characters in the LINQ portions of the code, but not in the XML portion? Yeah, I hate it, too. But it does generate nice

XML. If you look at the *books.xml* file generated by this code, it contains success-fully merged content from the XML and our original collections. It's also nicely indented.

```
<?xml version="1.0" encoding="utf-8"?>
<booklist>
  <book>
    <title>Anna Karenina</title>
    <author>Tolstoy, Leo</author>
    <pages>976</pages>
  </book>
  <book>
    <title>Ben-Hur</title>
    <author>Wallace, Lew</author>
    <pages>544</pages>
  </book>
  <book>
    <title>Peter Pan</title>
    <author>Barrie, J. M.</author>
    <pages>192</pages>
  </book>
  <book>
    <title>War and Peace</title>
    <author>Tolstoy, Leo</author>
    <pages>1424</pages>
  </book>
</booklist>
```

The key to intermixing XML and LINQ is correctly placing the <%= and %> markers around the LINQ-specific code. If you look at the sample carefully, you will see that there are two sets of markers, one inside the other.

```
<%= From ...
      <title><%= bk.Title %></title>
... %>
```

The outer set of markers surrounds the entire LINQ query, whereas each inner set of markers identifies a replacement variable to include in the XML content.

As easy as it is to generate XML using LINQ, it's just as easy to query data from existing XML documents. Reloading the XML we just saved allows us to query a list of book titles by intermixing LINQ with XML axis properties.

```
Dim bookXML As XDocument = _
    XDocument.Load("books.xml")
Dim fromXML = From bx In bookXML...<book> _
              Select bx.<title>.Value
ShowResults(fromXML)
' Results --> Anna Karenina
'             Ben-Hur
'             Peter Pan
'             War and Peace
```

LINQ for ADO.NET-Related Data

With ADO.NET's focus on querying data, it's understandable that ADO.NET has declared all-out war on its new enemy, LINQ. Oh wait, a truce was called in Beta 1. ADO.NET and LINQ now work very well together. In fact, ADO.NET sports three LINQ providers.

LINQ to Entities

Soon after the launch of Visual Studio 2008, Microsoft released the ADO.NET Entity Framework. This interface between your programming code and a database will let you define a *logical* view of your system. For instance, you can create an entity called Order that includes your customer, vendor, order header, order detail, and product tables, all in one logical view. Related stored procedures can also be part of the package.

The framework does all of this magic by creating a set of go-between classes and related XML structural content that manage the link between the logical and physical views of the data. Those classes can then be used in LINQ queries, and the author of the queries need not be concerned with trivial matters such as database connections and foreign key references. In reality, programmers have been writing code like this for years, abstracting the physical data model into a logical view that is easier to program against. The Entity Framework simply makes this process quicker and easier to set up.

The framework includes several tools that help you build the entities from the source database structures. One key tool is the ADO.NET Entity Data Model Designer, a visual drag-and-drop tool that makes creating entities as easy as creating Visual Basic forms.

Because the ADO.NET Entity Framework comes out after Visual Studio 2008, I will not be demonstrating the framework in this book.

LINQ to DataSet

LINQ supports queries of records within ADO.NET data tables. ADO.NET DataTable objects do not directly support the IEnumerable interface, and fields within these tables are, by default, untyped, which really makes LINQ angry. The new *LINQ to DataSet* functionality overcomes both of these limitations so that querying of data sets works.

Earlier in this chapter, we saw LINQ examples that used a Book class. Let's keep that sample data, but pretend that the data now appears in an ADO.NET DataTable instance. The table will have four records (for the four books in our sample) and three columns: Title, AuthorID, and Pages.

```
Class Book
    Public Title As String
    Public AuthorID As String
    Public Pages As Integer
End Class
```

Instead of issuing a LINQ to Objects query like this:

```
Dim choices = From bk In Library _
              Where bk.Field(Of Integer)!Pages >= 1000 _
              Or (bk.Pages < 1000 _
              And InStr(bk.Title, "-") > 0) _
              Select bk.Title
```

LINQ to DataSet uses dataset-object-specific methods that coerce the ADO.NET objects into something that LINQ can interact with, and in a strongly typed fashion.

```
Dim choices = _
    From bk In bookTable.AsEnumerable() _
    Where bk.Field(Of Integer)("Pages") >= 1000 _
    Or (bk.Field(Of Integer)("Pages") < 1000 _
    And InStr(bk.Field(Of String)("Title"), "-") > 0) _
    Select New With _
        {.Title = bk.Field(Of String)("Title")}
```

It looks really different, but it is the same query. The bookTable DataTable instance is first forced to look like an IEnumerable instance through its AsEnumerable method. Then, as each field is involved in the query, its data type is declared through generic Of clauses, followed by the name of the field in quotes. Finally, because the query doesn't have direct access to field names, the results set is created using the object initializer syntax. It's much more roundabout than LINQ to Objects. But if you already have data sitting in ADO.NET in-memory objects, LINQ to DataSet is the way to go.

LINQ to DataSet also includes support for "typed" data sets, data sets that include the necessary metadata to fully describe the data type of each field. With typed data sets, you don't need to constantly hold LINQ's hand through Of datatype clauses; LINQ will figure out the field types on its own. For information about creating typed data sets, see the MSDN documentation that comes with Visual Studio.

LINQ to SQL

LINQ to SQL is the provider that lets LINQ queries interact with SQL Server databases. Since the Library Project uses SQL Server, we will spend a little more time on this technology. As with LINQ to Entities, LINQ to SQL works through go-between classes.

Although you could provide a different logical view of your physical data tables using LINQ to SQL, there is more of an expectation that your LINQ to SQL objects will more closely resemble the underlying database tables.

LINQ to SQL includes a tool, the *Object Relational (O/R) Designer*, which will assist us in creating the go-between classes. You can take a quick peek at Figure 17-2 to see what it looks like, but I warn you, it's no Rembrandt. Still, it does a respectable job at making the needed database link. The O/R Designer is drag-and-drop simple, and is suitable for databases that aren't too terribly large. If you need to create the link classes for a database that has, say, hundreds of tables, you should read up on the *SqlMetal.exe* tool that comes with Visual Studio. You'll find full details in the MSDN documentation that comes with Visual Studio.

Using LINQ to SQL is done in five easy steps. You can follow along in a new Windows Forms project if you want:

1. *Add a new "dbml" file.* This file—actually, a few files that Visual Studio displays as one—describes your *data context*, the master class that contains link code for each database table that you will use in your application. To create this file from a Visual Studio project, use the Project → Add New Item menu command to display the Add New Item form. From the Data category, select the LINQ to SQL Classes template, change the name of the file to *Library.dbml* from the default, and click the Add button (see Figure 17-1).

Figure 17-1. Adding a new dbml class

A new Library.dbml item appears in your project, which opens the O/R Designer, shown in Figure 17-2. If you examine its properties, you'll see that its name is LibraryDataContext.

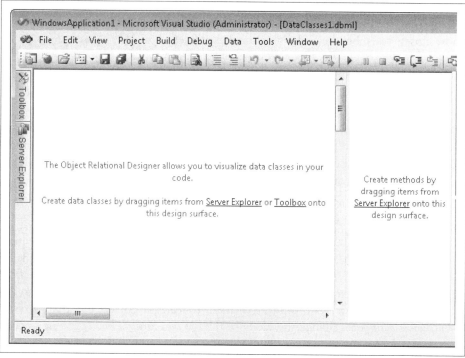

Figure 17-2. The O/R Designer; not much to look at right now

2. *Add tables to the O/R Designer.* Open the Server Explorer in Visual Studio. (Select the View → Server Explorer menu command to find it.) You should already see a link to the *Library* database in the Data Connections portion of the Server Explorer tree, since we created it in an earlier chapter. It will be called something like *myserver\sqlexpress.Library.dbo.* Expand that branch of the tree, and then the Tables branch below it. All of the tables in the *Library* database should appear.

Drag and drop the Activity table from the Server Explorer to the left half of the O/R Designer. Sooner or later, an image of the table should appear on-screen (see Figure 17-3).

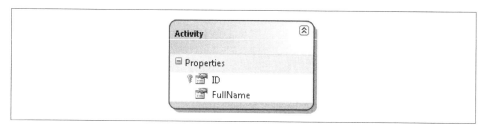

Figure 17-3. The familiar Activity table and its fields (properties)

3. *Build your application.* I've found that this step is necessary in some installs of Visual Studio, but not in others. It refreshes Visual Basic's view of the new LibraryDataContext classes. To build the application, select the Build → Build WindowsApplication1 menu command.

4. *Open your custom data context.* The code generated by the O/R Designer defines the interaction between your program and the database, but you should still specify the database connection when you run your application, just in case anything changes down the road. Add a new Button control to Form1, then add the following code to that button's Click event handler:

```
Dim LibraryDB As New SqlClient.SqlConnection( _
    "Data Source=myserver\sqlexpress;" & _
    "Initial Catalog=Library;Integrated Security=true")
Dim libraryLink = New LibraryDataContext(LibraryDB)
```

Replace *myserver* in the code with the name of your own system, and update the security settings if you use SQL Server authentication.

5. *Write queries.* You're ready to design your LINQ queries. Here's some code that gets the first five activities from the Activity table and sorts them:

```
Dim activities = From act In libraryLink.Activities _
                 Where act.ID <= 5 _
                 Order By act.FullName
For Each oneItem In activities
    MsgBox(oneItem.ID & ": " & oneItem.FullName)
Next oneItem
' Messages --> 2: Manage author and name types
'               1: Manage authors and names
'               3: Manage copy status codes
'               4: Manage media types
'               5: Manage series
```

If you click the Show All Files button in the Solution Explorer, you can access the *.dbml* file's underlying designer file, *Library.designer.vb*. This file contains the generated go-between classes used by LINQ to SQL. As far as using the Activity table in our LINQ queries, here are the relevant parts of the auto-generated source code:

```
<System.Data.Linq.Mapping.DatabaseAttribute(Name:="Library")> _
Partial Public Class LibraryDataContext
    Inherits System.Data.Linq.DataContext

    Public ReadOnly Property Activities() _
            As System.Data.Linq.Table(Of Activity)
        Get
            Return Me.GetTable(Of Activity)
        End Get
    End Property
End Class

<Table(Name:="dbo.Activity")> _
Partial Public Class Activity
    Private _ID As Long
    Private _FullName As String
```

```
<Column(Storage:="_ID", DbType:="BigInt NOT NULL", _
    IsPrimaryKey:=true)> _
Public Property ID() As Long
    Get
        Return Me._ID
    End Get
End Property

<Column(Storage:="_FullName", _
    DbType:="VarChar(50) NOT NULL", CanBeNull:=false)> _
Public Property FullName() As String
    Get
        Return Me._FullName
    End Get
End Property
End Class
```

The `LibraryDataContext` class implements a custom LINQ data context class that looks like, well, a mini version of my database. It contains references to those tables that I chose to include in the linkup; all of the Library tables would have appeared in this class if I had selected them. So, when I referenced `libraryLink.Activities` in the sample LINQ query, it was referencing the public `Activities` member from the data context.

The `Activity` table exposes distinct properties that match up with the underlying database fields. So really, it's no surprise that I'm able to query these classes through LINQ just like I do with any LINQ to Objects-type class. But there is that strange part about how the class actually gets the data from the database. That's the hidden LINQ to SQL part, handled through the base `DataContext` class and the associated attributes from the `System.Data.Linq.Mapping` namespace.

 Behind the scenes, LINQ to SQL is regularly generating SQL statements to query and even update records in the actual database tables. You can examine these generated queries using the SQL Query Debug Visualizer tool. It doesn't come with Visual Studio, but you can download it from Microsoft's MSDN web site.

Deferred Execution

When you build a LINQ query, Visual Basic does not process the query immediately. Instead, it *defers execution*, running the query only when you request a record from the results. This allows you to build up a query in parts, and not have it consume CPU cycles until you actually need the final data.

```
' WARNING: Simplistic example.
Dim someBooks = From bk In Library _
                Select bk.Title, bk.Pages
Dim orderedTitles = From bk In someBooks _
                Order By bk.Title
```

In this code, the ordering of the records doesn't happen until the second statement. But that doesn't matter since nothing was actually processed by the first statement. Remember that LINQ is really just converting your queries into extension methods and lambda expressions. The assignment of someBooks is doing something like this:

```
someBooks = Library.Select("Title, Pages")
```

The assignment of orderedTitles simply extends someBooks:

```
orderedTitles = _
    Library.Select("Title, Pages").OrderBy("Title")
```

Actual processing occurs when you request a record from orderedTitles. By "processing" I mean that each extension method is executed on the original Library data source in order, from left to right. For orderedTitles, the original Library data is reduced through the Select method, and then further modified by the OrderBy method.

Having methods processed from left to right explains why the order of clauses such as Skip and Take is so important. The expression

```
Library.Take(2).Skip(2)
```

is different from

```
Library.Skip(2).Take(2)
```

Summary

That was a fast overview of LINQ with some of its first-release permutations. It seems like a lot, but I covered only the basics. Besides querying data, you can also update the underlying data store through specially crafted LINQ statements. And the ability to craft your own LINQ provider means that the types of data stores that LINQ can process are unlimited.

The major downside of LINQ is that, especially for LINQ to SQL, the SQL statements and MSIL code that LINQ ultimately generates based on your query will probably not be as efficient as those that you could craft on your own. Some of your LINQ queries may run so slowly that you have no choice but to replace them with pre-LINQ alternatives. But for most common querying purposes, especially across divergent data sources, LINQ is a giant step forward.

Project

This chapter finally adds what many consider to be the heart of a library system: the lookup of books and other library items by patrons.

PROJECT ACCESS

Load the Chapter 17 (Before) Code project, either through the New Project templates or by accessing the project directly from the installation directory. To see the code in its final form, load Chapter 17 (After) Code instead.

Looking Up Library Items

When we built the main Library form back in Chapter 7, we included fields that allowed a patron to search for library items. But that's about all we did; we didn't enable the fields or make them usable. We also didn't include any place to display a list of matching items. Let's complete those components in this chapter. We'll start with the matching items list.

I've added a form to the project named *ItemLookup.vb* that displays the results of a search for library items. It includes a few buttons at the top of the form, and three main display panels:

PanelMatches

Contains a large listbox that displays non-item matches. For instance, it displays a list of matching author or publisher names as searched for by the patron. When this panel appears, the patron selects a match from the MatchingGeneral list, and clicks the Lookup button to display items tied to that selected author, publisher, or other entry.

PanelItem

Contains a large listbox that displays items from the NamedItem database table. That is, it displays a list of library items matching some criteria. Selecting an item from the MatchingItems list and clicking the Lookup button displays the details of that item.

PanelOneItem

Contains a WebBrowser control that displays details about a single library item. The detail content is built using standard HTML, and may contain links that return you to the PanelItems panel with a new set of matching items displayed. For instance, if you are viewing the details of an award-winning (one can hope) Visual Basic 2008 programming book and click on the publisher name for that item, the PanelItems panel appears, listing all items made by that publisher.

The form also includes a set of Back buttons (in the upper-left corner) that work like the Back button in your web browser, a Close button that returns to the main form, and a menu (BackMenu), used to support the Back button feature. Figure 17-4 shows the form with the PanelItems panel out in front, since it looks a little more interesting than the other two panels.

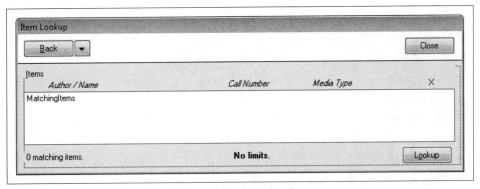

Figure 17-4. The panel of matching items, with column headings

The associated source code weighs in at around 1,000 lines, much of it focused on filling in the two listboxes and the HTML detail content. The search performed on the main form calls into this lookup form through the InitiateSearch method. The actual database search for matching items occurs in the PerformLookup method, which is called by InitiateSearch. PerformLookup includes LINQ queries that travel to the *Library* database and back via the LINQ to SQL provider. Queries for all different types of searches are included: title, author, subject, keyword, publisher, series, bar code, and some ID number searches, mostly for internal use. The type of search performed determines which of the three panels gets displayed (via the resultType variable). An author search displays PanelMatches with a list of matching author names; a title lookup displays matching items on the PanelItems panel.

Before we look at that LINQ code, we need to set some things up in the rest of the application to support these new LINQ queries. I've disabled the *ItemLookup.vb* file from compiling for now since it would just generate gobs of errors.

As amazing as LINQ to SQL is, it still requires the human touch (that's you) to help it locate the SQL Server database tables. We'll use the Object Relational Designer that we played with earlier in this chapter. Select the Project → Add New Item command from the Visual Studio menus. On the Add New Item form, select Data from the Categories list, select LINQ to SQL Classes from the Templates field, and set the Name field to "Library.dbml" before clicking the Add button. A blank O/R Designer window appears.

Open the Server Explorer and browse down to the *Library* database. From the Tables branch, drag and drop the following tables onto the left half of the O/R Designer window:

- Author
- CodeMediaType
- CodeSeries
- ItemAuthor
- ItemCopy
- ItemKeyword
- ItemSubject
- Keyword
- NamedItem
- Publisher
- Subject

The designer will correctly analyze the relationships between the tables and show link lines between foreign references. You can rearrange the tables as needed to better see the tables, or keep them in a heap if you like; I'm not your mother. But we do have to do a little renaming of the tables. The O/R Designer tries to be really smart, changing any plural table names it finds into their singular equivalent. (By tradition, singular names are preferred when designing database tables.) Unfortunately, it botched the conversion of the CodeSeries table, changing it to CodeSery. It's cute, but meaningless. Select that table and change its Name property to CodeSeries in the Properties panel.

That resets the table names to their roots, but it's still no good. The problem is that we used some of those table names for form names in the Library application. The conflicting classes are in different namespaces, so the code could compile, but we'd have to type a lot of namespaces when identifying these classes, and I'm just too lazy for that. To eliminate the conflicts, I arbitrarily decided to add the letter Q to the start of each LINQ to SQL table name. In the designer, select each table and rename them, adding a Q to the start. CodeSeries becomes QCodeSeries; ItemAuthor becomes QItemAuthor, and so on. When you are finished, you should have a designer view that looks something like Figure 17-5.

Despite working so hard to ensure that all the names avoid conflicts and that they are singular, when we use the library data context in our LINQ queries, we'll find that all of the class names for these LINQ-to-SQL-generated tables are somehow pluralized (QPublishers instead of QPublisher). Amazing.

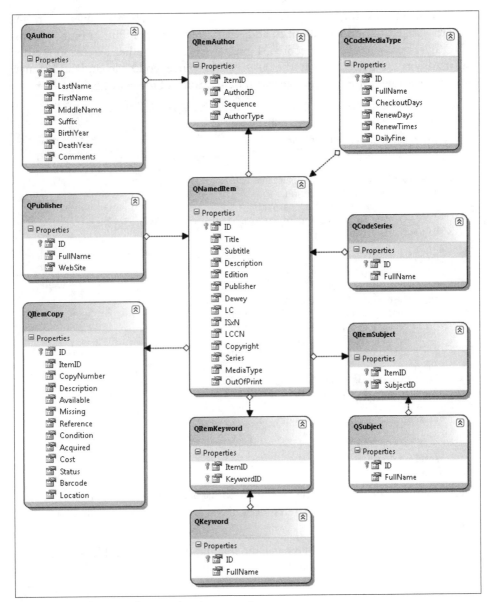

Figure 17-5. Why aren't they standing in a queue?

Back in the project code for Chapter 12, we added an extension method to the SqlClient.SqlDataReader class that formats an author name from a database query.

```
<System.Runtime.CompilerServices.Extension()> _
Public Function FormatAuthorName( _
    ByRef dbInfo As SqlClient.SqlDataReader) As String
```

Unfortunately, this routine is usable only with SqlDataReader objects. In the PerformLookup routine we're about to add, we'll need to format author names from a LINQ query of QAuthor table records. I guess we'll need another extension method for that type of object. Open the *General.vb* source code file and add a new FormatAuthorName method to the General module. Some of the code appears here.

INSERT SNIPPET

Insert Chapter 17, Snippet Item 1.

```
<System.Runtime.CompilerServices.Extension()> _
Public Function FormatAuthorName( _
    ByVal author As QAuthor) As String
    ' ----- Given an author record, return the formatted name.
    Dim authorName As String

    On Error Resume Next

    ' ----- Format the name.
    authorName = CStr(author.LastName)
    If (author.FirstName IsNot Nothing) Then
        authorName &= ", " & author.FirstName
        If (author.MiddleName IsNot Nothing) Then _
            authorName &= " " & author.MiddleName
    End If
    If (author.Suffix IsNot Nothing) Then _
        authorName &= ", " & author.Suffix

    ...some code omitted for brevity...

    ' ----- Finished.
    Return authorName
End Function
```

If you compare this source code to the SqlDataReader version, you'll find that this version is much cleaner since it references class members instead of database fields through a reader. Thanks LINQ!

That's it for the LINQ support changes. Enable the *ItemLookup.vb* file by selecting it in the Solution Explorer panel and changing its Build Action property from None to Compile. Now let's return to the code in that file.

The PerformLookup routine consists mostly of a giant If statement, with different conditions for most of the different types of searches. The last Else clause handles all of the searches that will fill in the list on the form's PanelItems panel. That's the list that shows actual items. It's got a lot of If statements, too. But what's really cool is its LINQ query. Instead of just being a simple query, it's a complex query that is built up little by little. The query starts with the basics, requesting matching records from the database's NamedItem table. (The libraryDC variable is the opened data context for the *Library* database.)

```
Dim itemQuery = From ni In libraryDC.QNamedItems
```

Next, if the user requested items of a specific media type ("just show me matching DVDs, not books"), the query is updated with the appropriate Where clause.

```
If (LimitByMedia <> -1) Then
    ' ----- Limit to a specific media type.
    itemQuery = From ni In itemQuery _
                Where ni.MediaType = LimitByMedia
End If
```

The type of search also adjusts the query. For instance, a keyword search adds user-specified keywords as the criteria.

```
keywordSet = New Generic.List(Of String)
keywordSet.AddRange(Split(searchText.ToUpper, ","))
itemQuery = From ni In itemQuery _
            Let keySet = (Aggregate ik In ni.QItemKeywords _
                Into Any(keywordSet.Contains( _
                ik.QKeyword.FullName.ToUpper))) _
            Where keySet = True _
            Select ni
```

That addition used an Aggregate subquery within the main query. The Let keyword, part of LINQ, assigns a subquery or other type of result to a temporary variable within the query (keySet in this case) so that it can be referenced elsewhere in the query.

Once the Where clauses have been added, the entire query is sorted and used.

```
itemQuery = From ni In itemQuery _
            Order By ni.Title, ni.Subtitle
```

Some of the LINQ queries in the PerformLookup routine are very straightforward. Here's the code that does a publisher-name search:

```
' ----- Prepare the query for a publisher lookup.
holdText = Trim(searchText)
If (InStr(holdText, "*") = 0) Then holdText &= "*"
Dim publisherQuery = From pb In libraryDC.QPublishers _
                     Where pb.FullName Like holdText _
                     Order By pb.FullName
```

It doesn't look that different from what you would expect in a SQL query. One nice thing is that wildcards use the * character instead of the SQL standard % character.

After processing this query, the LINQ results are scanned, and records are moved into the MatchingGeneral list.

```
For Each publishItem In publisherQuery
    MatchingGeneral.Items.Add(New ListItemData( _
        publishItem.FullName, CInt(publishItem.ID)))
    matches += 1
Next publishItem
```

This is just more of the same code you've seen in previous chapters. It loads the ListBox control with ListItemData objects, each containing a display name and an ID number from the database. That's fine for a list with simple display requirements. But if you look back at Figure 17-4, it's clear we want something a little more interesting for the list of matching items. We want columns, and columns require reasonable data.

To store this data, we'll make up a new class, called MatchingItemData, which works just like ListItemData, but has more data fields.

```
Private Class MatchingItemData
    Public ItemID As Integer   ' NamedItem.ID
    Public Title As String
    Public Subtitle As String
    Public Author As String
    Public MediaType As String
    Public CallNumber As String

    Public Overrides Function ToString() As String
        ' ----- Build a simple display string.
        If (Subtitle = "") Then
            Return Title & ", by " & Author
        Else
            Return Title & ": " & Subtitle & ", by " & Author
        End If
    End Function
End Class
```

Since this class will be used only to display matching items on this form, I've made it a subordinate class within the larger ItemLookup form class. The ToString method outputs the text that appears in the list. We won't generate the actual columnar output until the next chapter. For now, we'll just display the title and author.

The PanelMatches and PanelItems panels each include a Lookup button that initiates a new call to PerformLookup based on the item selected in the list. The Lookup button on the PanelItems panel retrieves the selected MatchingItemData object from the list, and performs the new search.

```
Private Sub ActItemLookup_Click( _
        ByVal sender As System.Object, _
        ByVal e As System.EventArgs) _
        Handles ActItemLookup.Click
    ' ----- Look up the item with the selected ID.
    Dim itemID As Integer

    ' ----- Ignore if no match is selected.
    If (MatchingItems.SelectedIndex = -1) Then Return
    itemID = CType(MatchingItems.SelectedItem, _
        MatchingItemData).ItemID
```

```
'  ----- Perform the lookup.
   If (PerformLookup(LookupMethods.ByDatabaseID, _
      CStr(itemID), False) = False) Then Return

'  ----- Store the history.
   AddLookupHistory(LookupMethods.ByDatabaseID, CStr(itemID))
End Sub
```

The call to PerformLookup starts the process all over again.

Maintaining Search History

Let's say you have a patron with a lot of time on his hands, and he wants to look up the book *War and Peace*.

- Starting from InitiateSearch and moving on to the PerformLookup code, the initial title search ("War and Peace") displays a list of matching titles on the PanelItems panel.

- The patron locates the book in this list, and clicks the Lookup button, which calls the ActItemLookup_Click event handler.

- This event handler in turn calls PerformLookup again, this time doing a precise lookup based on a database ID within the NamedItem table.

- The detail of the item appears on the PanelOneItem panel. (I'll discuss how it's done later in this chapter.)

- The detail includes a link to "Tolstoy, Leo," the long-suffering author of the book. When the patron clicks on this link, it initiates another call to PerformLookup, this time by author ID.

- We're back to the PanelItems panel, viewing a list of books and other items by Tolstoy, assuming he had time to write anything else.

So, the patron now has an experience with three search panels: (1) a "general" list of titles matching the name "War and Peace"; (2) the "detail" display for the selected "War and Peace" item; and (3) an "items" list of books written by Leo Tolstoy. The history feature included in this form lets the patron return to any previous search page, just like the feature in your web browser.

It's possible that some of the searches performed could return hundreds of results. We don't want to store all of that content in memory, since it's possible the patron will never use the Back button. Instead, we will do just what your web browser does: store the minimum information needed to perform the query again. Your web browser maintains just the name and URL of visited paths in its "back" list. (File and image caching is not part of the history feature.) The *ItemLookup.vb* form needs to store only those values that PerformLookup needs to do the search again: the type of search, and the numeric or text criteria used in the search.

Patron history is accessed on a "last-in, first-out" basis. The most recent page viewed is the one the patron wants to see first when using the Back button. We discussed just such a last-in, first-out, or "LIFO," structure in Chapter 16: the stack. Each time the user views a panel, we'll make note of it, *pushing* just those values we will need later onto the stack. When the user wants to view history, we will *pop* the most recent lookup content off the stack and update the display.

The `ItemLookupHistory` class, another subordinate class within the `ItemLookup` class, stores the values we need to manage history in the stack.

```
Private Class ItemLookupHistory
    Public HistoryDisplay As String
    Public LookupType As Library.LookupMethods
    Public LookupData As String
End Class
```

`HistoryDisplay` provides a short display name to help the user scan through history. `LookupType` and `LookupData` are the values that get passed to `PerformLookup`. It's all nice and neat. To make things even neater, we'll use a generic stack for actual storage. It's declared as a field of the `ItemLookup` class.

```
Private LookupHistorySet As _
    Collections.Generic.Stack(Of ItemLookupHistory)
```

As the patron visits each panel, calls to the `AddLookupHistory` method populate the stack with each new visited item.

```
Private Sub AddLookupHistory( _
        ByVal searchType As Library.LookupMethods, _
        ByVal searchText As String)
    ' ----- Add an item to the lookup history.
    Dim newHistory As ItemLookupHistory
    Dim displayText As String

    ' ----- Build the text for display in the new item.
    displayText = BuildDisplayText(searchType, searchText)

    ' ----- Build the new history item.
    newHistory = New ItemLookupHistory
    newHistory.LookupType = searchType
    newHistory.LookupData = searchText
    newHistory.HistoryDisplay = displayText
    LookupHistorySet.Push(newHistory)

    ' ----- Update the back button.
    RefreshBackButtons()
End Sub
```

Later, when the patron clicks one of the Back buttons, the `BackMenuItems_Click` event handler examines the history stack, and calls `PerformLookup` as needed. And because we stored the `ItemLookupHistory` objects in a generic stack, we don't have to specifically convert them from `System.Object`; the program just knows what data type they are.

```
Private Sub BackMenuItems_Click( _
      ByVal sender As System.Object, _
      ByVal e As System.EventArgs) _
      Handles BackMenu1.Click, ..., BackMenu10.Click
   ' ----- One of the back menu items was clicked.
   Dim whichItem As Integer
   Dim counter As Integer
   Dim scanHistory As ItemLookupHistory

   ' ----- Determine the clicked item.
   whichItem = CInt(DigitsOnly(CType(sender, _
      System.Windows.Forms.ToolStripMenuItem).Name))
   If (whichItem >= LookupHistorySet.Count) Then Return

   ' ----- Get rid of the in-between items.
   For counter = 1 To whichItem
      LookupHistorySet.Pop( )
   Next counter

   ' ----- Perform a lookup as requested.
   scanHistory = LookupHistorySet.Peek
   If (PerformLookup(scanHistory.LookupType, _
      scanHistory.LookupData, False) = False) Then Return
   RefreshBackButtons( )
End Sub
```

Showing Item Detail

The BuildHTMLAndLinks function builds the HTML content that appears on the
PanelOneItem panel. This panel includes SingleItemDetail, a WebBrowser control
included with .NET. It's basically a version of Internet Explorer that you embed in
your applications. Normally, you supply it with a URL to display, but you can also
provide custom content through the control's DocumentText property. The
ByDatabaseID and ByBarcode lookup methods within the PerformLookup routine assign
this property with content returned from BuildHTMLAndLinks.

```
SingleItemDetail.DocumentText = _
   BuildHTMLAndLinks(CInt(idQuery.ToArray(0)))
```

The content supplied by this routine is standard HTML, but with some specially
crafted links that let the library program perform additional lookups based on the
details of the displayed library item.

Most of the HTML is boilerplate, and it seems a shame to waste brain cells doing
string concatenation just to include it. So instead, I stored much of the HTML as a
text file resource through the Resources panel of the project properties. On that
panel, I clicked the Add Resource button, clicked the Add New Text File menu item,
and entered "ItemLookupBody" as the name for the new text file (see Figure 17-6).

Figure 17-6. Adding a new text file resource

In the text editor window that appeared, I added the following HTML content:

```
<html>
<head>
<style type="text/css">
body { font-family: "Arial"; }
h1 { font-family: "Arial"; margin-top: 0px;
    margin-bottom: 0px; font-size: 18pt; font-weight: bold; }
h2 { font-family: "Arial"; margin-top: 20px;
    margin-bottom: 0px; font-size: 15pt; font-weight: normal; }
h3 { font-family: "Arial"; margin-top: 0px;
    margin-bottom: 0px; font-size: 15pt; font-weight: normal;
    font-style: italic; }
p { margin-top: 2px; margin-bottom: 2px;
    margin-left: 15px; font-family: "Arial"; font-size: 12pt; }
table { border: solid black 1px; margin-left: 15px; }
th { border: solid black 1px; background-color: black;
    color: white; white-space: nowrap; text-align: left; }
td { border: solid black 1px; white-space: nowrap; }
a:visited { color: blue; }
</style>
</head>
<body>
```

If you're familiar with HTML, you'll recognize most of the content as an embedded Cascading Style Sheet (CSS). Its various formatting rules will bring a specific and consistent look and feel to the browser content that appears within the item lookup form. This is not a book on CSS, but there are some good books at your local bookstore that can talk you through the rules and syntax if you're interested.

You can find the HTML content portion in the Solution Explorer, within the Resources branch. You've probably already noticed that the closing `</body>` and `</html>` tags aren't included. We'll attach those in the `BuildHTMLAndLinks` method. Since string concatenation is notoriously slow, I chose to use a `StringBuilder` class, a special string-like class that is custom-designed for speed when repeatedly adding content to a base string. You attach content to the end of the StringBuilder using its Append and AppendLine methods, and retrieve the entire string through the standard ToString method.

We'll begin the content with the boilerplate HTML listed previously. Since we added it as a resource, it already appears in the My.Resources object under the name we gave it.

```
Dim detailBody As New System.Text.StringBuilder
detailBody.Append(My.Resources.ItemLookupBody)
```

Most of the code adds plain text to the detailBody string builder using its AppendLine method. Here's the code that adds the main book title:

```
sqlText = "SELECT Title, Subtitle FROM NamedItem " & _
    "WHERE ID = " & itemID
dbInfo = CreateReader(sqlText)
dbInfo.Read()
detailBody.AppendLine("<h1>" & _
    HTMLEncode(CStr(dbInfo!Title)) & "</h1>")
```

The HTMLEncode function, called in this block, is included in the ItemLookup class. It does some simple modification of special characters as required by HTML. It's called repeatedly throughout BuildHTMLAndLinks.

So, that's the HTML, but what about the links? If I put a standard link to, say, *http://www.microsoft.com*, the embedded browser will jump to that page when the link is clicked. But that doesn't help me do database lookups. The WebBrowser control doesn't really expose a "link clicked" event, but it has a Navigating event that is close. This event fires whenever the browser is about to move to a new page. Fortunately, one of the data values passed to the event handler is the target URL. So, all we have to do is build a link that contains the information we need to perform the database lookup.

I decided to store the relevant database lookup details as a collection (similar to the history stack), and create fake URL-like links that indicate which item in the collection to use. After a lot of thought and contemplation, I decided on the format of my fake URL links:

```
library://x
```

where *x* gets replaced by an index into the collection of links. It's simple, and it works. The collection of search details is a generic dictionary stored as a field within the form class.

```
Private Class SingleItemLink
    Public LinkType As Library.LookupMethods
    Public LinkID As Integer
End Class

Private ItemLinkSet As Collections.Generic.Dictionary( _
    Of Integer, SingleItemLink)
```

Then back in the HTML-building code, I add fake URLs and SingleItemLink objects in tandem. Here's some of the code used to add in author links, given a data reader with author name fields. (The entryID value supplies the *x* in library://x.)

```
Do While dbInfo.Read
    ' ----- Add in this one author name.
    holdText = FormatAuthorName(dbInfo)
    entryID += 1
    detailBody.AppendLine("<p><a href=""library://" & _
        entryID & """>" & HTMLEncode(holdText & " [" & _
        CStr(dbInfo!AuthorTypeName) & "]") & "</a></p>")

    ' ----- Add in an author link.
    newLink = New SingleItemLink
    newLink.LinkType = General.LookupMethods.ByAuthorID
    newLink.LinkID = CInt(dbInfo!ID)
    ItemLinkSet.Add(entryID, newLink)
Loop
```

When the user clicks on a link in the embedded web browser, it triggers the Navigating event handler.

```
Private Sub SingleItemDetail_Navigating( _
        ByVal sender As Object, ByVal e As System.Windows. _
        Forms.WebBrowserNavigatingEventArgs) _
        Handles SingleItemDetail.Navigating
    ' ----- Follow the clicked link.
    If (e.Url.Scheme = "library") Then _
        FollowItemLink(CInt(e.Url.Host()))
End Sub
```

The e.Url.Scheme property returns the portion of the URL before the :// characters, while e.Url.Host returns the first slash-delimited component just after these characters. That's where we stored the index into the ItemLinkSet dictionary. The FollowItemLink method extracts the lookup details from ItemLinkSet, and calls our trusty PerformLookup method, resulting in a new search that gets stored in the search history.

```
Private Sub FollowItemLink(ByVal entryID As Integer)
    ' ----- Given a character position in the single item
    '       text panel, follow the link indicated by that item.
    Dim scanLink As SingleItemLink

    ' ----- Access the link.
    scanLink = ItemLinkSet.Item(entryID)
    If (scanLink Is Nothing) Then Return

    ' ----- Perform a lookup as requested.
    If (PerformLookup(scanLink.LinkType, _
        CStr(scanLink.LinkID), False) = False) _
        Then Return

    ' ----- Store the history.
    AddLookupHistory(scanLink.LinkType, CStr(scanLink.LinkID))
End Sub
```

Enabling the Search Features

The ItemLookup form is ready to use. We just need to call it from the search fields on the main form. The PanelLibraryItem panel in *MainForm.vb* includes several ComboBox selection controls, but there is no code to fill them in. Let's add that code now. Access the source code for *MainForm.vb*, and locate the MainForm_Load event. There's already some code there that adjusts the form elements. Append the new list-filling code to the end of this routine.

INSERT SNIPPET

Insert Chapter 17, Snippet Item 2.

Here's the portion of that new code that fills in the list of search methods:

```
' ----- Load in the list of search types.
SearchType.Items.Add(New ListItemData( _
   "Lookup By Title", LookupMethods.ByTitle))
SearchType.SelectedIndex = 0
SearchType.Items.Add(New ListItemData( _
   "Lookup By Author", LookupMethods.ByAuthor))
SearchType.Items.Add(New ListItemData( _
   "Lookup By Subject", LookupMethods.BySubject))
SearchType.Items.Add(New ListItemData( _
   "Lookup By Keyword (Match Any)", _
   LookupMethods.ByKeywordAny))
SearchType.Items.Add(New ListItemData( _
   "Lookup By Keyword (Match All)", _
   LookupMethods.ByKeywordAll))
SearchType.Items.Add(New ListItemData( _
   "Lookup By Publisher", LookupMethods.ByPublisher))
SearchType.Items.Add(New ListItemData( _
   "Lookup By Series Name", LookupMethods.BySeries))
SearchType.Items.Add(New ListItemData( _
   "Lookup By Barcode", LookupMethods.ByBarcode))
```

The Clear button on the search panel resets all of the search fields and prepares them for a new search. Add a new ActSearchClear_Click event handler either by using the method selection fields just above the code editor window, or by double-clicking on the Clear button on the form itself. Then add the following code to the handler.

INSERT SNIPPET

Insert Chapter 17, Snippet Item 3.

```
' ----- Clear the current search criteria.
SearchType.SelectedIndex = SearchType.Items.IndexOf( _
   CInt(LookupMethods.ByTitle))
SearchText.Text = ""
SearchMediaType.SelectedIndex = _
```

```
SearchMediaType.Items.IndexOf(-1)
SearchLocation.SelectedIndex = _
    SearchLocation.Items.IndexOf(-1)
```

Since the Library application will probably be used by many different patrons throughout the day, we should assume that a different person is using the program each time the form returns to the search panel. Let's simulate a click on the Clear button whenever the user views the search panel. Locate the existing TaskLibraryItem method, and add the following code to the end of the routine, just before the SearchText.Focus( ) statement.

INSERT SNIPPET

Insert Chapter 17, Snippet Item 4.

```
ActSearchClear.PerformClick( )
If (ActSearchLimits.Top = LabelMoreLimitsTop.Top) Then _
    ActSearchLimits.PerformClick( )
```

In the interest of being as user-friendly as possible, let's add some "help text" to the search panel that varies based on the search type selected in the Search Type dropdown list. Add a new SearchType_SelectedIndexChanged event handler, and then add its code.

INSERT SNIPPET

Insert Chapter 17, Snippet Item 5.

I won't list it all here since it's rather repetitive. The code simply examines the current selection in the SearchType control, and sets the LabelSearchHintsData label to some helpful descriptive text.

We're getting close. The only thing left to do is to perform the search when the user clicks the Lookup button. Add an event handler for ActSearch_Click, and then add its code.

INSERT SNIPPET

Insert Chapter 17, Snippet Item 6.

Most of this routine checks for valid input before calling the ItemLookup form through its InitiateSearch public method.

```
Call (New ItemLookup).InitiateSearch( _
    CType(searchMethod, Library.LookupMethods), _
    Trim(SearchText.Text), mediaLimit, locationLimit)
```

You've done it, doctor. You've added a heart to the patient. The program is ready to run and use for item lookups! If you've already added some named items, you can locate them using any of the relevant search methods. Try doing a title search, using just the * wildcard character for the search criteria.

Although the search feature works, you will find that some of the display elements on the ItemLookup form don't work perfectly. We never did get those columns working on the item results panel. Improvements are coming soon. With the next chapter's focus on user interface techniques, we'll soon be able to customize the display to our heart's content.

CHAPTER 18

User Interface

A picture is worth a thousand words—or several thousand lines of source code, if you're generating a bitmap image of it. Writing code to manipulate images of varying color depths, or to trace out multilayer vector art, can be a nightmare of geometric contortions and linear algebra. It makes one yearn for those days of prescreen computers. The first programming class I took used a *DECWriter*, a printer-based terminal that had no screen, and included the graphics capabilities of a jellyfish. It was perfect for me. I couldn't draw a straight line anyway, and I didn't need some fancy schmancy "video display terminal" reminding me of it.

The graphics included in early display systems weren't much better. "Dumb terminals," such as the popular *VT100*, included some simple character graphics that displayed basic lines and blocks. Each graphic part was exactly one character in size, and any images you sought to display had to fit in a clunky 80×24 grid.

Fortunately for art aficionados everywhere, computers have come a long way in the graphics department. *GDI+*, the standard .NET drawing system, includes complex drawing features that would make a DECWriter cry. Built upon the older Windows "Graphics Device Interface" (GDI) technology, GDI+ includes commands for drawing lines, text, and images in the Picasso-enhanced world of 2D graphics.

Beyond GDI+, .NET also provides support for the newer *Windows Presentation Foundation* (WPF), a rich user interface and multimedia presentation system based in part on XML. WPF includes display and interaction features that go way beyond GDI+, although there are a few GDI+ features absent from WPF. Although I will give a brief overview of WPF in this chapter, most of the chapter (and all of the Library Project's user interface code) will focus on GDI+.

Overview of GDI+

Before .NET, Windows programmers depended on the GDI system to draw pretty much anything on the screen, even if they didn't know that GDI existed. In addition to bitmap images, all controls, labels, window borders, and icons appeared on the screen thanks to GDI. It was a giant step forward from character graphics. GDI presented a basic set of drawing features from which you could potentially output any type of complex image. But it wasn't easy. The graphics primitives were—well—primitive, and you had to build up complex systems from the parts. Most programmers weren't into making things beautiful, so they tried to avoid the complexities of GDI. But sometimes you had to draw a line or a circle, and there was no way around it.

GDI+, new with .NET, builds on GDI, providing the basic primitives of GDI, but also supplying some more complex groupings of graphics features into easy-to-use functions. This simplicity has brought about a renaissance of programmer-initiated graphics work. Take a look at Figure 18-1, which shows an image that was drawn using the older GDI, and that same image generated with just a few quick commands in GDI+.

Figure 18-1. The marvel that is GDI+

The GDI+ system makes its home in the System.Drawing namespace, and includes multitudes of classes that represent the drawing objects, surfaces, and embellishment features that enable display graphics. But it's not just about display. GDI+ generalizes bitmap and vector drawing on all available output surfaces: bitmaps or line drawings on the screen (including form and control surfaces), report output on a printer, graffiti on the back wall of your local supermarket, image content destined for a JPEG file—they are all the same to GDI+. All destinations use the same drawing methods and objects, making it easier for you to generalize your drawing code.

GDI+'s features include surfaces, drawing inks, drawing elements, and transformations.

- GDI+ generalizes drawing *surfaces* through the System.Drawing.Graphics class. This object represents a drawing canvas, with attributes for color depth and size (width and height). The canvas may link to a region of the workstation screen, an internal holding area for final output to the printer, or a general graphics canvas for manipulating content in-memory before outputting it to a display or a file. Another type of surface, the *path* (System.Drawing.Drawing2D.GraphicsPath), is like a macro recorder for vector (line) graphics. Drawing done within a path can be "replayed" on a standard drawing surface, or used to supply boundaries for other drawing commands.

- Colors and inks appear in the form of *colors* (opaque or semitransparent color values), *brushes* (bitmap-based pseudo-pens used for fills and tiling), and *pens* (colored line-drawing objects with a specific thickness).

- *Drawing elements* include rectangles, ellipses, lines, and other standard or custom-edge shapes. They also include fonts, both bitmapped and outline-based versions.

- *Transformations* let you resize, rotate, and skew drawings as you generate them. When a transformation is applied to a surface, you can draw objects as though there were no transformation applied, and the changes will happen in real time.

The Windows Forms controls that you use in desktop applications generally take care of their own display features. However, some controls let you take over some or all of the drawing responsibilities. For instance, the ListBox control displays simple single-color text for each list item. However, you can override the drawing of each list item, providing your own custom content, which may include multicolor text or graphics. This ability to supply some of the drawing code to a control is known as *owner draw*, and it works through the same generalized Graphics object used for other drawing. We'll include some owner draw code in the Library Project.

In the interest of full disclosure, you should know that this chapter will cover probably only 1% of the available GDI+ features, if even that. GDI+ is complex and vast, and you could spend years delving into every little feature, just in time for your eventual switch over to WPF. I'll give you a brief overview of the GDI+ system so that you get a feel for some of the basics. If you need to manipulate images and text beyond what is listed here (and you probably will), try the MSDN documentation or another resource dedicated to deciphering GDI+.

Selecting a Canvas

Most drawing in .NET occurs in the context of a Graphics object. (For those familiar with pre-.NET development in Windows, this is similar to a *device context*.) Graphics objects provide a canvas on which you draw lines, shapes, bitmap images, and prerecorded drawing macros. Graphics object do not contain the graphics surface itself; they are simply generic conduits to the actual canvas.

There is always some surface behind the `Graphics` object, whether it is a portion of the screen, a `Bitmap` object, or the simulated surface of a printed page. Any drawing that is done to the `Graphics` object immediately impacts the underlying surface.

The `Graphics` object includes dozens of methods that let you draw shapes and images on the graphics surface, and perform other magical 2D activities. We'll cover many of them in this chapter.

Obtaining and Creating Graphics Objects

Getting a `Graphics` object for an on-screen form or control is as easy as calling the form's or control's `CreateGraphics` method.

```
Dim wholeFormGraphics As Graphics = _
   Me.CreateGraphics( )
Dim buttonOnlyGraphics As Graphics = _
   Button1.CreateGraphics( )
```

Some events, most notably the `Paint` event for forms and controls, provide access to a `Graphics` object through the event arguments.

```
Private Sub PictureBox1_Paint(ByVal sender As Object, _
      ByVal e As System.Windows.Forms.PaintEventArgs) _
      Handles PictureBox1.Paint
   Dim paintCanvas As Graphics = e.Graphics
End Sub
```

You can also create a `Graphics` object that is unrelated to any existing display area by associating it to a bitmap.

```
Dim trueBitmap As New Bitmap(50, 50)
Dim canvas = Graphics.FromImage(trueBitmap)
```

Remember, all changes made to the canvas instance will impact the `trueBitmap` image.

Disposing of Graphics Objects Properly

When you are finished with a `Graphics` object *that you create*, you must dispose of it by calling its `Dispose` method. (This rule is true for many different GDI+ objects.) Don't keep it around for a rainy day because it won't be valid later. You must, must, must dispose of it when you are finished with it. If you don't, it could result in image corruption, memory usage issues, or worse yet, international armed conflict. So, please dispose of all `Graphics` objects properly.

```
canvas.Dispose( )
```

If you create a `Graphics` object within an event, you really need to dispose of it before exiting that event handler. There is no guarantee that the `Graphics` object will still be valid in a later event. Besides, it's easy to re-create another `Graphics` object at any time.

If you use a Graphics object that is passed to you from another part of the program (like that e.Graphics reference in the preceding Paint event handler), you should not dispose of it. Each creator is responsible for disposing of its own objects.

Choosing Pens and Brushes

A lot of graphics work involves drawing primitives: using lines, ellipses, rectangles, and other regular and irregular shapes to build up a final display. As in real life, you draw these primitives using a Pen object. For those primitives that result in a fillable or semifillable shape, a Brush object specifies the color or pattern to use in that filled area. GDI+ includes many predefined pens and brushes, or you can create your own.

Pens

Pens are line-drawing tools used with the drawing commands of a Graphics object. A basic pen has a solid color and a thickness.

```
' ----- A red pen five units wide.
Dim redPen As New Pen(Color.Red, 5)
```

As with Graphics objects, any Pen you create using the New keyword *must be disposed of properly* when you are finished with it.

```
redPen.Dispose( )
```

Several predefined pens are made available through the System.Drawing.Pens class, all named by their color, as in Pens.Red. If you use one of these pens, you don't have to dispose of it.

You can create a lot of interesting pens that vary by line styles, end decorations, and color variations. The following code generates the image displayed in Figure 18-2:

```
Private Sub PictureBox1_Paint(ByVal sender As Object, _
      ByVal e As System.Windows.Forms.PaintEventArgs) _
      Handles PictureBox1.Paint
   ' ----- Draw some fancy lines.
   Dim usePen As Pen

   ' ----- Blank out the background.
   e.Graphics.Clear(Color.White)

   ' ----- Draw a basic 1-pixel line using the title
   '       bar color.
   usePen = New Pen(SystemColors.ActiveCaption, 1)
   e.Graphics.DrawLine(usePen, 10, 10, 200, 10)
   usePen.Dispose( )

   ' ----- Draw a thicker dashed line with arrow and ball
   '       end caps. Each dashed segment has a triangle end.
   usePen = New Pen(Color.FromName("Red"), 5)
   usePen.DashCap = Drawing2D.DashCap.Triangle
```

```
      usePen.StartCap = Drawing2D.LineCap.ArrowAnchor
      usePen.EndCap = Drawing2D.LineCap.RoundAnchor
      usePen.DashStyle = Drawing2D.DashStyle.Dash
      e.Graphics.DrawLine(usePen, 10, 30, 200, 30)
      usePen.Dispose( )

      ' ----- A semitransparent black pen with three line
      '       parts, two thin and one thick.
      usePen = New Pen(Color.FromArgb(128, 0, 0, 0), 10)
      usePen.CompoundArray = _
         New Single( ) {0.0, 0.1, 0.4, 0.5, 0.8, 1.0}
      e.Graphics.DrawLine(usePen, 10, 55, 200, 55)
      usePen.Dispose( )
   End Sub
```

Figure 18-2. Yes sir, yes sir, three lines full

The code shows that there are a few different ways to specify a color, by either its predefined name (Color.White and SystemColors.ActiveCaption), a string name (using Color.FromName), or its Alpha-Red-Green-Blue value (Color.FromArgb). That last version lets you supply distinct values for the "alpha blend" (which sets the transparency level, from 0 for fully transparent to 255 for fully opaque), red, green, and blue components of the full color.

Most of the pen-specific properties I demonstrated here are somewhat self-explanatory. As with most of GDI+, the mind-numbing amount of available features makes it impossible to completely document in a small chapter, let alone provide a good night's sleep for authors designing such chapters. I will simply refer you to the online documentation for the Pen class to get all of the luscious details.

Brushes

Brushes are used for filling in spaces between drawn lines, even if you make those lines fully invisible. GDI+ includes a variety of brush types, including *solid brushes* (your basic single-color brush), *hatch brushes* (pattern brushes that are pleasant but general), *texture brushes* (where a custom bitmap is used for the brush), and *gradient brushes* (which slowly fade from one color to another across the brush). The System.Drawing.Brushes class includes some predefined solid brushes based on color name. As with pens, you must dispose of brushes that you create, but not the solid system-defined brushes.

The following block of code draws some simple rectangles with a variety of brush styles. The results appear in Figure 18-3.

```
Private Sub PictureBox1_Paint(ByVal sender As Object, _
    ByVal e As System.Windows.Forms.PaintEventArgs) _
    Handles PictureBox1.Paint
  ' ----- Draw some fancy rectangles.
  Dim useBrush As Brush

  e.Graphics.Clear(Color.White)

  ' ---- Draw a filled rectangle with a solid color.
  e.Graphics.FillRectangle(Brushes.Cyan, 10, 10, 150, 50)

  ' ----- Draw a hatched rectangle. Use black for the
  '       background, and white for the pattern foreground.
  useBrush = New Drawing2D.HatchBrush( _
    Drawing2D.HatchStyle.LargeConfetti, _
    Color.White, Color.Black)
  e.Graphics.FillRectangle(useBrush, 10, 70, 150, 50)
  useBrush.Dispose()

  ' ----- Draw a left-to-right linear gradient rectangle.
  '       The gradient's own rectangle determines the
  '       starting offset, based on the Graphics surface
  '       origin.
  useBrush = New Drawing2D.LinearGradientBrush( _
    New Rectangle(200, 10, 75, 25), Color.Blue, _
    Color.Yellow, Drawing2D.LinearGradientMode.Horizontal)
  e.Graphics.FillRectangle(useBrush, 200, 10, 150, 50)
  useBrush.Dispose()

  ' ----- Use an image for the brush. I'm using the
  '       "LookupItem.bmp" graphic used in the Library
  '       Project.
  useBrush = New TextureBrush(Image.FromFile( _
    "LookupItem.bmp"))
  e.Graphics.FillRectangle(useBrush, 200, 70, 150, 50)
  useBrush.Dispose()
End Sub
```

Figure 18-3. Kind of square, if you ask me

Flowing Text from the Font

Circles and squares are OK, but they don't always communicate much, unless you are Joan Miró. Most of us depend on text to say what we mean. Fortunately, GDI+ has features galore that place text on your graphics surface.

Before graphical user interfaces were all the rage, text wasn't really an issue; either you used the characters built into the system, or you used nothing. On the screen, each letter of the alphabet was designed into the hardware of the computer or monitor, and any particular character could appear only within each square of the predefined 80×24 grid. Printers were a little better, since you could backspace and retype over previously typed positions to generate either bold or underscore text. Still, you were generally limited to one font, or just a small handful of basic fonts embedded in the printer's memory.

Such limitations are a thing of the past. All text in Microsoft Windows appears courtesy of *fonts*, descriptions of character shapes that can be resized or stretched or emphasized to meet any text need. And because the user can add fonts to the system at any time, and from any third-party source, the variety of these fonts is amazing. But you already know all this. Let's get on to the code.

To gain access to a font for use in your graphics, create an instance of the System. Drawing.Font class, passing it at least the font name and point size, and an optional style reference:

```
Dim basicFont As New Font("Arial", 14, FontStyle.Italic)
```

Naturally, the list of available fonts varies by system; if you're going to go beyond the basic preinstalled fonts supplied with Windows, you should confirm that a named font is really available, and have a fallback option if it is not. You can get a list of all fonts by asking GDI+ nicely. All fonts appear in "families," where each named family may have bold, italic, and other variations installed as separate font files. The following code block adds a list of all installed font families to a ListBox control:

```
Dim allFonts As New Drawing.Text.InstalledFontCollection()
For Each oneFamily As Drawing.FontFamily In allFonts.Families
   ListBox1.Items.Add(oneFamily.Name)
Next oneFamily
```

If the font you need isn't available and you aren't sure what to use, let GDI+ choose for you. It includes a few generic fonts for emergency use.

```
Drawing.FontFamily.GenericMonospace
Drawing.FontFamily.GenericSansSerif
Drawing.FontFamily.GenericSerif
```

Getting back to using fonts in actual drawing, the Graphics object includes a DrawString method that blasts out some text to the canvas.

```
Private Sub PictureBox1_Paint(ByVal sender As Object, _
    ByVal e As System.Windows.Forms.PaintEventArgs) _
    Handles PictureBox1.Paint
  Dim basicFont As New Font("Arial", 14, FontStyle.Italic)
  e.Graphics.DrawString("This is a test", basicFont, _
    Brushes.Black, 0, 0)
  basicFont.Dispose()
End Sub
```

Figure 18-4 shows the output for this code block. In most of the sample code in this chapter, I'll be outputting content to a PictureBox control named PictureBox1 that I've placed on the form of a new Windows Forms application. I've also set that control's BorderStyle property to FixedSingle, and its BackColor property to White so that I can visualize the edges of the canvas. Drawing occurs in the Paint event handler, which gets called whenever the picture box needs to be refreshed, as when another window obscures it and then goes away. In the remaining code examples, I won't be including the Sub PictureBox1_Paint method definition, just the code that goes inside it.

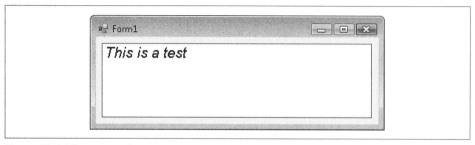

Figure 18-4. This is a test for sure

Of course, you can mix and match fonts on a single output canvas. This code includes text using Arial 14 and Arial 18:

```
Dim basicFont As New Font("Arial", 14)
Dim strongFont As New Font("Arial", 18, FontStyle.Bold)
Dim offset As Single = 0.0
Dim showText As String
Dim textSize As Drawing.SizeF

showText = "This is some "
textSize = e.Graphics.MeasureString(showText, basicFont)
e.Graphics.DrawString(showText, basicFont, _
   Brushes.Black, offset, 0)
offset += textSize.Width

showText = "strong"
textSize = e.Graphics.MeasureString(showText, strongFont)
e.Graphics.DrawString(showText, strongFont, _
   Brushes.Black, offset, 0)
offset += textSize.Width
```

```
showText = "text."
textSize = e.Graphics.MeasureString(showText, basicFont)
e.Graphics.DrawString(showText, basicFont, _
   Brushes.Black, offset, 0)
offset += textSize.Width

strongFont.Dispose( )
basicFont.Dispose( )
```

The output of this code appears in the top box of Figure 18-5, and it's OK. But I want the bottom edges of the main body parts of each text block—that is, the *baselines* of each block—to line up properly, as shown in the lower box of Figure 18-5.

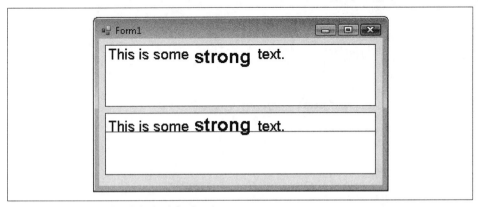

Figure 18-5. The good and the bad; both ugly

Doing all of the fancy font-lining-up stuff is kind of a pain in the neck. You have to do all sorts of measuring based on the original font design as extrapolated onto the pixel-based screen device. Then you connect the knee bone to the thigh bone, and so on. Here's the code I used to generate the second lined-up image:

```
Dim basicFont As New Font("Arial", 14)
Dim strongFont As New Font("Arial", 18, FontStyle.Bold)
Dim offset As Single = 0.0
Dim showText As String
Dim textSize As Drawing.SizeF
Dim basicTop As Single
Dim strongTop As Single
Dim strongFactor As Single
Dim basicFactor As Single

' ----- The Font Family uses design units, probably
'         specified by the original designer of the font.
'         Map these units to display units (points).
strongFactor = strongFont.FontFamily.GetLineSpacing( _
   FontStyle.Regular) / strongFont.Height
basicFactor = basicFont.FontFamily.GetLineSpacing( _
   FontStyle.Regular) / basicFont.Height
```

```
' ----- Determine the location of each font's baseline.
strongTop = (strongFont.FontFamily.GetLineSpacing( _
   FontStyle.Regular) - strongFont.FontFamily.GetCellDescent( _
   FontStyle.Regular)) / strongFactor
basicTop = (basicFont.FontFamily.GetLineSpacing( _
   FontStyle.Regular) - basicFont.FontFamily.GetCellDescent( _
   FontStyle.Regular)) / basicFactor

' ----- Draw a line that proves the text lines up.
e.Graphics.DrawLine(Pens.Red, 0, strongTop, _
   e.ClipRectangle.Width, strongTop)

' ----- Show each part of the text.
showText = "This is some "
textSize = e.Graphics.MeasureString(showText, basicFont)
e.Graphics.DrawString(showText, basicFont, _
   Brushes.Black, offset, strongTop - basicTop)
offset += textSize.Width

showText = "strong"
textSize = e.Graphics.MeasureString(showText, strongFont)
e.Graphics.DrawString(showText, strongFont, _
   Brushes.Black, offset, 0)
offset += textSize.Width

showText = "text."
textSize = e.Graphics.MeasureString(showText, basicFont)
e.Graphics.DrawString(showText, basicFont, _
   Brushes.Black, offset, strongTop - basicTop)
offset += textSize.Width

strongFont.Dispose( )
basicFont.Dispose( )
```

There's a lot more calculating going on in that code. And I didn't even try to tackle things like kerning, ligatures, or anything else having to do with typography. Anyway, if you need to perform complex font manipulation, GDI+ does expose all of the details so that you can do it properly. If you just want to output line after line of text using the same font, call the font's GetHeight method for each line displayed:

```
verticalOffset += useFont.GetHeight(e.Graphics)
```

Enough of that complex stuff. There are easy and cool things to do with text, too. Did you notice that text output uses brushes and not pens? This means you can draw text using any brush you can create. This block of code uses the Library Project's LookupItem bitmap brush to display some bitmap-based text.

```
Dim useBrush As Brush = New TextureBrush( _
   Image.FromFile("LookupItem.bmp"))
Dim useFont As New Font("Arial", 60, FontStyle.Bold)
e.Graphics.DrawString("Wow!", useFont, useBrush, 0, 0)
useFont.Dispose( )
useBrush.Dispose( )
```

The output appears in Figure 18-6.

Figure 18-6. The merger of text and graphics

Imagining Images

Probably more than anything else, the Internet has fueled the average computer user's need for visual stimuli. Web sites are awash with GIF, JPG, TIFF, and a variety of other image formats. Even if you deal with non-web applications, it's likely that you, as a programmer, will come into more frequent contact with graphical images. Fortunately, GDI+ includes features that let you manage and manipulate these images with ease.

The "BMP" file format is the native bitmap format included in Microsoft Windows, but it's not all that common in the web world. But none of that matters to GDI+. It can load and manage files using the following graphics formats:

- Windows "BMP" bitmap files of any color depth and size.
- CompuServe Graphics Interchange Format ("GIF") files, commonly used for non-photo images on the Internet.
- Joint Photographic Experts Group ("JPEG") files, commonly used for photos and other images on the Internet. JPEG files are compressed internally to reduce file size, but with the possible loss of image quality.
- Exchangeable Image File ("EXIF") files, a variation of JPEG that stores professional photographs.
- Portable Network Graphics ("PNG") files, which are similar to GIF files, but with some enhanced features.
- Tag Image File Format ("TIFF") files, which are kind of a combination of all other file formats. Some government organizations store scanned images using TIFF.
- Metafiles, which store vector line art instead of bitmap images.
- Icon ("ICO") files, which are used for standard Microsoft Windows icons. You can load them as bitmaps, but there is also a distinct Icon class that lets you treat them in more icon-like ways.

Three primary classes are used for images: Image (an abstract base class for the other two classes), Bitmap, and Metafile. I'll discuss the Metafile class a little later.

Bitmaps represent an image as drawn on a grid of bits. When a bit in the grid is *on*, that grid cell is visible or filled. When the bit is *off*, the grid cell is invisible or empty. Figure 18-7 shows a simple image using such a bitmap grid.

Figure 18-7. An 8×8 monochrome bitmap containing great art

Since a bit can support only two states, "1-bit bitmap files" are monochrome, displaying images using only black and white. To include more colors, bitmaps add additional "planes." The planes are stacked on each other so that a cell in one plane matches up with that same position cell in all other planes. A set of eight planes results in an "8-bit bitmap image," and supports 256 colors per cell (because $2^{planes} = 2^8 = 256$). Some images include as many as 32 or even 64 bits (planes), although some of these bits may be reserved for "alpha blending," which makes perceived transparency possible.

Unless you are a hardcore graphics junkie, manipulating all of those bits is a chore. Fortunately, you don't have to worry about it since it's all done for you by the Bitmap class. You just need to worry about loading and saving bitmaps (using simple Bitmap methods, of course), using a bitmap as a brush or drawing object (as we did in some sample code in this chapter already), or writing on the bitmap surface itself by attaching a Graphics object to it.

If you have a bitmap in a file, you can load it via the Bitmap class constructor.

```
Dim niceImage As New Bitmap("LookupItem.bmp")
```

To save a bitmap object to a file, use its Save method.

```
niceImage.Save("LookupItem.jpg", Imaging.ImageFormat.Jpeg)
```

Another constructor lets you create new bitmaps in a variety of formats.

```
' ---- Create a 50-50 pixel bitmap, using 32 bit-planes
'      (eight each for the amounts of red, green, and blue
'      in each pixel, and eight bits for the level of
'      transparency of each pixel, from 0 to 255).
Dim niceImage As New Bitmap(50, 50, _
   Drawing.Imaging.PixelFormat.Format32bppArgb)
```

To draw a bitmap on a graphics surface, use the Graphics object's DrawImage method.

```
e.Graphics.DrawImage(niceImage, leftOffset, topOffset)
```

That statement draws the image to the graphics surface as is, but that's kind of boring. You can stretch and crop the image as you draw it, or even generate a thumbnail. I'll try all these methods using the image from the Library Project's "splash" welcome form (*SplashImage.jpg*).

```
Dim splashImage As New Bitmap("SplashImage.jpg")

' ----- Draw it at half width and height.
e.Graphics.DrawImage(splashImage, New RectangleF(10, 50, _
   splashImage.Width / 2, splashImage.Height / 2))

' ----- Stretch it with fun!
e.Graphics.DrawImage(splashImage, New RectangleF(200, 10, _
   splashImage.Width * 1.25, splashImage.Height / 4))

' ----- Draw the middle portion.
e.Graphics.DrawImage(splashImage, 200, 100, New RectangleF( _
   0, splashImage.Height / 3, splashImage.Width, _
   splashImage.Height / 2), GraphicsUnit.Pixel)
```

Figure 18-8 shows the output for the previous block of code. But that's not all the drawing you can do. The DrawImage method includes 30 overloads. That would keep me busy for 37 minutes at least!

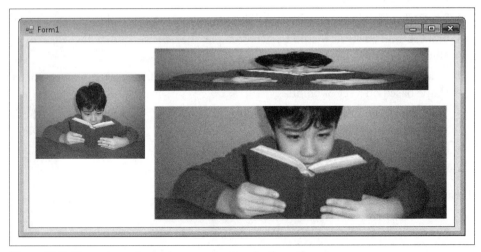

Figure 18-8. Three views of a reader: a masterpiece by the author

Exposing Your True Artist

OK, we've covered most of the basic GDI+ features used to draw images. Now it's all just a matter of issuing the drawing commands for shapes, images, and text on a graphics surface. Most of the time, you'll stick with the methods included on the Graphics object, all 12 bazillion of them. Perhaps I overcounted, but there are quite a few. Here's just a sampling:

- `Clear` method. Clear the background with a specific color.
- `CopyFromScreen` method. If the Prnt Scrn button on your keyboard falls off, this is the method for you.
- `DrawArc` method. Draw a portion of an arc along the edge of an ellipse. Zero degrees starts at three o'clock. Positive arc sweep values move in a clockwise direction; use negative sweep values to move counterclockwise.
- `DrawBezier` and `DrawBeziers` methods. Draw a Bézier spline, a formula-based curve that uses a set of points, plus directionals that guide the curve through the points.
- `DrawCurve`, `DrawClosedCurve`, and `FillClosedCurve` methods. Draw "cardinal" curves (where points define the path of the curve), with an optional brush fill.
- `DrawEllipse` and `FillEllipse` methods. Draw an ellipse or a circle (which is a variation of an ellipse).
- `DrawIcon`, `DrawIconUnstretched`, `DrawImage`, `DrawImageUnscaled`, and `DrawImageUnscaledAndClipped` methods. Different ways of drawing images and icons.
- `DrawLine` and `DrawLines` methods. Draw one or more lines with lots of options for making the lines snazzy.
- `DrawPath` and `FillPath` methods. I'll discuss "graphic paths" a little later.
- `DrawPie` and `FillPie` methods. Draw a pie slice border along the edge of an ellipse.
- `DrawPolygon` and `FillPolygon` methods. Draw a regular or irregular geometric shape based on a set of points.
- `DrawRectangle`, `DrawRectangles`, `FillRectangle`, and `FillRectangles` methods. Draw squares and rectangles.
- `DrawString` method. We used this before to output text to the canvas.
- `FillRegion` method. I'll discuss regions later in the chapter.

Here's some sample drawing code:

```
' ----- Line from (10, 10) to (40, 40).
e.Graphics.DrawLine(Pens.Black, 10, 10, 40, 40)

' ----- 90degree clockwise arc for 40-pixel diameter circle.
e.Graphics.DrawArc(Pens.Black, 50, 10, 40, 40, 0, -90)

' ----- Filled 40x40 rectangle with a dashed line.
e.Graphics.FillRectangle(Brushes.Honeydew, 120, 10, 40, 40)
Using dashedPen As New Pen(Color.Black, 2)
   dashedPen.DashStyle = Drawing2D.DashStyle.Dash
   e.Graphics.DrawRectangle(dashedPen, 120, 10, 40, 40)
End Using
```

```
' ----- A slice of elliptical pie.
e.Graphics.FillPie(Brushes.BurlyWood, 180, 10, 80, 40, _
   180, 120)
```

And so on. You get the idea. Figure 18-9 shows the output for this code.

Figure 18-9. Some simple drawings

Paths: Drawings on Macro-Vision

The GraphicsPath class lets you collect several of the more primitive drawing objects (such as lines and arcs, and even rectangles) into a single grouped unit. This full path can then be replayed onto a graphics surface as a macro.

```
Using thePath As New Drawing2D.GraphicsPath
   thePath.AddEllipse(0, 0, 50, 50)
   thePath.AddArc(10, 30, 30, 10, 10, 160)
   thePath.AddRectangle(New Rectangle(15, 15, 5, 5))
   thePath.AddRectangle(New Rectangle(30, 15, 5, 5))

   e.Graphics.DrawPath(Pens.Black, thePath)
End Using
```

This code block draws a smiley face on the canvas (see Figure 18-10).

Figure 18-10. Drawing with a GraphicsPath object

That's cute. Fortunately, there are other uses for graphics paths, some of which I'll discuss in the next section.

Keeping It Regional

Usually, when you draw images, you have the entire visible canvas to work with. (You can draw images and shapes off the edge of the canvas if you want, but if a tree draws an image in the forest and no one is there to admire it, does it appear?) But there are times when you may want only a portion of what you draw to appear. Windows uses this method itself to save time. When you obscure a window with another one, and then expose the hidden window, the application has to redraw everything that appeared on the form or window. But if only a portion of that background window was hidden and then made visible again, why should the program go through the trouble of drawing everything again? It really has to redraw only the part that was hidden, the part that was in the hidden region.

A *region* specifies an area to be drawn on a surface. And regions aren't limited to boring rectangular shapes. You can design a region based on simple shapes, or you can combine existing regions into more complex regions. For instance, if you have two rectangular regions, you can overlap them and request a new combined region that contains (1) all of the original two regions; (2) the original regions but without the overlapped parts; or (3) just the overlapped parts. Figure 18-11 shows these combinations.

Figure 18-11. Different combinations of regions

During drawing operations, regions are sometimes referred to as "clipping regions" because any content drawn outside the region is clipped off and thrown away. The following code draws an image, but masks out an ellipse in the middle by using (ta-da!) a graphics path to establish a custom clipping region:

```
' ----- Load the image. We'll show it smaller than normal.
Dim splashImage As New Bitmap("SplashImage.jpg")
Dim thePath As New Drawing2D.GraphicsPath()

' ----- Create an elliptical path that is the size of the
'       output image.
thePath.AddEllipse(20, 20, splashImage.Width \ 2, _
    splashImage.Height \ 2)

' ----- Replace the original clipping region that covers
'       the entire canvas with just the rectangular region.
e.Graphics.SetClip(thePath, Drawing2D.CombineMode.Replace)
```

```
' ----- Draw the image, which will be clipped.
e.Graphics.DrawImage(splashImage, 20, 20, _
    splashImage.Width \ 2, splashImage.Height \ 2)

' ----- Clean up.
thePath.Dispose()
```

The output for this code appears in Figure 18-12.

Figure 18-12. Ready to hang in your portrait gallery

Regions are also useful for "hit testing." If you draw a non-rectangular image on a form, and you want to know when the user clicks on the image, but not on any pixel just off the image, you can use a region that is the exact shape of the image to test for mouse clicks.

Twisting and Turning with Transformations

Normally, anything you draw on the graphics canvas is laid down directly on the bitmap surface. It's like a giant grid, and your drawing commands are basically dropping colored inks directly into each grid cell. The Graphics object also gives you the ability to pass your drawing commands through a geometric transformation before their output goes to the canvas surface. For instance, a rotation transformation would rotate your lines, shapes, and text by the amount you specify (in degrees), and then apply the result to the surface. Figure 18-13 displays the results of the following code, which applies two translations: (1) moving the (0, 0) origin right by 100 pixels and down by 75 pixels; and (2) adding a clockwise rotation of 270 degrees.

```
e.Graphics.DrawString("Normal", _
    SystemFonts.DefaultFont, Brushes.Black, 10, 10)
e.Graphics.TranslateTransform(100, 75)
e.Graphics.RotateTransform(270)
e.Graphics.DrawString("Rotated", _
    SystemFonts.DefaultFont, Brushes.Black, 10, 10)
e.Graphics.ResetTransform()
```

Figure 18-13. Normal and rotated text

Transformations are cumulative; if you apply multiple transformations to the canvas, any drawing commands will pass through all of the transformations before arriving at the canvas. The order in which transformations occur is important. If the code we just ran had reversed the TranslateTransform and RotateTransform statements, the rotation would have altered the x, y coordinates for the entire canvas world. The subsequent translation of (100, 75) would have moved up the origin 100 pixels and then to the right 75 pixels.

The Graphics class includes these methods that let you apply transformations to the "world view" of the canvas during drawing:

RotateTransform

Rotates the world view in clockwise degrees, from 0 to 359. The rotation can be positive or negative.

ScaleTransform

Sets a scaling factor for all drawing. Basically, this increases or decreases the size of the canvas grid when drawing. Changing the scale impacts the width of pens. If you scale the world by a factor of two, not only do distances appear to be twice as far apart, but all pens draw twice as thick as when unscaled.

TranslateTransform

Repositions the origin based on an *x* and *y* offset.

MultiplyTransform

A sort of master transformation method that lets you apply transforms through a Matrix object. It has more options than just the standard transforms included in the Graphics object. For instance, you can apply a shearing transformation that skews all output in a rectangle-to-parallelogram type of change.

ResetTransform

Removes all applied transformations from a canvas.

Save

Saves the current state of the transformed (or untransformed) graphics surface to an object for later restoration. This allows you to apply some transformations, save them, apply some more, and then restore the saved set, wiping out any transformations applied since that set was saved.

Restore

Restores a saved set of transformations.

Enhancing Controls Through Owner Draw

A lot more GDI+ drawing features are included in .NET, but what we've seen here should be enough to whet your appetite. You can do a lot of fancy drawing with GDI+, but let's face it: you and I are programmers, not artists. If we were artists, we'd be raking in six figures using a floor mop to draw traditional abstract cubist Italian landscapes with Bauhausian accents.

Fortunately, there are practical semi-artistic things you can do with GDI+. One important drawing feature is owner draw, a sharing of drawing responsibilities between a control and you, the programmer. (You are the "owner.") The ComboBox control supports owner drawing of the individual items in the drop-down portion of the list. Let's create a ComboBox control that displays color names, including a small sample of the color to the left of the name. Create a new Windows Forms application, and add a ComboBox control named ComboBox1 to Form1. Make these changes to ComboBox1:

1. Change its DropDownStyle property to DropDownList.

2. Change its DrawMode property to OwnerDrawFixed.

3. Alter its Items property, adding multiple color names as distinct text lines in the String Collection Editor window. I added Red, Green, and Blue.

Now, add the following code to the source code area of Form1's class:

```
Private Sub ComboBox1_DrawItem(ByVal sender As Object, _
      ByVal e As System.Windows.Forms.DrawItemEventArgs) _
      Handles ComboBox1.DrawItem
   ' ----- Ignore the unselelected state.
   If (e.Index = -1) Then Return

   ' ----- Create a brush for the display color, based on
   '       the name of the item.
   Dim colorBrush As New SolidBrush(Color.FromName( _
      CStr(ComboBox1.Items(e.Index))))
```

```
' ----- Create a text brush. The color varies based on
'        whether this item is selected or not.
Dim textBrush As Brush
If ((e.State And DrawItemState.Selected) = _
      DrawItemState.Selected) Or _
      ((e.State And DrawItemState.HotLight) = _
      DrawItemState.HotLight) Then
   textBrush = New SolidBrush(SystemColors.HighlightText)
Else
   textBrush = New SolidBrush(SystemColors.ControlText)
End If

' ----- Get the shape of the color display area.
Dim colorBox As New Rectangle(e.Bounds.Left + 4, _
   e.Bounds.Top + 2, (e.Bounds.Height - 4) * 2, _
   e.Bounds.Height - 4)

' ----- Draw the selected or unselected background.
e.DrawBackground()

' ----- Draw the custom color area.
e.Graphics.FillRectangle(colorBrush, colorBox)
e.Graphics.DrawRectangle(Pens.Black, colorBox)

' ----- Draw the name of the color to the right of
'        the color.
e.Graphics.DrawString(CStr(ComboBox1.Items(e.Index)), _
   ComboBox1.Font, textBrush, 8 + colorBox.Width, _
   e.Bounds.Top + ((e.Bounds.Height - _
   ComboBox1.Font.Height) / 2))

' ----- Draw a selected rectangle around the item,
'        if needed.
e.DrawFocusRectangle()

' ----- Clean up.
textBrush.Dispose()
colorBrush.Dispose()
End Sub
```

Run the code and play with the combo box, as shown in Figure 18-14.

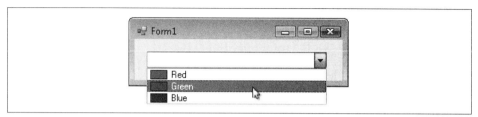

Figure 18-14. Our custom color combo box

Windows Presentation Foundation

Graphical user interfaces are a relatively new phenomenon. The first programmers didn't have all of the glitzy bling-bling that adorns many a modern UI. They had to make do with naval semaphore flags and Morse code. Here in the 21st century, having passed through the epochs of text-based and stick-figure interfaces, computers are finally able to present information in a way that totally confuses the end-user, yet in a beautiful and highly interactive style.

Microsoft's latest tool for building active, next-generation user interfaces is Windows Presentation Foundation, or WPF. As in LINQ, WPF melds together many different technologies into a unified whole. Some of those technologies have been with us for many years, such as Microsoft's Direct3D system that displays and manipulates 3D elements. WPF condenses all of these technologies, and makes them available through an XML-based descriptive language known as *XAML* (eXtensible Application Markup Language).

WPF includes features and elements that deal with many areas of presentation, including on-screen controls, 2D drawings (like GDI+), 3D graphics (from Direct3D), static images (such as JPEG pictures), interactive multimedia (video and audio), and WYSIWYG document presentation (similar to PDF documents). Individual elements and entire user interfaces can be animated automatically, or in response to user interactions.

When it comes time to display your WPF content, you can present it to the user in a few common ways. XAML files and related .NET code can be built into a standalone application, much like a typical .NET Windows Forms application, but with the amazing Cary Grant looks normally inaccessible to developers.

WPF can also be used to generate web-based applications hosted within a user's browser. In fact, elements that you design for use in desktop-style applications can be used on the Web generally without any modifications. As expected, security limitations put a damper on some of the things you can do when running in this type of host.

Browser-based WPF programs require that the .NET Framework and the WPF libraries be installed and accessible on the client workstation. Microsoft is bundling up much of that technology and packaging it in a product called *Silverlight*. Designed to compete with the likes of Adobe's Flash platform and Sun Microsystems' new JavaFX system, Silverlight will eventually allow XAML and .NET linked content to run on non-Windows platforms, such as the Macintosh.

A third variation uses a subset of XAML to define a PDF-like static document. Such documents are known as *XPS* (XML Paper Specification) documents, and are actually ZIP files that contain all of the XAML pages, graphics, and other page elements in distinct files within the archive.

WPF and XAML

One of the hallmarks of application design in WPF is the separation of logic from presentation. This is a common goal expressed in many newer technologies, including XML and ASP.NET (see Chapter 23). All application logic—all event handlers triggered by user input and system actions—is written in standard .NET code. The user interface can also appear as .NET code, with objects created out of the WPF-specific System.Windows namespace. But it's more common to design user interface elements and derived controls through XAML, an XML schema that can be generated by you in Visual Studio or Notepad, or by third-party tools.

Because XAML content can be built outside its application, a user interface design specialist with limited programming knowledge can build the UI components independently from the developer's work on the application logic. Microsoft offers a tool for such designers, called *Microsoft Expression Blend*, one of a handful of Expression design products. Other vendors also offer tools to generate rich XAML content.

Visual Studio 2008 lets you create complete WPF applications based on XAML content. To build a WPF application, start Visual Studio, create a new project, and from the New Project dialog select the WPF Application template within the Visual Basic Project type. Then click OK. Windows immediately creates a new WPF Forms project, displaying the starting form, Window1 (see Figure 18-15).

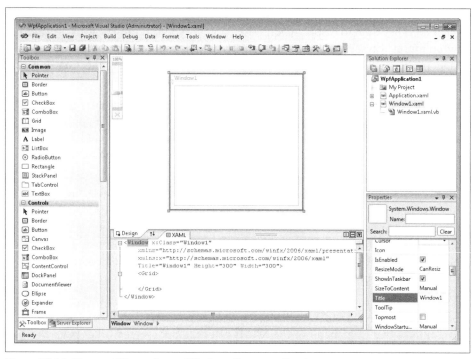

Figure 18-15. Not too different from a Windows Forms application

The user interface is defined entirely by the XML set displayed at the bottom of the form. Currently, it defines the eventual application window itself.

```
<Window x:Class="Window1"
    xmlns="http://schemas.microsoft.com
    ↳/winfx/2006/xaml/presentation"
    xmlns:x="http://schemas.microsoft.com/winfx/2006/xaml"
    Title="Window1" Height="300" Width="300">
    <Grid>

    </Grid>
</Window>
```

This code defines the window, Window1, which has as its real class System.Windows. Window. The attributes of the XAML Window tag, including Title, Height, and Width, map back to properties of the same name in the Window class.

Let's spice up this form a little more. I'll add a button that includes a rainbow on the button's face, plus add a yellow glow around the button. I'll also add an event handler that shows a message box. As with standard Windows Forms application, you use the controls in the toolbox to build your form. I'll drag a button onto the form's surface and use the XAML text area to bring new life to the window.

```
<Window x:Class="Window1"
    xmlns="http://schemas.microsoft.com/winfx/2006/xaml/presentation"
    xmlns:x="http://schemas.microsoft.com/winfx/2006/xaml"
    Title="Window1" Height="160" Width="411">
    <Grid>
        <Button Margin="95,26,99,35" Name="Button1">
            <Button.Foreground>White</Button.Foreground>
            <Button.FontSize>18</Button.FontSize>
            <Button.FontWeight>Bold</Button.FontWeight >
            <Button.Background>
                <LinearGradientBrush>
                    <LinearGradientBrush.GradientStops>
                    <GradientStopCollection>
                        <GradientStop Color="Red" Offset="0" />
                        <GradientStop Color="Orange" Offset="0.1425"/>
                        <GradientStop Color="Yellow" Offset="0.285"/>
                        <GradientStop Color="Green" Offset="0.4275"/>
                        <GradientStop Color="Blue" Offset="0.57"/>
                        <GradientStop Color="Indigo" Offset="0.7325"/>
                        <GradientStop Color="Violet" Offset="0.875"/>
                    </GradientStopCollection>
                    </LinearGradientBrush.GradientStops>
                </LinearGradientBrush>
            </Button.Background>
            <Button.BitmapEffect>
                <OuterGlowBitmapEffect />
            </Button.BitmapEffect> Click Me
        </Button>
    </Grid>
</Window>
```

I'll also add an event handler, using the same point-and-click simplicity that I've used in Windows Forms projects.

```
Private Sub Button1_Click(ByVal sender As Object, _
      ByVal e As System.Windows.RoutedEventArgs) _
      Handles Button1.Click
   MsgBox("Hello, World")
End Sub
```

Running this program with the F5 key gives us the expected form and button, but oh, what a complex-looking button it is (see Figure 18-16).

Figure 18-16. Click somewhere on the rainbow

Although the colors don't appear in this grayscale book, the form does indeed have a rainbow button.

Enhancing Classes with Attributes

Class-modifying attributes are something we discussed way back in Chapter 1, and they have nothing to do with GDI+. I just wanted to refresh your memory since they will be used in this chapter's project code.

Class- or member-modifying attributes appear just before the definition of the class or member, and within angle brackets. This code attaches the ObsoleteAttribute attribute to the SomeOldClass class:

```
<ObsoleteAttribute> _
Class SomeOldClass
   ...class details here...
End Class
```

(You can leave the "Attribute" part of an attribute's name off if the first part of the name doesn't conflict with any Visual Basic keyword.) Attributes appear as metadata in the final compiled assembly, and they are used by classes and applications that, by design, extract meaning from specific attributes. In this chapter's code, we'll make use of the `PropertyGrid` control, the control that implements the Properties panel within the Visual Studio development environment, and is often used to modify `Form` and `Control` properties. This control is available for your use in your own applications. To use it, assign a class instance to the control's `SelectedObject` property. Then, magically, all of the object's properties appear in the control's list of properties.

Nice as this is, it's not always desirable. Your object may have properties that should not be displayed. The `PropertyGrid` control is designed to be generic; it doesn't know about your object's needs, so it doesn't know which properties to exclude. That is, it doesn't know until you tell it through attributes. By adding specific attributes to your class's properties, you tell the `PropertyGrid` control how to treat members of your object. For instance, the `BrowsableAttribute` attribute tells the `PropertyGrid` to include (`True`) or exclude (`False`) the property.

```
<Browsable(False)> _
Public Property SecretProperty( ) As String...
```

I'll supply additional details about this when we use the `PropertyGrid` control later in this chapter.

Summary

Although many parts of GDI+ are pretty much wrappers around the old GDI system, GDI+ still manages to provide power and simplicity that go way beyond the original implementation. In business development, you won't always have a need to use the more interesting aspects of the `System.Drawing` namespace. But when you do, you'll encounter a simple and coherent system for displaying images, text, and custom vector elements on the screen or other output medium.

And speaking of simple and coherent, look for WPF at a computer near you. As more and more programmers cozy up to the new system, it may eventually supplant both the Windows Forms and the ASP.NET page system as the primary presentation layer in .NET desktop and web applications.

Project

The Library Project has used features of GDI+ since the moment the first form appeared in the newly created project, but it all came for free through code included in the framework. Now it's time for you, the programmer, to add your own GDI+ contribution to the application. In this chapter's project code, we'll use GDI+ to enhance the normal display of a control through owner draw features. Plus, we'll finally begin to implement some of the bar code features I tempted you with in earlier chapters. I'm sorry to say that we won't be using the cool XML drawing experience that is WPF.

Install the Bar Code Font

If you haven't yet obtained a bar code font, now is the time to do it. The features
included in this chapter's project code will require you to use such a font. The publisher web site for this book (listed in Appendix A) includes suggested resources for
obtaining a font at little or no cost for your personal use. You may also purchase a
professional bar code font. Make sure the font you obtain is a TrueType font.

Using Owner Draw

In the previous chapter, we added the *ItemLookup.vb* form with its multiple views of
library items. One of those views included the MatchingItems control, a multicolumn
listbox displaying Author/Name, Call Number, and Media Type columns. Although we
stored the column-specific data within each item already, we didn't actually display
the individual columns to the user.

The thing about multicolumn lists and other limited-space text displays is that some
of the text is bound to overrun its "official" area if you let it. For instance, the text in
one list column may overlap into another column of text. In such cases, it has
become the tradition to chop off the extended content and replace it with an ellipsis
("…"). So, we'll need a routine that will determine whether a string is too long for its
display area, and perform the chopping and ellipsizing as needed. Add the
FitTextToWidth method to the *General.vb* file's module code.

_____

INSERT SNIPPET

Insert Chapter 18, Snippet Item 1.

_____

```
Public Function FitTextToWidth(ByVal origText As String, _
      ByVal pixelWidth As Integer, _
      ByVal canvas As System.Drawing.Graphics, _
      ByVal useFont As System.Drawing.Font) As String
   ' ----- Given a text string, make sure it fits in the
   '       specified pixel width. Truncate and add an
   '       ellipsis if needed.
   Dim newText As String
```

```
      newText = origText
      If (canvas.MeasureString(newText, useFont).Width( ) > _
            pixelWidth) Then
         Do While (canvas.MeasureString(newText & "...", _
               useFont).Width( ) > pixelWidth)
            newText = Left(newText, newText.Length - 1)
            If (newText = "") Then Exit Do
         Loop
         If (newText <> "") Then newText &= "..."
      End If
      Return newText
   End Function
```

The *ItemLookup.vb* form has a web-browser-like Back button with a drop-down list
of recent entries. The items added to this list may include long book titles and author
names. Let's use the new FitTextToWidth method to limit the size of text items in this
list. Open the source code for the ItemLookup form and locate the RefreshBackButtons
method. About halfway through this routine is this line of code:

```
whichMenu.Text = scanHistory.HistoryDisplay
```

Replace this line with the following lines instead.

INSERT SNIPPET

Insert Chapter 18, Snippet Item 2.

```
whichMenu.Text = FitTextToWidth(scanHistory.HistoryDisplay, _
   Me.Width \ 2, useCanvas, whichMenu.Font)
```

That will limit any menu item text to half the width of the form, which seems reasonable to me. That useCanvas variable is new, so add a declaration for it at the top of
the RefreshBackButtons method.

INSERT SNIPPET

Insert Chapter 18, Snippet Item 3.

```
Dim useCanvas As Drawing.Graphics = Me.CreateGraphics( )
```

Also, we need to properly dispose of that created graphics canvas at the very end of
the method.

INSERT SNIPPET

Insert Chapter 18, Snippet Item 4.

```
useCanvas.Dispose( )
```

Now let's tackle owner draw list items. ListBox controls allow you to use your own custom drawing code for each visible item in the list. You have two options when you are managing the item drawing by yourself: you can keep every item a consistent height, or you can make each list item a different height based on the content for that item. In the MatchingItems listbox, we'll use the same height for every list item.

To enable owner draw mode, open the ItemLookup form design editor, select the MatchingItems listbox on the form or through the Properties panel, and change its DrawMode property to OwnerDrawFixed.

Each matching list item will include two rows of data: (1) the title of the matching item, in bold; and (2) the three columns of author, call number, and media type data. Add the following code to the form's Load event handler that determines the entire height of each list item, and the position of the second line within each item.

INSERT SNIPPET

Insert Chapter 18, Snippet Item 5.

```
' ----- Prepare the form.
Dim formGraphics As System.Drawing.Graphics

' ----- Set the default height of items in the matching
'       items listbox.
formGraphics = Me.CreateGraphics()
MatchingItems.ItemHeight = CInt(formGraphics.MeasureString( _
   "A" & vbCrLf & "g", MatchingItems.Font).Height()) + 3
SecondItemRow = CInt(formGraphics.MeasureString("Ag", _
   MatchingItems.Font).Height()) + 1
formGraphics.Dispose()
```

I used the text "Ag" to make sure that the height included all of the font's ascenders and descenders (the parts that stick up and stick down from most letters). I think the calculation would include those values even if I used "mm" for the string, but better safe than sorry, I always say. Setting the MatchingItems.ItemHeight property here indicates the size of all items in the list. If we had decided to use variable-height items instead of fixed-height items, we would have handled the control's MeasureItem event. With fixed items, we can ignore that event, and move on to the event that does the actual drawing: DrawItem.

Here is what the code is going to do for each list item: (1) create the necessary brushes and font objects we will use in drawing; (2) draw the text strings on the list item canvas; and (3) clean up. Since list items can also be selected or unselected, we'll call some framework-supplied methods to draw the proper background and foreground elements that indicate item selections.

When we draw the multiple columns of text, it's possible that one column of text will be too long, and intrude into the next column area. This was why we wrote the

FitTextToWidth function earlier. But it turns out that GDI+ already includes a feature that adds ellipses to text at just the right place when it doesn't fit. It's found in a class called StringFormat, in its Trimming property. Setting this property to EllipsisCharacter and using it when drawing the string will trim the string when appropriate. When we draw the string on the canvas, we will provide a rectangle that tells the string what its limits are. Here is the basic code used to draw one column of truncated text:

```
Dim ellipsesText As New StringFormat
ellipsesText.Trimming = StringTrimming.EllipsisCharacter
e.Graphics.DrawString("Some Long Text", e.Font, someBrush, _
    New Rectangle(left, top, width, height), ellipsesText)
```

The code we'll use to draw each list item in the MatchingItems list will use code just like this. Let's add that code now to the MatchingItems.DrawItem event handler.

INSERT SNIPPET

Insert Chapter 18, Snippet Item 6.

```
' ----- Draw the matching items on two lines.
Dim itemToDraw As MatchingItemData
Dim useBrush As System.Drawing.Brush
Dim boldFont As System.Drawing.Font
Dim ellipsesText As StringFormat

' ----- Draw the background of the item.
If (CBool(CInt(e.State) And CInt(DrawItemState.Selected))) _
    Then useBrush = SystemBrushes.HighlightText _
    Else useBrush = SystemBrushes.WindowText
e.DrawBackground( )

' ----- The title will use a bold version of the main font.
boldFont = New System.Drawing.Font(e.Font, FontStyle.Bold)

' ----- Obtain the item to draw.
itemToDraw = CType(MatchingItems.Items(e.Index), _
    MatchingItemData)
ellipsesText = New StringFormat
ellipsesText.Trimming = StringTrimming.EllipsisCharacter

' ----- Draw the text of the item.
e.Graphics.DrawString(itemToDraw.Title, boldFont, useBrush, _
    New Rectangle(0, e.Bounds.Top, _
    ItemColEnd.Left - MatchingItems.Left, _
    boldFont.Height), ellipsesText)
e.Graphics.DrawString(itemToDraw.Author, e.Font, useBrush, _
    New Rectangle(ItemColAuthor.Left, _
    e.Bounds.Top + SecondItemRow, _
    ItemColCall.Left - ItemColAuthor.Left - 8, _
    e.Font.Height), ellipsesText)
```

```
e.Graphics.DrawString(itemToDraw.CallNumber, e.Font, _
    useBrush, New Rectangle(ItemColCall.Left, _
    e.Bounds.Top + SecondItemRow, _
    ItemColEnd.Left - ItemColType.Left, _
    e.Font.Height), ellipsesText)
e.Graphics.DrawString(itemToDraw.MediaType, e.Font, _
    useBrush, New Rectangle(ItemColType.Left, _
    e.Bounds.Top + SecondItemRow, _
    ItemColType.Left - ItemColCall.Left - 8, _
    e.Font.Height), ellipsesText)

' ----- If the ListBox has focus, draw a focus rectangle.
e.DrawFocusRectangle( )
boldFont.Dispose( )
```

See, it's amazingly easy to draw anything you want in a listbox item. In this code, the actual output to the canvas via GDI+ amounted to just the four DrawString statements. Although this library database doesn't support it, we could have included an image of each item in the database, and displayed it in this listbox, just to the left of the title. Also, the calls to e.DrawBackground and e.DrawFocusRectangle let the control deal with properly highlighting the right item (although I did have to choose the proper text brush). Figure 18-17 shows the results of our hard labor.

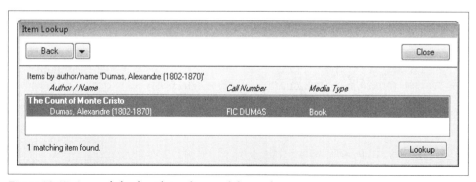

Figure 18-17. A sample book with two lines and three columns

Bar Code Design

The Library Project includes generic support for bar code labels. I visited a few libraries in my area and compared the bar codes added to both their library items (such as books) and their patron ID cards. I found that the variety was too great to shoehorn into a single predefined solution. Therefore, the Library application allows an administrator or librarian to design sheets of bar code labels to meet their specific needs. (There are businesses that sell preprinted bar code labels and cards to libraries that don't want to print their own. The application also supports this method, since bar code generation and bar code assignment to items are two distinct steps.)

To support generic bar code design, we will add a set of design classes and two forms to the application:

BarcodeItemClass.vb

This class file contains six distinct classes, one of which is a base class for the other five derived classes. The derived classes design the static text elements, bar code images, bar code numbers, lines, and rectangles that the user will add to the surface of a single bar code label.

BarcodePage.vb

This is an editor form derived from `BaseCodeForm`, the same base form used for the various code editors in the application. This form specifies the arrangement of label sheets. The user will probably purchase label sheets from his local office supply store. By entering the number of label rows and columns, the size of each label, and any spacing between and around each label, the user can design on pretty much any regular sheet of labels.

BarcodeLabel.vb

Another editor based on `BaseCodeForm`, this form lets the user design a single bar code label by adding text, bar codes, lines, and rectangles to a preview area.

In a future chapter, we'll add label printing, where labels and pages are joined together in one glorious print job.

Since these three files together include around 2,000 lines of source code, I will show you only key sections of each one. I've already added all three files to your project code, so let's start with *BarcodeItemClass.vb*. It defines each type of display item that the user will add to a label template in the *BarcodeLabel.vb* form. Here's the code for the abstract base class, BarcodeItemGeneric:

```
Imports System.ComponentModel
Public MustInherit Class BarcodeItemGeneric
    <Browsable(False)> Public MustOverride ReadOnly _
        Property ItemType( ) As String
    Public MustOverride Overrides _
        Function ToString( ) As String
End Class
```

Not much going on here. The class defines two required members: a read-only String property named ItemType, and a requirement that derived classes provide their own implementation for ToString. The other five derived classes in this file enhance the base class to support the distinct types of display elements included on a bar code label. Let's look briefly at one of the classes, BarcodeItemRect. It allows an optionally filled rectangle to appear on a bar code label, and includes private members that track the details of the rectangle.

```
Public Class BarcodeItemRect
    ' ----- Includes a basic rectangle element in a
    '       bar code label.
    Inherits BarcodeItemGeneric
```

```
' ----- Private store of attributes.
Private StoredRectLeft As Single
Private StoredRectTop As Single
Private StoredRectWidth As Single
Private StoredRectHeight As Single
Private StoredRectColor As Drawing.Color
Private StoredFillColor As Drawing.Color
Private StoredRectAngle As Short
```

The rest of the class includes properties that provide the public interface to these private members. Here's the code for the public `FillColor` property:

```
<Browsable(True), DescriptionAttribute( _
"Sets the fill color of the rectangle.")> _
Public Property FillColor() As Drawing.Color
    ' ----- The fill color.
    Get
        Return StoredFillColor
    End Get
    Set(ByVal Value As Drawing.Color)
        StoredFillColor = Value
    End Set
End Property
```

Like most of the other properties, it just sets and retrieves the related private value. Its declaration includes two attributes that will be read by the `PropertyGrid` control later on. The `Browsable` property says, "Yes, include this property in the grid," and `DescriptionAttribute` sets the text that appears in the bottom help area of the `PropertyGrid` control.

When you've used the Properties panel to edit your forms, you've been able to set colors for a color property using a special color selection tool built into the property. Just having a property defined using `System.Drawing.Color` is enough to enable this same functionality for your own class. How does it work? Just as the `FillColor` property has attributes recognized by the `PropertyGrid` control, the `System.Drawing.Color` class also has such properties, one of which defines a custom property editor class for colors. Its implementation is beyond the scope of this book, but it's cool anyway. If you're interested in doing this for your own classes, you can read an article I wrote about property grid editors a few years ago.[*]

Before we get to the editor forms, I need to let you know about four supporting functions I already added to the *General.vb* module file:

`BuildFontStyle` *function*

Font styles (such as bold and italic) are set in `Font` objects using members of the `System.Drawing.FontStyle` enumeration. But when storing font information in the database, I chose to store these style settings using letters (such as B for bold). This function converts the letters back to a `FontStyle` value.

---

[*] You can find the article referenced on my web site, *http://www.timaki.com*, in the Articles section.

ConvertPageUnits *function*

The label editors let you position items in a few different measurement systems, including inches and centimeters. This function converts measurements between the different systems.

DBFontStyle *function*

This is the opposite of the BuildFontStyle function, preparing a FontStyle value for insertion into a database record.

GetBarcodeFont *function*

This returns the name of the bar code font, if configured.

The BarcodePage form lets the user define a full sheet of labels. Not the labels themselves, but the positions of multiple labels on the same printed page. Figure 18-18 shows the fields on the form with some sample data.

Figure 18-18. The BarcodePage form

Collectively, the fields on the form describe the size of the page and the size of each label that appears on the page. As the user enters the values, the Page Preview area instantly refreshes with a preview of what the page will look like.

As a code editor derived from BaseCodeForm, the logic in the form is already familiar to you; it manages the data found in a single record from the BarcodeSheet table. What's different is the GDI+ code found in the PreviewArea.Paint event handler. Its first main block of code tries to determine how you scale down an 8.5×11 piece of paper to make it appear in a small rectangle that is only 216×272 pixels in size. It's a lot of gory calculations that, when complete, determine the big-to-small-paper ratio, and lead to the drawing of the on-screen piece of paper with a border and a drop shadow.

```
e.Graphics.FillRectangle(SystemBrushes.ControlDark, _
    pageLeft + 1, pageTop + 1, pageWidth + 2, pageHeight + 2)
e.Graphics.FillRectangle(SystemBrushes.ControlDark, _
    pageLeft + 2, pageTop + 2, pageWidth + 2, pageHeight + 2)
e.Graphics.FillRectangle(Brushes.Black, pageLeft - 1, _
    pageTop - 1, pageWidth + 2, pageHeight + 2)
e.Graphics.FillRectangle(Brushes.White, pageLeft, _
    pageTop, pageWidth, pageHeight)
```

Then, before drawing the preview outlines of each rectangular label, it repositions the grid origin to the upper-left corner of the on-screen piece of paper, and transforms the world scale based on the ratio of a real-world piece of paper and the on-screen image of it.

```
e.Graphics.TranslateTransform(pageLeft, pageTop)
e.Graphics.ScaleTransform(useRatio, useRatio)
```

There are a few more calculations for the size of each label, followed by a double loop (for both rows and columns of labels) that does the actual printing of the label boundaries (detail calculations omitted for brevity).

```
For rowScan = 1 To CInt(BCRows.Text)
    For colScan = 1 To CInt(BCColumns.Text)
        leftOffset = ...
        topOffset = ...
        e.Graphics.DrawRectangle(Pens.Cyan, _
            leftOffset, topOffset, _
            oneWidthTwips, oneHeightTwips)
    Next colScan
Next rowScan
```

The BarcodeLabel form is clearly the more interesting and complex of the two bar code editing forms. While the BarcodePage form defines an entire sheet of labels with nothing inside each label, BarcodeLabel defines what goes inside each of those labels. Figure 18-19 shows this form with a sample label.

The BarcodeLabel form does derive from BaseCodeForm, so much of its code deals with the loading and saving of records from the BarcodeLabel and BarcodeLabelItem database tables. Each bar code label is tied to a specific bar code page template (which we just defined through the BarcodePage form), and stores its primary record in the BarcodeLabel table. This table defines the basics of the label, such as its name and measurement system. The text and shape items placed on that label are stored as records in the related BarcodeLabelItem table.

Figure 18-19. The BarcodeLabel form

The `PrepareFormFields` routine loads existing label records from the database, creating instances of classes from the new *BarcodeItemClass.vb* file, and adds them to the `DisplayItems` ListBox control. Here's the section of code that loads in a "bar code image" (the actual displayed bar code) from an entry in the `BarcodeLabelItems` table:

```
newBarcodeImage = New Library.BarcodeItemBarcodeImage
newBarcodeImage.Alignment = CType(CInt(dbInfo!Alignment), _
    System.Drawing.ContentAlignment)
newBarcodeImage.BarcodeColor = _
    System.Drawing.Color.FromArgb(CInt(dbInfo!Color1))
newBarcodeImage.BarcodeSize = CSng(dbInfo!FontSize)
newBarcodeImage.Left = CSng(dbInfo!PosLeft)
newBarcodeImage.Top = CSng(dbInfo!PosTop)
newBarcodeImage.Width = CSng(dbInfo!PosWidth)
newBarcodeImage.Height = CSng(dbInfo!PosHeight)
newBarcodeImage.RotationAngle = CShort(dbInfo!Rotation)
newBarcodeImage.PadDigits = _
    CByte(DBGetInteger(dbInfo!PadDigits))
DisplayItems.Items.Add(newBarcodeImage)
```

The user can add new shapes, text elements, and bar codes to the label by clicking on one of the five Add Items buttons that appear just below the DisplayItems control. Each button adds a default record to the label, which the user can then modify. As each label element is selected from the DisplayItems, its properties appear in the ItemProperties control, an instance of a PropertyGrid control. Modification of a label element is a matter of changing its properties. Figure 18-20 shows a color property being changed.

Figure 18-20. Modifying a label element property

As with the BarcodePage form, the real fun in the BarcodeLabel form comes through the Paint event of the label preview control, PreviewArea. This 300+ line routine starts out drawing the blank surface of the label with a drop shadow. Then it processes each element in the DisplayItems list, one by one, transforming and drawing each element as its properties indicate. As it passes through the element list, the code applies transforms to the drawing area as needed. To keep things tidy for each element, the state of the surface is saved before changes are made, and restored once changes are complete.

```
For counter = 0 To DisplayItems.Items.Count - 1
    ' ----- Save the current state of the graphics area.
    holdState = e.Graphics.Save( )

    ...main drawing code goes here, then...
```

```
' ----- Restore the original transformed state of
'       the graphics surface.
    e.Graphics.Restore(holdState)
Next counter
```

Each element type's code performs the various size, position, and rotation transformations needed to properly display the element. Let's take a closer look at the code that displays static text elements (code that is also called to display bar code text). After scaling down the world view to the label surface preview area, any user-requested rotation is performed about the upper-left corner of the rectangle that holds the printed text.

```
e.Graphics.TranslateTransform(X1, Y1)
e.Graphics.RotateTransform(textAngle)
```

Next, a gray dashed line is drawn around the text object to show its selected state.

```
pixelPen = New System.Drawing.Pen(Color.LightGray, _
    1 / e.Graphics.DpiX)
pixelPen.DashStyle = Drawing2D.DashStyle.Dash
e.Graphics.DrawRectangle(pixelPen, X1, Y1, X2, Y2)
pixelPen.Dispose()
```

After setting some flags to properly align the text vertically and horizontally within its bounding box, the standard `DrawString` method thrusts the text onto the display.

```
e.Graphics.DrawString(textMessage, useFont, _
    New System.Drawing.SolidBrush(textColor), _
    New Drawing.RectangleF(X1, Y1, X2, Y2), textFormat)
```

We will somewhat duplicate the label drawing code included in the `BarcodeLabel` class when we print actual labels in a later chapter.

The only thing left to do is to link up these editors to the main form. Since I've had so much fun with these forms, I'll let you play for a while in the code. Open the code for `MainForm`, locate the event handler for the `AdminLinkBarcodeLabel.LinkClicked` event, and add the following code.

INSERT SNIPPET

Insert Chapter 18, Snippet Item 7.

```
' ----- Let the user edit the list of bar code labels.
If (SecurityProfile( _
        LibrarySecurity.ManageBarcodeTemplates) = False) Then
    MsgBox(NotAuthorizedMessage, MsgBoxStyle.OkOnly Or _
    MsgBoxStyle.Exclamation, ProgramTitle)
    Return
End If
```

```
' ----- Edit the records.
ListEditRecords.ManageRecords(New Library.BarcodeLabel)
ListEditRecords = Nothing
```

Do the same for the `AdminLinkBarcodePage.LinkClicked` event handler. Its code is almost identical except for the class instance passed to `ListEditRecords`.

INSERT SNIPPET

Insert Chapter 18, Snippet Item 8.

```
' ----- Let the user edit the list of bar code pages.
If (SecurityProfile( _
     LibrarySecurity.ManageBarcodeTemplates) = False) Then
   MsgBox(NotAuthorizedMessage, MsgBoxStyle.OkOnly Or _
   MsgBoxStyle.Exclamation, ProgramTitle)
   Return
End If

' ----- Edit the records.
ListEditRecords.ManageRecords(New Library.BarcodePage)
ListEditRecords = Nothing
```

Fun with Graphics

GDI+ isn't all about serious drawing stuff; you can also have some fun. Let's make a change to the *AboutProgram.vb* form so that it fades out when the user clicks its Close button. This involves altering the form's `Opacity` property to slowly increase the transparency of the form. From our code's point of view, no GDI+ is involved. But it's still involved through the hidden code that responds to the `Opacity` property.

Open the source code for the *AboutProgram.vb* file, and add the following code to the end of the `AboutProgram.Load` event handler.

INSERT SNIPPET

Insert Chapter 18, Snippet Item 9.

```
' ----- Prepare the form for later fade-out.
Me.Opacity = 0.99
```

Although this statement isn't really necessary, I found that the form tended to blink a little on some systems when the opacity went from 100% (1.0) to anything else (99%, or 0.99, in this case). This blink was less noticeable when I made the transition during the load process.

In the event handler for the `ActClose.Click` event, include this code.

```
' ----- Fade the form out.
Dim counter As Integer

For counter = 90 To 10 Step -20
   Me.Opacity = counter / 100
   Me.Refresh( )
   Threading.Thread.Sleep(50)
Next counter
Me.DialogResult = Windows.Forms.DialogResult.Cancel
```

This code slowly fades out the form over the course of 250 milliseconds, in five distinct steps. So that the form doesn't close abruptly before the cool fade-out, open the form designer, select the ActClose button, and change its DialogResult property to None.

Another thing we never did was to set the primary icon for the application. Although this isn't strictly GDI+, it does involve graphics display, which impacts the user's perception of the program's quality. I've included an icon named *Book.ico* in the project's file set. Open the project properties, select the Application tab, and use the Icon field to browse for the *Book.ico* file.

While testing out the icon, I noticed that the splash window appeared (with the default Visual Studio icon) in the Windows task bar. In fact, each opened form appeared in the task bar, right alongside the main form's entry. This is non-standard, and it's all due to the ShowInTaskbar property setting included in each form. I've taken the liberty of going through all the forms (except for MainForm) and setting this property to False. Most of the forms were already set properly, so I altered the dozen or so that were set improperly.

The Library application is really starting to bulk up with features. In fact, by the next chapter, we will have added more than 95% of its total code. I can see the excitement on your face. Go ahead, turn the page, and add to your coding enjoyment.

Localization and Globalization

Bienvenue à chapitre dix-neuf! My apologies to those of you who don't speak French—and also to those who actually do. I took four full years of the language in high school, but for some reason, it didn't stick. I can still remember a few important sentences, such as «*Je suis un garçon*» and «*Où est le crayon?*», but that's about it. We even read *Candide* and *Le Petit Prince* in class, but to no avail. I did take Japanese in college, and found it much easier to digest than French. So, perhaps I should instead say 第十九章にようこそ.

In an attempt to expand this book beyond the shores of English-speaking nations, I localized that previous paragraph. In an attempt to expand the appeal of your own applications beyond the English-speaking world, .NET provides features that let you *localize* your project in another language, even after your software has been compiled and released.

Coverage of all localization features in .NET would include lunar- and emperor reign-based calendars, and right-to-left writing systems. This chapter covers only some of the more common user interface localization features. Hopefully, it will entice you to push the language limits of your own applications, reaching out to *les étoiles*.

Defining Globalization and Localization

Microsoft has hundreds of for-sale and freely available software applications, and the company makes a lot of money worldwide providing these software products to consumers. Most of its products are developed in the United States, written by programmers who speak mainly English, directed by technical leads and product managers who make decisions in English, marketed by a sales team that plans out campaigns in English, and dogged by competitors and detractors who blast the motives and business practices behind each product in English. So, how is it possible that Microsoft can sell software to non-English speakers around the globe?

The key lies in the globalization and localization of its products. Sure, Microsoft or any other company could develop distinct yet identical products, each in a different language, and sell them in the appropriate markets. But that would be expensive and time-consuming. Instead, it writes a single program, and then enhances it with language- and culture-specific features.

Globalization is the process of preparing software so that it can be easily adjusted for each language and culture market. No foreign terms are added to software during the globalization process. Instead, the developers design the application so that all relevant English (in my case) terms and American cultural elements (such as currency displays in U.S. dollars) can be quickly and easily replaced by foreign substitutes, all without impacting the core software elements.

Windows applications have traditionally used *resources* to keep applications globally generic. Resources contain text strings, images, and other non-code elements that are replaced at runtime based on the active language and culture of the operating system. On a German-language system, the application loads its German-language resources (if available) and displays them instead of the default resources. The .NET Framework continues to use resources for this purpose, although it enhances resource development through XML-based resource files and tools.

Localization adds the actual non-native language and culture elements to an application. It is in this step that, say, English-language form labels get translated into Swahili, or some other target language. Visual Studio lets you localize an application within the development environment itself, or through external tools that translators who have no access to the application source code can use.

The good news for .NET developers is that Microsoft pretty much took care of the globalization part for you. You mainly need to focus on localizing your application. Your local community college offers foreign language instruction in a dozen or so languages, so I'll let you choose your first localization target.

Resource Files

Resource files are the key to language localization in .NET programs. Visual Studio will write the files for you, but it's good to know something about how they work, since you may want to craft your own resource files (if you have a lot of time on your hands). The life of a resource moves through three phases, as determined by the type of file in which it appears:

Source

An application's resources start their lives in a resource source file. Before .NET, resources appeared in "resource script" files, which merged all the best of C-language development and UPPER CASE SCRIPT COMMANDS, and used an *.rc* file extension. In Visual Basic 2008, you use XML-based *.resx* files. Every new Windows Forms application already includes a *Resources.resx* file just waiting to be joyfully filled with your application resources.

Beyond the core resource source files, other file types can be included as resources, although they are still referenced through the *.resx* file content. Common external resource files include image files (such as *.gif* and *.jpg* files) and plain-text files (*.txt*). The Library Project uses a file named *SplashImage.jpg* as a resource for the splash screen, and another file named *ItemLookupBody.txt* that contains HTML content used when displaying items through the *ItemLookup.vb* form.

Intermediate

Once you have your resource sources ready, they are converted into an inter-mediate form, and stored with a *.resources* file extension, through a process called *resource generation*. Visual Studio normally does this step behind the scenes for you, but you can also use a tool supplied with the .NET SDK (called *resgen.exe*) to generate these files yourself. Intermediate resource files include binary content only, and are not designed for browsing in Notepad.

Compiled

Intermediate resource files aren't much use to your deployed application. The term *intermediate* kind of gave this secret away, didn't it? Before employing the resources in your program, they need to be compiled into a DLL or EXE file. Per-haps you already knew that these files contained multiple sections, including dis-tinct code and data sections. A compiled resource file contains only a data section with the resources; there is no code in a compiled resource file, although standard compiled code files may also include compiled resources.

In .NET, compiled resource files are satellite assemblies. They support your pri-mary application assembly, and are not generally useful apart from that master assembly.

Figure 19-1 shows the lifetime of a resource through these three stages.

Some standard resource types are stored in .NET resource (*.resx*) files:

Strings

We'll focus primarily on string resources in this chapter. Each string resource includes a name and a string value.

Images

Visual Basic applications can include JPEG, GIF, TIFF, PNG, and BMP image files. Each image, as with all resources, includes an associated name, which may differ from the original name of the graphics file.

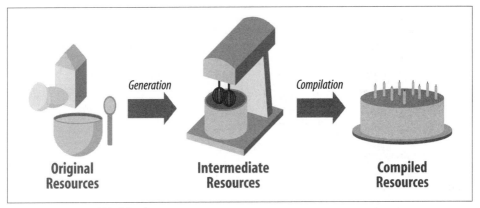

Figure 19-1. The edible life of a resource

Icons

Program icons used with forms and the application itself appear as standard resources. Icons have an *.ico* file extension.

Audio

Resources can include named audio files, based on WAV audio content.

Files

If the file types listed so far don't meet your needs, you can include whole files of any type as a named resource.

Other

Beyond files, you can store the content of any valid .NET data type as a resource. The resources in a *.resx* file are actually strongly typed to .NET types, so there's really no limit to the type of data you can place there. You can also modify the underlying *.resx* file to include "non-standard" resources. Non-standard resources are beyond the scope of this chapter.

The project properties window includes a manager for application-wide resources (see Figure 19-2). The IDE also includes special editors that let you edit standard and a few non-standard resource types.

The My.Resources Object

We discussed this in earlier chapters, but as a reminder, you can access an application's resources through the `My.Resources` object. If you have a string resource named `MainFormCaption`, the following reference returns its value:

```
My.Resources.MainFormCaption
```

All resources are strongly typed. In this case, `MainFormCaption` is of type `System.String`. The `SplashImage` image resource included in the Library Project is declared as type `System.Drawing.Bitmap`. Because each resource is strongly typed, you can use the `My.Resources` reference in your code just like any data of the resource's type.

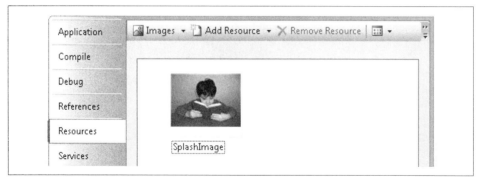

Figure 19-2. The resource manager for the Library Project in Visual Studio

In new Windows Forms applications, all application-wide resources appear in the *Resources.resx* file, found in the *My Project* directory within the application's source code directory. You can view it in Notepad if you want. It's a pretty big XML file that doesn't immediately interest me, except that it works! Here's the portion of the Library Project's *Resources.resx* file that specifies our two existing resources. (I've wrapped some of the lines to make it fit on the page.) I've highlighted the name of each resource, and their strong data types.

```
<data name="ItemLookupBody"
  type="System.Resources.ResXFileRef, System.Windows.Forms">
  <value>..\Resources\ItemLookupBody.txt;System.String,
    mscorlib, Version=2.0.0.0, Culture=neutral,
    PublicKeyToken=b77a5c561934e089;Windows-1252</value>
</data>

<data name="SplashImage"
  type="System.Resources.ResXFileRef, System.Windows.Forms">
  <value>..\Resources\SplashImage.jpg;System.Drawing.Bitmap,
    System.Drawing, Version=2.0.0.0, Culture=neutral,
    PublicKeyToken=b03f5f7f11d50a3a</value>
</data>
```

Each form you add to your project also has its own private resource file. The one for `Form1` is called *Form1.resx*. These files end up being a big plus in the localization of Windows Forms applications.

Behind the scenes, your application is taking an object-oriented approach to resource management. It's using the `System.Resources.ResourceManager` class to locate and return instances of each resource when you need it. And this same class makes decisions about which language-specific or culture-specific resources—from the dozens I'm sure you'll have added to your application—will be made visible to the user.

Localizing Forms Within Visual Studio

There's no sense in postponing the introduction to the localization features of Visual Studio, since they are so easy to use. You already know about the application-wide project properties resource editor. Instead, let's look at the amazing part: localizing forms and controls right in the Visual Studio form editor. You might as well start up Visual Studio and try it out with me, because it's just so fun.

Here's a cute but relatively harmless Windows Forms application that writes your name upside down. I added some `Label` controls, a `TextBox` control, and a `PictureBox` control to a form, as shown in Figure 19-3.

Figure 19-3. A typical Windows Forms application

Then I added the following source code to the form:

```
Private Sub TextBox1_TextChanged( _
      ByVal sender As System.Object, _
      ByVal e As System.EventArgs) _
      Handles TextBox1.TextChanged
   ' ----- Force a redraw.
   PictureBox1.Invalidate( )
End Sub

Private Sub PictureBox1_Paint(ByVal sender As Object, _
      ByVal e As System.Windows.Forms.PaintEventArgs) _
      Handles PictureBox1.Paint
   ' ----- Draw the blank background.
   e.Graphics.Clear(SystemColors.Window)
   e.Graphics.DrawRectangle(SystemPens.InactiveCaption, _
      0, 0, PictureBox1.Width - 1, PictureBox1.Height - 1)

   ' ----- Change the orientation of the display.
   Dim saveState As Drawing2D.GraphicsState = _
      e.Graphics.Save( )
   Dim mirrorMatrix As New Drawing2D.Matrix( _
      1, 0, 0, -1, 0, PictureBox1.Height)
   e.Graphics.Transform = mirrorMatrix
```

```
' ----- Draw the text.
e.Graphics.DrawString(TextBox1.Text, TextBox1.Font, _
   SystemBrushes.WindowText, 1, 4)

' ----- Put everything back.
e.Graphics.Restore(saveState)
End Sub
```

When you run the program, it creates a mirror image of whatever you type in the TextBox control using GDI+ features. Figure 19-4 shows me playing with the program instead of meeting this chapter's submission deadline.

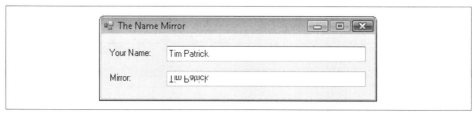

Figure 19-4. Look Ma, I'm upside down

As interesting as this program may be, it is neither fully globalized nor localized. It's *almost* globalized. All we need to do to fully globalize it is to "throw the switch" on the form that enables later localization. We do this through the form's Localizable property. Change this property from False to True. Ta-da! Your form is globalized!

Now for part 2: localization. Here are the steps to localize the form:

1. Determine which language or language-culture combination you want to localize.

2. Select that language or language-culture from the form's Language property. When you open this property list, it includes languages alone, such as "French," and languages combined with a culture or country, as with "French (Canada)." The language-alone entries are known as "neutral language" entries. You can use either type for localization. If you select, for instance, "French," users of your application in either France or French-speaking Canada will use the French resources. If you localize using "French (Canada)," French Canadian users will access the localized resources, but not French-language users in France.

3. Modify any of the properties of the form or its controls.

That's it. Whenever the form's Language property is changed to something other than (Default), Visual Studio starts recording all form and control changes into a separate form-specific *and* language- or language-culture-specific resource file.

You can localize the form with multiple languages. Each time you change the Language property to another language or language-culture selection, the changes to the form or controls apply only to that selection. Whatever you change gets saved in a separate resource file.

Let's try it with the sample mirror program. I'm going to choose Japanese for the localization language. First, I set the form's Language property to "Japanese." The form momentarily blinks, but there is no other noticeable change. It looks just as it did in Figure 19-3.

Next, I change the Text properties of the form and of each label control to their Japanese language equivalents (see Figure 19-5).

Figure 19-5. The name-mirror program in Japanese

Do you notice how the shorter Japanese language labels are farther away from the text and mirror display fields? Does it bother you as much as it bothers me? To get it out of my mind, I will resize the two fields a little larger by stretching them to the left, as I've done in Figure 19-6.

Figure 19-6. The Japanese version with adjusted fields

The amazing part is that if you set the form's Language property back to (Default), not only will the labels return to English, but the resized text and mirror fields will return to their "natural" sizes. Although I haven't checked out every property, the localization feature seems to impact all display elements of each control.

The program is now fully localized for English (the default language) and Japanese. Normally, the Japanese resource would be used only on a system running the Japanese version of Microsoft Windows. But we can force the program to use Japanese by changing its "user interface culture." In the application's startup code (the MyApplication_Startup routine in the *ApplicationEvents.vb* file), I add the following code:

```
Private Sub MyApplication_Startup(ByVal sender As Object, _
    ByVal e As Microsoft.VisualBasic.ApplicationServices. _
    StartupEventArgs) Handles Me.Startup
  If (MsgBox("Switch from English to Japanese?", _
      MsgBoxStyle.Question Or MsgBoxStyle.YesNo) = _
      MsgBoxResult.Yes) Then
```

```
            My.Application.ChangeUICulture("ja-JP")
        End If
    End Sub
```

And sure enough, running the program and saying "Yes" to the "Switch to Japanese" prompt presents a form in Japanese, as shown in Figure 19-7. (If you answer "No" to the question, the default language, English, appears.)

Figure 19-7. Look Ma, I'm Japanese

Let's look at the files created in this project. (Look in the installation directory of this book's code for the *Foreign Names* subdirectory. I've placed a copy of this mirror-text project there for you.) The source code directory includes a *Form1.resx* file, added by default to all new Windows Forms applications. But there is also a *Form1.ja.resx* file, the *Form1* resource file for the Japanese language. Visual Studio will compile this file into a language-specific resource when it builds the project. At that time, the code's *bin\Release* subdirectory will contain a further *ja* subdirectory with a file named *ForeignNames.resources.dll*. This is the satellite assembly that contains all of the Japanese language resources. If the application had included multiple forms, all of the Japanese resources for all forms would appear in that single DLL file.

Adding Resources Outside Visual Studio

Visual Studio makes localization quite easy. But it's rare that the developer of a major application would also be fluent in multiple target languages. And you certainly don't want non-programmers gaining access to your forms and code in Visual Studio, where they can do who-knows-what to its logic.

To keep foreign-language eyes and fingers where they belong, Microsoft wrote the Windows Resource Localization Editor, and included it with the Software Development Kit supplied with .NET. (On my system, it's located at Start → [All] Programs → Microsoft Windows SDK v6.0A → Tools → Windows Resource Localization Editor. Its command-line name is *winres.exe*.) When you are ready to have a translator convert a form to a specific language, you only need to provide them with this program, and the form's *.resx* file (such as *Form1.resx*). The program simulates the display of the form as it appears in Visual Studio, and lets the translator modify any relevant form or control properties for a specific language. Figure 19-8 shows ForeignNames's Form1 in the Localization Editor.

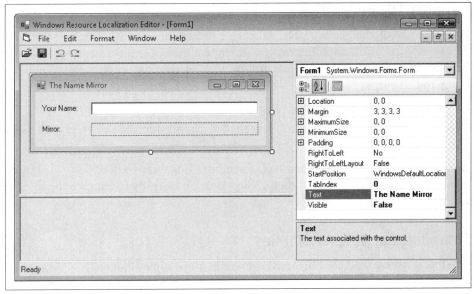

Figure 19-8. An amazing likeness of Form1, ready for translation

The program prompts for the target language or language-culture when you try to save changes. It outputs a language-specific *.resx* file (such as *Form1.ja.resx* for Japanese) that can be used in your application. Once you get the foreign resource files back from the translators, store them (the files, not the translators) in the project's source directory, and rebuild the project to generate the correct satellite assemblies.

Manually Compiling Resources

It's possible to generate the satellite assemblies manually from the source *.resx* files without rebuilding the entire project in Visual Studio. You will have to use the Windows command line (*cmd.exe*), and you will need access to the main assembly's EXE or DLL file. It's not for the faint of heart, and a single mistyped character could cost American taxpayers millions.

Figure 19-1 summarized the steps needed to move a *.resx* file into a satellite assembly. The "generate" and "compile" steps can be done using two command-line utilities: *resgen.exe* and *al.exe*. Doesn't that sound like great fun?

As with other .NET command-line tools, these tools need the command-line environment to be set up just so, or they will have a snit and refuse to run. To ensure that you have the correct environment, you need to open the special .NET version of the command line. The .NET SDK was installed when you installed the framework, so you should be able to find a Start-menu entry for it at Start → [All] Programs → Microsoft Visual Studio 2008 → Visual Studio Tools → Visual Studio 2008 Command Prompt.

Resource File Generation

Once you have a *.resx* file available, either by creating it manually or by using the Windows Resource Localization Editor, you generate a *.resources* file using *resgen.exe*, the Resource Generator command-line utility, part of the SDK toolset. It accepts an input and an output filename as its arguments.

```
resgen.exe Form1.ja.resx Form1.ja.resources
```

If you omit the output filename, *resgen* will simply replace the *.resx* extension with *.resources*.

If you have multiple foreign-language assemblies (for multiple forms, for instance), generate resource files for all of them. Then you will be ready to compile the satellite assembly.

Compiling Satellite Assemblies

.NET uses *al.exe*, the Assembly Linker program, to compile all of your .NET applications to their final assembly files. We'll use this same program to generate the satellite assemblies. Its command-line arguments were designed by a secret society, so getting them just right will take some work. Let's look at the command first, and then I'll explain it.

```
al.exe /target:lib
 ↳/embed:Form1.ja.resources,ForeignNames.Form1.ja.resources
 ↳/culture:ja
 ↳/out:ForeignNames.resources.dll
 ↳/template:bin\Release\ForeignNames.exe
```

You should enter these lines as one long line. I had to wrap them in the book because the publisher didn't want to do one of those fold-out pages that you see in some children's books. They didn't like my interactive "pop-up" Visual Studio environment idea, either (something about keeping the book at less than $100 per copy).

The options provided to *al.exe* work all of the magic:

/target:lib
    The lib part says, "Output a DLL-style file."

/embed
    This option indicates which source files you want to include in the output assembly. The first comma-delimited part indicates the source *filename*. The second part indicates the *name* by which this resource will be known in the application. The *name* must be in the format *basename.cultureName*.resources, where *basename* is the application name (for application-wide resources) or the class name (qualified with its namespace) for a specific class, such as Form1. Since my application and its default top-level namespace are both "ForeignNames," I've included that in the name component. You can add as many /embed options as you have resource files to include.

`/culture`

Although you will eventually put the satellite assembly in a folder named for the target culture, Visual Basic doesn't trust you. Instead, it wants a record of the culture embedded in the assembly itself. You do that through this command-line option.

`/out`

This option specifies the output name of the satellite file. You really need to use the name *application.resources.dll* for the file, where *application* is the same as your application's name before the *.exe* part. If you don't do this, it won't work. Well, you could still get it to work by adjusting the application's *app.config* file, but that file is just plain scary, so you don't want to go there.

`/template`

This is the option that says, "I'm making a satellite assembly, and the related primary assembly is *x*."

To use the satellite assembly, locate the directory that contains the main EXE assembly. Create a new subdirectory right there, giving it the name of the language or language-culture key used to create the assembly ("ja" in my case; "ja-JP" would have been an option if I created the assembly using "Japanese (Japan)"). Then put the new satellite assembly in that subdirectory.

Other Localization Features

Localization is more than just words on a screen. There are also issues of how you display times, dates, and monetary values to the user. The good news is that these features will work automatically if you *globalize* your program properly. Just as each .NET program maintains a "user interface culture" (which we played with in the sample program previously), it also has a "general culture" used for string manipulation of times, dates, financial values, and other similar culture-dependent things.

If you use core methods such as CDate to extract date values, instead of scanning through a user-entered date string by hand, you get culture-specific date processing for free. Also for output, if you use the predefined formats for the Format method (and other similar string output methods), you get correct culture-specific formatting for no additional effort on your part. Let's try a quick sample that displays money using the local currency.

I'm creating a new Windows Forms application. I'll add the following code to the *ApplicationEvents.vb* file:

```
Private Sub MyApplication_Startup(ByVal sender As Object, _
      ByVal e As Microsoft.VisualBasic.ApplicationServices. _
      StartupEventArgs) Handles Me.Startup
   If (MsgBox("Switch from English to Japanese?", _
      MsgBoxStyle.Question Or MsgBoxStyle.YesNo) = _
      MsgBoxResult.Yes) Then
```

```
    My.Application.ChangeCulture("ja-JP")
  End If
End Sub
```

This code block is almost identical to the one we used in the previous sample, but I'm calling `My.Application.ChangeCulture` instead of `My.Application.ChangeUICulture` (the `UI` part is missing). This changes the string-manipulation culture instead of the user interface culture.

Now I'll add the following code to `Form1`'s class:

```
Private Sub Form1_Load(ByVal sender As System.Object, _
    ByVal e As System.EventArgs) Handles MyBase.Load
  MsgBox(Format("500", "Currency"))
End Sub
```

Figure 19-9 shows the results of this code when run in both English and Japanese modes.

Figure 19-9. Spending money in two places at once

The Framework Class Libraries (FCLs) include even more culture management features in the `System.Globalization` namespace. The classes in this namespace let you manually adjust the output of culture-sensitive strings to meet your needs. Most of them are pretty esoteric and are intended for specific culture groups, so I won't be discussing them here.

Summary

It's a small world, after all. And the culture-specific features in .NET have helped to make it that way, at least for your software. I'm still amazed that I'm able to use Japanese on my English version of Microsoft Windows. (I first had to enable support for East Asian languages in the Control Panel's Regional and Language Options applet.) And now it's not just Windows or Microsoft Office that can automatically shift with the current culture. Politicians can do it, too. Oops, I mean that your own applications can do it, too. By taking advantage of culture-specific resources and the automatic and manual formatting features included with .NET, you'll soon be selling your snazzy business application in six of the seven continents.

Project

I know you're expecting me to localize all of the forms in the Library Project into Greek, and it is a tempting idea. But in the interest of brevity (and my sanity), I'll leave that as an exercise for the reader. (Muffled laughter.)

What we will do in this chapter's project code is to enable the remaining patron-specific tracking and management features. Those features include the management of fines for naughty patrons who don't return their library books on time. We'll use the generic currency formatting features discussed in this chapter to make the application as globally accessible as possible.

PROJECT ACCESS

Load the Chapter 19 (Before) Code project, either through the New Project templates or by accessing the project directly from the installation directory. To see the code in its final form, load Chapter 19 (After) Code instead.

Tracking Patron Payments

Let's create a class that exposes the important features of each set of payments applied to a specific checked-in item. Of course, they'll all be stored in the Library database. But keeping a summary of payments temporarily cached in memory simplifies some processing.

Add a new class item to the Library Project, giving it the name *PaymentItem.vb*. Define it using the following code.

INSERT SNIPPET

Insert Chapter 19, Snippet Item 1.

```
Public Class PaymentItem
    ' ----- Used to track and print payment tickets.
    Public ItemTitle As String
    Public PatronCopyID As Integer
    Public FeesPaid As Decimal
    Public BalanceDue As Decimal
End Class
```

Each instance of this class identifies the collected fines and payments for a specific library item (ItemTitle) and for the patron who turned in the item late (PatronCopyID).

Calculating Patron Fines

We also need to know the total fines owed by a patron for all items, even when we're not showing the details. Add the `CalculatePatronFines` function to the *General.vb* module.

INSERT SNIPPET

Insert Chapter 19, Snippet Item 2.

```
Public Function CalculatePatronFines( _
      ByVal patronID As Integer) As Decimal
   ' ----- Given a patron ID, calculate the fines due.
   Dim sqlText As String

   On Error GoTo ErrorHandler

   ' ----- Retrieve the fine records for the patron.
   sqlText = "SELECT SUM(Fine - Paid) FROM PatronCopy " & _
      "WHERE Patron = " & patronID
   Return DBGetDecimal(ExecuteSQLReturn(sqlText))

ErrorHandler:
   GeneralError("CalculatePatronFines", Err.GetException())
   Return 0@
End Function
```

It's pretty basic code, actually, since the database does all of the work of adding up the values. I checked the database documentation and confirmed that `Fine` and `Paid` are required fields, and will never be `NULL`. This keeps the SQL code terse.

Patron Record Access

Before reviewing a patron's record, the user must identify the patron. This is done through a Patron Record Access form, sort of a login form for patrons. Each patron is assigned a password, which must be supplied before the patron can access his or her record. Administrators can access a patron's record without providing the password.

I've already added the *PatronAccess.vb* form to your project; it appears in Figure 19-10.

This form's code is a lot like that found in the *ChangeUser.vb* form, a form that provides administrative access to the program, and that we added back in Chapter 11. The Patron Access form behaves a little differently for administrators and regular patrons.

- Regular patrons must either provide their bar code, or supply their name (full last name, optional wildcards on the first name) *and* their password. If they use a partial name instead of a bar code, and a search of that name results in multiple matches, they will have to provide a more correct entry of their name. (If two patrons have the same name, they will have to depend on bar codes; but this program is for a *small* library, so name conflicts should be rare.)

Figure 19-10. The Patron Access form, PatronAccess.vb

- Administrators enter the patron's name or bar code, but no password is needed. If there are multiple name matches, the form presents all matching names in a list, and the administrator can select the correct entry from the list. This gives an administrator full access to all patron records. It's obviously important for an administrator to log out when finished using a workstation that is available to patrons.

The `PatronAccess` form's `SelectPatron` method provides the interface to the form for both administrators and ordinary patrons. The function returns the ID of the selected patron, or –1 if the user didn't successfully access a patron record.

Patron Password Modification

Although administrators can change the password of each patron through the *Patron.vb* form, we don't want to give ordinary patrons access to that form and all of its raw, unadulterated power. But we still want the patrons to be able to change their own passwords, because it's the nice and secure thing to do. I've added the *PatronPassword.vb* form to your project to fulfill this purpose (see Figure 19-11).

Figure 19-11. The Patron Password form, PatronPassword.vb

The form is basically a dramatically reduced subset of the full *Patron.vb* form. Since it needs to deal with only active patrons, it doesn't have a lot of the *Patron.vb* code that differentiates between new and existing patron records. The focus of the Patron Password form is the update statement that sets the patron's password, in the SaveFormData method.

```
sqlText = "UPDATE Patron SET [Password] = " & _
   DBText(EncryptPassword("patron", _
   Trim(RecordPassword.Text))) & _
   " WHERE ID = " & ActiveID
ExecuteSQL(sqlText)
```

The word *Password* is a reserved keyword in SQL Server, so we need to "escape" it with square brackets when referring to the field in SQL statements.

Collecting Patron Payments

In a perfect world, patrons would never let their books and other library items reach the overdue state. Of course, in a perfect world, libraries would let you keep books you like indefinitely. And give me a break with those incessant overdue notices. What's up with that?

But for those small libraries that insist on charging fines for overdue items, the Library Project includes features for assigning and tracking fines. In a later chapter, we'll add the code that automatically calculates the fines for overdue items. Right now, we'll implement the form that lets you document patron payments and other financial adjustments to items in the patron's record.

I've added the PatronPayment form to the collection of project files, but it's not yet integrated into the project. Select the *PatronPayment.vb* file in the Solution Explorer, and then change its Build Action property (in the Properties panel) from None to Compile. Figure 19-12 shows the controls on this form.

Fines that are automatically added to an overdue item appear in the PatronCopy.Fine database field. Although that value is displayed on the Patron Payment form, it's not the primary focus of that form. Instead, the form exists to allow a librarian to enter charges and payments for a previously checked-out item, storing these updates in the PatronPayment database table. This table tracks four types of financial events for each item checked out by a patron:

- Additional fines imposed by a librarian or administrator. For example, a librarian may add the value of an item as a fine if it turns out that the patron has lost the item. Additional fine entries use the letter *F* in the PatronPayment.EntryType database field.
- Payments made by the patron for an overdue item. *P* is the entry type.
- A dismissal of some or all of the pending fines for an overdue item, indicated by a *D* entry type.
- If the entry type is *R*, the record indicates a refund paid to the patron by the library.

Figure 19-12. The Patron Payment form, PatronPayment.vb

Each PatronPayment table record includes a transaction date, the amount of the transaction, optional comments, and the identity of the administrative user recording the entry. To make the code a little clearer, the letter codes in the database table are converted into enumeration values from the EventEntryType enumeration.

```
Private Enum EventEntryType
    NotDefined
    PatronPayment
    FineAdded
    FineDismissal
    RefundToPatron
    OverdueFines
End Enum
```

The OverdueFines entry allows the PatronCopy.Fines value to be part of the displayed financial history on the form.

The librarian uses the fields in the New Payment Event section of the PatronPayment form to add charge and payment records. All previously added records appear in the EventHistory list, in the Payment Event History section of the form.

The calling form (added later in this chapter) needs to pass in the PatronCopy.ID value to identify the proper record. But the plan is to have payments added on this form flow back to the parent form. The two forms will share a set of PaymentItem objects using the class we added a few sections earlier in this chapter. We'll store it in a local member variable as a generic set.

```
Private PaymentsOnly As Generic.List(Of PaymentItem)
```

The entry point into the form will be a public method named `ManagePayments`. Add that code now to the `PatronPayment` class.

INSERT SNIPPET

Insert Chapter 19, Snippet Item 3.

```
Public Sub ManagePayments(ByVal patronCopyID As Integer, _
      ByVal sessionPayments As Generic.List(Of PaymentItem))
   ' ----- Manage the payments for an item.
   ActivePatronCopyID = patronCopyID
   PaymentsOnly = sessionPayments
   Me.ShowDialog()
End Sub
```

This method records the patron-copy ID number and the collection of payments for that checked-out item. Processing then moves on to the form's `Load` event handler. It's in this routine that we will add our localized financial management code. In the `PatronPayment_Load` routine, scan down about one-third of the way through the method to the code that loads in the "summary details" from the database. Just after the line:

```
RecordItem.Text = CStr(dbInfo!Title)
```

add the statements that will globally format currency values for the Fines, Payments, and Balance summary labels that appear near the top of the form.

INSERT SNIPPET

Insert Chapter 19, Snippet Item 4.

```
originalFine = CDec(dbInfo!Fine)
RecordFine.Text = Format(originalFine, "Currency")
RecordPayments.Text = Format(CDec(dbInfo!Paid), "Currency")
balanceDue = originalFine - CDec(dbInfo!Paid)
RecordBalance.Text = Format(balanceDue, "Currency")
```

The rest of the `Load` event handler's code loads existing records from the `PatronPayment` table, plus the original overdue fine, if any, from the `PatronCopy.Fine` database field.

Later, when the user clicks the Add button to add a new financial event to the patron-and-item-copy entry, the `SaveEventData` routine—equivalent to the `SaveFormData` method in most of the other forms we've developed so far—saves the updated information in the database. This routine needs to save the new charge or payment in the `PatronPayment` table, plus update the charge and payment summary in the `PatronCopy` record. Add the code that writes out these records, just after the calculations for the `fineAmount` and `paidAmount` variables in the `SaveEventData` method.

Insert Chapter 19, Snippet Item 5.

```
' ----- Add the entry to the database.
TransactionBegin()
sqlText = "INSERT INTO PatronPayment (PatronCopy, " & _
    "EntryDate, EntryType, Amount, Comment, UserID) " & _
    "OUTPUT INSERTED.ID VALUES (" & ActivePatronCopyID & _
    ", GETDATE(), " & DBText(entryCode) & ", " & _
    RecordAmount.Text & ", " & _
    DBText(Trim(RecordComment.Text)) & _
    ", " & LoggedInUserID & ")"
newID = CInt(ExecuteSQLReturn(sqlText))

sqlText = "UPDATE PatronCopy SET Fine = " & fineAmount & _
    ", Paid = " & paidAmount & " WHERE ID = " & _
    ActivePatronCopyID
ExecuteSQL(sqlText)
TransactionCommit()
```

I've wrapped up both database statements in a transaction to help ensure the integrity of the data. Once the database is up-to-date, it's time to update the screen. The on-screen list of charges and payments needs this new record. That list uses the local EventHistoryItem class, a variation of the application-wide ListItemData class that we usually use in ListBox controls. EventHistoryItem has fields that are specific to displaying financial information in the EventHistory listbox. Add the code that builds an EventHistoryItem record and add it to the EventHistory list, immediately after the database update code we just added.

Insert Chapter 19, Snippet Item 6.

```
' ----- Add an item to the entry list.
historyItem = New EventHistoryItem
historyItem.PaymentID = newID
historyItem.EntryDate = Today
historyItem.PaymentAmount = CDec(RecordAmount.Text)
historyItem.Comments = Trim(RecordComment.Text)
historyItem.EntryType = entryType
EventHistory.Items.Add(historyItem)
```

This code block is followed by similar code that updates the PaymentsOnly list, the Generic.List(Of PaymentItem) that was passed in from the calling form. The code either updates the existing payment summary record, or adds a new record to the generic list.

```
' ----- Add a new payment.
scanPayment = New PaymentItem
scanPayment.PatronCopyID = ActivePatronCopyID
scanPayment.ItemTitle = RecordItem.Text
scanPayment.FeesPaid = paidAmount
scanPayment.BalanceDue = fineAmount - paidAmount
PaymentsOnly.Add(scanPayment)
```

Before leaving this function, we need to refresh the three financial summary values near the top of the form, the ones we set when the form first loaded. Add this code just after the update to the PaymentOnly list.

INSERT SNIPPET

Insert Chapter 19, Snippet Item 7.

```
' ----- Update the on-screen values.
RecordFine.Text = Format(fineAmount, "Currency")
RecordPayments.Text = Format(paidAmount, "Currency")
RecordBalance.Text = Format(fineAmount - paidAmount, _
    "Currency")
```

The EventHistory list is a variable-line-height owner draw control, similar to one we designed in Chapter 18. Its MeasureItem event handler sets the height of each list item (comments appear on a second line when available), and its DrawItem event handler does the actual drawing of each data column and the comments.

Managing All Fines and Payments

The Patron Payment form lets a librarian enter individual fines and payments, but the program still needs a form to manage all fines and payments for a single patron, a form that calls up the Patron Payment form when needed. The new *PatronRecord.vb* form fulfills this need. I've added this form to your project, although you need to enable it. Select it in the Solution Explorer, and change its Build Action property (in the Properties panel) from None to Compile. Figure 19-13 shows the controls on this form.

This form is available to both administrators and patrons, although some of the fields are hidden from patron view.

The Password button leads to the Change Patron Password form we added earlier in this chapter. The Edit button, available only to administrators, provides access to the full *Patron.vb* form. The main section of the Patron Record form displays a list of all items the patron currently has checked out. It includes a Renew button that lets a patron extend the due date for a checked-out item. We'll add the code for that feature in a later chapter.

The form also displays a summary of all pending fines and payments. Figure 19-14 shows the Fines tab and its fields.

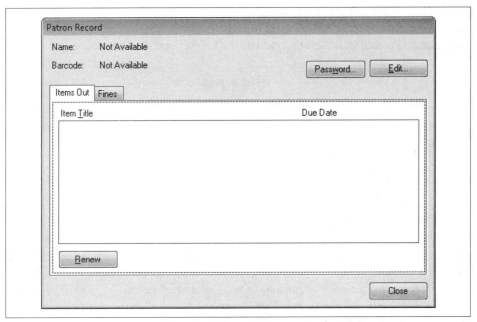

Figure 19-13. The Patron Record form, PatronRecord.vb

Figure 19-14. The Fines panel on the Patron Record form

The Print Balance Ticket button generates a printed receipt of all fines and payments for the patron. We'll add its code in a later chapter.

Most of the code in this form exists to manage fines and payments. To add a charge or payment, the librarian selects an item from the Fines list, and then clicks the Fines and Payments button. This brings up the just-added Patron Payment form.

The two main lists on the Patron Record form will each forgo the standard ListItemData class, and use a more property-rich class to support the display needs of each list. We'll add this `PatronDetailItem` as a separate public class since (as we'll see in a later chapter) it will be used elsewhere in the Library Project. Create a new class named *PatronDetailItem.vb*, and use the following code for its content.

INSERT SNIPPET

Insert Chapter 19, Snippet Item 8.

```
Private Class PatronDetailItem
    Public DetailID As Integer
    Public TitleText As String
    Public DueDate As Date
    Public FineAmount As Decimal
    Public PaidAmount As Decimal
    Public BalanceDue As Decimal
End Class
```

Now back to the `PatronRecord` form. As you can tell from looking at the form, the Fines list displays several columns of currency values. Let's add the code that correctly formats the currency according to the regional monetary settings. First, locate the `RefreshPaymentFines` method. This routine adds up all fines and payments, and displays the result through the `BalanceDue Label` control.

Near the top of this routine is a comment that states, "Clear the current list." Add the following code just after this comment.

INSERT SNIPPET

Insert Chapter 19, Snippet Item 9.

```
Fines.Items.Clear()
totalBalance = 0@
BalanceDue.Text = Format(0@, "Currency")
Me.Cursor = Windows.Forms.Cursors.WaitCursor
```

We could have just set the `BalanceDue` field to "$0.00," but this would not be properly globalized. Using the `Format` function with "Currency" as the formatting rule still results in "$0.00" when used in America, but properly adjusts for other cultures as well.

The `RefreshPaymentFines` method does a whole bunch of calculations, and ends up with the remaining patron balance in the `totalBalance` local variable. Locate the comment that reads, "Show the total balance," and add the following code just after it.

INSERT SNIPPET

Insert Chapter 19, Snippet Item 10.

```
BalanceDue.Text = Format(totalBalance, "Currency")
```

The Fines list, an owner draw ListBox implementation, also displays currency values. This is another list that forgoes the standard ListItemData class, using the local PatronDetailItem class instead for its item management. Locate the Fines_DrawItem event handler, and the "Extract the details from the list item" comment within that handler. Add the following code just after the comment.

INSERT SNIPPET

Insert Chapter 19, Snippet Item 11.

```
itemDetail = CType(Fines.Items(e.Index), PatronDetailItem)
titleText = itemDetail.TitleText
fineText = Format(itemDetail.FineAmount, "Currency")
paidText = Format(itemDetail.PaidAmount, "Currency")
balanceText = Format(itemDetail.BalanceDue, "Currency")
If (itemDetail.BalanceDue = 0@) Then useNotice = useBrush
```

This block properly formats each currency value. By default, all due amounts appear in red in the list. The last line in this code block resets the color to the neutral list item color if no balance is due.

Connecting Patron Features to the Main Form

That does it for the new patron-specific forms. Let's enable access to them through the main Library form. Wow! It's been awhile since I really looked at this form. I've forgotten what it looks like. Ah, yes. One of the main icons provides access to a patron's record (see Figure 19-15).

Figure 19-15. Accessing patron records from the main form

All we need to do is add an event handler for the Patron button. Locate the ActAccessPatron_Click event handler in the form's source code. Then add the following code to that handler.

INSERT SNIPPET

Insert Chapter 19, Snippet Item 12.

```
' ----- Look up the record of an active patron.
Dim patronID As Integer

' ----- Get the ID of the patron.
patronID = (New PatronAccess).SelectPatron( )
If (patronID = -1) Then Return

' ----- Show the patron record.
Call (New PatronRecord).ViewPatronRecord(patronID, True)
```

This code makes direct calls to two of the forms we added in this chapter: PatronAccess and PatronRecord. It first prompts the user to select a patron record, and then displays its details through the Patron Record form.

Dueling Patron Management Forms

Let's make one more change regarding patron records. Way back in an earlier chapter, we included a Manage Patron Items button on the *Patron.vb* form. This button existed to provide access to the future *PatronRecord.vb* form, but it's pretty much been dead weight until now. But with the *PatronRecord.vb* form in place, we're ready to make patron management history.

Open the source code for the *Patron.vb* form, and locate the ActItems_Click event handler. Then add the following code to it.

INSERT SNIPPET

Insert Chapter 19, Snippet Item 13.

```
Call (New PatronRecord).ViewPatronRecord(ActiveID, False)
```

This is all well and good, but you are probably thinking to yourself, "The Patron form now lets you open the Patron Record form. And that form has an Edit button that lets you once again open the Patron form. If you get a rogue librarian, there may be millions of patron management forms on the screen at once." And that's all true. So, we had to add some code to prevent that from happening. The second False argument to PatronRecord.ViewPatronRecord is a flag that says, "Don't show the Edit button on the Patron Record form." Similar code exists in the Patron Record form that stops the recursion.

```
Private Sub ActEditPatron_Click...
   If ((New Patron).EditRecordLimited( _
      ActivePatronID) <> -1) Then...
```

The EditRecordLimited method hides the Manage Patron Items button on the *Patron.vb* form. Whichever form you start with, you can access the other form, but you won't be able to generate a new copy of the initial form.

There was a lot of new code in this chapter, but it was all very pedestrian. We could have made even more culturally sensitive changes. For example, the Due Date column in the list of checked-out items on the *PatronRecord.vb* form uses a hardcoded date format for its display.

```
dueDate = Format(itemDetail.DueDate, "MMM d, yyyy")
```

You could change this to Short Date or another culture-neutral setting. Whichever method you choose really depends on your target audience. And if that target audience likes to see things spelled out on paper, the next chapter on printing is just for you.

CHAPTER 20

Printing

When Microsoft released its original version of MS-DOS, it included printing features that supported the then-available printers: chisel and stone. Fortunately, printing has come a long way since then. These days, advanced color laser printers and even "paperless" printing systems (such as Adobe Acrobat and XPS) provide printer support that rivals that of professional four-color offset printing facilities.

Although the .NET Framework does not replace the print spooler system built into each copy of Windows, it makes it greatly accessible. As you'll read in this chapter, a printer is now treated like any other .NET drawing surface. The statements you use to draw on a form or control can be copied and pasted directly into your printing code.

As I mentioned in Chapter 18, Windows Presentation Foundation (WPF) includes features that let you generate XPS files, designed for eventual WYSIWYG printing. I will not be discussing that technology in this chapter since the XPS files are actually an interim step between your printing code and the physical printer. The GDI+ based printing techniques shown in this chapter provide for more direct integration between your code and the printer.

This chapter provides a general discussion of .NET printing support. A discussion of report printing appears in the next chapter. If you are reading this chapter in its electronic format through the Safari publishing system, you can still rush right out and plunk down the funds for a hardcopy version of this book. Having that tactile response from the surface of the page should get you in the mood for this chapter's discussion of ink and paper.

Printing in Windows

Printers are a lot like people. Oh, I don't mean that they are cantankerous, or that they quickly run out of ink. Like the people of the world, printers speak many different languages. At the basic end of the language scale, some printers simply output the characters they receive. Others add "escape sequences," special combinations of characters that enable enhanced features such as font selection and double-wide text. At the complex end of the scale are PostScript and XPS, full-scale printer languages with commands that are somewhat similar to those in GDI+.

It would be every programmer's worst nightmare to adjust application code so that it targets all likely printers that a user may have. Each new printer language would mean another bout of development and testing. And printer makers are just giddy enough to come up with new language variations on a monthly basis.

Fortunately, Windows implements a system of printer-specific drivers that shield the developer from most printer variations. These drivers all speak a common language—let's call it "Printish"—which the driver translates into the printer's native tongue. As developers, we need only design software that speaks Printish.

The .NET Framework's printing system adds yet another level of language translation. .NET programs do not directly communicate with the printer drivers. Instead, they use GDI+ commands—the same commands used for screen updates—to output content to an in-memory printer canvas. The framework then converts these commands to Printish and sends the output on to the appropriate printer driver, and finally to the printer. Figure 20-1 shows a summary of the steps involved in .NET printing.

Figure 20-1. From programmer to canvas: printing with .NET

Printing in .NET

Having both screen and printer output generated through identical GDI+ commands means that I can make this a really short chapter, referring you back to Chapter 18 for details. But it also means that there needs to be a canvas—a System.Drawing.Graphics object—where the printer-specific GDI+ commands target their output. The System.Drawing.Printing.PrintDocument class provides you with the output canvas you need for both ordinary printing and "print preview" output. There are three ways to use the PrintDocument class:

- Add a PrintDocument control to a form from the Windows Forms toolbox. This control appears by default in the toolbox's Printing section. Assign its properties and respond to its events as with any other control.

- Create a field-level instance of the PrintDocument class. Include the With Events clause in the definition to get event management.

- Create a local instance of PrintDocument, and connect any events using AddHandler.

These are standard methods in .NET, but having a control variation makes the class that much more convenient. We'll get into the actual printing code a little later.

Four other printer-specific controls are available for Windows Forms projects:

PageSetupDialog

> This control presents a standard Windows printer settings dialog that lets the user configure a specific print job, or all print jobs for the application. The control's ShowDialog method displays the form shown in Figure 20-2. The control also exposes properties related to the user's selection. Its PageSettings member exposes specific user preferences as defined on the form, and the PrinterSettings member identifies the selected printer and its properties. You can retain these members and later assign them to other printer-specific classes that include similar members.

PrintDialog

> Figure 20-3 shows this control's dialog, the standard dialog that appears in most programs when the user selects the File → Print menu command. This control also exposes a PrinterSettings member used to assign or retrieve the selected printer and related options.

PrintPreviewDialog

> This control's dialog displays a preview of your printed document to the user. It includes standard preview presentation features, including zoom level and a pages-to-see-at-once control. The included Print button sends the preview content to the default printer (without prompting for printer selection). This control directly interacts with your PrintDocument instance, which drives the actual display content. Figure 20-4 shows the Print Preview dialog, although with no page-specific content.

Figure 20-2. The Page Setup dialog

PrintPreviewControl

The PrintPreviewDialog control includes basic preview management features (such as the zoom feature) that meet the needs of most applications. Unfortunately, that control is a sealed black box, and you cannot easily add your own custom features to it, or remove features that you don't want. The PrintPreviewControl control provides an alternative interface that lets you fully customize the print preview experience. Instead of a full dialog, it implements just the page-display portion of the form. You must implement all toolbars and other features, and link their functionality with the preview control. I won't be discussing this control in this chapter. If you're interested in using this advanced control, you can read an article I wrote about print preview a few years ago.[*]

Before you print, you need to know which printer your user wants to target for the output. You may also need to know about available features of the printer, such as whether it supports color. If you used to be a Visual Basic 6.0 developer, you were accustomed to the convenient Printers collection. The absence of that collection in Visual Basic 2008 means that we must use more indirect means to access the printers.

---

[*] You can find the article referenced on my web site, *http://www.timaki.com*, in the Articles section.

Figure 20-3. The Print dialog

Figure 20-4. The Print Preview dialog

The System.Drawing.Printing.PrinterSettings class includes a shared InstalledPrinters string collection that lists the path to each configured printer. You can assign any of these strings to the PrinterSettings' PrinterName member, making the specific printer available within the application. The following code chunk lets the user select from the list of printers, and displays some basic information about the selected printer:

```
Private Sub Form1_Load(ByVal sender As System.Object, _
      ByVal e As System.EventArgs) Handles MyBase.Load
    ' ----- Display the list of printers.
    Dim scanPrinter As String

    For Each scanPrinter In Drawing.Printing. _
          PrinterSettings.InstalledPrinters
      ListBox1.Items.Add(scanPrinter)
    Next scanPrinter
End Sub

Private Sub Button1_Click(ByVal sender As System.Object, _
      ByVal e As System.EventArgs) Handles Button1.Click
    ' ----- Display information about the selected printer.
    Dim selectedPrinter As Drawing.Printing.PrinterSettings

    If (ListBox1.SelectedIndex = -1) Then Return
    selectedPrinter = New Drawing.Printing.PrinterSettings()
    selectedPrinter.PrinterName = ListBox1.Text
    MsgBox(selectedPrinter.ToString)
End Sub
```

Printing a Document

Earlier we saw that many Windows components work together to generate your printed output. Within your .NET code, you will also use many components (classes) to drive the printing process. Four main steps are involved (at least directly) in printing a document from your code:

1. Create an instance of a PrintDocument class (or add it as a control to your form).

2. Set the PrintDocument's various printer settings, either by using a PrintDialog (or related) class/control, or by using the default or manual settings.

3. Add an event handler for the PrintDocument's PrintPage event. This event is called once for each page, and receives a System.Drawing.Graphics object for the printer canvas. Your event handler code prints a single page, and updates a flag telling the document whether there are more pages to come.

4. Call the PrintDocument's Print method to start the ball rolling.

Let's try a little code to see how this printing beast eats. Or prints. Or whatever it does. How about a simple program that prints a five-page document on the user's selected printer? The output will be a large single-digit page number, perfect for the Sesame Street set. First, let's create a new Windows Forms application, and add a single button to Form1 named ActPrint. We'll also add a PrintDocument control (named CountingDoc), and a PrintDialog control (named UserPrinter). Figure 20-5 shows the form and its supporting controls.

Figure 20-5. A program with only printing on its mind

These controls implement the first two steps of our four-step printing process. Next, we'll add the source code.

```
Public Class Form1
    Private WhichPage As Integer

    Private Sub ActPrint_Click(ByVal sender As System.Object, _
        ByVal e As System.EventArgs) Handles ActPrint.Click
        ' ----- Prompt the user for printer settings, and
        '       start printing.
        UserPrinter.Document = CountingDoc
        If (UserPrinter.ShowDialog() = _
            Windows.Forms.DialogResult.OK) Then _
            CountingDoc.Print()
    End Sub

    Private Sub CountingDoc_BeginPrint(ByVal sender As Object, _
        ByVal e As System.Drawing.Printing.PrintEventArgs) _
        Handles CountingDoc.BeginPrint
        ' ----- Start the counting over.
        WhichPage = 1
    End Sub

    Private Sub CountingDoc_PrintPage(ByVal sender As Object, _
        ByVal e As System.Drawing.Printing. _
        PrintPageEventArgs) Handles CountingDoc.PrintPage
        ' ----- Print a single page.
        Dim hugeFont As Font
        Dim centeredText As StringFormat
```

```
             ' ----- Let's go overboard on the font: 256 points!
             hugeFont = New Font("Arial", 256)

             ' ----- Center the text on the page.
             centeredText = New StringFormat( )
             centeredText.Alignment = StringAlignment.Center
             centeredText.LineAlignment = StringAlignment.Center

             ' ----- Print the number.
             e.Graphics.DrawString(CStr(WhichPage), hugeFont, _
                Brushes.Black, e.MarginBounds, centeredText)

             ' ----- Draw the page margins to make it clear where
             '       they are.
             e.Graphics.DrawRectangle(Pens.Blue, e.MarginBounds)

             ' ----- Limit the output to five pages.
             WhichPage += 1
             If (WhichPage <= 5) Then e.HasMorePages = True _
                Else e.HasMorePages = False
        End Sub
     End Class
```

This code implements steps 3 (ActPrint_Click) and 4 (CountingDoc_PrintPage). The ActPrint button's Click event handler links the document and the Print dialog so that they both refer to the same settings. It then prompts the user to select a printer and various options through the ShowDialog call. If the user clicks the OK button on that dialog, it triggers a call to the document's Print method.

The action then moves to the events of the PrintDocument instance. I've implemented two of the events: a BeginPrint event handler that performs some initialization, and a PrintPage event handler that does the hard work. (Other events include EndPrint, used to clean up when printing is complete, and QueryPageSettings, where you can change the orientation and settings of each page of the document.) Actually, it's not all that hard, especially since we saw similar code in Chapter 18. The biggest difference is the amount of space available on a printed page, allowing us to play with fonts in the hundreds of point sizes.

Figure 20-6 shows page 2 of the output from this program. I printed to the pseudo-printer installed for capturing print jobs as XPS documents. You can see in the bottom-left corner that it did properly record five output pages.

Print Preview

Adding a print preview interface is so easy, you should probably ask your boss for a really hard project to do first, and then come back when you're worn out. Let's build on our simple number-printing application, adding a new Button control named ActPreview. We will also add a PrintPreviewDialog control named UserPreview. Once these are in place, add the following preview button Click event handler:

Figure 20-6. This page is brought to you by the number 2

```
Private Sub ActPreview_Click(ByVal sender As System.Object, _
    ByVal e As System.EventArgs) Handles ActPreview.Click
  ' ----- Display a preview of the document.
  UserPreview.Document = CountingDoc
  UserPreview.ShowDialog()
End Sub
```

Hey, that's even simpler than the code that initiates printing to a real printer, even though print preview technology seems to be more complex than plain printing. There almost ought to be a law against code that simple. Fortunately, there's not. Figure 20-7 shows the preview window, after using the two-pages-at-once toolbar button.

Let's dwell just a little longer on how simple that code was. I can accept that the PrintPreviewDialog class includes a lot of amazing code for previewing printed output. But the remarkable part of the code is that we didn't have to rewrite the custom GDI+ drawing logic. The same set of GDI+ statements now drives the preview display and the actual output. All we had to do was assign the PrintDocument object to the correct dialog control.

Figure 20-7. The preview displays multiple pages at once with no extra effort on our part

Counting and Numbering Pages

During the printing (or preview) process, the `PrintDocument`'s `PrintPage` event handler gets called once for each output page. But here's the tricky thing: when the `PrintPage` handler was called the first time, it was not to print "page 1" of the document, but to print "the first page in need of printing," whatever its page number. Search all you want through the properties of the `PrintDocument` class, but you will never find a `PageNumber` property. The `PrintDocument` class does not know about the page numbers in your document, and—despite all of the nice things it does for you—it does not care. All it knows is that you have a bunch of pages to print, and it will call your `PrintPage` event handler until you say "enough!"

If you turn back to Figure 20-3, you'll see that the Print dialog includes a Page Range section, although most of its controls are disabled by default. The `PrintDialog` control includes three Boolean properties that let you enable specific controls in that section: `AllowCurrentPage`, `AllowSomePages`, and `AllowSelection`. Setting any of these properties to `True` enables the matching option control. Later, after the user has made a choice, you can query the `PrintDocument` object's `PrinterSettings.PrintRange` property to determine which choice it is.

Let's add code that enables page range selection. We'll still limit the allowed pages to just those numbered one to five, but the user will be able to choose a subrange within that set. Return to the Click event handler for the ActPrint button, and insert a few new lines of code (the ones in bold):

```
Private Sub ActPrint_Click(ByVal sender As System.Object, _
    ByVal e As System.EventArgs) Handles ActPrint.Click
    ' ----- Prompt the user for printer settings, and
    '       start printing.
    UserPrinter.Document = CountingDoc

    UserPrinter.AllowSomePages = True
    CountingDoc.PrinterSettings.MinimumPage = 1
    CountingDoc.PrinterSettings.MaximumPage = 5
    CountingDoc.PrinterSettings.FromPage = 1
    CountingDoc.PrinterSettings.ToPage = 5

    If (UserPrinter.ShowDialog() = _
        Windows.Forms.DialogResult.OK) Then _
        CountingDoc.Print()
End Sub
```

When the user clicks on the Print button this time, the Print Range section of the dialog has enabled the Pages field, and it's already filled in with the minimum and maximum pages in the range "1–5" (see Figure 20-8).

Figure 20-8. Support for page ranges

If the user adjusts this field to "1–6," an error occurs stating that the valid range is somewhere within "1–5" only. But whether the user selects All Pages or 1–5 or 1–4 or 2–3 or Current Page or Selection, the PrintPage event handler will be called in exactly the same manner. In fact, the handler will be called dozens, even hundreds, of times until you tell it to stop. The user's selection impacts the PrinterSettings.PrintRange property and some other properties, but it does not directly impact the print process. It is up to you to alter the print behavior based on these settings.

Let's pretend that the user entered a print range of 2–3. We cannot let the PrintDocument fire the PrintPage event for all five pages because, even if we generated output for only pages 2 and 3, we would still get three other blank pages out of the printer. What we want is to have the event fire only twice, once for page 2 and once for page 3. We'll need to adjust the use of the WhichPage class-level tracking variable to compensate for the indicated range. First, let's change the BeginPrint handler to use the correct starting page number.

```
Private Sub CountingDoc_BeginPrint(ByVal sender As Object, _
      ByVal e As System.Drawing.Printing.PrintEventArgs) _
      Handles CountingDoc.BeginPrint
   ' ----- Start the counting over.
   WhichPage = CountingDoc.PrinterSettings.FromPage
End Sub
```

In the PrintPage event handler, we must modify the code that determines when to quit the print process.

```
WhichPage += 1
If (WhichPage <= CountingDoc.PrinterSettings.ToPage) _
   Then e.HasMorePages = True Else e.HasMorePages = False
```

Since the print preview code shares the same document settings, we need to adjust the preview code to force it to always print all pages.

```
Private Sub ActPreview_Click(ByVal sender As System.Object, _
      ByVal e As System.EventArgs) Handles ActPreview.Click
   ' ----- Display a preview of the document.
   UserPreview.Document = CountingDoc
   CountingDoc.PrinterSettings.PrintRange = _
      Printing.PrintRange.AllPages
   UserPreview.ShowDialog()
End Sub
```

If you run the program and adjust the print range, you should get just the pages you requested. I've placed a copy of this program in the book's installation directory. You'll find it in the *Print Preview Test* subdirectory.

Printing in "Raw" Mode

Using GDI+ to generate printed pages is pretty straightforward. For complex pages, you may have to do a lot of positioning and measuring of text strings and whatnot, but it all boils down to "draw this text or this shape at this position."

Sadly, not all printers support the application-to-printer-via-GDI-and-Printish way of doing things. This is especially true of printers used to print thermal credit card receipts at your favorite pizza place. Although some of these printers may have Windows drivers, they are really designed for direct communication with an application via their special "escape sequence" language. For such printers, you need to write directly to the printer in "raw" mode, where you control exactly which characters get sent to the printer. (Actually, you don't have to go directly to the printer. You can still write to the printer's queue, and let Windows manage the scheduling of the print job.)

It is with even more sadness that I must inform you of .NET's lack of raw printer support. Although a DLL is included with Windows that enables this direct printing method, a managed .NET wrapper for it does not ship with the framework. You, and other overburdened programmers everywhere, must take up the charge yourselves.

Well, it's not all that bad. Microsoft and other developers have published code that maps the unmanaged DLL calls to managed equivalents. We'll be using a variation of some of this code in the Library Project in this chapter to support the printing of checkout slips, paper receipts that let a patron know which items were just checked out and when they are all due back.

Summary

I recommend that you peruse the printer-specific classes and controls discussed in this chapter. They include many properties that let you fine-tune the output of your printed page based on the user's specified settings. For instance, I promised you earlier in the chapter that you could discover whether a printer supported color. The `PrinterSettings.SupportsColor` property gives you a straight-up yes or no answer to this feature question. If you know that a printer does not support color, you can adjust your `PrintPage` code to present the page content in a slightly different format.

Project

As advertised, this chapter's project focuses on the printing of checkout and fine-payment receipts. But we'll also add all of the code that lets patrons and librarians check in and check out books and other library items.

PROJECT ACCESS

Load the Chapter 20 (Before) Code project, either through the New Project templates or by accessing the project directly from the installation directory. To see the code in its final form, load Chapter 20 (After) Code instead.

Supporting Raw Printing

In the interest of frank and honest discussion, I must tell you that I didn't come up with the basic code for raw printing in this section. Oh, some of the code is mine, both stylistically and imaginatively. But I didn't figure out all of the links between the application and the *winspool.drv* file. That code originally came from Microsoft Knowledge Base article number 322090, which describes raw printing support from .NET applications. It uses a feature of .NET known as "interop" that allows .NET code to "interoperate" with older unmanaged COM-based components and applications.

Boy, am I glad that I got that off my chest. I mean, if anyone thought I was the one who came up with the code you are about to see, there would be angry mobs storming my house nightly, and general turmoil in the streets. The code, contained in the RawPrinterHelper class, is just plain ugly. Well, there's no sense in postponing it any longer. Create a new class named *RawPrinterHelper.vb*, and use the following code for its definition.

INSERT SNIPPET

Insert Chapter 20, Snippet Item 1.

```vb
Imports System.Runtime.InteropServices

Public Class RawPrinterHelper
    ' ----- The code in this class is based on Microsoft
    '       knowledge base article number 322090.
    '       Web: http://support.microsoft.com/?id=322090

    ' ----- Structure and API declarations.
    <StructLayout(LayoutKind.Sequential, _
    CharSet:=CharSet.Unicode)> _
    Private Structure DOCINFOW
        <MarshalAs(UnmanagedType.LPWStr)> _
            Public pDocName As String
        <MarshalAs(UnmanagedType.LPWStr)> _
            Public pOutputFile As String
        <MarshalAs(UnmanagedType.LPWStr)> _
            Public pDataType As String
    End Structure

    <DllImport("winspool.Drv", EntryPoint:="OpenPrinterW", _
        SetLastError:=True, CharSet:=CharSet.Unicode, _
        ExactSpelling:=True, _
        CallingConvention:=CallingConvention.StdCall)> _
    Private Shared Function OpenPrinter(ByVal src As String, _
        ByRef hPrinter As IntPtr, ByVal pd As Long) As Boolean
    End Function

    <DllImport("winspool.Drv", EntryPoint:="ClosePrinter", _
        SetLastError:=True, CharSet:=CharSet.Unicode, _
        ExactSpelling:=True, _
        CallingConvention:=CallingConvention.StdCall)> _
    Private Shared Function ClosePrinter( _
        ByVal hPrinter As IntPtr) As Boolean
    End Function

    <DllImport("winspool.Drv", EntryPoint:="StartDocPrinterW", _
        SetLastError:=True, CharSet:=CharSet.Unicode, _
        ExactSpelling:=True, _
        CallingConvention:=CallingConvention.StdCall)> _
```

```
Private Shared Function StartDocPrinter( _
   ByVal hPrinter As IntPtr, ByVal level As Int32, _
   ByRef pDI As DOCINFOW) As Boolean
End Function

<DllImport("winspool.Drv", EntryPoint:="EndDocPrinter", _
   SetLastError:=True, CharSet:=CharSet.Unicode, _
   ExactSpelling:=True, _
   CallingConvention:=CallingConvention.StdCall)> _
Private Shared Function EndDocPrinter( _
   ByVal hPrinter As IntPtr) As Boolean
End Function

<DllImport("winspool.Drv", EntryPoint:="StartPagePrinter", _
   SetLastError:=True, CharSet:=CharSet.Unicode, _
   ExactSpelling:=True, _
   CallingConvention:=CallingConvention.StdCall)> _
Private Shared Function StartPagePrinter( _
   ByVal hPrinter As IntPtr) As Boolean
End Function

<DllImport("winspool.Drv", EntryPoint:="EndPagePrinter", _
   SetLastError:=True, CharSet:=CharSet.Unicode, _
   ExactSpelling:=True, _
   CallingConvention:=CallingConvention.StdCall)> _
Private Shared Function EndPagePrinter( _
   ByVal hPrinter As IntPtr) As Boolean
End Function

<DllImport("winspool.Drv", EntryPoint:="WritePrinter", _
   SetLastError:=True, CharSet:=CharSet.Unicode, _
   ExactSpelling:=True, _
   CallingConvention:=CallingConvention.StdCall)> _
Private Shared Function WritePrinter( _
   ByVal hPrinter As IntPtr, ByVal pBytes As IntPtr, _
   ByVal dwCount As Int32, ByRef dwWritten As Int32) _
   As Boolean
End Function

Public Shared Function SendStringToPrinter( _
      ByVal targetPrinter As String, _
      ByVal stringContent As String, _
      ByVal documentTitle As String) As Boolean
   ' ----- Send an array of bytes to a printer queue.
   '       Return True on success.
   Dim printerHandle As IntPtr
   Dim errorCode As Int32
   Dim docDetail As DOCINFOW = Nothing
   Dim bytesWritten As Int32
   Dim printSuccess As Boolean
   Dim contentBytes As IntPtr
   Dim contentSize As Int32
```

```
On Error Resume Next

' ----- Set up the identity of this document.
With docDetail
    .pDocName = documentTitle
    .pDataType = "RAW"
End With

' ----- Convert the string to ANSI text.
contentSize = stringContent.Length( )
contentBytes = Marshal.StringToCoTaskMemAnsi( _
    stringContent)

' ----- Open the printer and print the document.
printSuccess = False
If OpenPrinter(targetPrinter, printerHandle, 0) Then
    If StartDocPrinter(printerHandle, 1, docDetail) Then
        If StartPagePrinter(printerHandle) Then
            ' ----- Send the content to the printer.
            printSuccess = WritePrinter(printerHandle, _
                contentBytes, contentSize, bytesWritten)
            EndPagePrinter(printerHandle)
        End If
        EndDocPrinter(printerHandle)
    End If
    ClosePrinter(printerHandle)
End If

' ----- GetLastError may provide information on the
'        last error. For now, just ignore it.
If (printSuccess = False) Then errorCode = _
    Marshal.GetLastWin32Error( )

' ----- Free up unused memory.
Marshal.FreeCoTaskMem(contentBytes)

' ----- Complete.
Return printSuccess
    End Function
End Class
```

Although ugly, the code is relatively clear-cut. The SendStringToPrinter method prepares a string for printing by forcing it to a standard ANSI format. It then uses the
functions in the *winspool.drv* library to open a new print job, and send the prepared
content to it. There's a whole lot of "marshalling" going on in the code through
members of the Marshal class. Since *winspool.drv* is an unmanaged library, all data
must be shuttled indirectly between the managed Library application and the
unmanaged *winspool.drv* library.

Printing Tickets

Now that we have a convenient class that will send any raw content to any specific printer, let's add some code to use it. First, we need to add a helper class for a portion of the ticket printing. Create a new class file named *CheckedOutItem.vb*, and replace its empty class template with the following code.

INSERT SNIPPET

Insert Chapter 20, Snippet Item 2.

```
Public Class CheckedOutItem
    ' ----- Used to store the details of each checked-out
    '       item on the main form, although it also supports
    '       receipt printing.
    Public ItemTitle As String
    Public CopyNumber As Integer
    Public Barcode As String
    Public DueDate As Date
End Class
```

We'll use this class to convey the details to be printed on the receipt when checking out items. Speaking of ticket printing, let's add the class that does the actual printing. Create a new module file (not a class) named *TicketPrinting.vb*. Replace its empty module definition with the snippet code.

INSERT SNIPPET

Insert Chapter 20, Snippet Item 3.

The code includes three methods that drive printing: PrintCheckoutTicket, PrintBalanceTicket, and PrintPaymentTicket. These methods are called from other parts of the application when it's time to present a printed ticket to the user. The TicketPrinting module also includes a few other methods that support these three primary methods. Since these three methods are somewhat similar in structure, let's just look at PrintCheckoutTicket.

```
Public Sub PrintCheckoutTicket(ByVal patronID As Integer, _
    ByVal checkedOutItems As ListBox)
    ' ----- Print out a ticket of what the patron checked
    '       out. The supplied ListBox control contains
    '       objects of type CheckedOutItem.
    Dim ticketWidth As Integer
    Dim ticketText As System.Text.StringBuilder
    Dim counter As Integer
    Dim patronFines As Decimal
    Dim itemDetail As CheckedOutItem

    On Error GoTo ErrorHandler
```

```
    ' ----- Ignore if there is nothing to print.
    If (patronID = -1) Or (checkedOutItems.Items.Count = 0) _
        Then Return

    ' ----- Get the width of the ticket.
    ticketWidth = My.Settings.ReceiptWidth
    If (ticketWidth <= 0) Then ticketWidth = 40

    ' ----- Build the heading.
    ticketText = GetTicketHeader(patronID, ticketWidth)
    If (ticketText Is Nothing) Then Return

    ' ----- Process each checked-out item.
    For counter = 0 To checkedOutItems.Items.Count - 1
        ' ----- Extract the detail from the list.
        itemDetail = CType(checkedOutItems.Items(counter), _
            CheckedOutItem)

        ' ----- Add the item name.
        ticketText.AppendLine(Left(itemDetail.ItemTitle, _
            ticketWidth))

        ' ----- Add the bar code number and due date.
        ticketText.AppendLine(LeftAndRightText( _
            itemDetail.Barcode, "Due: " & _
            Format(itemDetail.DueDate, "MMM d, yyyy"), _
            ticketWidth))
        ticketText.AppendLine( )
    Next counter

    ' ----- If there are fines due, print them here.
    patronFines = CalculatePatronFines(patronID)
    If (patronFines > 0@) Then
        ticketText.AppendLine("Fines Due: " & _
            Format(patronFines, "Currency"))
        ticketText.AppendLine( )
    End If

    ' ----- Add the bottom display text.
    ticketText.Append(GetTicketFooter(ticketWidth))

    ' ----- Send the ticket to the printer.
    RawPrinterHelper.SendStringToPrinter( _
        My.Settings.ReceiptPrinter, _
        ticketText.ToString( ), "Checkout Receipt")
    Return

ErrorHandler:
    GeneralError("TicketPrinting.PrintCheckoutTicket", _
        Err.GetException( ))
    Return
End Sub
```

The code builds a string (actually a `StringBuilder`) of display content, adding details about each checked-out item to a string buffer. Then it calls `SendStringToPrinter` to send the content to the configured receipt printer (`My.Settings.ReceiptPrinter`).

We'll add the code that calls `PrintCheckoutTicket` later. Right now, let's add code that calls the two other methods. When the Payment Record form closes, we want to automatically print a receipt of all payments made while the form was open. Add the following code to the `PatronRecord.ActClose_Click` event handler, just before the code already found in that handler.

INSERT SNIPPET

Insert Chapter 20, Snippet Item 4.

```
' ----- Print out a ticket if needed.
If (SessionPayments.Count > 0) Then _
   PrintPaymentTicket(ActivePatronID, SessionPayments)
SessionPayments.Clear()
SessionPayments = Nothing
```

Then, add some code to the `ActBalanceTicket_Click` event handler, also in the `PatronRecord` class, that prints a balance ticket when the user requests it.

INSERT SNIPPET

Insert Chapter 20, Snippet Item 5.

```
' ----- Print a ticket of all balances.
PrintBalanceTicket(ActivePatronID, Fines)
```

Printing Bar Codes

The Library Project prints three types of bar codes: (1) item bar codes that you can stick on books, CDs, and anything else that can be checked out or managed by the system; (2) patron bar codes that can be made into patron identification cards; and (3) miscellaneous bar codes that a library can use for any other purpose. All three bar code types are printed through the new `BarcodePrint` form. Figure 20-9 shows the controls included on this form.

I've already added this form to the project, including its code. Here's the code for the Preview button, which should look familiar after I beat its concepts into you throughout this chapter.

```
Private Sub ActPreview_Click(ByVal sender As System.Object, _
      ByVal e As System.EventArgs) Handles ActPreview.Click
   ' ----- The user wants to preview the labels.
   On Error Resume Next
```

Figure 20-9. One form, three bar code types, many happy labels

```
    ' ----- Make sure the user supplied valid data.
    If (VerifyFields() = False) Then Return

    ' ----- Load in all of the page-specific details to be
    '       used in printing.
    If (LoadPageDetails() = False) Then Return

    ' ----- Create the preview dialog.
    Me.Cursor = Windows.Forms.Cursors.WaitCursor
    PageSoFar = 0
    PreviewMode = True
    BarcodeDoc = New System.Drawing.Printing.PrintDocument

    ' ----- Display the preview.
    BarcodePreview.Document = BarcodeDoc
    BarcodePreview.ShowDialog()
    BarcodeDoc = Nothing
    Me.Cursor = Windows.Forms.Cursors.Default
End Sub
```

The Print button's code is almost exactly the same, but it uses a `PrintDialog` instance instead of `PrintPreviewDialog`. It also keeps track of the final printed bar code number so that it can help avoid overlaps the next time they are printed.

The `BarcodeDoc_PrintPage` event handler does the actual bar code printing. Its code combines the `BarcodeLabel.PreviewArea_Paint` and `BarcodePage.PreviewArea_Paint` event handlers into one glorious printing machine.

To enable use of the bar code printing form, add the following statements to the `ActReportsBarcode_Click` event handler in the `MainForm` class.

INSERT SNIPPET

Insert Chapter 20, Snippet Item 6.

```
' ----- Make sure the user is allowed to do this.
If (SecurityProfile(LibrarySecurity. _
        ManageBarcodeTemplates) = False) Then
    MsgBox(NotAuthorizedMessage, MsgBoxStyle.OkOnly Or _
        MsgBoxStyle.Exclamation, ProgramTitle)
    Return
End If

' ----- Show the bar code label printing form.
Call (New BarcodePrint).ShowDialog()
```

Renewal of Checked-Out Patron Items

For a library patron, the only thing more important than checking items out and in is being able to read those items. The Library Project won't help anyone with that, but it will do that check-in, checkout transaction thing through the code we add in this chapter. Let's start by adding the renewal code for currently checked-out items. The Renew button on the Patron Record form initiates the process. Add the code to the PatronRecord.ActRenewItemsOut_Click event handler that does the renewal.

INSERT SNIPPET

Insert Chapter 20, Snippet Item 7.

The code does some calculations to determine the new due date (avoiding holidays), and then updates the database in a transaction.

```
TransactionBegin()

' ----- Update the record.
sqlText = "UPDATE PatronCopy SET DueDate = " & _
    DBDate(dueDate) & ", Renewal = " & renewsSoFar & _
    " WHERE ID = " & itemDetail.DetailID
ExecuteSQL(sqlText)

' ----- Update the patron record.
sqlText = "UPDATE Patron SET LastActivity = GETDATE() " & _
    "WHERE ID = " & ActivePatronID
ExecuteSQL(sqlText)

TransactionCommit()
```

Support for Check-In and Checkout

If a library adds bar code labels to all of its items, check-in and checkout will be via a bar code reader. But a very small library using the program may not have the staff time available to bar code everything on the shelves. Therefore, the Library Project needs to support check-in and checkout by title. During checkout or check-in, the user enters either a bar code or a title (partial or complete). Non-numeric entries are assumed to be titles, and initiate a title search. The new *CheckLookup.vb* form, pictured in Figure 20-10, displays all matches for the entered title.

Figure 20-10. A title matching form for both check-in and checkout

Although the fields on the form initially indicate that they are for checkout only, the form does double duty, altering its visage for check-in purposes. Additionally, check-in listings are limited to only those items already checked out.

I've already added this form to the project, along with its source code. Most of the code queries the database for matching library items and displays the results using an owner draw listbox. It is a subset of the code found in the *ItemLookup.vb* form. The only real difference between check-in and checkout occurs in the PerformLookup method. This code block starts to build the main item selection SQL command, and then ends it with these statements:

```
If (asCheckIn) Then sqlText &= " AND IC.ID IN" _
    Else sqlText &= " AND IC.ID NOT IN"
sqlText &= " (SELECT ItemCopy FROM PatronCopy " & _
    "WHERE Returned = 0)"
```

So, the difference is "IN" versus "NOT IN."

The CheckItemByTitle function is the main interface to the form's logic.

```
Public Function CheckItemByTitle(ByVal CheckIn As Boolean, _
    ByVal searchText As String) As Integer
```

You pass this function the user-supplied title (searchText) and a flag indicating check-in or checkout, and it returns the ItemCopy.ID database field for the selected library item.

All of the remaining changes in this chapter occur in the MainForm class, so let's go there now. The UpdateDisplayForUser method adjusts the main form's features when an administrator logs in or out. One feature we didn't take into account before is the administrator-defined ability for patrons to check out their own items without librarian assistance. To support that feature, we need to change some of the code in the UpdateDisplayForUser method. About 10 lines into the code, in the conditional section that sets up the display for patrons, you'll find these four lines:

```
LabelTasks.Visible = False
LineTasks.Visible = False
PicCheckOut.Visible = False
ActCheckOut.Visible = False
```

Replace these four lines with the following code.

INSERT SNIPPET

Insert Chapter 20, Snippet Item 8.

```
' ----- See if patrons can check out items by themselves.
Dim userCanCheckOut As Boolean = _
   CBool(Val(GetSystemValue("PatronCheckOut")))

LabelTasks.Visible = userCanCheckOut
LineTasks.Visible = userCanCheckOut
PicCheckOut.Visible = userCanCheckOut
ActCheckOut.Visible = userCanCheckOut
```

We also need to add similar security-related code to the TaskCheckOut method. Here are the first few lines of code from that method:

```
' ----- Update the display.
AllPanelsInvisible()
If (SecurityProfile(LibrarySecurity.CheckOutItems)) Then _
   PanelCheckOut.Visible = True
```

Replace these lines with the following code.

INSERT SNIPPET

Insert Chapter 20, Snippet Item 9.

```
' ----- Check Out mode.
Dim userCanCheckOut As Boolean

' ----- See if patrons can check out items by themselves.
userCanCheckOut = CBool(Val(GetSystemValue("PatronCheckOut")))

' ----- Update the display.
AllPanelsInvisible()
If (userCanCheckOut Or _
   SecurityProfile(LibrarySecurity.CheckOutItems)) Then _
   PanelCheckOut.Visible = True
```

The actual checkout of items occurs on the main form itself. First, a patron is identified, and then the items to check out get processed. Let's add a class-level variable to MainForm to keep track of the patron. And as long as we're adding definitions, we'll also add two constants that refer to images stored in the MainForm.StatusImages control.

These constants will be used in some check-in-related code added a little later. Add the following code to the start of the class definition.

INSERT SNIPPET

Insert Chapter 20, Snippet Item 10.

```
Private ActiveCheckOutPatron As Integer = -1

Private Const StatusImageBad As Integer = 0
Private Const StatusImageGood As Integer = 1
```

When the user identifies the patron to use for checkout, and then starts checking items out, the last step is a click of the Finish button, indicating the end of the checkout process for that patron. (Skip ahead to Figure 20-11 if you want to see the Finish button now.) However, there is nothing to stop the user from jumping to another part of the program, or from exiting the program completely, without first clicking the Finish button. We must anticipate this rude behavior so typical of software users. To ensure that checkout completes properly, we will add some code to three places in MainForm that should catch any such discourteous actions by the user. Add the following code to *the start* of these three methods: (1) the MainForm_FormClosing event handler; (2) the ShowLoginForm method; and (3) the AllPanelsInvisible method.

INSERT SNIPPET

Insert Chapter 20, Snippet Item 11 *three times*.

```
' ----- Finish the in-process check-out if needed.
If (ActiveCheckOutPatron <> -1) Then _
    ActFinishCheckOut.PerformClick()
```

Checking Out Items

All of the checkout code (except for the code in the *CheckLookup.vb* form) appears in the main form's class. Checkout is one of the eight main display panels accessed through this form (see Figure 20-11).

Here's the process for checking out items from the checkout panel:

1. The user clicks the Patron button and identifies the patron who will check out items.

2. The user enters the title or bar code for each item to check out, and clicks the Check Out button for each one.

3. The user clicks the Finish button when checkout is complete.

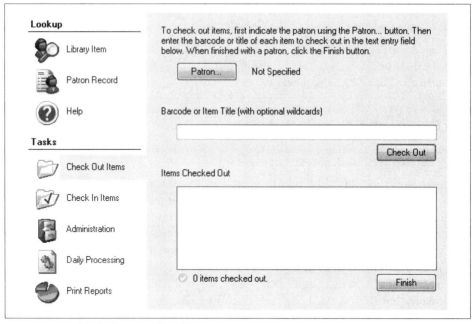

Figure 20-11. The checkout panel on the main form

Let's add the code for each of these three buttons. First, add code to the ActCheckOutPatron_Click event handler.

INSERT SNIPPET

Insert Chapter 20, Snippet Item 12.

This code prompts the user for patron selection, and displays the remaining fields if successful. Here's the part of the code that does the prompting:

```
' ----- Get the ID of the patron.
patronID = (New PatronAccess).SelectPatron( )
If (patronID = -1) Then Return

' ----- Get the patron name.
sqlText = "SELECT FirstName + ' ' + LastName FROM Patron " & _
   "WHERE ID = " & patronID
patronName = CStr(ExecuteSQLReturn(sqlText))

' ----- Is this patron active?
sqlText = "SELECT Active FROM Patron WHERE ID = " & patronID
If (CBool(ExecuteSQLReturn(sqlText)) = False) Then
   MsgBox("Patron '" & patronName & _
      "' is marked as inactive.", MsgBoxStyle.OkOnly Or _
      MsgBoxStyle.Exclamation, ProgramTitle)
   Return
End If
```

Add code to the ActDoCheckOut_Click event handler, which processes each item through the Check Out button.

INSERT SNIPPET

Insert Chapter 20, Snippet Item 13.

As I mentioned before, this code differentiates between numeric entry (bar codes) and other entries (titles).

```
If (IsNumeric(Trim(CheckOutBarcode.Text))) Then
    ' ----- Probably a bar code supplied. Get the related ID.
    sqlText = "SELECT ID FROM ItemCopy WHERE Barcode = " & _
        DBText(Trim(CheckOutBarcode.Text))
    copyID = DBGetInteger(ExecuteSQLReturn(sqlText))
    If (copyID = 0) Then
        ' ----- Invalid bar code.
        MsgBox("Bar code not found.", MsgBoxStyle.OkOnly Or _
            MsgBoxStyle.Exclamation, ProgramTitle)
        CheckOutBarcode.Focus()
        CheckOutBarcode.SelectAll()
        Return
    End If
Else
    ' ----- Lookup by title.
    copyID = (New CheckLookup).CheckItemByTitle(False, _
        Trim(CheckOutBarcode.Text))
    If (copyID = -1) Then Return
End If
```

Eventually, after verifying that the item is available for patron use, the code checks out the item by updating the relevant records in the database.

```
TransactionBegin()

' ----- Update patron copy record.
sqlText = "INSERT INTO PatronCopy (Patron, ItemCopy, " & _
    "CheckOut, Renewal, DueDate, Returned, Missing, " & _
    "Fine, Paid) VALUES (" & ActiveCheckOutPatron & ", " & _
    copyID & ", " & DBDate(Today) & ", 0, " & _
    DBDate(untilDate) & ", 0, 0, 0, 0)"
ExecuteSQL(sqlText)

' ----- Update the patron record.
sqlText = "UPDATE Patron SET LastActivity = GETDATE() " & _
    "WHERE ID = " & ActiveCheckOutPatron
ExecuteSQL(sqlText)

TransactionCommit()
```

The last of the three buttons is the Finish button. Add code to the ActFinishCheckOut_Click event handler.

Insert Chapter 20, Snippet Item 14.

This code simply resets the display fields in preparation for the next patron checkout.

The listbox on the checkout panel needs to display two columns of data: (1) the due date; and (2) details of the item, such as title and bar code. These values were added to the list using the CheckedOutItem class we added a little earlier in the chapter. Add code to the CheckedOutItems_DrawItem event handler.

Insert Chapter 20, Snippet Item 15.

Checking In Items

Checking in items is much simpler since we don't need to first identify the patron. The bar code or title of the check-in item is sufficient to complete all processing. Figure 20-12 shows the check-in panel.

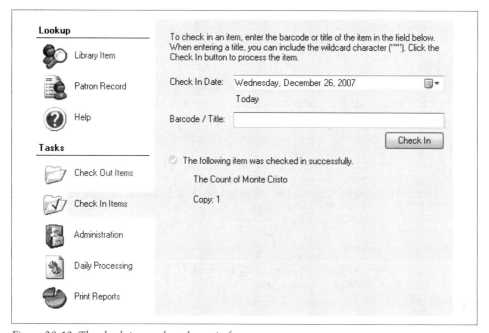

Figure 20-12. The check-in panel on the main form

This panel includes a date indicating when the item will be checked in. Normally, that's today, but if library items are turned in through a nighttime repository after business hours, the librarian might want to adjust the date to "Yesterday," just in case any of these items were turned in before midnight. Let's add some code so that the panel indicates "Today" or "Yesterday" or some other day when the date changes. Add the following code to the CheckedInDate_ValueChanged event handler.

INSERT SNIPPET

Insert Chapter 20, Snippet Item 16.

```
' ----- Adjust the day in the display.
Select Case DateDiff(DateInterval.Day, _
      CheckInDate.Value, Today)
   Case 0    ' ----- Today
      CheckInDay.Text = "Today"
      CheckInDay.BackColor = SystemColors.Control
      CheckInDay.ForeColor = SystemColors.ControlText
   Case 1    ' ----- Yesterday
      CheckInDay.Text = "Yesterday"
      CheckInDay.BackColor = Color.Red
      CheckInDay.ForeColor = Color.White
   Case Else ' ----- X days ago
      CheckInDay.Text = DateDiff(DateInterval.Day, _
      CheckInDate.Value, Today) & " days ago"
      CheckInDay.BackColor = Color.Red
      CheckInDay.ForeColor = Color.White
End Select
```

The actual check-in occurs when the user enters a bar code or title in the text field, and clicks the Check In button. Add code to the ActDoCheckIn_Click event handler.

INSERT SNIPPET

Insert Chapter 20, Snippet Item 17.

After performing some lookups and confirmation checks, the code checks in the item through database updates.

```
' ----- Do the check-in in a transaction.
TransactionBegin( )

' ----- Update patron copy record.
sqlText = "UPDATE PatronCopy SET CheckIn = " & _
   DBDate(CheckInDate.Value) & _
   ", Returned = 1 WHERE ID = " & patronCopyID
ExecuteSQL(sqlText)
```

```
' ----- Update the patron record.
sqlText = "UPDATE Patron SET LastActivity = " & _
    "GETDATE() WHERE ID = " & patronID
ExecuteSQL(sqlText)

TransactionCommit()
```

That's it for the check-in and checkout procedures, and all ticket printing. It's pretty good code, but not yet perfect. What we haven't yet added is code to properly process fines on items before they are checked in, or as they are adjusted in other ways. We will postpone this logic until Chapter 22. Until then, let's look at another application printing feature: reports.

Reporting

For the business application developer, reports are a fact of life. You may want to spend your time developing cool user interfaces or figuring out the core algorithms used in Generally Accepted Accounting Principles. But instead, you invest many boring hours each week turning out report after report. And these reports take a significant toll on the programming community. In America alone, the Centers for Disease Control and Prevention estimates nearly 850 report-related deaths each year—and that doesn't even count those who read the reports. I once had a customer that printed off 20 copies of a 600-page report every month for its top-level managers. Clearly stupefied by the amount of tree pulp used to generate this report, the staff was unable to come up with a more interesting name than "the monthly report."

So, if you are a business programmer, reports are in your future. But whereas your forebears had to deal with languages such as RPG III, you get to use .NET. Hey, reports won't be so bad after all. And even without resorting to third-party reporting tools, Visual Studio and .NET include several report-focused features and tools you can use right out of the box.

This chapter discusses some of those reporting resources, and delves a little deeper into the reporting controls used in the Library Project.

Report Options in .NET

Reporting involves displaying and printing basic or summarized data to the user for specific business purposes. Visual Basic 2008 Professional Edition includes six primary methods of accomplishing this goal. Other editions add to or reduce this set of choices, and you can always enhance this list using third-party tools.

PrintDocument-Based Printing

As we learned in the previous chapter, the .NET Framework includes a full object-based printing system that uses GDI+ commands to draw text and graphics on each printed page. Since you can put anything you want on each page, you could develop your own custom reports using this method. The responsibility for positioning each label and calculated field on the page, and determining when to move to a new page, will rest entirely on your shoulders. Still, the GDI+ commands are straightforward, and developing some basic reports using this method would not be overwhelming.

If you want to take this route for your reports, I refer you back to Chapter 20 and the basic printing concepts presented there.

HTML/Web Pages

Besides being a significant timewaster, the Internet (and its HTML-based page description language) is a great medium for data-report communication. The table-formatting tags in HTML (such as <td>) let you organize tabular output without much effort. Sure, it's a chore stringing all of those baby-size text strings together to build the page, but there are ways around that, too.

Back in Chapter 13, I discussed XSLT (XSL Transformations), a way to take XML-based data and reshape it into any form you want—including great works of art by Michelangelo, or nicely crafted HTML. However you obtain the HTML, you have a choice of display methods as well. The most direct method involves storing the generated HTML in a disk file, and starting the user's default browser to display it using a command such as:

```
Process.Start("c:\temp\MyReport.htm")
```

If you want the report to have a more "integrated" look in your application, you can display the HTML content in a web browser control. We did this in the project code for Chapter 17, when we displayed the details of a library item as HTML.

XPS Documents

Windows Presentation Foundation (WPF) is used primarily to make your user interface dance with color and action. But a portion of that technology exists to generate XML-based static documents known as *XPS* (XML Paper Specification). Just as you can generate reports using HTML, you can generate them using the XPS standard.

Chapter 18 includes a brief discussion of WPF and XPS. If the generation of XPS-based reports is of interest to you, check out the documentation included with Visual Studio.

Reporting Services and Controls

Visual Studio includes a set of classes in the `Microsoft.Reporting` namespace that are specifically designed to report data. The key class in this namespace is the `ReportViewer` class (identified as `MicrosoftReportViewer` in its control alter-ego). Actually, it is two controls: one for Windows Forms and one for Web Forms. These controls are based, in part, on the technology found in Microsoft SQL Server Reporting Services, although you can use the controls without SQL Server.

The Library Project will use the `WinForms.ReportViewer` control for its built-in reports. We'll spend most of this chapter discussing the control and its use in Windows Forms applications. I won't be discussing the Web Forms version of the control here, although its use closely parallels that of the Windows Forms version.

You'll see how simple it is to add the `MicrosoftReportViewer` control to an existing project. But Visual Studio also includes a new project template that focuses on the `MicrosoftReportViewer` control. Creating a new "Reports Application" project uses a project wizard to help you set up a custom report. The final result can be your complete report application, or you can use it as the basis for further customization.

Crystal Reports

If you have at least the Professional Edition of Visual Studio 2008, you received a complimentary copy of Crystal Reports. The included version is a functional subset of the official Crystal Reports 2008 release. If you are new to Visual Basic, you have missed out on the previous versions of Crystal Reports that have been included with the language since its earliest releases. Because of this long-time relationship with Visual Basic, Crystal Reports has become one of the most widely used reporting packages on the market.

Crystal Reports is a third-party product, currently owned by a company called Business Objects. The product has changed ownership hands several times since it was first paired with Visual Basic, but Business Objects seems to be taking care of it for now. I won't be discussing Crystal Reports any further in this book.

Integration with Microsoft Office

Visual Basic has been the primary macro language of the Microsoft Office suite of applications since the untimely death of WordBasic. But I'm talking about pre-.NET Visual Basic, which is so unmanaged. Fortunately, you can also use the managed world of Visual Basic 2008 to interact with Microsoft Office applications. How you interact with Office depends on whether the Office document or the Visual Basic application is the primary focus for the user.

If your goal is to enhance a "line of business" application by using various Office applications as the portal to that application—for example, showing the latest sales figures from within Microsoft Outlook—consider building an *Office Business Application* (OBA). OBAs represent a new way of designing integrated programs using Visual Studio, Microsoft Office, Microsoft SharePoint Services, and other related systems. From the Visual Studio side of the world, your development work happens through Visual Studio Tools for Office (abbreviated as VSTO, or "visto"), included with the Professional and Team System editions of Visual Studio.

If your goal is to create your own "task bar" add-ins within Office applications, use the new Office Add-In project templates included with Visual Studio. These easy-to-develop extensions let you customize the user experience by customizing the Office feature set. Add-ins are also considered part of VSTO, and are available only with Visual Studio 2008 Professional and Team System editions.

If the user will access Office features only indirectly through your Visual Basic application (e.g., if you want your program to initiate a Microsoft Word mail merge), use the Microsoft Office Primary Interop Assemblies (PIA) supplied by Microsoft. These libraries provide access to Office application-specific features through the `Microsoft.Office` namespace. Like VSTO, these libraries link up your .NET code to Microsoft Office, but with the focus on your code instead of on the Office document.

Using Reporting Controls in .NET

Let's spend the remainder of this chapter discussing the standard reporting tools provided in Visual Studio. As mentioned earlier, two `ReportViewer` classes are included in Visual Studio: one for desktop development and one for web development. I'll be talking about only the desktop variation in this chapter. The designer used to develop these reports does not differentiate between the report target (desktop or browser). There are some differences in deployment, but I'll have to leave the web deployment to a future best-selling programming book, or to your own research.

The `MicrosoftReportViewer` control integrates directly with Microsoft SQL Server Reporting Services, displaying whole pages generated by that server-based system. Since we're assuming that you are using SQL Server Express Edition for your development (which does not include Reporting Services), I'll focus instead on the control's "local" mode presentation. This lets you display any data from any source you choose on each report display page, including SQL Server.

In the vein of "those who can, do; those who can't, teach," let me walk you through the steps needed to visually design a simple report using the `ReportViewer` class. We'll create a report that lists the records in the Library Project's `Activity` table, a table that will have data in it even if you haven't used the Library program yet. This works best if you follow along in front of your computer, because reading about report design is a lot like reading about brain surgery: it's more interesting if you actually do it. Start by creating a new Windows Forms application.

Adding the Data Source

Add a data source to the project that refers to the Activity database table. We already did this back in Chapter 10, in the "Creating a Data Source" section. Select the Data → Add New Data Source menu command, and use the Data Source Configuration Wizard to locate your Library database. When you reach the list of database objects, check the box next to the Activity table, and click the Finish button. You should now have a data source named LibraryDataSet. Figure 21-1 shows the elements added to the Solution Explorer and the Data Sources panel by this action.

Figure 21-1. The LibraryDataSet as a data source, and as an XML ".xsd" file

Adding a Report Design Surface

Use the Project → Add New Item menu command to add a new "Report" item. Figure 21-2 shows the item report in the Add New Item dialog. Make sure you choose Report and not Crystal Report from the list.

Figure 21-2. Adding a new report to the project

Click the Add button to insert the report into the project. A new *Report1.rdlc* file appears in your project, and its designer opens automatically. "RDLC" is short for "Report Definition Language – Client," and files of this type contain XML content that describes the layout of a locally designed report. Figure 21-3 shows the designer for the added *Report1.rdlc* file, plus the controls in the toolbar that you can add to the report surface. I will refer to reports created through this designer as "RDLC reports" throughout the rest of this chapter.

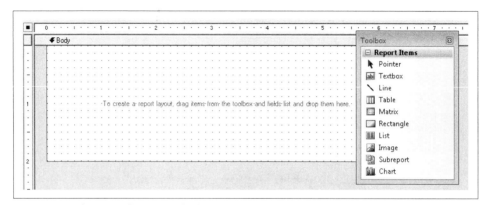

Figure 21-3. The report designer and related toolbar

Designing the Report Surface

If you've written reports in Microsoft Access or in some other common reporting tool, you are probably familiar with "banded" reports. These reports have separate "bands" or stripes that represent a portion of the printed page. Bands include page headers and footers, report headers and footers, the record detail section, and group headers and footers used to visually and logically group the detail entries. As the report runs, an imaginary horizontal page-wide line runs from the top to the bottom of the page. As the line hits each band, the report processes the fields in that band until there are no more records to process.

RDLC reports are a little bit different from those banded reports. There are only three bands: page header, page footer, and everything else (a band called "Body"). Instead of adding bands for records and groups, you add fields to *data regions*. These special controls process the records linked to the report according to the shape of the data region. There are four data region controls in the toolbox:

Table
> This region presents an unlimited number of data rows, but with a predefined set of data columns. It's designed for tabular presentation of data records, with each column generally displaying a single source or calculated data field. Each row of the table represents a source data record.

Matrix
> This control is similar to the Table region, but it allows for a flexible number of data columns, not just rows.

List
> The List region provides a free-form display section for each incoming record. You can add any number of fields or display controls to the record section.

Chart
> Charts use the collected data of the report to present line, bar, and pie charts to the user.

Records from data sets are always tied to a data region. If your report includes data from multiple distinct data sources, each data source will link to exactly one report region, and all regions appear in the Body band. We'll use a List data region for this sample report. Go ahead and add the List control to the Body band on the report surface. You can now add other items either to the band surface itself, or to the List control surface. Items added to the List control are reprocessed for each record in the incoming data source. These items can be either controls from the toolbox, or database fields displayed in the Data Sources panel. Using the Activity table in the Data Sources panel, drag the FullName field to the List control surface. Figure 21-4 shows the display just after performing this drag operation.

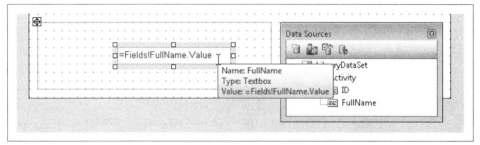

Figure 21-4. A List control with a field from the data set

When we dragged the field from the data source to the List control, Visual Studio established a link between them. The list1 control's DataSetName field now refers to LibraryDataSet_Activity, the name of the data source. It also added a TextBox control to the list's surface, and added an expression (=Fields!FullName.Value) that displays the contents of that field from the database for each processed record.

I'm going to resize the List control, the text box, and the Body band so that the FullName text box field is pretty much all there is in the report (see Figure 21-5).

Figure 21-5. A resized version of the report

The report is ready to use. As we designed the report surface, Visual Studio was busy generating XML and storing it in the *Report1.rdlc* file.

Using a Report Control

The RDLC file is only an XML definition of a report; it doesn't have any ability to display itself. To view the report, we must add a report control to a form or web page that knows how to properly merge the XML design content with the data from the specified data source. Return to Form1, and add a MicrosoftReportViewer control to its surface from the toolbox (it's in the Reporting section of the toolbox on my system).

The added control includes a small "smart tags" button in its upper-right corner. Clicking this button displays the ReportViewer Tasks fly-out window, which appears in Figure 21-6.

The MicrosoftReportViewer control presents a form-based experience for displaying reports. Most of the control is a blank area where the report appears. It also includes a toolbar used to navigate through the pages of the report. The user can also initiate an export or a printout of the report through these controls. If you don't need the toolbar or one of its controls, use the various Show... properties of the MicrosoftReportViewer control to hide the unneeded elements.

Figure 21-6. The MicrosoftReportViewer control on the form surface

The report viewer is generic and report-independent. If you have several RDLC files in your project, you can display any of them (one at a time) through the same report viewer. We have only one report in our project, so let's connect it (*SimpleReport.Report1.rdlc*) to the viewer by using the Choose Report task from the report viewer's smart tag button. Also, click on the "Dock in parent container" task in the fly-out window to expand the report to the form's size.

The RDLC report, the data from the data source, and the MicrosoftReportViewer control are all joined in one glorious report display by the magic of data binding. When you linked the report to the viewer control, three more controls appeared on the form: LibraryDataSet, ActivityBindingSource, and ActivityTableAdapter. LibraryDataSet is a reference to the actual data source we added earlier. The other two controls wrap up that data in a form that can be bound to the report viewer. Although you can't see it in the designer, the hidden form code connects up these controls and the XML report to the viewer.

```
ReportDataSource1.Name = "LibraryDataSet_Activity"
ReportDataSource1.Value = Me.ActivityBindingSource
Me.ReportViewer1.LocalReport.DataSources.Add( _
    ReportDataSource1)
Me.ReportViewer1.LocalReport.ReportEmbeddedResource = _
    "SimpleReport.Report1.rdlc"
```

Yeah, I don't really get it, either. But that's OK. Visual Studio connected it all up for us.

Running the Report

Press F5 and see the results of your efforts. In Figure 21-7, I adjusted the view by clicking on the Page Layout toolbar button, and setting the zoom level to Page Width.

Well, that report is fine as far as Activity table reports go, but we could spruce it up a bit more.

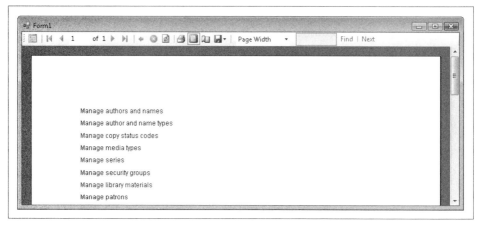

Figure 21-7. Reporting the essential contents of the Activity table

Adding a Page Header and Footer

I think the report needs a meaningful title at the top of each page, plus a page number in the bottom-right corner. Let's return to the RDLC report designer and add them. Once there, right-click on the background of the report (not the body, which has the grid marks on it), as shown in Figure 21-8.

Figure 21-8. Adding page headers and footers

From this menu, select Page Header, then bring up the menu again and select Page Footer. Each new band appears on the report surface.

Whether it's static, unchanging text or text that's dynamically generated from a data source, the TextBox control is the control of choice for showing text content. Add a TextBox control from the toolbox to both the header and footer sections. Click inside the header's text box, and type the following:

```
="The Activity Table Report"
```

You can use the Properties panel to adjust the look of this control, including its display font.

In the footer text box, add this text:

```
="Page " & Globals!PageNumber
```

The `Globals` pseudo-object includes a few members that you can use in the report. How did I know to use `Globals!PageNumber`? I built the expression visually using the Expression Editor. To access it, right-click on the `TextBox` control and select Expression from the shortcut menu. The editor, shown in Figure 21-9, lets you build up an expression using lists of functions and field names. The actual functions just happen to be—hooray—Visual Basic functions.

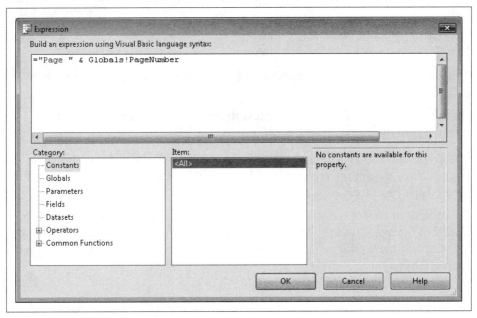

Figure 21-9. The Expression Editor

Support for Grouping and Sorting

Grouping of data is common in printed reports. To add grouping to our report, we need to embed our existing `List` control (the detail record) within another `List` control (the group), and set various properties on the group `List` control to determine the method of data grouping.

Let's try it. Add another `List` control (called `list2`) to the report body, and give it twice the height as the existing `List` control (called `list1`). Then, drag `list1` (the detail record) into `list2` (the new group), placing it toward the bottom. Your report should look like Figure 21-10.

To configure the group, right-click on it and select Properties from the shortcut menu. The List Properties form appears. On its General tab, click the "Edit details group" button, which sets the grouping. On the Grouping and Sorting Properties form that appears, enter the following text into the first row of the "Group on" field:

```
=Left(Fields!FullName.Value, 1)
```

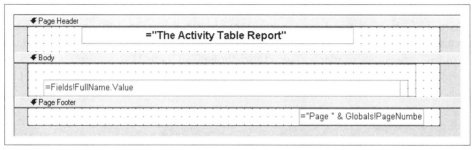

Figure 21-10. A grouping list added to the report

This expression tells the list2 control to group its detail results by the first character of the first name field.

On this same form, add the following text to the "Document map label" field:

```
="Letter: " & Left(Fields!FullName.Value, 1)
```

The document map enables a clickable hyperlink list into the different groups of the report. When we run the report a little later, we'll see this map just to the left of the report display surface.

The records in the Activity table are ordered for the convenience of the programmer (me). But the report user probably wants to see them sorted in some reasonable fashion. Click on the Sorting tab, and add the following text to the "Sort on" field, in the Expression column:

```
=Fields!FullName.Value
```

As expected, this will sort the data by the FullName field. Click the OK buttons all the way out, and return to the report surface.

We still need to add something that will make each group stand out. Add a TextBox control to the list2 grouping control. Put it in the upper-left corner of that parent control, and type the following text into it (or into its Value property):

```
=Left(Fields!FullName.Value, 1)
```

I also set its BackgroundColor property to "Black," its Color property to "White," and its Font property to "Normal, Arial, 12pt, Bold" just for looks.

Running the report gives the results in Figure 21-11. Notice the document map along the left edge of the window, and the grouped single-letter titles before each grouped section.

Enhanced Style Formatting

Probably the coolest feature of RDLC reports is that many of the properties for items placed on the report surface can include conditional expressions. This means that you can conditionally alter, say, the visual properties of a TextBox control based on the value of a field in the current record.

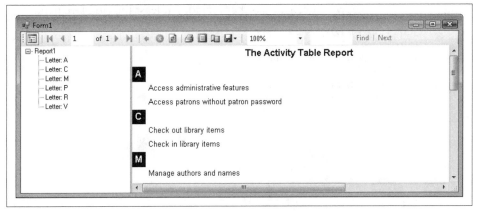

Figure 21-11. The full report, with grouping and sorting enabled

In the "Project" section of this chapter, we'll write a report that uses due dates for items currently checked out. If the item is past due, I want to show the due date in red. Normally, a `TextBox` control's `Color` property (which controls font color) is "Black." To have that field respond to overdue items, I will replace "Black" with the following expression:

```
=IIf(Fields!DueDate.Value < Today, "Red", "Black")
```

Using Custom Data

Although it is very common to generate reports from databases, you can actually use data from virtually any source. When using the `MicrosoftReportViewer` control, any data source that implements the `IEnumerable` interface is good enough. That includes all collections, arrays, and LINQ query results. The report isn't that picky, as long as the data is formatted as it expects. For the report we just made, we can ditch the actual data and supply our own fake data. This intercepting and substituting data is like something out of a spy thriller. But we must follow a few rules to make it work:

- When we dragged the `Activity.FullName` field from the data source to the report surface, the report (actually, the `list1` control) got this funny idea that all data had to come from a data source named `LibraryDataSet_Activity`. Any data source we use in place of the real one must keep this name.
- The fake data source must include the `FullName` field, since that is what the report fields expect.

Those rules aren't so bad. So, here's what we need to do: create a fake data source, intercept the report just before it tries to get the data from the Library database, and insert our own data instead.

For a fake data source, we'll need a class that includes at least the `FullName` field.

```
Public Class FakeActivityRecord
   Private StoredID As Long
   Private StoredFullName As String

   Public Sub New(ByVal whatID As Long, _
         ByVal whatFullName As String)
      StoredID = whatID
      StoredFullName = whatFullName
   End Sub

   Public Property ID() As Long
      Get
         Return StoredID
      End Get
      Set(ByVal value As Long)
         StoredID = value
      End Set
   End Property

   Public Property FullName() As String
      Get
         Return StoredFullName
      End Get
      Set(ByVal value As String)
         StoredFullName = value
      End Set
   End Property
End Class
```

The exposed fields must be properties, and not just public fields; the report viewer doesn't recognize standard member fields.

If you look at the source code for Form1, you'll find that the following code was added to the Form_Load event handler when we linked the report viewer with the RDLC report:

```
Me.ActivityTableAdapter.Fill(Me.LibraryDataSet.Activity)
Me.ReportViewer1.RefreshReport()
```

It's that first line that loads the data from the Library database's Activity table and links it to the report. We need to replace those two wizard-generated lines with code that cuts off the real data at the pass.

```
' ----- Create a fake table of fake records.
Dim fakeSource As New Collections.Generic.List( _
   Of FakeActivityRecord)

' ----- Add each of the fake records.
fakeSource.Add(New FakeActivityRecord(1, "Do some work"))
fakeSource.Add(New FakeActivityRecord(2, "Take a nap"))
fakeSource.Add(New FakeActivityRecord(3, "Write a program"))
```

```
'----- The report was already bound to the true
'       data source. Delete it.
Me.ReportViewer1.LocalReport.DataSources.Clear( )

'----- Build a new data source. Remember, it must have
'       the same name.
Dim fakeReportSource As New _
    Microsoft.Reporting.WinForms.ReportDataSource
fakeReportSource.Name = "LibraryDataSet_Activity"
fakeReportSource.Value = fakeSource

'----- Connect the data source to the report, and we're done.
Me.ReportViewer1.LocalReport.DataSources.Add(fakeReportSource)
Me.ReportViewer1.RefreshReport( )
```

Figure 21-12 shows the report with the fake data on display.

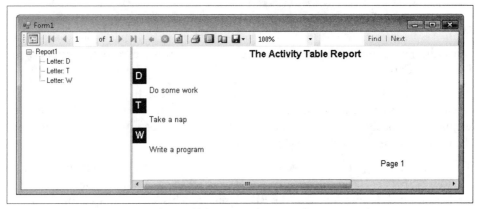

Figure 21-12. This fake data will not self-destruct in five seconds

Supplying Custom Data Sources

Substituting data at the last second is fine and all, but what if you want to design a report that doesn't depend on a database at all? You can do that, too, by supplying a fully custom data source. RDLC reports require some sort of data source schema at design time; you just can't supply fully custom data on the fly when running the report. But you can supply a custom schema based on a class in your application.

For the class, we'll stick with the FakeActivityRecord we created in the previous section. Then we will design a data source from this class. Select the Data → Add New Data Source menu command. When the Data Source Configuration Wizard has appeared in the past, you have always selected Database as the source for the data. This time, select Object, as shown in Figure 21-13.

When you click the Next button, a hierarchy of all the classes in your application appears. Expand the classes, then locate and select the FakeActivityRecord class.

Figure 21-13. Creating a data source based on a custom object

Click the Finish button. FakeActivityRecord now appears as a data source in the Data Sources panel.

Now you can drag and drop this data source's FullName field onto a new RDLC report design surface. Add a new report to your project, and follow the same steps we used previously to design the first report. This time, use the FakeActivityRecord data source instead of the LibraryDataSet source.

To test this new report, I removed the original Form1 from the project and added a brand-new Form1. I also added a MicrosoftReportViewer control to its surface and docked it, but I did not link it to the RDLC report. This keeps things a lot cleaner as there are no binding source controls and whatnot to worry about. Then I added this code to the form's Load event handler:

```
' ----- Link to the RDLC report design.
Me.ReportViewer1.LocalReport.ReportEmbeddedResource = _
   "SimpleReport.Report2.rdlc"

' ----- Create a fake table of fake records.
Dim fakeSource As New Collections.Generic.List( _
   Of FakeActivityRecord)

' ----- Add each of the fake records.
fakeSource.Add(New FakeActivityRecord(1, "Breakfast"))
fakeSource.Add(New FakeActivityRecord(2, "Lunch"))
fakeSource.Add(New FakeActivityRecord(3, "Dinner"))

' ----- Build a new data source. Remember, it must have
'       the same name.
Dim fakeReportSource As New _
   Microsoft.Reporting.WinForms.ReportDataSource
fakeReportSource.Name = "SimpleReport_FakeActivityRecord"
fakeReportSource.Value = fakeSource
```

```
' ----- Connect the data source to the report, and we're done.
Me.ReportViewer1.LocalReport.DataSources.Add(fakeReportSource)
Me.ReportViewer1.RefreshReport()
```

It's pretty similar to the previous custom code, although the data source name is now `SimpleReport_FakeActivityRecord`, the name this new report expects (which I found out by running the report and reading the error message).

I've saved a copy of both custom reports in the installation directory for the book's source code samples. Look in the subdirectory named *SimpleReport*.

Summary

Although this chapter included many pretty pictures and a lot of instructions, we only scratched the surface of the features available in the reporting controls included with .NET. I think I bruised my brain when I tried to study up on every available feature, but perhaps your brain is better prepared for the task. Still, if you don't find it exactly to your liking, you can use one of the other reporting features I listed at the start of the chapter, or even opt for a third-party solution.

Reports are an important part of the business developer's daily life. Finding the right reporting tool and getting comfortable with its features is not only a good suggestion, it's a necessity in the world of report-hungry software users.

Project

When we last left the Technical Resource Kit document for the Library Project, it listed five "built-in" reports:

- Report #1: Items Checked Out Report
- Report #2: Items Overdue Report
- Report #3: Items Missing Report
- Report #4: Fines Owed by Patrons Report
- Report #5: Library Database Statistics Report

We'll add these five reports to the project in this chapter. Before we write any code, we need to figure out how we're going to get the data. Since the data will come from the Library database, we just need to craft the SQL statement for each report that will link to the designed report.

The fifth report, "statistics," will report things such as the number of items, the number of patrons, and other similar statistical values from the Library database. Since this data can't really come from a single SQL statement, we'll extract the data from the database and build a custom data source that feeds into the report.

Crafting the SQL Statements

The first report, "items checked out," lists the patron name and item title for every item currently checked out by the patron. It involves the Patron table (to get the patron name), the PatronCopy table (the checkout event), the ItemCopy table (the actual item checked out), and the NamedItem table (where the item title appears). We'll also include the CodeMediaType table, which tells us whether the item is a book, a CD, or some other media type.

Microsoft SQL Server Management Studio Express includes a visual Query Designer that we can use to design the query. Figure 21-14 shows the five needed tables as linked together by the designer.

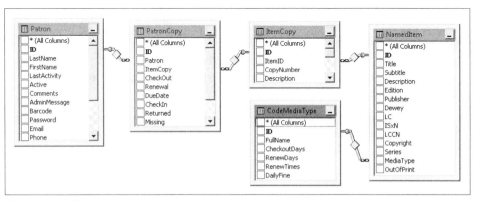

Figure 21-14. The five tables in the checked-out items query

Whether you use the Query Designer or build the SQL statement by hand, you eventually come up with something similar to the following, which we'll use within the Library application:

```
/* ----- Report #1: Items checked out report. */
SELECT PA.LastName + ', ' + PA.FirstName AS PatronName,
   PA.Barcode AS PatronBarcode,
   PC.DueDate, IC.CopyNumber, IC.Barcode AS ItemBarcode,
   NI.Title, CMT.FullName AS MediaName
FROM Patron AS PA
   INNER JOIN PatronCopy AS PC ON PA.ID = PC.Patron
   INNER JOIN ItemCopy AS IC ON PC.ItemCopy = IC.ID
   INNER JOIN NamedItem AS NI ON IC.ItemID = NI.ID
   INNER JOIN CodeMediaType AS CMT ON NI.MediaType = CMT.ID
WHERE PC.Returned = 0
   AND PC.Missing = 0
   AND IC.Missing = 0
ORDER BY NI.Title, IC.CopyNumber, PA.LastName, PA.FirstName
```

This query links up all of the tables, and then requests every record that has not been returned (PC.Returned = 0). It ignores any item marked as missing (PC.Missing = 0 AND

IC.Missing = 0). This query will eventually drive the report. But for now, keep in mind that RDLC reports don't actually need a real SQL statement or database table for the report schema. We can also build a compatible schema by hand using a class. This turns out to be a lot cleaner since we won't have a lot of dataset-related files strewn throughout the project source code. (The LibraryDataSet data source we created in the sample report earlier in this chapter added four source files and nearly 50 KB of source code to the project, not counting the RDLC report! The class-based data source didn't add any code other than the class definition itself, and a little bit of XML in the RDLC file.)

As for the data source schema, we can extrapolate it from the SELECT clause of the SQL query. If we were to design a class with a matching schema, it would look like this (without the property detail code):

```
Class Report1Schema
    Public Property PatronName As String
    Public Property PatronBarcode As String
    Public Property DueDate As Date
    Public Property CopyNumber As Integer
    Public Property ItemBarcode As String
    Public Property Title As String
    Public Property MediaName As String
End Class
```

The next two reports are for "overdue items" and "missing items." For me, the schema for report #1 is exactly what I want to see in these other two reports, so let's just use the same SQL statement. All we need to do is change the WHERE clause. For the overdue items report, use this WHERE clause:

```
WHERE PC.Returned = 0
    AND PC.Missing = 0
    AND IC.Missing = 0
    AND PC.DueDate < GETDATE()
```

The missing items report will use this WHERE clause:

```
WHERE PC.Missing = 1
    OR IC.Missing = 1
```

The fourth report displays the amount of fines still owed by patrons, so it will require a different schema. Here's its SQL statement, which uses some aggregate grouping features:

```
/* ----- Report #4: Fines owed by patron. */
SELECT PA.LastName + ', ' + PA.FirstName AS PatronName,
    PA.Barcode AS PatronBarcode,
    SUM(PC.Fine - PC.Paid) AS FinesDue
FROM Patron AS PA
    INNER JOIN PatronCopy AS PC ON PA.ID = PC.Patron
GROUP BY PA.LastName + ', ' + PA.FirstName, PA.Barcode
HAVING SUM(PC.Fine - PC.Paid) > 0
ORDER BY PatronName
```

Here's the schema that goes with report #4:

```
Class Report4Schema
    Public Property PatronName As String
    Public Property PatronBarcode As String
    Public Property FinesDue As Decimal
End Class
```

For the final report, we'll just use a schema with two string values: a statistic name, and its related value. Here's its schema:

```
Class Report5Schema
    Public Property EntryName As String
    Public Property EntryValue As String
End Class
```

Well, that's enough preparation. Let's start coding.

PROJECT ACCESS

Load the Chapter 21 (Before) Code project, either through the New Project templates or by accessing the project directly from the installation directory. To see the code in its final form, load Chapter 21 (After) Code instead.

Adding Report Schemas

The *ReportSchemas.vb* file, already added to the project, includes the three schemas used for the five built-in reports. Just to remind us of the members, here are the public property definitions included in each class, minus the Get and Set accessors, and minus the private class members:

```
Public Class ReportSchemaPatronItems
    ' ----- Used for the following reports:
    '          Report #1: Items checked out report
    '          Report #2: Items overdue report
    '          Report #3: Items missing report
    Public Property PatronName() As String
    Public Property PatronBarcode() As String
    Public Property DueDate() As Date
    Public Property CopyNumber() As Integer
    Public Property ItemBarcode() As String
    Public Property Title() As String
    Public Property MediaName() As String
End Class

Public Class ReportSchemaPatronFines
    ' ----- Used for the following reports:
    '          Report #4: Fines owed by patron
    Public Property PatronName() As String
    Public Property PatronBarcode() As String
    Public Property FinesDue() As Decimal
End Class
```

```
Public Class ReportSchemaStatistics
   ' ----- Used for the following reports:
   '         Report #5: Library database statistics report
   Public Property EntryName() As String
   Public Property EntryValue() As String
End Class
```

Once the schema classes are in the project, you will need to build the project before those classes can be used in RDLC reports as data sources. In the Library Project, build the project now with the Build → Build Library menu command. All three schemas should then appear as sources in the Data Sources panel (see Figure 21-15). If the Data Sources panel is closed, open it using the Data → Show Data Sources menu command.

Figure 21-15. The three data source schemas

Adding Reports

Since we already jointly created an RDLC report earlier in the chapter, I went ahead and added the five built-in reports for you:

ReportCheckedOut.rdlc

This file implements report #1, the "items checked out" report. It uses the ReportSchemaPatronItems class schema, and includes three columns in the main data list: patron name/bar code, item name/bar code/details, and due date. For the item name field, I wanted to present additional information when available. The item name, copy number, and media type are required values, but item bar code is optional. Here's the format I desired:

```
Item Name (#CopyNumber, MediaType, Barcode)
```

To get this result, I had to concatenate the various source fields together, and use a conditional function (IIf) to optionally include the bar code and its comma:

```
=Fields!Title.Value & " (#" &
↳CStr(Fields!CopyNumber.Value) & ", " &
↳Fields!MediaName.Value &
↳IIf(IsNothing(Fields!ItemBarcode.Value), "",
↳", " & Fields!ItemBarcode.Value) & ")"
```

As mentioned earlier, the due date field has an expression in its Color property that turns the text red when the item is overdue.

ReportOverdue.rdlc

This report shows a list of all overdue items in the system. Since everything will be overdue, I set the due date field to always use red for its font color. Other than that and the title, the report is basically identical to the checked-out items report.

ReportMissing.rdlc

This report shows a list of all items marked as missing. Even though the schema includes a due date field, I don't use it in this report. The rest of the report is basically identical to the checked-out items report.

ReportPatronFines.rdlc

This report lists all patrons that still owe fines, and the amount of the fine due. It uses the ReportSchemaPatronFines class schema. The field that displays the fine has a "C" in its Format property. This formatting code forces the decimal value to display as currency using the culture settings on the local system. This Format property uses the same codes recognized by the String.Format method.

ReportStatistics.rdlc

Report #5 displays record counts from some of the tables in the Library database. This is the only report that uses the ReportSchemaStatistics class schema. The report itself just displays two strings per record: a name and a value. It depends on the calling code to format those fields properly.

Adding a Report Viewer

It's time to add a MicrosoftReportViewer control. Since a single MicrosoftReportViewer control can display any type of RDLC report, we'll just add a single form to handle all five built-in reports.

Add a new form named *ReportBuiltinViewer.vb* to the project. Set its Text property to Library Report and its WindowState property to Maximized. Also, load the project's icon (*Book.ico*) into the Icon property. You'll find a copy of this file in the project installation directory. If you want, you can size the form to some reasonable starting point for a report (I used "680, 400"), but each report will start out maximized when used.

Add a `MicrosoftReportViewer` control named `ReportContent` to the form, and set its Dock property to `Fill`. Set both the `ShowBackButton` and `ShowDocumentMapButton` properties to `False`.

The code we will add to this form is a variation of code we wrote earlier in this chapter. The code that starts each report will pass to this form the name of the report RDLC file, the name of the data schema used, and the actual data. Since these reports will be modeless (you can keep them open while still using other parts of the Library program), we can't let the calling code wait around for the user to close the report before we discard the report data. We'll let the report dispose of the data itself. To do this, we need to keep a reference to that data. Add the following statement to the `ReportBuiltinViewer` form class.

INSERT SNIPPET

Insert Chapter 21, Snippet Item 1.

```
Private StoreDataTable As Object
```

Remember, reports can use a variety of data source formats, including true database connections, arrays, and collections. Reports #1 through #4 will use a `System.Data.DataTable` instance, and report #5 will pass a generic `List` collection.

The best time to dispose of the data is when the report is closing. Add the following event handler to the form, which confirms that the data supports the disposal process before calling the `Dispose` method.

INSERT SNIPPET

Insert Chapter 21, Snippet Item 2.

```
Private Sub ReportBuiltinViewer_FormClosing( _
      ByVal sender As Object, ByVal e As _
      System.Windows.Forms.FormClosingEventArgs) _
      Handles Me.FormClosing
   ' ----- Get rid of the data.
   If (TypeOf StoreDataTable Is IDisposable) Then
      CType(StoreDataTable, IDisposable).Dispose()
   End If
End Sub
```

The code that opens this display form will pass in the essential report values through a public method named `StartReport`. Add its code now.

INSERT SNIPPET

Insert Chapter 21, Snippet Item 3.

```
Public Sub StartReport(ByVal whichReport As String, _
    ByVal whichDataSchema As String, _
    ByVal whichData As Object)
  ' ----- Run one of the built-in reports. whichReport is
  '       the name of the RDLC report file, in the format
  '       "Library.xxx.rdlc." whichDataSchema provides the
  '       name of the schema to use, in the format
  '       "Library_xxx." whichDataSet is the actual data
  '       to link to the report, which must match the schema.
  Dim customDataSource As New _
      Microsoft.Reporting.WinForms.ReportDataSource

  ' ----- Connect the viewer, the report, and the data.
  ReportContent.LocalReport.ReportEmbeddedResource = _
      whichReport
  customDataSource.Name = whichDataSchema
  customDataSource.Value = whichData
  ReportContent.LocalReport.DataSources.Add( _
      customDataSource)

  ' ----- Display the report.
  StoreDataTable = whichData
  Me.Show( )
End Sub
```

This code tells the viewer which report to use as an embedded resource, and then attaches the data as a custom data source. "Local" in these property names indicates a local (client) report instead of a "server" report that runs within SQL Server.

When we were playing with the reports before, we saw that the default display mode was the "fill-the-entire-screen-with-page-content" mode. Personally, I like to see those fake page boundaries. The MicrosoftReportViewer control doesn't include a property that lets us change this default view (why not?), but we can still adjust the initial display style through methods on the control. When we added the report viewer to the form, Visual Studio also added the following statement to the form's Load event handler:

```
ReportContent.RefreshReport( )
```

Add the following code just before that statement.

INSERT SNIPPET

Insert Chapter 21, Snippet Item 4.

```
' ----- Generate and display the report.
ReportContent.SetDisplayMode( _
    Microsoft.Reporting.WinForms.DisplayMode.PrintLayout)
ReportContent.ZoomMode = _
    Microsoft.Reporting.WinForms.ZoomMode.Percent
ReportContent.ZoomPercent = 100
```

Adding Built-in Reports

I forget how long ago we added the *ReportSelect.vb* form that drives reporting, but it is already there in the project. In case you forgot what it looked like (I did), Figure 21-16 gives us a refresher.

Figure 21-16. The report selection form

We previously added support for our five built-in reports in this form's code. In a tribute to the never-ending reality of forgetting to finish all of the code, we need to add some code that we overlooked earlier. If you use an XML report configuration file to populate the report list, and you provide a description for each report in the XML, each entry displays that description in the lower half of the report selection form. But if you don't use a configuration file, and just depend on the form to add the five built-in reports by default (which it does), the form won't display associated descriptions, because we forgot to add them. Add a function to the ReportSelect class that returns a short description for each of the five reports.

INSERT SNIPPET

Insert Chapter 21, Snippet Item 5.

```
Private Function GetBuiltinReportDescription( _
      ByVal whichReport As ReportItemEnum) As String
   ' ----- Return a predefined description for the
   '       built-in reports.
   Select Case whichReport
      Case ReportItemEnum.BuiltInCheckedOut
         Return "Displays all items currently checked " & _
            "out, sorted by name."
      Case ReportItemEnum.BuiltInOverdue
         Return "Displays all overdue items, sorted by name."
      Case ReportItemEnum.BuiltInMissing
```

```
         Return "Displays all missing items, sorted by name."
      Case ReportItemEnum.BuiltInFinesOwed
         Return "Displays all unpaid fines owed by " & _
            "patrons, sorted by patron name."
      Case ReportItemEnum.BuiltInStatistics
         Return "Displays some record counts from the " & _
            "Library database."
      Case Else
         Return "There is no description for this report."
   End Select
End Function
```

We'll call this code from two places. The first is in the `LoadReportGroup` method. This code loads in the XML report configuration file. If that file includes one of the built-in reports, but doesn't supply a description with it, we'll supply the description ourselves. About halfway through that code, you'll find these lines:

```
' ----- So, what type of entry is it?
If (scanNode.Attributes("type").Value = "built-in") Then
```

About five lines below this is the following statement:

```
reportEntry.ItemType = CType(CInt( _
   reportEntry.ReportPath), ReportItemEnum)
```

Add the following code just after that statement.

INSERT SNIPPET

Insert Chapter 21, Snippet Item 6.

```
If (reportEntry.Description = "") Then _
   reportEntry.Description = _
   GetBuiltinReportDescription(reportEntry.ItemType)
```

The second need for the built-in descriptions appears in the `RefreshReportList` method. This method makes the call to `LoadReportGroup` to retrieve the XML configuration. But if after that the report list is still empty, `RefreshReportList` adds in the five default reports, which each require a description. Near the end of the method, within a `For...Next` loop, you'll find this closing statement:

```
' ----- Add the report entry to the list.
AllReports.Items.Add(reportEntry)
```

Add the following code just before that statement.

INSERT SNIPPET

Insert Chapter 21, Snippet Item 7.

```
reportEntry.Description = GetBuiltinReportDescription( _
   reportEntry.ItemType)
```

OK, that's it for the fix-up code. Now back to writing the actual reports. The code to start each of the five reports already exists in the ReportSelect form's ActRun_Click event handler. Most of that code includes a Select Case statement that acts as a switchboard for the selected report. Here's the part that calls the five built-in reports:

```
Case ReportItemEnum.BuiltInCheckedOut
   ' ----- Items Checked Out
   ' TODO: Write BasicReportCheckedOut( )
Case ReportItemEnum.BuiltInOverdue
   ' ----- Items Overdue
   ' TODO: Write BasicReportOverdue( )
Case ReportItemEnum.BuiltInMissing
   ' ----- Items Missing
   ' TODO: Write BasicReportMissing( )
Case ReportItemEnum.BuiltInFinesOwed
   ' ----- Fines Owed by Patrons
   ' TODO: Write BasicReportFines( )
Case ReportItemEnum.BuiltInStatistics
   ' ----- Library Database Statistics
   ' TODO: Write BasicReportStatistics( )
```

Clearly, this code isn't accomplishing much. Change each of the TODO lines, removing the TODO: Write portion of the statement. So, in the line that says:

```
' TODO: Write BasicReportCheckedOut( )
```

change the code to:

```
BasicReportCheckedOut( )
```

Do that for each of the five TODO lines.

Exposing these five method calls means that we have to write those methods, darn it. These methods will retrieve the data for the report, and send that data to the report viewer, along with the name of the RDLC file. They're actually quite short and simple, considering the beautiful reports you will get out of them. Let's start by adding the BasicReportCheckedOut method to the ReportSelect class.

INSERT SNIPPET

Insert Chapter 21, Snippet Item 8.

```
Private Sub BasicReportCheckedOut( )
   ' ----- Run built-in report #1: Items checked out report.
   Dim sqlText As String
   Dim reportData As Data.DataTable
   Dim reportForm As ReportBuiltinViewer

   On Error GoTo ErrorHandler

   ' ----- Retrieve the data as a dataset.
   sqlText = "SELECT PA.LastName + ', ' + " & _
      "PA.FirstName AS PatronName, " & _
```

```
          "PA.Barcode AS PatronBarcode, " & _
          "PC.DueDate, IC.CopyNumber, " & _
          "IC.Barcode AS ItemBarcode, " & _
          "NI.Title, CMT.FullName AS MediaName " & _
          "FROM Patron AS PA " & _
          "INNER JOIN PatronCopy AS PC ON PA.ID = PC.Patron " & _
          "INNER JOIN ItemCopy AS IC ON PC.ItemCopy = IC.ID " & _
          "INNER JOIN NamedItem AS NI ON IC.ItemID = NI.ID " & _
          "INNER JOIN CodeMediaType AS CMT ON " & _
          "NI.MediaType = CMT.ID " & _
          "WHERE PC.Returned = 0 " & _
          "AND PC.Missing = 0 " & _
          "AND IC.Missing = 0 " & _
          "ORDER BY NI.Title, IC.CopyNumber, " & _
          "PA.LastName, PA.FirstName"
      reportData = CreateDataTable(sqlText)

      ' ----- Check for no data.
      If (reportData.Rows.Count = 0) Then
         reportData.Dispose()
         MsgBox("No items are checked out.", MsgBoxStyle.OkOnly _
            Or MsgBoxStyle.Exclamation, ProgramTitle)
         Return
      End If

      ' ----- Send the data to the report.
      reportForm = New ReportBuiltinViewer
      reportForm.StartReport("Library.ReportCheckedOut.rdlc", _
         "Library_ReportSchemaPatronItems", reportData)
      Return

   ErrorHandler:
      GeneralError("ReportSelect.BasicReportCheckedOut", _
         Err.GetException())
      Return
   End Sub
```

The code retrieves the report-specific records from the database, and makes sure that
at least one record was included. (We could have added the SQL statement to the
Library database as either a stored procedure or a view, and called that instead. For
the purposes of this tutorial, it was simpler to store the statement directly in code.) It
then calls the report viewer, passing the name of the RDLC file, the schema name (in
the format ProjectName_ClassName), and the data table.

Next, add the BasicReportOverdue and BasicReportMissing methods. I won't show
the code here since, except for the name of the RDLC file and the WHERE clause in the
SQL statement, they are identical to BasicReportCheckedOut.

INSERT SNIPPET

Insert Chapter 21, Snippet Item 9.

Add in the BasicReportFines method, which handles built-in report #4.

INSERT SNIPPET

Insert Chapter 21, Snippet Item 10.

It's also quite similar to the BasicReportCheckedOut method, but it uses the SQL statement we designed earlier for patron fine retrieval. It also uses a different schema and report name.

```
reportForm.StartReport("Library.ReportPatronFines.rdlc", _
   "Library_ReportSchemaPatronFines", reportData)
```

The last method to add to *ReportSelect.vb* is BasicReportStatistics, which handles built-in report #5. It's a little different from the other four because it gathers data from six different tables, one at a time. In each case, it retrieves a count of the number of records in a database table. The results are then stored in a generic collection (System.Collections.Generic.List), where each list entry is an instance of ReportSchemaStatistics, the class we used for the fifth report's data schema. What a coincidence!

Here's the code for BasicReportStatistics for you to add now to the ReportSelect form class.

INSERT SNIPPET

Insert Chapter 21, Snippet Item 11.

```
Private Sub BasicReportStatistics()
   ' ----- Run built-in report #5: Library database
   '       statistics report.
   Dim sqlText As String
   Dim reportData As Collections.Generic.List( _
      Of ReportSchemaStatistics)
   Dim oneEntry As ReportSchemaStatistics
   Dim reportForm As ReportBuiltinViewer
   Dim resultValue As Integer
   Dim counter As Integer
   Const tableSets As String = "Author,Publisher," & _
      "Subject,NamedItem,ItemCopy,Patron"
   Const tableTitles As String = "Authors,Publishers," & _
      "Subject Headings,Items,Item Copies,Patrons"

   On Error GoTo ErrorHandler

   ' ----- Build the report data. It's all counts from
   '       different tables.
   reportData = New Collections.Generic.List( _
      Of ReportSchemaStatistics)
```

```
        For counter = 1 To CountSubStr(tableSets, ",") + 1
            ' ----- Process one table.
            sqlText = "SELECT COUNT(*) FROM " & _
                GetSubStr(tableSets, ",", counter)
            resultValue = DBGetInteger(ExecuteSQLReturn(sqlText))

            ' ----- Add it to the report data.
            oneEntry = New ReportSchemaStatistics
            oneEntry.EntryName = _
                GetSubStr(tableTitles, ",", counter)
            oneEntry.EntryValue = CStr(resultValue)
            reportData.Add(oneEntry)
        Next counter

        ' ----- Send the data to the report.
        reportForm = New ReportBuiltinViewer
        reportForm.StartReport("Library.ReportStatistics.rdlc", _
            "Library_ReportSchemaStatistics", reportData)
        Return

    ErrorHandler:
        GeneralError("ReportSelect.BasicReportStatistics", _
            Err.GetException())
        Return
    End Sub
```

Since we really need to get the same information (`COUNT(*)`) for each of the six tables involved, I just implemented the code as a loop, and built the SQL statement for each one as I passed through the loop. A friendly table name and the record count are then stored in the generic list, which is eventually sent to the report.

You can now run the application and use the five built-in reports. You must log in as a librarian or administrator, and then access the Print Reports panel on the main form.

Believe it or not, we're almost finished with the application. The only big thing left to do is to process past-due patron items to see whether fines are required. We'll add this code in the next chapter, and also take a look at licensing.

Licensing Your Application

Proper .NET content licensing can mean the difference between marketplace dominance and financial bankruptcy. And I'm just talking about trying to understand the license agreement that comes with Visual Studio. You still have to figure out a licensing method for your own application before you send it to your customers.

Licensing and license agreements are an essential means of protecting the intellectual property you've worked so hard to develop. How does licensing work? The key is found in the roots of the word itself: *license* comes from "li-" (to tell a lie) and "-cense" (from "cents" as in "pennies"). Together, these roots mean "to tell lies about small units of currency." The confusion brought about in trying to figure out what this means keeps the bad guys perplexed and occupied long enough so that they don't steal your application.

If this method doesn't work, there are software solutions, some of which I'll review in this chapter. Part of the discussion focuses on designing a licensing system that will appear in the Library Project. The .NET Framework does include classes for component licensing but they are primarily used for designers of controls used by other programmers within the Visual Studio IDE, and not for end-user applications. We will not be covering these licensing features in this chapter. If you're curious about such features, start by reading about the License Compiler (*lc.exe*) in the Visual Studio online help.

Software Licensing Options

Back in the early days of software, licensing wasn't an issue: if you could get to the computer, it was because you were authorized. All user interaction with the system was through the programmers and technicians. If some user wanted to steal something, it would be in the form of 20 tons of steel, wires, and vacuum tubes. Fun? Yes. Easy? No.

Today, it's a different story. Most users are non-technical, and some are unethical. So, now we have licensing agreements and teams of lawyers to back it all up. But we also have software, software that can delicately enforce some of the rules. For a particular piece of software, there is still the question of "How much licensing enforcement code do I add to my application?" The amount of software control you include will fall somewhere in the "Freedom–Security" continuum shown in Figure 22-1.

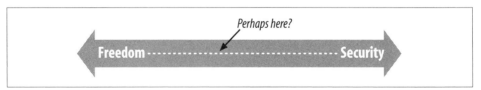

Figure 22-1. The licensing enforcement continuum: where are you on it?

If you go for the Freedom end of the spectrum ("convenient for users and hackers"), you will have to go on the trustworthiness of your users, and any armed guards you have dispatched to their offices, to keep the program in compliance. At the Security end of the scale ("secure for programmers and highly paid law firms"), the software implements practices and policies that ensure that only licensed users of the application ever use or install it; no armed guards needed.

The rest of this section discusses some possible options you could choose within the Freedom–Security range.

License Agreement Only

The license agreement-only method clearly opts for freedom over security. When you supply the user with software, it comes with a carefully crafted license agreement that lays out the terms of use for both the user and the software supplier. It generally gives the user certain rights as to installation, use, and distribution of the software.

When you write an application for use only within a specific organization or by a small group of users who you will have regular contact with, the license agreement-only method may be just what you need. In fact, I would bet that most Visual Basic applications are in this vein. Microsoft has announced over the years that the vast majority of Visual Basic programmers target their applications for use in a specific business organization, tied to a specific custom database. Such systems often require very little in the way of license enforcement, since the application is useless when carried outside the building where it was meant to reside.

Even if your software achieves widespread distribution, this licensing scheme may still be the way to go. Many open source applications, including a major operating system that rhymes with "Plinux," use the Free Software Foundation's GNU General Public License (*http://www.fsf.org/licensing/licenses/gpl.html*) as their primary licensing and distribution policy.

Generated General License Key

If you need a bit more control over the distribution, installation, and use of an application, you can impose a *generated general license key*—basically a password that allows the application to be installed or used. Such keys are often entered at the start of the installation process, with the user prompted for a specific key. Without the key, it's goodbye installation.

The software vendor will need a way to generate a good set of unique installation keys. There are a couple of options:

- Just generate a sequential serial number, and mix into it a product ID and version number. The great thing about such a key is that it is easy to generate. The installation program doesn't need to perform any complex verification logic on the key. It only needs to ensure that the general format is correct. One of the products I used to develop online help documentation for my older Visual Basic 6.0 applications used such a license key. In a way, it's not much more secure than using just a license agreement, since anyone who knows the general format can make up his own key.

- Use a hashed or scrambled key, based on some original serial number or formula that can be verified by the installation program. A well-crafted hashing algorithm can generate a wide range of keys, but makes it difficult for others who don't know the formula to generate their own fake keys. Although I am not privy to Microsoft's internal processes, this appears to be the method it uses for its 25-character "CD Keys," including the one supplied with Visual Studio. Although it is difficult for keys to be invented out of whole cloth, the public nature of the keys makes them subject to sharing. For some of its products, Microsoft combines a CD key with an online or phone-based registration process to enhance security.

- Supply a hashed or encrypted key based on a serial number that is (secretly) supplied with the installation program or distribution media. When the user enters the key, it is unencrypted or otherwise prepared, and then compared with the serial number. Only if it matches will the software installation complete properly.

Generated Custom License Key

A custom-generated license key is similar to a general generated key, but uses personal information supplied by the user as part of the generation process. Such a key is more interactive, and requires that the end-user specifically communicate with the software vendor (or an application on its web site) to complete the installation process.

During the purchase or installation process, the user makes specific information (such as the owner's name and the date of purchase) available to the software vendor. The vendor then uses public-private key encryption (asymmetric cryptography) to either fully encrypt or digitally sign the relevant information. The encrypted signature is then returned to the end-user for installation. The installation process uses the public portion of the key pair to ensure that the signature is valid.

We will use this license key method in the Library Project, so I'll have more to say about it a little later.

License Key with Hardware Identity or Lock

For paranoid software vendors, or for those who have a legitimate need to keep a tight rein on their installation base, there are solutions that involve regular access to hardware or services to confirm that previously installed software is legal and valid. One popular method uses a "dongle," typically a USB port-based device that the software must have access to each time it runs. The software vendor supplies a dongle with the licensed software, and may encode it with date-based or use-based limits.

With the prevalence of the Internet, software vendors also have the option of real-time verification over the Web. Each time the program runs, it could access a known vendor site to engage in a usage verification process. Such a system allows for ongoing monitoring of the software by vendors who may have a business or governmental reason to limit use of the software.

For one of my customer projects, I must access a third-party web site on a monthly basis and download proprietary data for use with that vendor's software. The vendor requires that I always access their web site from a specific machine with a specific IP address. It will refuse to supply the data if I attempt to connect from any other machine. If I have a real need to use a fresh IP address (if, for example, I change Internet service providers), I must submit paperwork to the vendor informing them of the new IP address. It seems pesky, and it is an irritation. But the data they supply is unique and valuable, and they feel they have a business need to protect that investment. Since my customer requires the data, I have no choice but to comply with the monthly verification procedures.

Controlled Access

The highest level of security requires a blatant distrust of the user, although there may be good reason for this. For highly sensitive applications, the software vendor may make their product available to only a limited number of customers, and then only on a lease basis. As part of the lease agreement, the customer agrees to have a trained staff member of the software vendor on-site, running and maintaining the application for the customer. At the very least, the vendor will require that one of its employees be immediately available to the customer whenever the application is used.

In a world of off-the-shelf software applications, it seems unconscionable that such a system could exist. But in high-risk situations, security concerns are raised to such a level that neither party is willing to fully assume the risks of installing and using the application apart from the other.

Although I was tempted to use this system for the Library Project, I think we'll stick with our original plan of employing a custom-generated license key.

License Agreements

A *license agreement* is a document wherein the party of the first part hereby and does amicably render to the party of the second part certain rights, quid pro quos, treasury bonds, and other benefits; in exchange, the party of the second part will do the same for the party of the first part without respect for any other party or festival.

Let's try that again. A license agreement tells a user "Go ahead, install and use the software, but you have to follow these rules." Although they are often written in legalese, they can also appear in a real language, such as English. They also range in granted rights, from "You can use this, but when you're finished, you must destroy all copies" to "Use it, and feel free to pass a copy of the program and its source code to your friends and relations."

The Library software provided with this book comes with a license agreement. (I've included it in Appendix B.) When you installed the sample code, you agreed to the terms of the license agreement, including the part about supporting my family financially well into my retirement years. But enough about me; let's talk about license agreements you may want to use for your applications.

If you're developing a DVD catalog program for your cousin Fred, you can probably skip the license agreement part. But any software you craft in a business capacity for use outside your own company should include some sort of agreement between you (or your company) and the user of the software. This agreement could be defined as part of the contract that established the software development project (this is typical for software consulting), or you could include the agreement as a component of the software (common for off-the-shelf programs).

Whichever method you choose, it is important that you state it in written form because it can save you grief down the road. I once had a customer who insisted that I fork over a copy of the source code for an application I wrote for them so that they could enhance it and sell the new version to other businesses (the nerve!). Fortunately, we had a written contract that stated the rules of engagement. They were entitled to a copy of the source code for archive purposes, but they could not use it or derive products from it without written consent from me. This granted a level of safety for them while still providing the means for me to provide the best support possible for their organization. Fortunately, it all came to a happy conclusion, and since that Visual Basic 3.0 code doesn't even run anymore, it's a moot point.

A license agreement usually exists to protect the rights of the software vendor, but it would be useless if it didn't also grant meaningful rights to the user—and some of the rights can be rather generous. Did you know that the standard consumer licensing agreement for Microsoft Office allows you to install the product on two different systems using a single licensed copy of the program? It's not a complete install-fest. Both computers must belong to the same person, and one must be a desktop whereas the other is a portable device (a laptop). But it's still a meaningful benefit to the typical user.

The legal department at O'Reilly Media wants to remind you that Tim Patrick does not have a sufficient understanding of the law, and cannot advise you on the contents of any licensing agreement you may want to craft for your projects.

Obfuscation

I hinted a little about the obfuscation features in Visual Studio 2008 in Chapters 1 and 5, but it's high time we actually took a look at the features. Visual Studio includes a stripped-down version of Dotfuscator from a company named PreEmptive Solutions (not a part of Microsoft—yet). To access the program, use the Tools → Dotfuscator Community Edition menu command in Visual Studio. The main interface appears in Figure 22-2.

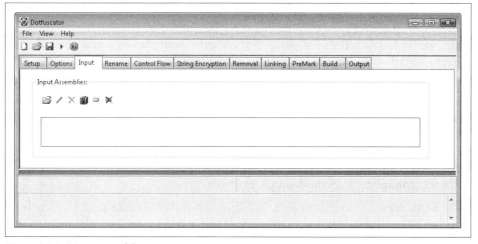

Figure 22-2. It's time to obfuscate!

 As of this writing, Dotfuscator Community Edition is not included with Visual Basic 2008 Express Edition.

Even though this is the basic version of the product, you can see that it has a gazillion options. If you want to dive into its enhanced features for your project, that's fantastic. I'll just cover the basic usage here.

Let's recall quickly why you would want to obfuscate your code, or even use the word *obfuscate* in mixed company. Here's some code from the Library Project:

```
Public Function CenterText(ByVal origText As String, _
    ByVal textWidth As Integer) As String
  ' ----- Center a piece of text in a field width.
  '       If the text is too wide, truncate it.
  Dim resultText As String

  resultText = Trim(origText)
  If (Len(resultText) >= textWidth) Then
    ' ----- Truncate as needed.
    Return Trim(Left(origText, textWidth))
  Else
    ' ----- Start with extra spaces.
    Return Space((textWidth - Len(origText)) \ 2) & _
      resultText
  End If
End Function
```

This code is quite easy to understand, especially with the comments and the meaningful method and variable names. Although .NET obfuscation works at the MSIL level, let's pretend that the obfuscator worked directly on Visual Basic code. Obfuscation of this code might produce results similar to the following:

```
Public Function A(ByVal AA As String, _
    ByVal AAA As Integer) As String
  Dim AAAA As String
  AAAA = Trim(AA)
  If (Len(AAAA) >= AAA) Then
    Return Trim(Left(AA, AAA))
  Else
    Return Space((AAA - Len(AA)) \ 2) & AAAA
  End If
End Function
```

In such a simple routine, we could still figure out the logic, but with more effort than in the original version. Naturally, true obfuscation goes much further than this, scrambling the readability of the code at the IL level, and confounding code readers and hackers alike.

To obfuscate an assembly:

1. Build your project in Visual Studio using the Build → Build [Project Name] menu command.

2. Start Dotfuscator using the Tools → Dotfuscator Community Edition menu command in Visual Studio.

3. When prompted for a project type, select Create New Project, and click the OK button.

4. On the Input tab of the Dotfuscator application window, click the "Browse and add assembly to list" toolbar button. This is the leftmost button—the one that looks like a file folder with a small arrow above it—on the panel shown in Figure 22-2.

5. When prompted for an assembly file, browse for your compiled application, and click the OK button. The assembly to use will be in the *bin\Release* subdirectory within your project's source code directory.

6. Select the File → Build menu command to generate the obfuscated assembly. You will be prompted to save the Dotfuscator project file (an XML file) before the build begins. Save this file to a new directory. When the build occurs, it will save the output assembly in a *Dotfuscated* subdirectory in the same directory that contains the XML project file.

7. The build completes, and a summary appears as shown in Figure 22-3. Your obfuscated file is ready to use. The process also generates a *Map.xml* file that documents all the name changes made to types and members within your application. It would be a bad thing to distribute this file with the assembly. It is for your debugging use only.

To prove that the obfuscation took place, use the IL Disassembler tool that comes with Visual Studio to examine each assembly. (On my system, this program is accessed via Start → [All] Programs → Microsoft Windows SDK v6.0A → Tools → IL Disassembler.) Figure 22-4 shows the global variables included in the Library Project's *General.vb* file. The obfuscated version of these same variables appears in Figure 22-5.

I will not be performing obfuscation on the Library Project through this book's tutorial sections. Feel free to try it out on your own.

The Library Licensing System

The tools and procedures we will use to design the Library Project's licensing system can be built from featuresMapMap.xml file.xml file alreaMap.xml filedy Map.xml filediscussed in previous chapters:

- The license file contains XML content. (Chapter 13)

- The license appears as a separate file in the same directory as the *Library.exe* assembly. The Library software reads content from the license file. (Chapter 15)

- The license will include a digital signature, which is based on public-private key encryption. (Chapter 11)

Figure 22-3. Summary of the obfuscation, with some advertising thrown in

- AllHolidays : public static class [mscorlib]System.Collections.Generic.List`1<class Library.HolidaySet>
- DefaultItemLocation : public static int32
- FineGraceDays : public static int32
- HoldTransaction : public static class [System.Data]System.Data.SqlClient.SqlTransaction
- LibraryDB : public static class [System.Data]System.Data.SqlClient.SqlConnection
- LoggedInGroupID : public static int32
- LoggedInUserID : public static int32
- LoggedInUserName : public static string
- MainAdminHelpFile : public static string
- MainHelpFile : public static string
- MatchNone : public static literal int32
- MatchPresent : public static literal int32
- MaxLibrarySecurity : public static literal valuetype Library.General/LibrarySecurity
- NotAuthorizedMessage : public static literal string
- ProgramTitle : public static literal string
- SearchMatchLimit : public static int32
- SecurityProfile : public static bool[]
- UseDBVersion : public static literal int32

Figure 22-4. Global variables before obfuscation

```
⬥ a : public static literal string
⬥ b : public static literal string
⬥ c : public static literal int32
⬥ d : public static literal int32
⬥ e : public static literal int32
⬥ f : public static literal valuetype x/a
⬥ g : public static class [System.Data]System.Data.SqlClient.SqlConnection
⬥ h : public static class [System.Data]System.Data.SqlClient.SqlTransaction
⬥ i : public static int32
⬥ j : public static string
⬥ k : public static int32
⬥ l : public static bool[]
⬥ m : public static int32
⬥ n : public static int32
⬥ o : public static string
⬥ p : public static string
⬥ q : public static int32
⬥ r : public static class [mscorlib]System.Collections.Generic.List`1<class aa>
```

Figure 22-5. Global variables after obfuscation

Each time the Library application runs, it attempts to read the license file. If the file doesn't exist, or if it contains invalid data or an invalid signature, the program downgrades its available features, disabling those features that are considered licensed.

Designing the License File

The Library Project's license file contains some basic ownership and rights information related to the user who purchased rights to the software. Here's the XML content I've come up with:

```
<?xml version="1.0" encoding="utf-8"?>
<License>
  <Product>Library Project</Product>
  <LicenseDate>1/1/2000</LicenseDate>
  <ExpireDate>12/31/2999</ExpireDate>
  <CoveredVersion>1.*</CoveredVersion>
  <Licensee>John Q. Public</Licensee>
  <SerialNumber>LIB-123456789</SerialNumber>
</License>
```

That seems sufficient. The process that builds the digital signature also stores an encrypted signature within the XML content.

Generating the License File

In the "Project" section of this chapter, we'll build a new application that exists solely to generate license files for the Library application. It will have three primary components:

1. Generate and manage the public and private keys used in the signature process.

2. Prompt the user for the license date, expiration date, covered version, licensee name, and serial number for a single license. These are the values that appear in the license file's XML content.

3. Output the XML license file and digitally sign it using the private key.

Installing the License File

The "Project" section of this chapter will show you how to generate a generic license file. This XML file will be distributed and installed with the Library application using the setup program that we will build in Chapter 25. The file will be named *LibraryLicense.lic* (by default) and will always appear in the same directory as the *Library.exe* application file.

If I were developing a real application for paying customers, and I had a web site that supported a web service (which I'll talk about in Chapter 23), here is one design for installing the license file that I might use:

1. Run the setup program to install the application on the user's workstation.

2. During installation, the setup program prompts the user for the license details that will ultimately appear in the XML license file.

3. The setup program contacts the web service on my vendor web site, and passes the user-supplied values to that registration service.

4. The registration service returns a digitally signed XML file that contains the licensing content.

5. The setup program installs this file along with the application.

6. If for any reason the licensing cannot complete successfully during setup, the main application contains identical licensing code, and can communicate with the registration service itself.

Using the License File

Whenever the Library application runs, it reads in the XML license file and performs many checks to ensure that the license is valid for the current application installation. If the license is invalid for any reason, the application blocks access to the enhanced administrative features included in the Library system.

Summary

Since you will often spend dozens or hundreds of hours designing and developing a quality Visual Basic application, it is important to use appropriate licensing and obfuscation technology to protect your hard work. Licensing is another one of those common programming tasks that didn't make it into the .NET Framework as an easy-to-use class—unless you are building and distributing design-time controls. For the rest of us, it's make-it-up-as-you-go time. Fortunately, .NET has great support tools, so adding licensing support isn't too difficult.

Project

In this chapter's project code, we'll follow two of the four licensing steps discussed in the section "The Library Licensing System," earlier in this chapter: *generating the license file* and *using the license file*. The design we created previously is good enough for our needs, although we still need to record it in the project's technical documentation. We won't formally install the license file until we create the setup program in Chapter 25.

Update Technical Documentation

Since we'll be adding a new external file that will be processed by the Library Project, we need to document its structure in the project's Technical Resource Kit. Let's add the following new section to that document.

License File

The Library Project reads a customer-specific license file generated by the Library License Generation support application. That program generates a digitally signed XML license file that includes licensee information. Here is a sample of the license file content:

```
<?xml version="1.0"?>
<License>
  <Product>Library Project</Product>
  <LicenseDate>1/1/2000</LicenseDate>
  <ExpireDate>12/31/2999</ExpireDate>
  <CoveredVersion>1.*</CoveredVersion>
  <Licensee>John Q. Public</Licensee>
  <SerialNumber>LIB-123456789</SerialNumber>
  <Signature>
    Digital signature appears here (not shown)
  </Signature>
</License>
```

The `<LicenseDate>` and `<ExpireDate>` tags indicate the first and last valid dates of the license. `<Licensee>` indicates the name of the license owner. `<SerialNumber>` includes the vendor-defined serial number associated with this license. The `<CoveredVersion>` tag contains data similar to the assembly version number included in .NET applications. It has up to four dot-delimited parts:

```
<major>.<minor>.<build>.<revision>
```

Each component can include a number from 0 to 9999, or the * character, which indicates all valid values for that position.

The <Signature> section contains the generated digital signature. Its format is dependant on the XML Cryptography tools in .NET that generate this section. To ensure a proper digital signature, always use the Library License Generation support application to build license files.

That support application generates a public and private key pair for use in digital signing. The public portion of this key (as an XML file) must be added as a resource named LicensePublicKey to the Library application. The private portion must be kept private. For consistency, the same key pair should be used throughout the lifetime of the Library Project's availability.

We will also store the location of the license file as an application setting in the main program. We need to record that setting with the other application settings already added to the User Settings section of the Resource Kit.

LicenseFileLocation

> The path to the Library License file on this workstation. If not supplied, the program will look for a file named *LibraryLicense.lic* in the same folder as the application.

Library License Helper Application

Generating license files and digital signatures by hand using Notepad would be...well, let's not even think about it. Instead, we'll depend on a custom application to create the files and signatures for us. I've already developed that custom tool for you. You'll find it in the installation directory for this book's code, in the *LibraryLicensing* subdirectory.

This support application includes two main forms. The first (*KeyLocationForm.vb*, shown in Figure 22-6) locates or creates the public-private key files used in the digital signature process.

Figure 22-6. Support form for digital signatures

Most of the form's code helps to locate and verify the folder that will contain the two key files (one private, one public). Some of the code in the ActGenerate_Click event handler creates the actual files.

```
Dim twoPartKey As RSA
Dim publicFile As String
Dim privateFile As String

...some code skipped here, then...

' ----- Generate the keys.
twoPartKey = New RSACryptoServiceProvider
twoPartKey = RSA.Create( )

' ----- Save the public key.
My.Computer.FileSystem.WriteAllText(publicFile, _
   twoPartKey.ToXmlString(False), False)

' ----- Save the private key.
My.Computer.FileSystem.WriteAllText(privateFile, _
   twoPartKey.ToXmlString(True), False)
```

That's really simple! The System.Security.Cryptography.RSA class and the related RSACryptoServiceProvider class do all the work. All you have to do is call the RSA.Create method, and then generate the relevant XML keys using the ToXmlString method, passing an argument of False for the public key and True for the private key. If you want to look at some sample keys, open the *LicenseFiles* subdirectory in this book's source installation directory. You'll find two files, one for the public key and one for the private key. I'd print one of them here, but it all just looks like random characters.

The other support form is *MainForm.vb*, which generates the actual end-user license file, and appears in Figure 22-7.

Figure 22-7. Support form for license file generation

As with the first form, most of this form's code simply ensures that the public and private key files are intact, and that the user entered valid data before generation. The ActGenerate_Click event handler is where the real fun is. First, we need some XML content, which we build in the BuildXmlLicenseContent method. It creates the content element by element, using the methods we learned about in Chapter 13. For instance, here's the part of the code that adds the serial number:

```
dataElement = result.CreateElement("SerialNumber")
dataElement.InnerText = Trim(SerialNumber.Text)
rootElement.AppendChild(dataElement)
```

Then comes the digital signature, via the SignXmlLicenseContent function, most of which appears here:

```
Private Function SignXmlLicenseContent( _
        ByVal sourceXML As XmlDocument) As Boolean
    ' ----- Add a digital signature to an XML document.
    Dim privateKeyFile As String
    Dim privateKey As RSA
    Dim signature As SignedXml
    Dim referenceMethod As Reference

    ' ----- Load in the private key.
    privateKeyFile = My.Computer.FileSystem.CombinePath( _
        KeyLocation.Text, PrivateKeyFilename)
    privateKey = RSA.Create()
    privateKey.FromXmlString( _
        My.Computer.FileSystem.ReadAllText(privateKeyFile))

    ' ----- Create the object that generates the signature.
    signature = New SignedXml(sourceXML)
    signature.SignedInfo.CanonicalizationMethod = _
        SignedXml.XmlDsigCanonicalizationUrl
    signature.SigningKey = privateKey

    ' ----- The signature will appear as a <reference>
    '        element in the XML.
    referenceMethod = New Reference("")
    referenceMethod.AddTransform(New _
        XmlDsigEnvelopedSignatureTransform(False))
    signature.AddReference(referenceMethod)

    ' ----- Add the signature to the XML content.
    signature.ComputeSignature()
    sourceXML.DocumentElement.AppendChild(signature.GetXml())

    ' ----- Finished.
    Return True
End Function
```

Digital signing occurs via the SignedXml class (in the System.Security.Cryptography.Xml namespace). This class uses a few different signing methods; the one I chose (XmlDsigCanonicalizationUrl) is used for typical XML and ignores embedded comments.

This signature appears as tags and values in the XML output, added through the AppendChild statement near the end of the routine. Since we don't want the signature itself to be considered when we later scan the XML file for valid content, the SignedXml class adds the signature as a <reference> tag. This occurs in code by adding a Reference object that is programmed for that purpose. It's added through the signature.AddReference method call.

Once we have the signature in the XML content, we write it all out to a file specified by the user via the standard XmlDocument.Save method (in the ActGenerate_Click event handler).

```
licenseXML.Save(LicenseSaveLocation.FileName)
```

Here's a sample XML license file that includes a digital signature. This is the one that I have included in the *LicenseFiles* directory in the book's source installation directory (with some lines wrapped to fit this page).

```
<?xml version="1.0"?>
<License>
  <Product>Library Project</Product>
  <LicenseDate>1/1/2000</LicenseDate>
  <ExpireDate>12/31/2999</ExpireDate>
  <CoveredVersion>1.*</CoveredVersion>
  <Licensee>John Q. Public</Licensee>
  <SerialNumber>LIB-123456789</SerialNumber>
  <Signature xmlns="http://www.w3.org/2000/09/xmldsig#">
    <SignedInfo>
      <CanonicalizationMethod Algorithm=
        "http://www.w3.org/TR/2001/REC-xml-c14n-20010315" />
      <SignatureMethod Algorithm=
        "http://www.w3.org/2000/09/xmldsig#rsa-sha1" />
      <Reference URI="">
        <Transforms>
          <Transform Algorithm="http://www.w3.org/2000/09/
            xmldsig#enveloped-signature" />
        </Transforms>
        <DigestMethod Algorithm="http://www.w3.org/2000/09/
          xmldsig#sha1" />
        <DigestValue>Dn6JYIBI/qQudmvSiMvuOvnVBGU=
          </DigestValue>
      </Reference>
    </SignedInfo>
    <SignatureValue>NULghI4WbzDLroIcf2u9aoybfSjXPJRN5
      OUMrCPYa5bup+c7RJnqTM+SzP4jmfJWPPs7pOvDC/fbdNY
      VMaoyXWOjL3Lk8du3X4JXpW3xp9Nxq31y/Ld8E+RkoiPO6
      KRGDI+RRZ8MAQda8WS+L2fMyenRAjo+fR9KL3sQ/hOfQX8=
      </SignatureValue>
  </Signature>
</License>
```

The digital signature appears as the scrambled content within the <SignatureValue> tag. Now, if anyone tries to modify any of the license values, the license will no longer match the signature, and the entire license will become invalid.

Instead of using a digital signature, we could have just encrypted the entire licensing file with the private key, and later used the public key to decrypt it and examine its contents. But I like the digital signature better, since it allows anyone to open the license file and check the parameters of the license itself while still preventing any changes.

Adding the License to the Library Program

Let's return to the Library application already in progress.

PROJECT ACCESS

Load the Chapter 22 (Before) Code project, either through the New Project templates or by accessing the project directly from the installation directory. To see the code in its final form, load Chapter 22 (After) Code instead.

The program will adjust its behavior depending on whether it is licensed or not. But to make that determination, it needs to ensure that the contents of the licensing file are valid and haven't been tampered with. To do this, it needs a way to unscramble the signature and compare it with the rest of the license to make sure it matches. We built the signature using the private key; we must unscramble it using the public key.

We could store the public key in its own file outside the program, but then it might get lost (just like my real keys). Instead, we'll store the public key as an application resource, found externally in the source code's *Resources* folder. I've already added the resource to your copy of the program, and named it `LicensePublicKey`. With this key embedded in the application, *any regeneration of the public and private keys will require modification of this resource*. In code, we refer to the XML content of the public key using its resource name:

```
My.Resources.LicensePublicKey
```

Some of the security features use classes found in the `System.Security.Cryptography.Xml` namespace. This is not one of the namespaces included by default in new Visual Basic applications, so we'll have to add it ourselves. Open the project properties window and select the References tab. Just below the list of References, click the Add button, and then select System.Security from the .NET tab of the Add Reference window that appears.

Since we have the project properties window still open, click over to the Settings tab. Add a new String setting and use "LicenseFileLocation" for its name. We'll use this setting to store the path to the license file. Save and close the project properties window.

Our general licensing needs throughout the application are pretty simple. We only need to know the current status of the licensing file, and have access to a few of the licensing values so that we can display a short message about the license. We may need to do this in various parts of the program, so let's add some useful generic code to the *General.vb* module. Open that module now.

Right at the top of that file, the code already includes a reference to the System. Security.Cryptography namespace, since we include code that encrypts user passwords. But this doesn't cover the standard or secure XML stuff. So add two new Imports statements as well.

INSERT SNIPPET

Insert Chapter 22, Snippet Item 1.

```
Imports System.Xml
Imports System.Security.Cryptography.Xml
```

We'll use an enumeration to indicate the status of the license. Add it now to the General module.

INSERT SNIPPET

Insert Chapter 22, Snippet Item 2.

```
Public Enum LicenseStatus
    ValidLicense
    MissingLicenseFile
    CorruptLicenseFile
    InvalidSignature
    NotYetLicensed
    LicenseExpired
    VersionMismatch
End Enum
```

Let's also add a simple structure that communicates the values extracted from the license file. Add this code to the General module.

INSERT SNIPPET

Insert Chapter 22, Snippet Item 3.

```
Public Structure LicenseFileDetail
    Public Status As LicenseStatus
    Public Licensee As String
    Public LicenseDate As Date
    Public ExpireDate As Date
    Public CoveredVersion As String
    Public SerialNumber As String
End Structure
```

By default, the license file appears in the same directory as the application, using the name *LibraryLicense.lic*. Add a global constant to the General module that identifies this default name.

INSERT SNIPPET

Insert Chapter 22, Snippet Item 4.

```
Public Const DefaultLicenseFile _
    As String = "LibraryLicense.lic"
```

All we need now is some code to fill in the LicenseFileDetail structure. Add the new ExamineLicense function to the General module.

INSERT SNIPPET

Insert Chapter 22, Snippet Item 5.

```
Public Function ExamineLicense() As LicenseFileDetail
    ' ----- Examine the application's license file, and
    '       report back what's inside.
    Dim result As New LicenseFileDetail
    Dim usePath As String
    Dim licenseContent As XmlDocument
    Dim publicKey As RSA
    Dim signedDocument As SignedXml
    Dim matchingNodes As XmlNodeList
    Dim versionParts() As String
    Dim counter As Integer
    Dim comparePart As String

    ' ----- See if the license file exists.
    result.Status = LicenseStatus.MissingLicenseFile
    usePath = My.Settings.LicenseFileLocation
    If (usePath = "") Then usePath = _
        My.Computer.FileSystem.CombinePath( _
        My.Application.Info.DirectoryPath, DefaultLicenseFile)
    If (My.Computer.FileSystem.FileExists(usePath) = False) _
        Then Return result

    ' ----- Try to read in the file.
    result.Status = LicenseStatus.CorruptLicenseFile
    Try
        licenseContent = New XmlDocument()
        licenseContent.Load(usePath)
    Catch ex As Exception
        ' ----- Silent error.
        Return result
    End Try
```

```
' ----- Prepare the public key resource for use.
publicKey = RSA.Create()
publicKey.FromXmlString(My.Resources.LicensePublicKey)

' ----- Confirm the digital signature.
Try
   signedDocument = New SignedXml(licenseContent)
   matchingNodes = licenseContent.GetElementsByTagName( _
      "Signature")
   signedDocument.LoadXml(CType(matchingNodes(0), _
      XmlElement))
Catch ex As Exception
   ' ----- Still a corrupted document.
   Return result
End Try
If (signedDocument.CheckSignature(publicKey) = False) Then
   result.Status = LicenseStatus.InvalidSignature
   Return result
End If

' ----- The license file is valid. Extract its members.
Try
   ' ----- Get the licensee name.
   matchingNodes = licenseContent.GetElementsByTagName( _
      "Licensee")
   result.Licensee = matchingNodes(0).InnerText

   ' ----- Get the license date.
   matchingNodes = licenseContent.GetElementsByTagName( _
      "LicenseDate")
   result.LicenseDate = CDate(matchingNodes(0).InnerText)

   ' ----- Get the expiration date.
   matchingNodes = licenseContent.GetElementsByTagName( _
      "ExpireDate")
   result.ExpireDate = CDate(matchingNodes(0).InnerText)

   ' ----- Get the version number.
   matchingNodes = licenseContent.GetElementsByTagName( _
      "CoveredVersion")
   result.CoveredVersion = matchingNodes(0).InnerText

   ' ----- Get the serial number.
   matchingNodes = licenseContent.GetElementsByTagName( _
      "SerialNumber")
   result.SerialNumber = matchingNodes(0).InnerText
Catch ex As Exception
   ' ----- Still a corrupted document.
   Return result
End Try

' ----- Check for out-of-range dates.
If (result.LicenseDate > Today) Then
   result.Status = LicenseStatus.NotYetLicensed
```

```
            Return result
        End If
        If (result.ExpireDate < Today) Then
            result.Status = LicenseStatus.LicenseExpired
            Return result
        End If


        ' ----- Check the version.
        versionParts = Split(result.CoveredVersion, ".")
        For counter = 0 To UBound(versionParts)
            If (IsNumeric(versionParts(counter)) = True) Then
                ' ----- The version format is
                '           major.minor.build.revision.
                Select Case counter
                    Case 0 : comparePart = _
                        CStr(My.Application.Info.Version.Major)
                    Case 1 : comparePart = _
                        CStr(My.Application.Info.Version.Minor)
                    Case 2 : comparePart = _
                        CStr(My.Application.Info.Version.Build)
                    Case 3 : comparePart = _
                        CStr(My.Application.Info.Version.Revision)
                    Case Else
                        ' ----- Corrupt version number.
                        Return result
                End Select
                If (Val(comparePart) <> _
                        Val(versionParts(counter))) Then
                    result.Status = LicenseStatus.VersionMismatch
                    Return result
                End If
            End If
        Next counter


        ' ----- Everything seems to be in order.
        result.Status = LicenseStatus.ValidLicense
        Return result
    End Function
```

That's a lot of code, but most of it just loads and extracts values from the XML license file. The signature-checking part is relatively short.

```
publicKey = RSA.Create()
publicKey.FromXmlString(My.Resources.LicensePublicKey)
signedDocument = New SignedXml(licenseContent)
matchingNodes = licenseContent.GetElementsByTagName( _
    "Signature")
signedDocument.LoadXml(CType(matchingNodes(0), XmlElement))
If (signedDocument.CheckSignature(publicKey) = False) Then
    ' ----- Invalid
End If
```

The SignedXml object—which we also used to generate the original license file—needs to know exactly which XML tag in its content represents the digital signature.

You would think that having an element named <Signature> would be a big tip-off, but perhaps not. Anyway, once you've assigned that node using the SignedXml.LoadXml method, you call the CheckSignature method, passing it the public key. If it returns True, you're good. I mean, not in a moral sense; the code doesn't know anything about you. But the signature is good.

Display the License on the About Form

When we added the About form to the project a few hundred pages ago, we included a Label control named LabelLicensed. It currently always displays "Unlicensed," but now we have the tools to display a proper license, if available. Open the source code for the *About.vb* form, and add the following code to the start of the AboutProgram_Load event handler.

INSERT SNIPPET

Insert Chapter 22, Snippet Item 6.

```
' ----- Prepare the form.
Dim licenseDetails As LicenseFileDetail

' ----- Display the licensee.
licenseDetails = ExamineLicense()
If (licenseDetails.Status = LicenseStatus.ValidLicense) Then
    LabelLicensed.Text = _
        "Licensed to " & licenseDetails.Licensee & vbCrLf & _
        "Serial number " & licenseDetails.SerialNumber
End If
```

Figure 22-8 shows the About form in use with details displayed from the license file.

Just for fun, I changed the version number in my license file from "1.*" to "2.*" without updating the digital signature. Sure enough, when I displayed the About form again, it displayed "Unlicensed," since the check of the signature failed. How did I test the code this early? I copied the *LibraryLicense.lic* file from the book's installed *LicenseFiles* subdirectory and placed that copy in the *bin\Debug* subdirectory of the project's source code. Later on, you'll be able to put the file anywhere you want and browse for it, but we're getting ahead of ourselves.

Enforcing the License

At some point, a missing or invalid license should have a negative impact on the use of the application. When that happens, we should give the user a chance to correct the problem by locating a valid license file. We'll do this through the new *LocateLicense.vb* form. I've already added the form to your project. It appears in Figure 22-9.

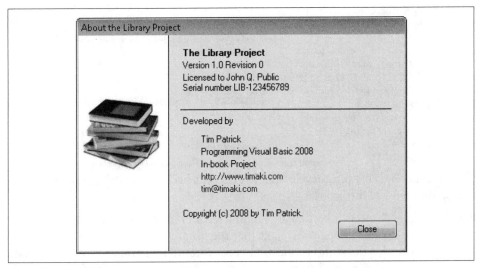

Figure 22-8. Displaying a valid license

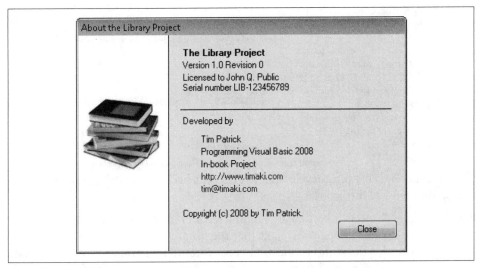

Figure 22-9. The gentle way to enforce a product license

This form starts up with a call to its public ChangeLicense function, which returns True if the user changes the license. Most of this form's code manages the display, presenting detailed reasons why a license is valid or invalid using the results of the ExamineLicense function. If for any reason the license is invalid, a click on the Locate button lets the user browse for a better version.

```
Private Sub ActLocate_Click(ByVal sender As System.Object, _
      ByVal e As System.EventArgs) Handles ActLocate.Click
   ' ----- Prompt the user for a new license file.
```

```
        If (LocateLicenseDialog.ShowDialog() <> _
            Windows.Forms.DialogResult.OK) Then Return

        ' ----- Store the new path.
        My.Settings.LicenseFileLocation = _
            LocateLicenseDialog.FileName
        LocationModified = True

        ' ----- Update the display.
        DisplayLicenseStatus()
        LicensePath.Text = My.Settings.LicenseFileLocation
    End Sub
```

The `LocationModified` form-level variable gets sent back to the caller as a trigger to refresh the status of the license.

For the Library Project in particular, I didn't see a point in enforcing the license on startup, since it's not the patrons' fault that the library stole this important work of software. Instead, I delay the verification process until an administrator or librarian tries to access the enhanced features of the application. Then, if the license check fails, the user should be able to browse the disk for a valid license file.

I think the best place to add the license check is just after the administrator successfully supplies a password. If we checked before that point, it would give ordinary patrons the ability to browse the disk, which is probably a no-no, since anyone and her uncle can walk up and use a patron workstation. Open the source code for the *ChangeUser.vb* form, locate the `ActOK_Click` event handler, and locate the "Successful login" comment.

```
    ' ----- Successful login.
    LoggedInUserID = CInt(dbInfo!ID)
    LoggedInUserName = CStr(dbInfo!LoginID)
    ...
```

Just *before* this block of code, add the following license-checking code.

INSERT SNIPPET

Insert Chapter 22, Snippet Item 7.

```
    ' ----- Don't allow the login if the program is unlicensed.
    Do While (ExamineLicense().Status <> _
            LicenseStatus.ValidLicense)
        ' ----- Ask the user what to do.
        If (MsgBox("This application is not properly licensed " & _
                "for administrative use. If you have access to " & _
                "a valid license file, you can verify it now. " & _
                "Would you like to locate a valid license file " & _
                "at this time?", MsgBoxStyle.YesNo Or _
                MsgBoxStyle.Question, ProgramTitle) <> _
                MsgBoxResult.Yes) Then
            dbInfo.Close()
```

```
            dbInfo = Nothing
            Return
        End If

        ' ----- Prompt for an updated license.
        Call LocateLicense.ChangeLicense( )
        LocateLicense = Nothing
    Loop
```

This code gives the user an unlimited number of chances to locate a valid license file. Once the license is validated, the code moves forward and enables administrative access.

Daily Item Processing

The last major set of code to be added to the Library Project isn't related to licensing, but it's important nonetheless: the processing of fines for overdue items. We'll add a common method that will perform the processing, and then call it where needed throughout the application.

Add the new DailyProcessByPatronCopy method to the General module.

INSERT SNIPPET

Insert Chapter 22, Snippet Item 8.

```
Public Sub DailyProcessByPatronCopy( _
        ByVal patronCopyID As Integer, ByVal untilDate As Date)
    ' ----- This routine does the most basic work of
    '        processing overdue fines. All other daily
    '        processing routines eventually call this routine.
    Dim sqlText As String
    Dim dbInfo As SqlClient.SqlDataReader
    Dim daysToFine As Integer
    Dim lastProcess As Date
    Dim fineSoFar As Decimal

    On Error GoTo ErrorHandler

    ' ----- Get all of the basic values needed to process
    '        this entry.
    sqlText = "SELECT PC.DueDate, PC.ProcessDate, " & _
        "PC.Fine, CMT.DailyFine FROM PatronCopy AS PC " & _
        "INNER JOIN ItemCopy AS IC ON PC.ItemCopy = IC.ID " & _
        "INNER JOIN NamedItem AS NI ON IC.ItemID = NI.ID " & _
        "INNER JOIN CodeMediaType AS CMT ON " & _
        "NI.MediaType = CMT.ID " & _
        "WHERE PC.ID = " & patronCopyID & _
        " AND PC.DueDate <= " & DBDate(Today) & _
        " AND PC.Returned = 0 AND PC.Missing = 0 " & _
        "AND IC.Missing = 0"
```

```
    dbInfo = CreateReader(sqlText)
    If (dbInfo.Read = False) Then
        ' ----- Missing the patron copy record. Oh well.
        '         It was probably because this item was not
        '         yet overdue, or it was missing, or something
        '         valid like that where fines should not increase.
        dbInfo.Close()
        dbInfo = Nothing
        Return
    End If

    ' ----- If we have already processed this record for today,
    '         don't do it again.
    If (IsDBNull(dbInfo!ProcessDate) = False) Then
        If (CDate(dbInfo!ProcessDate) >= untilDate) Then
            dbInfo.Close()
            dbInfo = Nothing
            Return
        End If
        lastProcess = CDate(dbInfo!ProcessDate)
    Else
        lastProcess = CDate(dbInfo!DueDate)
    End If

    ' ----- Fines are due on this record. Figure out how much.
    daysToFine = CInt(DateDiff(DateInterval.Day, _
        CDate(dbInfo!DueDate), untilDate) - _
        DateDiff(DateInterval.Day, CDate(dbInfo!DueDate), _
        lastProcess) - FineGraceDays)
    If (daysToFine < 0) Then daysToFine = 0
    fineSoFar = 0@
    If (IsDBNull(dbInfo!Fine) = False) Then _
        fineSoFar = CDec(dbInfo!Fine)
    fineSoFar += CDec(dbInfo!DailyFine) * CDec(daysToFine)
    dbInfo.Close()
    dbInfo = Nothing

    ' ----- Update the record with the latest fine and
    '         processing information.
    sqlText = "UPDATE PatronCopy SET " & _
        "ProcessDate = " & DBDate(untilDate) & _
        ", Fine = " & Format(fineSoFar, "0.00") & _
        " WHERE ID = " & patronCopyID
    ExecuteSQL(sqlText)
    Return

ErrorHandler:
    GeneralError("DailyProcessByPatronCopy", Err.GetException())
    Resume Next
End Sub
```

This code examines a PatronCopy record—the record that marks the checking out of a single item by a patron—to see whether it is overdue, and if so, what penalty needs to be added to the record. Each record includes a `ProcessDate` field. We don't want to charge the patron twice on the same day for a single overdue item (no, we don't), so we use the `ProcessDate` to confirm which days are uncharged.

There are a few places throughout the application where we want to call this processing routine without bothering the user. The first appears in the `PatronRecord` form, the form that displays the fines a patron still owes. Just before showing that list, we should refresh each item checked out by the patron to make sure we display the most up-to-date fine information. Open that form's source code, locate the `PatronRecord_Load` event handler, and add the following code, just before the call to `RefreshPatronFines(-1)` that appears halfway through the routine.

INSERT SNIPPET

Insert Chapter 22, Snippet Item 9.

```
' ----- Make sure that each item is up-to-date.
For counter = 0 To ItemsOut.Items.Count - 1
   newEntry = CType(ItemsOut.Items(counter), PatronDetailItem)
   DailyProcessByPatronCopy(newEntry.DetailID, Today)
Next counter
```

The overdue status for an item must also be refreshed just before it is checked in. Open the source code for the `MainForm` form and locate the `ActDoCheckIn_Click` event handler. About halfway through its code, you'll find a comment that starts with "Handle missing items." Just before that comment, insert the following code.

INSERT SNIPPET

Insert Chapter 22, Snippet Item 10.

```
' ----- Bring the status of the item up-to-date.
DailyProcessByPatronCopy(patronCopyID, CheckInDate.Value)
```

Checkout needs to refresh the patron's fines as well, just before letting the patron know whether there are, in fact, any fines due. Move to the `MainForm.ActCheckOutPatron_Click` event handler, and add the following declarations to the top of the routine.

INSERT SNIPPET

Insert Chapter 22, Snippet Item 11.

```
Dim dbTable As Data.DataTable
Dim dbRow As Data.DataRow
```

In this same method, find a comment that starts with "Show the patron if there are any fines due." As usual, it's about halfway through the routine. Insert the following code just before that comment.

INSERT SNIPPET

Insert Chapter 22, Snippet Item 12.

```
' ----- Bring the patron record up-to-date.
sqlText = "SELECT ID FROM PatronCopy WHERE Returned = 0 " & _
    "AND Missing = 0 AND DueDate < " & DBDate(Today) & _
    " AND (ProcessDate IS NULL OR ProcessDate < " & _
    DBDate(Today) & ") AND Patron = " & patronID
dbTable = CreateDataTable(sqlText)
For Each dbRow In dbTable.Rows
    DailyProcessByPatronCopy(CInt(dbRow!ID), Today)
Next dbRow
dbTable.Dispose()
dbTable = Nothing
```

In addition to automatic fine processing, the Library Project also allows an administrator or librarian to perform daily processing of all patron items at will. This occurs through the Daily Processing panel on the main form (see Figure 22-10).

Figure 22-10. Daily administrative processing

Currently, the panel doesn't do much of anything, so let's change that. The first task is to update the status label that appears at the top of the panel. Add a new method named RefreshProcessLocation to the MainForm form's class.

INSERT SNIPPET

Insert Chapter 22, Snippet Item 13.

I won't show its code here, but it basically checks the `CodeLocation.LastProcessing` database field either for all locations, or for the user-selected location, and updates the status display accordingly.

The user selects a location for processing with the `ProcessLocation` drop-down list, but we haven't yet added any code to populate that list. Find the `TaskProcess` method in the main form's source code, and add these declarations to the top of its code.

INSERT SNIPPET

Insert Chapter 22, Snippet Item 14.

```
Dim sqlText As String
Dim dbInfo As SqlClient.SqlDataReader

On Error GoTo ErrorHandler
```

Then add these statements to the end of the method.

INSERT SNIPPET

Insert Chapter 22, Snippet Item 15.

```
' ----- Refresh the list of locations.
ProcessLocation.Items.Clear()
ProcessLocation.Items.Add(New ListItemData( _
   "<All Locations>", -1))
ProcessLocation.SelectedIndex = 0
sqlText = "SELECT ID, FullName FROM CodeLocation " & _
   "ORDER BY FullName"
dbInfo = CreateReader(sqlText)
Do While dbInfo.Read
   ProcessLocation.Items.Add(New ListItemData( _
      CStr(dbInfo!FullName), CInt(dbInfo!ID)))
Loop
dbInfo.Close()
dbInfo = Nothing
RefreshProcessLocation()
Return

ErrorHandler:
   GeneralError("MainForm.TaskProcess", Err.GetException())
   Resume Next
```

Each time the user selects a different location from the list, we need to update the status display. Add the following code to the ProcessLocation_SelectedIndexChanged event handler.

INSERT SNIPPET

Insert Chapter 22, Snippet Item 16.

```
' ----- Update the status based on the current location.
RefreshProcessLocation( )
```

Daily processing occurs when the user clicks on the Process button. Add the following code to the ActDoProcess_Click event handler.

INSERT SNIPPET

Insert Chapter 22, Snippet Item 17.

```
' ----- Process all of the checked-out books.
Dim sqlText As String
Dim dbTable As Data.DataTable
Dim dbRow As Data.DataRow
Dim locationID As Integer

On Error GoTo ErrorHandler
Me.Cursor = Cursors.WaitCursor

' ----- Get the list of all items that likely need processing.
sqlText = "SELECT PC.ID FROM PatronCopy AS PC " & _
   "INNER JOIN ItemCopy AS IC ON PC.ItemCopy = IC.ID "& _
   "WHERE PC.Returned = 0 AND PC.Missing = 0 " & _
   "AND IC.Missing = 0 AND PC.DueDate < " & DBDate(Today) & _
   " AND (PC.ProcessDate IS NULL OR PC.ProcessDate < " & _
   DBDate(Today) & ")"
If (ProcessLocation.SelectedIndex <> -1) Then
   locationID = CInt(CType(ProcessLocation.SelectedItem, _
      ListItemData))
   If (locationID <> -1) Then sqlText &= _
      " AND IC.Location = " & locationID
Else
   locationID = -1
End If
dbTable = CreateDataTable(sqlText)
For Each dbRow In dbTable.Rows
   DailyProcessByPatronCopy(CInt(dbRow!ID), Today)
Next dbRow
dbTable.Dispose( )
dbTable = Nothing
Me.Cursor = Cursors.Default
MsgBox("Processing complete.", MsgBoxStyle.OkOnly Or _
   MsgBoxStyle.Information, ProgramTitle)
```

```
' ----- Update the processing date.
sqlText = "UPDATE CodeLocation SET LastProcessing = " & _
   DBDate(Today)
If (locationID <> -1) Then sqlText &= _
   " WHERE ID = " & locationID
ExecuteSQL(sqlText)

' ----- Update the status display.
ProcessStatus.Text = "     Processing is up to date."
ProcessStatus.ImageIndex = StatusImageGood
Return

ErrorHandler:
   GeneralError("MainForm.ActDoProcess_Click", Err.GetException())
   Resume Next
```

To try out the code, run it, locate a valid license file, and test out the different administrative features.

This marks the end of primary coding for the Library Project. Congratulations! But there's still plenty to do, as you can tell by the presence of four more chapters. Now would *not* be the time to close the book and call it a day. But it would be a good time to learn about ASP.NET, the topic of the next chapter.

Web Development

When Sir Tim Berners-Lee (knighted in 2004!) invented the World Wide Web in 1989, it really wasn't a big deal. As the primary designer of HTTP and HTML, he certainly was no slouch. But most of the technologies that went into structuring and transporting web pages had been around for years, even decades. SGML (the basis of HTML) and hyper-linking systems had been around since the 1960s, and Internet-based transmission of data between clients and servers was already common among university campuses and some businesses. Still, here we are in the 21st century, and the World Wide Web is the focus of so much computer technology that it makes my head spin. Thank you, Mr. B-L.

Microsoft promotes .NET as *the* system for developing web pages and related software. And it really is a great system. As we get into the code, you'll find that about 90% of what you do to write web applications in Visual Studio is identical to what you do when writing desktop applications. It's easy to do, and kind of fun, so you'll probably want to write some programs using it. And that's what we'll do in this chapter. But first, let's briefly review what happens in the world of client-server World Wide Web communication.

How the Internet Works

Before .NET, developing applications for "the Web" was cumbersome and boring. And with good reason: the World Wide Web was not designed as a programming or logic-processing platform. It was originally all about sending specially formatted text files from one computer to another. No programming languages to learn, no custom logic; just plain text, and maybe a binary graphics image or two.

Early web browsers were really just glorified file-copy programs. When you started up the Mosaic browser (pretty much all there was back then) and requested a web page from another computer, here is what would happen:

1. The web browser determined the IP address of the remote system.

2. The web browser contacted the remote system via TCP/IP port number 80.

3. The remote system accepted the connection.

4. The web browser said, "Hey, I'm looking for a file named *index.html*. Could you send it to me?"

5. The remote system said, "I have it," and immediately sent it.

6. The remote system closed the connection.

Much of this process is hidden from view, but you can actually see it happen. If you're interested, open the Windows command prompt and type the following command:

```
telnet www.google.com 80
```

This runs the Telnet program, a terminal emulation program that lets you connect to remote systems through a text interface. (Telnet is installed on Windows XP by default, but it is optional in Windows Vista. You can add it to Vista through the Control Panel's Programs and Features applet.) Telnet usually connects to TCP/IP port 23, but you can specify any port you want, as we did here with the default WWW port of 80.

Your screen may go blank, or it may just sit there, looking dead. If you're lucky, you'll see a "connected" message, but perhaps not. And that's OK. Your system is connected to Google's web server. Type the following command:

```
GET / HTTP/1.0
```

Don't miss the spaces surrounding the first slash. Follow this command with two light taps on the Enter key. This command asks the remote system to send the default web page at the top of that server's web hierarchy. And because you asked, it will.

```
HTTP/1.0 200 OK
Cache-Control: private
Content-Type: text/html; charset=ISO-8859-1
Set-Cookie: PREF=ID=1c1dd342e463f3f1:TM=1199325226
↳:LM=1199325226:S=Pl-4f1fg4yh8Mvw7;
↳expires=Sat, 02-Jan-2010 01:53:46 GMT;
↳path=/; domain=.google.com
Server: gws
Date: Tue, 01 Jan 2008 01:30:00 GMT
Connection: Close

<html><head>
    ...rest of HTML web page content here...
</body></html>

Connection to host lost.
```

Of course, you do not normally see all this. The web browser carries on this dialog for you, and nicely formats the response as a web page. This is actually all there is to the World Wide Web. You have just experienced the major features involved: the transfer of basic data through a TCP/IP port. So, where does programming come in?

Programming the Internet

Static pages were good for a while, but then the Internet became humdrum. Finally someone had a bright idea: "We have a program running on our web server that is responding to clients, and feeding them requested pages. What if we could enhance that program so that, for certain pages, it would call a program or script that would generate the HTML content on the fly, and have that content returned to the client?" So, they changed the server process. Now, when the client asked for a web page ending with the extension *.cgi*, the web server process ran a separate script that generated the content. The system also provided a means for some client-supplied content to make its way to the script, making possible customization and personalization features.

From there it was a short step to a generic solution. On the Microsoft platform, *Internet Information Server* supported add-ins that could be called based on the file extension of the requested file. This led to *Active Server Pages* (ASP), a solution that allowed developers to embed server-side script (often using VBScript, a variation of Visual Basic) right in the HTML content, and have it adjust the content before it was sent to the client.

Someone else said, "If we can write scripts on the server side, couldn't we also include a 'client-side script' right in the HTML content that a smart web browser could process?" Before long, client-side and server-side developers were battling it out in the streets, but the battle didn't get very far because all the programmers were exhausted. The cause? Programming in script! Whether it's embedding script in HTML (the client side) or generating HTML from script (the server side), script programming is cumbersome, slow, high in "bad" cholesterol, and almost impossible to debug interactively.

Some web script programmers hadn't used a language compiler for years, and were on the verge of lapsing into fatal script-induced comas. You could compile some server-side logic into a DLL and use it to process web pages, but it was far from easy, and these DLLs were still often linked into the HTML content via short scripts.

Then came .NET and its support for compiled server-side application development. Script programmers breathed a collective sigh of relief from their hospital beds; they could now use the full power of Visual Studio and .NET languages to build HTML content. And this new system, ASP.NET, was designed so that you could craft entire web applications without even looking at a single HTML tag. The design goal: to make web development nearly identical to desktop application development.

And Microsoft largely succeeded. It didn't solve the client scripting problem (maybe soon!), but some of the new server-side features included in ASP.NET greatly reduced the need for custom client-side scripts.

The pages you build in ASP.NET are called Web Forms, and because they are so closely tied together, I sometimes use ASP.NET and Web Forms interchangeably. But they aren't exactly the same thing: ASP.NET includes Web Forms.

ASP.NET Features

ASP.NET includes many new advances in web development technology. Here are just a few of the more famous ones:

Compiled code
> All of the code you write for ASP.NET applications is fully compiled into standard .NET DLL assemblies. When the client makes a request for a file with an *.aspx* extension, Internet Information Server locates this file (which contains HTML or combined HTML/ASP.NET content) and the associated compiled DLL, and uses them together to process the page content. You can precompile the DLL before deployment, or you can let ASP.NET compile it on the fly the first time the *.aspx* file gets called (although this incurs a bit of a performance hit).

.NET support
> ASP.NET applications can access the full .NET Framework Class Libraries (FCLs), except those that specifically target desktop development. Any of the cool features and classes you have in desktop .NET applications are right there in web applications as well.

Object-based
> HTML tags, such as the <textarea> tag, are really just text strings within a larger HTML text file. Pre-.NET server-side scripting was an exercise in string concatenation, building up a larger file from smaller content strings. ASP.NET treats all web-page elements as true objects, complete with properties and events. And some of these objects implement complex client-side controls, backed up by hundreds of lines of client-side script that you get for free.

Deployment simplicity
> Managing server-side scripts and custom DLLs before .NET was not very fun. Certain types of changes required a full shutdown of Internet Information Server, or at least of the portion that controlled the application being changed. ASP.NET lets you make changes on a production system without impacting active users. If you replace a compiled DLL, ASP.NET will start using it immediately, but will still keep the older version around until all existing clients have detached from it.

Browser independence

The web-page objects that you use in ASP.NET take responsibility for generating their own HTML and client-side script content. Many of them take the client's browser type and version into account, enhancing or reducing features automatically when needed. As an ASP.NET developer, you don't even have to know which browser is being used.

Extensibility

If you want to enhance a web-page element, you can derive from its class and add the new enhanced features, just as you do with any other .NET class.

Of course, there are more great features than the few I listed here. But you're probably ready to see ASP.NET in action. Let's get started.

Trying Out ASP.NET

Let's build a very simple ASP.NET application, and examine it and its parts to discover what it's all about.

 If you are using Visual Basic 2008 Express Edition, you will not be able to fully follow these instructions directly since that product does not include any ASP.NET or web development features. Instead, you need to download Visual Web Developer 2008 Express Edition from the Microsoft MSDN web site (*http://msdn.microsoft.com/express*). Its user interface, though streamlined, offers much of the same functionality as the full Visual Studio product. The tutorial included here was written using Visual Studio 2008 Professional Edition.

Start Visual Studio and select the File → New Web Site menu command. The New Web Site form appears (see Figure 23-1). Unlike desktop applications, you must immediately tell Visual Studio where you are going to store the files. We'll choose a location on the local filesystem, but this form also lets you work on a remote web site via FTP or HTTP. Choose the ASP.NET Web Site template, enter a directory path where you want to store the files, and click the OK button.

Figure 23-2 shows Visual Studio ready to start your new web application (the toolbars displayed are per my preferences).

The Solution Explorer panel already shows three files and a folder included in the project. If you browse to the project's directory—the default location in Windows Vista is *C:\Users\username\Documents\Visual Studio 2008\WebSites\WebSite1*—you'll see these same files. The *web.config* file is an XML file that contains application-specific settings; it's related to the *app.config* file used in desktop applications. *Default.aspx* is the web page itself, which will contain a mixture of HTML and special ASP.NET tags and directives. The related *Default.aspx.vb* file contains the Visual Basic "code behind" source code that will eventually be compiled to a DLL.

Figure 23-1. Creating a new ASP.NET application

Figure 23-2. A blank form is sometimes a good sign

Visual Studio also creates another folder at *C:\Users\username\Documents\Visual Studio 2008\Projects\WebSite1*. This folder contains the solution files normally created with any Visual Studio project. They're put out of the way so that they don't get included with the deployed web site.

The blank area you see in Visual Studio is a web page, just waiting for text and control content. If you want proof, click the Source section button in the bottom-left corner of the display, or use the View → Markup menu command. The window changes to HTML source code.

```
<%@ Page Language="VB" AutoEventWireup="false"
↳CodeFile="Default.aspx.vb" Inherits="_Default" %>

<!DOCTYPE html PUBLIC "-//W3C//DTD XHTML 1.0 Transitional//EN"
↳"http://www.w3.org/TR/xhtml1/DTD/xhtml1-transitional.dtd">

<html xmlns="http://www.w3.org/1999/xhtml">
<head runat="server">
    <title>Untitled Page</title>
</head>
<body>
    <form id="form1" runat="server">
    <div>

    </div>
    </form>
</body>
</html>
```

Well, *most* of it is HTML. There's a line at the top that starts with <%@ that doesn't look like real HTML—and it's not. This is an ASP.NET *page directive*. It includes properties that help guide ASP.NET in the processing of the page. Borrowing a standard from its ASP predecessor, ASP.NET uses the <%...%> bracket pair to mark ASP.NET-specific commands and code. (You might also recognize these markers from Chapter 13, since they are used in XML Literals.)

That's enough HTML. Who wanted to see it anyway? Click the Design section button, or use the View → Designer menu command to return to the blank page.

Let's create an application that multiplies two user-supplied numbers together and displays the product. For such a simple feature, we could just write some JavaScript and include it as a client-side script, but we're trying to avoid doing stuff like that. Type the following into the web page:

```
To multiply two values together, enter them in the
↳text fields, and click the Multiply button.
```

I made the word *Multiply* bold by using the Ctrl-B key sequence, just as I would do in a word processor. Press Enter once. By default, the web page lays out all elements like a word processing document, a method called *flow layout mode*. You can also use *absolute positioning* of individual elements to place them at a specific location on the page.

There's another way to organize elements on the page: through an HTML table. Let's add one now. Use the Table → Insert Table menu command. When the Insert Table dialog appears, specify a custom table that is three rows by two columns. Then click OK. The table should immediately appear in the body of the web page.

Type **Operand 1:** in the upper-left cell and type **Operand 2:** in the cell just below it. Your page should look like Figure 23-3.

To multiply two values together, enter them in the text fields, and click the **Multiply** button.

Operand 1:
Operand 2:

Figure 23-3. Just getting started on this application

It's not much to look at, but it will get better. So far, we haven't done much more than we could do in Notepad. But now we're ready to add some controls. If you open the toolbox, you'll see controls that look a lot like those found in a Windows Forms application (see Figure 23-4).

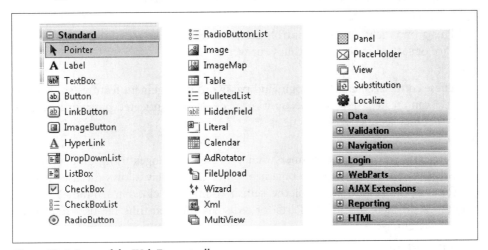

Figure 23-4. Some of the Web Forms toolbox

The controls are grouped by functionality:

Standard

> You will generally use the controls in this section to build the user interface of your web page. Many of these controls represent standard windows controls, with direct parallels in the Windows Forms world. For instance, the ListBox entry implements a standard Windows ListBox control within the web page. To you, the programmer, these controls look like standard .NET control classes, with properties, methods, and events. To the end-user, they look like standard web-page controls, delivered using ordinary HTML. Some of these controls are composite controls, which are single controls built from multiple HTML controls working together, possibly with client-side scripting doing some of the work.

Data

The data controls handle bound database interactions. As you may remember from previous chapters, I am not a big fan of bound controls in standard applications. But when you are communicating static data through a web page, they actually turn out to be a great timesaver. Some of these controls perform the data binding, while others perform the actual data presentation.

Validation

Users are a lot of fun, especially when they enter wacky data into your quality software. Verifying the data they enter is hard enough in desktop applications, but it's even more cumbersome when the client system talks to the application host only a few dozen seconds per hour. The validation controls remove some of the burden. They test for the most common types of data entry mistakes, and notify the user of problems, all without extra code on your part. When you do need to perform some custom validation logic, the `CustomValidator` control lets you add this logic as an event handler or client-side script.

Navigation

This group includes a few controls designed to help the user move from page to page or section to section within your web site.

Login

These controls encapsulate login and password management features so that the user can create a new user account, provide an authenticated password, or perform other security-related actions.

WebParts

WebParts are control containers that the user rearranges using drag-and-drop within the web page. This reorganization of the display allows the user to personalize the display to fulfill the selfish wants that cloud his mind. You can record the state of the WebParts for redisplay the next time the user returns to the site or page.

AJAX Extensions

The handful of controls in this section helps to support ASP.NET's Ajax functionality. Ajax (Asynchronous JavaScript and XML) is a set of web-based technologies that can help make web pages more responsive, especially through partial-page updates. Ajax is beyond the scope of this book.

Reporting

Here you'll find the `ReportViewer` control, the web version of the report technology we discussed in Chapter 21. It displays reports using the same RDLC files you built for your desktop application.

HTML

These are the standard HTML controls, such as `<textarea>`, that web page developers have been using for years. Visual Studio does provide some IntelliSense and property validation for you, but using these controls is identical to typing the matching HTML tag directly into the page markup.

Let's add a few controls from the Standard section of the toolbox to the web page. In the bottom-left cell of the table we added earlier, add a Button control, give it the name ActMultiple, and set its Text property to Multiply.

Add two TextBox controls to the top two cells in the righthand table column. Name one of them FirstOperand and name the other one SecondOperand.

Add a Label control to the bottom-right corner cell of the table. Name it Product, and set its Text property to 0 (that is, zero).

Did you notice how setting each property for these controls was no different from what you did in the main Library application? Simple! By now, your web page should look like the one in Figure 23-5.

Figure 23-5. The completed user interface

Return briefly to the HTML markup for this page by clicking on the Source section button at the bottom of the page. If you're familiar with HTML, you'll notice the `<table>` tag for the table we added. But you'll also find something unfamiliar within the first table row.

```
<table class="style1">
  <tr>
    <td>
      Operand 1:
    </td>
    <td>
      <asp:TextBox ID="FirstOperand"
        runat="server"></asp:TextBox>
    </td>
  </tr>
```

It's that `<asp:TextBox>` tag. It looks something like other HTML tags, but there are no HTML tags that start with "asp." This is a special ASP.NET tag that represents a Web Forms control class. These controls, and the `runat="server"` attributes strewn throughout the markup, are what make ASP.NET pages what they are. As ASP.NET processes the *.aspx* page, it strips out these custom control tags and calls on the related controls to generate their own browser-neutral HTML.

The user interface is done; let's add the logic. We want the program to multiply the two operands together when we click on the Multiply button. Return to the web page design and double-click on the Multiply button. It jumps to the code template for a button's Click event, just as you expected it to do.

```
Partial Class _Default
    Inherits System.Web.UI.Page

    Protected Sub ActMultiple_Click(ByVal sender As Object, _
            ByVal e As System.EventArgs) Handles ActMultiple.Click

        End Sub
End Class
```

The design goal of ASP.NET was to have code that was as close to desktop application code as possible, and this is it. Add the following logic to the event handler:

```
' ----- Multiply the two numbers.
Product.Text = Val(FirstOperand.Text) * _
    Val(SecondOperand.Text)
If (Val(Product.Text) < 0) Then
    Product.ForeColor = Drawing.Color.Red
Else
    Product.ForeColor = Drawing.Color.Black
End If
```

As you were typing, did you notice all of the IntelliSense responding to your every keystroke? I couldn't tell that this was a web-based application, and that's great.

Press the F5 key to start the application. You'll be prompted to turn on debugging, which you want to do. This will modify the application's *web.config* file to support debugging. Later, you'll want to disable that feature so that your users won't be able to debug the application. If you open the *web.config* file, you'll see this line:

```
<compilation debug="true" strict="false" explicit="true"/>
```

Just change the debug attribute to false to turn off debugging.

ASP.NET is a server application; it requires a living, breathing web server before pages can be processed. You may or may not have Internet Information Server installed on your system, but that's OK. Visual Studio 2008 includes its own "ASP.NET Development Server" that exists just so that you can test your ASP.NET applications. Figure 23-6 shows it popping up in the system tray.

Figure 23-6. Your built-in web server endeavors to give good service

Figure 23-7 shows the application running in my default web browser, Internet Explorer. (Dear web browser companies, for information on product placement in this page, contact me directly.)

Figure 23-7. Wow, a whole web application in fewer than 10 lines of code

If you don't like how the table spreads way across the page, you can adjust it using the CSS Properties panel. Back in Visual Studio, select the View → CSS Properties menu command. The panel opens, and adjusts itself depending on which page element you currently have selected. To eliminate the table's love affair with the right border, select the table itself, scroll down to the Position/Width property, and remove the "100%" value from that property entry.

More About Events

So far, our application looks just like a desktop application; the form displayed our initial drag-and-drop and property settings, and it responded to a button click by returning to the processing computer for the logic. But let's be honest. There's no way that a web application can ever be truly as responsive to events as a desktop application. What happens when the Internet connection goes down or it is just plain slow? How do you handle things such as TextChanged events in text fields? You can't have the web page go back to the web server every time the user presses a key.

The ASP.NET TextBox control has a TextChanged event, but it does not trigger for each keystroke. In fact, it doesn't trigger at all (by default) until something (such as a button click) causes the page to go back to the server. And there are a lot of other control events that work like this. They are all saved up until the user does something to bring the whole page back to the web server for processing. At that time, these delayed events finally fire, and processing continues as normal.

So, there are really two types of events: regular and premium. I mean postback and non-postback. *Postback events* are those that cause the web page to immediately return to the server for processing. *Non-postback events* delay their event handlers until something else causes a return to the server. Most events are one or the other, but some can be changed. The CheckBox control has a CheckedChanged event that fires in a non-postback way when the user alters the state of the checkbox. However, if you set the control's AutoPostBack property to True, the page will immediately return to the server anytime the user clicks the checkbox.

Besides control events, the entire page has a few events. The most significant is the Page_Load event. This is analogous to Windows Forms' Form_Load event; it's a great place to configure initial control properties, fill in drop-down lists, and so on. I'm going to add the following code to my page's Load event:

```
Protected Sub Page_Load(ByVal sender As Object, _
      ByVal e As System.EventArgs) Handles Me.Load
   ' ----- Initialize the data.
   Product.Text = "No Data"
End Sub
```

Now the Product label will display "No Data" the first time the page appears. The thing about the Load event handler is that *it runs every single time the web page is displayed*. Since this test application keeps using the same page over and over again for its results, the Load event handler will run afresh each time. For this test program, it's not really a big deal; the code in the ActMultiply_Click event handler overrides its initial "No Data" value. But in other applications, you might not want to keep reinitializing the data. Fortunately, the Load event will let you know whether this is the first time through via a page-level member called IsPostBack.

```
   ' ----- Initialize the data, but only the first time.
   If (Me.IsPostBack = False) Then Product.Text = "No Data"
```

State and View State

Wait a minute. If I am reloading the page from scratch every time with the need to initialize values in the Page_Load event handler, how is it that the two text boxes kept the user-entered values when the page reloaded? We didn't add any code to save and restore those values during initialization.

Here's the story. Although the Page_Load event does give you the opportunity to initialize the page every time the page loads, for most fields the page will remember what was in each field. Remember, ASP.NET is designed so that you think it is running just like a Windows Forms application. You would never be happy if the fields on your desktop form kept clearing out every time the user clicked a button. You wouldn't be happy if they cleared out in a Web Forms application either.

Because web pages are disconnected from the web server most of the time, each web page needs some way to retain the *state*—the current property and data settings—of each control between page loads. The Web Forms system does this through a feature called *View State*. Here's how it works: each ASP.NET web page includes a hidden static field that contains a serialized version of all important state information for the controls. When the user makes changes to each control and triggers some event that returns the page to the web server, it returns with both the embedded View State (built up from the previous construction of the page) and all the current settings for every control. Using this combined information, ASP.NET is able to reconstruct the true client-visible state of every control, and communicate that correctly to you in your server-side event handler code.

When you run an ASP.NET application, use the View → Source menu command in Internet Explorer or your favorite browser of the month, and you'll see something like the following:

```
<input type="hidden" name="__VIEWSTATE" id="__VIEWSTATE"
↳ value="/wEPDwUKMTEyMTc3MTQwNg9kFgICAw9kFgICBw8P
↳ FgIeBFRleHQFB05vIERhdGFkGFkZGQME+xLedutk85TvXy9OJd
↳ kQFO2YA==" />
```

That's the View State. Don't ask me how it works; I won't tell you (since I don't know). But it's not important to know how it works. It's only important that ASP.NET knows how it works so that it can keep your application working like the Windows Forms system it truly isn't.

As you add controls to your page, the View State will increase in size. Since all of the web page's content must be transported repeatedly over the Internet, a larger View State results in longer transmission times. It is possible to turn off View State for specific controls using their EnableViewState property. If you don't need a control's value retained from page use to page use, it's a good idea to turn it off.

Data Validation

Because this sample code uses the Visual Basic Val function to preprocess the user-supplied data, it almost always works without error. Any data considered invalid is simply converted to zero. Another option would be to chastise the user for invalid entry before processing occurs, to *validate* the supplied values. The five validators in the Validation section of the Web Forms toolbox help you do just that:

- The RequiredFieldValidator confirms that the user supplied any value at all in a control.
- The RangeValidator complains if a control's value does not fall between two values.
- The RegularExpressionValidator lets you compare a control's value against a regular expression pattern. For instance, you could compare the user's entry of a serial number to a pattern to ensure that it included two letters followed by five digits.

- The CompareValidator involves two controls, comparing the value between them. The control also doubles as a data type validator, confirming that a single field contains the proper type of data, such as a date value or an integer.

- The CustomValidator lets you perform any type of validation you want through code you supply.

All of these controls perform server-side validation, and they optionally do their data check using client-side scripts (the default). Having the client-side check reduces the need to go back to the web server just to ensure that a required field has data. Having the server-side check ensures that the data is valid even if the client has disabled scripting support.

The validators display their own error messages, so you place them on the page where you want the error message to appear. You can also have multiple validators display their collective issues in a single location by using a ValidationSummary control.

Let's add some validation to the two input fields in the multiplication sample. We want to ensure that the data is supplied, and that both values are valid integers. To do this, we must add both a RequiredFieldValidator and a CompareValidator for each field. Right-click in the bottom-right cell of the table, just after the Product label, and choose Insert → Column to the Right from the shortcut menu that pops up. In the new upper-right cell, add a RequiredFieldValidator control. Set the following properties:

- Set ControlToValidate to FirstOperand.

- Set Display to Dynamic. This lets the size of the validator shrink to nothing when there is no error to display.

- Set ErrorMessage to Missing.

Just to the right of that validator, in the same table cell, add a CompareValidator, and set these properties:

- Set ControlToValidate to FirstOperand.

- Set Display to Dynamic.

- Set ErrorMessage to Must be an integer.

- Set Operator to DataTypeCheck.

- Set Type to Integer.

Add a similar pair of validators to the second table row, using SecondOperand for the ControlToValidate. Your web page should look like Figure 23-8.

Run the program and just try to enter faulty data in the input cells. The page will complain immediately when you click the Multiply button.

That's all the multiplying we'll do for now. I've saved a copy of the project for you in the *WebSite1* subdirectory in the main directory where you installed this book's sample code.

To multiply two values together, enter them in the text fields, and click the **Multiply** button.

Operand 1: [   ] Missing. Must be an integer.
Operand 2: [   ] Missing. Must be an integer.
[Multiply] 0

Figure 23-8. Bulking up on the validation support

Database Integration

Connecting ASP.NET pages to a database, especially if you use some of the wizard-style features of Visual Studio, is extremely easy. That's because many of the controls included with ASP.NET are specifically designed to display and interact with data from tabular data sources. We'll try out a quick wizard example here, and do a lot more database integration in this chapter's "Project" section.

In Chapter 20, the first of the five built-in reports we created for the Library system displayed a list of all checked-out items. We designed an RDLC report for it, and since ASP.NET includes an RDLC Report Viewer control, we could reuse that for a web-based report. But instead we'll display the report using one of the Web Forms controls, GridView. Here's the query that retrieves the checked-out items:

```
SELECT PA.LastName + ', ' + PA.FirstName AS PatronName,
    PA.Barcode AS PatronBarcode,
    PC.DueDate, IC.CopyNumber, IC.Barcode AS ItemBarcode,
    NI.Title, CMT.FullName AS MediaName
FROM Patron AS PA
    INNER JOIN PatronCopy AS PC ON PA.ID = PC.Patron
    INNER JOIN ItemCopy AS IC ON PC.ItemCopy = IC.ID
    INNER JOIN NamedItem AS NI ON IC.ItemID = NI.ID
    INNER JOIN CodeMediaType AS CMT ON NI.MediaType = CMT.ID
WHERE PC.Returned = 0
    AND PC.Missing = 0
    AND IC.Missing = 0
ORDER BY NI.Title, IC.CopyNumber, PA.LastName, PA.FirstName
```

That should look familiar. Create a new ASP.NET web site through Visual Studio. Type the following line at the top of the content page:

```
ACME Library Checked Out Items
```

Feel free to embellish it to make it look nicer. I added <h1> tags around it in the markup to make it stand out. Below that title line, add a new GridView control to the page. I found it in the Data section of my Visual Studio Toolbox. The control's smart tag opens and shows a panel of GridView Tasks, as shown in Figure 23-9.

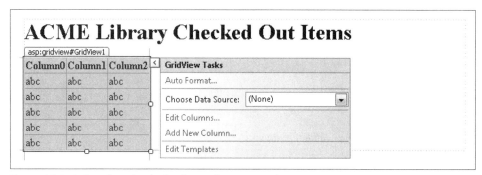

Figure 23-9. A short list of tasks for the GridView control

If you want to click on the Auto Format task and change the look of the grid, you can, but the important task for now is Choose Data Source. Select <Add New Source> from the list. Our old friend the Data Source Configuration Wizard appears again, although with some changes specific to ASP.NET. Select Database for the data source type and click the OK button. When prompted for the connection, you should already have a Library database connection in the list. Select it (or create a new connection) and click Next.

You'll be asked to save the connection string in the application configuration file. If you do, it will add an entry to the <connectionStrings> section of the *web.config* file created for the ASP.NET application. If you like to play power games with your system administrator, leave the field unchecked. But if you want an easy way to modify the connection information later, you had better leave the field as it is, giving the entry a reasonable name. Then click Next.

The wizard prompts you for table and field details. Select "Specify a custom SQL statement or stored procedure," click Next, and type in the checked-out-item query shown a few paragraphs back. Click Next again. The wizard gives you one last chance to test the query before you click the Finish button.

Now here's the simple part. Visual Studio connects to the database, reads the schema, and creates columns in the grid perfectly designed for the query. Your application is complete. Press F5 to run it.

We're going to stop there for now and pick this up in the "Project" section.

Windows Communication Foundation

Have you ever wanted to extract one piece of data from a web site for use in your Visual Basic application? No? Well let me tell you: it's called "screen scraping," and it's a pain in the neck. Most web sites with valuable content are designed by selfish people, programmers who think only about their own company's needs and nothing about other developers who need to pilfer essential data from—I mean, who need to add value to their own applications by enhancing it with content from a trusted third party.

Screen scraping is generally a bad thing. Not only is the HTML content ludicrously difficult to parse, but you never know when the web site owner is going to up and change the content without the courtesy of contacting you first. Fortunately, Windows Communication Foundation provides a solution to this problem. This core Microsoft technology, formerly code-named Indigo, exists to transport meaningful data between applications and systems, local or remote.

Windows Communication Foundation, usually abbreviated as WCF, joins several previously distinct technologies into a unified whole: message queues (such as MSMQ), web services (see the upcoming note), distributed transactions (such as MSDTC), and .NET Remoting. Since each of these technologies involved moving information from one application to another, it was a no-brainer for Microsoft to spend more money than you'll ever see on a merged service.

If a site has content or processes that need to be used by external applications, it can include a "service" on the site that makes screen scraping unnecessary. WCF implements the intersystem-based equivalent of function calls, complete with parameters and return values, all of which can be accessed remotely. They are based on published standards such as Simple Object Access Protocol (SOAP) that use plain text and XML to simulate the function call between two systems.

 Before Visual Studio 2008, .NET developers used a system called *XML Web Services* that provided functionality similar to the services portion of WCF. If you want to use XML Web Services, it is still available in Visual Studio 2008. However, Microsoft is recommending that new software use WCF instead of XML Web Services.

A lot of technologies are involved in making WCF possible, but you don't really need to know them. Instead, you will implement one or more Visual Basic methods based on an interface you define. This interface, marked up with WCF-specific attributes, establishes the "service contract" that makes the functional communication between two systems possible.

WCF services appear as *.svc* files on your web site. In Visual Studio, you can either create a new web site and select WCF Service as the project type, or add a WCF Service item to an existing web site project. When you do, Visual Studio adds the necessary files to your project. The first is the actual *.svc* file. It's a smart interface conduit between the web site and the actual web service code. Here's what I found in my *Service.svc* file:

```
<%@ ServiceHost Language="VB" Debug="true" Service="Service"
↳CodeBehind="~/App_Code/Service.vb" %>
```

This directive refers the caller to the Service class in the associated *Service.vb* source code file. That file is much more interesting. Here's a portion of that file:

```
Public Class Service
    Implements IService

    Public Function GetData(ByVal value As Integer) _
        As String Implements IService.GetData
        Return String.Format("You entered: {0}", value)
    End Function
End Class
```

This looks like sample code to me, and you'll replace it when you write your own service. The Service class in the code implements the members of the IService interface, found in the related *IService.vb* file.

```
<ServiceContract()> _
Public Interface IService
    <OperationContract()> _
    Function GetData(ByVal value As Integer) As String
End Interface
```

As shown, this interface also contains a meaningless sample member, GetData, which must be replaced. It's marked up with the WCF-focused attribute <OperationContract> which, along with the interface's <ServiceContract> attribute, declare, "There be WCF Services here." Remember that an attribute adds metadata to an assembly so that the compiler or some other program will do something special with the marked items. In this case, the <OperationContract> attribute tells WCF to treat the GetData method (when implemented) as a service member. WCF responds by connecting up all of the plumbing code that makes the service possible.

I'm going to replace the GetData function with another one that at least pretends to do some real work. First, I'll change the IService interface so that it defines the contract.

```
<ServiceContract()> _
Public Interface IService
    <OperationContract()> _
    Function NumberToText(ByVal sourceNumber _
        As Integer) As String
End Interface
```

Then, in the Service class, I'll implement the interface and its NumberToText member.

```
Public Class Service
    Implements IService

    Public Function NumberToText(ByVal sourceNumber As Integer) _
        As String Implements IService.NumberToText
        Select Case sourceNumber
            Case 0 : Return "Zero"
            Case 1 : Return "One"
            Case 2 : Return "Two"
            Case 3 : Return "Three"
            Case 4 : Return "Four"
```

```
            Case 5 : Return "Five"
            Case 6 : Return "Six"
            Case 7 : Return "Seven"
            Case 8 : Return "Eight"
            Case 9 : Return "Nine"
            Case Else : Return "Out of range"
        End Select
    End Function
End Class
```

If you run this application in Visual Studio, your web browser opens with the (partial) page shown in Figure 23-10.

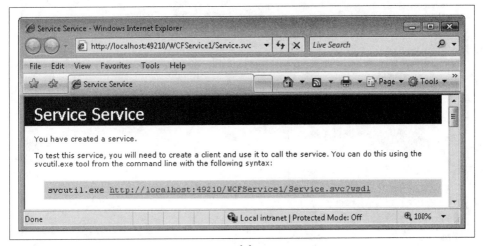

Figure 23-10. A WCF service running in your web browser

WCF services are methods, and a web browser isn't a typical medium for running subroutines and functions, so the page in Figure 23-10 appears instead. Its informational content shows you how you can test or use the service, either through a utility designed for that purpose, or through Visual Basic or C# code.

Since I have this service running on my system using my test ASP.NET web server, I'll write a desktop application to call the NumberToText method. Start a separate instance of Visual Studio and create a new Windows Forms project. Select the Project → Add Service Reference menu command. The Add Service Reference form appears; it's a tool you use to locate local and remote WCF services.

You can specifically request the service if you know its address. To determine this, double-click on the ASP.NET Development Web Server icon in the system tray. The Root URL field will provide the base of the address. On my system at this particular moment, it says "http://localhost:49210/WebSite2," although by default it will change port numbers if I restart the service. Add to this the name of the *.svc* file for your service.

```
http://localhost:49210/WCFService1/Service.svc
```

Enter this address in the Add Service Reference form's Address field, and click Go. If successful, the form locates the service and displays its contracts in the Services field. Figure 23-11 shows the located NumberToText operator. You can provide named access to the service in your code by changing the Namespace field. Then click the OK button.

Figure 23-11. A recognized web service

To test out the service, I added a TextBox control and a Button control to Form1, and added the following code (I used the default service namespace of ServiceReference1):

```
Private Sub Button1_Click(ByVal sender As System.Object, _
    ByVal e As System.EventArgs) Handles Button1.Click
  MsgBox((New ServiceReference1.ServiceClient). _
    NumberToText(CInt(Val(TextBox1.Text))))
End Sub
```

Running the program, typing in a number from 0 to 9, and then clicking the button correctly calls the web service and returns the English version of the number. And it would have worked just as well if the NumberToText service were running on a web server at one of the research facilities at the South Pole.

Summary

I really used to hate writing ASP applications. It was a pain to embed VBScript within HTML content. Although ASP.NET still supports a variation of this method, it's much better to use the code behind features of Web Forms. This makes web development only slightly more difficult than desktop application development. Windows Communication Foundation also makes interactions between web server-housed code and desktop code as easy as developing a class with methods.

When Microsoft first came out with the .NET Framework, its marketing department really went full strength on the web development aspects of Visual Studio. I was dubious. And although I am still mainly a desktop application developer, I no longer lose up to a week of sleep when I contemplate the building of Internet applications.

Project

For this chapter's project, I built a simple multipage web site that (1) lets the user look up items in the Library database; and (2) duplicates the Library Statistics report created in Chapter 21, but without the RDLC component. I went ahead and included the completed project in your installed source code directory, in the *LibraryWebSite* subdirectory. You can open it by locating its directory with the File → Open Web Site menu command in Visual Studio.

As shown in Figure 23-12, the project includes 11 files and two subdirectories.

Figure 23-12. The Library web site project files

Here's a quick rundown of each file and subdirectory:

App_Code

The directory for all project code that is not code behind for an actual ASP.NET web page. All of your general modules and classes for a project appear here.

General.vb

A code module with six methods that I stole almost verbatim from the main Library Project's *General.vb* file. I made just a few changes, mostly to deal with not having the LibraryDB global variable sitting around with its connection information.

BoundSchemas.vb

When we started the checked-out-item report earlier in this chapter, we bound a GridView control to a database query. The GridView control, like most of the Web Forms controls, can also bind to any class that supports the IList interface, including the generic collection classes. The classes in this file will be used for instances within a generic collection in two of the web pages.

App_Data

This directory normally contains data needed by the application. It was created automatically by Visual Studio. I don't use it in this project.

Default.aspx and Default.aspx.vb

This is the entry point of the Library web site. The client browser requests the *Default.aspx* web page to start the library experience. The page includes a link to the statistics report, plus fields that let you look up library items by title or author.

SearchResults.aspx and SearchResults.aspx.vb

Searches performed from the *Default.aspx* page end up here, with queries processed in code and then bound to a grid.

SearchDetail.aspx and SearchDetail.aspx.vb

Each search result includes a link to this page. It provides additional detail for an item, in the same format used in the main Library project's *ItemLookup.vb* file.

Statistics.aspx and Statistics.aspx.vb

This page displays the Library Statistics report as a bound web page.

web.config

Every ASP.NET project includes a *web.config* file used to specify project-specific settings in the development and production environments.

Configuring the Database

The *web.config* file contains a place for database connection strings. I've added an entry within it for the Library database.

```
<connectionStrings>
  <add name="LibraryConnection" connectionString=
  ↳"Data Source=MYSERVER\SQLEXPRESS;
  ↳Initial Catalog=Library;Integrated Security=True" />
</connectionStrings>
```

Modify the "MYSERVER\SQLEXPRESS" portion to the name of your SQL Server database instance, and modify the other parts of the connection string as needed. All four of the web pages use the Library database, and they all access the connection string from this entry, via the ConfigurationManager object:

```
Public LibraryDB As System.Data.SqlClient.SqlConnection
```

...and later...

```
LibraryDB = New SqlClient.SqlConnection( _
    ConfigurationManager.ConnectionStrings( _
    "LibraryConnection").ConnectionString)
LibraryDB.Open( )
```

...and later still...

```
LibraryDB.Close( )
```

The Default Page

The *Default.aspx* page is the starting point for the Library web application, and appears in Figure 23-13.

ACME Library

Item Search

To search for a library item, enter the search criteria, then click **Search**. You may include the "*" character as a wildcard in the title or name fields.

Item Title:	
Author (Last, First):	
Media Type:	Unbound ▼
	Search

Library Statistics

To view the general holding statistics of the library, click here.

Figure 23-13. The Library web site's default page

Its code is not much to talk about. It simply fills in the Media Type drop-down list with the available types from the database.

```
sqlText = "SELECT ID, FullName FROM CodeMediaType " & _
    "ORDER BY FullName"
dbInfo = CreateReader(sqlText, LibraryDB)
Do While dbInfo.Read
    SearchMediaType.Items.Add(New WebControls.ListItem( _
        CStr(dbInfo!FullName), CStr(dbInfo!ID)))
Loop
dbInfo.Close()
```

The page itself is a little more interesting. When we built the sample ASP.NET web application earlier, each click on the Multiply button sent the page back *to itself*. It was a one-page application. Most web applications would be useless with only a single page, so button clicks and links need to jump elsewhere in the project. The report link at the bottom of this page is a standard hyperlink to *Statistics.aspx*, another page within the application. In the search portion of the page, the Search button (ActSearch) also jumps to another project page, *SearchResults.aspx*. It does this through its PostBackUrl property, which is set to ~/SearchResults.aspx. The new page will have indirect access to all of the field selections on this starting page.

Search Results

The *SearchResults.aspx* page displays any matching results from the *Default.aspx* item search section. As shown in Figure 23-14, it includes a GridView control for the listing of results, plus a Label control that shows a count of the matches.

Figure 23-14. The Library web site's search results page

Unlike the GridView populated earlier, this one does not connect directly to a database query. Instead, I hand-build instances of the BoundSchemaSearchResults class (from *BoundSchemas.vb*), collect them into a generic List, and bind them to the fields in the GridView. Actually, binding in this way is a snap. Each column I configured in the GridView control looks for a property in the incoming records that matches a specific field name. These columns are defined through the Column Editor (see Figure 23-15), accessed via the control's Columns property.

Figure 23-15. Editing columns in a GridView control

Figure 23-15 shows the properties for the first bound data column, "Item Name." It's bound to a field in the data named ItemData via the DataField property. The next two columns are configured similarly but use the incoming data fields AuthorName and MediaType. The fourth column provides a hyperlink to the *SearchDetail.aspx* for each matching record. To build this column, I added it as a HyperLinkField column instead of a BoundField column. I set its Text property to Detail, which will appear on every record. Clicking on the link will pass the ID of the matching item (I set the DataNavigateUrlFields to ID) to the target page via a query string.

The `DataNavigateUrlFormatString` property contains a string that will be sent to the `String.Format` method, along with the fields listed in `DataNavigateUrlFields`. Here is the format string:

```
SearchDetail.aspx?ID={0}
```

The {0} part gets replaced with the value of each record's `ID` field.

This page's `Load` event handler is triggered by a call from the Search button on the *Default.aspx* page. When a Web Forms page calls itself, it can directly examine the values in its controls. But the controls on the *Default.aspx* page don't exist here in the *SearchResults.aspx* page. Fortunately, the previous page's controls are sent as data to the new page. You can access them through the `PreviousPage` object. The following code extracts the values from each of the search fields:

```
' ----- Get the title search text.
sourceTextBox = CType(PreviousPage.FindControl( _
   "SearchTitle"), TextBox)
If (sourceTextBox IsNot Nothing) Then _
   useTitle = Trim(sourceTextBox.Text)

' ----- Get the last name search text.
sourceTextBox = CType(PreviousPage.FindControl( _
   "SearchLastName"), TextBox)
If (sourceTextBox IsNot Nothing) Then _
   useLastName = Trim(sourceTextBox.Text)

' ----- Get the first name search text.
sourceTextBox = CType(PreviousPage.FindControl( _
   "SearchFirstName"), TextBox)
If (sourceTextBox IsNot Nothing) Then _
   useFirstName = Trim(sourceTextBox.Text)

' ----- Get the media type value.
sourceMediaType = CType(PreviousPage.FindControl( _
   "SearchMediaType"), DropDownList)
If (sourceMediaType IsNot Nothing) Then _
   useMediaType = sourceMediaType.SelectedValue
```

Amazingly, the previous page didn't just send its fields as string values. Instead, they retained their existence as true objects. Using the `CType` function to convert them to `TextBox` and `DropDownList` controls was enough to access their control properties.

I use the user-supplied values to build a SQL statement and query the database for results. If there are any, the resultant data is massaged into a list of objects.

```
Dim oneEntry As BoundSchemaSearchResults
Dim reportData As Collections.Generic.List( _
   Of BoundSchemaSearchResults)

Do While dbInfo.Read
   ' ----- Add it to the report data.
   oneEntry = New BoundSchemaSearchResults
   oneEntry.ID = CInt(dbInfo!ID)
```

```
    oneEntry.ItemName = CStr(dbInfo!Title)
    If (IsDBNull(dbInfo!LastName) = True) Then _
       useLastName = "" Else _
       useLastName = CStr(dbInfo!LastName)
    If (IsDBNull(dbInfo!FirstName) = True) Then _
       useFirstName = "" Else _
       useFirstName = CStr(dbInfo!FirstName)
    If (useFirstName <> "") Then
       If (useLastName <> "") Then useLastName &= ", "
       useLastName &= useFirstName
    End If
    oneEntry.AuthorName = useLastName
    oneEntry.MediaType = CStr(dbInfo!MediaName)

    reportData.Add(oneEntry)
Loop
```

The results are bound to the grid, and a count is displayed to the user.

```
ResultsGrid.DataSource = reportData
ResultsGrid.DataBind( )
MatchCount.Text = reportData.Count & " matching items."
```

You must call the `GridView` control's `DataBind` method or you won't see any results.

Search Detail

When the user clicks on one of the Detail links in the search results, it sends the ID of the selected `NamedItem` record to the *SearchDetail.aspx* page as a query string. The page itself, which I won't show here, includes many `Label` controls that attempt to mimic the output on the detail panel of the *ItemLookup.vb* form in the main Library application. I even use almost the same Cascading Style Sheet (CSS) instructions in this page that I use in the application.

When the page's `Load` event handler fires, it first examines the query string to extract the supplied `NamedItem` ID. A missing ID results in a return to the main search form.

```
itemID = Val(Page.Request.QueryString("ID"))
If (itemID <= 0) Then
    Response.Redirect("Default.aspx")
    Return
End If
```

Most of the formatting code for this page comes from the *ItemLookup.vb* file in the main application. It queries the database for details of the specified `NamedItem` record, and updates each label using these values. The only thing that is interesting—besides the fact that this seems all too easy for web-page development—is the creation of the table of item copies near the bottom of the page. In the *ItemLookup.vb* version of the code, I hand-crafted an HTML `<table>` set and filled in its columns with the status of each available copy of the named library item. I thought it was a shame to ignore all of that great code, so I just copied it nearly unchanged into the code for *SearchDetail.aspx.vb*.

So far, I haven't had to do anything with HTML itself, except when I wanted to add <h1> tags around the page titles. But since I had written the HTML-generating code, and since ASP.NET applications target HTML, I thought I could use it.

And I can. One of the Web Forms controls is Literal, a control that exists only so that you can set its Text property to properly formatted HTML content. After building up the table structure in a StringBuilder object named copyTable, I assign that HTML content to the Literal control.

```
' ----- Add the table to the output.
PutTableHere.Text = copyTable.ToString( )
```

Statistics Report

The *Statistics.aspx* page displays the same summary information included in one of the reports from Chapter 21. In the original statistics report, I displayed record counts from six different tables, and presented them as a list in an RDLC report format. In this web page, I do those same six queries, build a generic list of the results, and bind that list to—surprise—a GridView control, which is quickly becoming our favorite. Here's the code for the page in its entirety:

```
Imports System.Data

Partial Class Statistics
    Inherits System.Web.UI.Page

    Public LibraryDB As System.Data.SqlClient.SqlConnection

    Protected Sub Page_Load(ByVal sender As Object, _
            ByVal e As System.EventArgs) Handles Me.Load
        ' ----- Prepare the data for the report.
        Dim sqlText As String
        Dim reportData As Collections.Generic.List( _
            Of BoundSchemaStatistics)
        Dim oneEntry As BoundSchemaStatistics
        Dim resultValue As Integer
        Dim counter As Integer
        Dim tableSets( ) As String = {"Author", "Publisher", _
            "Subject", "NamedItem", "ItemCopy", "Patron"}
        Dim tableTitles( ) As String = {"Authors", "Publishers", _
            "Subject Headings", "Items", "Item Copies", "Patrons"}

        ' ----- Connect to the database.
        LibraryDB = New SqlClient.SqlConnection( _
            ConfigurationManager.ConnectionStrings( _
            "LibraryConnection").ConnectionString)
        LibraryDB.Open( )
```

```
' ----- Build the report data. It's all counts from
'         different tables.
reportData = New Collections.Generic.List( _
   Of BoundSchemaStatistics)
For counter = 0 To UBound(tableSets)
   ' ----- Process one table.
   sqlText = "SELECT COUNT(*) FROM " & _
      tableSets(counter)
   resultValue = CInt(ExecuteSQLReturn(sqlText, _
      LibraryDB))

   ' ----- Add it to the report data.
   oneEntry = New BoundSchemaStatistics
   oneEntry.EntryName = tableTitles(counter)
   oneEntry.EntryValue = CStr(resultValue)
   reportData.Add(oneEntry)
Next counter

' ----- Finished with the connection.
LibraryDB.Close( )

StatisticsGrid.DataSource = reportData
StatisticsGrid.DataBind( )
   End Sub
End Class
```

I included only a minimum set of features in this web site, and don't start cracking jokes about my web page design skills. If I were planning to deploy this web site, I would certainly enable some links on the *SearchDetail.aspx* page so that the user could click to search for other items by the same author, publisher, series, and so on. I would also add patron-specific features that would let users check their current checked-out items and any fines due. Another great feature to add would be online help content that told the patron or administrator how to use the system. And that just happens to be the topic for the next chapter. Lucky you.

Adding Online Help

If there's one thing I've learned in nearly 25 years of programming, it's that users often need some help to run software on their systems. Programmers need help, too, but getting back to computers: it's rare that you find a technically conversant user. If you write applications that target businesses and departments within organizations (that's what I do), you find that the users are very skilled at their jobs, but not necessarily skilled at using a computer. That's why it is imperative that you make your programs as straightforward to use as possible.

You should also add online help to your applications. These ready documents act as the first wave of support for your users' software needs. Of course, they seldom read it, and so you (or your technical support staff) will actually become the first wave of support. But it's somewhat refreshing to be able to say, "Did you check the online help, which covers this issue in detail?"

In this chapter, we'll discuss the online help options available to you in Visual Basic and focus in on HTML Help 1.x, Microsoft's standard Windows XP help system.

Windows Online Help Options

Online help has been a part of Windows since its initial release, back in the days when applications and operating systems still shipped with printed manuals and never required more than two floppy disks. I really miss those days. That sense of touch; the cold, smooth pages in my hands. I remember the first Windows software I ever purchased, a newly released "Personal Information Manager." It had everything I needed, including a 400-page user's guide and reference manual. Sheer delight.

Those days are gone, replaced by online help systems and HTML readme files. Now you buy books such as this one to bring back that included-user's-guide feeling. But you can do a lot with online help, especially these days with the ability to include dynamic, active content in online help pages.

WinHelp

The original Windows help system was *WinHelp*. It included simple formatted help pages with hyperlinks to other pages. A separate "contents" file added table-of-contents support; you had to ship the *.cnt* contents file with the *.hlp* file as a set. These basic help files were (and in many ways, still are) good enough for most users' needs, and they are still supported by all releases of Microsoft Windows.

WinHelp files were designed using Rich Text Format (RTF), a word-processing format supported by many vendors. Because of this, the content was easy to build, although hyperlinks and other help-specific features required bizarre text and formatting combinations. But WinHelp met the needs of Windows users for years.

HTML Help

RTF documents are so 1980s. When the Internet started sweeping the world with its ability to generate beautifully formatted pages through the common HTML tag-based language, Microsoft decided to upgrade its help system to one that used standard HTML documents: *HTML Help*. As its name implies, HTML Help is truly HTML-based. Anything that generates HTML can generate HTML Help content: third-party web-page designer tools, word processors, your own custom applications, even Notepad. As expected, some vendors designed tools specifically targeting the HTML Help system.

HTML Help is better than WinHelp, due to its dependence on HTML and other related technologies. Each page of your online help file is a separate HTML page/file. Hyperlinks to other help pages are standard HTML hyperlinks. And HTML Help employs most of the features used in any web page, including Cascading Style Sheets (CSS) and Java scripting.

Compiled HTML Help files have a *.chm* extension, and a single file includes primary content, the table of contents, and a predefined index of terms. We will use HTML Help technology to add online help content to the Library Project. I'll skip the details of the system until a little later in the chapter.

Microsoft Help 2

Most applications sold as of this writing use HTML Help, but not all. One big exception is Visual Studio itself. Its help system—*Microsoft Help 2* (a.k.a. HTML Help 2.*x*)—combines HTML and XML content into a set of collections that work together as one. If you've installed the full version of SQL Server on a system with Visual Studio, they together share a common help interface. You can even search for pages in both collections at the same time.

Microsoft makes a "Help Integration Kit" available for developers who wish to merge their own content into the Microsoft Help 2 system. This is most useful for vendors who develop third-party controls and tools that integrate with .NET or SQL Server. Microsoft Help 2 is rarely used for typical end-user software.

Assistance Platform

Windows Vista uses a new help system called *Assistance Platform* (AP). All of the online help that comes with Vista is written using AP, but not much else is. That's because Microsoft decided not to release the file format for other vendors to use. Well, there are a few big companies and OEMs using AP as guided by Microsoft, but you and I are not two of them.

Other Methods

Not every application uses these Microsoft-defined help systems. Some applications include no online help at all because they are designed by bad people. No, I'm just kidding. There may be instances where online help adds no value to a program. But it's usually best to include some sort of written assistance.

Standalone HTML pages are just one step down from HTML Help files, and are a viable alternative for simple applications, or those hosted on a web site. You can use other standard formats, such as word processing or text documents, if you just don't have the resources to generate true online help files. And of course there are books, which will get my attention.

Visual Studio includes a feature that lets you generate documentation from the XML comments added to each member of your class. (I don't discuss this in this book; see the Visual Studio online help—aren't you glad it's there?—for additional information on "XML Comments.") Don't even consider using this for your own user documentation needs unless you are developing class-based components for use by other developers.

Designing HTML Help

HTML Help files are built from multiple source files:

- *Content files*, especially standard HTML files, communicate core information to the user, either through static text and graphics or through advanced web-page-style behaviors and scripts normally available in web pages.

- *The Help Contents file* uses *.hhc* for its file extension. Using standard HTML <ul> and <li> tags, the file specifies the hierarchical table of contents used by the help file.

- *The Help Keywords file* uses an *.hhk* file extension, and documents the index used to access help pages from specific predefined keywords.
- *The Help Project file*, using an *.hhp* file extension, defines an entire help project and its target *.chm* file. This INI-style text file identifies all the other files that will be compiled into the target help file. It also defines a few project-wide options.

You can build the primary content files by hand using any standard HTML tool you wish, as long as the output format matches what is expected by the HTML Help Compiler (supplied by Microsoft). For the content files, it generally doesn't matter what tool you use since standard HTML is sufficient. Any hyperlinks that you include in the content to other help pages in the same directory will become standard help links in the compiled help file.

The non-content files require a very precise format; they are all based on HTML, except the Help Project file, which is an INI file. You will need to either design these files by hand using the expected format, or use a tool that can generate these files for you in the right format.

Microsoft provides a free tool that helps you create the non-content files, and joins together the content files with them for final compilation. You can download *HTML Help Workshop* directly from Microsoft's web site. Go to the Microsoft Download Center at *http://www.microsoft.com/downloads* and search for "HTML Help Workshop." You will receive a few results, but the first one in the list (when sorted by popularity) should be the one you need. Figure 24-1 shows the main page of the HTML Help Workshop application with an active project file open.

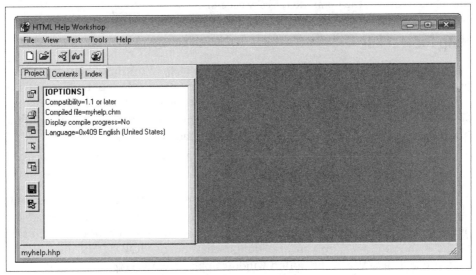

Figure 24-1. Giving help to those who really need it

In the rest of this section, we'll use HTML Help Workshop to build a simple HTML Help file that contains two pages: a welcome page and a "more information" page. You can find this sample help project in the *HTMLHelpSample* subdirectory of the book's installation directory.

Content Files

Our mini project includes two content files: *welcome.htm* and *moreinfo.htm*. Ever the technology maven, I crafted them in Notepad. Here's the content for *welcome.htm*:

```
<html>
  <head><title>Welcome to My Help</title></head>
  <body>
    Welcome to My Help. For more information,
    <a href="moreinfo.htm">click here</a>.
  </body>
</html>
```

The *moreinfo.htm* file is a lot like it.

```
<html>
  <head><title>My Help Additional Info</title></head>
  <body>
    Not much more to say. For a greeting,
    <a href="welcome.htm">click here</a>.
  </body>
</html>
```

You can add graphics files (such as JPEG and GIF files) and link them in as you normally would in a web page. Be sure to store the graphics files in the same directory (or subdirectory) as the main file for easy access.

Help Project File

Let's generate the remaining files through HTML Help Workshop. Start it up, and use the File → New menu command to create a new project. Using the New Project Wizard, identify the location and name of your new *.hhp* file. I'll create a file named *Simple.hhp* in the same folder as the two content files. The wizard prompts you for files already created. Check the "HTML files" field, as shown in Figure 24-2.

Add the two HTML files in the next step and complete the wizard. The project file is created with references to your two files.

The project is pretty empty; it doesn't even have a window title defined for the compiled help file. You can set the title and other general settings through the project options, accessed through the topmost button in the toolbar that runs on the left side of the main window. You can also double-click on the [OPTIONS] item in the project details list. When the option window appears, enter **Simple Help** in the Title field, and then click OK.

Figure 24-2. Locate the files now, or you can do it later

Here is what the project file contains at this point:

```
[OPTIONS]
Compatibility=1.1 or later
Compiled file=Simple.chm
Default topic=welcome.htm
Display compile progress=No
Language=0x409 English (United States)
Title=Simple Help

[FILES]
welcome.htm
moreinfo.htm

[INFOTYPES]
```

The file will change as we add the other two non-content files, but not by much.

Compiling the file right now (using the File → Compile menu command) and running it displays a very simple help window, as shown in Figure 24-3.

Help Contents File

A table of contents will help the user peruse this massive online help experience. To add a contents file, click on the Contents tab on the left side of the main form, and respond to the prompt that you wish to create a new file, naming it *Simple.hhc*. The form changes to display a table-of-contents editor. Another way to create the contents file is by using the File → New menu command, and choosing Table of Contents from the New selection form. This is less direct, as it doesn't immediately connect the contents file with the project.

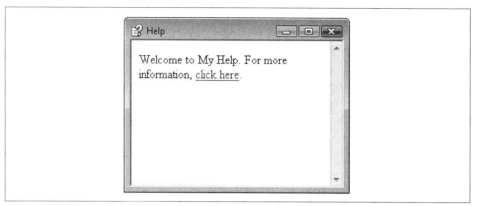

Figure 24-3. A little help; very little

Use the new toolbar buttons running down the left side of the window to add and modify content entries. First, use the top button ("Contents properties") to edit the options for the table of contents. On the Table of Contents Properties form, uncheck the "Use folders instead of books" field and click OK.

The next two buttons—the book button ("Insert a heading") and the page/question mark button ("Insert a page")—are the main buttons used to add new entries to the contents. I clicked the "Insert a page" button to get to the Table of Contents Entry form shown in Figure 24-4.

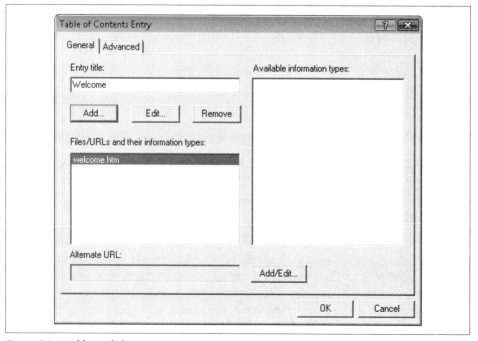

Figure 24-4. Adding a help page

As shown in the figure, I set the entry title ("Welcome"), and selected the Welcome to My Help (*welcome.htm*) file through the Add button. I did the same for the *moreinfo.htm* file, giving it a title of "More Information." I also added a heading entry using the "Insert a heading" toolbar button on the main form, naming it "Other Pages." I used the arrow toolbar buttons to move the *moreinfo.htm* entry into this heading section. Then I took a much-needed break and looked at my completed table of contents in Figure 24-5.

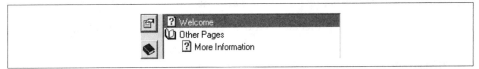

Figure 24-5. The full table of contents

If you compile and run the file, it now includes the table of contents in a separate panel, plus a toolbar (see Figure 24-6).

Figure 24-6. New and improved TOC; same great content

Help Keywords (Index) File

An index file lets the user access specific pages by searching for a concept or subject from a list. There is a many-to-many relationship between these keywords and the help pages: one keyword can lead to one or more pages, and a single page can be the target of multiple keywords.

Create an index by clicking on the Index tab on the left half of the main form, and respond to the prompt that you want to create a new index file, calling it *Simple. hhk*. As with the Contents editor, the Index editor includes a small vertical toolbar.

Use the second button in the toolbar, the one with the key image, to create new keyword entries. I will add three keywords:

- basic, linking to *welcome.htm*
- advanced, linking to *moreinfo.htm*
- everything, linking to both pages

The Index Entry editor form works just like the Table of Contents Entry form, allowing you to specify the target pages for each keyword.

Saving and compiling the project adds index features to the compiled help file.

Formatting Help Windows

On my system, running the compiled help file displayed the content in a little window in the upper-right corner of the screen. But my help content is important; I want it to appear much closer to the middle of the screen, and in a larger window. Fortunately, you can control the windows used to display the content. Return to the Project tab and click on the third toolbar button down on the left side of the window. This "Add/modify window definitions" button lets you define one or more windows to use for distinct help pages in your file. When prompted, add a New Window Type named SimpleWindow.

The Window Types dialog that appears has many options for getting just the window you want, although you're probably being too picky if you need more than, say, 243 different window types. The Position tab is a lot of fun. It includes an Autosizer button that lets you drag a window to the desired size. Adjust the size to something reasonable, add a "Title bar text" of "Simple Help" back on the General tab, and click OK. Since this is the only defined window, it becomes the default, and will be used for the main help display the next time you compile and run the file.

Accessing HTML Help

Visual Studio provides two primary methods of integrating online help into desktop applications. The first uses the HelpProvider control, found in the Components section of the Visual Studio Toolbox. The second uses the Help.ShowHelp method of the Windows Forms package. Both methods let you display specific pages or portions of a compiled HTML Help file.

HelpProvider Control

The HelpProvider control can be added to a form to enable access to online help. It provides two primary online help experiences: (1) standard access to compiled HTML Help files; and (2) pop-up help. Both methods put the focus on individual controls of a form, and on the specific help features to be tied to each control.

Accessing HTML help files

To use the HelpProvider control with compiled HTML Help files, set the control's HelpNamespace property to the location of a valid help file. Then adjust the properties of other controls on the form to refer to specific features within the help file. The HelpProvider control impacts other controls by adding several additional properties to each. Figure 24-7 shows the four additional properties (HelpKeyword, HelpNavigator, HelpString, and ShowHelp) automatically added to a Button control.

Figure 24-7. Adding help support to individual controls

The HelpNavigator property added to each control defines what features of the help file to access when the user presses the F1 key while that control has the focus. To access a specific page within the help file (such as *welcome.htm*), you set the target control's HelpNavigator property to Topic and set the related HelpKeyword property to the filename of the page (welcome.htm).

The HelpNavigator property for a control can be set to access non-page sections of the online help file as well. The value TableOfContents displays the file's contents outline; Index jumps to the keyword index. There are a few other choices as well.

Showing pop-up help

The HelpProvider control also enables "pop-up" help on individual controls. This help variation causes a small tool tip window to appear just above a control, displaying a short message that provides usage information for that control, as shown in Figure 24-8.

Figure 24-8. Pop-up help on a button control

Pop-up help works when you enable the "Pop-up button" in the form's title bar. To set pop-up help for a control, follow these steps:

1. Add a `HelpProvider` control to the form, but don't bother setting its `HelpNamespace` property to a file.

2. Set the form's `HelpButton` property to `True`.

3. Set the form's `MaximizeBox` and `MinimizeBox` properties to `False`.

4. Set the `HelpString on HelpProvider1` property to some informational text on each control that will display its own pop-up help.

The user displays pop-up help by first clicking on the question-mark "help" button in the form's title bar, and then clicking on a control.

ShowHelp Method

The `System.Windows.Forms.Help.ShowHelp` method displays specific portions of a compiled HTML Help file based on the arguments passed to the method. It's quite similar to the file-based help portion of the `HelpProvider` control, but in method form. To display a specific page within a help file, use this syntax:

```
Windows.Forms.Help.ShowHelp(Me, "Simple.chm", _
    HelpNavigator.Topic, "moreinfo.htm")
```

The first argument is a reference to the form calling the method.

A common way to use this method is to monitor the form for the F1 key, and call `ShowHelp` from the form's `KeyDown` event handler.

```
Private Sub Form1_KeyDown(ByVal sender As Object, _
        ByVal e As System.Windows.Forms.KeyEventArgs) _
        Handles Me.KeyDown
    ' ----- Call online help.
    If (e.KeyCode = Keys.F1) Then
        Windows.Forms.Help.ShowHelp(Me, "Simple.chm", _
            HelpNavigator.Topic, "moreinfo.htm")
    End If
End Sub
```

You must set the form's `KeyPreview` property to `True` to trigger the form-level `KeyDown` event. Otherwise, all keys go to the active control and bypass the form-level events.

The `ShowHelp` method offers a lot more control over the user's online help experience since you (and not the `HelpProvider` control) determine exactly when to access the help file.

Summary

If it is your plan to stand over the shoulder of each user and give running verbal instructions while they sit before your software, by all means skip the writing of any online help or other user documentation. But if you plan to have a life, make it easier by including usage support right in the application. These are not the bad old days when you had to provide your own method of online help display, or needed to dig through the Windows API library to find the function that accessed the help file. This is .NET! It has all the help features you need built right in.

Crafting compiled HTML files is not too difficult with the HTML Help Workshop tool. But if you will work on any sizable help file, or if you want to add enhanced features consistently, you should think about plunking down a few hundred dollars on a third-party help development tool.

Project

Once you have access to an online help file, you have access to every page of it. That's usually a good thing, because users are curious. (I mean that they are inquisitive and not merely objects of curiosity.) But in the case of the Library Project, that curiosity could lead to topics that are really no business of ordinary patrons. Most of the features in the Library application are for administrative use only. To keep things as calm as possible, the Library Project includes two online help files:

- *LibraryBasic.chm*, a patron-focused help file that describes only the parts of the program the patron can access
- *LibraryAdmin.chm*, a file targeting administrators and librarians that fully describes the features of the application

This section builds both of these online help files, and integrates them into the Library application.

Building the Help Files

I've written the content for both online help files for you. You'll find it all in the *Online Help* subdirectory in the primary install directory for this book, with distinct directory branches for Basic and Admin files. Figures 24-9 and 24-10 list the files found in each directory.

Figure 24-9. The files for patron-level online help

Figure 24-10. The files for administrator-level online help

Most of the HTML files have a one-to-one link with specific forms in the application. For instance, the *ItemLookup.htm* file contains the online help content for the *ItemLookup.vb* form in the application. And this help page shows up in both the basic and administrative versions of the file. When the user presses F1 from the Item Lookup form, the application tries to show the online help page *ItemLookup.htm*. If the user is a standard patron, it accesses this page in the *LibraryBasic.chm* file; administrative users access the same page name, but from the *LibraryAdmin.chm* file instead.

Each help source folder contains *.hhp*, *.hhc*, and *.hhk* files that define the project, the contents, and the index details, respectively. The administrative version also includes a few GIF graphics files.

I've already compiled each file and placed a copy of the *.chm* file in these directories.

Adding Help Support to the Application

To keep things simple and somewhat centralized, we'll employ the ShowHelp method described earlier to display online help for each form in the application. Because of the busywork nature of the changes involved in this chapter's project code, I've already made all of the updates to the project. Most of the changes involve making the same change to every form in the project, all of which I'll describe soon.

PROJECT ACCESS

Load the Chapter 24 (After) Code project, either through the New Project templates or by accessing the project directly from the installation directory. This chapter does not include a "Before" variation of the project code.

The *Maintenance.vb* form already provides a way for the administrator to specify the location of each online help file. It updates two settings through the My.Settings object.

```
My.Settings.HelpFile = Trim(RecordBasicHelp.Text)
My.Settings.HelpFileAdmin = Trim(RecordAdminHelp.Text)
```

Those settings also get stored in two global variables.

```
MainHelpFile = RecordBasicHelp.Text
MainAdminHelpFile = RecordAdminHelp.Text
```

That means we only need to call ShowHelp from each form and access one of the two files whenever the user presses F1.

But what if the administrator never uses the *Maintenance.vb* form to configure the locations of the help files? Since the help files will probably be installed in the same folder as the *Library.exe* program file, we should look there automatically. The InitializeSystem method in *General.vb* already sets the two global variables to the values stored in the settings.

```
' ----- Locate the online help files.
MainHelpFile = My.Settings.HelpFile & ""
MainAdminHelpFile = My.Settings.HelpFileAdmin & ""
```

Just in case these settings don't exist, let's add some code just after these lines to provide default access to the files.

```
If (MainHelpFile = "") Then MainHelpFile = _
    My.Computer.FileSystem.CombinePath( _
    My.Application.Info.DirectoryPath, "LibraryBasic.chm")
If (MainAdminHelpFile = "") Then MainAdminHelpFile = _
    My.Computer.FileSystem.CombinePath( _
    My.Application.Info.DirectoryPath, "LibraryAdmin.chm")
```

Since we need to continuously adapt to the current user state of the application (whether the user is a patron or an administrator), a centralized routine that displays help from the correct file seems best. Here's the code for OnlineHelp, a new method in the *General.vb* file:

```
Public Sub OnlineHelp(ByVal whichForm As _
        System.Windows.Forms.Form, _
        ByVal contextName As String)
    ' ----- Show the online help. Differentiate between the
    '       basic and the administrative online help usage.
    Dim fileToUse As String
```

```
' ----- Which file to use.
If (LoggedInUserID = -1) Then
    fileToUse = MainHelpFile
Else
    fileToUse = MainAdminHelpFile
End If
If (fileToUse = "") Then
    MsgBox("Online help is not properly configured.", _
        MsgBoxStyle.OkOnly Or MsgBoxStyle.Exclamation, _
        ProgramTitle)
    Return
End If

' ----- Show the online help.
Try
    Help.ShowHelp(whichForm, fileToUse, _
        HelpNavigator.Topic, contextName)
Catch
    MsgBox("An error occurred while trying to access " & _
        "the online help file.", MsgBoxStyle.OkOnly Or _
        MsgBoxStyle.Exclamation, ProgramTitle)
End Try
End Sub
```

The biggest task in this chapter involves going to each form in the project and making these two changes:

- Set the form's KeyPreview property to True.
- Add a call to OnlineHelp from the form's KeyDown event handler.

Here's the code added to the *ChangeUser.vb* form:

```
Private Sub ChangeUser_KeyDown(ByVal sender As Object, _
        ByVal e As System.Windows.Forms.KeyEventArgs) _
        Handles Me.KeyDown
    ' ----- F1 shows online help.
    If (e.KeyCode = Keys.F1) Then _
        OnlineHelp(Me, "ChangeUser.htm")
End Sub
```

A few of the forms process online help requests a little differently from the others. *About.vb* doesn't include its own online help page. Instead, it displays *Welcome.htm*. *Splash.vb* doesn't show any online help since the user isn't really supposed to interact with it. *ReportBuiltInViewer.vb*, the form that shows each of the five built-in reports, displays help for a related form via *ReportSelect.htm*. The *CheckLookup.vb* form has two associated online help pages: one for checkout and one for check-in of items. Its KeyDown event handler chooses the right page based on the current mode of the form.

```
If (e.KeyCode = Keys.F1) Then
    If (CheckInMode = True) Then
        OnlineHelp(Me, "CheckLookup_In.htm")
    Else
```

```
        OnlineHelp(Me, "CheckLookup_Out.htm")
      End If
    End If
```

The *Main.vb* form is even more diverse, choosing from among nine distinct online help pages when in administrative mode. Each panel on the main form is like a whole separate form, so I added an online help page for each panel. Code in the form's KeyDown event handler shows the right page based on the currently displayed panel.

```
If (PanelLibraryItem.Visible = True) Then
    OnlineHelp(Me, "MainForm_Library.htm")
ElseIf (PanelPatronRecord.Visible = True) Then
    OnlineHelp(Me, "MainForm_Patron.htm")
ElseIf (PanelHelp.Visible = True) Then
    OnlineHelp(Me, "MainForm_Help.htm")
ElseIf (PanelCheckOut.Visible = True) Then
    OnlineHelp(Me, "MainForm_Out.htm")
ElseIf (PanelCheckIn.Visible = True) Then
    OnlineHelp(Me, "MainForm_In.htm")
ElseIf (PanelAdmin.Visible = True) Then
    OnlineHelp(Me, "MainForm_Admin.htm")
ElseIf (PanelProcess.Visible = True) Then
    OnlineHelp(Me, "MainForm_Daily.htm")
ElseIf (PanelReports.Visible = True) Then
    OnlineHelp(Me, "MainForm_Print.htm")
Else
    OnlineHelp(Me, "MainForm_Basic.htm")
End If
```

The Help panel on the main form includes buttons designed to jump to the table of contents and index of the current online help file. I added event handlers for these buttons. The code for both MainForm.ActHelpContents_Click and MainForm.ActHelpIndex_Click is just like the code in the generic OnlineHelp routine, except for the final call to ShowHelp.

```
Private Sub ActHelpContents_Click(ByVal sender As Object, _
      ByVal e As System.EventArgs) _
      Handles ActHelpContents.Click
   ' ----- Show the online help table of contents.
   ...
   Help.ShowHelp(Me, fileToUse, _
      HelpNavigator.TableOfContents)
   ...
End Sub

Private Sub ActHelpIndex_Click(ByVal sender As Object, _
      ByVal e As System.EventArgs) _
      Handles ActHelpIndex.Click
   ' ----- Show the online help index.
   ...
   Help.ShowHelp(Me, fileToUse, HelpNavigator.Index)
   ...
End Sub
```

Once the online help (*.chm*) files are in place, and once the application is properly configured to locate those files on the workstation, the user can access help from any form by pressing the F1 key. Figure 24-11 shows help accessed from the Library Items panel of the main form.

Figure 24-11. Answering the call for help

Speaking of correctly configuring the *.chm* files, we still have to figure out how to get the entire application—including the online help files—onto the client workstation, and at a cost that will put food on the table. We'll look at these deployment issues in the next chapter.

Deployment

Although Aesop lived thousands of years ago, he has much to tell us about software development. His story of the boy who cried wolf is a perfect example. It concerns a young shepherd boy who tricks nearby villagers repeatedly by shouting, "Wolf!" when no such danger exists. The trick was good for a few laughs, but then the boy found out the consequences of his actions: he couldn't get any villagers to buy his sheep and he had to eat them all by himself. Yuck! If only the boy had learned how to properly deploy his flock into the hands of the villagers instead of making up wolf-based lies, he would never have come to such a tragic end.

So, Aesop clearly shows us how important deployment is. And Microsoft took this lesson to heart by including several different options right in Visual Studio that let you install your compiled applications and supporting files onto a target workstation. We'll look at these methods in this chapter, and use one of the methods to build a "setup" program for the Library Project.

What's Involved in Deployment?

In the days before Microsoft Windows, deployment wasn't so difficult. Many programs were nothing more than an MS-DOS executable file, with perhaps one or two supporting data and help files. That was it. Once you copied those files into some folder on the client workstation and updated the PATH environment variable, you were done.

Microsoft Windows applications (and large and complex MS-DOS programs) were not as easy to install. They often had these DLL file things hanging off them—files that had to be put in the proper places. And sometimes you didn't know what that proper place was, since a third-party vendor may have supplied the DLL without sufficient documentation. Then there were the configuration files, supporting data files, user-specific and workstation-specific changes to the system registry, shortcuts on the desktop and in the Start menu, uninstall settings and programs, two sets of forms (in triplicate) to the Library of Congress, online help files, the readme and license agreement files for the distribution CD, special fonts that may be required for the program, and on and on and on.

I don't think I even included half the files you need to deploy a full-bodied Windows application, but you can already see how involved it is. Fortunately, Visual Studio will share the burden with you in exchange for some simple configuration on your part.

The deployment features in Visual Studio provide you with the basic functionality you need to distribute standard desktop and web-based applications. If your deployment needs are complex, you can also purchase a third-party "setup and deployment" tool that includes advanced features such as scripting support.

Deployment Methods Within Visual Studio

With the early releases of Visual Basic, if you wanted to install your custom software using a setup program, you had to either write it yourself or use a purchased tool. Deployment tools did eventually appear in Visual Basic, especially the infamous "Package and Deployment Wizard." This canned setup program was written in Visual Basic, and you could enhance it to meet your own custom deployment needs. But it wasn't easy. And the rest of the world was already adopting the new "Windows Installer" platform for standardized deployment via *.msi* files. The Package and Deployment Wizard used the older *.cab* file format. Even for someone like me who actually enjoyed programming, the need to write effective installation programs sometimes made life ugly.

When Visual Basic .NET 2002 came out, life became beautiful again. Visual Studio included tools that let you target the Windows Installer technology, just like the big boys used. Sure, it was a stripped-down version that let you release only the simplest of applications, but third-party vendors have to have some fun.

These days, Visual Studio includes several deployment methods, a tribute to the different types of applications, the different types of users, and the different types of secure environments that a programmer may need to target. Read through each of the available methods to see which one best meets the needs of your program. I've already made my selection for the Library Project, which I'll reveal in a public ceremony about halfway through this chapter.

Direct ASP.NET Deployment

ASP.NET applications are clearly different from desktop applications. One big difference is that, for the final user, ASP.NET applications don't really have any deployment. You just browse to the right web site and you're using the application. But deployment still is needed for the hosting web server.

If your web server has Microsoft FrontPage Extensions installed, you can install a compiled ASP.NET application right from the comfort and safety of your development environment. I just glossed over it back in Chapter 23, but Visual Studio presents you with the option of putting a web application on a real live web site when you first try to create the ASP.NET application. In the New Web Site form, you can select an HTTP URL as the development location, as shown in Figure 25-1.

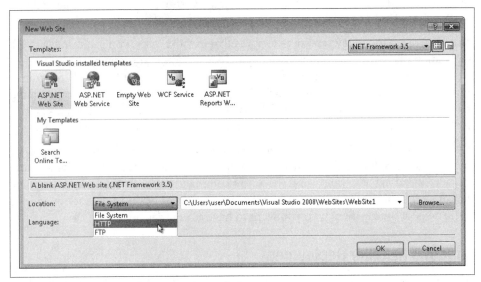

Figure 25-1. Getting an early start on that web site

Since you will be interactively developing your web site, you might not want to use this method on a production server. Instead, you can develop locally in a directory or on a development web server, and then later *publish* the site to the production server. This is just as easy as setting the HTTP location from the start. With the web site open in Visual Studio, select the Build → Publish Web Site menu command, and specify the URL of the new web site. No separate setup program is required.

ASP.NET is careful about how it handles the files in your application. It will not publish your source code. It will copy your *web.config* file to the server (it's a required file), which may contain your database connection string. But a properly configured ASP.NET web server will keep this file from prying eyes.

XCopy Deployment

Compiled .NET assemblies contain a manifest that fully describes the assembly and its needs. This means that you can copy any assembly to another system that has the correct version of the .NET Framework installed, and as long as the other files the assembly needs are copied as well, the program will run. This is called "XCopy deployment" because you can use the command-line XCopy command to move the files.

You may be thinking, "Well, duh! An EXE assembly is a real Windows program. Of course it will run when I copy it to a new system." Well, that's true. But it wasn't true for older Visual Basic applications. The ActiveX controls used by COM-based Visual Basic applications had to be registered in the Windows Registry before they could be accessed at runtime. Older Visual Basic programs also required that the Visual Basic runtime libraries be installed. The .NET Framework must also be installed for .NET programs, but since the framework is managed automatically by the Windows Update system, this is not as big of a headache.

What I've taken too many sentences to say is that in most cases, you can install a .NET application on a workstation just by copying the program, and maybe a few support files, to a directory. I'm not saying that this is how you should install programs. Actually, I would be shocked—shocked!—if I discovered any of my programming friends using this method in a real business environment. But .NET makes this deployment option available to you if you don't want to be my friend anymore.

If you do use XCopy deployment, you probably won't have any issues with security or administrative limitations that may be imposed on the workstation. Chances are, if you're installing software using the XCopy command or by dragging-and-dropping files, it's probably because you are friends with the owner of the workstation, and it's really none of my business who you want to have as your friends.

Windows Installer Deployment

Windows Installer is the official installation system provided by Microsoft. It serves as the base system for standard Visual Studio-generated installation packages, and also provides the underpinnings for most popular third-party installation tools.

Before Windows Installer, each installation package vendor pretty much did things as they saw fit. But this meant that installed products sometimes clobbered one another, since one software package didn't necessarily look out for files installed by another tool. Repairing such damage was difficult for the user, who usually didn't even know which files were installed or updated.

Microsoft sought to change that with Windows Installer. One of the key features of the system is its database of installed and updated files. It also supports a full uninstall/restore and rollback capability so that any failure can be fully undone, restoring the system to its previous state. Other features include support for patching, rebooting, custom enhancements, some limited user interface and prompt design, the ability to repair or "heal" a previously installed but damaged program, and install-on-demand, which keeps features or full applications on the installation media until the user tries to use that feature.

Windows Installer Version 4.x is the latest version for Windows Vista and other parallel Windows systems. (You can still get version 3.x for Windows XP, or 2.x for some older Windows systems such as Windows 98.)

The heart of the Windows Installer system is the "MSI" file (with an *.msi* file extension), the single file that contains all the files and instructions needed to install, update, and uninstall a software product. Visual Studio can create setup projects based on the MSI standard, although you can't use some of the more advanced features of Windows Installer through Visual Studio. Still, if your needs are simple—and most business-level software written in Visual Basic has simple installation needs—Visual Studio is probably all you require.

Building a setup project is just as easy as creating regular Visual Studio development projects. But first, I need something to set up. For the discussion in this section, I've created a desktop application. Well, not a very good one. I simply created a new *WindowsApplication1* project with its default Form1, and saved it to my *C:\temp* folder. All it does when you run it is display Form1.

To create an MSI installation file for a Visual Basic project, open that project in Visual Studio and use the File → Add → New Project menu command to add a setup project to the entire solution that contains your original project. Figure 25-2 shows the Add New Project dialog. Select the Setup and Deployment project type, and then the Setup Wizard template to create a setup program for the active project. Set the Name and Location fields according to your needs, and then click OK.

Figure 25-2. Adding a setup project to your solution

The Setup Wizard appears, leading you through five steps to peace, harmony, and a working MSI file.

Step 1

The first wizard step just says "Welcome," so click Next and get on with the real work.

Step 2

Step 2 asks you for the type of setup project to generate. Personally, I think it could have figured this out from the content of the already-loaded projects, but if the wizard did everything, why would the world need programmers like us? There are four choices, shown in Figure 25-3.

Figure 25-3. Choosing the type of setup program

The first two choices create full setup files for either desktop or web-based applications. (The web-based setup would be delivered to a web site administrator for installation on the server.) *Merge modules* let you create a portion of an installation that can later be merged into a full MSI file. This is a good choice if you are designing a library that will be used for multiple applications, but it's useless on its own. The CAB file option creates an archive of files that can be installed using slightly older file distribution technology. It's also the distribution system used for handheld devices. Since I'm targeting a desktop application, I'll choose "Create a setup for a Windows application" and click Next.

Step 3

Although you can create a setup program that simply installs miscellaneous files scavenged from your hard disk, you usually build a setup project based on the files or compiled output of other projects. The third wizard step prompts you to include elements from the other projects found in the active Visual Studio solution. I've chosen to include the compiled EXE file from my desktop project, as shown in Figure 25-4.

I generally don't want to include my source code in the setup project, so I'll leave that element unchecked. But the Content Files item may be useful. If my project had a compiled online help file (with a *.chm* file extension), I could have added it as a standard content file to the main project via the Project → Add Existing Item menu command.

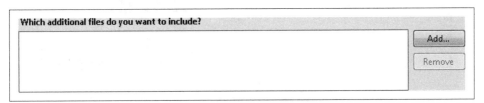

Which project output groups do you want to include?

- [ ] Localized resources from WindowsApplication1
- [ ] XML Serialization Assemblies from WindowsApplication1
- [ ] Content Files from WindowsApplication1
- [x] Primary output from WindowsApplication1
- [ ] Source Files from WindowsApplication1
- [ ] Debug Symbols from WindowsApplication1
- [ ] Documentation Files from WindowsApplication1

Description:

Contains the DLL or EXE built by the project.

Figure 25-4. Choosing project elements to include in the setup

That file would be classified as Content, and could move into this setup project through the Content Files selection. But there are other ways to include online help in the installation, which we'll see in the next step. For now, I'll stick with the "Primary output" selection, and click the Next button.

Step 4

In this step, you can add any other non-project-specific files you want to the setup project (see Figure 25-5). Readme files, online help content, license agreements, pictures of your kids, and pretty much anything else can be included here. I've got nothing more to add. Click Next.

Which additional files do you want to include?

Add...
Remove

Figure 25-5. Add those other files that have always wanted a chance at setup project stardom

Step 5

The final step displays a summary of the choices you made (see Figure 25-6). Well, that wizard was pretty easy. We had to do work in only three of the five steps. Click Finish to complete the wizard.

Figure 25-6. Confirming our choices for the setup project

After the wizard

Once the wizard completes, the primary interface for Visual Studio setup project design appears in the development window. Figure 25-7 shows Visual Studio displaying the newly generated setup project for *WindowsApplication1*, another project that also appears in the Solution Explorer panel.

Figure 25-7. A setup project within the development environment

The main window in Figure 25-7 is one of several "editors" that let you customize the setup project. You can access each editor through the View → Editor menu command, or by using the toolbar buttons in the Solution Explorer panel.

File System Editor

That's the editor you already saw in Figure 25-7. It presents a standard folder/ item view of portions of the target system's filesystem. Through this hierarchy, you place files (the EXE output from your main project, help files, configuration files, shortcuts to any of these files, etc.) into special folders (Application folder, Desktop, 32- or 64-bit Program Files, Fonts, the Start Menu folder, and others). If you don't see a folder you want in the File System on Target Machine panel, use the Action → Add Special Folder menu command to include it in the list. Besides the standard special folders, the Add Special Folder menu includes a Custom Folder option that lets you create a specific folder anywhere on the target system.

Registry Editor

This editor displays a truncated hierarchy of the registry hives. Any keys or values added here will be created in the user's registry during installation.

File Types Editor

This editor lets you define associations between a file extension (such as *.txt*) and specific programs or actions. Any custom action, such as Open or Print, can be linked to any command text you wish, including commands that target the primary assembly being installed.

User Interface Editor

The default setup project includes a few forms that prompt for things such as installation location and confirmation that the installation should occur. You can insert additional dialog boxes into the flow of the installation. But beware: you will not be adding full Visual Basic-enabled forms. Instead, you will choose from a few predefined dialogs (such as the License Agreement dialog, or the 4 Radio Buttons dialog), and set the dialog properties to configure the display text of each dialog field or prompt. Each user entry field/control includes a named value that you use in the other editors to limit a specific installation action. For instance, you could monitor the value of a user-prompted checkbox, and if the user didn't check it, you could withhold the installation of certain files that were associated with that checkbox.

Custom Actions Editor

If you need the ultimate level of control, you can add a custom action, a call to an external program or script, that runs at a certain point in the install (or uninstall) process.

Launch Conditions Editor

If the target workstation must be in a certain state before you can successfully install the project, this editor lets you define the limiting conditions. By default, the installer adds the .NET Framework as an installation condition; the framework must be installed before the project can be installed. You can look for specific files or registry keys that must be present before installation begins. For instance, you might want to confirm that the target database drivers are on the system before you install a database-dependent application.

Generating the MSI file

Once you've set up your project through the various editors, you output the final MSI file by building the solution via the Build → Build Solution menu command. The MSI file appears in the location specified in the setup project's properties (Project → Properties). This file contains all the instructions and content required to fully install the application on the target workstation.

ClickOnce Deployment

Visual Studio 2008 includes a deployment method called *ClickOnce*. It is designed to provide the ultimate in setup deployment ease for desktop (Windows Forms) applications. It still involves a wizard, darn it, but for basic installations, that's all there is to it. Once your application is "published" through ClickOnce, the user can install it directly from a web site or other stored location.

This sounds like a standard MSI installation, but it is different in several ways:

- ClickOnce deployments can be installed even if the current user does not have local administrative privileges. Many software installs affect key files in the *Windows* and *Windows\System32* folders, or in other important but restricted folders. If you are a developer, it's likely that you never experience this problem because you are the administrator on your own workstation. But in IT department-managed organizations with many users, there is a benefit to reducing the privilege level of individual users. One negative side effect of this is that an administrator must be present to install any software. But that's not the case with ClickOnce. Is your entire IT department out to lunch? (I mean that literally.) No problem. Any ClickOnce-published application can be installed by any user. The software is installed in a "sandbox" that protects the system and other applications from the ClickOnce-installed program's villainous intents.

- A ClickOnce-deployed application can trigger its own automatic software updates. If configured in this way, the program will check the original deployment location for a new version each time it runs. If there is a new version, it will be installed automatically without the user having to do a thing.

- ClickOnce applications are designed for ease of installation. With an MSI-deployed application, you need to download the MSI file and process it through the Windows Installer system. Although you also have to download a ClickOnce deployment, it happens more or less transparently. A ClickOnce-published application can be configured so that it looks like an extension of a web page: click a link, and the program immediately runs, displaying its main form to the user. (There may be some delay as the program is downloaded over the Internet.)

That sounds great. But it's not all peaches and cream. Since ClickOnce-enabled applications (by default) run in their own sandbox, they are limited in their access to some local resources. Also, to fully support all of the automatic-updating features, you must add code to your application that performs the actual update. (The My.Application.Deployment property provides access to these features.)

To deploy your project via ClickOnce, use the Build → Publish menu command in Visual Studio. After asking you some very basic questions about where the user will obtain the deployment file (from a web site, a network folder, or a CD/DVD), Visual Studio generates the installation file and makes it immediately available for use.

Of course, that method gives you only the most basic installation options. It makes the primary EXE or DLL of your project (and its dependencies) available for installation on the target workstation, but that's about it. If you want more control over the publishing process and the components it will include, use the Publish tab of your project's properties, as shown in Figure 25-8.

Figure 25-8. The world of publishing, just a mouse click away

This panel includes fields that let you set the version number for the published installation package. If you modify this version number and republish the application, the custom deployment code you added to the application can detect the new version and initiate an update from the distribution location.

Summary

It's really nice that Visual Studio provides a few different deployment methods for your custom applications. Visual Basic and the larger Visual Studio environment were designed as general-purpose programming systems that allow you to solve almost any development problem facing you or your users. But that doesn't mean that every single feature in the system is applicable to all environments. By having a few different deployment options available, Visual Studio is even more general-purpose than before, and I think that's just great. Sure, you have to take five minutes and decide between MSI and ClickOnce. But in most projects, the needs of the users will push you in one direction or the other.

I promised you earlier in the chapter that I would tell you my choice for the Library Project's deployment method. I have decided on a standard Windows Installer deployment with an MSI file. I'll explain some of my reasons for choosing this method in the next section.

Project

I chose a standard Windows Installer deployment because I thought it would match more closely with the needs of the typical Library system user. The Library application is meant to be a permanent feature on the target workstation, so it's likely that someone with IT knowledge or administrative privileges will perform the actual installation. As it is a licensed product, there is little chance that I would be putting copies of the Library installation out on my public web site. A CD distribution—common for MSI installations—is the expected medium. Also, since it's a quality piece of software from a trusted vendor (that's me), there isn't a need for a protective sandbox. Still, the application does include several files, including two online help files, so an XCopy installation would be a burden. All in all, a standard MSI installation is the best deployment plan.

Planning the Deployment

The Setup Wizard automatically adds my project assembly to the MSI file, but I am sure other files are needed to properly deploy the Library Project. A quick look through the previous chapters reveals the following list of file requirements:

The .NET Framework 3.5
> This must be installed on the target system to run the Library application. The setup program will need to automatically install the framework if it isn't already on the target system.

Library.exe
> This is the primary assembly. The install would be useless without it.

LibraryBasic.chm and LibraryAdmin.chm

These online help files will be installed in the same folder as the primary application.

The bar code font

If you have obtained distribution rights for a bar code font, your setup program can copy it directly to the target system's *Fonts* folder.

LibraryLicense.lic

Ah, the license file—remember that this hand-generated file needs to be custom-crafted for each customer purchasing the Library application. Compiling it directly into the setup program seems extreme, since I would have to regenerate Setup for each customer. Instead, I will put the file on the distribution media (the CD), and have the user locate it when running the Library program.

ACME Library Resource Kit.pdf

This administrator-level file shouldn't be installed by default on a workstation. It will remain on the distribution CD instead.

Database Creation Script.sql

If I were developing a full end-user application, I would build a separate setup system for the server portion, focusing mainly on the database setup. Since this book is designed as an introduction only, I will just copy the database build script to the distribution CD and assume that a qualified IT representative or database administrator will take charge of this installation step.

The Library web site

As with the database creation script, I am just going to copy the web site files to the CD and let the administrator figure things out.

Readme.htm

The CD should include an informational file right at the root that will tell the user how to use the files on the CD. I haven't written this file yet, but I will before the chapter ends.

The generated Setup file will include only the first four items in that list (three if you are excluding the font), and the first two are added automatically by the Setup Wizard. This won't be too difficult.

Building the Setup Project

Earlier in the chapter, we added a new setup project to an existing project, combining them into a single solution. It is possible to build a setup project that appears alone within Visual Studio. In such projects, you need to browse for the target assembly (*release\Library.exe*) to include it in the Setup output. However, the Setup Wizard doesn't do much for you if you go that route. So, for the Library project, let's add a new setup project to a Library project already loaded into Visual Studio.

The first few steps parallel those we performed earlier in this chapter. Once you have the Library project loaded and saved to its target folder, add a new setup project using the File → Add → New Project menu command. Select Setup Wizard as the template, enter **LibrarySetup** for the Name, and use the just-saved Library project's folder as the Location. Apply the following settings within the wizard:

- In step 2, select "Create a setup for a Windows application".
- In step 3, select "Primary output from Library" from the list.
- In step 4, locate and add the *LibraryBasic.chm* and *LibraryAdmin.chm* files. In this book's installation directory, you can find them in the subdirectory named *Online Help*.

Complete the wizard and use the File → Save All menu command. When prompted to save the solution file (*Library.sln*), just store it in the Library project directory, which should already be selected.

As before, the setup project opens to the File System Editor. Before making any changes within the editor, let's set some Setup-wide properties. Click on Library-Setup in the Solution Explorer panel, and modify the following properties in the Properties panel:

- Set the Author property to "Tim Patrick" or your own name.
- Set the Manufacturer property to "ACME".
- Set the ManufacturerURL property to "http://www.timaki.com" or any web site you wish to use.
- Set the ProductName property to "ACME Library".
- Set the Title property to "ACME Library Setup".

Since the File System Editor is open, let's make a few changes there. When we added the *Library.exe* assembly through the wizard, it figured out all of the required dependencies. Not only do the main program and help file items appear in the Application Folder section, but three additional DLLs appear, all used to run the library reports (see Figure 25-9).

Figure 25-9. A lot more files than we bargained for

Since these three DLLs are supplied by Microsoft as part of .NET, it doesn't make much sense to store them in my own application's installation directory. They should go in the Global Assembly Cache (GAC), the special system folder that maintains shared .NET assemblies. The GAC isn't one of the folder choices displayed in the editor, but it can be. Make sure that the lefthand panel of the File System Editor is selected (the one with File System on Target Machine) and then use the Action → Add Special Folder → Global Assembly Cache Folder menu command. A new folder, Global Assembly Cache Folder, appears in the left-side panel. Select the Application Folder item again, and then drag the three DLL items into the new Global Assembly Cache Folder item, as shown in Figure 25-10.

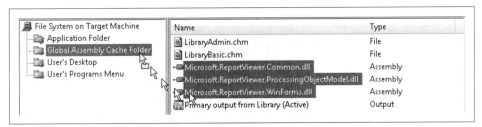

Figure 25-10. Make the three DLL files someone else's responsibility

Let's add two shortcuts to the user's system during installation: one on the desktop and one in the Start menu's Programs section. Both shortcuts point to the main *Library.exe* assembly. The Setup Wizard anticipated our needs by adding the *User's Desktop* and *User's Programs Menu* folders to the File System Editor. All we have to do is add a shortcut to each folder.

Let's start with the desktop. Select the *User's Desktop* folder and then right-click in the right-side panel (where the files would appear). From the context menu, choose the Create New Shortcut menu command. (This same command is available from the main Action menu when the right-side panel is active.) The Select Item in Project dialog, shown in Figure 25-11, appears. Browse into the Application Folder item and select Primary Output from Library (Active). The new shortcut appears in the right-side panel, waiting for you to give it a more meaningful name. Give it the name "ACME Library".

Figure 25-11. Adding a new shortcut to a target filesystem folder

To create the same shortcut in the Start menu, follow all the steps in the previous paragraph, but start from the *User's Programs Menu* folder instead of the *User's Desktop* folder.

Adding those shortcuts was a good idea, but whenever I install new software, I always immediately delete any shortcut that was added to the desktop. Adding an icon to the Start menu's *Programs* folder makes sense, but I like keeping a nice, clean desktop. Laugh if you want, but keeping that desktop free from clutter is what helps make me a world-famous author and developer.

What we need is a way to alter the behavior of the setup program so that it doesn't create the desktop icon if the user doesn't want one. The setup project provides a way to do this. First, we need to add a prompt where the user indicates a desktop-icon preference, and then we need to act on that preference. The first step involves altering the user interface of the setup program. Such changes occur through the User Interface Editor. Display this editor with the View → Editor → User Interface menu command. The User Interface Editor appears, as shown in Figure 25-12.

The User Interface Editor is divided into two main installation types: Install and Administrative Install. The administrative branch is used only when an administrator wants to store the setup image on a shared network folder. It doesn't allow the types of changes we want to make. So, let's focus on the standard Install branch, which manages standard user installations on a client workstation. Both branches

Figure 25-12. The user interface editor displays each dialog and each prompt

include step-by-step prompts that appear to the user during the setup process. Custom data collection prompts can only be added to the Start entry in the Install main branch.

During actual setup, the user interface prompts the user in a wizard-like fashion. During the initial Start phase, the setup program collects the user's desires for the remainder of the process. Once this section ends, the installation proceeds until it completes or fails. What we want to do is insert a new step in the wizard process, displaying a checkbox to the user that asks whether the desktop icon should appear or not. Additional data collection fields such as these are added through new "dialogs." And there just happens to be a dialog that includes a customizable checkbox. In the Install branch, right-click on the Start item and select Add Dialog from the context menu. The Add Dialog window, shown in Figure 25-13, displays the available dialogs. Select the Checkboxes (A) item from the list and click OK.

The new Checkboxes (A) item appears in the Install/Start section. Use the mouse to drag it up until it appears between the Welcome and Installation Folders dialogs. The Checkboxes dialog lets you display up to four checkbox selections with custom captions. Make sure it is selected in the dialog outline, and then use the Properties panel to set this new dialog's properties:

- Set the BannerText property to "Installation Options". This text appears near the top of the dialog window, displaying a large main title.

- Set the BodyText property to "Select the options you wish to use for this installation".

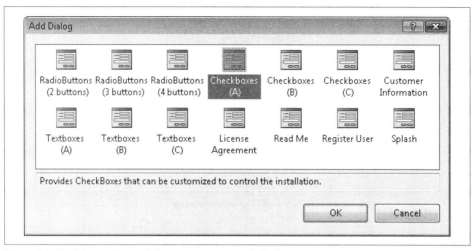

Figure 25-13. A few different dialog options are available for setup customization

- Set the Checkbox1Label property to "Add an icon for ACME Library to the desktop". This defines the custom text for the first checkbox control.
- Set the Checkbox1Property property to "LIBRARY_DESKTOP_LINK". This gives the checkbox a name that we can use later to alter the install process.
- Set the Checkbox1Value property to "Checked". This defaults the installation to include the desktop icon.
- Set the Checkbox2Visible, Checkbox3Visible, and Checkbox4Visible properties to "False", hiding the other three unused checkboxes.

During the setup process, the user sees the new dialog prompt in Figure 25-14. It includes the banner text, the body text, and the single checkbox as configured in the custom dialog's properties.

Now it's time to use that checkbox setting. Close the User Interface Editor and return to the File System Editor. Select the *User's Desktop* folder in the left-side panel, and then go to the Properties panel. One of the few listed properties is Condition, which lets you define a Boolean condition that, when true, installs the associated files on the user's desktop. However, if the condition is false, no associated files will be placed on the user's desktop during installation. Set this property to the following text:

```
LIBRARY_DESKTOP_LINK
```

This is the name we gave to the first checkbox back in the dialog design. During installation, the setup program checks the user's selection, and alters the desktop update as requested.

One thing I won't be adding to my version of the setup program is the bar code font. Sadly, I have not acquired a license to distribute a third-party font to you or anyone

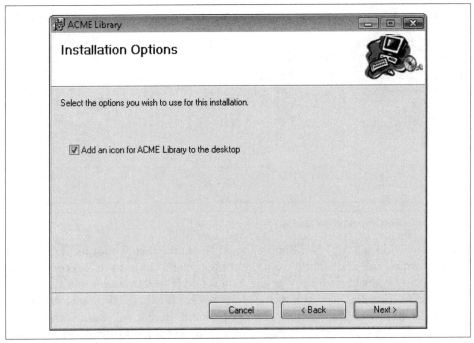

Figure 25-14. The sparse but useful checkbox dialog in action

else reading this book. The good news is that I just saved you $10 on the cost of the book. The bad news is that I will have to tell you how to add the font, but not actually do it.

Actually, you can probably already guess how to do it. The *Fonts* folder is one of the special folders available in the File System Editor. When the File System on Target Machine item on the left-side panel is active, use the Action → Add Special Folder → Fonts Folder menu command. Then add the original font file (a TrueType *.ttf* file) to the *Fonts* folder section. You won't be able to add this font directly from your *Windows\Fonts* folder. Instead, you will need to get the original *.ttf* file and use that. On the target workstation, the setup program properly installs and registers the font for use in Windows.

The setup project is complete. The only thing left to do is to generate the MSI file. You might not have noticed it, but Visual Studio includes different "compilation configurations" in every project. The two default configurations are Debug and Release, and they each generate a different set and flavor of final output files when you compile your application. Normally, your project is set to Debug, but you can change it by using the Configuration Manager. In Visual Studio, select the Build → Configuration Manager menu command to display the manager's form (see Figure 25-15). In this form, change the "Active solution configuration" setting from Debug to Release, then click the Close button.

Figure 25-15. The Configuration Manager form

It's time to build the MSI file. Right-click on the LibrarySetup root in the Solution Explorer panel, and select Build from the context menu. In just a few seconds, your MSI file will be baked and ready to eat. You'll find it in the setup project's *Release* subdirectory. This directory also includes a *Setup.exe* file that acts as a bootstrapper. Any workstation with the Windows Installer system present will work with just the plain MSI file, but providing a *Setup.exe* file may add a level of comfort to novice users.

The Distribution Media

I hate it when users come over to my office and try to copy the MSI file directly from my hard drive. I find that providing the file on a CD tends to improve the vendor-customer relationship. So, let's build a CD for client use.

The distribution CD contains all of the content needed by the library IT staff to support the application. It contains distinct directories for each type of content. Here's what I am planning to put in the root of the CD:

- *Readme.htm*, an HTML file that displays information about the contents of the CD.
- *Database*, a directory containing the database creation script, *Database Creation Script.sql*.
- *License*, a directory containing the specific user's license file, *LibraryLicense.lic*.
- *Setup*, a directory containing the main MSI file, *LibrarySetup.msi*.
- *Technical*, a directory containing the technical support documentation, *ACME Library Resource Kit.pdf*.
- *Web*, a directory containing the full source code for the Library web site that we created in Chapter 22. The administrator can use this as the basis for an expanded Library web site.

I've put all these directories and their files in the book's installation directory, in a subdirectory named *Library CD Contents*.

The *Readme.htm* file contains the following administrator-friendly content.

Acme Library 1.0

Welcome to the Acme Library system. This product was developed as part of the *Programming Visual Basic 2008* book project, written by Tim Patrick. When installed and configured properly, the application should give you years of library management value.

The installation CD includes the following folders:

Database
>   The *Database Creation Script.sql* file contains a SQL Server script that you can use to build a new ACME Library database.

License
>   The *LibraryLicense.lic* file contains the license for your site. Once you have installed the Library application on a workstation, copy the license file to that workstation. Using the Library application, log in as an administrator. You will be prompted for the license file path at that time.

Setup
>   The *LibrarySetup.msi* file performs a standard client installation of the Library product.

Technical
>   The *ACME Library Resource Kit.pdf* file contains technical information about the ACME Library system, its configuration files, and its database.

Web
>   This directory contains a sample ASP.NET web-based application that you can modify to allow patrons to interact with the ACME Library database through a web browser.

This CD and its contents are © 2008 by Tim Patrick.

I want this file to appear automatically when the user inserts the CD into the workstation drive. This requires one additional file named *autorun.inf* at the root of the CD. This simple INI-style file supports the Auto Run feature used by Windows CDs. Here is the content of the file that will display the *Readme.htm* file automatically:

```
[Autorun]
Open=explorer.exe Readme.htm
```

Copying all of these directories and files to a CD and adding a pretty label should result in a happy librarian.

We're quickly approaching the end of the book. Only one chapter remains. Turn the page to find out what exciting content you'll find there.

Project Complete

You've done it! You've completed the Library Project and met with acclaim from users and fellow programmers alike. And you've also accomplished something that few thought was possible: you slogged through all 26 chapters of this book. You're probably anxious to get on with your life as a highly paid software consultant, working just six months per year as the programmer who other programmers call when systems fail. Well, I won't keep you too long. But there are a few more issues to discuss concerning the Library Project and programming in general.

The Library Project

The Library Project is filled with features that target small library-style organizations. But it may not meet everyone's needs. And that's OK. The users know your address and phone number; you'll hear from them. When they call, you can tell them that the software wasn't designed for everyone; no software can be. All software, even general-purpose applications such as Visual Studio, can never meet the needs of every person or organization. What is important is that the features included in the project meet the needs of the intended audience. That audience may be the card-catalog-using public, or it may just be a small library with one part-time staff member.

Still, there is always room for improvement. Because the Library Project's real target audience was you—the student of Visual Basic and .NET—it did not have all the features that most libraries would require. Looking quickly back through the source code, I came up with at least the following changes that could be made to the project to bring a lot more value to library administrators and users:

Error logging
> The application includes rudimentary error detection and handling features, but they could definitely be improved. The logging feature used in the application's GeneralError method (which includes a call to My.Application.Log.WriteException) sends the written content to any registered log listener. We just used the default listeners, but we could have added listeners to centrally collect error reports and details in a database or file for later analysis.

Error handling

When an error does occur, most of the Library code simply reports the error and moves on. Some methods ignore errors completely. In general, the code could do a better job of processing error results. Some errors are more fatal than others, and specific errors should include additional options that the user can access to better recover from the fault.

Multithreading

We did not discuss or take advantage of any of the threading features included in the .NET Framework. Processor-intensive activities tend to kill the responsiveness of the user interface, but there are ways to mitigate the impact. In the Library Project, two specific areas would benefit from the use of background worker threads, either using the features of the System.Threading namespace directly, or by using the BackgroundWorker control: (1) searching for library items through the ItemLookup form; and (2) processing overdue and fine data for a single day at all locations through the MainForm.ActDoProcess_Click event handler.

User interface and presentation

Although I included some cute graphics on the main Library Project form and the Splash form, I didn't do much beyond that. Mostly it was an issue of time and effort, but I also have very little talent for the graphic arts. The program could use an update in its general look and presentation. And with the new graphics features available through the Windows Presentation Foundation (WPF), you could enable some really amazing effects with little programming effort.

User interface consistency

Although I tried to be careful, there are probably labels, controls, and error messages that use two different names for the same thing. Perhaps I used the word *book* or *DVD* when I should have used the more general term *item*. Although tracking down such inconsistencies is a lot of work, it increases the level of professionalism in your application. It also makes the task of foreign-language translation easier when localizing the program.

Testing new databases

The *LocateDatabase.vb* form builds a connection string from the fields supplied by the user, but it does not test the connection to see whether it works. Providing an option to test the entered values could reduce long-term errors. An even better option would be to let the user search for the database, similar to the way that SQL Server itself sniffs out and presents located servers and databases.

Numeric title searches

The checkout and check-in features let you locate an item either by name or by bar code. If you enter a number, the program assumes that you have entered a bar code and retrieves the matching item. But some book titles are numeric.

For instance, David McCullough's book *1776* would cause the program some difficulty if each copy did not include its own bar code. An enhancement to the program would provide the user additional disambiguation options when a numeric entry matched both a bar code and a title.

Enhanced item searches

Although I have much reason to be impressed by my item lookup code, the program could do so much more. When you use the card catalog systems at larger libraries, the lookup features include "proximity searches" that return results that are alphabetically close to the search terms provided by the user. SQL Server also has a "full text search" option that could be used to broaden the item lookups.

Reserves and holds

I started to add a "reserves" feature to the Library Project so that patrons could add their names to a waiting list for checked-out library items, and have those items placed aside by the library staff when they were returned by the previous patron. Although this would be a cool and useful feature for a library, it didn't add any pedagogic value to the book, so I left it out. But I still hear the software sniffling and crying once in a while when it thinks of the feature that might have been. This would be a great enhancement for "version 2."

Incomplete item history

On the *PatronRecord.vb* form, the Fines list shows a patron's previously checked-out library items only if those items had once been overdue and had incurred fines. Items that were returned on time cannot be displayed in the list using the current form logic. A satisfying change would add a "Show all returned items" checkbox that would include these checked-in items. This would allow a librarian to charge for things such as damage on items that were otherwise free of fines.

Return of missing items

If an item is marked as missing, the library staff may charge the patron for the loss of the book. If the patron later returns that item, the librarian can process a reimbursement to the patron. But the program could make this task easier by automatically marking the item as eligible for such a refund. This would require a new status field on the PatronCopy database table to track this status.

Bar code design interaction

The *BarcodeLabel.vb* form is, I think, pretty amazing with its graphics preview of the bar code. But the preview is unidirectional only; the user is not able to select a display element by clicking on that element in the preview. Instead, it is necessary to click on the related item in the DisplayItems list. Enhancing the program to detect clicks on the preview and to translate those clicks into item selections would make the program much more like other applications that support basic drawing features.

Database setup features

Although we built the setup program for the main Library application, we skimped on the server side, only providing the database creation scripts as text files on the installation media. A more professional system would provide a separate installation program that could build and configure a new database from an existing SQL Server installation.

Support for library standards

Just as the software development world has standard formats and protocols such as XML, library systems also share common standards. Two accepted standards are MARC (Machine-Readable Cataloging, a standard card catalog data format) and the Z39.50 interface (a communications protocol used for inter-computer searches and data retrieval). Incorporating these standards into a small library system may be overkill, but they would bring a much higher level of automation and convenience to the library staff.

Bug fixes

I probably left a few bugs in the application. No, wait. I think I put them in there on purpose to test you, to see whether you were learning and growing in your programming skills. Did you find them?

These are just some of the improvements that I thought of off the top of my head. If I had gone all the way down to my shoulders, I could have come up with even more. If your software will target the general population of users, you will probably release updates on a regular schedule, such as annually, and charge appropriately for the improved features. If you wrote the application for one specific customer, the updates may be more frequent, even weekly or daily in some cases. Whatever the audience size, your opportunities to improve and enhance the software will be regular and ongoing.

Visual Basic Flexibility

I started using Visual Basic back when version 2.0 of the product was still in vogue. As a result, I picked up some pre-.NET coding habits that have been hard to break, even with my full-time focus on .NET code. I've reached a level of comfort in my Visual Basic coding, and that comfort shows in my .NET programming style.

As I mentioned in earlier chapters, many of the features that previously existed in Visual Basic before .NET were moved out of the language and into Framework classes. The most noticeable of these were the mathematics features now found in the `System.Math` class. But there were other non-math Visual Basic language keywords that also became class methods. Many of these appear in the `Microsoft.VisualBasic` namespace, including methods such as `Left`, `Trim`, and `MsgBox`.

When I wrote the Library Project code, I freely used some features found in the `Microsoft.VisualBasic` namespace. Although I don't have a problem with this practice, you may encounter other Visual Basic developers who don't agree with how I've written the code. They point out that most, and possibly all, of the features in `Microsoft.VisualBasic` have Framework Class Library (FCL) equivalents, and these should be used for reasons of compatibility with other .NET languages and systems.

A key example is the `MsgBox` function. I've used it throughout the Library source code. The keyword `MsgBox` has always been a part of the Visual Basic language, but beyond its continued existence in `Microsoft.VisualBasic`, it is not a part of the Framework classes. Instead of `MsgBox`, other programmers (including C# programmers) use the `System.Windows.Forms.MessageBox.Show` method. It does offer more options than `MsgBox`, and it displays a message box that is every bit as beautiful as the Visual Basic version. But for me, my fingers have gotten used to typing the short six-character `MsgBox` keyword. (`MessageBox.Show` has 15 characters!) Also, the arguments passed to `MessageBox.Show` are slightly rearranged from those used in `MsgBox`. Using both of them in a single program could result in some confusion.

Supporters of `MessageBox.Show` emphasize that if you ever needed to convert Visual Basic code to C#, the presence of `MsgBox` would slow down the conversion. Although I understand this and other concerns, I have not yet been fully convinced that there is any problem using `MsgBox`. Any conversion tool that existed to change Visual Basic code into C# would certainly know how to handle `MsgBox`.

Beginning with the 2008 edition, Visual Basic includes something called "runtime agility." This is a fancy marketing way of saying that you can now compile and deploy Visual Basic applications without the need for the `Microsoft.VisualBasic` namespace and related assembly. Although this isn't a big deal for most desktop or ASP.NET applications, the ability to compile a Visual Basic program with fewer dependencies, and hence a smaller "footprint," does have implications for the quick download of custom logic over the Web through Microsoft's Silverlight product. If you will target this platform, it will be a good idea to omit all references to features found in `Microsoft.VisualBasic`.

As another example, consider the older `Exit Sub` statement. It still exists in Visual Basic for .NET, but the new `Return` keyword performs the same job of immediately exiting from the current method. (`Return` had a different meaning in Visual Basic before .NET, but now it only exits methods.) You can use either `Exit Sub` or `Return` in your code; they are identical in functionality. There are programmers who consider the older `Exit Sub` statement to be—well—older. But unlike my reticence to leave my favored `MsgBox` method, I have wholeheartedly embraced the new `Return` statement. If it were just an issue of `Exit Sub` versus `Return`, I might not have made the switch.

But there is the related issue of Exit Function versus Return. I was never happy with the way that pre-.NET Visual Basic functions obtained their return values through an assignment statement to the name of the function. I was ready to make the switch to the newer Return statement. I did so for clarity; keeping the return value as close as possible to the statement that triggers the return to the calling code is a good thing. Before .NET, you might assign the return value, and then not leave the function for dozens of lines. Combining the assignment and the return in a single statement makes sense to me. From there, it was a short trip to replacing Exit Sub with Return. You will not find (I hope) a single Exit Sub statement in the Library Project. My transformation in this area is complete.

Why do I bring all this up? I do it to encourage you to make flexibility your friend when it comes to the different coding variations that exist in Visual Basic. If two different ways of developing a block of code seem to be morally equivalent and you can make the logic clear no matter which method you pick, choose and enjoy the coding style that you are most comfortable with. Some programmers may tell you to do it one way or another, and that's OK. (If you are part of a development team, the entire team should agree on a common style.) Remember that Visual Basic is a "general-purpose" programming language, and it has a certain amount of flexibility built into the language and related features. Experiment with the variations, and find patterns that you enjoy and that increase your effectiveness as a developer.

The Programming Mindset

As you enter deeper into the world of software development, you will quickly discover that the application-building process is about much more than syntax, statements, and logic. It is also about who you are as a programmer. The way that you think about software, and the care with which you approach the task of programming, have a direct impact on the quality of the code you write. This is certainly true in other areas of life. If you are a portrait painter, but you don't take your strokes seriously, or if you are sloppy in your use of paints and brushes, it will show in the low quality of your work.

In one of my previous books, *The Visual Basic .NET Style Guide* (Prentice Hall), I wrote about three traits that provide a strong basis for the programming life:

Discipline
> The act of self-training with a goal of increasing order, focus, and quality in your projects and work ethic

Planning
> The careful analysis and implementation of procedures and standards that scream out for quality

Ethics
> The inner character drive that shows itself through public and private honesty in attitudes and actions

If you are deficient in any of these three areas of your programming life, your applications and code will also be deficient by a similar factor. I have tried to sprinkle some humor and fun throughout the pages of this book. But on this point, I make no jokes. You need these three elements in your work life.

If you are serious about a career in software development, take the time to ask yourself questions that focus on these three aspects. Do I employ regular discipline on the way that I craft my software? Do I create reasonable and reliable plans, and then stick to them during a project? Do I exhibit ethical standards in the way I communicate with my customers, my employer, my coworkers, and even myself? If you are not able to answer these questions to your satisfaction, find resources that can help you overcome the lapses. It will make your programming work so much easier, and it will positively impact the other areas of your life as well.

Summary

Now you've really reached the end of the book. You can read through the appendixes and the index if you're still hungry for more. But a better solution would be to find out if I've come out with the next edition of the book and buy it. Ha!

I thank you for taking the time to read through *Programming Visual Basic 2008*. I wrote it so that you might expand your understanding and expertise of a very practical and enjoyable subject: Visual Basic. And *enjoyable* is the key word. Nobody has to be a computer programmer, no matter what historians say. You should take on the role of a Visual Basic developer only if you truly take pleasure in helping other people become more productive through specialized or general software. If, even after reading this book, you find coding to be a bore and sheer drudgery, I recommend the food services industry as an alternative.

For those of you still excited about Visual Basic programming, have as much fun with it as possible. Microsoft is constantly updating the language and its Visual Studio shell so that you can really enjoy yourself as you program. Why do you think Microsoft put in all of those animation features? Take time to go beyond the mundane in your code and in your user interfaces. Challenge yourself by trying out new features within the language and in the framework. And above all, smile each time you successfully complete a project. Your author, and your users, will thank you.

Installing the Software

You are holding more than just a book. You are holding an idea. No wait, that's what you get when you hold a philosophy book. In this case, what you also get is software—free software. And it's all found on the publisher's web site for this book:

http://www.oreilly.com/catalog/9780596518431/

When you download and run the setup program provided on the web site, the following items are added to your system:

- A directory structure with all chapter-specific source code and documentation.
- A "vsi" file that installs a set of Visual Studio Project templates. Each template creates a new project based on "before" or "after" source code images for most chapters in the book. Once you install this file, you will have the option of accessing chapter-specific projects using the File → New Project menu command in Visual Studio.
- A directory of "code snippets" that let you follow along with the action in each chapter's "Project" section, all without the need to retype every line of code printed in the book.

The installation requires approximately 50 MB of disk space. This appendix discusses the download and installation procedures.

Download the Software

To obtain the software for the book, browse to the book's web site:

http://www.oreilly.com/catalog/9780596518431/

Locate the Source Code link on this page and click it. When prompted, save the download file to your system using the standard file download features of your browser. You can save the file, named *Programming Visual Basic 2008.exe*, to a temporary area of your system. Once you complete installation, you will no longer need this file, unless you wish to retain it as a backup.

Install the Software

Double-click or run the downloaded *Programming Visual Basic 2008.exe* file. When prompted, indicate the target directory to use for the installation of all project files. Once the files are extracted, a readme file appears describing the final installation steps.

Install Project Templates

One of the files installed in the target directory is named *Programming Visual Basic 2008 Templates.vsi*. Double-click or open this file to install the project templates for the book. The Visual Studio Content Installer window appears, as shown in Figure A-1.

Figure A-1. The Visual Studio Content Installer

To complete the installation, click the Next button, followed by a click on the Finish button. The next time you run Visual Studio, all of the installed project templates will appear when you use the File → New Project menu command.

Install Code Snippets

Code snippets are installed from within the Visual Studio application. Start Visual Studio, and run the Tools → Code Snippets Manager menu command. The Code Snippets Manager window appears, as shown in Figure A-2.

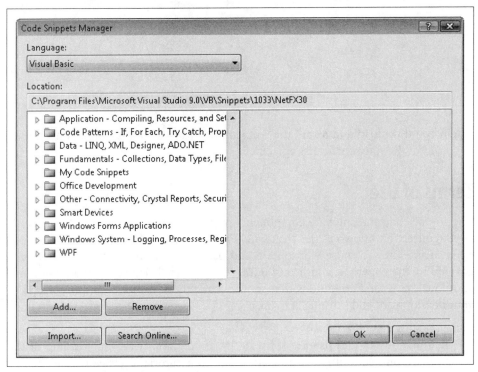

Figure A-2. The Code Snippets Manager

Click the Add button and browse to the directory where you extracted this book's downloaded content. Browse within the *Code Snippets* directory, select the *Programming Visual Basic 2008* subdirectory, and click the Select Folder button. When control returns to the Code Snippets Manager form, click the OK button to complete the installation.

Bar Code Support

The web site that hosts the project content also contains information on locating and obtaining bar code font information. You may use one of the bar codes mentioned on this site with the project code, or you may obtain your own valid bar code font.

APPENDIX B

Software License Agreement

When you download and install the software provided with this book, you agree to the terms of the software license agreement.

Terms of Use

The source code and software components provided with *Programming Visual Basic 2008* (collectively known as the "software") are designed for use with that book, and are available only to those who obtain and use the book. As such, the software is covered by the copyright and licensing of the book itself. However, there are a few additional terms and conditions that should make the software even more useful to your development and learning activities:

Using the software with the book
> You may install and use the software in conjunction with your reading of the text. If you use multiple workstations in your tutorial endeavors, feel free to install the software on each of those systems.

Distributing the supplied software
> You may not package, distribute, sell, or otherwise make available to others the partial or complete applications provided with the book. Claiming that this work is your own, and attempting to distribute or sell it as such, is wrong and an all-around bad idea.

Using portions of the software in your projects
> You may use portions of this software in your own applications and development projects. If you include significant portions of the software in your derived work, please give credit where credit is due, and make it known that your application employs the useful content provided with *Programming Visual Basic 2008*.

Acknowledgments
> The software was developed by Tim Patrick, author of *Programming Visual Basic 2008*. Tim Patrick and O'Reilly Media, Inc. gladly make this software available to you for your education and enjoyment.

Warranty

No warranty is provided with the software. Although every attempt has been made to keep the software safe and benign when installed on any target system, such safety is not guaranteed. Tim Patrick and O'Reilly Media, Inc. shall not be liable for any harm or damage that comes to your system or to any data stored on your system as a result of installing this software.

Other terms and conditions

There may be additional terms and conditions instituted on the download web site where you obtained this software. Please read those carefully as they contain important information concerning downloads accessed from the web site.

Enjoy

I hope that these terms and conditions didn't scare you off. The software exists to help you learn and to advance your understanding of Visual Basic software development concepts. I think you'll find the software to be quite useful in your training, so download and enjoy.

Index

Symbols

& (ampersand)
  &= (concatenation and assignment)
    operator, 34, 172
  button shortcuts, 148
  string concatenation operator, 36, 48,
    169
    overloading, 334
< and > (angle brackets)
  < (less than) operator, 170
    overloading, 334
  < > (not equal to) operator, 48, 170
    overloading, 334
  << (shift left) operator, 48, 170
    overloading, 335
  <<= (shift left and assignment)
    operator, 172
  <= (less than or equal to) operator, 48,
    170
    overloading, 334
  > (greater than) operator, 48, 170
  >= (greater than or equal to)
    operator, 48, 170
    overloading, 334
  >> (shift right) operator, 48, 170
    overloading, 335
  >>= (shift right and assignment)
    operator, 172
<%@, ASP.NET page directives, 648
<%…%> bracket pair for ASP.NET-specific
    commands and code, 648

<%= and %> symbols
  bracketing LINQ-specific code, 462
  embedded XML expressions, 376
<?xml…?>, XML document
    declaration, 372
* (asterisk)
  *= (multiplication and assignment)
    operator, 171
  multiplication operator, 48, 168
    overloading, 332, 333
\ (backslash)
  \= (integer division and assignment)
    operator, 171
  integer division operator, 48, 168
    overloading, 333
^ (caret)
  ^= (exponentiation and assignment)
    operator, 171
  exponentiation operator, 48, 168
    overloading, 334
{ } (curly braces)
  enclosing array elements, 175
  enclosing multiple generic
    constraints, 438
. (dot)
  descendant-member XML axis, 377
  instance member access, 233
  separating nodes in type hierarchy, 11
  SQL syntax, 101
= (equals sign)
  assignment operator, 47, 171
  equal to operator, 48, 170
    overloading, 334

We'd like to hear your suggestions for improving our indexes. Send email to *index@oreilly.com*.

B

banded reports, 587
bar codes
    fonts, 431, 721
    support for reading, 349
Base Class Library (see BCL)
base classes, 27, 222
    implementation of specific members,
        forced in derived classes, 237
    inheritance of members by derived
        classes, 230
    passing instance variables between derived
        classes and, 233
    shadowing members in derived class, 232
baselines of text blocks, 495
BASIC language, 31, 49
    defining an object containing an entire
        function, 253
BCL (Base Class Library), 11
    namespace hierarchy and, 13
    obsolete features, 14
BeginPrint event handler, 559
    changing to correct starting page
        number, 563
Berners-Lee, Tim, 642
beta versions, 87
bidirectional encryption, 306
bigint and smallint data types, 101
binary comparisons, 46
binary files, 361
binary operators, 47, 167, 331
binary values, 151
    for characters, 153
BinaryReader class, 421
BinaryWriter class, 421
binding (see data binding)
bitmaps
    associating Graphics object to, 489
    Bitmap object, 489, 497
    BMP files, 497
    creating in a variety of formats, 498
    drawing on a graphics surface, 498
    drawing with GDI+, 487
    image as drawn on a grid of bits, 498
    loading and saving, 498
    native BMP file format in Windows, 497
    stretching, cropping, and generating
        thumbnail while drawing, 499
    text based on, 496
    texture brushes, 491
bitwise conjunction operator (see And
    operator)

bitwise disjunction operator (see Or
    operator)
bitwise exclusion operator (see Xor operator)
bitwise negation operator (see Not operator)
bitwise operators
    overloading, 335
    (see also individual operators, under
        Symbols)
black boxes, 222
block statements, 165
block-level scope, 165
body of a procedure, 59
Boolean algebra, 37
Boolean data type, 39, 156
    conversions between integer values
        and, 156
    .NET, 153
Boolean values
    compiler constant, 135
    conditional statements resulting in, 51
    representing in binary form, 153
bound settings, 400
    main form position setting, 404
    (see also data binding)
boundaries, array, 174
BoundField column, GridView control, 667
BoundSchemaSearchResults class, 667
boxing and unboxing, 158
branches in code, 51
    If statements, 51
BrowsableAttribute attribute, 511
browser-based WPF programs, 507
brushes, 488, 491
    Brush object, 490
    drawing simple rectangles (example), 492
    using in text output, 496
buffer overrun issues, 3
BufferedStream object, 419
business-level software, xvi
Button class, 15
Button control, 141
    Click event handler, 208
    Click event in Visual Basic, 207
    monitoring event notifications, 208
    source code (example), 208
    typical event handler, 206
ByRef keyword, 58
Byte data type, 39, 154
    conversions, 337
ByVal keyword, 58
    parameters of partial methods, 240

C

c (denoting character literals), 36
C language, 49
C#, 31
    Boolean values, 41
      conversion to integers, 157
    conversions of Visual Basic code, MsgBox
      and, 715
Camel Casing, 166
CancelButton property, 141
canvas
    generalization by GDI+, 488
    Graphics objects, 488
    in-memory printer canvas, 553
CAPI (Cryptography API), 311
Cartesian join, 106
CAS (Code Access Security), 304
Cascading Style Sheets (see CSS)
Case clauses, Select Case statement, 52
Case Else condition, 53
casing methods, String class, 341
casing rules for variables, 166
Catch clause, Try...Catch...Finally
    statement, 266
CD distributions, 708
    installation keys, 613
CDate operator, 537
Char data type, 40, 156
character literals, 36
characters
    conversion to binary values, 153
    data types in .NET, 153
CheckBox controls
    Checkboxes dialog, 705
    CheckedChanged event firing as
      non-postback, 654
    installation process checkbox, 705–707
checksums, 306
child-member XML axis property, 377
Church, Alonzo, 253
CInt operator, 339, 342
Class and End Class keywords, 214
Class keyword, 225
Class Library projects, 23
classes, 6, 9, 225
    abstract classes defined by interfaces, 237
    anonymous types, 451
    attributes, 14, 510
    class libraries, .NET, 10–13
    constraining generic types, 437, 438
    constructors, 28, 163

    containing fields, local variables, and
      constants, 164
    creating instances of, 28, 232
    data type, 153
    derivation from System.Object, 157
    dividing single class among multiple
      source code files, 27
    extension methods, 340
    firing an event (example), 65
    forms, 142
    inheritance, 230–232, 244
    killing instances, 235
    members, 225–228
      overloaded, and optional
        arguments, 229
      shared, 228
    namespaces, 66
    naming, 12
    Object as root, 39
    partial, 225
    properties, 60
    referencing a library of, 68
    support by reference types, 158
Click event, 144
    adding to a form, 198
    Button control
      adding SQL Server data source, 290
      handler definition, 208
    errors stemming from, 269
ClickOnce deployment, 698
client-side data validation, 656
client-side record sets, 282
client-side scripting, 644
clipping regions, 502
closure classes, 258
CLR (Common Language Runtime), 7, 35
    final just-in-time (JIT) compilation of
      MSIL assembly, 17
CLS (Common Language Specification), 8
Codd, Edgar, 95
Code Access Security (CAS), 304
code behind features of Web Forms, 646,
    663
code examples from this book
    "Before" and "After" version, 70
    license agreement, 722
code snippets
    inserting, 71
    installing, 721
Code Snippets feature (Visual Studio), 70
collections, 440
    converting LINQ results to, 459

J

Japanese language, form
    localization, 533–534
JavaScript, 648
    Ajax, 650
    IntelliSense and debugging support,
        Visual Studio 2008, 21
    joins, 105
    LINQ query sources, 456
Joint Photographic Experts Group (see JPEG
        files)
JPEG files, 497
    GDI+, 487

K

Kemeny, John, 31
key user, 75
keyboard events, 66, 189
KeyDown event handler, 217, 686
KeyPreview property, 217, 686
Keys enumeration, 217
keywords
    Help Keywords file, 675
    LINQ, 452
    statement, 52
Kill command, 134
Kurtz, Thomas, 31

L

Label control, 139
    simulating lines and rectangles, 140
labels, line, 61
lambda calculus, 253
lambda expressions, 253–259
    complex, 257
    defining a variable as a simple
        function, 254
    expression trees, 256
    with inferred types, 255
    support for LINQ, 450
    variable lifting and closure classes, 258
Language Integrated Query (see LINQ)
language-culture selections, 532
languages, 527
    Language property, 532
    language settings, 129
    translator converting a form to a specific
        language, 534
last in, first out (LIFO), 440

Launch Conditions Editor, 697
Left function, 183
left outer joins, 105
Len function, 183
Length property, Stream object, 418
less than operators (see < and > [angle
        brackets], under Symbols)
Let keyword (LINQ), 475
libraries
    browser-based WPF programs, 507
    (see also BCL; FCLs)
license agreements, 615
    software for this book, 722
license-checking code (example), 634
LicenseStatus enumeration (example), 628
licensing, 611–641
    controlled access, 614
    custom-generated license key, 613
    license key with hardware identity or
        lock, 614
    license-agreement-only method, 612
    software, options for, 611
lifetime of a variable, 165
Like operator, 48, 170
    overloading, 335
line continuation characters, LINQ to XML
        code, 461
line labels, 61
linear approach to project management, 84
lines and shapes, adding to a form, 140
lines, geometric transformations, 503
LinkClicked event, 325
LinkLabel controls, 141
    multiple web-style links, 145
links, 144
    HTML Help files, 675
LINQ (Language Integrated Query), 32,
        448–485
    advantages of, 449
    aggregate queries, 459
    anonymous types, 450
    conversions of query results, 459
    deferred execution of queries, 468
    disadvantages of, 449
    LINQ for ADO.NET data, 463–468
        LINQ to DataSet, 463
        LINQ to Entities, 463
        LINQ to SQL, 464–468
    LINQ to Objects, 451
    LINQ to XML, 461

System.Windows.Forms.Application.Run method, 191
System.Windows.Forms.Control class, 191, 197
System.Windows.Forms.dll, 68
System.Windows.Forms.Form class, 142
System.Windows.Window class, 509
System.Xml namespace, 295, 371
System.Xml.Linq namespace, 371, 376
System.Xml.XPath namespace, 374

T

tab order, 141
tables, 95
    abbreviations for names, 105
    joining, 97, 105
    (see also database tables)
Tag Image File Format ("TIFF") files, 497
tags
    ASP.NET, 651
    XML, 366
Take clause, LINQ queries, 458
Take While clause, LINQ queries, 458
Team Foundation Server, 20
Team System 2008, Visual Studio, 20
Technical Resource Kit, 109
television (TV), considered as an object, 5
Telnet program, 643
templates
    chapter-specific project templates, 23
    installing project templates for this book, 720
ternary operator (If), 54
testing (acceptance criteria), 88
text
    aligning with bounding box, 523
    comparisons, 46
    data types, 156
    before graphical user interfaces, 493
    placing on graphics surface, 493–496
    string data, 34
    transformations before output to graphics surface, 503
    variables for, 34
TextBox controls
    adding to report header and footer, 590
    ASP.NET, TextChanged event, 653
    Color property, 593
TextReader class, 421
texture brushes, 491

TextWriter class, 421
The Rule (XML), 367
Then keyword, 51
Throw statement, 270
TIFF files, 497
Timer control, 191
ToArray method, 459
ToDictionary method, 459
ToList method, 459
ToLower method, String class, 341
toolbox (Visual Studio), 138
ToString method, 245
    ListBox control, 382
ToUpper method, String class, 341
TRACE constant, 136
Transaction property, SQLCommand object, 293
transactions, 292
transformations
    geometric, of graphics objects, 503
    rotations, 523
    (see also XSLT)
transparency
    setting level, 491
    slowly increasing for, 524
Trim function, 184
Trimming property, StringFormat class, 515
Triple DES encryption algorithm, 307
True value, 37
    conversion to integers, 157
TrueType fonts, 512
Try clause, Try…Catch…Finally statement, 266
Try…Catch…Finally statement, 266
T-SQL scripting language, 98
TV considered as an object, 5
type (data values), 36
type inference, 376
    combining with lambda expressions, 255
    use by anonymous types, 451
type parameters, 436
typed data sets, 282, 464
TypeOf operator, 171
types, 9
    CTS (Common Type System), 9
    namespace referencing, 67
    placing in subordinate namespaces from root namespace, 69
    variable, 38
    (see also data types)

W

WCF (Windows Communication Foundation), 658–662
  services, 659–662
web browsers, 642
  independence of ASP.NET applications, 646
  running a web service, 661
web development, 642–671
  ASP.NET features, 645
  creating an ASP.NET application, 646–653
  data validation, 655–656
  database integration, 657
  enhanced, .NET Framework, 3
  events, 653
  how the Internet works, 642
  Library Project web site, 663–671
  programming the Internet, 644
  state and View State, 654
  WCF (Windows Communication Foundation, 658–662
Web Forms, 583, 645
  code behind features, 646, 663
  control class, represented by ASP.NET tag, 651
  controls, 649–651
  GridView control, viewing RDLC report, 657
  Literal control, 670
  retaining page state with View State feature, 655
  validation of data, 655
Web namespace, 11
web page for this book, xviii, 719
web servers
  ASP.NET Development Server, 652, 661
  ASP.NET, deployment, 690
  connecting to Google web server, 643
  IIS (Internet Information Server), 652
  processing of web page changes, 653
  server-side scripting, 644
web services (see WCF)
Web Site template, 646
web.config file, 393, 646
  connection string for Library database, 664
  connection strings, 658
  copied to ASP.NET server, 691

web-based applications, hosted within a user's browser, 507
WebBrowser control, 470, 479
  custom content through DocumentText property, 479–481
  links through Navigating event, 481–482
WebParts control containers, 650
web-style links, 144
WHERE clause
  DELETE statement, 104
  SELECT statement, 599
  UPDATE statement, 104
Where clause, LINQ queries, 455
While clauses, Do…Loop, 55
While…End loop, 56
widening conversions, 46, 337
Widening keyword, 338
win.ini file, 393
Window class, 509
window procedures (see WndProc)
Window Types dialog, 680
windows, 188–189
  forms and controls, 189, 191
  HTML Help, 680
  redrawing after obscuring or exposing, 502
Windows Communication Foundation (see WCF)
Windows folder, 393
Windows Forms, 187–218, 288
  Add Service Reference form, 661
  Button control Click event, adding SQL Server data source, 290
  ClickOnce deployment of applications, 698
  controls, 198–205, 488
    available in Visual Studio, 200–205
  creating applications, 191–194
  default namespace, 69
  events and delegates, 206–209
  Help.ShowHelp method, 682
  localization of applications, 530
  My.Forms class, 70
  printer controls, 554
  properties, setting, 195–198
  System.Windows.Forms namespace, 68
Windows Forms applications, 23

About the Author

Tim Patrick is a software architect and developer with 25 years of experience in designing and building custom software solutions. A Microsoft MVP and Microsoft Certified Solution Developer, Tim has published five tutorials and references on Visual Basic development, along with several articles. His books include *Visual Basic 2005 in a Nutshell* and *Visual Basic 2005 Cookbook*, both by O'Reilly.

Colophon

The animal on the cover of *Programming Visual Basic 2008* is a bufflehead duck (*Bucephala albeola*). The name bufflehead derives from the words "buffalo" and "head," referring to the bulbous head shape distinctive to this species. Male buffleheads are black and white with a large white patch extending from the eye to the back of the head; females are paler, smaller, and have a small white cheek patch. Both sexes are characterized by short necks and narrow gray bills.

Ranging in size from 13 to 16 inches and 9 to 22 ounces, buffleheads are the smallest diving ducks in North America. Unlike other diving ducks, they are able to take flight directly from the water without having to run along the surface. They live by lakes, rivers, and bays in Canada and the northen U.S., migrating to coastal water on the Atlantic, Pacific, and Gulf coasts as far south as Mazatlan in the winter months. They nest in aspen and poplar cavities excavated by northern flickers and pileated woodpeckers.

The bufflehead diet consists of fresh- and saltwater insects, snails, crustaceans, and plants. They dive for their food and swallow it underwater. Bufflehead ducks tend to stay in a group, one or two of them feeding while the others stand watch for any potential danger. Although not prized among duck hunters, buffleheads are hunted for sport in the U.S. and Canada and comprise approximately two percent of North American waterfowl hunting. Their status is not currently threatened, but habitat degradation is an increasing concern. Because the ducks return to the same breeding ground each year, overharvesting and deforestation could have a devastating impact on their population if not carefully monitored.

The cover image is from Johnson's *Natural History*. The cover font is Adobe ITC Garamond. The text font is Linotype Birka; the heading font is Adobe Myriad Condensed; and the code font is LucasFont's TheSansMonoCondensed.

Related Titles from O'Reilly

.NET and C#

ADO.NET Cookbook

ADO.NET 3.5 Cookbook, *2nd Edition*

ASP.NET 2.0 Cookbook, *2nd Edition*

ASP.NET 2.0: A Developer's Notebook

Building an ASP.NET Web 2.0 Portal

C# 3.0 in a Nutshell, *3rd Edition*

C# Cookbook, *2nd Edition*

C# Design Patterns

C# in a Nutshell, *2nd Edition*

C# Language Pocket Reference

Exchange Server 2007 Administration: The Definitive Guide

Head First C#

Learning ASP.NET 2.0 with AJAX

Learning C# 2005, *2nd Edition*

Learning WCF

MCSE Core Elective Exams in a Nutshell

.NET and XML

.NET Gotchas

Programming Atlas

Programming ASP.NET, *3rd Edition*

Programming ASP.NET AJAX

Programming C#, *4th Edition*

Programming MapPoint in .NET

Programming .NET 3.5

Programming .NET Components, *2nd Edition*

Programming .NET Security

Programming .NET Web Services

Programming Visual Basic 2005

Programming WCF Services

Programming WPF, *2nd Edition*

Programming Windows Presentation Foundation

Programming the .NET Compact Framework

Visual Basic 2005: A Developer's Notebook

Visual Basic 2005 Cookbook

Visual Basic 2005 in a Nutshell, *3rd Edition*

Visual Basic 2005 Jumpstart

Visual C# 2005: A Developer's Notebook

Visual Studio Hacks

Windows Developer Power Tools

XAML in a Nutshell

O'REILLY®

The O'Reilly Advantage

Stay Current and Save Money